Lecture Notes in Computer Science 8797

Commenced Publication in 1973
Founding and Former Series Editors:
Gerhard Goos, Juris Hartmanis, and Jan van Leeuwen

T0212916

Peter Mika   Tania Tudorache
Abraham Bernstein   Chris Welty
Craig Knoblock   Denny Vrandečić
Paul Groth   Natasha Noy
Krzysztof Janowicz   Carole Goble (Eds.)

The Semantic Web – ISWC 2014

13th International Semantic Web Conference
Riva del Garda, Italy, October 19-23, 2014
Proceedings, Part II

 Springer

Volume Editors

Peter Mika, Yahoo Labs, Barcelona, Spain
E-mail: pmika@yahoo-inc.com

Tania Tudorache, Stanford University, CA, USA
E-mail: tudorache@stanford.edu

Abraham Bernstein, University of Zurich, Switzerland
E-mail: bernstein@ifi.uzh.ch

Chris Welty, IBM Research, Yorktown Heights, NY, USA
E-mail: welty@us.ibm.com

Craig Knoblock, University of Southern California, Los Angeles, CA, USA
E-mail: knoblock@isi.edu

Denny Vrandecic, Natasha Noy, Google, USA
E-mail: vrandecic@google.com; natashafn@acm.org

Paul Groth, VU University Amsterdam, The Netherlands
E-mail: p.t.groth@vu.nl

Krzysztof Janowicz, University of California, Santa Barbara, CA, USA
E-mail: jano@geog.ucsb.edu

Carole Goble, The University of Manchester, UK
E-mail: carole.goble@manchester.ac.uk

ISSN 0302-9743   e-ISSN 1611-3349
ISBN 978-3-319-11914-4   e-ISBN 978-3-319-11915-1
DOI 10.1007/978-3-319-11915-1
Springer Cham Heidelberg New York Dordrecht London

Library of Congress Control Number: 2014949616

LNCS Sublibrary: SL 3 – Information Systems and Application,
incl. Internet/Web and HCI

Typesetting: Camera-ready by author, data conversion by Scientific Publishing Services, Chennai, India

Printed on acid-free paper

Springer is part of Springer Science+Business Media (www.springer.com)

Preface

The Semantic Web is now a maturing field with a significant and growing adoption of semantic technologies in a variety of commercial, public sector, and scientific fields. Linked Data is pervasive: from enabling government transparency, to helping integrate data in life sciences and enterprises, to publishing data about museums, and integrating bibliographic data. Significantly, major companies, such as Google, Yahoo, Microsoft, and Facebook, have created their own "knowledge graphs" that power semantic searches and enable smarter processing and delivery of data: The use of these knowledge graphs is now the norm rather than the exception. The schema.org effort led by the major search companies illustrates the industry interest and support of the Semantic Web. Commercial players such as IBM, Siemens, BestBuy, and Walmart are seeing the value of semantic technologies and are regular presenters at Semantic Web conferences. The papers and the research topics covered in these proceedings follow directly from the requirements of this large adoption, and contribute greatly to the continuing success of the field.

The International Semantic Web Conference is the premier forum for Semantic Web research, where cutting-edge scientific results and technological innovations are presented, where problems and solutions are discussed, and where the future of this vision is being developed. It brings together specialists in fields such as artificial intelligence, databases, social networks, distributed computing, Web engineering, information systems, human–computer interaction, natural language processing, and the social sciences for tutorials, workshops, presentations, keynotes, and ample time for detailed discussions.

This volume contains the main proceedings of the 13th International Semantic Web Conference (ISWC 2014), which was held in Riva del Garda, Trentino, Italy, in October 2014. We received tremendous response to our calls for papers from a truly international community of researchers and practitioners. Indeed, several tracks of the conference received a record number of submissions this year. The careful nature of the review process, and the breadth and scope of the papers finally selected for inclusion in this volume, speak to the quality of the conference and to the contributions made by researchers whose work is presented in these proceedings. As such, we were all honored and proud that we were invited to serve the community in the stewardship of this edition of ISWC.

The proceedings include papers from four different tracks: the Research Track, the Semantic Web In-Use Track, the newly added Replication, Benchmark, Data and Software (RBDS) Track, and a selection of Doctoral Consortium papers. For the first time since we started publishing the LNCS proceedings, the papers are organized by their topic rather than by their track and correspond closely to the sessions in the conference schedule. The topics of the accepted papers reflect the broad coverage of the Semantic Web research and application: Linked Data, its quality, link discovery, and application in the life sciences; data integration, search and query answering, SPARQL, ontology-based data access and query rewriting and reasoning; natural language processing and information extraction; user interaction and personalization, and social media; ontology alignment and modularization; and sensors and streams.

Creating the program for ISWC 2014 would not have been possible without the tireless and fantastic work of the Senior Program Committees (SPC), the Program Committees (PC), as well as of the many sub-reviewers in the different tracks, several of whom volunteered to provide high-quality emergency reviews. To acknowledge this work, the Research Track and the Semantic Web In-Use Track each offered a best reviewer award. The decision on the awards was taken with the input of the SPC members, of the fellow reviewers from the PC, of the authors, and also using objective measures about the reviews provided by EasyChair, the conference management system.

The Research Track of the conference attracted 180 submissions, 38 of which were accepted, resulting in a 21% acceptance rate. Each paper received at least three, and sometimes as many as five, reviews from members of the PC. After the first round of reviews, authors had the opportunity to submit a rebuttal, leading to further discussions among the reviewers, a metareview and a recommendation from a member of the SPC. The SPC held a 10-hour virtual meeting in order to select the final set of accepted papers, paying special attention to papers that were borderline or had at least one recommendation for acceptance. In many cases, additional last-minute reviews were sought out to better inform the SPC's decision.

The best paper nominations for the Research Track reflect the broad range of topics that were submitted to this track:

Best paper nominations:

- AGDISTIS - "Graph-Based Disambiguation of Named Entities Using Linked Data" by Ricardo Usbeck, Axel-Cyrille Ngonga Ngomo, Michael Röder, Daniel Gerber, Sandro Athaide Coelho, Sören Auer and Andreas Both
- "Expressive and Scalable Query-based Faceted Search over SPARQL Endpoints" by Sébastien Ferré
- "Explass: Exploring Associations Between Entities via Top-K Ontological Patterns and Facets" by Gong Cheng, Yanan Zhang and Yuzhong Qu
- "Querying Factorized Probabilistic Triple Databases" by Denis Krompaß, Maximilian Nickel and Volker Tresp

Best student paper nominations:

- "OBDA: Query Rewriting or Materialization? In Practice, Both!" by Juan F. Sequeda, Marcelo Arenas and Daniel P. Miranker
- "SYRql: A Dataflow Language for Large Scale Processing of RDF Data" by Fadi Maali, Padmashree Ravindra, Kemafor Anyanwu and Stefan Decker
- "Pushing the Boundaries of Tractable Ontology Reasoning" by David Carral, Cristina Feier, Bernardo Cuenca Grau, Pascal Hitzler and Ian Horrocks

The Semantic Web In-Use Track received 46 submissions. Fifteen papers were accepted – a 33% acceptance rate. The papers demonstrated how semantic technologies are applied in a variety of domains, including: biomedicine and drug discovery, smart cities, sensor streams, multimedia, visualization, link generation, and ontology development. The application papers demonstrated how semantic technologies are applied in diverse ways, starting from using linked data in mobile environments to employing fully fledged artificial intelligence methods in real-time use cases. At least three members of the In-Use PC provided reviews for each paper. After the first round of reviews, authors had the opportunity to submit a rebuttal, leading to further discussions among the reviewers, a metareview and a recommendation from a member of the SPC.

The best paper nominations for the Semantic Web In-Use Track are:

- "Web Browser Personalization with the Client Side Triplestore" by Hitoshi Uchida, Ralph Swick and Andrei Sambra
- "Semantic Traffic Diagnosis with STAR-CITY: Architecture and Lessons Learned from Deployment in Dublin, Bologna, Miami and Rio", by Freddy Lecue, Robert Tucker, Simone Tallevi-Diotallevi, Rahul Nair, Yiannis Gkoufas, Giuseppe Liguori, Mauro Borioni, Alexandre Rademaker and Luciano Barbosa
- "Adapting Semantic Sensor Networks for Smart Building Analytics" by Joern Ploennigs, Anika Schumann and Freddy Lecue

This year we introduced the Replication, Benchmark, Data and Software (RBDS) track that provides an outlet for papers of these four categories. It extended and transformed last year's evaluations and experiments track to incorporate new categories of contributions. The four types of papers had very clearly specified scope and reviewing criteria that were described in the Call for Papers: (1) Replication papers focus on replicating a previously published approach in order to shed light on some important, possibly overlooked aspect; (2) benchmark papers make available to the community a new class of resources, metrics or software that can be used to measure the performance of systems in some dimension; (3) data papers introduce an important data set to the community; and (4) software framework papers advance science by sharing with the community software that can easily be extended or adapted to support scientific study and experimentation. The RBDS track received 39 submissions (18 benchmark studies, eight data papers, eight software framework papers, and four replication studies), and accepted 16 papers (five benchmark studies, five data papers, four software framework papers, and two replication studies), corresponding to an acceptance rate of 41%. Each paper was reviewed by at least three members of the PC and discussed thoroughly. The papers address a range of areas, such as linked stream data, federated query processing, tag recommendation, entity summarization, and mobile semantic web.

The Doctoral Consortium is a key event at the ISWC conference. PhD students in the Semantic Web field get an opportunity to present their thesis proposals and to interact with leading academic and industrial scientists in the field, who act as their mentors. The Doctoral Consortium received 41 submissions, a record number compared to previous years. Each paper received two reviews, one from an SPC member, and one from a co-chair. Out of 41 submissions, six were selected to be both included in these proceedings and for presentation at the Doctoral Consortium, while an additional 11 were selected for presentation. The Doctoral Consortium day is organized as a highly interactive event, in which students present their proposals and receive extensive feedback and comments from mentors as well as from their peers.

A unique aspect of the ISWC conference is the Semantic Web Challenge, now in its 12th year, with the goal of demonstrating practical progress toward achieving the vision of the Semantic Web. The overall objective of the challenge is to apply Semantic Web techniques in building online end-user applications that integrate, combine, and deduce information needed to assist users in performing tasks. Organized this year by Andreas Harth and Sean Bechhofer, the competition enables practitioners and scientists to showcase leading-edge real-world applications of Semantic Web technology. The Semantic Web Challenge is advised by a board of experts working at universities and in industry. The advisory board also acts as a jury and awards the best applications at the conference.

The keynote talks given by leading scientists or practitioners in their field further enriched the ISWC program. Prabhakar Raghavan, Vice-President of Engineering at Google, discussed "Web Search – From the Noun to the Verb." Paolo Traverso, Director of the Center for Information Technology at Fondazione Bruno Kessler, talked about "To Be or to Do?: The Semantics for Smart Cities and Communities." Yolanda Gil, Associate Director of the Intelligent Systems Division at ISI University of South California, discussed the "Semantic Challenges in Getting Work Done" addressing the application of semantics to scientific tasks. The industry track featured a plenary keynote on "The Semantic Web in an Age of Open Data" by Sir Nigel Shadbolt, Chairman and Co-Founder of the UK's Open Data Institute and Professor of Artificial Intelligence at the University of Southampton.

As in previous ISWC editions, the conference included an extensive tutorial and workshop program. Johanna Völker and Lora Aroyo, the chairs of this track, created a stellar and diverse collection of eight tutorials and 23 workshops, where the only problem that the participants faced was which of the many exciting workshops and tutorials to attend. This year, we hosted for the first time the Developers' Workshop, a dedicated event for software developers discussing implementations, methods, techniques, and solutions to practical problems of Semantic Web and Linked Data. The main topic of the Developers' Workshop was "Semantic Web in a Browser."

We would like to thank Matthew Horridge, Marco Rospocher, and Jacco van Ossenbruggen for organizing a lively poster and demo session. This year, the track got a record 156 submissions, a 50% increase compared with previous years. Moreover, 71 posters and 50 demos were introduced in a "minute madness session," where each presenter got 45 seconds to provide a teaser for their poster or demo. Axel Polleres, Alexander Castro, and Richard Benjamins coordinated an exciting Industry Track with presentations both from younger companies focusing on semantic technologies and from large enterprises, such as British Telecom, IBM, Oracle, and Siemens, just to name a few. With a record number of 39 submissions (seven of which were selected for full presentations and 23 for short lightning talks) in the industry track this year, the mix of presentations demonstrated the success and maturity of semantic technologies in a variety of industry- and business-relevant domains. The extended abstracts for posters, demos, and industry talks will be published in separate companion volumes in the CEUR workshop proceedings series.

We are indebted to Krzysztof Janowicz, our proceedings chair, who provided invaluable support in compiling the volume that you now hold in your hands (or see on your screen) and who put in many hours of additional work to create a completely new structure for these proceedings based on the topic rather than the tracks, as in previous years. Many thanks to Oscar Corcho and Miriam Fernandez, the student coordinators, for securing and managing the distribution of student travel grants and thus helping students who might not have otherwise attended the conference to come to Riva. Roberta Cuel, Jens Lehmann, and Vincenzo Maltese were tireless in their work as sponsorship chairs, knocking on every conceivable virtual "door" and ensuring an unprecedented level of sponsorship this year. We are especially grateful to all the sponsors for their generosity.

As has been the case in the past, ISWC 2014 also contributed to the Linked Data cloud by providing semantically annotated data about many aspects of the conference. This contribution would not have been possible without the efforts of Li Ding and Jie Bao, our metadata chairs.

Mauro Dragoni, our publicity chair, tirelessly tweeted, sent old-fashioned announcements on the mailing lists, and updated the website, creating more lively "buzz" than ISWC has had before.

Our very special thanks go to the local organization team, led by Luciano Serafini and Chiara Ghidini. They did a fantastic job of handling local arrangements, thinking of every potential complication way before it arose, often doing things when members of the Organizing Committee were only beginning to think about asking for them. Many thanks to the Rivatour Agency for providing great service for local arrangements.

Finally, we would like to thank all members of the ISWC Organizing Committee not only for handling their tracks superbly, but also for their wider contribution to the collaborative decision-making process in organizing the conference.

October 2014

Peter Mika
Tania Tudorache
Abraham Bernstein
Chris Welty
Craig Knoblock
Denny Vrandečić
Paul Groth
Natasha Noy
Krzysztof Janowicz
Carole Goble

Conference Organization

Organizing Committee

General Chair

Carole Goble   University of Manchester, UK

Local Chairs

Chiara Ghidini   Fondazione Bruno Kessler, Italy
Luciano Serafini   Fondazione Bruno Kessler, Italy

Program Committee Chairs

Peter Mika   Yahoo Labs, Spain
Tania Tudorache   Stanford University, USA
Abraham Bernstein   University of Zurich, Switzerland
Chris Welty   IBM Research, USA
Craig Knoblock   University of Southern California, USA
Denny Vrandečić   Google, USA

Research Track Chairs

Peter Mika   Yahoo Labs, Spain
Tania Tudorache   Stanford University, USA

In-Use Track Chairs

Craig Knoblock   University of Southern California, USA
Denny Vrandečić   Google, USA

Industry Track Chairs

Richard Benjamins   Telefonica, Spain
Alexander G. Castro   LinkingData I/O LLC, USA
Axel Polleres   Vienna University of Economics and
                                Business, Austria

Replication, Benchmark, Data and Software Track Chairs

Abraham Bernstein   University of Zurich, Switzerland
Chris Welty   IBM Research, USA

Workshops and Tutorials Chairs

Lora Aroyo   VU University Amsterdam,
                              The Netherlands
Johanna Völker   University of Mannheim, Germany

Posters and Demos Chairs

Matthew Horridge   Stanford University, USA
Marco Rospocher   Fondazione Bruno Kessler, Italy
Jacco van Ossenbruggen   Centrum voor Wiskunde en Informatica,
                              The Netherlands

Doctoral Consortium Chairs

Paul Groth   VU University Amsterdam,
                              The Netherlands
Natasha Noy   Google, USA

Proceedings Chair

Krzysztof Janowicz   University of California, Santa Barbara,
                              USA

Semantic Web Challenge Chairs

Sean Bechhofer   The University of Manchester, UK
Andreas Harth   Karlsruhe Institute of Technology,
                              Germany

Sponsorship Chairs

Roberta Cuel   University of Trento, Italy
Jens Lehmann   University of Leipzig, Germany
Vincenzo Maltese   DISI - University of Trento, Italy

Publicity Chairs

Mauro Dragoni   Fondazione Bruno Kessler, Italy

Metadata Chairs

Jie Bao   Memect, USA
Li Ding   Memect, USA

Student Coordinators

Oscar Corcho   Universidad Politécnica de Madrid,
                              Spain
Miriam Fernandez   KMI, Open University, UK

Senior Program Committee – Research

Harith Alani	The Open University, UK
Lora Aroyo	VU University Amsterdam, The Netherlands
Sören Auer	Bonn Universität, Germany
Philipp Cimiano	Bielefeld University, Germany
Oscar Corcho	Universidad Politécnica de Madrid, Spain
Philippe Cudré-Mauroux	University of Fribourg, Switzerland
Claudio Gutierrez	Chile University, Chile
Jeff Heflin	Lehigh University, USA
Ian Horrocks	University of Oxford, UK
Lalana Kagal	MIT, USA
David Karger	MIT, USA
Spyros Kotoulas	IBM Research, Ireland
Diana Maynard	University of Sheffield, UK
Natasha Noy	Google, USA
Jeff Pan	University of Aberdeen, UK
Terry Payne	University of Liverpool, UK
Marta Sabou	MODUL University Vienna, Austria
Uli Sattler	The University of Manchester, UK
Steffen Staab	University of Koblenz-Landau, Germany
Hideaki Takeda	National Institute of Informatics, Japan

Program Committee – Research

Karl Aberer	Paolo Bouquet
Sudhir Agarwal	Loris Bozzato
Faisal Alkhateeb	John Breslin
Pramod Anantharam	Christopher Brewster
Sofia Angeletou	Paul Buitelaar
Kemafor Anyanwu	Gregoire Burel
Marcelo Arenas	Andrea Calì
Manuel Atencia	Diego Calvanese
Medha Atre	Amparo E. Cano
Isabelle Augenstein	Iván Cantador
Nathalie Aussenac-Gilles	Soumen Chakrabarti
Jie Bao	Pierre-Antoine Champin
Payam Barnaghi	Gong Cheng
Sean Bechhofer	Key-Sun Choi
Klaus Berberich	Smitashree Choudhury
Christian Bizer	Michael Compton
Roi Blanco	Isabel Cruz
Eva Blomqvist	Bernardo Cuenca Grau
Kalina Bontcheva	Claudia D'Amato

Mathieu D'Aquin
Danica Damljanovic
Stefan Decker
Stefan Dietze
John Domingue
Jérôme Euzenat
Lujun Fang
Nicola Fanizzi
Anna Fensel
Miriam Fernandez
Lorenz Fischer
Achille Fokoue
Enrico Franconi
Fabien Gandon
Aldo Gangemi
Raúl García-Castro
Anna Lisa Gentile
Yolanda Gil
Birte Glimm
Jose Manuel Gomez-Perez
Olaf Görlitz
Alasdair Gray
Tudor Groza
Michael Gruninger
Christophe Guéret
Giancarlo Guizzardi
Peter Haase
Armin Haller
Harry Halpin
Siegfried Handschuh
Lynda Hardman
Manfred Hauswirth
Sandro Hawke
Tom Heath
Cory Henson
Martin Hepp
Pascal Hitzler
Rinke Hoekstra
Aidan Hogan
Matthew Horridge
Andreas Hotho
Geert-Jan Houben
Wei Hu
Bo Hu
Eero Hyvönen

Krzysztof Janowicz
Mustafa Jarrar
Hanmin Jung
Jaap Kamps
Yevgeny Kazakov
Maria Keet
Hong-Gee Kim
Matthias Klusch
Jacek Kopecky
Manolis Koubarakis
Markus Krötzsch
Werner Kuhn
Agnieszka Lawrynowicz
Freddy Lecue
Lei Li
Yuefeng Li
Juanzi Li
Chengkai Li
Vanessa Lopez
Pasquale Lops
David Martin
Robert Meusel
Alessandra Mileo
Iris Miliaraki
Riichiro Mizoguchi
Dunja Mladenic
Luc Moreau
Boris Motik
Enrico Motta
Mark Musen
Ekawit Nantajeewarawat
Axel-Cyrille Ngonga Ngomo
Nadeschda Nikitina
Andriy Nikolov
Lyndon Nixon
Kieron O'Hara
Beng Chin Ooi
Massimo Paolucci
Bijan Parsia
Carlos Pedrinaci
Silvio Peroni
H. Sofia Pinto
Dimitris Plexousakis
Valentina Presutti
Guilin Qi

Yves Raimond
Ganesh Ramakrishnan
Maya Ramanath
Chantal Reynaud
Riccardo Rosati
Marco Rospocher
Matthew Rowe
Sebastian Rudolph
Harald Sack
Satya Sahoo
Hassan Saif
Manuel Salvadores
Francois Scharffe
Ansgar Scherp
Stefan Schlobach
Daniel Schwabe
Juan F. Sequeda
Amit Sheth
Michael Sintek
Milan Stankovic
Markus Strohmaier
Rudi Studer
Gerd Stumme
Jing Sun

Vojtěch Svátek
Valentina Tamma
Kerry Taylor
Krishnaprasad Thirunarayan
Ioan Toma
Nicolas Torzec
Thanh Tran
Raphaël Troncy
Giovanni Tummarello
Anni-Yasmin Turhan
Jacopo Urbani
Victoria Uren
Jacco van Ossenbruggen
Maria-Esther Vidal
Johanna Völker
Haofen Wang
Kewen Wang
Zhichun Wang
Yong Yu
Fouad Zablith
Qingpeng Zhang
Antoine Zimmermann

Additional Reviewers – Research

Nitish Aggarwal
Muhammad Intizar Ali
Carlos Buil Aranda
Mihael Arcan
Estefanía Serral Asensio
Andrew Bate
Wouter Beek
Konstantina Bereta
David Berry
Nicola Bertolin
Leopoldo Bertossi
Dimitris Bilidas
Stefano Bortoli
Adrian Brasoveanu
Volha Bryl
Jean-Paul Calbimonte
Diego Calvanese

Delroy Cameron
Michele Catasta
Sam Coppens
Julien Corman
Jérôme David
Jana Eggink
Jae-Hong Eom
Ju Fan
Jean-Philippe Fauconnier
Daniel Fleischhacker
Andre Freitas
Riccardo Frosini
Irini Fundulaki
Stella Giannakopoulou
Jangwon Gim
Kalpa Gunaratna
Andreas Harth

Julia Hoxha
Gao Huan
Armen Inants
Ernesto Jimenez-Ruiz
Zoi Kaoudi
Patrick Kapahnke
Mario Karlovcec
Robin Keskisärkkä
Taehong Kim
Magnus Knuth
Haridimos Kondylakis
Aljaz Kosmerlj
Egor V. Kostylev
Adila A. Krisnadhi
Sarasi Lalithsena
Christoph Lange
Sungin Lee
Zhixing Li
Juanzi Li
Nuno Lopes
Yongtao Ma
Andre de Oliveira Melo
Albert Meroño-Peñuela
Ankush Meshram
Hyun Namgoong
Radim Nedbal
Hai Nguyen
Quoc Viet Hung Nguyen
Vinh Nguyen
Inna Novalija
Andrea Giovanni Nuzzolese
Francesco Osborne
Matteo Palmonari
Bianca Pereira
Jorge Pérez
Catia Pesquita
Robert Piro
Camille Pradel

Freddy Priyatna
Jay Pujara
Jean-Eudes Ranvier
David Ratcliffe
Martin Rezk
Laurens Rietveld
Petar Ristoski
Giuseppe Rizzo
Víctor Rodríguez-Doncel
Yannis Roussakis
Tong Ruan
Brigitte Safar
Andreas Schwarte
Kunal Sengupta
Chao Shao
Philipp Singer

Panayiotis Smeros
Kostas Stefanidis
Andreas Steigmiller
Nenad Stojanovic
Aynaz Taheri
Vahid Taslimitehrani
Veronika Thost
Alberto Tonon
Trung-Kien Tran
Tran Quoc Trung
Jung-Ho Um
Joerg Waitelonis
Simon Walk
Zhigang Wang
Zhe Wang
Guohui Xiao
Nasser Zalmout
Eva Zangerle
Dmitriy Zheleznyakov
Zhiqiang Zhuang

Senior Program Committee – Semantic Web In-Use

Yolanda Gil	University of South California, USA
Paul Groth	VU University Amsterdam, The Netherlands
Peter Haase	fluid Operations, Germany
Siegfried Handschuh	Digital Enterprise Research Institute (DERI), Ireland
Andreas Harth	Karlsruhe Institute of Technology, Germany
Krzysztof Janowicz	University of California, Santa Barbara, USA
Natasha Noy	Google, USA
Matthew Rowe	Lancaster University, UK
Uli Sattler	University of Manchester, UK

Program Committee – Semantic Web In-Use

Dean Allemang
Phil Archer
Isabelle Augenstein
Sean Bechhofer
Christian Bizer
Sebastian Blohm
Dan Brickley
Iván Cantador
Vinay Chaudhri
Michelle Cheatham
Paolo Ciccarese
Michael Compton
Oscar Corcho
Mathieu D'Aquin
Brian Davis
Mike Dean
Leigh Dodds
Basil Ell
Fabian Floeck
Alasdair Gray
Tudor Groza
Giancarlo Guizzardi
Armin Haller
Sebastian Hellmann
Martin Hepp
Matthew Horridge
Wei Hu
Prateek Jain
Anja Jentzsch
Benedikt Kämpgen

Pavel Klinov
Matthias Klusch
Christoph Lange
Yuan-Fang Li
Thorsten Liebig
Antonis Loizou
Markus Luczak-Roesch
Pablo Mendes
Hannes Mühleisen
Lyndon Nixon
Daniel Oberle
Massimo Paolucci
Carlos Pedrinaci
Héctor Pérez-Urbina
Edoardo Pignotti
Yves Raimond
Marco Rospocher
Manuel Salvadores
Miel Vander Sande
Marc Schaaf
Michael Schmidt
Oshani Seneviratne
Juan F. Sequeda
Evren Sirin
William Smith
Milan Stankovic
Thomas Steiner
Nenad Stojanovic
Pedro Szekely
Ramine Tinati

Nicolas Torzec
Giovanni Tummarello
Jacco van Ossenbruggen
Ruben Verborgh
Holger Wache
Jesse Jiaxin Wang
Kewen Wang

Zhe Wu
Fouad Zablith
Amrapali Zaveri
Qingpeng Zhang
Amal Zouaq

Additional Reviewers – Semantic Web In-Use

Ana Sasa Bastinos
Anila Sahar Butt
Charles Vardeman II

Gwendolin Wilke
Zhe Wang

Program Committee – Replication, Benchmark, Data and Software

Sören Auer
Jie Bao
Cosmin Basca
Chris Biemann
Philipp Cimiano
Oscar Corcho
Philippe Cudré-Mauroux
Richard Cyganiak
Claudia D'Amato
Victor de Boer
Gianluca Demartini
Jérôme Euzenat
Javier D. Fernández
Alfio Gliozzo
Martin Grund

Siegfried Handschuh
Matthew Horridge
Jens Lehmann
Alejandro Llaves
Axel Polleres
Marta Sabou
Thomas Scharrenbach
Heiner Stuckenschmidt
Jamie Taylor
Jürgen Umbrich
Gerhard Weikum
Stuart Wrigley
Josiane Xavier Parreira

Additional Reviewers – Replication, Benchmark, Data and Software

Judie Attard
Mihaela Bornea
Yu Chen
Souripriya Das
Sarthak Dash
Michael Glass
Tatiana Lesnikova

Michael Luggen
Christian Meilicke
Niels Ockeloen
Matthew Perry
Roman Prokofyev
Stephan Radeck-Arneth
Eugen Ruppert

Joerg Schoenfisch
Claus Stadler
Wei Tai
Alberto Tonon
Joerg Unbehauen

Han Wang
Marcin Wylot
Seid Muhie Yimam

Program Committee – Doctoral Consortium

Harith Alani
Lora Aroyo
Abraham Bernstein
Oscar Corcho
Philippe Cudré-Mauroux
Fabien Gandon
Paul Groth
Pascal Hitzler

Lalana Kagal
Diana Maynard
Enrico Motta
Natasha Noy
Terry Payne
Guus Schreiber
Elena Simperl

Sponsors

Student Travel Award Sponsor
Semantic Web Science Association (SWSA)
National Science Foundation (NSF)

Invited Speakers Sponsor
Artificial Intelligence Journal

Semantic Web Challenge Sponsor
Elsevier

Platinum
Yahoo! Labs
Elsevier

Gold
Telefonica
Parlance project
Google
IBM Research
Microsoft Research
LinkedUp project
The Open PHACTS Foundation
Systap
Semantic Valley

Silver
OpenLink software
Poolparty
fluid Operations
News Reader project
Synerscope
Okkam
SICRaS
Bpeng
Centro Ricerche GPI
Expert System
Informatica Trentina s.p.a.
Institute of Cognitive Sciences
  and Technologies - CNR

Doctoral Consortium Sponsor
iMinds

Video Sponsor
Videolectures

Organizing Institution/Foundation
Fondazione Bruno Kessler
Semantic Web Science Association

Keynote Talk (Abstracts)

Web Search - From the Noun to the Verb (Keynote Talk)

Prabhakar Raghavan

Vice President Engineering
Google, USA

Abstract. This talk examines the evolution of web search experiences over 20 years, and their impact on the underlying architecture. Early web search represented the adaptation of methods from classic Information Retrieval to the Web. Around the turn of this century, the focus shifted to triaging the need behind a query - whether it was Navigational, Informational or Transactional; engines began to customize their experiences depending on the need. The next change arose from the recognition that most queries embodied noun phrases, leading to the construction of knowledge representations from which queries could extract and deliver information regarding the noun in the query. Most recently, three trends represent the next step beyond these "noun engines": (1) "Queryless engines" have begun surfacing information meeting a user's need based on the user's context, without explicit querying; (2) Search engines have actively begun assisting the user's task at hand - the verb underlying the noun query; (3) increasing use of speech recognition is changing the distribution of queries.

"To Be or to DO?": The Semantics for Smart Cities and Communities (Keynote Talk)

Paolo Traverso

Director
Center for Information Technology
Fondazione Bruno Kessler, Italy

Abstract. The major challenge for so-called smart cities and communities is to provide people with value added services that improve their quality of life. Massive individual and territorial data sets – (open) public and private data, as well as their semantics which allows us to transform data into knowledge about the city and the community, are key enablers to the development of such solutions. Something more however is needed. A "smart" community needs "to do things" in a city, and the people need to act within their own community. For instance, not only do we need to know where we can find a parking spot, which cultural event is happening tonight, or when the next bus will arrive, but we also need to actually pay for parking our car, buy a bus ticket, or reserve a seat in the theater. All these activities (paying, booking, buying, etc.) need semantics in the same way as data does, and such a semantics should describe all the steps needed to perform such activities. Moreover, such a semantics should allow us to define and deploy solutions that are general and abstract enough to be "portable" across the details of the different ways in which activities can be implemented, e.g., by different providers, or for different customers, or for different cities. At the same time, in order to actually "do things", we need a semantics that links general and abstract activities to the possibly different and specific ICT systems that implement them. In my talk, I will present some of the main problems for realizing the concept of smart city and community, and the need for semantics for both understanding data and "doing things". I will discuss some alternative approaches, some lessons learned from applications we have been working with in this field, and the still many related open research challenges.

Semantic Challenges in Getting Work Done (Keynote Talk)

Yolanda Gil

Associate Director
Information Sciences Institute and Department of Computer Science
University of Southern California, USA

Abstract. In the new millennium, work involves an increasing amount of tasks that are knowledge-rich and collaborative. We are investigating how semantics can help on both fronts. Our focus is scientific work, in particular data analysis, where tremendous potential resides in combining the knowledge and resources of a highly fragmented science community. We capture task knowledge in semantic workflows, and use skeletal plan refinement algorithms to assist users when they specify high-level tasks. But the formulation of workflows is in itself a collaborative activity, a kind of meta-workflow composed of tasks such as finding the data needed or designing a new algorithm to handle the data available. We are investigating "organic data science", a new approach to collaboration that allows scientists to formulate and resolve scientific tasks through an open framework that facilitates ad-hoc participation. With a design based on social computing principles, our approach makes scientific processes transparent and incorporates semantic representations of tasks and their properties. The semantic challenges involved in this work are numerous and have great potential to transform the Web to help us do work in more productive and unanticipated ways.

The Semantic Web in an Age of Open Data (Keynote Talk)

Nigel Shadbolt

Professor of Artificial Intelligence
The University of Southampton
and
Chairman of the Open Data Institute

Abstract. The last five years have seen increasing amounts of open data being published on the Web. In particular, governments have made data available across a wide range of sectors: spending, crime and justice, education, health, transport, geospatial, environmental and much more. The data has been published in a variety of formats and has been reused with varying degrees of success. Commercial organisations have begun to exploit this resource and in some cases elected to release their own open data. Only a relatively small amount of the data published has been linked data. However, the methods and techniques of the semantic web could significantly enhance the value and utility of open data. What are the obstacles and challenges that prevent the routine publication of these resources as semantically enriched open data? What can be done to improve the situation? Where are the examples of the successful publication and exploitation of semantically enriched content? What lessons should we draw for the future?

Table of Contents – Part II

Reasoning

Semantic Infrastructures and Streams

Sensors

Social Media

SPARQL Extensions

User Interaction and Personalization

Doctoral Consortium

Table of Contents – Part I

Large-Scale RDF Processing and Dataset Availability

Linked Data

Linked Data and Data Quality

Mobile Reasoning and SPARQL Updates

Natural Language Processing and Information Extraction

OBDA and Query Rewriting

Detecting and Correcting Conservativity Principle Violations in Ontology-to-Ontology Mappings

Alessandro Solimando[1], Ernesto Jiménez-Ruiz[2], and Giovanna Guerrini[1]

[1] Dipartimento di Informatica, Università di Genova, Italy
[2] Department of Computer Science, University of Oxford, UK

Abstract. In order to enable interoperability between ontology-based systems, ontology matching techniques have been proposed. However, when the generated mappings suffer from logical flaws, their usefulness may be diminished. In this paper we present an approximate method to detect and correct violations to the so-called conservativity principle where novel subsumption entailments between named concepts in one of the input ontologies are considered as unwanted. We show that this is indeed the case in our application domain based on the EU Optique project. Additionally, our extensive evaluation conducted with both the Optique use case and the data sets from the Ontology Alignment Evaluation Initiative (OAEI) suggests that our method is both useful and feasible in practice.

1 Introduction

Ontologies play a key role in the development of the Semantic Web and are being used in many diverse application domains, ranging from biomedicine to energy industry. An application domain may have been modeled with different points of view and purposes. This situation usually leads to the development of different ontologies that intuitively overlap, but they use different naming and modeling conventions.

In particular, this is the case we are facing in the EU Optique project.[1] Optique aims at facilitating scalable end-user access to big data in the oil and gas industry. The project is focused around two demanding use cases provided by *Siemens* and *Statoil*. Optique advocates for an Ontology Based Data Access (OBDA) approach [24] so that end-users formulate queries using the vocabulary of a domain ontology instead of composing queries directly against the database. Ontology-based queries (*e.g.*, SPARQL) are then automatically rewritten to SQL and executed over the database.

In Optique two independently developed ontologies co-exist. The first ontology has been directly bootstrapped from one of the relational databases in Optique and it is linked to the database via *direct ontology-to-database mappings*;[2] while the second ontology is a domain ontology based on the Norwegian Petroleum Directorate (NPD) FactPages[3] [41] and it is currently preferred by Optique end-users to feed the visual query formulation interface[4] [42]. This setting requires the "query formulation" ontology to be linked to the relational database. In Optique we follow two approaches that

---

[1] http://www.optique-project.eu/
[2] http://www.w3.org/TR/rdb-direct-mapping/
[3] http://factpages.npd.no/factpages/
[4] The query formulation interface has been evaluated with end-users at Statoil.

P. Mika et al. (Eds.) ISWC 2014, Part II, LNCS 8797, pp. 1–16, 2014.

will complement each other: *(i)* creation of ontology-to-database mappings between the query formulation ontology and the database; *(ii)* creation of *ontology-to-ontology* mappings between the bootstrapped ontology and the query formulation ontology. In this paper we only deal with ontology-to-ontology mappings (or mappings for short). The creation, analysis and evolution of ontology-to-database mappings are also key research topics within Optique, however, they fall out of the scope of this paper.

The problem of (semi-)automatically computing mappings between independently developed ontologies is usually referred to as the *ontology matching problem*. A number of sophisticated ontology matching systems have been developed in the last years [11, 40]. Ontology matching systems, however, rely on lexical and structural heuristics and the integration of the input ontologies and the mappings may lead to many undesired logical consequences. In [19] three principles were proposed to minimize the number of potentially unintended consequences, namely: *(i) consistency principle*, the mappings should not lead to unsatisfiable classes in the integrated ontology, *(ii) locality principle*, the mappings should link entities that have similar *neighbourhoods*, *(iii) conservativity principle*, the mappings should not introduce new semantic relationships between concepts from one of the input ontologies.

The occurrence of these violations is frequent, even in the reference mapping sets of the Ontology Alignment Evaluation Initiative[5] (*OAEI*). Also manually curated alignments, such as *UMLS-Metathesaurus* [3] (*UMLS*), a comprehensive effort for integrating biomedical knowledge bases, suffer from these violations. Violations to these principles may hinder the usefulness of ontology mappings. In particular, in the Optique's scenario, violation of the consistency or conservativity principles will directly affect the quality of the query results, since queries will be rewritten according to the ontology axioms, the ontology-to-ontology mappings and the ontology-to-database mappings.

These principles has been actively investigated in the last years (*e.g.*, [31, 30, 15, 19, 17, 29, 37]). In this paper we focus on the conservativity principle and we explore a variant of violation of this principle which we consider appropriate for the application domain in Optique. Furthermore, this variant of the conservativity principle allows us to reduce the problem to a consistency principle problem. We have implemented a method which relies on the projection of the input ontologies to Horn propositional logic. This projection allows us to be efficient in both the reduction to the consistency principle and the subsequent repair process. Our evaluation suggests that our method is feasible even with the largest test cases of the OAEI campaign.

The remainder of the paper is organised as follows. Section 2 summarises the basics concepts and definitions we will rely on along the paper. In Section 3 we introduce our motivating scenario based on Optique. Section 4 describes our method. In Section 5 we present the conducted evaluation. A comparison with relevant related work is provided in Section 6. Finally, Section 7 gives some conclusions and future work lines.

2   Preliminaries

In this section, we present the formal representation of ontology mappings and the notions of semantic difference, mapping coherence and conservativity principle violation.

---

[5] http://oaei.ontologymatching.org/

2.1　Representation of Ontology Mappings

Mappings are conceptualised as 5-tuples of the form $\langle id, e_1, e_2, n, \rho \rangle$, with id a unique identifier, e_1, e_2 entities in the vocabulary or signature of the relevant input ontologies (i.e., $e_1 \in \mathrm{Sig}(\mathcal{O}_1)$ and $e_2 \in \mathrm{Sig}(\mathcal{O}_2)$), n a confidence measure between 0 and 1, and ρ a relation between e_1 and e_2, typically subsumption, equivalence or disjointness [10].

RDF Alignment [8] is the main format used in the OAEI campaign to represent mappings containing the aforementioned elements. Additionally, mappings are also represented as OWL 2 subclass, equivalence, and disjointness axioms [6]; mapping identifiers (id) and confidence values (n) are then represented as axiom annotations. Such a representation enables the reuse of the extensive range of OWL 2 reasoning infrastructure that is currently available. Note that alternative formal semantics for ontology mappings have been proposed in the literature (e.g., [4]).

2.2　Semantic Consequences of the Integration

The ontology resulting from the integration of two ontologies $\mathcal{O}_1$ and $\mathcal{O}_2$ via a set of mappings $\mathcal{M}$ may entail axioms that do not follow from $\mathcal{O}_1$, $\mathcal{O}_2$, or $\mathcal{M}$ alone. These new semantic consequences can be captured by the notion of *deductive difference* [25].

Intuitively, the deductive difference between $\mathcal{O}$ and $\mathcal{O}'$ w.r.t. a signature Σ (i.e., set of entities) is the set of entailments constructed over Σ that do not hold in $\mathcal{O}$, but do hold in $\mathcal{O}'$. The notion of deductive difference, however, has several drawbacks in practice. First, there is no algorithm for computing the deductive difference in expressive DLs [25]. Second, the number of entailments in the difference can be infinite.

Definition 1 (Approximation of the Deductive Difference). *Let A, B be atomic concepts (including $\top, \bot$), Σ be a signature, $\mathcal{O}$ and $\mathcal{O}'$ be two OWL 2 ontologies. We define the approximation of the Σ-deductive difference between $\mathcal{O}$ and $\mathcal{O}'$ (denoted $\mathrm{diff}_{\Sigma}^{\approx}(\mathcal{O}, \mathcal{O}')$ as the set of axioms of the form $A \sqsubseteq B$ satisfying: (i) $A, B \in \Sigma$, (ii) $\mathcal{O} \not\models A \sqsubseteq B$, and (iii) $\mathcal{O}' \models A \sqsubseteq B$.*

In order to avoid the drawbacks of the deductive difference, in this paper we rely on the *approximation* given in Definition 1. This approximation only requires comparing the classification hierarchies of $\mathcal{O}$ and $\mathcal{O}'$ provided by an OWL 2 reasoner, and it has successfully been used in the past in the context of ontology integration [18].

2.3　Mapping Coherence and Mapping Repair

The consistency principle requires that the vocabulary in $\mathcal{O}_{\mathcal{U}} = \mathcal{O}_1 \cup \mathcal{O}_2 \cup \mathcal{M}$ be satisfiable, assuming the union of input ontologies $\mathcal{O}_1 \cup \mathcal{O}_2$ (without the mappings $\mathcal{M}$) does not contain unsatisfiable concepts. Thus $\mathrm{diff}_{\Sigma}^{\approx}(\mathcal{O}_1 \cup \mathcal{O}_2, \mathcal{O}_{\mathcal{U}})$ should not contain any axiom of the form $A \sqsubseteq \bot$, for any $A \in \Sigma = \mathrm{Sig}(\mathcal{O}_1 \cup \mathcal{O}_2)$.

Definition 2 (Mapping Incoherence). *A set of mappings $\mathcal{M}$ is incoherent with respect to $\mathcal{O}_1$ and $\mathcal{O}_2$, if there exists a class A, in the signature of $\mathcal{O}_1 \cup \mathcal{O}_2$, such that $\mathcal{O}_1 \cup \mathcal{O}_2 \not\models A \sqsubseteq \bot$ and $\mathcal{O}_1 \cup \mathcal{O}_2 \cup \mathcal{M} \models A \sqsubseteq \bot$.*

An incoherent set of mappings $\mathcal{M}$ can be fixed by removing mappings from $\mathcal{M}$. This process is referred to as *mapping repair* (or repair for short).

Definition 3 (Mapping Repair). *Let $\mathcal{M}$ be an incoherent set of mappings w.r.t. $\mathcal{O}_1$ and $\mathcal{O}_2$. A set of mappings $\mathcal{R} \subseteq \mathcal{M}$ is a mapping repair for $\mathcal{M}$ w.r.t. $\mathcal{O}_1$ and $\mathcal{O}_2$ iff $\mathcal{M} \setminus \mathcal{R}$ is coherent w.r.t. $\mathcal{O}_1$ and $\mathcal{O}_2$.*

A trivial repair is $\mathcal{R} = \mathcal{M}$, since an empty set of mappings is trivially coherent (according to Definition 2). Nevertheless, the objective is to remove as few mappings as possible. Minimal (mapping) repairs are typically referred to in the literature as *mapping diagnoses* [29] — a term coined by Reiter [36] and introduced to the field of ontology debugging in [39]. A repair or diagnosis can be computed by extracting the justifications for the unsatisfiable concepts (*e.g.*, [38, 22, 43]), and selecting a hitting set of mappings to be removed, following a minimality criteria (*e.g.*, the number of removed mappings). However, justification-based technologies do not scale when the number of unsatisfiabilities is large (a typical scenario in mapping repair problems [16]). To address this scalability issue, mapping repair systems usually compute an *approximate repair* using incomplete reasoning techniques (*e.g.*, [17, 29, 37]). An approximate repair $\mathcal{R}^{\approx}$ does not guarantee that $\mathcal{M} \setminus \mathcal{R}^{\approx}$ is coherent, but it will (in general) significantly reduce the number of unsatisfiabilities caused by the original set of mappings $\mathcal{M}$.

2.4 Conservativity Principle

The conservativity principle (general notion) states that the integrated ontology $\mathcal{O}_{\mathcal{U}} = \mathcal{O}_1 \cup \mathcal{O}_2 \cup \mathcal{M}$ should not induce any change in the concept hierarchies of the input ontologies $\mathcal{O}_1$ and $\mathcal{O}_2$. That is, the sets $\text{diff}_{\Sigma_1}^{\approx}(\mathcal{O}_1, \mathcal{O}_{\mathcal{U}})$ and $\text{diff}_{\Sigma_2}^{\approx}(\mathcal{O}_2, \mathcal{O}_{\mathcal{U}})$ must be empty for signatures $\Sigma_1 = \text{Sig}(\mathcal{O}_1)$ and $\Sigma_2 = \text{Sig}(\mathcal{O}_2)$, respectively.

In [19] a lighter variant of the conservativity principle was proposed. This variant required that the mappings $\mathcal{M}$ alone should not introduce new subsumption relationships between concepts from one of the input ontologies. That is, the set $\text{diff}_{\Sigma}^{\approx}(\mathcal{O}_1, \mathcal{O}_1 \cup \mathcal{M})$ (resp. $\text{diff}_{\Sigma}^{\approx}(\mathcal{O}_2, \mathcal{O}_2 \cup \mathcal{M})$) must be empty for $\Sigma = \text{Sig}(\mathcal{O}_1)$ (resp. $\Sigma = \text{Sig}(\mathcal{O}_2)$).

In this paper we propose a different variant of the conservativity principle where we require that the integrated ontology $\mathcal{O}_{\mathcal{U}}$ does not introduce new subsumption relationships between concepts from one of the input ontologies, unless they were already involved in a subsumption relationship or they shared a common descendant. Note that we assume that the mappings $\mathcal{M}$ are coherent with respect to $\mathcal{O}_1$ and $\mathcal{O}_2$.

Definition 4 (Conservativity Principle Violations). *Let A, B, C be atomic concepts (not including $\top, \bot$), let $\mathcal{O}$ be one of the input ontologies, let $\text{Sig}(\mathcal{O})$ be its signature, and let $\mathcal{O}_{\mathcal{U}}$ be the integrated ontology. We define the set of conservativity principle violations of $\mathcal{O}_{\mathcal{U}}$ w.r.t. $\mathcal{O}$ (denoted $\text{consViol}(\mathcal{O}, \mathcal{O}_{\mathcal{U}})$) as the set of axioms of the form $A \sqsubseteq B$ satisfying: (i) $A, B, C \in \text{Sig}(\mathcal{O})$, (ii) $A \sqsubseteq B \in \text{diff}_{\text{Sig}(\mathcal{O})}^{\approx}(\mathcal{O}, \mathcal{O}_{\mathcal{U}})$, (iii) $\mathcal{O} \not\models B \sqsubseteq A$, and (iv) there is no C s.t. $\mathcal{O} \models C \sqsubseteq A$, and $\mathcal{O} \models C \sqsubseteq B$.*

This variant of the conservativity principle follows the *assumption of disjointness* proposed in [38]. That is, if two atomic concepts A, B from one of the input ontologies are not involved in a subsumption relationship nor share a common subconcept (excluding $\bot$) they can be considered as disjoint. Hence, the conservativity principle can be reduced to the consistency principle, if the input ontologies are extended with sufficient disjointness axioms. This reduction will allow us to reuse the available infrastructure and techniques for mapping repair.

Table 1. Fragments of the ontologies used in Optique

Ontology $\mathcal{O}_1$	Ontology $\mathcal{O}_2$
α_1 WellBore $\sqsubseteq \exists$belongsTo.Well	β_1 Exploration_well $\sqsubseteq$ Well
α_2 WellBore $\sqsubseteq \exists$hasOperator.Operator	β_2 Explor_borehole $\sqsubseteq$ Borehole
α_3 WellBore $\sqsubseteq \exists$locatedIn.Field	β_3 Appraisal_exp_borehole $\sqsubseteq$ Explor_borehole
α_4 AppraisalWellBore $\sqsubseteq$ WellBore	β_4 Appraisal_well $\sqsubseteq$ Well
α_5 ExplorationWellBore $\sqsubseteq$ WellBore	β_5 Field $\sqsubseteq \exists$hasFieldOperator.Field_operator
α_6 Operator $\sqsubseteq$ Owner	β_6 Field_operator $\sqcap$ Owner $\sqsubseteq$ Field_owner
α_7 Operator $\sqsubseteq$ Company	β_7 Company $\sqsubseteq$ Field_operator
α_8 Field $\sqsubseteq \exists$hasOperator.Company	β_8 Field_owner $\sqsubseteq$ Owner
α_9 Field $\sqsubseteq \exists$hasOwner.Owner	β_9 Borehole $\sqsubseteq$ Continuant $\sqcup$ Occurrent

Table 2. Ontology mappings for the vocabulary in $\mathcal{O}_1$ and $\mathcal{O}_2$

	Mappings $\mathcal{M}$			
id	e_1	e_2	n	ρ
m_1	$\mathcal{O}_1$:Well	$\mathcal{O}_2$:Well	0.9	$\equiv$
m_2	$\mathcal{O}_1$:WellBore	$\mathcal{O}_2$:Borehole	0.7	$\equiv$
m_3	$\mathcal{O}_1$:ExplorationWellBore	$\mathcal{O}_2$:Exploration_well	0.6	$\sqsubseteq$
m_4	$\mathcal{O}_1$:ExplorationWellBore	$\mathcal{O}_2$:Explor_borehole	0.8	$\equiv$
m_5	$\mathcal{O}_1$:AppraisalWellBore	$\mathcal{O}_2$:Appraisal_exp_borehole	0.7	$\equiv$
m_6	$\mathcal{O}_1$:Field	$\mathcal{O}_2$:Field	0.9	$\equiv$
m_7	$\mathcal{O}_1$:Operator	$\mathcal{O}_2$:Field_operator	0.7	$\sqsupseteq$
m_8	$\mathcal{O}_1$:Company	$\mathcal{O}_2$:Company	0.9	$\equiv$
m_9	$\mathcal{O}_1$:hasOperator	$\mathcal{O}_2$:hasFieldOperator	0.6	$\equiv$
m_{10}	$\mathcal{O}_1$:Owner	$\mathcal{O}_2$:Owner	0.9	$\equiv$

3   Conservativity Principle Violations in Practice

In this section, we show the problems led by the violation of the conservativity principle when integrating ontologies via mappings in a real-world scenario. To this end, we consider as motivating example a use case based on the Optique's application domain.

Table 1 shows the fragments of two ontologies in the context of the oil and gas industry. The ontology $\mathcal{O}_1$ has been directly bootstrapped from a relational database in Optique, and it is linked to the data via direct ontology-to-database mappings. The ontology $\mathcal{O}_2$, instead, is a domain ontology, based on the NPD FactPages, preferred by Optique end-users to feed the visual query formulation interface.[6]

The integration via ontology matching of $\mathcal{O}_1$ and $\mathcal{O}_2$ is required since the vocabulary in $\mathcal{O}_2$ is used to formulate queries, but only the vocabulary of $\mathcal{O}_1$ is connected to the database.[7] Consider the set of mappings $\mathcal{M}$ in Table 2 between $\mathcal{O}_1$ and $\mathcal{O}_2$ generated by an off-the-shelf ontology alignment system. As described in Section 2.1, mappings are represented as 5-tuples; for example the mapping m_2 suggests an equivalence relationship between the entities $\mathcal{O}_1$:WellBore and $\mathcal{O}_2$:Borehole, with confidence 0.7.

The integrated ontology $\mathcal{O}_{\mathcal{U}} = \mathcal{O}_1 \cup \mathcal{O}_2 \cup \mathcal{M}$, however, violates the conservativity principle, according to Definition 4, and introduces non desired subsumption relationhips (see Table 3). Note that the entailments σ_4 and σ_5 are not included in our variant of conservativity violation, since $\mathcal{O}_1$:Company and $\mathcal{O}_1$:Operator (resp. $\mathcal{O}_2$:Field_operator and $\mathcal{O}_2$:Company) are involved in a subsumption relationship in $\mathcal{O}_1$ (resp. $\mathcal{O}_2$).

---

[6] In Optique we use OWL 2 QL ontologies for query rewriting, while the query formulation may be based on much richer OWL 2 ontologies. The axioms that fall outside the OWL 2 QL profile are either approximated or not considered for the rewriting.

[7] As mentioned in Section 1, in this paper we only focus on ontology-to-ontology mappings.

Table 3. Example of conservativity principle violations

σ	Entailment:	follows from:	Violation?
σ_1	$\mathcal{O}_2$:Explor_borehole $\sqsubseteq$ $\mathcal{O}_2$:Exploration_well	m_3, m_4	YES
σ_2	$\mathcal{O}_1$:AppraisalWellBore $\sqsubseteq$ $\mathcal{O}_1$:ExplorationWellBore	β_3, m_4, m_5	YES
σ_3	$\mathcal{O}_2$:Field_operator $\sqsubseteq$ $\mathcal{O}_2$:Field_owner	$\alpha_6, \beta_6, m_7, m_{10}$	YES
σ_4	$\mathcal{O}_1$:Company $\equiv$ $\mathcal{O}_1$:Operator	$\alpha_7, \beta_7, m_7, m_8$	NO (*)
σ_5	$\mathcal{O}_2$:Field_operator $\equiv$ $\mathcal{O}_2$:Company		
σ_6	$\mathcal{O}_1$:Company $\sqsubseteq$ $\mathcal{O}_1$:Owner	σ_4, α_6	YES
σ_7	$\mathcal{O}_2$:Company $\sqsubseteq$ $\mathcal{O}_2$:Field_owner	σ_3, σ_5	YES

However, these entailments lead to other violations included in our variant (σ_6 and σ_7), and may also be considered as violations. These conservativity principle violations may hinder the usefulness of the generated ontology mappings since may affect the quality of the results when performing OBDA queries over the vocabulary of $\mathcal{O}_2$.

Example 1. Consider the following conjunctive query $CQ(x) \leftarrow \mathcal{O}_2$:Well(x). The query asks for wells and has been formulated from the Optique's query formulation interface, using the vocabulary of $\mathcal{O}_2$. The query is rewritten, according to the ontology axioms and mappings $\beta_1, \beta_4, m_1, m_3, m_4$ in $\mathcal{O}_\mathcal{U} = \mathcal{O}_1 \cup \mathcal{O}_2 \cup \mathcal{M}$, into the following union of conjunctive queries $UCQ(x) \leftarrow \mathcal{O}_2$:Well(x)$\cup\mathcal{O}_1$:Well(x)$\cup\mathcal{O}_2$:Exploration_well(x)$\cup$ $\mathcal{O}_2$:Appraisal_well(x)$\cup\mathcal{O}_1$:ExplorationWellBore(x)$\cup\mathcal{O}_2$:Explor_borehole(x). Since only the vocabulary of $\mathcal{O}_1$ is linked to the data, the union of conjunctive queries could be simplified as $UCQ(x) \leftarrow$ Well(x) $\cup$ ExplorationWellBore(x), which will clearly lead to non desired results. The original query was only asking for wells, while the rewritten query will also return data about exploration wellbores.

We have shown that the quality of the mappings in terms of conservativity principle violations will directly affect the quality of the query results. Therefore, the detection and repair of these violations arise as an important quality assessment step in Optique.

4   Methods

We have reduced the problem of detecting and solving conservativity principle violations, following our notion of conservativity (see Section 2), to a mapping (incoherence) repair problem. Currently, our method relies on the indexing and reasoning techniques implemented in *LogMap*, an ontology matching and mapping repair system [17, 20, 21].

Algorithm 1 shows the pseudocode of the implemented method. The algorithm accepts as input two OWL 2 ontologies, $\mathcal{O}_1$ and $\mathcal{O}_2$, and a set of mappings $\mathcal{M}$ which are coherent[8] with respect to $\mathcal{O}_1$ and $\mathcal{O}_2$. Additionally, an optimised variant to add disjointness axioms can be selected. The algorithm outputs the number of added disjointness during the process $disj$, a set of mappings $\mathcal{M}'$, and an (approximate) repair $\mathcal{R}^\approx$ such that $\mathcal{M}' = \mathcal{M} \setminus \mathcal{R}^\approx$. The (approximate) repair $\mathcal{R}^\approx$ aims at solving most of the conservativity principle violations of $\mathcal{M}$ with respect to $\mathcal{O}_1$ and $\mathcal{O}_2$. We next describe the techniques used in each step.

Module Extraction. In order to reduce the size of the problem our method extracts two locality-based modules [7], one for each input ontology, using the entities involved

---

[8] Note that $\mathcal{M}$ may be the result of a prior mapping (incoherence) repair process.

Algorithm 1. Algorithm to detect and solve conservativity principle violations

Input: $\mathcal{O}_1, \mathcal{O}_2$: input ontologies; $\mathcal{M}$: (coherent) input mappings; $Optimization$: Boolean value
Output: $\mathcal{M}'$: output mappings; $\mathcal{R}^\approx$: approximate repair; $disj$: number of disjointness rules

1: $\langle \mathcal{O}_1', \mathcal{O}_2' \rangle$:= ModuleExtractor$(\mathcal{O}_1, \mathcal{O}_2, \mathcal{M})$
2: $\langle \mathcal{P}_1, \mathcal{P}_2 \rangle$:= PropositionalEncoding$(\mathcal{O}_1', \mathcal{O}_2')$
3: SI_1 := StructuralIndex$(\mathcal{O}_1')$
4: SI_2 := StructuralIndex$(\mathcal{O}_2')$
5: **if** $(Optimization = \text{true})$ **then**
6:      $SI_\mathcal{U}$:= StructuralIndex$(\mathcal{O}_1' \cup \mathcal{O}_2' \cup \mathcal{M})$
7:      $\langle \mathcal{P}_1^d, disj_1 \rangle$:= DisjointAxiomsExtensionOptimized$(\mathcal{P}_1, SI_1, SI_\mathcal{U})$ ▷ See Algorithm 3
8:      $\langle \mathcal{P}_2^d, disj_2 \rangle$:= DisjointAxiomsExtensionOptimized$(\mathcal{P}_2, SI_2, SI_\mathcal{U})$
9: **else**
10:     $\langle \mathcal{P}_1^d, disj_1 \rangle$:= DisjointAxiomsExtensionBasic$(\mathcal{P}_1, SI_1)$ ▷ See Algorithm 2
11:     $\langle \mathcal{P}_2^d, disj_2 \rangle$:= DisjointAxiomsExtensionBasic$(\mathcal{P}_2, SI_2)$
12: **end if**
13: $\langle \mathcal{M}', \mathcal{R}^\approx \rangle$:= MappingRepair$(\mathcal{P}_1^d, \mathcal{P}_2^d, \mathcal{M})$ ▷ See Algorithm 2 in [21]
14: $disj := disj_1 + disj_2$
15: **return** $\langle \mathcal{M}', \mathcal{R}^\approx, disj \rangle$

in the mappings $\mathcal{M}$ as seed signatures for the module extractor (step 1 in Algorithm 1). These modules preserve the semantics for the given entities, can be efficiently computed, and are typically much smaller than the original ontologies.

Propositional Horn Encoding. The modules $\mathcal{O}_1'$ and $\mathcal{O}_2'$ are encoded as the Horn propositional theories, $\mathcal{P}_1$ and $\mathcal{P}_2$ (step 2 in Algorithm 1). This encoding includes rules of the form $A_1 \wedge \ldots \wedge A_n \rightarrow B$. For example, the concept hierarchy provided by an OWL 2 reasoner (*e.g.*, [32, 23]) will be encoded as $A \rightarrow B$ rules, while the explicit disjointness relationships between concepts will be represented as $A_i \wedge A_j \rightarrow$ false. Note that the input mappings $\mathcal{M}$ can already be seen as propositional implications. This encoding is key to the mapping repair process.

Example 2. Consider the ontologies and mappings in Tables 1 and 2. The axiom β_6 is encoded as Field_operator∧Owner $\rightarrow$ Field_owner, while the mapping m_2 is translated into rules $\mathcal{O}_1$:WellBore $\rightarrow$ $\mathcal{O}_2$:Borehole, and $\mathcal{O}_2$:Borehole $\rightarrow$ $\mathcal{O}_1$:WellBore.

Structural Index. The concept hierarchies provided by an OWL 2 reasoner (excluding $\bot$) and the explicit disjointness axioms of the modules $\mathcal{O}_1'$ and $\mathcal{O}_2'$ are efficiently indexed using an interval labelling schema [1] (steps 3 and 4 in Algorithm 1). This structural index exploits an optimised data structure for storing directed acyclic graphs (DAGs), and allows us to answer many entailment queries over the concept hierarchy as an index lookup operation, and hence without the need of an OWL 2 reasoner. This kind of index has shown to significantly reduce the cost of answering taxonomic queries [5, 33] and disjointness relationships queries [17, 20].

Disjointness Axioms Extension. In order to reduce the conservativity problem to a mapping incoherence repair problem following the notion of *assumption of disjointness*, we need to automatically add sufficient disjointness axioms into each module $\mathcal{O}_i'$. However, the insertion of additional disjointness axioms δ may lead to unsatisfiable classes in $\mathcal{O}_i' \cup \delta$.

Example 3. Consider the axiom β_9 from Table 1. Following the *assumption of disjointness* a very naïve algorithm would add disjointness axioms between Borehole, Continuant and Occurrent, which would make Borehole unsatisfiable.

Algorithm 2. Basic disjointness axioms extension

Input: $\mathcal{P}$: propositional theory; SI: structural index
Output: $\mathcal{P}^d$: extended propositional theory; $disj$: number of disjointness rules
1: $disj := 0$
2: $\mathcal{P}^d := \mathcal{P}$
3: **for each** pair $\langle A, B \rangle \in$ OrderedVariablePairs($\mathcal{P}$) **do**
4:     **if not** (areDisj(SI, A, B) **or** inSubSupRel(SI, A, B) **or** shareDesc(SI, A, B)) **then**
5:         $\mathcal{P}^d := \mathcal{P}^d \cup \{A \wedge B \rightarrow false\}$
6:         $SI :=$ updateIndex($SI, A \sqcap B \rightarrow \bot$)
7:         $disj := disj + 1$
8:     **end if**
9: **end for**
10: **return** $\langle \mathcal{P}^d, disj \rangle$

In order to detect if each candidate disjointness axiom leads to an unsatisfiability, a non naïve algorithm requires to make an extensive use of an OWL 2 reasoner. In large ontologies, however, such extensive use of the reasoner may be prohibitive. Our method, in order to address this issue, exploits the propositional encoding and structural index of the input ontologies. Thus, checking if $\mathcal{O}'_i \cup \delta$ contains unsatisfiable classes is restricted to the Horn propositional case.

We have implemented two algorithms to extend the propositional theories $\mathcal{P}_1$ and $\mathcal{P}_2$ with disjointness rules of the form $A \wedge B \rightarrow \bot$ (see steps 5-12 in Algorithm 1). These algorithms guarantee that, for every propositional variable A in the extended propositional theory $\mathcal{P}_i^d$ (with $i \in \{1, 2\}$), the theory $\mathcal{P}_i^d \cup \{true \rightarrow A\}$ is satisfiable. Note that this does not necessarily hold if the disjointness axioms are added to the OWL 2 ontology modules, $\mathcal{O}'_1$ and $\mathcal{O}'_2$, as discussed above.

Algorithm 2 presents a (basic) algorithm to add as many disjointness rules as possible, for every pair of propositional variables A, B in the propositional theory $\mathcal{P}$ given as input. In order to minimize the number of necessary disjointness rules, the variables in $\mathcal{P}$ are ordered in pairs following a top-down approach. The algorithm exploits the structural index SI to check if two propositional variables (*i.e.*, classes in the input ontologies) are disjoint (areDisj(SI, A, B)), they keep a sub/super-class relationship (inSubSupRel(SI, A, B)), or they share a common descendant (shareDesc(SI, A, B)) (step 4 in Algorithm 2). Note that the structural index is also updated to take into account the new disjointness rules (step 6 in Algorithm 2).

The addition of disjointness rules in Algorithm 2, however, may be prohibitive for large ontologies (see Section 5). Intuitively, in order to reduce the number of disjointness axioms, one should only focus on the cases where a conservativity principle violation occurs in the integrated ontology $\mathcal{O}_\mathcal{U} = \mathcal{O}'_1 \cup \mathcal{O}'_2 \cup \mathcal{M}$, with respect to one of the ontology modules $\mathcal{O}'_i$ (with $i \in \{1, 2\}$); *i.e.*, adding a disjointness axiom between each pair of classes $A, B \in \mathcal{O}'_i$ such that $A \sqsubseteq B \in$ consViol($\mathcal{O}'_i, \mathcal{O}_\mathcal{U}$), as in Definition 4. Algorithm 3 implements this idea for the Horn propositional case and extensively exploits the structural indexing to identify the conservativity principle violations (step 3 in Algorithm 3). Note that this algorithm also requires to compute the structural index of the integrated ontology, and thus its classification with an OWL 2 reasoner (step 6 in Algorithm 1). The classification of the integrated ontology is known to be typically much higher than the classification of the input ontologies individually [16]. However, this was not a bottleneck in our experiments, as shown in Section 5.

Algorithm 3. Optimised disjointness axioms extension

Input: $\mathcal{P}$: propositional theory; SI: structural index $SI_{\mathcal{U}}$: structural index of the union ontology
Output: $\mathcal{P}^d$: extended propositional theory; $disj$: number of disjointness rules

1: $disj := 0$
2: $\mathcal{P}^d := \mathcal{P}$
3: **for** $A \rightarrow B \in$ ConservativityViolations$(SI, SI_{\mathcal{U}})$ **do**
4:     **if not** (areDisj(SI, A, B)) **then**
5:         $\mathcal{P}^d := \mathcal{P}^d \cup \{A \wedge B \rightarrow false\}$
6:         $SI :=$ updateIndex$(SI, A \sqcap B \rightarrow \perp)$
7:         $disj := disj + 1$
8:     **end if**
9: **end for**
10: **return** $\langle \mathcal{P}^d, disj \rangle$

Mapping Repair. The step 13 of Algorithm 1 uses the mapping (incoherence) repair algorithm presented in [17, 21] for the extended Horn propositional theories $\mathcal{P}_1^d$ and $\mathcal{P}_2^d$, and the input mappings $\mathcal{M}$. The mapping repair process exploits the Dowling-Gallier algorithm for propositional Horn satisfiability [9] and checks, for every propositional variable $A \in \mathcal{P}_1^d \cup \mathcal{P}_2^d$, the satisfiability of the propositional theory $\mathcal{P}_A = \mathcal{P}_1^d \cup \mathcal{P}_2^d \cup \mathcal{M} \cup \{true \rightarrow A\}$. Satisfiability of $\mathcal{P}_A$ is checked in worst-case linear time in the size of $\mathcal{P}_A$, and the number of Dowling-Gallier calls is also linear in the number of propositional variables in $\mathcal{P}_1^d \cup \mathcal{P}_2^d$. In case of unsatisfiability, the algorithm also allows us to record *conflicting* mappings involved in the unsatisfiability, which will be considered for the subsequent repair process. The unsatisfiability will be fixed by removing some of the identified mappings. In case of multiple options, the mapping confidence will be used as a differentiating factor.[9]

Example 4. Consider the propositional encoding $\mathcal{P}_1$ and $\mathcal{P}_2$ of the axioms of Table 1 and the mappings $\mathcal{M}$ in Table 2, seen as propositional rules. $\mathcal{P}_1^d$ and $\mathcal{P}_2^d$ have been created by adding disjointness rules to $\mathcal{P}_1$ and $\mathcal{P}_2$, according to Algorithm 2 or 3. For example, $\mathcal{P}_2^d$ includes the rule $\psi = \mathcal{O}_2$:Well $\wedge$ $\mathcal{O}_2$:Borehole $\rightarrow$ $false$. The mapping repair algorithm identifies the propositional theory $\mathcal{P}_1^d \cup \mathcal{P}_2^d \cup \mathcal{M} \cup \{true \rightarrow \mathcal{O}_1$:ExplorationWellbore$\}$ as unsatisfiable. This is due to the combination of the mappings m_3 and m_4, the propositional projection of axioms β_1 and β_2, and the rule ψ. The mapping repair algorithm also identifies m_3 and m_4 as the cause of the unsatisfiability, and discards m_3, since its confidence is smaller than that of m_4 (see Table 2).

Algorithm 1 gives as output the number of added disjointness rules during the process $disj$, a set of mappings $\mathcal{M}'$, and an (approximate) repair $\mathcal{R}^{\approx}$ such that $\mathcal{M}' = \mathcal{M} \setminus \mathcal{R}^{\approx}$. $\mathcal{M}'$ is coherent with respect to $\mathcal{P}_1^d$ and $\mathcal{P}_2^d$ (according to the propositional case of Definition 2). Furthermore, the propositional theory $\mathcal{P}_1 \cup \mathcal{P}_2 \cup \mathcal{M}'$ does not contain any conservativity principle violation with respect to $\mathcal{P}_1$ and $\mathcal{P}_2$ (according to the propositional case of Definition 4). However, our encoding is incomplete, and we cannot guarantee that $\mathcal{O}_1' \cup \mathcal{O}_2' \cup \mathcal{M}'$ does not contain conservativity principle violations with respect to $\mathcal{O}_1'$ and $\mathcal{O}_2'$. Nonetheless, our evaluation suggests that the number of remaining violations after repair is typically small (see Section 5).

---

[9] In scenarios where the confidence of the mapping is missing (*e.g.*, in reference or manually created mapping sets) or unreliable, our mapping repair technique computes fresh confidence values based on the locality principle [19].

Algorithm 4. Conducted evaluation over the Optique and OAEI data sets

Input: $\mathcal{O}_1, \mathcal{O}_2$: input ontologies $\mathcal{M}$: reference mappings for $\mathcal{O}_1$ and $\mathcal{O}_2$

1: $\mathcal{O}_\mathcal{U} := \mathcal{O}_1 \cup \mathcal{O}_2 \cup \mathcal{M}$
2: Store size of $\text{Sig}(\mathcal{O}_1)$ **(I)**, $\text{Sig}(\mathcal{O}_2)$ **(II)** and $\mathcal{M}$ **(III)**
3: Compute number of conservativity principle violations (our variant as in Definition 4): $\text{consViol} := |\text{consViol}(\mathcal{O}_1, \mathcal{O}_\mathcal{U})| + |\text{consViol}(\mathcal{O}_2, \mathcal{O}_\mathcal{U})|$ **(IV)**
4: Compute number of conservativity principle violations (general notion as in Section 2.4): $\text{diff}^{\approx} := |\text{diff}^{\approx}_{\text{Sig}(\mathcal{O}_1)}(\mathcal{O}_1, \mathcal{O}_\mathcal{U})| + |\text{diff}^{\approx}_{\text{Sig}(\mathcal{O}_2)}(\mathcal{O}_2, \mathcal{O}_\mathcal{U})|$ **(V)**
5: Compute two repairs $\mathcal{R}^{\approx}$ using Algorithm 1 for $\mathcal{O}_1, \mathcal{O}_2, \mathcal{M}$, with the *Optimization* set to false (see Table 5) and true (see Table 6)
6: Store number of added disjointness $disj$ **(VI and XII)**, size of repair $|\mathcal{R}^{\approx}|$ **(VII and XIII)**, time to compute disjointness rules t_d **(VIII and XIV)**, and time to compute the mapping repair t_r **(IX and XV)**
7: $\mathcal{O}_\mathcal{U} := \mathcal{O}_1 \cup \mathcal{O}_2 \cup \mathcal{M} \setminus \mathcal{R}^{\approx}$
8: Compute number of remaining conservativity principle violations (our variant): $\text{consViol} := |\text{consViol}(\mathcal{O}_1, \mathcal{O}_\mathcal{U})| + |\text{consViol}(\mathcal{O}_2, \mathcal{O}_\mathcal{U})|$ **(X and XVI)**
9: Compute number of remaining conservativity principle violations (general notion): $\text{diff}^{\approx} := |\text{diff}^{\approx}_{\text{Sig}(\mathcal{O}_1)}(\mathcal{O}_1, \mathcal{O}_\mathcal{U})| + |\text{diff}^{\approx}_{\text{Sig}(\mathcal{O}_2)}(\mathcal{O}_2, \mathcal{O}_\mathcal{U})|$ **(XI and XVII)**

---

5 Evaluation

In this section we evaluate the feasibility of using our method to detect and correct conservativity principle violations in practice. To this end we have conducted the evaluation in Algorithm 4 (the Roman numbers refer to stored measurements) over the Optique's use case and the ontologies and reference mapping sets of the OAEI 2013 campaign:[10]

  i *Optique*'s use case is based on the NPD ontology and a bootstrapped ontology (BootsOnto) from one of the Optique databases. The mappings between these ontologies were semi-automatically created using the ontology matcher *LogMap* [20]. Although the NPD ontology is small with respect to the size of the bootstrapped ontology, its vocabulary covers a large portion of the current query catalog in Optique.
 ii *LargeBio*: this dataset includes the biomedical ontologies FMA, NCI and (a fragment of) SNOMED, and reference mappings based on the UMLS [3].
iii *Anatomy*: the Anatomy dataset involves the Adult Mouse Anatomy (MO) ontology and a fragment of the NCI ontology (NCI$_{\text{Anat}}$), describing human anatomy. The reference alignment has been manually curated [48].
 iv *Library*: this OAEI dataset includes the real-word thesauri STW and TheSoz from the social sciences. The reference mappings have been manually validated.
  v *Conference*: this dataset uses a collection of 16 ontologies from the domain of academic conferences [46]. Currently, there are 21 manually created mapping sets among 7 of the ontologies.

Table 4 shows the size of the evaluated ontologies and mappings (**I, II** and **III**). For the Conference dataset we have selected only 5 pair of ontologies for which the reference mappings lead to more than five conservativity principle violations. Note that we count equivalence mappings as two subsumption mappings, and hence $\mathcal{M}$ represents subsumption mappings. Table 4 also shows the conservativity principle violations for

---

[10] Note that the reference mappings of the OAEI 2013 campaign are coherent with respect to the test case ontologies [13]. More information about the used ontology versions can be found in http://oaei.ontologymatching.org/2013/

Table 4. Test cases and violations with original reference mappings. BootsOnto contains around 3,000 concepts, and a large number of properties.

Dataset	$\mathcal{O}_1 \sim \mathcal{O}_2$	Problem size			Original Violations	
		I	II	III	IV	V
		$|\text{Sig}(\mathcal{O}_1)|$	$|\text{Sig}(\mathcal{O}_2)|$	$|\mathcal{M}|$	consViol	diff$^{\approx}$
Optique	NPD~BootsOnto	757	40,671	102	214	220
LargeBio	SNOMED~NCI	122,519	66,914	36,405	>525,515	>546,181
	FMA~SNOMED	79,042	122,519	17,212	125,232	127,668
	FMA~NCI	79,042	66,914	5,821	19,740	19,799
Anatomy	MO~NCI$_{\text{Anat}}$	2,747	3,306	3,032	1,321	1,335
Library	STW~TheSoz	6,575	8,376	6,322	42,045	42,872
Conference	cmt~confof	89	75	32	11	11
	conference~edas	124	154	34	8	8
	conference~iasted	124	182	28	9	9
	confof~ekaw	75	107	40	6	6
	edas~iasted	154	182	38	7	7

Table 5. Results of our basic method to detect and solve conservativity principle violations

Dataset	$\mathcal{O}_1 \sim \mathcal{O}_2$	Solution size		Times		Remaining Violations	
		VI	VII	VIII	IX	X	XI
		#disj	$|\mathcal{R}^{\approx}|$	$t_d(s)$	$t_r(s)$	consViol	diff$^{\approx}$
Optique	NPD~BootsOnto	4,716,685	49	9,840	121	0	0
LargeBio	SNOMED~NCI	–	–	–	–	–	–
	FMA~SNOMED	1,106,259	8,234	35,817	1,127	0	121
	FMA~NCI	347,801	2,176	2,471	38	103	112
Anatomy	MO~NCI$_{\text{Anat}}$	1,331,374	461	397	56	0	3
Library	STW~TheSoz	591,115	2,969	4,126	416	0	24
Conference	cmt~confof	50	6	0.01	0.01	0	0
	conference~edas	774	6	0.03	0.01	0	0
	conference~iasted	2,189	4	0.06	0.02	0	0
	confof~ekaw	296	6	0.02	0.01	0	0
	edas~iasted	1,210	4	0.06	0.02	1	1

the reference mappings (**IV** and **V**). For LargeBio and Library the number is expecially large using both our variant and the general notion of the conservativity principle.[11]

Tables 5 and 6 show the obtained results for our method using both the basic and optimised algorithms to add disjointness axioms.[12]

We have run the experiments on a desktop computer with an *AMD Fusion A6-3670K* CPU and allocating 12 GB of RAM. The obtained results are summarized as follows:

i The number of added disjointness rules $disj$ (**VI**), as expected, is very large in the basic algorithm and the required time prohibitive (**VIII**) when involving SNOMED (it did not finish for SNOMED-NCI). This is clearly solved in our optimised algorithm that considerably reduces the number of necessary disjoitness rules (**XII**) and it requires only 275 seconds to compute them in the SNOMED-NCI case (**XIV**).

---

[11] In the SNOMED-NCI case no OWL 2 reasoner could succeed in classifying the integrated ontology via mappings [16], so we used the OWL 2 EL reasoner ELK [23] for providing a lower bound on the number of conservativity principle violations.

[12] The computation times of Steps 1-4 in Algorithm 1 were negligible with respect to the repair and disjointness addition times (t_r and t_d) and thus they were not included in the result tables.

Table 6. Results of our optimised method to detect and solve conservativity principle violations

Dataset	$O_1 \sim O_2$	Solution size		Times		Remaining Violations	
		XII	XIII	XIV	XV	XVI	XVII
		#disj	$|\mathcal{R}^\approx|$	t_d(s)	t_r(s)	consViol	diff$^\approx$
Optique	NPD~BootsOnto	214	41	2.54	0.17	0	0
LargeBio	SNOMED~NCI	525,515	15,957	275	3,755	>411	>1,624
	FMA~SNOMED	125,232	8,342	30	251	0	131
	FMA~NCI	19,740	2,175	34	6.18	103	112
Anatomy	MO~NCI$_{Anat}$	1,321	491	1.39	0.53	0	3
Library	STW~TheSoz	42,045	3,058	4.93	41	0	40
Conference	cmt~confof	11	6	0.05	0.01	0	0
	conference~edas	8	6	0.07	0.01	0	0
	conference~iasted	9	1	0.22	0.01	0	0
	confof~ekaw	6	5	0.04	0.01	0	0
	edas~iasted	7	4	0.21	0.02	1	1

ii The computed repairs $\mathcal{R}^\approx$ (**VII** and **XIII**) using both the basic and optimised algorithms are of comparable size. This suggests that the large number of added disjointness in the basic algorithm does not have a negative impact (in terms of aggressiveness) on the repair process.

iii Repair times t_r (**IX** and **XV**) are small and they do not represent a bottleneck in spite of the large number of added disjointness rules.

iv The conservativity principle violations using both algorithms and considering our variant (**X** and **XVI**) are completely removed in the Optique, Anatomy and Library cases, and almost completely removed in the Conference and LargeBio datasets.

v The number of missed violations is only slightly higher when considering the general notion of the conservativity principle (**XI** and **XVII**), which suggests that our (approximate) variant is also suitable in practice. Furthermore, in several test cases these violations are also almost removed.

vi The computed repairs $\mathcal{R}^\approx$, using both algorithms (**VII** and **XIII**), are rather aggressive and they can remove from 16% (Anatomy) up to 48% (Optique) of the mappings. In the Optique's use case, however, we follow a *better safe than sorry* approach and we prefer to remove as many violations as possible, rather than preserving potentially conflicting mapping sets.

In summary, the results suggest that our method to repair conservativity principle violations is suitable for Optique, and it is feasible in practice, even when considering the largest datasets of the OAEI.

6   Related Work

The conservativity principle problem, although indirectly, has been actively studied in the literature. For example, the assumption of disjointness was originally introduced by Schlobach [38] to enhance the repair of ontologies that were underspecified in terms of disjointness axioms. In [30], a similar assumption is followed in the context of repairing ontology mappings, where the authors restricted the number of disjointness axioms by using learning techniques [45]. These techniques, however, typically require a manually created training set. In [12] the authors present an interactive system to guide the expert user in the manual enrichment of the ontologies with disjointness axioms. In this paper, as in [45, 30, 12], we have also focused on the addition of a small set of disjointness axioms, since adding all possible disjointness may be unfeasible for large ontologies. However, our method does not require manual intervention. Furthermore, to address the scalability problem when dealing with large ontologies and mapping sets, our method relies on the propositional projection of the input ontologies.

Ontology matching systems have also dealt with the conservativity principle in order to improve the precision (with respect to a reference mapping set) of the computed mappings. For example, systems such as *ASMOV* [15], *Lily* [47] and *YAM++* [34] have implemented different heuristics and patterns to avoid violations of the conservativity principle. Another relevant approach has been presented in [2], where a set of sanity checks and best practices are proposed for computing ontology mappings. In this paper we present an elegant way to detect and solve conservativity principle violations by reducing the problem to a consistency principle violation problem. Concretely, we have reused and adapted the infrastructure provided by *LogMap* [17, 20]. However, other mapping repair systems, such as *Alcomo* [29] or *AML* [37], could be considered. Note that, to the best of our knowledge, these mapping repair systems have only focused on solving violations of the consistency principle.

The work presented in [26, 14, 27] deserves a special attention since they propose an opposite approach with respect to ours. Authors consider the violations of the conservativity principle as false positives, based on the potential incompleteness of the input ontologies. Hence, the correction strategy does not aim at removing mappings but at inserting subsumption axioms to the input ontologies to enrich their concept hierarchies. Authors in [35] also suggest that removing mapping may not be the best solution in a mapping repair process, and fixing the input ontologies may be an alternative.

Currently, in the Optique use case, we consider that the input ontologies are not modifiable. The query formulation ontology is based on the NPD ontology, which includes knowledge already agreed by the community, while the bootstrapped ontology is *directly* linked to the information represented in the database. Nevertheless, future extensions in Optique may consider appropriate the extension of the input ontologies.

7 Conclusions and Future Work

In this paper we have presented an approximate and fully-automatic method to detect and correct conservativity principle violations in practice. We have characterised the conservativity principle problem, following the assumption of disjointness, as a consistency principle problem. We have also presented an elegant and scalable way to detect and repair violations in the Horn propositional case. Thus, our method is incomplete and it may fail to detect and repair all violations. However, the conducted evaluation suggests that our method produces competitive results in practice. In the close future we plan to consider extensions of the current projection to Horn propositional logic while keeping the nice scalability properties of the current method.

The implemented method follows a "better safe than sorry" approach, which we currently consider suitable for the Optique project since we do not want ontology-to-ontology mappings to lead to unexpected results for the OBDA queries, as motivated in Section 3. Hence, we currently delegate complex relationhips between ontology entities and the database to the (hand-crafted) schema-to-ontology mappings, which will also play an important role in Optique. Nevertheless we do not discard in the future to explore alternative methods to detect and repair conservative principle violations. In particular, we plan to study the potential application of approaches based on graph-theory, in order to extend the detection and repair of conservativity principle violations. Strongly connected compontents of a graph representation of the subsumption relation between named concepts (as defined in [29]), for instance, may be used to capture violations between pairs of concepts already involved in a subsumption relationship.

Additionally, we will also consider exploring the use of learning techniques for the addition of disjointness axioms [45], and to involve the domain experts in the assessment/addition of such disjointness [18, 12]. This manual assessment may also be used to consider violations as false positives, as proposed in [26, 14, 27], and suggest them as candidate extensions of the input ontologies.

We consider that the proposed method has also potential in scenarios others than Optique. For instance, the authors in [28] apply ontology matching in a multi-agent system scenario in order to allow the exchange and extension of ontology-based *action plans* among agents. In such a context, violations of the conservativity principle should be taken into account and highly critical tasks should not be performed if violations are detected. In [44], authors present an ontology-based data integration (OBDI) system, which integrates ontology mapping and query reformulation techniques. As in Optique, mappings violating the conservativity principle may compromise the quality of the query results in the proposed OBDI system.

Finally, we have short-term plans for deployment in the Optique industry partners Statoil and Siemens. The techniques described in this paper have already been integrated within the "ontology and mapping management module" (see [24] for details about the Optique architecture).

Acknowledgements. This work was supported by the EU FP7 IP project Optique (no. 318338), the MIUR project CINA (Compositionality, Interaction, Negotiation, Autonomicity for the future ICT society) and the EPSRC project Score!. We also thank the unvaluable help provided by Bernardo Cuenca and Ian Horrocks. Finally, we are also very grateful for the support of the Optique colleagues that facilitated our understanding of the domain, especially: Dag Hovland, Evgeny Kharlamov, Dmitry Zheleznyakov and Martin G. Skjæveland.

References

1. Agrawal, R., Borgida, A., Jagadish, H.V.: Efficient Management of Transitive Relationships in Large Data and Knowledge Bases. In: ACM SIGMOD Conf. on Manag. of Data (1989)
2. Beisswanger, E., Hahn, U., et al.: Towards valid and reusable reference alignmentsten basic quality checks for ontology alignments and their application to three different reference data sets. J. Biomed. Semant. 3(suppl. 1), S4 (2012)
3. Bodenreider, O.: The Unified Medical Language System (UMLS): integrating biomedical terminology. Nucleic Acids Research 32, 267–270 (2004)
4. Borgida, A., Serafini, L.: Distributed Description Logics: Assimilating Information from Peer Sources. J. Data Sem. 1, 153–184 (2003)
5. Christophides, V., Plexousakis, D., Scholl, M., Tourtounis, S.: On Labeling Schemes for the Semantic Web. In: Int'l World Wide Web Conf. (WWW), pp. 544–555 (2003)

6. Cuenca Grau, B., Horrocks, I., Motik, B., Parsia, B., Patel-Schneider, P.F., Sattler, U.: OWL 2: The next step for OWL. J. Web Sem. 6(4), 309–322 (2008)
7. Cuenca Grau, B., Horrocks, I., Kazakov, Y., Sattler, U.: Modular Reuse of Ontologies: Theory and Practice. J. Artif. Intell. Res. 31, 273–318 (2008)
8. David, J., Euzenat, J., Scharffe, F., Trojahn, C.: The Alignment API 4.0. J. Sem. Web 2(1), 3–10 (2011)
9. Dowling, W.F., Gallier, J.H.: Linear-Time Algorithms for Testing the Satisfiability of Propositional Horn Formulae. J. Log. Prog. 1(3), 267–284 (1984)
10. Euzenat, J.: Semantic Precision and Recall for Ontology Alignment Evaluation. In: Int'l Joint Conf. on Artif. Intell (IJCAI), pp. 348–353 (2007)
11. Euzenat, J., Meilicke, C., Stuckenschmidt, H., Shvaiko, P., Trojahn, C.: Ontology Alignment Evaluation Initiative: Six Years of Experience. J. Data Sem. 15, 158–192 (2011)
12. Ferré, S., Rudolph, S.: Advocatus Diaboli - Exploratory Enrichment of Ontologies with Negative Constraints. In: ten Teije, A., Völker, J., Handschuh, S., Stuckenschmidt, H., d'Acquin, M., Nikolov, A., Aussenac-Gilles, N., Hernandez, N. (eds.) EKAW 2012. LNCS (LNAI), vol. 7603, pp. 42–56. Springer, Heidelberg (2012)
13. Grau, B.C., Dragisic, Z., Eckert, K., et al.: Results of the Ontology Alignment Evaluation Initiative 2013. In: Ontology Matching (OM) (2013)
14. Ivanova, V., Lambrix, P.: A Unified Approach for Aligning Taxonomies and Debugging Taxonomies and their Alignments. In: Cimiano, P., Corcho, O., Presutti, V., Hollink, L., Rudolph, S. (eds.) ESWC 2013. LNCS, vol. 7882, pp. 1–15. Springer, Heidelberg (2013)
15. Jean-Mary, Y.R., Shironoshita, E.P., Kabuka, M.R.: Ontology Matching With Semantic Verification. J. Web Sem. 7(3), 235–251 (2009)
16. Jiménez-Ruiz, E., Cuenca Grau, B., Horrocks, I.: On the feasibility of using OWL 2 DL reasoners for ontology matching problems. In: OWL Reasoner Evaluation Workshop (2012)
17. Jiménez-Ruiz, E., Cuenca Grau, B.: LogMap: Logic-based and Scalable Ontology Matching. In: Aroyo, L., Welty, C., Alani, H., Taylor, J., Bernstein, A., Kagal, L., Noy, N., Blomqvist, E. (eds.) ISWC 2011, Part I. LNCS, vol. 7031, pp. 273–288. Springer, Heidelberg (2011)
18. Jiménez-Ruiz, E., Cuenca Grau, B., Horrocks, I., Berlanga, R.: Ontology integration using mappings: Towards getting the right logical consequences. In: Aroyo, L., et al. (eds.) ESWC 2009. LNCS, vol. 5554, pp. 173–187. Springer, Heidelberg (2009)
19. Jiménez-Ruiz, E., Cuenca Grau, B., Horrocks, I., Berlanga, R.: Logic-based Assessment of the Compatibility of UMLS Ontology Sources. J. Biomed. Semant. 2(suppl. 1), S2 (2011)
20. Jiménez-Ruiz, E., Cuenca Grau, B., Zhou, Y., Horrocks, I.: Large-scale Interactive Ontology Matching: Algorithms and Implementation. In: Eur. Conf. on Artif. Intell. (ECAI) (2012)
21. Jiménez-Ruiz, E., Meilicke, C., Grau, B.C., Horrocks, I.: Evaluating Mapping Repair Systems with Large Biomedical Ontologies. In: Description Logics, pp. 246–257 (2013)
22. Kalyanpur, A., Parsia, B., Horridge, M., Sirin, E.: Finding all justifications of OWL DL entailments. In: Aberer, K., et al. (eds.) ISWC/ASWC 2007. LNCS, vol. 4825, pp. 267–280. Springer, Heidelberg (2007)
23. Kazakov, Y., Krötzsch, M., Simančík, F.: Concurrent Classification of EL Ontologies. In: Aroyo, L., Welty, C., Alani, H., Taylor, J., Bernstein, A., Kagal, L., Noy, N., Blomqvist, E. (eds.) ISWC 2011, Part I. LNCS, vol. 7031, pp. 305–320. Springer, Heidelberg (2011)
24. Kharlamov, E., et al.: Optique: Towards OBDA Systems for Industry. In: Cimiano, P., Fernández, M., Lopez, V., Schlobach, S., Völker, J. (eds.) ESWC 2013. LNCS, vol. 7955, pp. 125–140. Springer, Heidelberg (2013)
25. Konev, B., Walther, D., Wolter, F.: The Logical Difference Problem for Description Logic Terminologies. In: Armando, A., Baumgartner, P., Dowek, G. (eds.) IJCAR 2008. LNCS (LNAI), vol. 5195, pp. 259–274. Springer, Heidelberg (2008)
26. Lambrix, P., Dragisic, Z., Ivanova, V.: Get My Pizza Right: Repairing Missing Is-a Relations in $\mathcal{ALC}$ Ontologies. In: Takeda, H., Qu, Y., Mizoguchi, R., Kitamura, Y. (eds.) JIST 2012. LNCS, vol. 7774, pp. 17–32. Springer, Heidelberg (2013)

27. Lambrix, P., Liu, Q.: Debugging the Missing Is-a Structure Within Taxonomies Networked by Partial Reference Alignments. Data Knowl. Eng. (DKE) 86, 179–205 (2013)
28. Mascardi, V., Ancona, D., Barbieri, M., Bordini, R.H., Ricci, A.: CooL-AgentSpeak: Endowing AgentSpeak-DL Agents with Plan Exchange and Ontology Services. Web Intelligence and Agent Systems 12(1), 83–107 (2014)
29. Meilicke, C.: Alignments Incoherency in Ontology Matching. Ph.D. thesis, University of Mannheim (2011)
30. Meilicke, C., Völker, J., Stuckenschmidt, H.: Learning Disjointness for Debugging Mappings between Lightweight Ontologies. In: Gangemi, A., Euzenat, J. (eds.) EKAW 2008. LNCS (LNAI), vol. 5268, pp. 93–108. Springer, Heidelberg (2008)
31. Melnik, S., Garcia-Molina, H., Rahm, E.: Similarity Flooding: A Versatile Graph Matching Algorithm and Its Application to Schema Matching. In: IEEE Int'l Conf. on Data Eng. (2002)
32. Motik, B., Shearer, R., Horrocks, I.: Hypertableau Reasoning for Description Logics. J. Artif. Intell. Res (JAIR) 36, 165–228 (2009)
33. Nebot, V., Berlanga, R.: Efficient Retrieval of Ontology Fragments Using an Interval Labeling Scheme. Inf. Sci. 179(24), 4151–4173 (2009)
34. Ngo, D., Bellahsene, Z.: YAM++: A Multi-strategy Based Approach for Ontology Matching Task. In: ten Teije, A., Völker, J., Handschuh, S., Stuckenschmidt, H., d'Acquin, M., Nikolov, A., Aussenac-Gilles, N., Hernandez, N. (eds.) EKAW 2012. LNCS, vol. 7603, pp. 421–425. Springer, Heidelberg (2012)
35. Pesquita, C., Faria, D., Santos, E., Couto, F.M.: To repair or not to repair: reconciling correctness and coherence in ontology reference alignments. In: Ontology Matching (OM) (2013)
36. Reiter, R.: A Theory of Diagnosis from First Principles. Artif. Intell. 32(1) (1987)
37. Santos, E., Faria, D., Pesquita, C., Couto, F.: Ontology Alignment Repair Through Modularization and Confidence-based Heuristics. arXiv:1307.5322 preprint (2013)
38. Schlobach, S.: Debugging and Semantic Clarification by Pinpointing. In: Gómez-Pérez, A., Euzenat, J. (eds.) ESWC 2005. LNCS, vol. 3532, pp. 226–240. Springer, Heidelberg (2005)
39. Schlobach, S., Cornet, R.: Non-standard Reasoning Services for the Debugging of Description Logic Terminologies. In: Int'l Joint Conf. on Artif. Intell. (IJCAI), pp. 355–362 (2003)
40. Shvaiko, P., Euzenat, J.: Ontology Matching: State of the Art and Future Challenges. IEEE Transactions on Knowl. and Data Eng. (TKDE) (2012)
41. Skjæveland, M.G., Lian, E.H., Horrocks, I.: Publishing the Norwegian Petroleum Directorate's FactPages as Semantic Web Data. In: Alani, H., et al. (eds.) ISWC 2013, Part II. LNCS, vol. 8219, pp. 162–177. Springer, Heidelberg (2013)
42. Soylu, A., Skjæveland, M.G., Giese, M., Horrocks, I., Jimenez-Ruiz, E., Kharlamov, E., Zheleznyakov, D.: A Preliminary Approach on Ontology-Based Visual Query Formulation for Big Data. In: Garoufallou, E., Greenberg, J. (eds.) MTSR 2013. CCIS, vol. 390, pp. 201–212. Springer, Heidelberg (2013)
43. Suntisrivaraporn, B., Qi, G., Ji, Q., Haase, P.: A Modularization-Based Approach to Finding All Justifications for OWL DL Entailments. In: Domingue, J., Anutariya, C. (eds.) ASWC 2008. LNCS, vol. 5367, pp. 1–15. Springer, Heidelberg (2008)
44. Tian, A., Sequeda, J.F., Miranker, D.P.: QODI: Query as Context in Automatic Data Integration. In: Alani, H., et al. (eds.) ISWC 2013, Part I. LNCS, vol. 8218, pp. 624–639. Springer, Heidelberg (2013)
45. Völker, J., Vrandečić, D., Sure, Y., Hotho, A.: Learning Disjointness. In: Franconi, E., Kifer, M., May, W. (eds.) ESWC 2007. LNCS, vol. 4519, pp. 175–189. Springer, Heidelberg (2007)
46. Šváb, O., Svátek, V., Berka, P., Rak, D., Tomášek, P.: OntoFarm: Towards an Experimental Collection of Parallel Ontologies. In: Int'l Sem. Web Conf. (ISWC). Poster Session (2005)
47. Wang, P., Xu, B.: Debugging Ontology Mappings: A Static Approach. Computing and Informatics 27(1), 21–36 (2012)
48. Zhang, S., Mork, P., Bodenreider, O.: Lessons Learned from Aligning two Representations of Anatomy. In: Int'l Conf. on Principles of Knowl. Repr. and Reasoning (KR) (2004)

Towards Annotating Potential Incoherences
in BioPortal Mappings

Daniel Faria[1], Ernesto Jiménez-Ruiz[2], Catia Pesquita[1,3],
Emanuel Santos[3], and Francisco M. Couto[1,3]

[1] LASIGE, Faculdade de Ciências, Universidade de Lisboa, Portugal
[2] Department of Computer Science, University of Oxford, UK
[3] Departamento de Informática, Faculdade de Ciências, Universidade de Lisboa, Portugal

Abstract. BioPortal is a repository for biomedical ontologies that also includes
mappings between them from various sources. Considered as a whole, these mappings may cause logical errors, due to incompatibilities between the ontologies
or even erroneous mappings.

We have performed an automatic evaluation of BioPortal mappings between
19 ontology pairs using the mapping repair systems of LogMap and Agreement-
MakerLight. We found logical errors in 11 of these pairs, which on average involved 22% of the mappings between each pair. Furthermore, we conducted a
manual evaluation of the repair results to identify the actual sources of error, verifying that erroneous mappings were behind over 60% of the repairs.

Given the results of our analysis, we believe that annotating BioPortal mappings with information about their logical conflicts with other mappings would
improve their usability for semantic web applications and facilitate the identification of erroneous mappings. In future work, we aim to collaborate with BioPortal
developers in extending BioPortal with these annotations.

1 Motivation

OWL ontologies are extensively used in biomedical information systems. Prominent
examples of biomedical ontologies are the Gene Ontology [1], the National Cancer
Institute Thesaurus (NCIT) [14] and the Foundational Model of Anatomy (FMA) [32].

Despite some community efforts to ensure a coordinated development of biomedical ontologies [38], many ontologies are being developed independently by different
groups of experts and, as a result, they often cover the same or related subjects, but
follow different modeling principles and use different entity naming schemes. Thus,
to integrate data among applications, it is crucial to establish correspondences (called
mappings) between the entities of the ontologies they use.

In the last ten years, the semantic web and bioinformatics research communities
have extensively investigated the problem of (semi-)automatically computing correspondences between independently developed ontologies, which is usually referred to
as the *ontology matching problem*. Resulting from this effort are the growing number of
ontology matching systems in development [8,7,37] and the large mapping repositories
that have been created (e.g., [2,10]).

P. Mika et al. (Eds.) ISWC 2014, Part II, LNCS 8797, pp. 17–32, 2014.

One such repository, BioPortal [10,33], is a coordinated community effort which currently provides access to more than 370 biomedical ontologies and over 12 million mappings between them.[1] While not all BioPortal ontologies were originally OWL ontologies (e.g., some were developed in OBO format[2]), many have been (or can be) converted to OWL [15]. Mappings in BioPortal are either generated automatically by a sophisticated lexical matcher [13] or added manually by domain experts through the Web interface or the REST APIs [29].

OWL ontologies have well-defined semantics [4] and thus the integration of independently developed ontologies via a set of mappings (i.e., an alignment) may lead to logical errors such as unsatisfiablities [25]. BioPortal, however, explicitly supports the idea that alternative (i.e., created for different purposes) mapping sets may co-exist and that they could potentially contradict each other [29].

While it is true that many logical errors in alignments are caused by incompatibilities between the ontologies they map [19,31], some may be caused by erroneous mappings. Furthermore, logical soundness may be critical to some semantic web applications that integrate two or more ontologies [31]. For these reasons, we consider that it would be advantageous to enrich BioPortal mappings with *annotations* about potential logical conflicts with other mappings. This would improve the usability of BioPortal mappings for semantic web applications and domain users, and facilitate the identification of erroneous mappings and potential errors in the ontologies themselves.

In this paper we quantify the logical errors in the BioPortal mappings among several ontologies by applying mapping repair algorithms. Furthermore, we manually analyze a subset of the identified conflicting mappings in order to qualify the causes of the errors. Our goal is to show the importance of identifying (and annotating) logical conflicts in BioPortal and the role ontology mapping repair algorithms may play in that task.

The rest of the paper is organized as follows: Section 2 describes how mappings are represented in BioPortal; Section 3 introduces the concept of mapping repair and presents the repair algorithms used in this study; Section 4 details the automatic and manual evaluations we conducted and presents and discusses their results; and finally, Section 5 presents some conclusions and future work lines.

2 Mappings in BioPortal

Mappings are treated as first-class citizens in BioPortal [29,12], as it enables the querying, upload, and retrieval of all mappings between all of its ontologies. A survey conducted in 2009 revealed that 33% of BioPortal ontologies had 50% of their entities mapped to other ontologies [12], which indicates that BioPortal ontologies are highly interconnected.

The number of mappings in BioPortal has grown quickly in recent years, from 30,000 mappings between 20 ontologies in 2008 [29] to 9 million mappings between 302 ontologies in 2012 [33]. At the time of writing this paper, there were approximately 13 million mappings between 373 ontologies.

---

[1] BioPortal: https://bioportal.bioontology.org/
[2] http://www.geneontology.org/GO.format.obo-1_4.shtml

Mappings in BioPortal are represented as a 4-tuple of the form $\langle e_1, e_2, Rel, Ann \rangle$, where e_1, e_2 are the URIs of two entities from the vocabulary of two BioPortal ontologies, Rel is the semantic relationship between them, and Ann is a set of annotations or metadata associated to the mapping. The relation Rel can be of one of the following types:[3] *skos:exactMatch, skos:relatedMatch, skos:closeMatch, skos:narrowMatch, skos:broadMatch. Ann* includes, among other details, important provenance information about the mapping such as: origin (e.g., user-defined or alignment system employed), application context, creator, and creation date.

According to BioPortal authors [33], the statistics about mapping origin are the following: *(i)* 64.96% of the mappings were created by the lexical matcher LOOM [13]; *(ii)* 32.48% of the mappings had UMLS [2] as origin; *(iii)* 2.41% represented mappings between entities with the same URI; *(iv)* 0.02% came from *Xref* OBO Mappings; *(v)* finally 0.13% of the mappings were submitted by users.

Mappings between entities with the same URI are labeled *skos:exactMatch* by BioPortal, LOOM and UMLS mappings are labeled *skos:closeMatch*, and *Xref* OBO Mappings are labeled *skos:relatedMatch*. User submitted mappings can be labeled with any of the relation types listed above.

BioPortal mappings can be retrieved via its REST API, being straightforward to identify the entities involved in the mapping, its origin, and the source ontologies.[4]

In this paper, we have focused only on *skos:closeMatch* mappings, which account for the large majority of BioPortal mappings. We represented these mappings as OWL 2 equivalence axioms since that is typically the semantic relation they convey (the tag *skos:closeMatch* is used to link concepts that can be used interchangeably, at least in a given context). Mapping annotations Ann have (optionally) been represented as OWL 2 axiom annotations. This representation of mappings enables the reuse of the extensive range of OWL 2 reasoning infrastructure that is currently available. Note that alternative formal semantics for ontology mappings have been proposed in the literature (e.g., [3,6,28]).

3 Mapping Repair

The ontology resulting from the integration of $\mathcal{O}_1$ and $\mathcal{O}_2$ via a set of mappings $\mathcal{M}$, may entail axioms that do not follow from $\mathcal{O}_1$, $\mathcal{O}_2$, or $\mathcal{M}$ alone. These new semantic consequences can be captured using the notion of *deductive difference* [24,18], and can be divided into desired and undesired entailments. Undesired entailments are typically introduced due to erroneous mappings in $\mathcal{M}$. However, even if all mappings in $\mathcal{M}$ are correct, undesired entailments may occur due to conflicting descriptions between the overlapping entities in $\mathcal{O}_1$ and $\mathcal{O}_2$. Undesired entailment can be divided into two groups: entailments causing unsatisfiable classes, which can be easily detected using (automatic) logical reasoning; and entailments not causing unsatisfiable classes, which require domain knowledge to decide whether they are indeed undesired. In this paper we only focus on the first group of undesired entailments.

---

[3] http://www.bioontology.org/wiki/index.php/BioPortal_Mappings
[4] http://data.bioontology.org/documentation#Mapping

A set of mappings that leads to unsatisfiable classes in $\mathcal{O}_1 \cup \mathcal{O}_2 \cup \mathcal{M}$ is referred to as *incoherent* w.r.t. $\mathcal{O}_1$ and $\mathcal{O}_2$ [26].

Definition 1 (Mapping Incoherence). *A set of mappings $\mathcal{M}$ is incoherent with respect to $\mathcal{O}_1$ and $\mathcal{O}_2$, if there exists a class A in the signature of $\mathcal{O}_1 \cup \mathcal{O}_2$ such that $\mathcal{O}_1 \cup \mathcal{O}_2 \not\models A \sqsubseteq \bot$ and $\mathcal{O}_1 \cup \mathcal{O}_2 \cup \mathcal{M} \models A \sqsubseteq \bot$.*

An incoherent set of mappings $\mathcal{M}$ can be fixed by removing mappings from $\mathcal{M}$. This process is referred to as *mapping repair* (or repair for short).

Definition 2 (Mapping Repair). *Let $\mathcal{M}$ be an incoherent set of mappings w.r.t. $\mathcal{O}_1$ and $\mathcal{O}_2$. A set of mappings $\mathcal{R} \subseteq \mathcal{M}$ is a mapping repair for $\mathcal{M}$ w.r.t. $\mathcal{O}_1$ and $\mathcal{O}_2$ if $\mathcal{M} \setminus \mathcal{R}$ is coherent w.r.t. $\mathcal{O}_1$ and $\mathcal{O}_2$.*

A trivial repair is $\mathcal{R} = \mathcal{M}$, since an empty set of mappings is obviously coherent. Nevertheless, the objective is to remove as few mappings as possible. Minimal (mapping) repairs are typically referred to in the literature as *mapping diagnosis* [25].

In the literature there are different approaches to compute a repair or diagnosis for an incoherent set of mappings. Early approaches were based on Distributed Description Logics (DDL) (e.g. [27,28,30]). The work presented in [30] deserves special mention, as it reports on a preliminary coherence evaluation of BioPortal mappings using DDL.[5] The authors, however, emphasized the problems of efficiency of the coherence checking task due to the reasoning complexity of DDL and suggest the use of approximate techniques in the future.

Alternatively, if mappings are represented as OWL 2 axioms, mapping repairs can also be computed using the state-of-the-art approaches for debugging and repairing inconsistencies in OWL 2 ontologies, which rely on the extraction of justifications for the unsatisfiable classes (e.g. [36,22,39,18]). However, justification-based technologies do not scale when the number of unsatisfiabilities is large (a typical scenario in mapping repair problems [16]).

To address this scalability issue, mapping repair systems usually compute an *approximate repair* using incomplete reasoning techniques (e.g. [17,25,9]). An approximate repair $\mathcal{R}^{\approx}$ does not guarantee that $\mathcal{M} \setminus \mathcal{R}^{\approx}$ is coherent, but it will (in general) reduce significantly the number of unsatisfiabilities caused by the original mappings $\mathcal{M}$. Indeed, approximate repair techniques have been successfully applied to audit the UMLS metathesaurus [19,17].

In this paper, we have applied the *approximate* mapping repair techniques implemented in LogMap [17,20,21] and AgreementMakerLight (AML) [9,35] to the BioPortal mappings. As described in Section 2, we have represented the BioPortal mappings as OWL 2 equivalence axioms. Note that, although both LogMap and AML were originally implemented as ontology matching systems, they can also operate as a standalone mapping repair systems. From this point onwards, we will refer to LogMap's and AML's repair modules as LogMap-Repair and AML-Repair respectively.

---

[5] To the best of our knowledge, no automatic repair was conducted.

Algorithm 1. AML-Repair algorithm

Input: $\mathcal{O}_1, \mathcal{O}_2$: input ontologies; $\mathcal{M}$: input mappings
Output: $\mathcal{M}'$: output mappings; $\mathcal{R}^{\approx}$: approximate mapping repair; $\mathcal{CS}$: identified conflicting sets; $\mathcal{M}_{CS}$: mappings involved in conflicting sets
1: $\mathcal{M}' := \mathcal{M}$
2: $\mathcal{R}^{\approx} := \emptyset$
3: $\langle \mathcal{O}'_1, \mathcal{O}'_2, \text{Checkset} \rangle := \text{BuiltCoreFragments}(\mathcal{O}_1, \mathcal{O}_2, \mathcal{M}')$
4: $\mathcal{CS} := \text{ConflictSets}(\mathcal{O}'_1, \mathcal{O}'_2, \mathcal{M}', \text{Checkset})$
5: $\mathcal{M}_{CS} := \text{MappingsInConflictSets}(\mathcal{CS})$
6: $\mathcal{CS}' := \mathcal{CS}$
7: **while** $|\mathcal{CS}'| > 0$ **do**
8:      $w := \text{SelectMappingToRemove}(\mathcal{CS}')$
9:      $\mathcal{CS}' := \text{RemoveMapping}(\mathcal{CS}', w)$
10:     $\mathcal{M}' := \mathcal{M}' \setminus \{w\};$
11:     $\mathcal{R}^{\approx} := \mathcal{R}^{\approx} \cup \{w\}$
12: **end while**
13: **return** $\langle \mathcal{M}', \mathcal{R}^{\approx}, \mathcal{CS}, \mathcal{M}_{CS} \rangle$

3.1 Mapping Repair Using AML-Repair

The pseudocode of the algorithm implemented by AML-Repair is described in Algorithm 1. The algorithm is divided in three main tasks:

1. The computation of the core fragments (see [34]) (step 3);
2. The search for all (minimal) conflicting sets of mappings $\mathcal{CS}$, i.e. mappings that lead to an incoherence (step 4);
3. The resolution of incoherences using a heuristic to minimize the set of mappings removed from every conflicting set (step 8 to 11);
4. The algorithm outputs a set of repaired mappings $\mathcal{M}'$, an approximate mapping repair $\mathcal{R}^{\approx}$, conflicting sets of mappings $\mathcal{CS}$, and the set of all mappings involved in at least one conflicting set $\mathcal{M}_{CS}$.

AML-Repair implementation is based on a modularization of the input ontologies, called core fragments, that only contains the necessary classes and relations to detect all existing incoherences [34]. This modularization is computed by the BuildCoreFragments method (Step 3 of Algorithm 1), which also computes a minimal set of classes (the Checkset) that need to be checked for incoherences.

AML-Repair determines subsumption relations between atomic classes syntactically (i.e., without using an OWL 2 Reasoner) and it also considers disjointness axioms between atomic classes. Unlike LogMap-Repair, equivalence mappings are considered indivisible units and are never split into two subsumption mappings. Thus, an input mapping is either removed or kept in the alignment during the repair procedure.

The ConflictSets method (step 4) returns all mapping sets that will lead to an incoherence by doing a full depth-first search in the core fragments structure for each class in the Checkset. This way, AML-Repair determines all minimal sets of mappings, called conflicting sets $\mathcal{CS}$, which cause the incoherences. Since conflicting sets are minimal, a

---

Algorithm 2. LogMap-Repair algorithm based on Horn propositional reasoning

Input: $\mathcal{O}_1, \mathcal{O}_2$: input ontologies; $\mathcal{M}$: input mappings
Output: $\mathcal{M}'$: output mappings; $\mathcal{R}^\approx$: approximate mapping repair; $\mathcal{CG}$: conflicting groups; $\overline{\mathcal{M}_{\mathcal{CG}}}$: mapping average in conflicting groups

1:   $\mathcal{M}' := \mathcal{M}$
2:   $\mathcal{R}^\approx := \emptyset$
3:   $\mathcal{CG} := \emptyset$
4:   $\langle \mathcal{P}_1, \mathcal{P}_2 \rangle := \mathsf{PropEncoding}(\mathcal{O}_1, \mathcal{O}_2)$
5:   **for each** $C \in \mathsf{OrderedVariables}(\mathcal{P}_1 \cup \mathcal{P}_2)$ **do**
6:      $\mathcal{P}_C := \mathcal{P}_1 \cup \mathcal{P}_2 \cup \mathcal{M}' \cup \{\mathsf{true} \to C\}$
7:      $\langle sat, \mathcal{M}_\perp \rangle := \mathsf{DowlingGallier}(\mathcal{P}_C)$
8:      **if** $sat = \mathsf{false}$ **then**
9:         $\mathcal{CG} := \mathcal{CG} \cup \{\mathcal{M}_\perp\}$
10:        $Rep := \emptyset$
11:       $rep\_size := 1$
12:       **repeat**
13:          **for each** subset $\mathcal{R}_C$ of $\mathcal{M}_\perp$ of size rep_size **do**
14:            $sat := \mathsf{DowlingGallier}(\mathcal{P}_C \setminus \mathcal{R}_C)$
15:            **if** $sat = \mathsf{true}$ **then** $Rep := Rep \cup \{\mathcal{R}_C\}$
16:          **end for**
17:         $rep\_size := rep\_size + 1$
18:       **until** $Rep \neq \emptyset$
19:       $\mathcal{R}_C :=$ element of Rep with minimum aggregated confidence.
20:       $\mathcal{M}' := \mathcal{M}' \setminus \mathcal{R}_C$
21:       $\mathcal{R}^\approx := \mathcal{R}^\approx \cup \mathcal{R}_C$
22:     **end if**
23: **end for**
24: $\overline{\mathcal{M}_{\mathcal{CG}}} := \mathsf{AverageMappingsInConflictGroups}(\mathcal{CG})$
25: **return** $\langle \mathcal{M}', \mathcal{R}^\approx, \mathcal{CG}, \overline{\mathcal{M}_{\mathcal{CG}}} \rangle$

---

conflicting set is resolved if at least one of its mappings is removed. The algorithm also keeps the set $\mathcal{M}_{\mathcal{CS}}$ containing all mappings involved in a conflicting set (Step 5).

AML-Repair aims to minimize the number of removed mappings by determining a minimal set of mappings that intersect all conflict sets. Given that computing this set is NP-Complete, AML-Repair uses an efficient heuristic procedure that consists of iteratively removing the mappings that belong to the highest number of conflicting sets (as identified in Step 8 of Algorithm 1), and in case of tie, those that have the lowest confidence values. This strategy typically produces near-optimal results.

3.2 Mapping Repair Using LogMap-Repair

Algorithm 2 shows the pseudocode of the algorithm implemented by LogMap-Repair. Steps 1-3 initialise the output variables. LogMap-Repair encodes the input ontologies $\mathcal{O}_1$ and $\mathcal{O}_2$ as Horn propositional theories $\mathcal{P}_1$ and $\mathcal{P}_2$ (Step 4) and exploits this encoding to subsequently detect unsatisfiable classes in an efficient and sound way during the repair process. The theory $\mathcal{P}_1$ (resp. $\mathcal{P}_2$) consists of the following Horn rules:

- A rule $A \rightarrow B$ for all distinct classes A, B such that A is subsumed by B in $\mathcal{O}_1$ (resp. in $\mathcal{O}_2$); subsumption relations can be determined using either an OWL 2 reasoner, or syntactically (in an incomplete way).
- Rules $A_i \wedge A_j \rightarrow$ false ($1 \leq i < j \leq n$) for each disjointness axiom of the form $DisjointClasses(A_1, \ldots, A_n)$.
- A rule $A_1 \wedge \ldots \wedge A_n \rightarrow B$ for each subclass or equivalence axiom having the intersection of $A_1, \ldots A_n$ as subclass expression and B as superclass.

In Step 5, propositional variables in $\mathcal{P}_1$ (resp. in $\mathcal{P}_2$) are ordered such that a variable C in $\mathcal{P}_1$ (resp. in $\mathcal{P}_2$) comes before D whenever D is subsumed by C in $\mathcal{O}_1$ (resp. in $\mathcal{O}_2$). This is a well-known repair strategy: subclasses of an unsatisfiable class are also unsatisfiable and hence before repairing an unsatisfiable class one first needs to repair its superclasses. Satisfiability of a propositional variable C is determined by checking satisfiability of the propositional theory $\mathcal{P}_C$ (Step 6) consisting of *(i)* the rule (true $\rightarrow$ C); *(ii)* the propositional representations $\mathcal{P}_1$ and $\mathcal{P}_2$; and *(iii)* the current set of output mappings $\mathcal{M}'$ (seen as propositional implications). Note that LogMap-Repair splits equivalence mappings into two equivalent subsumption mappings.

LogMap-Repair implements the classical Dowling-Gallier algorithm for propositional Horn satisfiability [5,11]. LogMap-Repair's implementation of Dowling-Gallier's algorithm also records all mappings potentially involved in an unsatisfiability. Thus, a call to Dowling-Gallier returns a satisfiability value *sat* and, optionally, the (overestimated) group of conflicting mappings $\mathcal{M}_\perp$ (see Steps 7 and 14). For statistical purposes, the set $\mathcal{CG}$ keeps all conflicting groups for the identified unsatisfiable classes (Step 9). An unsatisfiable class C is repaired by discarding conflicting mappings for C (Steps 10 to 21). Thus, subsets $\mathcal{R}_C$ of $\mathcal{M}_\perp$ of increasing size are then identified until a repair is found (Steps 12-18). Note that, LogMap-Repair does not compute a diagnosis for the unsatisfiable class C but rather the repairs of smallest size. If several repairs of a given size exist, the one with the lowest aggregated confidence is selected according to the confidence values assigned to mappings (Step 19). Steps 20 and 21 update the output mappings $\mathcal{M}'$ and the approximate mapping repair $\mathcal{R}^\approx$ by extracting and adding $\mathcal{R}_C$, respectively. Finally, Step 24 calculates the average number of mappings in each identified conflicting group $\mathcal{CG}$.

Algorithm 2 ensures that $\mathcal{P}_1 \cup \mathcal{P}_2 \cup \mathcal{M}' \cup \{\text{true} \rightarrow C\}$ is satisfiable for each C occurring in $\mathcal{P}_1 \cup \mathcal{P}_2$. The propositional encoding of $\mathcal{O}_1$ and $\mathcal{O}_2$ is, however, incomplete and hence the algorithm does not ensure satisfiability of each class in $\mathcal{O}_1 \cup \mathcal{O}_2 \cup \mathcal{M}'$. Nevertheless, the number of unsatisfiable classes remaining after computing an approximate repair $\mathcal{R}^\approx$ is typically small.

4   Evaluation

In order to evaluate the coherence of BioPortal mappings, we manually selected 19 ontology pairs from BioPortal such that *(i)* each pair had at least 500 mappings listed in BioPortal, *(ii)* at least one of the ontologies in the pair contained disjointness clauses between their classes, and *(iii)* the domain of both ontologies was biomedical. The purpose of the first two criteria is to exclude ontology pairs that are uninteresting from an (automatic) mapping repair perspective, whereas the third criterion ensures that we are

Table 1. Ontologies comprising the 19 ontology pairs selected

Ontology	Acronym	# Classes	Source
Bone Dysplasia Ontology	BDO	13,817	BioPortal
Cell Culture Ontology	CCONT	14,663	BioPortal
Experimental Factor Ontology	EFO	14,499	BioPortal
Human Developmental Anatomy Ontology, timed ver.	EHDA	8,340	OBO Foundry
Cardiac Electrophysiology Ontology	EP	81,957	BioPortal
Foundational Model of Anatomy	FMA	83,280	BioPortal
Mouse Adult Gross Anatomy Ontology	MA	3,205	OBO Foundry
NCI Thesaurus	NCIT	105,347	BioPortal
Online Mendelian Inheritance in Man	OMIM	76,721	BioPortal
Sleep Domain Ontology	SDO	1,382	BioPortal
SNP ontology	SNP	2,206	BioPortal
Sequence Types and Features Ontology	SO	2,021	BioPortal
Teleost Anatomy Ontology	TAO	3,372	OBO Foundry
Uber Anatomy Ontology	UBERON	15,773	OBO Foundry
Zebrafish Anatomy and Development Ontology	ZFA	2,955	OBO Foundry

Table 2. BioPortal mappings for the selected ontology pairs

Ontology Pair	Listed Mappings	Retrieved Mappings	Actual Mappings	Unsat. Classes
BDO-NCIT	1,637	1,636	1,636	34,341
CCONT-NCIT	2,815	2,813	2,097 (-19)	50,304
EFO-NCIT	3,289	3,287	2,507	60,347
EHDA-FMA	3,731	2,496	2,496	0
EP-FMA	79,497	78,489	78,489	210
EP-NCIT	2,468	2,465	2,465 (-1)	14,687 (-1)
MA-FMA	5,491	961	961	850
OMIM-NCIT	5,198	5,198	5,178	70,172
SDO-EP	662	135	135	44
SDO-FMA	593	529	529 (-1)	0
SNPO-SO	2,168	2,150	2,028 (-1)	0
UBERON-FMA	2,233	1,932	1,932	4,753
ZFA-CCONT	532	437	333	0
ZFA-EFO	773	538	427	913
ZFA-EHDA	2,595	1,809	1,809	0
ZFA-FMA	1,240	265	265	0
ZFA-MA	1,639	129	129	0
ZFA-TAO	1,737	1,524	1,521	0
ZFA-UBERON	817	724	724	104

able to manually evaluate the repair results as they lie within our domain of expertise. This selection was not exhaustive, as our goal was merely to select a substantial and representative set of ontology pairs.

Algorithm 3. Automatic repair evaluation of BioPortal mappings

Input: $\mathcal{O}_1$, $\mathcal{O}_2$: two BioPortal ontologies; $\mathcal{M}$: the set of BioPortal mappings between them
1: Compute all conflict sets of mappings $\mathcal{CS}$, the total number of mappings involved in conflicts $\mathcal{M}_{\mathcal{CS}}$, and the approximate repair $\mathcal{R}^{\approx}$ using AML-Repair system ▷ See Algorithm 1
2: Get unsatisfiable classes of $\mathcal{O}_1 \cup \mathcal{O}_2 \cup \mathcal{M} \setminus \mathcal{R}^{\approx}$ using ELK reasoner
3: Compute the conflicting mapping groups $\mathcal{CG}$ per unsatisfiability, the average number of mappings per conflict group $\mathcal{M}_{\mathcal{CG}}$, and the approximate repair $\mathcal{R}^{\approx}$ using LogMap-Repair system ▷ See Algorithm 2
4: Get unsatisfiable classes of $\mathcal{O}_1 \cup \mathcal{O}_2 \cup \mathcal{M} \setminus \mathcal{R}^{\approx}$ using ELK reasoner

The 15 ontologies comprising these 19 pairs are listed in Table 1. We retrieved the latest OWL version of each ontology from BioPortal, except for the ontologies that were only available in OBO format. Because AML is currently not set-up to handle ontologies in the OBO format, we retrieved the latter from the OBO Foundry[6] [38] in OWL format (making sure the versions matched those in BioPortal).

We implemented a script that, given a pair of ontologies, uses BioPortal's REST API to retrieve all mappings between those ontologies. We focused only on *skos:closeMatch* mappings and we represented them as OWL 2 equivalence axioms. We did not consider *skos:exactMatch* mappings since they represent correspondences between entities with the same URI, which in OWL ontologies are considered equivalent (even though the equivalence between them is not explicitly defined). We also excluded a few mappings that had only a *null* source or involved only one entity.

The mappings between the 19 selected ontology pairs are listed in Table 2. We verified that the number of retrieved mappings did not match the number of mappings listed in the BioPortal website, and that sometimes the discrepancy was large (i.e., not accounted for by the small fraction of mappings we excluded). BioPortal developers confirmed that there is indeed an inconsistency between the metrics and the available mappings. Furthermore, in several cases, some of the mappings retrieved pointed to classes that were not found in the ontologies (possibly obsolete classes), so the actual mappings between the ontologies were less than those retrieved. Additionally, in some cases less mappings were found when using the Jena API to read the ontologies (used by AML) than when using the OWL API (used by LogMap). The difference between the two is shown in parenthesis in Table 2.

Finally, we computed the satisfiability of each alignment with the OWL 2 EL reasoner ELK [23], finding several unsatisfiable classes in 11 of the alignments. We opted for ELK for the sake of efficiency, given the size of some of the ontologies. ELK is incomplete and thus the identified unsatisfiabilities represent a lower bound of the actual number of such logical errors.

4.1 Automatic Repair Evaluation

For each of the 11 ontology pairs that had incoherent mapping sets (as detected by ELK and listed in Table 2), we conducted the evaluation detailed in Algorithm 3. The results

---

[6] http://www.obofoundry.org/

Table 3. Automatic mapping repair using AML-Repair and LogMap-Repair

Ontology Pairs	$\mathcal{M}$	AML-Repair				LogMap-Repair			
		$|\mathcal{CS}|$	$|\mathcal{M_{CS}}|$	$|\mathcal{R}^{\approx}|$	Unsat.	$|\mathcal{CG}|$	$\mathcal{M_{CG}}$	$|\mathcal{R}^{\approx}|$	Unsat.
BDO-NCIT	1,636	1,649	1,374 (84%)	53	0	125	3.2	154	0
CCONT-NCIT	2,097	1,197	1,136 (55%)	55	3,630	125	2.7	119	75
EFO-NCIT	2,507	1,731	1,541 (61%)	143	3,687	311	4.3	353	73
EP-FMA	78,489	348	109 (0.1%)	16	0	168	11.0	168	0
EP-NCIT	2,465	363	307 (12%)	69	253	136	3.8	180	0
MA-FMA	961	21	22 (2%)	1	0	1	2.0	2	0
OMIM-NCIT	5,178	1,800	1,078 (21%)	154	0	396	10.2	536	0
SDO-EP	135	3	3 (2%)	1	0	1	3.0	3	0
UBERON-FMA	1,932	486	121 (6%)	19	25	70	6.3	85	25
ZFA-EFO	427	7	11 (3%)	5	0	10	2.6	10	0
ZFA-UBERON	724	0	0 (0%)	0	104	0	0	0	104
Average	8,777	691	518 (22%)	94	700	122	5	146	25

$\mathcal{M}$: number of BioPortal mappings; $|\mathcal{CS}|$: number of conflict sets; $|\mathcal{M_{CS}}|$: number of distinct mappings in conflict sets; $|\mathcal{CG}|$: number of conflict groups; $\mathcal{M_{CG}}$: average number of mappings per conflict group; $|\mathcal{R}^{\approx}|$: repair size in number of mappings (AML) or number of half-mappings (LogMap); **Unsat.**: unsatisfiable classes after repair.

we obtained are shown in Table 3. Note that LogMap-Repair splits equivalence mappings into two subsumption mappings, so the value of $\mathcal{R}^{\approx}$ is not directly comparable with AML-Repair (the latter should be doubled to compare it with the former).

The incoherence of the repaired mapping sets has been significantly reduced, and in many cases completely removed. The one exception was the ZFA-UBERON case, as neither AML-Repair nor LogMap-Repair could detect and repair any of the unsatisfiabilities in this alignment. Furthermore, the computed (approximate) repairs were not aggressive, as they removed at most 5.7% (AML-Repair) and 7% (LogMap-Repair) of the mappings (in the EFO-NCIT case).

In addition to producing a repair, AML-Repair also identifies the number of conflicting mapping sets $\mathcal{CS}$ and the total number of mappings that are involved in at least one conflict $\mathcal{M_{CS}}$. For example, in the BDO-NCIT case, AML-Repair identifies 1,649 conflicting sets which involve 84% of the mappings $\mathcal{M}$ in this alignment. Given that these mappings were leading to 34,341 unsatisfiable classes (see Table 2), the fact that only 53 equivalence mappings were removed indicates that (at least) some of these were causing several unsatisfiabilities, likely because they were in conflict with multiple other mappings.

LogMap-Repair, on the other hand, identifies groups of potentially conflicting mappings $\mathcal{CG}$ (which contain one or more $\mathcal{CS}$) involved in each unsatisfiability, and the average number of mappings in each conflicting group $\overline{\mathcal{M_{CG}}}$. $\mathcal{CG}$ represents a lower bound of the total number of groups, since LogMap-Repair repairs on-the-fly and removing one mapping may solve multiple unsatisfiabilities. For example, in the BDO-NCIT case, LogMap-Repair only identifies 125 conflicting groups with an average of

3.2 mappings per group. Note that solving the 125 unsatisfiabilities corresponding to the conflict groups is sufficient to repair the original 34,341 unsatisfiabilities, which again suggests that a few mappings in the conflict groups were causing many of these errors.

4.2 Manual Analysis

To complement the automatic repair evaluation and investigate the causes behind the incoherences identified therein, we analyzed manually the mappings removed by AML-Repair and LogMap-Repair (up to a maximum of 100 mappings per ontology pair, and in the case of LogMap-Repair, only the cases where the subsumption mappings were removed in both directions).

For each removed mapping, we assessed whether it was correct or erroneous (within the context of the ontologies). We deemed a mapping to be erroneous if it falls into one of the following categories:

1. At least one of the entities it maps is obsolete/retired, as in the mapping: BDO# HP_0001596 (Alopecia) ⇔ NCIT#C2865 (Alopecia), where the latter class is retired in NCIT.
2. The entities it maps are not directly related, as in the mapping: BDO#PATO_ 0001901 (Back) ⇔ NCIT#C13062 (Back), where the former class stands for the directional qualifier and the latter stands for the body part.
3. The entities it maps are related but the relationship between them should not be modeled as *skos:closeMatch*, as in the the mapping: BDO#G0000064 (CREBP) ⇔ NCIT#C17803 (CREB-Binding Protein), which maps entities that are related (the gene and corresponding protein) but semantically distinct. Moreover, this mapping conflicts with the correct (protein-protein) mapping: BDO#P000022 (CREB-Binding Protein) ⇔ NCIT#C17803 (CREB-Binding Protein).

Additionally, when the removed mapping was deemed to be correct, we analyzed the conflict sets CS in which the removed mapping was present (computed by AML-Repair, see Algorithm 3) and assessed whether the mappings in conflict with it were correct or erroneous. For the purpose of our evaluation, the main issue is not whether the repair algorithms remove erroneous mappings, but rather whether any of the unsatisfiabilities in which it is involved are caused by erroneous mappings. Thus, if either the removed mapping or at least one of its conflicting mappings was erroneous, we attributed the cause of removal to a mapping error. If the mapping itself and all of its conflicting mappings were correct, we considered the cause of removal to be an incompatibility between the ontologies.

The results of our manual analysis are summarized in Table 4. In total, over 40% of the mappings removed by both repair systems were indeed erroneous. Furthermore, errors in the mappings were the cause of removal of over 60% of the mappings.

We found that category 1 errors (i.e., mappings including obsolete/retired classes) were relatively common in all alignments that included NCIT. Furthermore, there were two common category 3 error patterns in these alignments: gene-protein matches, and human-mouse matches. The former pattern consists of a mapping between a gene and its corresponding protein or vice-versa, as exemplified above. The latter pattern consists

Table 4. Manual evaluation of the repaired BioPortal mappings

Ontology Pairs	AML-Repair			LogMap-Repair		
	Analyzed	Erroneous	Err. Cause	Analyzed	Erroneous	Err. Cause
BDO-NCIT	53	55%	83%	52	62%	83%
CCONT-NCIT	55	33%	62%	68	43%	59%
EFO-NCIT	100	53%	91%	100	54%	93%
EP-FMA	16	0%	0%	84	0%	0%
EP-NCIT	69	43%	71%	78	60%	73%
MA-FMA	1	100%	100%	1	100%	100%
OMIM-NCIT	100	48%	71%	100	49%	76%
SDO-EP	1	100%	100%	0	N/A	N/A
UBERON-FMA	19	0%	0%	20	0%	0%
ZFA-EFO	5	60%	100%	4	75%	100%
Total	419	44%	71%	507	42%	62%

of a mapping between a (Human) Health/Anatomy classes and a corresponding NCIT Mouse class (from the Mouse Pathologic Diagnoses or Mouse Anatomy Concepts sections) which naturally conflicts with the mapping to the main (Human) NCIT sections. One example of this pattern is the mapping: BDO#HP_0010786 (Urinary Tract Neoplasm) ⇔ NCIT#C25806 (Mouse Urinary Tract Neoplasm). Another pattern of this category that occurred in the OMIM-NCIT alignment consists of a mapping between a disease/symptom and a corresponding adverse event, such as: OMIM#MTHU023845 (Neck Pain) ⇔ NCIT#C56135 (Neck Pain Adverse Event).

Regarding category 2 errors, there were few patterns other than number mismatches, such as in the mapping: BDO#G0000133 (TBX4) ⇔ NCIT#C101638 (TBX3 Gene). While the cause of these mismatches was often clear, as in the 'back' example above, some defy reason as the case of: EFO#CHEBI_15366 (Acetic Acid) ⇔ NCIT#C37392 (C58 Mouse).

As for incompatibilities between the ontologies, one of the most interesting cases is the EP-FMA alignment, which is actually an alignment between the OBO version of FMA (which is imported by EP) and the BioPortal version of FMA. Indeed, it was surprising to find that the alignment is incoherent, given that all mappings are true equivalences. It turns out that there are a few structural differences between the two versions of the ontology which cause the incoherences, as some entities are modeled as 'Material Anatomical Entity' in the OBO version and as 'Immaterial Anatomical Entity' in the BioPortal version (with the latter appearing to be more correct in most cases). The same type of structural differences is also behind the incoherences in the UBERON-FMA alignment. Also interesting is the OMIM-NCIT alignment, as OMIM models diseases as subclasses of the anatomical structures where they occur, whereas NCIT models diseases as disjoint from anatomical structures, making it impossible to obtain a coherent alignment between the ontologies where both diseases and anatomical structures are mapped.

4.3 Discussion

The results of our study reveal that many sets of BioPortal mappings lead to logical incoherences when taken as a whole, and that many of these incoherences involve erroneous mappings. Thus, adding annotations to BioPortal mappings about potential logical incompatibilities with other mappings would not only improve their usability for semantic web applications, which require logical integrity, but also contribute to identify and discard erroneous mappings.

Our study also demonstrates that approximate repair algorithms such as AML-Repair and LogMap-Repair can effectively identify most of the logical conflicts in BioPortal mappings, as well as the mappings that cause them. Furthermore, unlike complete repair algorithms such as those based on DDL [30], AML-Repair and LogMap-Repair are feasible in practice (repair times in AML-Repair ranged from 10 seconds to 10 minutes, whereas in LogMap-Repair they ranged from 3 to 92 seconds, in a quad-core computer with 8 GB allocated RAM). Thus these algorithms could play a pivotal role in the task of identifying and annotating conflicts between BioPortal mappings.

Furthermore, in addition to the annotation of existing mappings, AML-Repair and LogMap-Repair could be employed to screen newly submitted mappings, so that those leading to logical conflicts can be reviewed before being integrated into BioPortal. This could effectively preclude the addition of some erroneous mappings, and would enable the immediate annotation of the mappings accepted for integration.

Regarding the categories of erroneous mappings found, the category 1 errors (i.e, mappings that include retired/obsolete entities) are straightforward to identify and handle automatically, even without the use of repair algorithms. These mappings should not be maintained as 'active' mappings in BioPortal given that retired/obsolete entities are no longer be considered an active part of the ontologies. However, it makes sense to keep track of such mappings, so the best solution would be to annotate the mappings themselves as obsolete.

Category 2 errors (i.e., mappings between unrelated classes) should definitely be excluded from BioPortal, whereas category 3 errors (i.e., mappings between classes that are related but not closely) can be addressed either by exclusion or by changing the semantic relationship. For instance, a gene and its corresponding protein could be considered *skos:relatedMatch* rather than *skos:closeMatch*, although ideally a more descriptive mapping relation should be used. However, if both ontologies describe the gene and the protein, at least one ontology describes the relation between them, and BioPortal includes both the gene-gene and the protein-protein mappings; then maintaining a gene-protein mapping is semantically redundant.

Although finding category 2 and 3 errors typically requires human intervention, the use of mapping repair algorithms is critical to facilitate their detection. Note that, not all erroneous mappings necessarily lead to logical conflicts, particularly when the ontologies lack disjointness definitions. Nevertheless, addressing conflict-causing errors will surely be a significant improvement, and the common error patterns thus identified can be employed to search for (non-conflict causing) errors, even in ontologies that lack disjointness restrictions.

The identification of logical conflicts caused by inherent incompatibilities between the ontologies is also critical to understand the limits of interoperability. For instance, integrating OMIM and NCIT requires excluding either mappings between anatomic entities or mappings between diseases (depending on the intended application), or ultimately relaxing the disjointness restrictions in the NCIT. Additionally, such incompatibilities may point to modeling errors in the ontologies, as in the EP-FMA case, and enable their correction.

5   Conclusions

BioPortal fulfills a critical need of the biomedical community by promoting integration and interoperability between the numerous biomedical ontologies with overlapping domains. However, the different scopes of these ontologies often lead to incompatible views of a given domain, placing restrictions on interoperability. Maintaining conflicting mappings may best serve the needs of the community, as a wider mapping coverage will satisfy more users and enable more applications. Nevertheless, if BioPortal mappings are to be usable on a large scale, and particularly by automatic applications, then identifying those that lead to logical errors is paramount.

Another issue that affects BioPortal are mapping errors, which are inevitable on this scale, particularly when most mappings are produced by automated ontology matching techniques. Finding and correcting these errors is a daunting task, but one of the utmost importance, as they are likely to propagate if used to draw inferences. While not all errors cause logical conflicts, many do, and as our evaluation illustrates, identifying these enables the discovery of error patterns that can be applied to identify further errors.

Identifying logical conflicts in BioPortal mappings thus serves the dual purpose of improving usability and facilitating error detection. Given that using complete reasoners for this task is unfeasible, due to the scale of BioPortal, approximate mapping repair systems such as AML-Repair and LogMap-Repair appear to be the ideal solution. Indeed, our study has shown that these systems are both effective and efficient in tackling large sets of mappings, and will be even more efficient considering that the goal is only to identify conflicts rather than to repair them.

Our proposal is that BioPortal mappings be enriched with annotations about other mappings they conflict with, a solution which fits into BioPortal's community-driven and multiple-perspective approach. While distinguishing mappings errors from incompatibilities will require manual analysis, this is a task that could be carried out gradually by the community once mappings are annotated with logical conflicts.

There is, however, one type of error that can be addressed immediately: mappings that include obsolete/retired entities. Despite the fact that there are different representations of these entities among BioPortal ontologies, identifying them (and their mappings) should be straightforward to do automatically. We propose that such mappings be annotated as obsolete, which would enable BioPortal and its users to keep track of them while allowing their automatic exclusion by applications.

Our next step will be to contact BioPortal developers and collaborate with them in the process of finding and annotating mappings with information about logical conflicts, by applying our repair algorithms to the whole BioPortal.

Acknowledgements. This work was supported by the EU FP7 IP project Optique (no. 318338) and the EPSRC project Score!, and by the Portuguese FCT through the

SOMER project (PTDC/EIA-EIA/119119/2010) and the LASIGE Strategic Project (PEst-OE/EEI/UI0408/2014).

We would like to thank the invaluable help provided by Bernardo Cuenca Grau and Ian Horrocks in the development of LogMap-Repair, and by Isabel F. Cruz in the development of AML-Repair.

References

1. Ashburner, M., Ball, C.A., Blake, J.A., Botstein, D., Butler, H., Cherry, J.M., Davis, A.P., Dolinski, K., Dwight, S.S., Eppig, J.T., et al.: Gene Ontology: tool for the unification of biology. Nature Genetics 25(1), 25–29 (2000)
2. Bodenreider, O.: The unified medical language system (UMLS): integrating biomedical terminology. Nucleic Acids Research 32, 267–270 (2004)
3. Borgida, A., Serafini, L.: Distributed description logics: Assimilating information from peer sources. J. Data Sem. 1, 153–184 (2003)
4. Cuenca Grau, B., Horrocks, I., Motik, B., Parsia, B., Patel-Schneider, P.F., Sattler, U.: OWL 2: The next step for OWL. J. Web Sem. 6(4), 309–322 (2008)
5. Dowling, W.F., Gallier, J.H.: Linear-time algorithms for testing the satisfiability of propositional Horn formulae. J. Log. Prog. 1(3), 267–284 (1984)
6. Euzenat, J.: Semantic precision and recall for ontology alignment evaluation. In: Int'l Joint Conf. on Artif. Intell (IJCAI), pp. 348–353 (2007)
7. Euzenat, J., Meilicke, C., Stuckenschmidt, H., Shvaiko, P., Trojahn, C.: Ontology alignment evaluation initiative: Six years of experience. J. Data Sem. 15, 158–192 (2011)
8. Euzenat, J., Shvaiko, P.: Ontology matching. Springer (2007)
9. Faria, D., Pesquita, C., Santos, E., Palmonari, M., Cruz, I.F., Couto, F.M.: The agreement-makerlight ontology matching system. In: Meersman, R., Panetto, H., Dillon, T., Eder, J., Bellahsene, Z., Ritter, N., De Leenheer, P., Dou, D. (eds.) ODBASE 2013. LNCS, vol. 8185, pp. 527–541. Springer, Heidelberg (2013)
10. Fridman Noy, N., Shah, N.H., Whetzel, P.L., Dai, B., Dorf, M., Griffith, N., Jonquet, C., Rubin, D.L., Storey, M.A.D., Chute, C.G., Musen, M.A.: BioPortal: ontologies and integrated data resources at the click of a mouse. Nucleic Acids Research 37(Web-Server-Issue) (2009)
11. Gallo, G., Urbani, G.: Algorithms for testing the satisfiability of propositional formulae. J. Log. Prog. 7(1), 45–61 (1989)
12. Ghazvinian, A., Noy, N.F., Jonquet, C., Shah, N., Musen, M.A.: What four million mappings can tell you about two hundred ontologies. In: Bernstein, A., Karger, D.R., Heath, T., Feigenbaum, L., Maynard, D., Motta, E., Thirunarayan, K. (eds.) ISWC 2009. LNCS, vol. 5823, pp. 229–242. Springer, Heidelberg (2009)
13. Ghazvinian, A., Noy, N.F., Musen, M.A.: Creating mappings for ontologies in biomedicine: Simple methods work. In: AMIA Annual Symposium (AMIA) (2009)
14. Golbeck, J., Fragoso, G., Hartel, F.W., Hendler, J.A., Oberthaler, J., Parsia, B.: The National Cancer Institute's Thésaurus and Ontology. J. Web Sem. 1(1), 75–80 (2003)
15. Golbreich, C., Horridge, M., Horrocks, I., Motik, B., Shearer, R.: OBO and OWL: Leveraging Semantic Web Technologies for the Life Sciences. In: Aberer, K., et al. (eds.) ISWC/ASWC 2007. LNCS, vol. 4825, pp. 169–182. Springer, Heidelberg (2007)
16. Jiménez-Ruiz, E., Cuenca Grau, B., Horrocks, I.: On the feasibility of using OWL 2 DL reasoners for ontology matching problems. In: OWL Reasoner Evaluation Workshop (2012)
17. Jiménez-Ruiz, E., Cuenca Grau, B.: LogMap: Logic-based and Scalable Ontology Matching. In: Aroyo, L., Welty, C., Alani, H., Taylor, J., Bernstein, A., Kagal, L., Noy, N., Blomqvist, E. (eds.) ISWC 2011, Part I. LNCS, vol. 7031, pp. 273–288. Springer, Heidelberg (2011)
18. Jiménez-Ruiz, E., Cuenca Grau, B., Horrocks, I., Berlanga, R.: Ontology integration using mappings: Towards getting the right logical consequences. In: Aroyo, L., et al. (eds.) ESWC 2009. LNCS, vol. 5554, pp. 173–187. Springer, Heidelberg (2009)

19. Jiménez-Ruiz, E., Cuenca Grau, B., Horrocks, I., Berlanga, R.: Logic-based Assessment of the Compatibility of UMLS Ontology Sources. J. Biomed. Semant. 2(suppl. 1), S2 (2011)
20. Jiménez-Ruiz, E., Cuenca Grau, B., Zhou, Y., Horrocks, I.: Large-scale interactive ontology matching: Algorithms and implementation. In: Europ. Conf. on Artif. Intell. (ECAI) (2012)
21. Jiménez-Ruiz, E., Meilicke, C., Grau, B.C., Horrocks, I.: Evaluating mapping repair systems with large biomedical ontologies. In: Description Logics, pp. 246–257 (2013)
22. Kalyanpur, A., Parsia, B., Horridge, M., Sirin, E.: Finding all justifications of OWL DL entailments. In: Aberer, K., et al. (eds.) ISWC/ASWC 2007. LNCS, vol. 4825, pp. 267–280. Springer, Heidelberg (2007)
23. Kazakov, Y., Krötzsch, M., Simančík, F.: Concurrent classification of EL ontologies. In: Aroyo, L., Welty, C., Alani, H., Taylor, J., Bernstein, A., Kagal, L., Noy, N., Blomqvist, E. (eds.) ISWC 2011, Part I. LNCS, vol. 7031, pp. 305–320. Springer, Heidelberg (2011)
24. Konev, B., Walther, D., Wolter, F.: The Logical Difference Problem for Description Logic Terminologies. In: Armando, A., Baumgartner, P., Dowek, G. (eds.) IJCAR 2008. LNCS (LNAI), vol. 5195, pp. 259–274. Springer, Heidelberg (2008)
25. Meilicke, C.: Alignments Incoherency in Ontology Matching. Ph.D. thesis, University of Mannheim (2011)
26. Meilicke, C., Stuckenschmidt, H.: Incoherence as a basis for measuring the quality of ontology mappings. In: Ontology Matching Workshop (2008)
27. Meilicke, C., Stuckenschmidt, H., Tamilin, A.: Repairing ontology mappings. In: Proc. of AAAI Conf. on Artif. Intell., pp. 1408–1413 (2007)
28. Meilicke, C., Stuckenschmidt, H., Tamilin, A.: Reasoning support for mapping revision. J. Log. Comput. 19(5) (2009)
29. Noy, N.F., Griffith, N., Musen, M.A.: Collecting community-based mappings in an ontology repository. In: Sheth, A.P., Staab, S., Dean, M., Paolucci, M., Maynard, D., Finin, T., Thirunarayan, K. (eds.) ISWC 2008. LNCS, vol. 5318, pp. 371–386. Springer, Heidelberg (2008)
30. Pathak, J., Chute, C.G.: Debugging Mappings between Biomedical Ontologies: Preliminary Results from the NCBO BioPortal Mapping Repository. In: Int'l Conf. on Biomedical Ontology (ICBO) (2009)
31. Pesquita, C., Faria, D., Santos, E., Couto, F.M.: To repair or not to repair: reconciling correctness and coherence in ontology reference alignments. In: Ontology Matching (OM) (2013)
32. Rosse, C., Mejino Jr., J.: A reference ontology for biomedical informatics: the Foundational Model of Anatomy. J. Biomed. Informatics 36(6), 478–500 (2003)
33. Salvadores, M., Alexander, P.R., Musen, M.A., Noy, N.F.: BioPortal as a dataset of linked biomedical ontologies and terminologies in RDF. Semantic Web 4(3), 277–284 (2013)
34. Santos, E., Faria, D., Pesquita, C., Couto, F.: Ontology alignment repair through modularization and confidence-based heuristics. arXiv:1307.5322 preprint (2013)
35. Santos, E., Faria, D., Pesquita, C., Couto, F.M.: Ontology alignment repair through modularization and confidence-based heuristics. CoRR abs/1307.5322 (2013)
36. Schlobach, S.: Debugging and semantic clarification by pinpointing. In: Gómez-Pérez, A., Euzenat, J. (eds.) ESWC 2005. LNCS, vol. 3532, pp. 226–240. Springer, Heidelberg (2005)
37. Shvaiko, P., Euzenat, J.: Ontology matching: State of the art and future challenges. IEEE Trans. Knowledge and Data Eng. (2012)
38. Smith, B., Ashburner, M., Rosse, C., Bard, J., Bug, W., Ceusters, W., Goldberg, L.J., Eilbeck, K., Ireland, A., Mungall, C.J., Leontis, N., Rocca-Serra, P., Ruttenberg, A., Sansone, S.A., Scheuermann, R.H., Shah, N., Whetzel, P.L., Lewis, S.: The OBO Foundry: coordinated evolution of ontologies to support biomedical data integration. Nat. Biotech. 25(11) (2007)
39. Suntisrivaraporn, B., Qi, G., Ji, Q., Haase, P.: A modularization-based approach to finding all justifications for OWL DL entailments. In: Domingue, J., Anutariya, C. (eds.) ASWC 2008. LNCS, vol. 5367, pp. 1–15. Springer, Heidelberg (2008)

Conference v2.0: An Uncertain Version of the OAEI Conference Benchmark

Michelle Cheatham and Pascal Hitzler

Data Semantics (DaSe) Laboratory, Wright State University, Dayton OH 45435, USA

Abstract. The Ontology Alignment Evaluation Initiative is a set of benchmarks for evaluating the performance of ontology alignment systems. In this paper we re-examine the Conference track of the OAEI, with a focus on the degree of agreement between the reference alignments within this track and the opinion of experts. We propose a new version of this benchmark that more closely corresponds to expert opinion and confidence on the matches. The performance of top alignment systems is compared on both versions of the benchmark. Additionally, a general method for crowdsourcing the development of more benchmarks of this type using Amazon's Mechanical Turk is introduced and shown to be scalable, cost-effective and to agree well with expert opinion.

1 Introduction

The Ontology Alignment Evaluation Initiative (OAEI) is now a decade old, and it has been extremely successful by many different measures: participation, accuracy, and the variety of problems handled by alignment systems have all increased, while runtimes have decreased [4]. The OAEI benchmarks have become *the* standard for evaluating general-purpose (and in some cases domain-specific or problem-specific) alignment systems. In fact, you would be hard-pressed to find a publication on an ontology alignment system in the last ten years that *didn't* use these benchmarks. They allow researchers to measure their system's performance on different types of matching problems in a way that is considered valid by most reviewers for publication. They also enable comparison of a new system's performance to that of other alignment systems without the need to obtain and run the other systems.

When a benchmark suite becomes so widely used and influential, it is important to re-evaluate it from time to time to ensure that it is still relevant and focused on the most important problems in the field. In this paper we do this for the Conference track within the OAEI benchmark suite. In particular, we examine the ramifications on ontology alignment system evaluation of the rather strong claims made by the reference alignments within the Conference track, in terms of both the number of matches and the absolute certainty of each match.

The paper is organized as follows: In Section 2 we discuss the current version of the OAEI Conference track, including the performance of automated alignment systems and a group of experts as evaluated with respect to the existing reference alignments. Section 3 introduces a new version of the Conference reference

P. Mika et al. (Eds.) ISWC 2014, Part II, LNCS 8797, pp. 33–48, 2014.

alignments that includes varying confidence values reflecting expert disagreement on the matches. Performance of current alignment systems is evaluated on this benchmark in terms of both traditional precision and recall and versions of these metrics that consider the confidence values of the matches. Because it is difficult to gather enough expert opinions to generate reference alignment benchmarks of this type, Section 4 analyzes the feasibility of using Amazon's Mechanical Turk webservice for this purpose and introduces an openly available software tool to automate the process. Finally, Section 5 discusses related work and Section 6 concludes the paper by summarizing the results of this research and describing how they can be used in the future.

The central contributions of this paper are:

- A new version of a popular ontology alignment benchmark that more fully reflects the opinion and degree of consensus of a relatively sizable group of experts.
- Evaluation of 15 state-of-the-art alignment systems against the current and proposed revision of the benchmark.
- A general method for creating more benchmarks of this type that is scalable, cost-effective, and agrees well with expert opinion.

2 The OAEI Conference Track

The OAEI Conference track contains 16 ontologies covering the domain of conference organization. These ontologies were created to reflect the material on conference websites, software tools used for organizing conferences, and the knowledge of people involved in conference administration. Alignment systems are intended to generate alignments between each pair of ontologies, for a total of 120 alignments. Each system's output is evaluated against reference alignments in terms of precision, recall, and f-measure. A subset of 21 reference alignments have been published. The intent of the track is to provide real-world matching problems over ontologies covering the same domain. More detail about the track can be found at the OAEI website: http://oaei.ontologymatching.org

The ontologies that comprise the Conference track were developed in 2005 as part of the OntoFarm project [17]. As explained in [4], the Conference track, together with the Anatomy track, was introduced to provide more realism and difficulty than that offered by the synthetically-generated Benchmark track. The history of the Conference track can be gleaned from the OAEI website. The track has been a part of every OAEI since 2006. For the first two years, reference alignments were unavailable and so alignments were evaluated using a combination of manual labeling by a group of experts (where each match was marked correct, incorrect, or unclear), data mining and logical reasoning techniques. Interesting or unclear matches were discussed in "Consensus Workshops." In 2008 the track organizers created a reference alignment for all possible pairs of five of the conference ontologies. The reference alignments were based on the majority opinion of three evaluators and were discussed during the consensus workshop

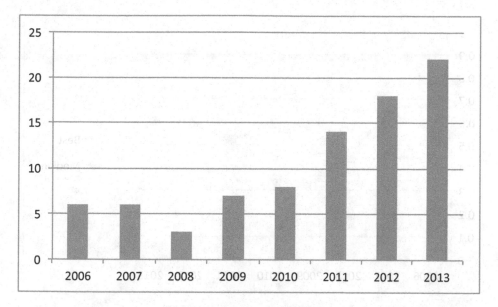

Fig. 1. Number of participating systems throughout the history of the Conference track

that year. The confidence value for all mappings in the reference alignments is 1.0. By 2009 the reference alignments contained all pairs for seven ontologies and the consensus workshop had been phased out.[1] Additionally, as the number of participating systems grew (see Figure 1), the manual labeling was scaled back from one of correct, incorrect, or unclear to simply correct or incorrect. Further, this labeling was performed on the 100 matches in which the alignment systems had the highest confidence. By 2011 manual labeling was eliminated entirely and evaluation relied completely on the reference alignments and logical coherence. Each step in this history, while understandable due to the increasing number of participating systems, resulted in a loss of nuance in evaluation.

Today the reference alignments for the Conference track are being used to report precision and recall values for nearly all ontology alignment systems being developed. As can be seen in Figure 2, performance has improved significantly over the existence of the track. Also, none of the matches in the reference alignments have been questioned in any of the ontology matching workshop papers submitted by tool developers from 2006 through 2013, and in the last three years of the ontology matching workshop none of the matches have come up for debate. However, it should be noted that these alignments were developed by just three individuals (with support from the consensus workshops). We wanted to determine the degree of consensus on these reference alignments from a group

---

[1] These reference alignments were revised slightly in 2012 by computing the transitive closure of the original alignments and manually resolving any logical conflicts. This revision was minor and did not significantly impact the performance of most alignment systems.

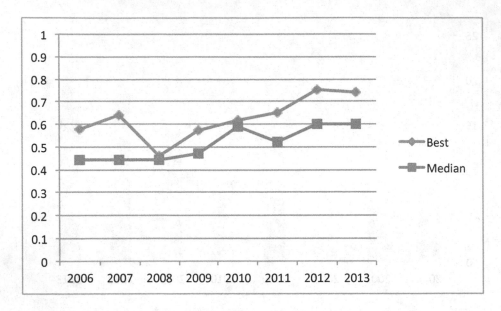

Fig. 2. Best and median f-measure throughout the history of the Conference track

of experts. Initially we collected all of the matches in the reference alignments together with any match that was produced by at least one alignment system that competed in the 2013 OAEI. This resulted in 757 matches. We asked a group of people familiar with both ontologies and academic conferences to indicate whether or not they agreed with each match. The experts politely refused to opine on so many matches. In order to prune the question set, we adopted the approach described in [15] by using the consensus of existing alignment systems as a filter. In our case the alignment systems we consulted were the 2013 OAEI competitors that performed better than the baseline string similarity metric edna. There were 15 such systems, which is a much larger sample than was used for the filtering step in [15]. We considered those matches in the reference alignments that at least one of the qualifying alignment systems disagreed on. This resulted in 168 matches that were presented to the experts for validation. The 141 matches that all of the alignment systems agreed upon were simple string equivalences. In fact, the Conference track seems quite challenging for current alignment systems, most of which are unable to identify the large majority of matches in the reference alignments that do not involve equivalent or nearly-equivalent strings. Additionally, there does not seem to be evidence of widespread overfitting despite the reference alignments being made available over five years ago. This is similar to the lack of overfitting discovered in an analysis of results on the Benchmark track after it had been available for a similar amount of time [14], and encouraging for the field of ontology alignment.

The experts were given a link to download a Java program and accompanying data files. See Figure 3 for a screenshot of the program during execution. Note

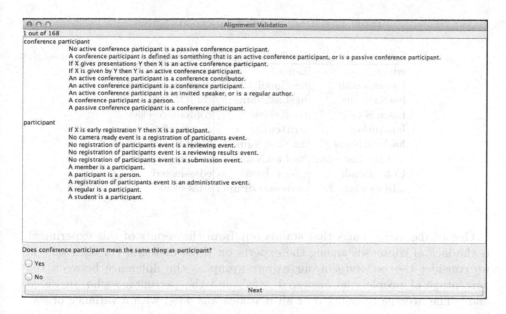

Fig. 3. Sample matching question presented to users

that the entity labels from each match were stripped of the URL, tokenized, and put into lower case. Additionally, in order to provide the experts with some context for the labels, all of the axioms in the ontologies were translated to English using Open University's SWAT Natural Language Tools.[2] Any axioms related to either of the entities in the match were displayed to the users. Users were then asked a question of the form "Does labelA mean the same thing as labelB?" and prompted to choose a yes or no answer.

We received input from 13 experts. Using a majority rules approach (i.e. considering any matches on which more than 50 percent of the experts agreed to be valid), the experts concurred with 106 of the 168 matches. Assuming that the experts would also have accepted all of the 141 matches that were not asked about because all of the alignment systems agreed upon them and that they would not have identified any additional mappings not in the reference alignments, their precision is 1.0. The second part of this assumption is admittedly more of a leap, but seems reasonable because no other matches were suggested by more than one of the top-performing alignment systems, and the developers of those systems are encouraged to bring matches that they believe to be correct but are not in the reference alignment to the attention of the track organizers. The expert recall is 0.80 and their f-measure is 0.89. The f-measure of the individual experts ranges from 0.78 to 0.95 when computed against the OAEI reference alignment. This compares to an f-measure of 0.74 for the top-performing automated alignment system in 2013, while the median of this group of systems was 0.64.

---

[2] http://swat.open.ac.uk/tools/

Table 1. Matches on which all experts agreed

Entity 1	Entity 2	Test Name
email	E-mail	cmt-sigkdd
has_an_email	hasEmail	conference-confOf
hasSurname	hasLastName	confOf-edas
has_a_review	hasReview	conference-ekaw
hasAuthor	writtenBy	cmt-confOf
hasFirstName	hasFirstName	confOf-edas
has_the_last_name	hasLastName	conference-edas
CoffeeBreak	Coffee_break	edas-iasted
isReviewing	reviewerOfPaper	edas-ekaw

One of the main things that stands out from the results of this experiment is the lack of consensus among the experts on these matches. For each match, we consider the *certainty* of our expert group as the difference between the percentage of people who answered "yes" and the percentage who answered "no." The average certainty over all matches was 43%, with a variance of 9%. There was total agreement on just 9 matches, while the experts were split 7-6 or 6-7 on 40 matches. Further, 6 of the 9 matches with complete consensus were exact or near lexical matches that were missed by one or more of the alignment systems for some reason (see Table 1). The experts deemed all of these matches to be valid – there were no cases in which the experts unanimously disagreed with a match.

3   Conference v2.0

In 2011 the developers of MapPSO pointed out that in the reference alignment for the Benchmark track (a separate testset offered alongside the Conference track) there were two matches resulting from the synthetic testset generation process that could not possibly be detected unequivocally from an information theoretic perspective. They argue that since neither humans nor machines could resolve these mappings, the confidence should be set at 50% for each [1]. We claim that our results on the experiment discussed in the previous section show that a similar issue is occurring with the Conference track. It is less than ideal to evaluate automated alignment systems against a reference alignment with confidence values for all matches equal to 1.0 when the degree of consensus among human experts is actually quite different. Therefore, we have established another version of the Conference track reference alignments which has confidence values that reflect the percentage of agreement for each match among our group of experts. This alignment is available in the Alignment API format from http://www.michellecheatham.com/files/ConferenceV2.zip.

The first six columns of Table 2 show the results of the 2013 alignment systems that performed better than the string edit distance baseline on both the original (v1) and our revised (v2) versions of this benchmark. These columns

Table 2. Results of qualifying 2013 OAEI alignment systems on the traditional and proposed revision of the Conference track

System	Pre v1	Rec v1	Fms v1	Pre v2	Rec v2	Fms v2	Pre_{cont}	Rec_{cont}	Fms_{cont}
AML	0.87	0.56	0.68	0.83	0.67	0.74	0.88	0.65	0.75
AMLback	0.87	0.58	0.70	0.81	0.68	0.74	0.88	0.68	0.76
CIDER_CL	0.74	0.49	0.59	0.74	0.61	0.67	0.75	0.60	0.67
HerTUDA	0.74	0.50	0.60	0.74	0.63	0.68	0.75	0.66	0.70
HotMatch	0.71	0.51	0.60	0.71	0.64	0.67	0.71	0.66	0.68
IAMA	0.78	0.48	0.59	0.78	0.60	0.68	0.78	0.64	0.70
LogMap	0.80	0.59	0.68	0.76	0.70	0.73	0.83	0.56	0.67
MapSSS	0.74	0.50	0.60	0.73	0.62	0.67	0.72	0.64	0.68
ODGOMS	0.76	0.51	0.61	0.76	0.64	0.70	0.78	0.67	0.72
ODGOMS1_2	0.74	0.60	0.66	0.70	0.72	0.71	0.71	0.73	0.72
ServOMap	0.72	0.55	0.63	0.68	0.65	0.67	0.71	0.67	0.69
StringsAuto	0.71	0.54	0.61	0.68	0.65	0.66	0.67	0.67	0.67
WeSeEMatch	0.85	0.47	0.60	0.85	0.58	0.69	0.84	0.61	0.70
WikiMatch	0.73	0.49	0.59	0.73	0.62	0.67	0.73	0.65	0.69
YAM++	0.80	0.69	0.74	0.73	0.79	0.76	0.80	0.54	0.65

show the traditional precision, recall, and f-measure metrics. In this evaluation approach, matches in the new version of the benchmark with a confidence of 0.5 or greater are considered fully correct and those with a confidence less than 0.5 are considered completely invalid. Thresholds for the matchers' results were set at a value that optimized f-measure for each system, in accordance with the evaluation procedure used by the OAEI. A hypothetical alignment system that perfectly agreed with the current version of the Conference track reference alignments would have a precision of 0.8 and a recall of 1.0 on this version, yielding an f-measure of 0.89. All of the qualifying 2013 alignment systems saw an increase in traditional f-measure. In fact, six systems saw a double-digit percentage improvement. In most cases precision remained constant or dropped slightly while recall increased significantly (see Figure 4). This is expected because no new matches were added to the reference alignments, but those that the experts did not agree on were removed. If we rank the systems in terms of f-measure, we see that the top five systems remain consistent across both versions. Also interesting to note, the rank of StringsAuto, the authors' own automated alignment system [2], dropped from the middle of the pack to next-to-last when evaluated under this version of the benchmark. This was by far the largest drop in rank of any system. StringsAuto approaches the ontology alignment problem solely through the use of string similarity metrics. The specific metrics used are chosen based on global characteristics of the particular ontologies to be matched. The relative success of this approach on the existing version of the Conference track may indicate a bias towards exact or near-exact lexical matches in the benchmark.

Intuitively, it seems desirable to penalize an alignment system more if it fails to identify a match on which 90% of the experts agree than one on which only

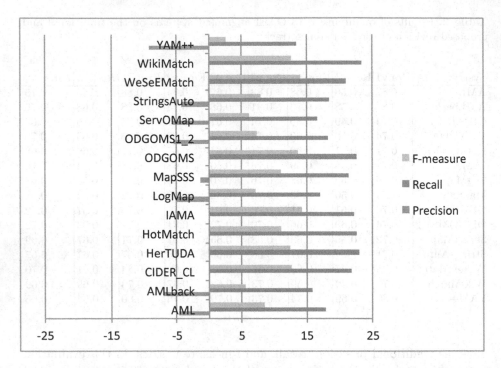

Fig. 4. Percent difference in traditional precision, recall, and f-measure between the current and proposed revision of the Conference track

51% of them agree. To do this, we evaluate the same group of 2013 systems based on modified precision and recall metrics that consider the confidence values of the matches, i.e., precision and recall metrics which are continuous versions of the traditional, discrete ones. Let us briefly reflect on how to do this. In order to follow the intuition of the discrete (Boolean, two-valued) case, we would like to retain the usual definitions of precision, recall, and f-measure in terms of the numbers of *true positives* (tp), *false positives* (fp), and *false negatives* (fn), which are as follows.

$$\text{Precision} = \frac{\text{tp}}{\text{tp} + \text{fp}}$$

$$\text{Recall} = \frac{\text{tp}}{\text{tp} + \text{fn}}$$

$$\text{F-measure} = \frac{2 \cdot \text{tp}}{2 \cdot \text{tp} + \text{fp} + \text{fn}} = \frac{2 \cdot \text{Precision} \cdot \text{Recall}}{\text{Precision} + \text{Recall}}$$

It remains to obtain tp, fp, and fn for the case where both the benchmark and the results of the system to be evaluated are expressed in terms of confidence values for each alignment.

Given a potential match i (say, between "conference participant" and "participant"), let $b(i) \in [0, 1]$ denote the confidence value assigned to this match by the benchmark, and let $s(i) \in [0,1]$ denote the confidence value assigned to this match by the system to be evaluated. Interpreting $b(i)$ and $s(i)$ as certainty values in the sense of fuzzy set theory [12] – which is reasonable from our perspective – we thus arrive at the formula

$$\mathsf{tp} = \sum_{i \in I} T(b(i), s(i)),$$

where T is some t-norm, i.e., a continuous-valued version of logical conjunction. The most obvious choices for the T-norm are arguably the product t-norm and the Gödel (or minimum) t-norm – it actually turns out that there is not much difference between these two with respect to our analysis. In fact the effect is within rounding error in most cases and maximally 3% (resulting in, e.g., f-measure of .65 rather than .67). In the following we will thus stick with the product t-norm.[3]

From this perspective, we thus arrive at the following.

$$\mathsf{tp} = \sum_{i \in I} b(i) \cdot s(i)$$

$$\mathsf{fp} = \sum_{i \in \{j \in I | b(j) < s(j)\}} |b(i) - s(i)|$$

$$\mathsf{fn} = \sum_{i \in \{j \in I | b(j) > s(j)\}} |b(i) - s(i)|$$

Note that all three revert to their original definition in a discrete (Boolean) setting in which only confidence values of 0 and 1 are used.

With these definitions, we thus obtain the following.

$$\text{Precision} = \frac{\mathsf{tp}}{\mathsf{tp} + \mathsf{fp}} = \frac{\sum_{i \in I} b(i) \cdot s(i)}{\sum_{i \in I} b(i) \cdot s(i) + \sum_{i \in \{j \in I | b(j) < s(j)\}} |b(i) - s(i)|}$$

$$\text{Recall} = \frac{\mathsf{tp}}{\mathsf{tp} + \mathsf{fn}} = \frac{\sum_{i \in I} b(i) \cdot s(i)}{\sum_{i \in I} b(i) \cdot s(i) + \sum_{i \in \{j \in I | b(j) > s(j)\}} |b(i) - s(i)|}$$

$$\text{F-measure} = \frac{2 \cdot \mathsf{tp}}{2 \cdot \mathsf{tp} + \mathsf{fp} + \mathsf{fn}} = \frac{2 \cdot \sum_{i \in I} b(i) \cdot s(i)}{2 \cdot \sum_{i \in I} b(i) \cdot s(i) + \sum_{i \in I} |b(i) - s(i)|}$$

Note that the f-measure is also rather intuitive: It is the sum $\sum_{i \in I} |b(i) - s(i)|$ of all differences in confidence, normalized (using tp) to a value between 0 and 1. The value for $(\mathsf{fp} + \mathsf{fn})$ is captured in this sum of differences.

A Java class that computes these metrics is included with the downloadable version of the reference alignments, together with a small driver program illustrating its use.

The last three columns of Table 2 show the results of the alignment systems when evaluated with these metrics. The continuous precision for most systems

---

[3] Note that the product t-norm also lends itself to a probabilistic interpretation.

was slightly higher than that of the traditional precision metric on Conference v2. The average increase was about 3%. The continuous recall measures were also slightly higher (generally 3-5%) than the traditional version. Half of the alignment systems evaluated here created alignments that consisted entirely or predominantly of matches with a confidence at or very near 1.0. If confidence values were stressed more as part of the alignment system evaluation, we would likely see larger differences between the continuous and discrete (traditional) precision and recall measures.

An interesting side note is that this method of evaluation does not involve setting any thresholds, either for the reference alignment or the matching systems. We argue that this is an improvement because it eliminates the need to artificially discretize a similarity assessment that is inherently continuous. It also considerably speeds up the evaluation process.

The performance of two systems in particular looks very different when these confidence-conscious versions of precision and recall are used to evaluate them. LogMap and YAM++ move from the top three to the bottom three systems when ranked by f-measure. These systems assign relatively low confidence values (e.g. 0.5-0.75) for many matches even when the labels of the entities involved are identical, which apparently does not correspond well to human evaluation of the match quality.

4   Using Mechanical Turk to Establish Benchmarks

While it is clearly valuable to have ontology alignment benchmarks that reflect the consensus opinions of a large number of experts, it is very difficult to persuade such experts to take the time necessary to create the required reference alignments. What if we could leverage the so-called "Wisdom of Crowds" for this task instead? We have investigated the use of Amazon's Mechanical Turk webservice for this purpose.

Amazon publicly released Mechanical Turk in 2005. It is named for a famous chess-playing "automaton" from the 1700s. The automaton actually concealed a person inside who manipulated magnets to move the chess pieces. Similarly, Amazon's Mechanical Turk is based on the idea that some tasks remain very difficult for computers but are easily solved by humans. Mechanical Turk therefore provides a way to submit these types of problems, either through a web interface or programmatically using a variety of programming languages, to Amazon's servers, where anyone with an account can solve the problem. In general, this person is compensated with a small sum of money, often just a cent or two. The solution can then be easily retrieved for further processing, again either manually or programmatically. While there are few restrictions on the type of problems that can be submitted to Mechanical Turk, they tend towards relatively simple tasks such as identifying the subject of an image, retrieving the contents of receipts, business cards, old books, or other documents that are challenging for OCR software, transcribing the contents of audio recordings, etc. As of 2010, 47% of Mechanical Turk workers, called "Turkers", were from the United States while 34% were from India. Most are relatively young (born after 1980), female, and have a Bachelors degree [8]. It is possible for individuals asking questions via Mechanical Turk (called Requesters) to impose qualifications on the Turkers who answer them. For instance, Requesters can specify that a person lives in a particular geographic area, has answered a given number of previous questions, has had a given percentage of their previous answers judged to be of high quality, or pass a test provided by the Requester. In addition, Requesters have the option to refuse to pay a Turker if they judge the Turker's answers to be of poor quality.

We used Mechanical Turk to ask 40 individuals their opinion on the same 168 matches presented to the group of experts. Each question was formatted in the same way as Figure 3, with the exception of the Next button. The questions were presented in 21 batches with 8 questions per batch. Respondents earned 16 cents for each batch and were paid regardless of the specific answers they gave. No qualifications were placed on who could work on the tasks.

We created alignments for the pairs of ontologies in the Conference track based on the results from the 40 Turkers. The confidence of each match was set to the percentage of Turkers who indicated the match was valid. These alignments were then evaluated against both the current and proposed revisions of the reference alignments. The results are shown in Table 3. The first line in the table shows that the recall is somewhat low on the current version of the Conference track. This is arguably an indication that the current version attempts to map too much. Remember from Section 2 that the performance of the experts, when taken as a group, was nearly identical (their precision was 1.0 and their recall was 0.80, yielding an f-measure of 0.89). Though further experimentation is necessary for confirmation, these results support the hypothesis that using Mechanical Turk to validate existing reference alignments yields essentially the same results as those produced by experts. Moreover, the third row in Table 3 indicates that the Turkers don't just agree with the experts in a binary context – the degree of consensus among them also closely corresponded to that of the experts, resulting in very similar confidence values. These results are quite encouraging – for $134.40 we generated a high-quality reference alignment in less than two days (over Easter weekend, no less). However, they may be somewhat overly optimistic, because the results were calculated on the reference alignments in their entirety, but 141 of the 309 matches in those alignments were trivial and therefore not included in our survey. If we compute the same metrics but restrict them to the subset of matches on which the Turkers and experts were surveyed, we arrive at the values in the last row of Table 3. These results are still quite strong, and we feel that this is a viable method of benchmark generation. This belief is supported by the fact that when the performance of the top alignment systems from the 2013 OAEI on the expert-generated reference alignments is compared to what it would be if the reference alignments were instead based solely on the results from the Turkers, there is little practical difference between the two. None of the continuous precision, recall, or f-measures differs by more than 0.02, and the vast majority are within 0.01.

Table 3. Performance of the Mechanical Turk-generated alignments on the traditional and proposed revision of the Conference track

Test Version	Prec.	Recall	F-meas.
Conference v1	1.00	0.81	0.90
Conference v2 (discrete)	0.88	0.89	0.88
Conference v2 (continuous)	0.98	0.96	0.97
Conference v2 subset (continuous)	0.94	0.88	0.91

Other researchers have mentioned a problem with spammers on Mechanical Turk, who will answer questions randomly or with some other time-saving strategy in order to maximize their profit-to-effort ratio [15]. While we did not have this issue during our experiments, it might be possible to further optimize the crowdsourcing of reference alignments by reducing the number of Turkers recruited for the effort. It stands to reason that the fewer inputs that are collected, the higher quality each one needs to be in order to reap reasonable results. Amazon's Mechanical Turk Requester Best Practices Guide[4] suggests several potential ways to find high-quality Turkers, including using qualification tests or "golden questions." In an effort to identify high-performing individuals, we implemented the golden question approach, in which a Turker's answers are validated against a set of questions for which the answers are obvious. In this case, there were nine questions on which all of the experts agreed. There were 10 Turkers who agreed on either 8 or 9 of these golden questions. We call these respondents "Super Turkers." We created alignments using only the results of these Super Turkers and evaluated them with respect to the expert-generated reference alignments. If we evaluate their results over the whole of the Conference v2 reference alignments, we arrive at essentially the same result we achieved using the 40 regular Turkers. However, if we evaluate the Super Turker results over the subset of unclear matches, the performance is slightly worse than that of the entire group. Actually, it is roughly the same as the performance of a sample of the same size drawn randomly (see Figure 5, which shows the continuous precision, recall, and f-measure for varying numbers of randomly selected Turkers). So it does seem that the wisdom lies in the crowd rather than a few individuals in this instance.

The Java code to interact with Mechanical Turk and generate the reference alignments is available at http://www.michellecheatham.com/files/MTurk.zip. The program can be run from the command line and requires the following input:

– The ontologies to be aligned, in OWL or RDF format.
– A text file specifying the particular matches to be verified. One option would be to use one or more automated alignment algorithms to arrive at a set of possibilities.

---

[4] http://mturkpublic.s3.amazonaws.com/docs/MTURK_BP.pdf

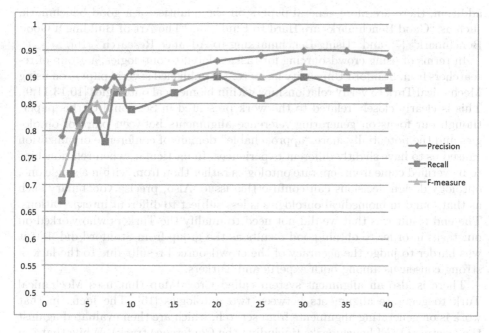

Fig. 5. Performance of varying-sized groups of Turkers randomly selected from the responses

- A text file containing the English translations of all of the axioms in both ontologies. This can be produced using the tool at http://swat.open.ac.uk/tools/.
- Two Mechanical Turk properties files containing information such as a Requester access key, the payment amount per question, and any qualifications required for Turkers to accept the assignments.

A Mechanical Turk Requester account with sufficient funds is required to submit questions to Amazon. There is a sandbox available from Amazon to test the assignments before submitting them.

5   Related Work

Most of the existing work on benchmark development for evaluation of ontology alignment systems has been conducted as part of the OAEI. The Benchmark track of the OAEI, which contains synthetically-generated tests to exercise different aspects of an alignment system, was revised in 2011 to increase its variability and difficulty [14]. The creation of a track within the OAEI in 2008 focused on evaluating the matching of instance data is described in [5]. There is also a system called TaxME 2 that generates large scale reference alignments to evaluate the scalability of alignment systems. These reference alignments were built semi-automatically from Google, Yahoo and Looskmart web directories [6]. In addition, there are more general papers on the qualities of a good benchmark, such as "Good Benchmarks are Hard to Find" [3], "The Art of Building a Good Benchmark" [7], and "Using Benchmarking to Advance Research" [16].

In terms of using crowdsourcing for tasks related to ontologies, a group of researchers from Stanford University has recently published several papers on using Mechanical Turk to verify relationships within biomedical ontologies [10,13,11,9]. This is clearly closely related to the work presented in Section 4 of this paper, though our focus on generating reference alignments between pairs of ontologies and the potentially more "approachable" domain of conference organization caused us to have slightly different experiences. In particular, when relationships to be verified come from separate ontologies rather than from within a single one, ontology design decisions can confuse this issue. Also, precise vocabulary such as that found in biomedical ontologies is less subject to different interpretations. The end result was that we did not need to qualify the Turkers who worked on our tasks in order to obtain good results as the group from Stanford did, but it was harder to judge the accuracy of the crowdsourced results due to the lack of strong consensus among both experts and Turkers.

There is also an alignment system called CrowdMap that uses Mechanical Turk to generate alignments between two ontologies [15]. The focus in that work is on generating alignments from scratch, which are then evaluated against the existing OAEI benchmarks (including the Conference track). While that is a topic we are interested in as well, we view the work presented here as complementary since our current goal is to establish a new version of the Conference track that more accurately reflects expert opinion. For instance, the authors of [15] indicated that some of the mappings from the reference alignments seemed suspect, including WelcomeTalk = Welcome_address, SocialEvent = Social_program and Attendee = Delegate (from the edas-iasted test case). Our work here has shown that the authors do indeed have a point in at least the last of these cases – our experts had a confidence of 0.85, 0.69, and 0.38, respectively, in those matches.

There has also been research into using crowdsourcing in other contexts that bear some similarity to ontology alignment, such as natural language processing, information retrieval, and audio processing [19,18].

6   Conclusions and Future Work

In this paper we show that the reference alignments in the current version of the OAEI Conference track do not reflect the high degree of discord present among experts familiar with both ontology design and conference organization. We suggest a revised version of this benchmark with confidence values that quantify the degree of consensus on each match. This benchmark can be used in the same manner as the current version by considering any matches with a confidence of 0.5 or greater to be fully correct and all other matches to be completely invalid. Alternatively, the revised version can be used with variants of the standard precision and recall metrics that consider the confidence levels in both the reference alignments and the alignments to be evaluated. We argue that this more clearly reflects the degree to which an alignment system's results match user expectations. A comparison of the top 15 performing alignment systems from the 2013 OAEI on the current and revised versions of the Conference track is presented. Finally, a general method of producing new reference alignments using crowdsourcing via Mechanical Turk is introduced and validated. A Java implementation of this system is available as open source software.

On a more general note, this paper stressed that alignments are used for a variety of purposes. For instance, an alignment used to query multiple datasets and merge the results has different requirements than one used to facilitate logical reasoning across datasets. The point here is that alignments are inherently biased (e.g. towards a particular viewpoint of the domain or a particular use case for the ontology). Crowdsourcing a reference alignment is one way to reflect the natural spectrum of different biases. The result of such crowdsourcing is meaningful confidence values for mappings between ontologies. It should also be noted that a lack of consensus on mappings, either on the part of experts or automated alignment systems, is not a sign that something is wrong. Rather, the degree of consensus is in some sense a reflection of both the reasonableness of the mapping and the breadth of situations in which it makes sense.

Our future work in this area will involve the further verification of the crowd-sourcing approach to reference alignment generation, and the creation of additional benchmarks. We also plan to integrate Mechanical Turk into an existing ontology alignment system with the specific goal of improving performance on property alignment, particularly in cases where a property in one ontology is related to a class in another ontology.

Acknowledgments. This work was supported by the National Science Foundation under award 1017225 "III: Small: TROn—Tractable Reasoning with Ontologies." The authors would also like to thank everyone who helped to generate this set of reference alignments.

References

1. Bock, J., Danschel, C., Stumpp, M.: Mappso and mapevo results for oaei 2011. In: Proc. 6th ISWC Workshop on Ontology Matching (OM), Bonn, DE, pp. 179–183 (2011)
2. Cheatham, M., Hitzler, P.: String similarity metrics for ontology alignment. In: Alani, H., et al. (eds.) ISWC 2013, Part II. LNCS, vol. 8219, pp. 294–309. Springer, Heidelberg (2013)
3. Dekhtyar, A., Hayes, J.H.: Good benchmarks are hard to find: Toward the benchmark for information retrieval applications in software engineering (2006)
4. Euzenat, J., Meilicke, C., Stuckenschmidt, H., Shvaiko, P., Trojahn, C.: Ontology alignment evaluation initiative: Six years of experience. In: Spaccapietra, S. (ed.) Journal on Data Semantics XV. LNCS, vol. 6720, pp. 158–192. Springer, Heidelberg (2011)
5. Ferrara, A., Lorusso, D., Montanelli, S., Varese, G.: Towards a benchmark for instance matching. In: The 7th International Semantic Web Conference, p. 37 (2008)

6. Giunchiglia, F., Yatskevich, M., Avesani, P., Shivaiko, P.: A large dataset for the evaluation of ontology matching. The Knowledge Engineering Review 24(02), 137–157 (2009)
7. Huppler, K.: The art of building a good benchmark. In: Nambiar, R., Poess, M. (eds.) TPCTC 2009. LNCS, vol. 5895, pp. 18–30. Springer, Heidelberg (2009)
8. Ipeirotis, P.G.: Demographics of mechanical turk (2010)
9. Mortensen, J.M.: Crowdsourcing ontology verification. In: Alani, H., et al. (eds.) ISWC 2013, Part II. LNCS, vol. 8219, pp. 448–455. Springer, Heidelberg (2013)
10. Mortensen, J.M., Musen, M.A., Noy, N.F.: Crowdsourcing the verification of relationships in biomedical ontologies. In: AMIA Annual Symposium (submitted, 2013)
11. Mortensen, J.M., Musen, M.A., Noy, N.F.: Ontology quality assurance with the crowd. In: First AAAI Conference on Human Computation and Crowdsourcing (2013)
12. Nguyen, H.T., Walker, E.A.: A First Course in Fuzzy Logic, 3rd edn. Chapman and Hall / CRC (2005)
13. Noy, N.F., Mortensen, J., Musen, M.A., Alexander, P.R.: Mechanical turk as an ontology engineer?: using microtasks as a component of an ontology-engineering workflow. In: Proceedings of the 5th Annual ACM Web Science Conference, pp. 262–271. ACM (2013)
14. Rosoiu, M., dos Santos, C.T., Euzenat, J., et al.: Ontology matching benchmarks: generation and evaluation. In: Proc. 6th ISWC workshop on ontology matching (OM), pp. 73–84 (2011)
15. Sarasua, C., Simperl, E., Noy, N.F.: Crowdmap: Crowdsourcing ontology alignment with microtasks. In: Cudré-Mauroux, P., et al. (eds.) ISWC 2012, Part I. LNCS, vol. 7649, pp. 525–541. Springer, Heidelberg (2012)
16. Sim, S.E., Easterbrook, S., Holt, R.C.: Using benchmarking to advance research: A challenge to software engineering. In: Proceedings of the 25th International Conference on Software Engineering, pp. 74–83. IEEE Computer Society (2003)
17. Šváb, O., Svátek, V., Berka, P., Rak, D., Tomášek, P.: Ontofarm: Towards an experimental collection of parallel ontologies. In: Poster Track of ISWC 2005 (2005)
18. Ul Hassan, U., ORiain, S., Curry, E.: Towards expertise modelling for routing data cleaning tasks within a community of knowledge workers. In: Proceedings of the 17th International Conference on Information Quality (2012)
19. Wichmann, P., Borek, A., Kern, R., Woodall, P., Parlikad, A.K., Satzger, G.: Exploring the crowdas enabler of better information quality. In: Proceedings of the 16th International Conference on Information Quality, pp. 302–312 (2011)

Fast Modularisation and Atomic Decomposition of Ontologies Using Axiom Dependency Hypergraphs[*]

Francisco Martín-Recuerda[1] and Dirk Walther[2]

[1] Universidad Politécnica de Madrid, Spain
fmartinrecuerda@fi.upm.es
[2] TU Dresden, Theoretical Computer Science
Center for Advancing Electronics Dresden, Germany
Dirk.Walther@tu-dresden.de

Abstract. In this paper we define the notion of an axiom dependency hypergraph, which explicitly represents how axioms are included into a module by the algorithm for computing locality-based modules. A locality-based module of an ontology corresponds to a set of connected nodes in the hypergraph, and atoms of an ontology to strongly connected components. Collapsing the strongly connected components into single nodes yields a condensed hypergraph that comprises a representation of the atomic decomposition of the ontology. To speed up the condensation of the hypergraph, we first reduce its size by collapsing the strongly connected components of its graph fragment employing a linear time graph algorithm. This approach helps to significantly reduce the time needed for computing the atomic decomposition of an ontology. We provide an experimental evaluation for computing the atomic decomposition of large biomedical ontologies. We also demonstrate a significant improvement in the time needed to extract locality-based modules from an axiom dependency hypergraph and its condensed version.

1 Introduction

A *module* is a subset of an ontology that includes all the axioms required to define a set of terms and the relationships between them. Computing minimal modules is very expensive (or even impossible) and cheap approximations have been developed based on the notion of *locality* [7]. Module extraction facilitates the reuse of existing ontologies. Moreover, some meta-reasoning systems such as MORe[1] and Chainsaw[2] also exploit module extraction techniques for improving the performance of some reasoning tasks.

The number of all possible modules of an ontology can be exponential wrt. the number of terms or axioms of the ontology [7]. *Atomic decomposition* was

---

[*] Partially supported by the German Research Foundation (DFG) via the Cluster of Excellence 'Center for Advancing Electronics Dresden'.
[1] http://www.cs.ox.ac.uk/isg/tools/MORe/
[2] http://sourceforge.net/projects/chainsaw/

P. Mika et al. (Eds.) ISWC 2014, Part II, LNCS 8797, pp. 49–64, 2014.
© Springer International Publishing Switzerland 2014

introduced as a succinct representation of all possible modules of an ontology [5]. Tractable algorithms for computing the atomic decomposition for locality-based modules have been defined [5], and subsequently improved further [14]. Moreover, it has been suggested that the atomic decomposition of an ontology can help to improve the performance of the locality-based module extraction algorithm [4].

In this paper we introduce the notion of an *axiom dependency hypergraph (ADH)* for OWL ontologies, which explicitly represents how axioms are included into a module by the locality-based module extraction algorithm [7]. This algorithm first identifies the axioms that are non-local wrt. a given signature Σ, and then it extends Σ with the symbols of the axioms selected. In this fashion, the algorithm iteratively includes in the module more axioms of the ontology that become non-local wrt. to the extended signature until no more axioms are added. The hyperedges of an ADH indicate which axioms become non-local wrt. a signature after one or more axioms of the ontology have been included in the module [9]. Unlike other hypergraph representations of ontologies [12,10], the relationship between atoms of an ontology and the strongly connected components (SCCs) of the ADH becomes apparent. This allows us to employ standard algorithms from graph theory to compute atoms and locality-based modules.

To speed up the computation of SCCs in a directed hypergraph, we first compute the SCCs of its graph fragment (only directed edges are considered), and subsequently we collapse them into a single nodes. Note that in directed graphs, the SCCs can be computed in linear time wrt. the size of the graph [13], whereas in directed hypergraphs, this process is at least quadratic [1]. In this way, we manage to reduce the size of the original hypergraph significantly, in some cases, which then reduces the time needed for computing the SCCs in the hypergraph. The result of computing and collapsing all SCCs of an axiom dependency hypergraph yields its condensed version, a *condensed* axiom dependency hypergraph. The graph fragment of this hypergraph corresponds to the atomic decomposition of the ontology as introduced in [5]. From the condensed axiom dependency hypergraph, it is also possible to compute locality-based modules using an adapted version of the modularization algorithm discussed in [7]. In this case, a module correspond to a connected component in the hypergraph.

We implemented our method in a Java prototype named HyS. We compared our prototype against state-of-the-art implementations for computing locality-based modules and atomic decomposition [14,15]. We confirm a significant improvement in running time for a selection of large biomedical ontologies from the NCBO Bioportal.[3]

The paper is organised as follows. In Section 2 we present relevant notions on syntactic locality, atomic decomposition, and hypergraphs. In Section 3 we introduce the notion of axiom dependency hypergraphs, and we use this notion to characterise locality-based modules and the atomic decomposition of any OWL ontology. We explain implementation details of HyS in Section 4, and we report on the result of the evaluation of our Java prototype in Section 5. We conclude this paper in a final section.

---

[3] http://bioportal.bioontology.org/

2   Preliminaries

We consider ontologies formulated in the expressive description logic $\mathcal{SROIQ}$ [8] which underlies the Web Ontology Language OWL 2.[4] For the evaluation of our algorithms for computing modules and the atomic decomposition as introduced in this paper, we consider prominent biomedical ontologies formulated in the light-weight description logic $\mathcal{EL}^{++}$ [2], which is at the core of the OWL 2 EL profile.[5] We refer to [3] for a detailed introduction to description logics.

2.1   Syntactic Locality-Based Modules

For an ontology $\mathcal{O}$ and a signature Σ, a module $\mathcal{M}$ is a subset of $\mathcal{O}$ that preserves all entailments formulated using symbols from Σ only. A signature Σ is a finite set of symbols, and we denote with $\text{sig}(X)$ the signature of X, where X ranges over any syntactic object.

Definition 1 (Module). $\mathcal{M} \subseteq \mathcal{O}$ *is a* module *of* $\mathcal{O}$ *wrt. a signature* Σ *if for all entailments* α *with* $\text{sig}(\alpha) \subseteq \Sigma$: $\mathcal{M} \models \alpha$ *iff* $\mathcal{O} \models \alpha$.   ⊣

Computing a minimal module is hard (or even impossible) for expressive fragments of OWL 2. The notion of *syntactic locality* was introduced to allow for efficient computation of approximations of minimal modules [7]. Intuitively, an axiom α is *local* wrt. Σ if it does not state anything about the symbols in Σ. In this case, an ontology can *safely* be extended with α, or it can *safely* import α, where 'safe' means not changing the meaning of terms in Σ. A locality-based module wrt. Σ of an ontology consists of the axioms that are non-local wrt. Σ and the axioms that become non-local wrt. Σ extended with the symbols in other non-local axioms. Typically the notions $\bot$-*locality* and $\top$-*locality* are considered [7]. We denote with $\text{Mod}_{\mathcal{O}}^{x}(\Sigma)$ the x-local module of an ontology $\mathcal{O}$ wrt. Σ, where $x \in \{\bot, \top\}$.

Checking for syntactic locality involves checking that an axiom is of a certain form (syntax), no reasoning is needed, and it can be done in polynomial time [7]. However, the state of non-locality of an axiom can also be checked in terms of signature containment [12]. To this end, we introduce the notion of minimal non-locality signature for $\mathcal{SROIQ}$ axioms.

Definition 2 (Minimal non-Locality Signature). *Let* $x \in \{\bot, \top\}$ *denote a locality notion. A* Minimal non-x-Locality Signature *for an axiom* α *is a signature* $\Sigma \subseteq \text{sig}(\alpha)$ *such that* α *is not* x-local *wrt.* Σ, *and* Σ *is minimal (wrt. set inclusion) with this property. The set of minimal non-x-locality signatures is denoted by* $MLS^{x}(\alpha)$.   ⊣

The notion of minimal non-locality signature turns out to be equivalent to the notion of minimal globalising signatures, which were introduced specifically for computing modules from an atomic decomposition [4].

---

[4] http://www.w3.org/TR/owl2-overview/
[5] http://www.w3.org/TR/owl2-profiles/#OWL_2_EL

The following example shows that there can be exponentially many minimal non-locality signatures for an axiom using merely conjunction and disjunction as logical operators.

Example 1. Let $\alpha = (X_{11} \sqcup X_{12} \sqcup \cdots \sqcup X_{1m}) \sqcap \cdots \sqcap (X_{n1} \sqcup X_{n2} \sqcup \cdots \sqcup X_{nm}) \sqsubseteq Y$ be an axiom. The minimal non-$\bot$-locality signature $\mathsf{MLS}(\alpha)$ of α is as follows:

$$\mathsf{MLS}^{\bot}(\alpha) = \{\{X_{1i_1}, X_{2i_2}, \ldots, X_{ni_n}\} \mid \\ i_1, i_2, \ldots, i_n \in \{1, \ldots, m\}\}$$

Then: $|\mathsf{MLS}^{\bot}(\alpha)| = m^n$.   ◁

However, exponentially many minimal non-locality signatures can be avoided if the axiom is normalised. An ontology $\mathcal{O}$ (that is formulated in the description logic $\mathcal{SRIQ}$) is normalised by applying the normalisation rules presented in [10], which are an extension of the normalisation for $\mathcal{EL}$ ontologies [12]. Axioms of a normalised ontology have one of the following forms, where $A_i \in \mathsf{N_C} \cup \{\top\}$, $B_i \in \mathsf{N_C} \cup \{\bot\}$, $R_i \in \mathsf{N_R} \cup \mathrm{inv}(\mathsf{N_R})$, $X, Y \in \{\exists R.B, (\geq n\, R.B), \exists R.Self \mid B \in \mathsf{N_C}, R \in \mathsf{N_R} \cup \mathrm{inv}(\mathsf{N_R}), n \geq 0\}$ and $\ell, m \geq 0$:

$$\alpha_1 : A_1 \sqcap \ldots \sqcap A_\ell \sqsubseteq B_1 \sqcup \ldots \sqcup B_m \qquad \alpha_5 : X \sqsubseteq Y$$
$$\alpha_2 : X \sqsubseteq B_1 \sqcup \ldots \sqcup B_m \qquad\qquad\quad \alpha_6 : R_1 \sqsubseteq R_2$$
$$\alpha_3 : A_1 \sqcap \ldots \sqcap A_\ell \sqsubseteq Y \qquad\qquad\quad\;\; \alpha_7 : Dis(R_1, R_2)$$
$$\alpha_4 : R_1 \circ \ldots \circ R_\ell \sqsubseteq R_{\ell+1}$$

where $\mathrm{inv}(\mathsf{N_R})$ is the set of inverse roles r^-, for $r \in \mathsf{N_R}$, and $\exists R.Self$ expresses the local reflexivity of R. The normalisation of an ontology $\mathcal{O}$ runs in linear time in the size of $\mathcal{O}$. The normalised ontology preserves Σ-entailments of $\mathcal{O}$ [10].[6] Notice that the normalisation rules can be applied backwards over normalised axioms to compute the original axioms of the ontology. However, denormalisation requires a careful application of the normalisation rules to ensure that we obtain the original axioms.

There are at most two minimal non-locality signatures for a normalised axiom.

Proposition 1. *Let α be a normalised axiom. Then:* $|MLS^{\bot}(\alpha)| = 1$ *and* $|MLS^{\top}(\alpha)| \leq 2$.   ⊣

We can apply additional normalisation rules to reduce the number of symbols on the left- and right-hand side of normalised axioms [9]. Bounding the number of symbols in an axiom results in bounding the size of the minimal non-locality signatures of the axiom.

We now give simple conditions under which normalised axioms are not syntactic local. Similar non-locality conditions are presented in the notions of $\bot$- and $\top$-reachability in [10].

---

[6] The normalisation in [10] can straightforwardly be extended to $\mathcal{SROIQ}$-ontologies. Then a normalised axiom can be of the forms as described, where A_i and B_i additionally range over nominals. However, nominals are not contained in any minimal non-locality signature of a normalised axiom.

Proposition 2 (Non-locality via Signature Containment). *Let α be a normalised axiom, and denote with $LHS(\alpha)$ and $RHS(\alpha)$ the left- and the right-hand side of α, respectively. Let Σ be a signature. Then: α is not $\perp$-local wrt. Σ iff one of the following holds:*

- $\mathsf{sig}(LHS(\alpha)) \subseteq \Sigma$ *if α is of the form $\alpha_1, \alpha_2, \alpha_3, \alpha_4, \alpha_5, \alpha_6$;*
- $\mathsf{sig}(\alpha) \subseteq \Sigma$ *if α is of the form α_7;*

Then: α is not $\top$-local wrt. Σ iff α is of the form α_7 or one of the following holds:

- $\mathsf{sig}(RHS(\alpha)) \cap \Sigma \neq \emptyset$ *if α is of the form $\alpha_3, \alpha_4, \alpha_5, \alpha_6$;*
- $\mathsf{sig}(RHS(\alpha)) \subseteq \Sigma$ *if α is of the form α_1, α_2.* ⊣

2.2 Atomic Decomposition

An atom is a set of highly related axioms of an ontology in the sense that they always co-occur in modules [5].

Definition 3 (Atom). *An atom $\mathfrak{a}$ is a maximal set of axioms of an ontology $\mathcal{O}$ such that for every module $\mathcal{M}$ of $\mathcal{O}$ either $\mathfrak{a} \cap \mathcal{M} = \mathfrak{a}$ or $\mathfrak{a} \cap \mathcal{M} = \emptyset$.* ⊣

Consequently, we have that two axioms α and β are contained in an atom $\mathfrak{a}$ iff $\mathsf{Mod}_{\mathcal{O}}^{x}(\mathsf{sig}(\alpha)) = \mathsf{Mod}_{\mathcal{O}}^{x}(\mathsf{sig}(\beta))$, where $\mathsf{sig}(\alpha)$ $(\mathsf{sig}(\beta))$ is the signature of the axiom α (β). We denote with $\mathsf{Atoms}_{\mathcal{O}}^{x}$ the set of all atoms of $\mathcal{O}$ wrt. syntactic x-locality modules, for $x \in \{\perp, \top\}$. The atoms of an ontology partition the ontology into pairwise disjoint subsets. All axioms of the ontology are distributed over atoms such that every axiom occurs in exactly one atom. A dependency relation between atoms can be established as follows [5].

Definition 4 (Dependency relation between atoms). *An atom $\mathfrak{a}_2$ depends on an atom $\mathfrak{a}_1$ in an ontology $\mathcal{O}$ (written $\mathfrak{a}_1 \succcurlyeq_{\mathcal{O}} \mathfrak{a}_2$) if $\mathfrak{a}_2$ occurs in every module of $\mathcal{O}$ containing $\mathfrak{a}_1$. The binary relation $\succcurlyeq_{\mathcal{O}}$ is a partial order.* ⊣

In other words, an atom $\mathfrak{a}_2$ depends on an atom $\mathfrak{a}_1$ in an ontology $\mathcal{O}$ if the module $\mathsf{Mod}_{\mathcal{O}}^{x}(\mathsf{sig}(\beta))$ is contained in the module $\mathsf{Mod}_{\mathcal{O}}^{x}(\mathsf{sig}(\alpha))$, for some α, β with $\alpha \in \mathfrak{a}_1$ and $\beta \in \mathfrak{a}_2$. For a given ontology $\mathcal{O}$, the poset $\langle \mathsf{Atoms}_{\mathcal{O}}^{x}, \succcurlyeq_{\mathcal{O}} \rangle$ was introduced as the *Atomic Decomposition (AD)* of $\mathcal{O}$, and it represents the modular structure of the ontology [5].

2.3 Directed Hypergraphs

A *directed hypergraph* is a tuple $\mathcal{H} = (\mathcal{V}, \mathcal{E})$, where $\mathcal{V}$ is a non-empty set of *nodes* (vertices), and $\mathcal{E}$ is a set of *hyperedges* (*hyperarcs*) [6]. A *hyperedge* e is a pair $(T(e), H(e))$, where $T(e)$ and $H(e)$ are non-empty disjoint subsets of $\mathcal{V}$. $H(e)$ $(T(e))$ is known as the *head* (*tail*) and represents a set of nodes where the hyperedge ends (starts). A *B-hyperedge* is a directed hyperedge with only one node in the head. We call a *B*-hyperedge e *simple* if $|T(e)| = 1$ (i.e., if e corresponds to a directed edge); otherwise, if $|T(e)| > 1$, e is called *complex*. Directed hypergraphs containing B-hyperedges only are called *directed B-hypergraphs*; these are the only type of hypergraphs considered in this paper.

A node v is *B-connected* (or forward reachable) from a set of nodes $\mathcal{V}'$ (written $\mathcal{V}' \geq_B v$) if (i) $v \in \mathcal{V}'$, or (ii) there is a B-hyperedge e such that $v \in H(e)$ and all tail nodes in $T(e)$ are B-connected from $\mathcal{V}'$. For a set of nodes $\mathcal{V}' \subseteq \mathcal{V}$, we denote with $\geq_B(\mathcal{V}')$ the set $\geq_B(\mathcal{V}') = \{v \in \mathcal{V} \mid \mathcal{V}' \geq_B v\}$ of B-connected nodes from $\mathcal{V}'$.

In a directed hypergraph $\mathcal{H}$, two nodes v_1 and v_2 are *strongly B-connected* if v_2 is B-connected to v_1 and *vice versa*. In other words, both nodes, v_1 and v_2, are *mutually connected*. A *strongly B-connected component (SCC)* is a set of nodes from $\mathcal{H}$ that are all mutually connected [1]. We allow an SCC to be a singleton set since the connectivity relation is reflexive, i.e., any axiom is mutually connected from itself.

3 Axiom Dependency Hypergraph

Directed B-hypergraphs can be used to explicitly represent the locality-based dependencies between axioms. *Axiom dependency hypergraphs* for ontologies wrt. the locality-based modularity notions are defined as follows.

Definition 5 (Axiom Dependency Hypergraph). *Let $\mathcal{O}$ be an ontology. Let $x \in \{\bot, \top\}$ denote a locality notion. The* Axiom Dependency Hypergraph $\mathcal{H}_{\mathcal{O}}^x$ *for $\mathcal{O}$ wrt. x-locality (x-ADH) is defined as the directed B-hypergraph $\mathcal{H}_{\mathcal{O}}^x = (\mathcal{V}^x, \mathcal{E}^x)$, where*

- *$\mathcal{V}^x = \mathcal{O}$; and*
- *$e = (T(e), H(e)) \in \mathcal{E}^x$ iff $T(e) \subseteq \mathcal{V}^x$ and $H(e) = \{\beta\}$, for some $\beta \in \mathcal{V}^x$, such that:*
  - *(i) $\beta \notin T(e)$, and*
  - *(ii) β is not x-local wrt. $\mathsf{sig}(T(e))$.*   ⊣

The nodes of the axiom dependency hypergraph are the axioms in the ontology. Hyperedges are directed and they might connect many tail nodes with one head node. Note that a head node of a hyperedge is not allowed to occur in its tail. Intuitively, the tail nodes of an hyperedge e correspond to axioms that provide the signature symbols required by the axiom represented by the head node of e to be non-local. We can think on reaching B-connected nodes as how the module extraction algorithm computes a module by successively including axioms into the module [9].

The notion of ADH for ontologies depends on the notion of syntactic locality. Using Prop. 2, we can similarly define this notion using minimal non-locality signatures by replacing Item (ii) of Def. 5 with:

(iib) $\Sigma \subseteq \mathsf{sig}(T(e))$, *for some* $\Sigma \in \mathsf{MLS}(\beta)$.

An ADH $\mathcal{H}_{\mathcal{O}}$ contains all locality-based dependencies between different axioms of the ontology $\mathcal{O}$. These dependencies are represented by the hyperedges in

$\mathcal{H}_\mathcal{O}$. Note that $\mathcal{H}_\mathcal{O}$ may contain exponentially many hyperedges, many of which can be considered redundant in the following sense.

Definition 6. *A hyperedge e in a directed B-hypergraph $\mathcal{H}$ is called* redundant *if there is a hyperedge e' in $\mathcal{H}$ such that $H(e) = H(e')$ and $T(e') \subsetneq T(e)$.* ⊣

A *compact* version of a directed B-hypergraph $\mathcal{H}$ is obtained from $\mathcal{H}$ by removing all redundant hyperedges while the B-connectivity relation between axioms is preserved. In the remainder of the paper, we consider ADHs that are compact. Notice that compact ADHs are unique and they may still contain exponentially many hyperedges. The number of hyperedges can be reduced to polynomially many by applying extra-normalisation rules that restrict the amount of signature symbols in each side of the axiom up to 2 symbols.

Next, we characterise modules and atoms together with their dependencies in terms of ADHs for which B-connectivity is crucial.

3.1 Locality-Based Modules in an ADH

B-connectivity in an ADH can be used to specify locality-based modules in the corresponding ontology. A locality-based module of an ontology $\mathcal{O}$ for the signature of an axiom α (or a subset of axioms $\mathcal{O}' \subseteq \mathcal{O}$) corresponds to the B-connected component in the ADH for $\mathcal{O}$ from α (or $\mathcal{O}'$) [9].

Proposition 3. *Let $\mathcal{O}$ be an ontology, $\mathcal{O}' \subseteq \mathcal{O}$ and $\Sigma = \mathsf{sig}(\mathcal{O}')$. Let $\geq_B$ be the B-connectivity relation of the x-ADH for $\mathcal{O}$, where $x \in \{\bot, \top\}$. Then: $Mod_\mathcal{O}^x(\Sigma) = \geq_B(\mathcal{O}')$.* ⊣

However, ADHs do not contain sufficient information for computing a module for *any* signature as the following simple example shows.

Example 2. Let $\mathcal{O} = \{\alpha_1 = A \sqsubseteq C, \alpha_2 = C \sqcap B \sqsubseteq D, \alpha_3 = D \sqsubseteq A\}$ and $\Sigma = \{A, B\}$. We have that $\mathsf{Mod}^\bot(\Sigma) = \{\alpha_1, \alpha_2, \alpha_3\}$. The $\bot$-ADH for $\mathcal{O}$ contains no hyperedge e with $H(e) = \{\alpha_2\}$ and, consequently, α_2 cannot be reached via a hyperedge. ◁

The problem can be solved by incorporating the signature Σ into the ADH. The *Σ-extension* $\mathcal{H}_{\mathcal{O},\Sigma}^x$ of an x-ADH $\mathcal{H}_\mathcal{O}^x$ for an ontology $\mathcal{O}$ wrt. x-locality, $x \in \{\bot, \top\}$, is defined as the ADH according to Def. 5 but with Item (*ii*) replaced with:

(*iii*) β is not x-local wrt. $\Sigma \cup \mathsf{sig}(T(e))$.

Intuitively, no symbol in Σ contributes to the dependencies between axioms. Consequently, less axioms in the tail are needed to provide the signature for non-locality of β. Note that non-redundant hyperedges in the original ADH may become redundant in the Σ-extended ADH. The remaining hyperedges represent the dependencies between axioms *modulo* Σ.

Example 3. Let $\mathcal{O}$ and Σ be as in Ex. 2. The Σ-extension of $\bot$-ADH for $\mathcal{O}$ contains the edge $e = \{\{\alpha_1\}, \{\alpha_2\}\}$. Hence, α_2 can be reached via the hyperedge e. Axiom α_1 is the only axiom that is not-$\bot$ local wrt. Σ. The B-connected nodes from α_1 are the axioms in $\mathsf{Mod}^\bot(\Sigma)$. ◁

Given the Σ-extension of an ADH for an ontology, B-connectivity can be used to determine the axioms that are not local wrt. to Σ and to compute the corresponding locality-based module.

Proposition 4. *Let $\mathcal{O}$ be an ontology, Σ a signature and $x \in \{\bot, \top\}$. Let $\mathcal{O}_{\Sigma}^{x}$ be the set of axioms from $\mathcal{O}$ that are not x-local wrt. Σ. Let $\geq_{B}$ be the B-connectivity relation of the Σ-extension of the x-ADH for $\mathcal{O}$. Then: $\mathsf{Mod}_{\mathcal{O}}^{x}(\Sigma) = \geq_{B}(\mathcal{O}_{\Sigma}^{x})$.* ⊣

Proof. The algorithm for computing the locality-based module $\mathsf{Mod}_{\mathcal{O}}^{x}(\Sigma)$ (see [9]) computes a sequence $\mathcal{M}_0, ..., \mathcal{M}_n$ such that $\mathcal{M}_0 = \emptyset$, $\mathcal{M}_i \subseteq \mathcal{M}_{i+1}$, for $i \in \{0, ..., n-1\}$, and $\mathcal{M}_n = \mathsf{Mod}_{\mathcal{O}}^{x}(\Sigma)$. We show by induction on $n > 0$ that $\mathcal{M}_1 \geq_{B} \alpha$, for every axiom $\alpha \in \mathcal{M}_n$.

For the direction from right to left of the set inclusion, we show that $\mathcal{O}_{\Sigma}^{x} \geq_{B} \beta$ implies $\beta \in \mathsf{Mod}_{\mathcal{O}}^{x}(\Sigma)$ by induction on the maximal length $n = \mathsf{dist}_{\mathcal{H}}(\mathcal{O}_{\Sigma}^{x}, \beta)$ of an acyclic hyperpath from an axiom α in $\mathcal{O}_{\Sigma}^{x}$ to β.   ⊣

3.2   ADH Atomic Decomposition

In the previous section, we have established that locality-based modules of an ontology $\mathcal{O}$ correspond to sets of B-connected nodes in the axiom dependency hypergraph for $\mathcal{O}$. An atom of $\mathcal{O}$ consists of axioms α that share the same modules wrt. the signature of α. It holds that for every x-local atom $\mathfrak{a} \subseteq \mathcal{O}$ with $x \in \{\bot, \top\}$: $\alpha, \beta \in \mathfrak{a}$ if, and only if, $\mathsf{Mod}_{\mathcal{O}}^{x}(\mathsf{sig}(\alpha)) = \mathsf{Mod}_{\mathcal{O}}^{x}(\mathsf{sig}(\beta))$ [5]. Together with Proposition 3, we can now characterise the notion of an atom with a corresponding notion in axiom dependency hypergraphs. We have that two nodes in an ADH represent axioms that are contained in the same atom if, and only if, the nodes agree on the set of nodes that are B-connected from them. Formally: $\alpha, \beta \in \mathfrak{a}$ if, and only if, $\geq_{B}(\alpha) = \geq_{B}(\beta)$, where $\geq_{B}$ be the B-connectivity relation of the ADH $\mathcal{H}_{\mathcal{O}}$ for $\mathcal{O}$. It follows that all axioms of an atom are mutually B-connected in $\mathcal{H}_{\mathcal{O}}$. Axioms that are mutually B-connected constitute strongly B-connected components of $\mathcal{H}_{\mathcal{O}}$. Consequently, the set of atoms for an ontology $\mathcal{O}$ corresponds to the set of strongly B-connected components in the axiom dependency hypergraph for $\mathcal{O}$. Let $\mathsf{SCCs}(\mathcal{H}_{\mathcal{O}}^{x})$ be the set of strongly connected components of the hypergraph $\mathcal{H}_{\mathcal{O}}^{x}$, where $x \in \{\bot, \top\}$.

Proposition 5. *Let $\mathcal{O}$ be an ontology and let $x \in \{\bot, \top\}$ denote a locality notion. Let $\mathcal{H}_{\mathcal{O}}^{x} = (\mathcal{V}_{\mathcal{O}}^{x}, \mathcal{E}_{\mathcal{O}}^{x})$ be the x-ADH for $\mathcal{O}$. Then: $\mathsf{Atoms}_{\mathcal{O}}^{x} = \mathsf{SCCs}(\mathcal{H}_{\mathcal{O}}^{x})$.*   ⊣

The condensed ADH is formed by collapsing the strongly B-connected components into single nodes and turning hyperedges between axioms into hyperedges between sets of axioms. The condensed ADH corresponds to the quotient hypergraph $\mathcal{H}_{\mathcal{O}}/_{\simeq_{B}}$ of $\mathcal{H}_{\mathcal{O}}$ under the mutual B-connectivity relation $\simeq_{B}$ in $\mathcal{H}_{\mathcal{O}}$. The $\simeq_{B}$-equivalence classes are the strongly B-connected components of $\mathcal{H}_{\mathcal{O}}$. The partition of a hypergraph under an equivalence relation is defined as follows.

Definition 7 (Quotient Hypergraph). *Let $\mathcal{H} = (\mathcal{V}, \mathcal{E})$ be a hypergraph. Let $\simeq$ be an equivalence relation over $\mathcal{V}$. The quotient of $\mathcal{H}$ under $\simeq$, written $\mathcal{H}/_{\simeq}$, is the graph $\mathcal{H}/_{\simeq} = (\mathcal{V}/_{\simeq}, \mathcal{E}_{\simeq})$, where*

- $\mathcal{V}/_\simeq = \{[x]_\simeq \mid x \in \mathcal{V}\}$; and
- $e = (T(e), H(e)) \in \mathcal{E}_\simeq$ iff there is an $e' \in \mathcal{E}$ such that $T(e) = \{[x]_\simeq \mid x \in T(e')\}$, $H(e) = \{[x]_\simeq \mid x \in H(e')\}$ and $T(e) \cap H(e) = \emptyset$. $\dashv$

We can now define the notion of a *condensed* ADH (cADH) as the partition of the ADH under the mutual B-connectivity relation. The cADH is formed by collapsing the strongly B-connected components into single nodes and turning hyperedges between axioms into hyperedges between the newly formed nodes.

Definition 8 (Condensed Axiom Dependency Hypergraph). *Let $\mathcal{H}_\mathcal{O}^x$ be the x-ADH for an ontology $\mathcal{O}$, where $x \in \{\bot, \top\}$. Let $\simeq_B$ be the mutual B-connectivity relation in $\mathcal{H}_\mathcal{O}^x$. The condensed axiom dependency hypergraph for $\mathcal{O}$ wrt. x-locality (x-cADH) is defined as the quotient $\mathcal{H}_\mathcal{O}^x/_{\simeq_B}$ of $\mathcal{H}_\mathcal{O}^x$ under $\simeq_B$.*
          $\dashv$

Similarly, it is also possible to compute the *partially condensed* ADH (pcADH) of an ADH. The idea is to identify and collapse the strongly connected components of the graph fragment of the ADH (Axiom Dependency Graph) such that only simple B-hyperedges are considered ($|T(e)| = 1$). The hyperedges of the ADH are re-calculated to consider the newly formed nodes.

Definition 9 (Partially Condensed Axiom Dependency Hypergraph). *Let $\mathcal{H}_\mathcal{O}^x = (\mathcal{V}_\mathcal{O}^x, \mathcal{E}_\mathcal{O}^x)$ be the x-ADH for an ontology $\mathcal{O}$, where $x \in \{\bot, \top\}$. Let $\mathcal{G}_{\mathcal{H}_\mathcal{O}^x} = (\mathcal{V}_{\mathcal{H}_\mathcal{O}^x}, \mathcal{E}_{\mathcal{H}_\mathcal{O}^x})$ be a directed graph such that $\mathcal{V}_{\mathcal{H}_\mathcal{O}^x} = \mathcal{V}_\mathcal{O}^x$ and $\mathcal{E}_{\mathcal{H}_\mathcal{O}^x} = \{(T(e), H(e)) \in \mathcal{E}_\mathcal{O}^x \mid |T(e)| = 1\}$.*

Let $\simeq_B$ be the mutual B-connectivity relation in $\mathcal{G}_{\mathcal{H}_\mathcal{O}^x}$. The partially condensed axiom dependency hypergraph for $\mathcal{O}$ wrt. x-locality (x-cADH) is defined as the quotient $\mathcal{H}_\mathcal{O}^x/_{\simeq_B}$ of $\mathcal{H}_\mathcal{O}^x$ under $\simeq_B$.
          $\dashv$

The dependency relation $\succsim_\mathcal{O}^x$ between x-local atoms of $\mathcal{O}$, for $x \in \{\bot, \top\}$, is defined as follows [5]. For atoms $\mathfrak{a}, \mathfrak{b} \in \mathsf{Atoms}_\mathcal{O}^x$ and axioms $\alpha \in \mathfrak{a}$ and $\beta \in \mathfrak{b}$: $\mathfrak{a} \succsim_\mathcal{O}^x \mathfrak{b}$ if, and only if, $\mathfrak{b} \subseteq \mathsf{Mod}_\mathcal{O}^x(\alpha)$ if, and only if, $\mathsf{Mod}_\mathcal{O}^x(\beta) \subseteq \mathsf{Mod}_\mathcal{O}^x(\alpha)$.

Proposition 6. *Let $\mathcal{O}$ be an ontology with $\alpha, \beta \in \mathcal{O}$. Let $\mathfrak{a}, \mathfrak{b} \in \mathsf{Atoms}_\mathcal{O}^x$ such that $\alpha \in \mathfrak{a}$ and $\beta \in \mathfrak{b}$, where $x \in \{\bot, \top\}$. Let $\simeq$ be the mutual B-connectivity relation in the x-locality ADH $\mathcal{H}$ for $\mathcal{O}$ and $\geq$ the B-connectivity relation in the x-cADH for $\mathcal{O}$. Then: $\mathfrak{a} \succsim_\mathcal{O}^x \mathfrak{b}$ iff $[\alpha]_\simeq \geq [\beta]_\simeq$.* $\dashv$

Example 4. Let $\mathcal{O} = \{\alpha_1, ..., \alpha_5\}$, where $\alpha_1 = A \sqsubseteq B$, $\alpha_2 = B \sqcap C \sqcap D \sqsubseteq E$, $\alpha_3 = E \sqsubseteq A \sqcap C \sqcap D$, $\alpha_4 = A \sqsubseteq X$, $\alpha_5 = X \sqsubseteq A$. The $\bot$-ADH $\mathcal{H}_\mathcal{O}^\bot$ contains the following hyperedges:

$e_1 = (\{\alpha_1, \alpha_3\}, \{\alpha_2\})$ $e_2 = (\{\alpha_1\}, \{\alpha_4\})$ $e_3 = (\{\alpha_2\}, \{\alpha_3\})$ $e_4 = (\{\alpha_3\}, \{\alpha_1\})$

$e_5 = (\{\alpha_3\}, \{\alpha_4\})$ $e_6 = (\{\alpha_4\}, \{\alpha_1\})$ $e_7 = (\{\alpha_4\}, \{\alpha_5\})$ $e_8 = (\{\alpha_5\}, \{\alpha_1\})$

$e_9 = (\{\alpha_5\}, \{\alpha_4\})$

We obtain the following $\perp$-local modules for the axioms:

$$\mathsf{Mod}_{\mathcal{O}}^{\perp}(\alpha_1) = \{\alpha_1, \alpha_4, \alpha_5\} \qquad \mathsf{Mod}_{\mathcal{O}}^{\perp}(\alpha_4) = \{\alpha_1, \alpha_4, \alpha_5\}$$
$$\mathsf{Mod}_{\mathcal{O}}^{\perp}(\alpha_2) = \{\alpha_1, \alpha_2, \alpha_3, \alpha_4, \alpha_5\} \quad \mathsf{Mod}_{\mathcal{O}}^{\perp}(\alpha_5) = \{\alpha_1, \alpha_4, \alpha_5\}$$
$$\mathsf{Mod}_{\mathcal{O}}^{\perp}(\alpha_3) = \{\alpha_1, \alpha_2, \alpha_3, \alpha_4, \alpha_5\}$$

The resulting atoms in $\mathsf{Atoms}_{\mathcal{O}}^{\perp}$ are $\mathfrak{a}_1 = \{\alpha_2, \alpha_3\}$ and $\mathfrak{a}_2 = \{\alpha_1, \alpha_4, \alpha_5\}$, where $\mathfrak{a}_1 \succcurlyeq \mathfrak{a}_2$, i.e. $\mathfrak{a}_2$ depends on $\mathfrak{a}_1$. The ADH $\mathcal{H}_{\mathcal{O}}^{\perp}$ with the SCCs and the condensed ADH $\mathcal{H}_{\mathcal{O}}^{\perp}/_{\simeq_B}$ is depicted in Figure 1.

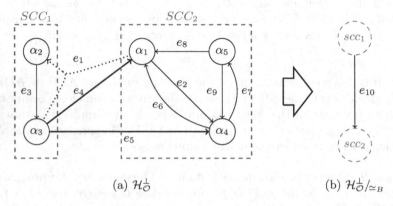

(a) $\mathcal{H}_{\mathcal{O}}^{\perp}$ \qquad\qquad (b) $\mathcal{H}_{\mathcal{O}}^{\perp}/_{\simeq_B}$

Fig. 1. Example 4: From the $\perp$-ADH to the condensed $\perp$-ADH

Consider the strongly connected components of $\mathcal{H}_{\mathcal{O}}^{\perp}$. Axiom α_1 is B-connected with the axioms α_4 and α_5, α_4 is B-connected with α_1 and α_5, and α_5 is B-connected with α_1 and α_4. Axiom α_2 is B-connected with α_3 and *vice versa*. Axioms α_2, α_3 are each B-connected with α_1, α_4 and α_5, but not *vice versa*. Hence, $\{\alpha_1, \alpha_4, \alpha_5\}$ and $\{\alpha_2, \alpha_3\}$ are the strongly connected components of $\mathcal{H}_{\mathcal{O}}^{\perp}$. Moreover, we say that the former component *depends* on the latter as any two axioms contained in them are unilaterally and not mutually B-connected. Note that the atoms $\mathfrak{a}_1$ and $\mathfrak{a}_2$ of $\mathcal{O}$ and their dependency coincide with the strongly connected components of $\mathcal{H}_{\mathcal{O}}^{\perp}$. $\triangleleft$

Analogously to the previous section, we can characterise modules in terms of B-connectivity in condensed axiom dependency hypergraphs. Proposition 4 can be lifted to cADHs as follows.

Proposition 7. *Let $\mathcal{O}$ be an ontology, Σ a signature and $x \in \{\perp, \top\}$. Let $\mathcal{O}_{\Sigma}^x$ be the set of axioms from $\mathcal{O}$ that are not x-local wrt. Σ. Let $\simeq$ be the mutual B-connectivity relation of the x-ADH for $\mathcal{O}$ and $\geq_B$ the B-connectivity relation of the Σ-extended x-cADH for $\mathcal{O}$. Then: $\mathsf{Mod}_{\mathcal{O}}^x(\Sigma) = \bigcup \geq_B(\{[\alpha]_{\simeq} \mid \alpha \in \mathcal{O}_{\Sigma}^x\})$.* $\dashv$

4   Implementation

The number of hyperedges of an ADH may be exponential in the size of the input ontology [9], which makes it impractical to represent the entire ADH explicitly. We implement an ADH $\mathcal{H} = (\mathcal{V}, \mathcal{E})$ as a directed labelled graph $\mathcal{G}_{\mathcal{H}} = (\mathcal{V}, \mathcal{E}', \mathcal{L})$ containing the simple hyperedges of $\mathcal{H}$ and encoding the complex hyperedges in the node labels as follows. A node v_α in $\mathcal{G}$ for an axiom α is labelled with the pair $\mathcal{L}(v_\alpha) = (\mathsf{MLS}^x(\alpha), \mathsf{sig}(\alpha))$ consisting of the minimal non-x-locality signatures of α and the signature of α, where $x \in \{\bot, \top\}$. In fact, not all symbols of $\mathsf{sig}(\alpha)$ are needed in the second component, only those symbols that occur in the minimal non-locality signature of some axiom in the ontology. Condensed axiom dependency hypergraphs are implemented in a similar way with the difference that nodes represent sets of axioms. A node v_S for a set S of axioms is labelled with the pair $\mathcal{L}(v_S) = (\mathsf{MLS}^x(S), \mathsf{sig}(S))$, where $\mathsf{MLS}^x(S) = \bigcup_{\alpha \in S} \mathsf{MLS}^x(\alpha)$ and $\mathsf{sig}(S) = \bigcup_{\alpha \in S} \mathsf{sig}(\alpha)$.

We introduce the notion of a graph representation of an axiom dependency hypergraph that may be (partially) condensed.

Definition 10. *Let $\mathcal{H} = (\mathcal{V}_{\mathcal{H}}, \mathcal{E}_{\mathcal{H}})$ be an ADH, pcADH or cADH. Let $x \in \{\bot, \top\}$ be a syntactic locality notion. The* graph representation $\mathcal{G}_{\mathcal{H}}$ *of $\mathcal{H}$ is the directed labelled graph $\mathcal{G}_{\mathcal{H}} = (\mathcal{V}, \mathcal{E}, \mathcal{L})$, where*

- $\mathcal{V} := \mathcal{V}_{\mathcal{H}}$;
- $\mathcal{E} := \{(v, v') \mid \Sigma_{v'} \subseteq \mathsf{sig}(v), \text{ for some } \Sigma_{v'} \in \mathsf{MLS}^x(v')\}$;
- $\mathcal{L}(v) := (\mathsf{MLS}^x(v), \mathsf{sig}(v))$, *for every $v \in \mathcal{V}$.*   ⊣

To define the graph representation $\mathcal{G}_{\mathcal{H}}$ of a hypergraph $\mathcal{H}$, we assume that every node v in $\mathcal{H}$ is associated with a set $\mathsf{MLS}^x(v)$ of minimal non-locality signatures, and a set $\mathsf{sig}(v)$ of signature symbols. Note that a node in $\mathcal{H}$ represents an axiom if $\mathcal{H}$ is an ADH, and a set of axioms if $\mathcal{H}$ is a pcADH or a cADH.

4.1   Atomic Decomposition

For a collection of well-known biomedical ontologies from the NCBO Bioportal, we observe that for many (if not all) axioms, the locality-based dependencies to other axioms can be represented using only *simple* directed hyperedges. For instance, the ADH for ontologies like CHEBI can be seen as a directed graph without *complex* hyperedges. Computing strongly connected components in a directed graph can be done in linear-time using standard algorithms from graph theory [11,13]. That is, for ontologies like CHEBI we compute the strongly connected components of the respective ADH in linear time.

For ADHs of ontologies $\mathcal{O}$ like SNOMED CT that contain both, simple and complex hyperedges, we compute the strongly connected components in four steps. First, we build the axiom dependency graph $\mathcal{G}_{\mathcal{H}_{\mathcal{O}}^x}$, which is the fragment of the ADH $\mathcal{H}_{\mathcal{O}}^x$ for $\mathcal{O}$ without complex hyperedges. Second, we compute the strongly connected components of $\mathcal{G}_{\mathcal{H}_{\mathcal{O}}^x}$ using a linear-time algorithm [11,13].

Note that the strongly connected components give rise to an equivalence relation $\simeq_{B_\mathcal{G}}$ on the nodes in $\mathcal{G}_{\mathcal{H}_\mathcal{O}^x}$. In the third step, we reduce the size of $\mathcal{H}_\mathcal{O}^x$ by computing the quotient graph $\mathcal{H}_\mathcal{O}^x/_{\simeq_{B_\mathcal{G}}}$ of $\mathcal{H}_\mathcal{O}^x$ using $\simeq_{B_\mathcal{G}}$ (cf. Def. 7). This corresponds to the computation of the pcADH, $\mathcal{H}_\mathcal{O}^x/_{\simeq_{B_\mathcal{G}}}$, for the ADH $\mathcal{H}_\mathcal{O}^x$. Finally, in step four, we obtain the strongly connected components of $\mathcal{H}_\mathcal{O}^x$ by determining for any two nodes in $\mathcal{H}_\mathcal{O}^x/_{\simeq_{B_\mathcal{G}}}$ whether they are mutually reachable. This last step produces the cADH, $\mathcal{H}_\mathcal{O}^x/_{\simeq_{B_\mathcal{H}}}$, where $\simeq_{B_\mathcal{H}}$ is the mutual B-connectivity relation in $\mathcal{H}_\mathcal{O}^x/_{\simeq_{B_\mathcal{G}}}$. Note that computing mutual connectivity this way is a quadratic process [1]. However, using $\mathcal{H}_\mathcal{O}^x/_{\simeq_{B_\mathcal{G}}}$ instead of $\mathcal{H}_\mathcal{O}^x$ it is usually more efficient as the number of nodes is typically reduced.

The function compute_condensed_hypergraph(.) provides a more succinct description of the previous process.

---

function compute_condensed_hypergraph($\mathcal{G} = (\mathcal{V}, \mathcal{E}, \mathcal{L})$) returns $\mathcal{G}_c$

1: $\mathcal{G}_{pc} :=$ collapse_SCCs($\mathcal{G}$, Tarjan($(\mathcal{V}, \mathcal{E})$))

2: if (contains_complex_Dependencies($\mathcal{G}_{pc}$) = false) then

3:      return $\mathcal{G}_c := \mathcal{G}_{pc}$

4: end if

5: $\mathcal{G}_c :=$ collapse_SCCs($\mathcal{G}_{pc}$, mutual_reach($\mathcal{G}_{pc}$))

6: return $\mathcal{G}_c$

Given the graph representation $\mathcal{G}$ of an ADH $\mathcal{H}_\mathcal{O}^x$, the function compute_condensed_ hypergraph($\mathcal{G}$) computes the graph representation, denoted with $\mathcal{G}_c$, of the cADH of $\mathcal{H}_\mathcal{O}^x$ in two main steps. In the first step, the function computes the graph representation of the pcADH, which we denote with $\mathcal{G}_{pc}$ (Line 1). Only simple directed hyperedges ($\mathcal{E}$) of $\mathcal{G}$ are considered. The strongly connected components are determined in linear time using the Tarjan algorithm [13] (Line 2). The computation of the strongly connected components when complex directed hyperedges are considered is done in Line 5. After the strongly connected components are identified, the function collapse_SCCs produces the graph representation $\mathcal{G}_c$ of the cADH for $\mathcal{H}_\mathcal{O}^x$.

4.2   Module Extraction

Modules correspond to connected components in the axiom dependency hypergraph or its (partially) condensed version. We now present the algorithm for computing the connected components in the graph representation of a directed hypergraph that can encode an ADH, pcADH or cADH for the input ontology.

The function $\mathsf{Mod}^x(\mathcal{G}, \Sigma)$ computes all Σ-reachable nodes in the labelled graph $\mathcal{G}$ and returns the axioms represented by these nodes. In Line 2, the algorithm determines the set $\mathcal{S}_1$ of initial nodes in $\mathcal{G}$. Every initial node $\mathcal{S}_1$ is associated with a minimal non-locality signature that is contained in Σ. In Line 5, the set of nodes is determined that are reachable via simple B-hyperedges that are explicitly given in $\mathcal{E}$. Note that $\mathcal{E}(v)$ denotes the set of nodes that are directly reachable in $\mathcal{G}$ from the node v using simple directed hyperedges.

---

function Mod$^x(\mathcal{G}_{\mathcal{H}_{\mathcal{O}}^x} = (\mathcal{V}, \mathcal{E}, \mathcal{L}), \Sigma)$ returns x-local module of $\mathcal{O}$ wrt. Σ
1: $\Sigma_0 := \Sigma$, $m := 1$
2: $\mathcal{S}_0 := \emptyset$, $\mathcal{S}_1 := \{v \in \mathcal{V} \mid \Sigma_v \subseteq \Sigma_0 \text{ for some } \Sigma_v \in \mathsf{MLS}^x(v)\}$
3: do
4:      $m := m + 1$
5:      $\mathcal{S}_m := \bigcup\{\mathcal{E}(v) \mid v \in \mathcal{S}_{m-1} \setminus \mathcal{S}_{m-2}\} \cup \mathcal{S}_{m-1}$
6:      $\Sigma_m := (\bigcup_{s \in \mathcal{S}_m \setminus \mathcal{S}_{m-1}} \mathsf{sig}(s)) \cup \Sigma_{m-1}$
7:      $\mathcal{S}_m := \mathcal{S}_m \cup \{v \in \mathcal{V} \mid \Sigma_v \subseteq \Sigma_m \text{ for some } \Sigma_v \in \mathsf{MLS}^x(v) \text{ with } |\Sigma_v| > 1\}$
8: until $\mathcal{S}_m = \mathcal{S}_{m-1}$
9: return get_axioms($\mathcal{S}_m$)

In Line 7, the input signature is extended with the symbols that are associated to the nodes reached so far. Using the extended signature Σ_m, the function Mod$^x(\cdot, \cdot)$ computes the nodes that can be reached using complex B-hyperedges implicitly represented by the labels $\mathcal{L}(v)$ of the nodes v in $\mathcal{S}_m$. The algorithm iterates until a fix point is reached and no more new nodes are added (Lines 3−8). Finally, in Line 9, the function get_axioms($\cdot$) computes the set of axioms that correspond to the nodes in $\mathcal{S}_m$.

5   Evaluation

The system HyS is a Java implementation of the approach described in the previous section. HyS can compute syntactic locality-based modules for a given input signature and the atomic decomposition of an ontology defined in $\mathcal{EL}^{++}$ extended with inverse and functional role axioms.[7] In the current version of HyS only syntactic $\perp$-locality is supported. We plan to extend the implementation to support both $\top$-locality and full $\mathcal{SROIQ}$-ontologies in the future.

For the evaluation, we have selected nine well-known biomedical ontologies. Seven of them are available in the NCBO Bioportal. The version of Full-Galen that we used is available in the Oxford ontology repository.[8]

We divide the ontologies into two groups: a group consisting of CHEBI, FMA-lite, Gazetteer, GO, NCBI and RH-Mesh, and another group consisting of CPO, Full-Galen and SNOMED CT. Every ontology in the former group consist of axioms whose $\perp$-locality dependencies between axioms can be represented using simple directed hyperedges only. This means that the ADH can be represented using a direct graph. On the other hand, each of the latter three ontologies contain axioms that require complex hyperedges to represent the dependencies.

We compare HyS against two systems for computing the atomic decomposition of OWL 2 ontologies which implement the same algorithm from [14]: FaCT++

---

[7] HyS supports all the constructors used in the ontology Full-Galen.
[8] http://www.cs.ox.ac.uk/isg/ontologies/

v1.6.2, which is implemented in C++ [14][9], and OWLAPITOOLS v1.0.0 which is implemented in Java [15][10] as an extension of the OWLAPI.[11]

Ontology $\mathcal{O}$	Properties of $\mathcal{O}$				Time for Atomic Dec. of $\mathcal{O}$		
	Signature size	#axioms $A \sqsubseteq C$	#axioms $C \equiv D$	#role axioms	FaCT++	OWLAPI TOOLS	HyS
CHEBI	37 891	85 342	0	5	137 s	1 619 s	4 s
FMA-lite	75 168	119 558	0	3	18 481 s	13 258 s	17 s
Gazetteer	517 039	652 355	0	6	31 595 s	–	24 s
GO	36 945	72 667	0	2	47 s	1 489 s	4 s
NCBI	847 796	847 755	0	0	49 228 s	–	66 s
RH-Mesh	286 382	403 210	0	0	6 921 s	9 159 s	17 s
CPO	136 090	306 111	73 461	96	9 731 s	26 480 s	2 283 s
Full-Galen	24 088	25 563	9 968	2 165	640 s	781 s	115 s
SNOMED CT	291 207	227 698	63 446	12	16 081 s	57 282 s	2 540 s

All experiments were conducted on an Intel Xeon E5-2640 2.50GHz with 100GB RAM running Debian GNU/Linux 7.3. We use Java 1.7.0_51 and the OWLAPI version 3.5.0. The table lists the time needed for each system to compute the atomic decomposition of the ontologies. The time values are the average of at least 10 executions. We applied a timeout of 24h, which aborted the executions of the OWLAPITOOLS on the ontologies Gazetteer and NCBI. Moreover, the table contains, for each ontology, the size of the signature, the number of axioms of the form $A \sqsubseteq C$, where A is a concept name, the number of axioms of the form $C \equiv D$, the number of role axioms contained in the ontology.

HyS consistently outperforms FaCT++ which in turn (considerably) outperforms the OWLAPITOOLS, with the exception of FMA-lite. In the case of the first group of six ontologies, an over 1 000-fold speedup could be achieved compared to the performance of FaCT++ on FMA-lite and Gazetteer. For the smallest ontology in this group, which is GO, HyS is 13 times faster than FaCT++. HyS also scales better than the other systems. For the second group of three ontologies, the speedup is reduced but HyS is still considerably faster. HyS is 4–7 times faster than FaCT++ and 11–23 faster than the OWLAPITOOLS. The computation of the partially condensed ADH nearly decreases 50% the number of nodes in the ADH. The use of a tree datastructure to represent the set of reachable nodes computed for each node of the ADH reduces the time needed to identify mutually reachable nodes.

We compare the performance of HyS for extracting ⊥-locality modules with the performance of FaCT++ and the OWLAPI. The following table presents for every method the time needed to extract a module from an ontology for a signature consisting of 500 symbols selected at random.

---

[9] http://code.google.com/p/factplusplus/
[10] http://owlapitools.sourceforge.net/
[11] http://owlapi.sourceforge.net/

Ontology $\mathcal{O}$	Time for Extraction of ⊥-local Modules from $\mathcal{O}$				
	FacT++	OWLAPI	HyS		
			ADH	pcADH	cADH
CHEBI	38.6 ms	175.8 ms	3.9 ms	2.4 ms	2.1 ms
FMA-lite	326.9 ms	1 042.3 ms	55.3 ms	3.9 ms	3.4 ms
Gazetteer	177.9 ms	1 503.0 ms	27.3 ms	16.1 ms	15.9 ms
GO	512.2 ms	1 398.7 ms	8.1 ms	6.2 ms	6.1 ms
NCBI	236.2 ms	9 193.6 ms	22.7 ms	15.8 ms	16.3 ms
RH-Mesh	91.2 ms	1 811.3 ms	10.6 ms	9.1 ms	8.9 ms
CPO	564.7 ms	3 026.8 ms	84.3 ms	53.4 ms	51.6 ms
Full-Galen	75.2 ms	215.4 ms	13.2 ms	3.7 ms	2.9 ms
SNOMED CT	525.0 ms	2 841.3 ms	93.6 ms	88.4 ms	84.4 ms

HyS outperforms FaCT++ and the OWLAPITOOLS in all cases. For the first group of six ontologies, the best speedup of over 90 times was achieved in the case of FMA-lite. Notice that module extraction times using the pcADH and the cADH (last two columns) are nearly the same as the two graphs are equivalent. The small variation in extraction time is due to noise in the execution environment. The differences in the times values in the third column and the last two columns correspond to the differences in size of the ADH and the pcADH/cADH. For the second group of three ontologies, the best performance improvement was realised in the case of Full-Galen with a speedup of over 20-times. However, we note that using the cADH instead of the pcADH does not yield a large performance difference despite the fact that the cADH is slightly smaller than the pcADH. In the particular case of Full-Galen, there appears to be a trade-off between condensation and increased time needed to perform signature containment checks. Computing the partially condensed ADH (using a linear time algorithm) is generally much faster than computing the condensed ADH (which is done in quadratic time). Given that the module extraction times are similar when using the pcADH and the cADH (cf. the times in the last two columns), it seems more efficient to only compute modules using the partially condensed ADH.

6   Conclusion

We have introduced the notion of an axiom dependency hypergraph that represents explicitly the locality-based dependencies between axioms. We have shown that locality-based modules of an ontology correspond to a set of connected nodes in the hypergraph, and atoms of an ontology to strongly connected components. We have implemented a prototype in Java that computes, based on axiom dependency hypergraphs, the atomic decomposition of $\mathcal{EL}^{++}$-ontologies wrt. ⊥-locality. Our prototype outperforms FaCT++ and the OWLAPITOOLS in computing the atomic decomposition of all biomedical ontologies tested. In some cases a staggering speedup of over 1 000 times could be realised. Moreover, the prototype significantly outperforms FaCT++ and the OWLAPI in extracting syntactic ⊥-locality modules.

We plan to extend the prototype implementation to support both T-locality and full $\mathcal{SROIQ}$-ontologies. Moreover, it would be interesting to investigate the possibility to compute strongly connected components in hypergraphs in less than quadratic time. Such a result would improve the performance of computing mutual connectivity in the axiom dependency hypergraph for ontologies whose locality-based dependencies can only be represented by hyperedges with more than one node in the tail.

References

1. Allamigeon, X.: On the complexity of strongly connected components in directed hypergraphs. Algorithmica 69(2), 335–369 (2014)
2. Baader, F., Brandt, S., Lutz, C.: Pushing the $\mathcal{EL}$ envelope further. In: In Proc. of the OWLED 2008 DC Workshop on OWL: Experiences and Directions (2008)
3. Baader, F., Calvanese, D., McGuinness, D.L., Nardi, D., Patel-Schneider, P.F. (eds.): The description logic handbook: theory, implementation, and applications. Cambridge University Press (2007)
4. Del Vescovo, C., Gessler, D.D.G., Klinov, P., Parsia, B., Sattler, U., Schneider, T., Winget, A.: Decomposition and modular structure of bioportal ontologies. In: Aroyo, L., Welty, C., Alani, H., Taylor, J., Bernstein, A., Kagal, L., Noy, N., Blomqvist, E. (eds.) ISWC 2011, Part I. LNCS, vol. 7031, pp. 130–145. Springer, Heidelberg (2011)
5. Del Vescovo, C., Parsia, B., Sattler, U., Schneider, T.: The modular structure of an ontology: Atomic decomposition. In: Proc. of IJCAI 2011, pp. 2232–2237 (2011)
6. Gallo, G., Longo, G., Pallottino, S., Nguyen, S.: Directed hypergraphs and applications. Discrete Applied Mathematics 42(2-3), 177–201 (1993)
7. Grau, B.C., Horrocks, I., Kazakov, Y., Sattler, U.: Modular reuse of ontologies: theory and practice. JAIR 31, 273–318 (2008)
8. Horrocks, I., Kutz, O., Sattler, U.: The even more irresistible SROIQ. In: Proc. of KR 2006, pp. 57–67. AAAI Press (2006)
9. Martín-Recuerda, F., Walther, D.: Towards fast atomic decomposition using axiom dependency hypergraphs. In: Proc. of WoMO 2013, pp. 61–72. CEUR-WS.org (2013)
10. Nortje, R., Britz, K., Meyer, T.: Reachability modules for the description logic SRIQ. In: McMillan, K., Middeldorp, A., Voronkov, A. (eds.) LPAR-19 2013. LNCS, vol. 8312, pp. 636–652. Springer, Heidelberg (2013)
11. Sharir, M.: A strong connectivity algorithm and its applications to data flow analysis. Computers & Mathematics with Applications 7(1), 67–72 (1981)
12. Suntisrivaraporn, B.: Polynomial time reasoning support for design and maintenance of large-scale biomedical ontologies. PhD thesis, TU Dresden, Germany (2009)
13. Tarjan, R.E.: Depth-first search and linear graph algorithms. SIAM J. Computation 1(2), 146–160 (1972)
14. Tsarkov, D.: Improved algorithms for module extraction and atomic decomposition. In: Proc. of DL 2012, vol. 846. CEUR-WS.org (2012)
15. Tsarkov, D., Vescovo, C.D., Palmisano, I.: Instrumenting atomic decomposition: Software APIs for OWL. In: Proc. of OWLED 2013, vol. 1080. CEUR-WS.org (2013)
16. Turlapati, V.K.C., Puligundla, S.K.: Efficient module extraction for large ontologies. In: Klinov, P., Mouromtsev, D. (eds.) KESW 2013. CCIS, vol. 394, pp. 162–176. Springer, Heidelberg (2013)

A Study on the Atomic Decomposition
of Ontologies

Matthew Horridge[1], Jonathan M. Mortensen[1],
Bijan Parsia[2], Ulrike Sattler[2], and Mark A. Musen[1]

[1] Stanford University, California, USA
[2] The University of Manchester, UK

Abstract. The Atomic Decomposition of an ontology is a succinct representation of the logic-based modules in that ontology. Ultimately, it reveals the modular structure of the ontology. Atomic Decompositions appear to be useful for both user and non-user facing services. For example, they can be used for ontology comprehension and to facilitate reasoner optimisation. In this article we investigate claims about the practicality of computing Atomic Decompositions for naturally occurring ontologies. We do this by performing a replication study using an off-the-shelf Atomic Decomposition algorithm implementation on three large test corpora of OWL ontologies. Our findings indicate that (a) previously published empirical studies in this area are repeatable and verifiable; (b) computing Atomic Decompositions in the vast majority of cases is practical in that it can be performed in less than 30 seconds in 90% of cases, even for ontologies containing hundreds of thousands of axioms; (c) there are occurrences of extremely large ontologies ($< 1\%$ in our test corpora) where the polynomial runtime behaviour of the Atomic Decomposition algorithm begins to bite and computations cannot be completed within 12-hours of CPU time; (d) the distribution of number of atoms in the Atomic Decomposition for an ontology appears to be similar for distinct corpora.

Keywords: OWL, Ontologies, Atomic Decomposition.

1 Introduction

The Atomic Decomposition of an ontology is essentially a *succinct representation of the modular structure* of that ontology. In this article we present an empirical study on the Atomic Decomposition of ontologies. We begin by introducing modularity in the context of ontologies and then move on to discuss the notion of Atomic Decomposition. We then present a replication study that we have performed, which thoroughly examines the performance of existing software and techniques for computing Atomic Decompositions.

Ontology Modularity. In recent years the topic of ontology modularity has gained a lot of attention from researchers in the OWL community. In the most general sense, a module of an ontology $\mathcal{O}$ is a subset of $\mathcal{O}$ that has some desirable (non-trivial) properties and is useful for some particular purpose. For example, given a biomedical ontology

P. Mika et al. (Eds.) ISWC 2014, Part II, LNCS 8797, pp. 65–80, 2014.

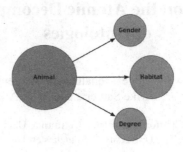

Fig. 1. The ε-connection Partition of the **Koala** Ontology

about anatomy one might extract a module for the class **Heart**. This module preserves all information about **Heart** from the original ontology and can therefore be used in place of the original ontology when a description of **Heart** is needed. In this case, the module that describes **Heart** is hopefully much smaller than the size of the original ontology, which makes reusing the description of **Heart** much easier (in terms of file size, editing and reasoning) than if it were necessary to import and reuse the original ontology in its entirety. For large biomedical ontologies, the difference in size between a module for a term and the size of ontology that the module was extracted from can be very large. For example, Suntisrivaraporn [7] determined that the average size of a module in SNOMED was around 30 axioms compared to the size of the ontology which is over 300,000 axioms. A key desirable property about the kinds of modules discussed here is that given a module $\mathcal{M}$ of an ontology $\mathcal{O}$, the entities in $\mathcal{M}$ are described exactly as they are in $\mathcal{O}$, and from the point of view of these entities, $\mathcal{M}$ is indistinguishable from $\mathcal{O}$.

From Modules to the Modular Structure of an Ontology. Although the above scenario of ontology reuse was the main driving force for the development of proper modularity definitions and practical module extraction techniques, modules have also been used for other purposes such as ontology comprehension. Here, the basic idea is that an ontology can be split up into modules that capture the different *topics* that are described by the complete ontology. Moreover, a dependency relation between topics specifies how they link together, and for a given topic, which other topics it depends upon. For example, in a medical ontology the topic (module) "diseases of the heart" may depend upon the topic "hearts", which may depend upon the topic "organs". Figure 1, taken from [10], shows how this idea could be used in a tool.[1] The circles in the diagram represent the various topics in the **Koala** ontology[2] with the lines between the circles representing the logical dependencies between these topics. For example, the topic **Animal** depends upon the topics **Gender**, **Habitat** and **Degree**. Each topic contains axioms that describe

---

[1] In this particular case, the modules are ε-connection modules, and the diagram has been produced by the ontology editor Swoop.

[2] The ontology can be found in the TONES ontology repository at
http://owl.cs.manchester.ac.uk/repository/

entities pertaining to that topic. It is easy to imagine that such a representation would be useful for getting an overview of, and browsing, an ontology.

As far as the latest modularisation techniques for OWL ontologies are concerned (efficient syntactic-locality-based techniques) there can be an exponential number of modules for any given ontology with respect to the size of the ontology. However, not all modules are necessarily interesting. This gives rise to the notion of *genuine modules*. A genuine module is essentially a module that is not made up of the union (disjoint union or otherwise) of two or more other modules. Genuine modules are of interest because they can be used to generate a topicality-based structuring of an ontology.

In terms of computing genuine modules, a straight forward algorithm for obtaining the set of genuine modules for an ontology is to compute all of the modules for the ontology and then to compare them with each other in order to eliminate non-genuine modules. However, since there can be an exponential number of modules for any given ontology this is, in general, not feasible. Fortunately, it is possible to efficiently compute the *Atomic Decomposition* of an ontology as a succinct representation[3] of the modules in that ontology. Ultimately, an Atomic Decomposition can be used to generate structures similar to the structure shown in Figure 1. Moreover, it is possible to generate these succinct representations in a runtime that is polynomial (actually quadratic) with respect to the size of the input ontology.

Atomic Decomposition. In short, the Atomic Decomposition of an ontology $\mathcal{O}$ is a pair consisting of a set of *atoms* of $\mathcal{O}$ and a directed dependency relation over these atoms [10]. An atom is a maximal set of axioms (statements from $\mathcal{O}$) which are tightly bound to each other. That is, for a given module $\mathcal{M}$ in $\mathcal{O}$, either *all* of the axioms in an atom belong to $\mathcal{M}$ or else none of them belong to $\mathcal{M}$. More precisely,

Definition 1 (Atom). *let $\mathcal{O}$ be an ontology. A non-empty set of axioms $S \subseteq \mathcal{O}$ is an atom in $\mathcal{O}$ if for any module $\mathcal{M} \subseteq \mathcal{O}$, it is the case that (a) either $S \subseteq \mathcal{M}$, or, $S \cap \mathcal{M} = \emptyset$; and (b) S is maximal, i.e. there is no S' strict superset of S that satisfies (a).*

For the notions of modules considered in this article, which are depleting modules, the set of atoms for an ontology $\mathcal{O}$ is *uniquely determined*, it partitions $\mathcal{O}$, and is called an *atomic decomposition* of $\mathcal{O}$.

Besides being used for end user facing tasks such as ontology comprehension, the technique of Atomic Decomposition can also be used in non-user facing services as an optimisation technique. For example, Klinov and colleagues use Atomic Decomposition based techniques for the offline computation of modules, in order to reduce memory requirements and speed up reasoning in Web services [11]. Similarly, Tsarkov et al use Atomic Decomposition based techniques for optimising reasoning in their CHAINSAW reasoner [9].

In terms of using Atomic Decomposition in 3rd party tools, there are off-the-shelf implementations of algorithms for computing the Atomic Decomposition of an ontology. These algorithms have been designed and implemented by Del Vescovo and colleagues [10], and further optimised by Tsarkov [8]. Assuming that the modularisation

---

[3] In this case succinct representation means a non-exponential representation that is linear in the size of the ontology.

sub-routines used by the algorithm have polynomial runtime behaviour (which is the case for the most widely used modularisation algorithms), the worst case complexity of these Atomic Decomposition algorithms is polynomial-time in the size of the input ontology.

Despite the fact that a polynomial-time algorithm is considered to be an efficient procedure, Del Vescovo points out that if a single invocation of the modularisation sub-routine takes 1 ms to perform, then it would take ten years to compute the Atomic Decomposition for an ontology the size of SNOMED (300,000 axioms in size). However, Del Vescovo performed a series of experiments on a restricted subset of the Bio-Portal [6] corpus of ontologies and her results indicate that, in practice, the algorithm performs well and is useable in tools.

Aims and Objectives. Given the potential of Atomic Decomposition techniques for use in both user-facing and non-user-facing tools, in this article we aim to check the claims of the practicality of the optimised algorithm for computing Atomic Decompositions. Del Vescovo's original experiments were performed on a subset of 253 ontologies from the NCBO BioPortal repository. Amongst various filtering criteria, Del Vescovo excluded ontologies from the experiment that were greater than 20,000 axioms in size. Clearly, this leaves some room for verification. We therefore replicate Del Vescovo's experiments, showing that they are repeatable, and we verify the claims made by extending the experiments using a current, and complete, snapshot of the BioPortal corpus. We also bolster our results with a much larger corpus of 4327 ontologies that includes non-biomedical ontologies—specifically, we use the Semantic Web corpus described by Matentzoglu and colleagues at ISWC 2013 in "A Snapshot of the OWL Web" [4].

We make the following contributions:

- We replicate Del Vescovo's Atomic Decomposition experiments. We show that they are repeatable and we verify the runtime performance results on the exact corpus used by Del Vescovo.
- We use the same methodology and software to extend the experiments on the complete BioPortal corpus. This includes ontologies that are an order of magnitude larger than the paired down corpus used by Del Vescovo. We do this to investigate the claims that the techniques are practical.
- We carry out another round of experiments on a third corpus of 4327 ontologies obtained from a Web-crawl. As well as being larger than the BioPortal corpus, this Web-crawl corpus contains non-biomedical ontologies, which may reflect different styles of modelling. We examine both the runtime performance of the Atomic Decomposition algorithm and also the number of atoms per ontology, comparing these result to the results from Del Vescovo's corpus.
- We discuss how the nature of the ontologies affects the results of the second and third experiments and make some recommendations for future work.

2   Preliminaries

In the work presented here, we deal with a corpus of ontologies written in the Web Ontology Language (OWL), and more specifically OWL 2, its latest version [5]. Throughout the rest of this article we refer to OWL 2 simply as OWL. In this section, we present the main OWL terminology that is useful in the context of this article. We assume that the reader has basic familiarity with ontologies and OWL.

OWL: Entities, Class Expressions, Axioms and Ontologies. An OWL ontology is a set of *axioms*. Each axiom makes a *statement* about the domain of interest. The building blocks of axioms are *entities* and *class expressions*. Entities correspond to the important terms in the domain of interest and include *classes*, *properties*, *individuals*, and *datatypes*. The *signature* of an ontology is the set of entities that appear in that ontology. OWL is a highly expressive language and features a rich set of class constructors that allow entities to be combined into more *complex class expressions*. As a convention, we use the letters A and B to stand for class names and the letters C and D to stand for (possibly complex) class expressions. We also use the word *term* (or *terms*) as a synonym for entity (entities).

Syntactic-Locality-Based Modularity. The most widely implemented form of modularity in available tools, and the type of modularity used by Del Vescovo and thus in the experiments in this article, is *syntactic-locality-based modularity*. Given an ontology $\mathcal{O}$ and a signature Σ which is a subset of the signature of $\mathcal{O}$, a syntactic-locality-based module $\mathcal{M} = \mathsf{Module}(\mathcal{O}, \Sigma) \subseteq \mathcal{O}$ can be extracted from $\mathcal{O}$ for Σ by inspecting the syntax of axioms in $\mathcal{O}$. Syntactic-locality-based-modules have the desirable property that given an entailment α expressed using terms from Σ, $\mathcal{M}$ behaves exactly the same as $\mathcal{O}$. That is, $\mathcal{M}$ entails α if and only if $\mathcal{O}$ entails α. Given $\mathcal{O}$ and Σ, it is possible to extract three three main types, or *notions*, of syntactic-locality-based modules: the $\bot$-module (pronounced "bottom module"), the $\top$-module (pronounced "top module") and the $\top\bot^*$-module (pronounced "star module"). To take a *very rough, over-simplistic view*, a $\bot$-module includes axioms that define relationships between terms in Σ and more general terms in $\mathcal{O}$, a $\top$-module includes axioms that define relationships between terms in Σ and more specific terms in $\mathcal{O}$, and a $\top\bot^*$-module includes axioms that define and preserve relationships between terms in Σ.

Atomic Decomposition. An atomic decomposition of an ontology $\mathcal{O}$ is a pair $(\mathcal{A}(\mathcal{O}), \succ)$, where $\mathcal{A}(\mathcal{O})$ is the set of *atoms* induced by the genuine modules of $\mathcal{O}$, and $\succ$ is a partial order (dependency relation) between the atoms. An atom is a set of axioms (from $\mathcal{O}$) all of which, for a given Σ and corresponding genuine module $\mathcal{M}$, are either contained within $\mathcal{M}$ or are not contained within $\mathcal{M}$. An atomic decomposition can be computed within a period of time that is polynomial with respect to the size of the ontology. For a given ontology $\mathcal{O}$ and each notion of syntactic-locality it is possible to compute an Atomic Decomposition of $\mathcal{O}$. This gives us a $\bot$ Atomic Decomposition (or $\bot$-AD for short), a $\top$ Atomic Decomposition (or $\top$-AD for short), and a $\top\bot^*$ Atomic Decomposition (or $\top\bot^*$-AD for short). The $\bot$-AD highlights dependencies of more specific atoms on more general atoms, the $\top$-AD highlights the dependencies of more general atoms on more specific atoms, and the $\top\bot^*$-AD highlights differences between atoms.

Class Expression, Axiom and Ontology Length. In line with the reporting of results in Del Vescovo's work [10], we use the notion of the "length" of an ontology to report the results in this article. In essence the length of an ontology is the number of steps required to parse the symbols in an ontology and reflects the number of operations required to compute a module for some signature. For example, the length of $C \sqsubseteq D$ is the length of C plus the length of D. The length of $C \sqcap D$ is the length of C plus the length of D. The length of the class name A is 1. The length of an ontology $\mathcal{O}$ is the sum of the lengths of the axioms in $\mathcal{O}$. For the sake of brevity we do not give a complete definition of length here. Instead we stick with the intuitive meaning and refer the reader to page 23 of Del Vescovo's thesis [10] for a complete definition.

3   Previous Studies on Atomic Decomposition

The most comprehensive study on Atomic Decomposition to date is presented in Del Vescovo 2013 [10]. In this work, Del Vescovo describes a series of experiments on 253 ontologies that were taken from a November 2012 snapshot of the NCBO BioPortal repository [6]. For each ontology Del Vescovo investigated the time to compute the ontology's $\bot$-AD, $\top$-AD, and $\top\bot^*$-AD and she also explored the makeup of the structure of each Atomic Decomposition.

The expressivity of ontologies contained in Del Vescovo's corpus, ranges from lightweight $\mathcal{EL}$ [1] (OWL2EL) and $\mathcal{AL}$ (56 ontologies), through $\mathcal{SHIF}$ (OWL-Lite, 51 ontologies) to $\mathcal{SHOIN}$ [3] (OWL-DL, 36 ontologies) and $\mathcal{SROIQ}$ [2] (OWL2DL, 47 ontologies). While this corpus does not contain ontologies that could not be downloaded or parsed from BioPortal, for obvious reasons, it also excludes BioPortal ontologies that are either (a) inconsistent or, (b) that are greater than 20,000 axioms in size.

Given that Del Vescovo's experiments are limited to a single filtered corpus, which has itself evolved since 2013, a replication study, which uses both the current BioPortal corpus and other ontology corpora, would be useful in order verify her results and help reduce threats to the external validity of her experiments. In what follows we therefore repeat and extend her experiments using three different corpora of ontologies.

4   Ontology Corpora

In our replication experiments which follow we use three different ontology corpora. The first, is the *exact* corpus used by Del Vescovo. We refer to this as the DEL-VESCOVO corpus. The second and third corpora, which contain much larger ontologies than the DEL-VESCOVO corpus, are made up from all parseable OWL (and OWL compatible syntaxes such as OBO) ontologies from the BioPortal ontology repository [6], and ontologies from a Web-crawl. We refer to these as the BIOPORTAL corpus and the WEB-CRAWL corpus respectively. BioPortal is a community-based repository of biomedical ontologies [6][4], which at the time of writing contains more than 360 biomedical ontologies written in various languages.

We now describe the three corpora in more detail. All three corpora, along with summary descriptions for each (sizes, expressivities etc.), may be found on-line.[5]

---

[4] http://bioportal.bioontology.org
[5] http://www.stanford.edu/ horridge/publications/2014/iswc/
    atomic-decomposition/data

The DEL-VESCOVO Corpus (242 Ontologies)

The corpus used by Del Vescovo is described in detail in Del Vescovo 2012 [10]. It contains a handful of ontologies that are well known ontologies in the area of modular-ontologies research, namely Galen, Koala, Mereology, MiniTambis, OWL-S, People, TambisFull, and University. It also contains a subset (234 ontologies) of the ontologies from a November 2012 snapshot of the NCBO BioPortal repository. Del Vescovo graciously provided us with the exact set of ontologies used in her experiment. For each ontology in the corpus, its imports closure was provided to us merged into a single OWL/XML ontology document.

The BIOPORTAL Corpus (249 Ontologies)

Since the DEL-VESCOVO corpus contains a subset of the ontologies from BioPortal, and in particular does not contain ontologies whose sizes are greater than 20,000 axioms, we decided to construct a corpus based on all of the downloadable, and parseable, OWL and OBO ontologies contained in BioPortal. The corpus was constructed as follows: We accessed BioPortal on the 5th of May 2014 using the NCBO Web services API. We downloaded all OWL compatible (OWL plus OBO) ontology documents. For each document in the corpus we parsed it using the OWL API version 3.5.0, merged the imports closure and then saved the merged imports closure into a single ontology document. We silently ignored missing imports and discarded any ontologies that would not parse. The total number of (root) ontology documents that could be parsed along with their imports closures was 249.

The WEB-CRAWL Corpus (4327 Ontologies)

The WEB-CRAWL corpus is based on a corpus obtained by crawling the Web for ontologies and is described by Matentzoglu in the ISWC 2013 article, "A Snapshot of the OWL Web" [4]. This is a large and diverse corpus containing ontologies from many different domains (including biomedicine). A "raw" version of the corpus was supplied to us by Matentzoglu as a zip file containing the exact collection of RDF ontology documents that were obtained by the Web-crawl. For each document in this collection, we parsed it using the OWL API version 3.5.0, merged its imports closure and then saved the merged imports closure into a single ontology document. We silently ignored missing imports and discarded any ontologies that would not parse.[6] The total number of (root) ontology documents that could be parsed along with their imports closures was 4327.

Corpora Summary

Table 1 shows ontology sizes (number of logical axioms) and lengths for the three corpora. Looking at the 90th and 99th percentiles, and also the max values of the BIOPORTAL corpus, and comparing these to those of the DEL-VESCOVO corpus, it is clear

---

[6] In the time between the Web-crawl and present day several imported ontologies have become unavailable.

Table 1. A summary of the three ontology corpora. For each corpus the 50th, 75th, 90th, 99th and 100th (Max) percentiles are shown for ontology size (number of logical axioms) and ontology length. For any given percentile Pn, the value represents the largest size (or length) of the smallest n percent of ontologies.

Corpus	P50	P75	P90	P99	Max
DEL-VESCOVO #Ax	691	2,284	4,898	12,821	16,066
Length	1,601	5,812	14,226	35,327	38,706
BIOPORTAL #Ax	1,230	4,384	25,942	324,070	433,896
Length	3,113	12,303	62,950	835,834	1,209,554
WEB-CRAWL #Ax	105	576	3,983	68,593	740,559
Length	255	1,427	11,374	184,646	2,720,146

to see that the BIOPORTAL corpus includes much larger ontologies, both in terms of size (an order of magnitude larger) and length (two orders of magnitude larger). Similarly, the WEB-CRAWL corpus is distinctively different in terms of size. It contains a lot of small and mid-sized ontologies (75% being 576 axioms or less), and a also some extremely large ontologies. For example, the largest ontology in the WEB-CRAWL corpus contains 740,559 axioms (it has a length of 2,720,146), which is two orders of magnitude larger than the largest ontology in the DEL-VESCOVO corpus.

5   Materials and Methods

Apparatus

All experiments were performed using Ubuntu GNU/Linux machines running 24-core 2.1 GHz AMD Opteron (6172) processors. The machines were running Java version 1.7.0_25 OpenJDK Runtime Environment (IcedTea 2.3.10).

Algorithm Implementation

For computing Atomic Decompositions we used the off-the-shelf implementation provided by Del Vescovo and Palmisano. The implementation is available via Maven Central (maven.org) with an artifactId of owlapitools-atomicdecomposition. We used version 1.1.1 dated 23-Jan-2014. For parsing and loading ontologies we used the OWL API version 3.5.0—also available via Maven Central.

Procedure

The algorithm implementation described above was used to compute the ⊥-AD, ⊤-AD and ⊤⊥*-AD of each ontology in each of the three corpora (DEL-VESCOVO, BIOPORTAL, WEB-CRAWL). Each Atomic Decomposition was run as a separate process with 8

Gigabytes of RAM set as the maximum available memory for the Java Virtual Machine (-Xmx8G).[7] A timeout of 12 hours was imposed for each kind of Atomic Decomposition on each ontology. The CPU-time required for each Atomic Decomposition was measured using the JavaThreadMX framework. Finally, for each Atomic Decomposition, the number atoms and the sizes of each atom were recorded.

6   Results

In what follows we present the main results that we obtained in this replication study. An analysis and interpretation of the results takes place in Section 7.

The times for computing each type of Atomic Decomposition are shown in Figures 2–7. To make comparison with Del Vescovo's work easier the results for the DEL-VESCOVO corpus have been repeated throughout the figures. Figures 2, 3 and 4 show CPU-times for the Atomic Decompositions of the DEL-VESCOVO corpus versus the BIOPORTAL corpus for $\perp$-AD, $\top$-AD and $\top\perp^*$-AD respectively. Figures 5, 6 and 7 show CPU-times for the Atomic Decompositions of the DEL-VESCOVO corpus versus the WEB-CRAWL corpus for $\perp$-AD, $\top$-AD and $\top\perp^*$-AD respectively. For each Figure, the x-axis plots the *length* of the ontology and the y-axis plots the time in milliseconds (ms) for the associated computation. It should be noted that the axes in all plots are logarithmic.

Summaries of CPU-times for each corpus are described below and presented in Tables 2, 3 and 5. Due to the large spread of times, some of the summaries that we present include percentile times (for the 90th, 95th and 99th percentiles). The time for the nth percentile represents the maximum time taken for n percent of ontologies in the relevant corpus. For example, the 95th percentile time for $\perp$-AD in the DEL-VESCOVO corpus (shown in Table 2) is 23,366ms. This means that 95 percent of ontologies in this corpus can be decomposed in 23,366ms or less.

The DEL-VESCOVO corpus All computations finished within the 12 hour time-out window. A summary of the CPU-time required to compute Atomic Decomposition over the corpus is shown in Table 2. All times are shown in milliseconds.

The BIOPORTAL Corpus Within this corpus 240 ontologies completed within the 12 hour timeout period. A summary of the CPU-time required to compute Atomic Decomposition over the corpus is shown in Table 3. All times are shown in milliseconds. There were 9 timeouts, with the ontologies that timed out being very large in size. Table 4 shows these ontologies, along with their sizes and lengths. Although these ontologies timed out, we note that there are other very large ontologies that do not time out. For example, three such ontologies are: one with 433,896 axioms and a length of 1,209,554; one with 356,657 axioms and a length of 891,619; and one with 227,101 axioms and a length of 726,421.

The WEB-CRAWL Corpus Within the WEB-CRAWL corpus Atomic Decompositions for 4,321 ontologies were completed within the timeout period. The Mean, Standard Deviation (StdDev), Median, 90th percentile, 95th percentile, 99th percentile and

---

[7] We chose 8 Gigabytes of RAM as this was the limit used in Del Vescovo's original work. We acknowledge that that there are other differences in the hardware used, but where possible we used the same parameters, for example, max available RAM.

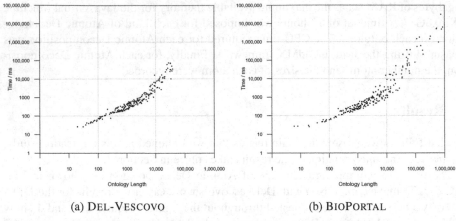

(a) DEL-VESCOVO   (b) BIOPORTAL

Fig. 2. The time (ms) to compute ⊥-AD versus ontology length

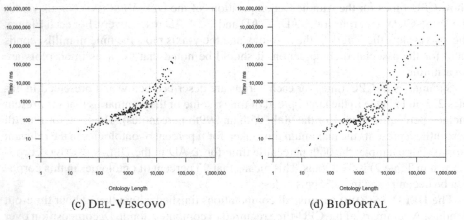

(c) DEL-VESCOVO   (d) BIOPORTAL

Fig. 3. The time (ms) to compute ⊤-AD versus ontology length

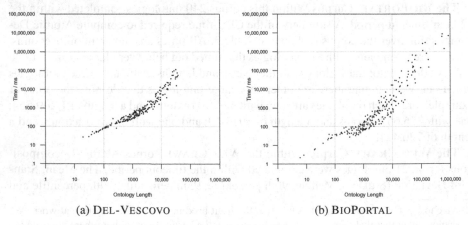

(a) DEL-VESCOVO   (b) BIOPORTAL

Fig. 4. The time (ms) to compute ⊤⊥*-AD versus ontology length

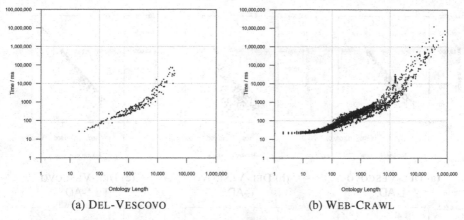

(a) DEL-VESCOVO
(b) WEB-CRAWL

Fig. 5. The time (ms) to compute ⊥-AD versus ontology length.

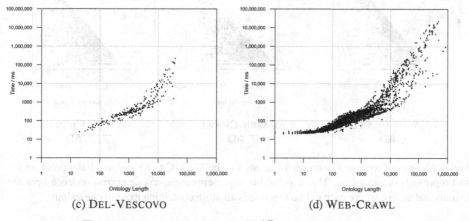

(c) DEL-VESCOVO
(d) WEB-CRAWL

Fig. 6. The time (ms) to compute ⊤-AD versus ontology length

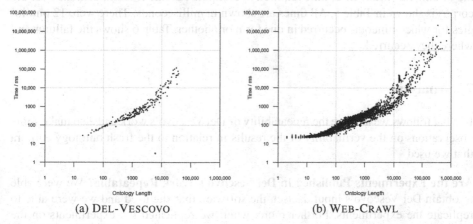

(a) DEL-VESCOVO
(b) WEB-CRAWL

Fig. 7. The time (ms) to compute ⊤⊥*-AD versus ontology length

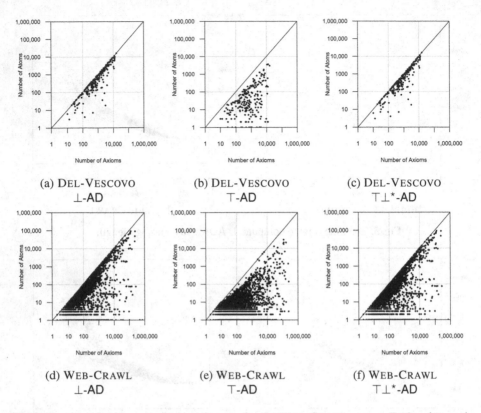

(a) DEL-VESCOVO ⊥-AD

(b) DEL-VESCOVO ⊤-AD

(c) DEL-VESCOVO ⊤⊥*-AD

(d) WEB-CRAWL ⊥-AD

(e) WEB-CRAWL ⊤-AD

(f) WEB-CRAWL ⊤⊥*-AD

Fig. 8. Number of axioms vs number of atoms for the WEB-CRAWL corpus. Each point on the plot represents one ontology. The diagonal line represents a one-to-one correspondence between axioms and atoms, where each dot on this line is an atom containing exactly one axiom.

the Maximum (Max) CPU-time required to compute Atomic Decompositions over the corpus is shown in Table 5. All times are shown in milliseconds. There were 12 ontologies for which timeouts occurred in one form or another. Table 6 shows the failures and where they occurred.

7   Analysis

In what follows we analyse the repeatability of Del Vescovo's work and also make some observations on the verifiability of the results in relation to the fresh ontology corpora that we used.

Are the Experiments Published in Del Vescovo's Work Repeatable? We were able to obtain Del Vescovo's input dataset, the software that she used and we were able to replicate the experiments. Further more, when we replicated the experiments on the DEL-VESCOVO corpus, all of the algorithms terminated on all inputs and, while we do not include an exact comparison of times due to hardware setup differences, our

Table 2. A Summary of the CPU-Time required for computing Atomic Decompositions on the DEL-VESCOVO corpus. All times are shown in milliseconds. Pn represents the maximum time for the nth percentile.

			CPU-Time / (milliseconds)				
Type	Mean	StdDev	Median	P90	P95	P99	Max
⊥-AD	3,756	10,597	461	8,424	23,366	64,586	72,499
⊤-AD	5,379	21,857	353	8,559	23,327	131,541	222,760
⊤⊥*-AD	5,633	16,275	564	13,051	35,783	93,090	113,581

Table 3. A Summary of the CPU-Time required for computing Atomic Decompositions on the BIOPORTAL corpus. All times are shown in milliseconds.

			CPU-Time / (milliseconds)				
Type	Mean	StdDev	Median	P90	P95	P99	Max
⊥-AD	31,592	164,585	575	27,988	102,048	587,664	1,778,371
⊤-AD	56,499	387,190	171	20,573	113,216	1,274,069	5,168,475
⊤⊥*-AD	52,687	288,363	306	44,074	155,289	1,053,092	3,046,087

times were in the same order of magnitude as the times computed by Del Vescovo. Figures 2(a) - 7(a) exhibit the same data spread as Figures 4.7, 4.8 and 4.9 in Del Vescovo's presentation of the results [10]. Del Vescovo observed that, over her complete corpus, times for computing ⊤-AD's are generally larger than those for computing ⊥-AD's. We also observed this aspect (Table 2), mainly for larger ontologies in the corpus. Overall, we therefore consider Del Vescovo's results to be repeatable. Moreover, we consider our results on the DEL-VESCOVO corpus to be a reliable proxy for her results.

What Are the Main Similarities and Differences That Can Be Observed between the DEL-VESCOVO Corpus the Other Two Corpora? The first thing to note are significant differences in the makeup of the DEL-VESCOVO corpus and our corpora. Both the BIOPORTAL corpus and the WEB-CRAWL corpus contain ontologies that are smaller and also ontologies that are (one or two orders of magnitude) larger than the ontologies found in the DEL-VESCOVO corpus (see Table 1). For some of the largest ontologies, certain types of Atomic Decompositions could not be computed within 12 hours (Table 4 and Table 6). Having said this, there are equally large ontologies for which it is possible to compute the Atomic Decompositions. Looking at these Figures 2(a) - 7(a) and comparing these with the corresponding 2(b) - 7(b) the distributions of points on the plots over the same length scales are obviously similar. For smaller ontology lengths and larger ontology lengths, the plots highlight the polynomial trend in computation time. For the largest ontologies, which have lengths in excess of 500,000 and up to 1,000,000, it is noticeable that the computation time strays above one hour (3,600,000ms). Ontologies of this size were not present in Del Vescovo's sample and these results begin to give some idea of what is possible with, and the boundaries of,

Table 4. Ontologies in the BIOPORTAL corpus that had timeouts

Ontology	Axioms	Length
OMIM	112,794	302,298
NPO	160,002	389,385
CVRGRID	172,647	431,713
SNMI	218,231	545,611
NCI	227,101	726,421
RXNORM	253377	759,955
PIERO	288,767	794,163
ICD	356,657	891,619
RADLEX	433,896	1,209,554

Table 5. A Summary of the CPU-Time required for computing Atomic Decompositions on the WEB-CRAWL corpus. All times are shown in milliseconds.

			CPU-Time / (milliseconds)				
Type	Mean	StdDev	Median	P90	P95	P99	Max
$\perp$-AD	35,617	732,890	105	968	11,018	21,915	54,340
$\top$-AD	72,124	832,698	100	2,732	21,291	982,399	21,793,805
$\top\perp^*$-AD	37,940	643,327	138	2,246	26,418	688,046	28,993,456

the current implementation. Obviously, whether or not these times are practical depends entirely upon the application in question.

Why Do Several Ontologies in the BIOPORTAL Corpus and the WEB-CRAWL Corpus Have Timeouts? The primary cause is the size of the ontology and the size of modules in these ontologies. On closer inspection we found that nearly all of these ontologies have extremely large ABoxes. Browsing through them in Protégé also revealed that these ABoxes are largely used for annotation purposes as their individual-signatures were puns of class names which participated in labelling property assertions (such as skos:notation, or name, where these properties are data properties rather than annotation properties). Ignoring these ABox assertions, which are essentially annotations, would bring many of the ontology lengths into the bounds whereby the Atomic Decompositons could be computed.

How Does the Number of Atoms Vary between the Different Corpora? Figure 8 shows how the number of atoms per ontology vary over the DEL-VESCOVO corpus and the WEB-CRAWL corpus.[8] The main thing to note is that variation over each corpus is similar for the different notions of Atomic Decomposition. For example, it is easy to see that the number of atoms in a $\top$-AD tend to be fewer and larger when compared to the

---

[8] For the sake of brevity we only compare these two corpora. The results are similar for the DEL-VESCOVO corpus and the BIOPORTAL corpus.

Table 6. Ontologies in the WEB-CRAWL corpus that had timeouts. Ontologies are sorted by length.

OntologyId	Axioms	Length
3631	117,135	234,268
3069	139,358	288,755
4093	119,560	327,946
3886	168,826	423,119
3147	230,477	474,265
4301	334,546	693,230
2245	277,039	816,406
1577	539,885	1,128,610
1123	238,310	1,495,684
496	714,789	1,892,611
47	740,559	2,122,416
2658	476,620	2,720,146

$\perp$-AD and $\top\perp$*-AD.[9] The other thing to note is that the majority of $\top$-AD and $\perp$-AD atoms are fine-grained. This phenomena is manifested as the points clustering around the diagonals in the plots for these types of decompositions. In this sense, ontologies in the WEB-CRAWL corpus exhibit similar modular structures to the ontologies in the DEL-VESCOVO corpus.

What Is the Practical Implication of These Results? The algorithm for computing Atomic Decompositions has a theoretical worst-case complexity of polynomial runtime behaviour. The polynomial runtime over all corpora is evident from looking at the plots of CPU-time vs ontology length. For the vast majority of ontologies, Del Vescovo's observation, that computing the Atomic Decompositions for naturally occurring ontologies is practical holds—over all corpora the Atomic Decompositions for 90% of ontologies could be computes in less than 30 seconds. For the handful of extremely large ontologies, the polynomial runtime behaviour of the algorithm begins to bite and there a small number of these ontologies for which it is not possible to compute the Atomic Decomposition within what one might regard as a reasonable time frame. For balance, we note that there are huge ontologies for which it is possible to compute the Atomic Decompositions including ontologies of sizes 433,896 axioms, 356,657 axioms and 227,101 axioms.

8   Conclusions

In this article we performed a replication study using an off-the-shelf Atomic Decomposition algorithm on three large test corpora of OWL ontologies. The main aim of this work was to replicate and verify previously published results. Our findings indicate that

---

[9] Recall that atoms are disjoint with each other and the complete set of atoms for an ontology covers that ontology.

(a) the previously published empirical studies in this area are repeatable; (b) computing Atomic Decompositions in the vast majority of cases is practical, in that they can be computed in less than 30 seconds in 90% of cases, even for ontologies containing hundreds of thousands of axioms; (c) there are occurrences of extremely large ontologies ($< 1\%$ in our test corpora) where the polynomial runtime behaviour of the Atomic Decomposition algorithm begins to bite, and computations cannot be completed within 12-hours of CPU time; (d) the distribution of number of atoms in the Atomic Decomposition for an ontology appears to be similar for distinct corpora. Finally, the ontology corpora, summary metrics for the corpora, experiment results and software used to run the experiments are available online at http://www.stanford.edu/~horridge/publications/2014/iswc/atomic-decomposition/data.

Acknowledgements. This work was funded by Grant GM103316 from the National Institute of General Medical Sciences at the United States National Institute of Health.

References

1. Baader, F., Brandt, S., Lutz, C.: Pushing the $\mathcal{EL}$ envelope. In: Proceedings of IJCAI (2005)
2. Horrocks, I., Kutz, O., Sattler, U.: The even more irresistible $\mathcal{SROIQ}$. In: Proceedings of KR 2006 (2006)
3. Horrocks, I., Patel-Schneider, P.F., van Harmelen, F.: From $\mathcal{SHIQ}$ and RDF to OWL: The making of a web ontology language. J. of Web Semantics 1(1), 7–26 (2003)
4. Matentzoglu, N., Bail, S., Parsia, B.: A snapshot of the OWL Web. In: Alani, H., et al. (eds.) ISWC 2013, Part I. LNCS, vol. 8218, pp. 331–346. Springer, Heidelberg (2013)
5. Motik, B., Patel-Schneider, P.F., Parsia, B.: OWL 2 Web Ontology Language structural specification and functional style syntax. Technical report, W3C – World Wide Web Consortium (October 2009)
6. Noy, N.F., Shah, N.H., Whetzel, P.L., Dai, B., Dorf, M.V., Griffith, N., Jonquet, C., Rubin, D.L., Storey, M.-A., Chute, C.G., Musen, M.A.: BioPortal: Ontologies and integrated data resources at the click of a mouse. Nucleic Acids Research 37 (May 2009)
7. Suntisrivaraporn, B.: Polynomial-Time Reasoning Support for Design and Maintenance of Large-Scale Biomedical Ontologies. PhD thesis, T.U. Dresden (2009)
8. Tsarkov, D.: Improved algorithms for module extraction and atomic decomposition. In: Proceedings of DL 2012 (2012)
9. Tsarkov, D., Palmisano, I.: Chainsaw: a metareasoner for large ontologies. In: Proceedings of ORE 2012 (2012)
10. Del Vescovo, C.: The Modular Structure of an Ontology: Atomic Decomposition and its applications. PhD thesis, The University of Manchester (2013)
11. Del Vescovo, C., Gessler, D.D.G., Klinov, P., Parsia, B., Sattler, U., Schneider, T., Winget, A.: Decomposition and modular structure of BioPortal ontologies. In: Aroyo, L., Welty, C., Alani, H., Taylor, J., Bernstein, A., Kagal, L., Noy, N., Blomqvist, E. (eds.) ISWC 2011, Part I. LNCS, vol. 7031, pp. 130–145. Springer, Heidelberg (2011)

Structural Properties as Proxy for Semantic Relevance in RDF Graph Sampling*

Laurens Rietveld[1], Rinke Hoekstra[1,2],
Stefan Schlobach[1], and Christophe Guéret[3]

[1] Dept. of Computer Science, VU University Amsterdam, NL
{laurens.rietveld,k.s.schlobach,rinke.hoekstra}@vu.nl
[2] Leibniz Center for Law, University of Amsterdam, NL
hoekstra@uva.nl
[3] Data Archiving and Network Services (DANS), NL
christophe.gueret@dans.knaw.nl

Abstract. The Linked Data cloud has grown to become the largest knowledge base ever constructed. Its size is now turning into a major bottleneck for many applications. In order to facilitate access to this structured information, this paper proposes an automatic sampling method targeted at maximizing answer coverage for applications using SPARQL querying. The approach presented in this paper is novel: no similar RDF sampling approach exist. Additionally, the concept of creating a sample aimed at maximizing SPARQL answer coverage, is unique. We empirically show that the relevance of triples for sampling (a semantic notion) is influenced by the topology of the graph (purely structural), and can be determined without prior knowledge of the queries. Experiments show a significantly higher recall of topology based sampling methods over random and naive baseline approaches (e.g. up to 90% for Open-BioMed at a sample size of 6%).

Keywords: subgraphs, sampling, graph analysis, ranking, Linked Data.

1 Introduction

The Linked Data cloud grows every year [4,10] and has turned the Web of Data into a knowledge base of unprecedented size and complexity. This poses problems with respect to the scalability of our current infrastructure and tools. Datasets such as DBPedia (459M triples) and Linked Geo Data (289M triples) are central to many Linked Data applications. Local use of such large datasets requires investments in powerful hardware, and cloud-based hosting is not free either. These costs are avoidable if we know which part of the dataset is needed for our application, i.e. if only we could pick the data a priori that is actually being used, or required to solve a particular task. Experience in the OpenPHACTS and

---

* This work was supported by the Dutch national program COMMIT, and carried out on the Dutch national e-infrastructure with the support of SURF Foundation.

P. Mika et al. (Eds.) ISWC 2014, Part II, LNCS 8797, pp. 81–96, 2014.

Data2Semantics projects[1] shows that for the purposes of prototyping, demoing or testing, developers and users are content with relevant subsets of the data. They accept the possibility of incomplete results that comes with it. A locally available subset is also useful when the connection to a cloud based server is inaccessible (something which happens frequently [10]). Since more users can host subsets of very large data locally, this will lift some of the burden for (often non-commercial) Linked Data providers, while links to the remaining parts on external servers remain in place.

Our analysis of five large datasets (>50M triples) shows that for a realistic set of queries, at most 2% of the dataset is actually used (see the 'coverage' column in Table 1): a clear opportunity for pruning RDF datasets to more manageable sizes.[2] Unfortunately, this set of queries is not always known: queries are not logged or logs are not available because of privacy or property rights issues. And even if a query set is available, it may not be representative or suitable, e.g. it contains queries that return the entire dataset.

We define *relevant sampling* as the task of finding those parts of an RDF graph that maximize a task-specific relevance function while minimizing size. For our use case, this relevance function relies on semantics: we try to find the smallest part of the data that entails as many of the original answers to typical SPARQL queries as possible. This paper investigates whether we can use structural properties of RDF graphs to predict the relevance of triples for typical queries.

To evaluate this approach, we represent "typical use" by means of a large number of SPARQL queries fired against datasets of various size and domain: *DB-pedia 3.9* [3], *Linked Geo Data* [5], *MetaLex* [19], *Open-BioMed*[3], *Bio2RDF* [8] and *Semantic Web Dog Food* [24] (see Table 1). The queries were obtained from server logs of the triple stores hosting the datasets and range between 800 and 5000 queries for each dataset. Given these datasets and query logs, we then 1) rewrite RDF graphs into directed unlabeled graphs, 2) analyze the topology of these graphs using standard network analysis methods, 3) assign the derived weights to triples, and 4) generate samples for every percentile of the size of the original graph. These steps were implemented as a scalable sampling pipeline, called *SampLD*.

Our results show that the topology of the hypergraph alone helps to predict the relevance of triples for typical use in SPARQL queries. In other words, we show in this paper that without prior knowledge of the queries to be answered, we can determine to a surprisingly high degree which triples in the dataset can safely be ignored and which cannot. As a result, we are able to achieve a recall of up to .96 with a sample size as small as 6%, using *only* the structural

---

[1] See http://openphacts.org and http://www.data2semantics.org, respectively.

[2] The figure of 2% depends on the assumption that the part of the graph touched by queries is relatively stable over time. We intend to investigate this further in future work.

[3] See http://www.open-biomed.org.uk/

properties of the graph. This means that we can use purely *structural* properties of a knowledge base as proxy for a *semantic* notion of relevance.

This paper is structured as follows. We first discuss related work, followed by the problem definition and a description of our approach. The fourth section discusses the experiment setup and evaluation, after which we present the results. Finally we discuss our conclusions.

2   Related Work

Other than naive random sampling [30], extracting relevant parts of Linked Data graphs has not been done before. However, there are a number of related approaches that deserve mentioning: relevance ranking for Linked Data, generating SPARQL benchmark queries, graph rewriting techniques, and non-deterministic network sampling techniques.

Network Sampling. [23] evaluates several non-deterministic methods for sampling networks: random node selection, random edge selection, and exploration techniques such as random walk. Quality of the samples is measured as the structural similarity of the sample with respect to the original network. This differs from our notion of quality, as we do not strive at creating a structurally representative sample, but rather optimize for the ability to answer the same queries. Nevertheless, the sampling methods discussed by [23] are interesting baselines for our approach; we use the random edge sampling method in our evaluation (See Section 5).

Relevance Ranking. Existing work on Linked Data relevance ranking focuses on determining the relevance of individual triples for answering a single query [2,7,12,20,22]. Graph summaries, such as in [11], are collections of important RDF *resources* that may be presented to users to assist them in formulating SPARQL queries, e.g. by providing context-dependent auto completion services. However, summarization does not produce a list of triples ordered by relevance.

TRank [32] ranks RDF entity types by exploiting type hierarchies. However, this algorithm still ranks entities and not triples. In contrast, TripleRank [12] uses 3d tensor decomposition to model and rank triples in RDF graphs. It takes knowledge about different link types into account, and can be seen as a multi-model counterpart to web authority ranking with HITS. TripleRank uses the rankings to drive a faceted browser. Because of the expressiveness of a tensor decomposition, TripleRank does not scale very well, and [12] only evaluate small graphs of maximally 160K triples. Lastly, TripleRank prunes predicates that dominate the dataset, an understandable design decision when developing a user facing application, but it has an adverse effect on the quality of samples as prominent predicates in the data are likely to be used in queries as well.

ObjectRank [7] is an adaptation of PageRank that implements a form of link semantics where every type of edge is represented by a particular weight. This approach cannot be applied in cases where these weights are not known beforehand. SemRank [2] ranks relations and paths based on search results. This approach can filter results based on earlier results, but it is not applicable to *a priori* estimation of the relevancy of the triples in a dataset. Finally, stream-based approaches such as [15] derive the schema. This approach is not suitable for retrieving the most relevant *factual* data either, regarding a set of queries.

Concluding, existing approaches on ranking RDF data either require prior knowledge such as query sets, a-priori assignments of weights, produce samples that may miss important triples, or focus on resources rather than triples.

Synthetic Queries. SPLODGE [14] is a benchmark query generator for arbitrary, real-world RDF datasets. Queries are generated based on features of the RDF dataset. SPLODGE-based queries would allow us to run the sampling pipeline on many more datasets, because we would not be restricted by the requirement of having a dataset *plus* corresponding query logs. However, *benchmark* queries do not necessarily resemble *actual* queries, since they are meant to test the performance of Linked Data storage systems [1]. Furthermore, SPLODGE introduces a dependency between the dataset features and the queries it generates, that may not exist for user queries.[4]

RDF Graph Rewriting. RDF graphs can be turned into networks that are built around a particular property, e.g. the social aspects of co-authorship, by extracting that information from the RDF data [33]. Edge labels can sometimes be ignored when they are not directly needed, e.g. to determine the context of a resource [20], or when searching for paths connecting two resources [17].

The networks generated by these rewriting approaches leave out *contextual* information that may be critical to assess the relevance of triples. The triples $\langle : bob, : hasAge,$ "50"$\rangle$ and $\langle : anna, : hasWeight,$ "50"$\rangle$ share the same literal ("50"), but it respectively denotes an *age* and a *weight*. Finally, predicates play an important role in our notion of *relevance*. They are crucial for answering SPARQL queries, which suggests that they should carry as much weight as subjects and objects in our selection methodology. Therefore, our approach uses different strategies to remove the edge labels, while still keeping the context of the triples.

In [18], RDF graphs are rewritten to a bipartite network consisting of subjects, objects and predicates, with a separate statement node connecting the three. This method preserves the role of predicates, but increases the number of edges and nodes up to a threefold, making it difficult to scale. Additionally, the resulting graph is no longer *directed*, disqualifying analysis techniques that take this into account.

3   Context

In the previous section, we presented related work on RDF ranking and network sampling, and showed that sampling for RDF graphs has not been done

---

[4] In an earlier stage of this work, we ran experiments against a synthetic data and query set generated by SP^{2}Bench [29]. The results were different from any of the datasets we review here, as the structural properties of the dataset were quite different, and the SPARQL queries (tailored to benchmarking triple-stores) are incomparable to regular queries as well.

before. This section introduces a very generic framework for such RDF sampling. We elaborate on different RDF sampling scenarios, and present the particular sampling scenario addressed by this paper.

3.1   Definitions

A *'sample'* is just an arbitrary subset of a graph, so we introduce a notion of *relevance* to determine whether a sample is a suitable replacement of the original graph. Relevance is determined by a relevance function that varies from application to application. The following definitions use the same SPARQL definitions as presented in [25].

Definition 1. *An RDF graph $\mathcal{G}$ is a set of triples. A sample $\mathcal{G}'$ of $\mathcal{G}$ is a proper subset of $\mathcal{G}$. A sample is relevant w.r.t. a relevance function $F(\mathcal{G}', \mathcal{G})$ if it maximizes F while minimizing its size.*

Finding a relevant sample is a multi-objective optimization problem: selecting a sample small enough, while still achieving a recall which is high enough. Moreover, there is no sample that fits all tasks and problems, and for each application scenario a specific relevance function has to be defined. In this paper, relevance is defined in terms of the *coverage of answers* with respect to SPARQL queries.

Definition 2. *The* relevance function for SPARQL querying $F_s(\mathcal{G}', \mathcal{G})$ *is the probability that the solution μ to an arbitrary SPARQL query Q is also a solution to Q w.r.t. $\mathcal{G}'$.*

As usual, all elements $T \in \mathcal{G}$ are triples of the form $(s, p, o) \in I \times I \times (I \cup L)$, where s is called the subject, p the predicate, and o the object of T. I denotes all IRIs, where L denotes all literals. For this paper, we ignore blank nodes.

In other words, a *relevant sample* of a RDF graph is a smallest subset of the graph, on the basis of which the largest possible number of answers that can be found with respect to the original RDF graph. As common in multi-objective optimization problems, the solution cannot be expected to be a single *best* sample, but a set of samples of increasing size.

3.2   Problem Description

The next step is to determine the method by which a sample is made. As briefly discussed in the introduction, this method is restricted mostly by the pre-existence of a suitable set of queries. To what extent can these queries be used to *inform* the sampling procedure? As we have seen in the related work, sampling without prior knowledge – *uninformed* sampling – is currently an unsolved problem. And in fact, even if we *do* have prior knowledge, a method that does not rely on prior knowledge is still useful.

With *informed* sampling, there is a complete picture of what queries to expect: we know exactly which queries we want to have answered, and we consequently know which part of the dataset is required to answer these queries. Given the size of Linked Data sets, this part can still be too large to handle. This indicates a need for heuristics or uninformed methods to reduce the size even more.

Table 1. Data and query set statistics

Dataset	#Tripl.	Avg. Deg.	Tripl. w/ literals	#Q	Coverage	Q w/ literals	#Triple patt. per query (avg / stdev)
DBpedia 3.9	459M	5.78	25.44%	1640	0.003%	61.6%	1.07 / 0.40
LGD	289M	4.06	46.35%	891	1.917%	70.7%	1.07 / 0.27
MetaLex	204M	4.24	12.40%	4933	0.016%	1.1%	2.02 / 0.21
Open-BioMed	79M	3.66	45.37%	931	0.011%	3.1%	1.44 / 3.72
Bio2RDF/KEGG	50M	6.20	35.06%	1297	2.013%	99.8%	1.00 / 0.00
SWDF	240K	5.19	34.87%	193	39.438%	62.4%	1.80 / 1.50

If we have an incomplete notion of what queries to expect, e.g. we only know part of the queries or only know their structure or features, we could still use this information to create a *semi-informed* selection of the data. This requires a deeper understanding of what features of queries determine relevance, how these relate to the dataset, and what sampling method is the best fit.

In this paper we focus on a comparison of methods for uninformed sampling, the results of which can be used to augment scenarios where more information is available. For instance, a comparison of query features as studied in [26,28], combined with performance of our uninformed sampling methods, could form the basis of a system for semi-informed sampling.

To reiterate, our hypothesis is that we can use standard network metrics on RDF graphs as useful proxies for the relevance function. To test this hypothesis, we implemented a scalable sampling pipeline, SampLD, that can run several network metrics to select the top ranked triples from RDF datasets and evaluate the quality of those samples by their capability to answer real SPARQL queries.

3.3 Datasets

We evaluate the quality of our sampling methods for the six datasets listed in the introduction: DBPedia, Linked Geo Data (LGD), MetaLex, Open-BioMed (OBM), Bio2RDF[5] and Semantic Web Dog Food (SWDF). These datasets were chosen based on the availablity of SPARQL queries. These datasets were the only ones with an available correponding large query set. The MetaLex query logs were made available by the maintainers of the dataset. In the other five cases, we used server query logs made available by the USEWOD workshop series [9].

Table 1 shows that the size of these dataset ranges from 240K triples to 459M triples. The number of available queries per dataset ranges between 193 and 4933. Interestingly, for all but one of our datasets, less than 2% of the triples is actually *needed* to answer the queries. Even though the majority of these queries are machine generated (see Section 7), this indicates that only a very small portion of the datasets is relevant, which corroborates our intuition that

---

[5] For Bio2RDF, we use the KEGG dataset [21], as this is the only Bio2RDF dataset for which USEWOD provides query logs. KEGG includes biological systems information, genomic information, and chemical information.

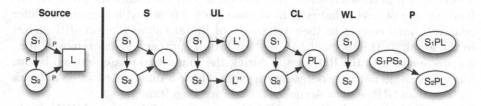

Fig. 1. Rewrite methods

the costs for using Linked Data sets can be significantly reduced by selecting only the relevant part of a dataset. However, these low numbers make finding this small set of relevant triples more difficult as well. Other relevant dataset properties shown in this table are the average degree of the subjects and objects, the percentage of triples where the object is a literal, the percentage of queries of which at least one binding uses a literal, and the average and standard deviation of the number of triple patterns per query.

4   Sampling Pipeline

The SampLD pipeline calculates and evaluates the quality of samples across different uninformed sampling methods for multiple large datasets.[6] The procedure consists of the following four phases:

1. *rewrite* an RDF graph to a directed unlabeled graph,
2. *analyze* the rewritten graph using standard network analysis algorithms,
3. *assign* the node weights to triples, creating a ranked list of triples,
4. *generate* samples from the ranked list of triples.

We briefly discuss each of the four phases here.

Step 1: Graph Rewriting. Standard network analysis methods, are not readily suited for *labeled* graphs, nor do they take into account that a data model may be reflected in the verbatim RDF graph structure in many ways [16]. Since the edge labels (predicates) play an important role in RDF, simply ignoring them may negatively impact the quality of samples (see the related work). For this reason, the SampLD pipeline can evaluate pairwise combinations of network analysis techniques and alternative representations of the RDF graph, and compare their performance across sample sizes.

SampLD implements five rewriting methods: a *simple* (S), *unique literals* (UL), *without literals* (WL), *context literals* (CL), and *path* (P). As can be seen in Figure 1, the first four methods convert every triple (s, p, o) to a directed edge

---

[6] The SampLD pipeline and evaluation procedure are available online at
   https://github.com/Data2Semantics/GraphSampling/

$s \rightarrow o$. If several triples result in the same edge (e.g. when only the predicate differs), we do not assert that edge more than once. These first four methods differ primarily with respect to their treatment of literal values (i.e. non-IRI nodes) in the graph. It is important to note that for all approaches, any removed literals are re-added to the RDF graph during the round-trip phase detailed below. Since literals do not have outgoing edges they have a different effect on network metrics than IRIs, e.g. by acting as a 'sink' for PageRank.

The Simple (S) method retains the exact structure of the original RDF graph. It treats every *syntactically* unique literal as a single node, taking the data type and language tag of the literal into account. Two occurrences of the literal "50"^^xsd:Integer result in a single node. The Unique literals (UL) method converts every occurrence of a literal as a separate node. The average degree drops, and the graph becomes larger but will be less connected. The Context literals (CL) approach preserves the context of literals, it groups literals that share the same predicate together in a single node. This allows us to make sure that the network metrics distinguish e.g. between integers that express weight, and those that express age. This also results in fewer connections and a lower average degree since predicate-literal pairs will be less frequent than literals. The Without literals (WL) method simply ignores all occurrences of literals. As a result the graph becomes smaller.

The fifth method, Path (P), is triple, rather than resource oriented. It represents every triple (s, p, o) as a single node, and two nodes are connected when they form a path of length 2, i.e. their subject and object must overlap. Asserting edges between triples that share *any* resource discards the direction of the triple, and produces a highly verbose graph, cf. [18], as a resource shared between n triples would generate $\frac{n(n-1)}{2}$ edges. Also, occurrences of triples with rdf:type predicates would result in an extremely large number of connections. The path method has the advantage that it results in a smaller graph with low connectedness, and that maintains directedness, where we can assign weights directly to *triples* rather than resources (as with the other methods).

Step 2: Network Analysis. In the second step, SampLD applies three common network analysis metrics to the rewritten RDF graph: *PageRank*, *in degree* and *out degree*. These are applied "as is" on the rewritten graphs.

Step 3: Assign Triple Weights. Once we have obtained the network analysis metrics for all nodes in the rewritten graph, the (aggregated) values are assigned as *weights* on the triples in the original graph. For method P, we simply assign the value of the node that corresponds to the triple. For the S, UL, WL and CL methods, we retrieve the values for the subject and object of each triple, and assign whichever is *highest* as weight to that triple[7]. When the object of a triple is a literal, it has no corresponding node in the graph produced through

---

[7] One can also use the minimum or average node weight. We found that the maximum value performs better.

the WL method: in such cases, the value of the *subject* will function as weight for the triple as a whole. The result of this assignment phase is a ranked list of triples, ordered by weight in descending order. The distribution of triple weights typically follows a 'long tail' distribution, where large numbers of triples may share the same weight. To prevent potential bias when determining a sample, these triples with equal weights are added to the ranked list in random order.

Step 4: Generating Samples. Given the ranked list of triples, generating the sample is a matter of selecting the desired top-k percent of the triples, and removing the weights. The 'best' k value can differ per use-case, and depends on both the minimum required quality of the sample, and the maximum desired sample size. For our current purposes SampLD produces samples for each accumulative percentile of the total number of triples, resulting in 100 samples *each* for every combination of dataset, rewrite method and analysis algorithm.

Implementation. Because the datasets we use are quite large, ranging up to 459 Million triples for DBPedia, each of these steps was implemented using libraries for scalable distributed computing (Pig [13] and Giraph [6]). Scale also means that we are restricted in the types of network metrics we could evaluate. For instance, Betweenness Centrality is difficult to paralellize because of the need for shared memory [31]. However many of the tasks *are* parallelizable, e.g. we use Pig to fetch the weights of all triples.

Given the large number of samples we evaluate in this paper (over 15.000, considering all sample sizes, datasets and sampling methods), SampLD uses a novel scalable evaluation method that avoids the expensive procedure (in terms of hardware and time) of loading each sample in triple-stores to calculate the recall.

5 Experiment Setup and Evaluation

The quality of a sample is measured by its ability to return answers on a set of queries: we are interested in the *average recall* taken over all queries. Typically, these queries are taken from publicly available server query logs, discarding those that are designed to return all triples in a dataset, and focusing on SELECT queries, as these are the most dominant. A naive approach would be to execute each query on both the original dataset and the sample, and compare the results. This is virtually impossible, given the large number of samples we are dealing with: 6 datasets means 15.600 samples (one, for every combination of dataset (6), sampling method (15) and baseline (1+10), and percentile(100)), or $1.4 \cdot 10^{12}$ triples in total.

Instead, SampLD (a.) executes the queries once on the original dataset and analyzes which triples are used to answer the query, (b.) uses a cluster to check which weight these triples have. It then (c.) checks whether these triples *would have been* included in a sample, and calculates recall. This avoids the need to load and query each sample. Below, we give a detailed description of this procedure.

Terminology. For each graph G we have a set of SELECT queries $\mathcal{Q}$, acting as our relevance measure. Each $Q \in \mathcal{Q}$ contains a set of variables $\mathcal{V}$, of which some may be projection variables $\mathcal{V}_p \subseteq \mathcal{V}$ (i.e. variables for which bindings are returned). Executing a query Q on G returns a result set R_q^g, containing a set of query solutions $\mathcal{S}$. Each query solution $S \in \mathcal{S}$ contains a set of bindings $\mathcal{B}$. Each binding $B \in \mathcal{B}$ is a mapping between a projection variable $V_p \in \mathcal{V}_p$ and a value from our our graph: $\mu : \mathcal{V}_p \to (I \cup L)$

Required Triples. Rewriting a SELECT query into a CONSTRUCT query returns a bag of *all* triples needed to answer the SELECT query. However, there is no way to determine what role individual triples play in answering the query: some triples may be essential in answering all query solutions, others just circumstantial. Therefore, SampLD extracts triples from the query on a *query solution* level. It instantiates each triple pattern, by replacing each variable used in the query triple patterns with the corresponding value from the query solution. As a result, the query contains triple patterns without variables, and only IRIs and literals. These instantiated triple patterns ('query triples') show us which triples are *required* to produce this specific query solution. This procedure is not trivial.

First, because not all variables used in a query are also projection variables, and blank nodes are inaccessible as well, we rewrite every SELECT query to the 'SELECT DISTINCT *' form and replace blank nodes with unique variable names. This ensures that all nodes and edges in the matching part of the original graph G are available to us for identifying the query triples. However, queries that already expected DISTINCT results need to be treated with a bit more care. Suppose we have the following query and dataset:

```
SELECT DISTINCT ?city  WHERE {          <university1> :inCity <London> .
  ?university :inCity ?city ;           <university1> :rating <high> .
              :rating :high .           <university2> :inCity <London> .
}                                       <university2> :rating <high> .
```

Rewriting the query to 'SELECT DISTINCT *' results in two query solutions, using all four dataset triples. However, we only either need at least the first two triples, or the last two, but not all four. SampLD therefore tracks each distinct combination of bindings for the projection variables $\mathcal{V}_p$.

Secondly, when the clauses of a UNION contain the same variable, but only one clause matches with the original graph G, the other clause should not be instantiated. We instantiate each clause following the normal procedure, but use an ASK query to check wether the instantiated clause exists in G. If it does not exist, we discard the query triples belonging to that clause.

Thirdly, we ignore the GROUP and ORDER solution modifiers, because they do not tell us anything about the actual triples required to answer a query. The LIMIT modifier is a bit different as it indicates that the user requests a specific number of results, but not exactly *which* results. The limit is used in recall calculation as a cap on the maximum number of results to be expected for a query. In other words, for these queries we don't check whether *every* query solution for G is present for the sample but only look at the proportion of query solutions.

Finally, we currently ignore negations in SPARQL queries since they are very scarce in our query sets. Negations may *increase* the result set for smaller sample sizes, giving us a means to measure precision, but the effect would be negligible.

Calculate Recall. For all query triples discovered in the previous step, and for each combination of rewrite method and network analysis algorithm, we find the weight of this triple in the ranked list of triples. The result provides us with information on the required triples of our query solutions, and their weights given by our sampling methods. SampLD can now determine whether a query solution would be returned for any given sample, given the weight of its triples, and given a k cutoff percentage. If a triple from a query solution is not included in the sample, we mark that solution as *unanswered*, otherwise it is *answered*.

Recall is then determined as follows. Remember that query solutions are grouped under distinct combinations of projection variables. For every such combination, we check each query solution, and whenever one of the grouped query solutions is marked as *answered*, the combination is marked answered as well. For queries with OPTIONAL clauses, we do not penalize valid query solutions that do not have a binding for the optional variable, even though the binding may be present for the original dataset.[8] If present, the value for the LIMIT modifier is used to cap the maximum number of answered query solutions.

The recall for the *query* is the number of answered projection variable combinations, divided by the total number of distinct projection variable combinations. For each *sample*, SampLD uses the average recall, or arithmetic mean over the query recall scores as our measure of relevance.

Baselines. In our evaluation we use two baselines: a *random selection* (rand) and using *resource frequency* (freq). Random selection is based on 10 random samples for each of our datasets. Then, for each corresponding query we calculate recall using the 10 sampled graphs, and average the recall over each query. The resource frequency baseline counts the number of occurrences of every subject, predicate and object present in a dataset. Each triple is then assigned a weight equal to the sum of the frequencies of its subject, predicate and object.

6   Results

This section discusses the results we obtained for each of the datasets. An interactive overview of these results, including recall plots, significance tests, and degree distributions for *every* dataset, is available online.[9] Figure 2a shows the best performing sample method for each of our datasets. An ideal situation would show a maximum recall for a low sample size.[10] For *all* the datasets, these best

---

[8] Queries with only OPTIONAL clauses are ignored in our evaluation.

[9] See http://data2semantics.github.io/GraphSampling/

[10] Note that all plots presented in this paper are clickeable, and point to the online interactive version.

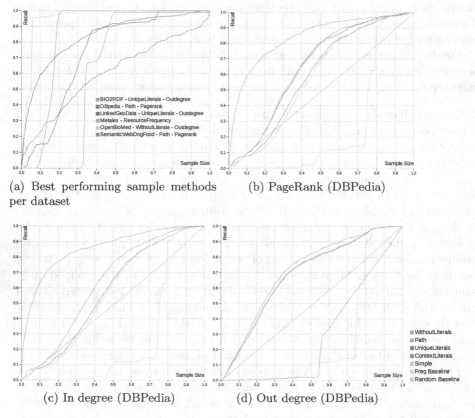

(a) Best performing sample methods per dataset

(b) PageRank (DBPedia)

(c) In degree (DBPedia)

(d) Out degree (DBPedia)

Fig. 2. Best samping methods per dataset (a) and comparison of methods for DBPedia (b,c,d)[12]

performing sampling methods outperform the random sample, with often a large difference in recall between both. The P rewrite method (see Figure 1) combined with a PageRank analysis performs best for Semantic Web Dog Food and DB-pedia (see also Figure 2). The UL method combined with an out degree analysis performs best for Bio2RDF and Linked Geo Data. For Open-BioMed the WL and out degree performs best, where the naive resource frequency method performs best for MetaLex. For each dataset, the random baseline follows an (almost) linear line from recall 0 to 1; a stark difference with the sampling methods.

Figure 2a also shows that both the sample *quality* and *method* differs between datasets. Zooming in on sample sizes 10%, 25% and 50%, the majority of the best performing sampling methods have significantly better average recall ($\alpha = 0.05$) than the random sample. Exceptions are LGD and Bio2RDF for sample size 10%, and MetaLex for sample size 10% and 25%.

The dataset properties listed in Table 1 help explain results for some sampling methods. The resource frequency baseline performs extremely bad for OBM[9]: for all possible sample sizes, the recall is almost zero. Of all objects in Open-BioMed triples, 45.37% are literals. In combination with 32% duplicate literals, this results in high rankings for triples that contain literals for this particular baseline. However, *all* of the queries use at least one triple pattern consisting *only* of IRIs. As most dataset triples contain a literal, and as these triples are ranked high, the performance of this specific baseline is extremely bad.

Another observation is the presences of 'plateaus' in Figure 2a, and for some sample sizes a steep increase in recall. This is because some triples are required for answering a large number of queries. Only once that triple is included in a sample, the recall can suddenly rise to a much higher level. For the Bio2RDF sample created using PageRank and the path rewrite method (viewable online), the difference in recall between a sample size of 1% and 40% is extremely small. In other words, choosing a sample size of 1% will result in more or less the same sample quality as a sample size of 40%.

Figure 2 (b,c,d) shows the performance of the sampling methods for DBpedia. The P method combined with either PageRank or in degree performs best on DB-pedia, where both baselines are amongst the worst performing sampling methods. A sample size of 7% based on the P and PageRank sampling method already results in an average recall of 0.5. Notably, this same rewrite method (P) performs worst on DBpedia when applied with out degree. This difference is caused by triples with literals acting as sink for the path rewrite method: because a literal can never occur in a subject position, that triple can never link to any other triple. This causes triples with literals to *always* receive an out degree of zero for the P rewrite method. Because 2/3 of the DBpedia queries require at least one literal, the average recall is extremely low. This 'sink' effect of P is stronger compared to other rewrite methods: the triple weight of these other methods is based on the weight of the subject and object (see section 4). For triples containing literals, the object will have an out degree of zero. However, the subject may have a larger out degree. As the subject and object weights are aggregated, these triples will often receive a non-zero triple weight, contrary to the P rewrite method.

Although our plots show striking differences between the datasets, there are similarities as well. First, the out degree combined with the UL, CL and S methods performs very similar across all datasets and sample sizes (See our online results[9]). The reason for this similarity is that these rewrite methods *only* differ in how they treat literals: as-is, unique, or concatenated with the predicate. These are exactly those nodes which *always* have an out degree of zero, as literals only have incoming edges. Therefore, this combination of rewrite methods and network analysis algorithms performs consistently the same. Second, the in degree of the S and CL rewrite methods are similar as well for all datasets with only a slight deviation in information loss for DBpedia. The main idea behind the CL is appending the predicate to the literal to provide context. The similarity for the in degree of both rewrite methods might indicate only a small difference between the literals in both rewrite methods regarding incoming links: adding context to these literals has no added value. DBpedia is the only dataset with a difference between both rewrite methods. This makes sense, as this dataset has many distinct predicates (53.000), which increases the chances of a single literal being used in multiple contexts, something the CL rewrite method is designed for.

What do these similarities buy us? They provide rules of thumb for applying SampLD to new datasets, as it shows which combinations of rewrite methods and network analysis algorithms you can safely ignore, restricting the number of samples to create and analyze for each dataset.

7 Conclusion

This paper tests the hypothesis as to whether we can use uninformed, network topology based methods to estimate semantic relevance of triples in an RDF graph. We introduced a pipeline that uses network analysis techniques for scalable calculation and selection of ranked triples, *SampLD*. It can use five ways to rewrite labeled, directed graphs (RDF) to unlabeled directed graphs, and runs a parallelized network analysis (indegree, outdegree and PageRank). We furthermore implemented a method for determining the recall of queries against our samples that does not require us to load every sample in a triple store (a major bottleneck). As a result, SampLD allows us to evaluate 15.600 different combinations of datasets, rewritten graphs, network analysis and sample sizes.

RDF graph topology, query type and structure, sample size; each of these can influence the quality of samples produced by a combination of graph rewriting and network analysis. This paper does not offer a definitive answer as to which combination is the best fit: we cannot yet predict the best performing sampling method given a data and query set. To make this possible, we plan to use Machine Learning on the results for several more independent data and query sets. Although SampLD provides the technical means, the number of publicly available query sets is currently too limited to learn significant correlations (6 query sets in total for USEWOD 2013, only 3 in 2014)[11].

In other work [27,28] we propose a SPARQL client (YASGUI), of which its logs allows us to gather and analyze queries for a wider range of datasets. [28] shows that these queries are quite different from the ones we can find in the publicly available server logs that we had access to for the purposes of this paper. In future work, we will use these query features in abstract, intermediate representations of queries and query sets. This allows us to better understand the effect of query types on our sampling methods, and forms the basis for sample quality prediction: a prerequisite for more informed sampling methods. Finally, a deeper analysis of the queries will also reveal information about the dynamics of Linked Data usage: does the part of the data touched by queries remain stable over time, or is it very volatile? In other words, is the 2% coverage from Table 1 predictive for future situations?

Our results, all of which are available online[12], indicate that the topology of RDF graphs *can* be used to determine good samples that, in many cases,

---

[11] See http://data.semanticweb.org/usewod/2013/challenge.html and http://usewod.org/reader/release-of-the-2014-usewod-log-data-set.html, respectively.

[12] Interactive plots of our results are available at http://data2semantics.github.io/GraphSampling/.

significantly outperform our baselines. Indeed, this shows that we can mimic *semantic* relevance through *structural* properties of RDF graphs, without an a-priori notion of relevance.

References

1. Angles Rojas, R., Minh Duc, P., Boncz, P.A.: Benchmarking Linked Open Data Management Systems. ERCIM News 96, 24–25 (2014)
2. Anyanwu, K., Maduko, A., Sheth, A.: SemRank: ranking complex relationship search results on the semantic web. In: Proceedings of the 14th International Conference on WWW, pp. 117–127. ACM (2005)
3. Auer, S., Bizer, C., Kobilarov, G., Lehmann, J., Cyganiak, R., Ives, Z.G.: Dbpedia: A nucleus for a web of open data. In: Aberer, K., et al. (eds.) ISWC/ASWC 2007. LNCS, vol. 4825, pp. 722–735. Springer, Heidelberg (2007)
4. Auer, S., Demter, J., Martin, M., Lehmann, J.: Lodstats–an extensible framework for high-performance dataset analytics. In: ten Teije, A., Völker, J., Handschuh, S., Stuckenschmidt, H., d'Acquin, M., Nikolov, A., Aussenac-Gilles, N., Hernandez, N. (eds.) EKAW 2012. LNCS (LNAI), vol. 7603, pp. 353–362. Springer, Heidelberg (2012)
5. Auer, S., Lehmann, J., Hellmann, S.: Linkedgeodata: Adding a spatial dimension to the web of data. In: Bernstein, A., Karger, D.R., Heath, T., Feigenbaum, L., Maynard, D., Motta, E., Thirunarayan, K. (eds.) ISWC 2009. LNCS, vol. 5823, pp. 731–746. Springer, Heidelberg (2009)
6. Avery, C.: Giraph: Large-scale graph processing infrastructure on hadoop. In: Proceedings of the Hadoop Summit, Santa Clara (2011)
7. Balmin, A., Hristidis, V., Papakonstantinou, Y.: Objectrank: Authority-based keyword search in databases. In: VLDB, pp. 564–575 (2004)
8. Belleau, F., Nolin, M.A., Tourigny, N., Rigault, P., Morissette, J.: Bio2rdf: towards a mashup to build bioinformatics knowledge systems. Journal of Biomedical Informatics 41(5), 706–716 (2008)
9. Berendt, B., Hollink, L., Luczak-Rösch, M., Möller, K., Vallet, D.: Usewod2013 3rd international workshop on usage analysis and the web of data. In: 10th ESWC - Semantics and Big Data, Montpellier, France (2013)
10. Buil-Aranda, C., Hogan, A., Umbrich, J., Vandenbussche, P.-Y.: Sparql web-querying infrastructure: Ready for action? In: Alani, H., et al. (eds.) ISWC 2013, Part II. LNCS, vol. 8219, pp. 277–293. Springer, Heidelberg (2013)
11. Campinas, S., Perry, T.E., Ceccarelli, D., Delbru, R., Tummarello, G.: Introducing RDF Graph Summary with application to Assisted SPARQL Formulation. In: 23rd International Workshop on Database and Expert Systems Applications (2012)
12. Franz, T., Schultz, A., Sizov, S., Staab, S.: Triplerank: Ranking semantic web data by tensor decomposition. In: Bernstein, A., Karger, D.R., Heath, T., Feigenbaum, L., Maynard, D., Motta, E., Thirunarayan, K. (eds.) ISWC 2009. LNCS, vol. 5823, pp. 213–228. Springer, Heidelberg (2009)
13. Gates, A.F., et al.: Building a high-level dataflow system on top of map-reduce: the pig experience. Proceedings of the VLDB Endowment 2(2), 1414–1425 (2009)
14. Görlitz, O., Thimm, M., Staab, S.: Splodge: systematic generation of sparql benchmark queries for linked open data. In: Cudré-Mauroux, P., et al. (eds.) ISWC 2012, Part I. LNCS, vol. 7649, pp. 116–132. Springer, Heidelberg (2012)
15. Gottron, T., Pickhardt, R.: A detailed analysis of the quality of stream-based schema construction on linked open data. In: Semantic Web and Web Science, pp. 89–102. Springer (2013)

16. Guéret, C., Wang, S., Groth, P., Schlobach, S.: Multi-scale analysis of the web of data: A challenge to the complex system's community. Advances in Complex Systems 14(04), 587 (2011)
17. Halaschek, C., Aleman-meza, B., Arpinar, I.B., Sheth, A.P.: Discovering and ranking semantic associations over a large rdf metabase. In: VLDB (2004)
18. Hayes, J., Gutierrez, C.: Bipartite Graphs as Intermediate Model for RDF. In: McIlraith, S.A., Plexousakis, D., van Harmelen, F. (eds.) ISWC 2004. LNCS, vol. 3298, pp. 47–61. Springer, Heidelberg (2004)
19. Hoekstra, R.: The MetaLex Document Server - Legal Documents as Versioned Linked Data. In: Aroyo, L., Welty, C., Alani, H., Taylor, J., Bernstein, A., Kagal, L., Noy, N., Blomqvist, E. (eds.) ISWC 2011, Part II. LNCS, vol. 7032, pp. 128–143. Springer, Heidelberg (2011)
20. Hogan, A., Harth, A., Decker, S.: Reconrank: A scalable ranking method for semantic web data with context. In: 2nd Workshop on Scalable Semantic Web Knowledge Base Systems (2006)
21. Kanehisa, M., et al.: From genomics to chemical genomics: new developments in kegg. Nucleic Acids Research 34(suppl. 1), D354–D357 (2006)
22. Kleinberg, J.M.: Authoritative sources in a hyperlinked environment. Journal of the ACM (JACM) 46(5), 604–632 (1999)
23. Leskovec, J., Faloutsos, C.: Sampling from large graphs. In: The 12th ACM SIGKDD International Conference on Knowledge Discovery and Data Mining, pp. 631–636 (2006)
24. Möller, K., Heath, T., Handschuh, S., Domingue, J.: Recipes for semantic web dog food. the eswc and iswc metadata projects. In: Aberer, K., et al. (eds.) ISWC/ASWC 2007. LNCS, vol. 4825, pp. 802–815. Springer, Heidelberg (2007)
25. Pérez, J., Arenas, M., Gutierrez, C.: Semantics of SPARQL. Technical Report TR/DCC-2006-17, Department of Computer Science, Universidad de Chile (2006)
26. Picalausa, F., Vansummeren, S.: What are real sparql queries like? In: International Workshop on Semantic Web Information Management, p. 7. ACM (2011)
27. Rietveld, L., Hoekstra, R.: YASGUI: Not Just Another SPARQL Client. In: Cimiano, P., Fernández, M., Lopez, V., Schlobach, S., Völker, J. (eds.) ESWC 2013. LNCS, vol. 7955, pp. 78–86. Springer, Heidelberg (2013)
28. Rietveld, L., Hoekstra, R.: Man vs. Machine: Differences in SPARQL Queries. In: ESWC, 4th USEWOD Workshop on Usage Analysis and the Web of Data (2014)
29. Schmidt, M., Hornung, T., Meier, M., Pinkel, C., Lausen, G.: Sp2bench: A sparql performance benchmark. In: Semantic Web Information Management, pp. 371–393. Springer (2010)
30. Sundara, S., et al.: Visualizing large-scale rdf data using subsets, summaries, and sampling in oracle. In: 2010 IEEE 26th International Conference on Data Engineering (ICDE), pp. 1048–1059. IEEE (2010)
31. Tan, G., Tu, D., Sun, N.: A parallel algorithm for computing betweenness centrality. In: Proc. of ICPP, pp. 340–347 (2009)
32. Tonon, A., Catasta, M., Demartini, G., Cudré-Mauroux, P., Aberer, K.: TRank: Ranking Entity Types Using the Web of Data. In: Alani, H., et al. (eds.) ISWC 2013, Part I. LNCS, vol. 8218, pp. 640–656. Springer, Heidelberg (2013)
33. Wang, S., Groth, P.: Measuring the dynamic bi-directional influence between content and social networks. In: Patel-Schneider, P.F., Pan, Y., Hitzler, P., Mika, P., Zhang, L., Pan, J.Z., Horrocks, I., Glimm, B. (eds.) ISWC 2010, Part I. LNCS, vol. 6496, pp. 814–829. Springer, Heidelberg (2010)

Holistic and Compact Selectivity Estimation for Hybrid Queries over RDF Graphs[*]

Andreas Wagner[1], Veli Bicer[2], Thanh Tran[3], and Rudi Studer[1]

[1] Karlsruhe Institute of Technology
[2] IBM Research Centre Dublin
[3] San Jose State University
{a.wagner,rudi.studer}@kit.edu, velibice@ie.ibm.com,
ducthanh.tran@sjsu.edu

Abstract. Many RDF descriptions today are *text-rich*: besides *structured* data they also feature much *unstructured* text. Text-rich RDF data is frequently queried via predicates matching structured data, combined with string predicates for textual constraints (*hybrid queries*). Evaluating hybrid queries efficiently requires means for *selectivity estimation*. Previous works on selectivity estimation, however, suffer from inherent drawbacks, which are reflected in efficiency and effectiveness issues. We propose a novel estimation approach, *TopGuess*, which exploits topic models as data synopsis. This way, we capture correlations between structured and unstructured data in a *holistic and compact* manner. We study TopGuess in a theoretical analysis and show it to guarantee a linear space complexity w.r.t. text data size. Further, we show selectivity estimation time complexity to be independent from the synopsis size. In experiments on real-world data, TopGuess allowed for great improvements in estimation accuracy, without sacrificing efficiency.

1 Introduction

RDF data contains descriptions of entities, with each description being a set of *triples*. Many RDF descriptions feature *textual data*: On the one hand, structured RDF data often comprises text via predicates such as `comment` or `description`. On the other hand, unstructured Web documents are frequently annotated with structured data (e.g., via RDFa or Microformats).

Hybrid Queries. Such text-rich RDF descriptions are often queried with queries, which comprise predicates that match *structured data* as well as *words* in text data (*hybrid queries*). Consider the following example (cf. Fig. 1-a/b):

```
SELECT * WHERE {
    ?m ex:title ?title .     ?p ex:name ?name .     ?l ex:name ?name2 .
    ?m ex:starring ?p .      ?p ex:bornIn ?l .
    ?m a Movie .             ?p a Person .
    FILTER (contains(?title,"Holiday") && contains(?name,"Audrey") &&
            contains(?name2,"Belgium")) }
```

[*] This work was supported by the European Union through project XLike (FP7-ICT-2011-288342).

P. Mika et al. (Eds.) ISWC 2014, Part II, LNCS 8797, pp. 97–113, 2014.

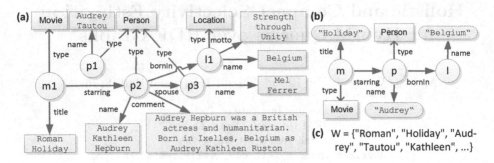

Fig. 1. (a) RDF graph about "Audrey Hepburn" and her movie "Roman Holiday". (b) Hybrid query graph asking for movies with title "Holiday" and starring a person with name "Audrey", who was born in "Belgium". (c) Vocabulary W comprising all words from attributes values in the data graph.

Hybrid queries are highly relevant for RDF stores with SPARQL fulltext extension, e.g., LARQ[1] or Virtuoso[2]. In fact, every store that supports FILTER clauses on texts faces hybrid queries.

Selectivity Estimation. For finding an optimal query plan, RDF stores rely on *selectivity estimates* to approximate the result size of a query (fragment) [19]. Various selectivity estimation techniques have been proposed for relational data [1,7,9,17,18,21] as well as for RDF data [10,16,19,20,23]. These techniques summarize the data via a *data synopsis* (e.g., histograms, join synopses, tuple-graph synopses, or probabilistic relational models (PRM)) to capture data correlations/statistics. Based on these synopses, different estimation approaches have been proposed to efficiently approximate the query's selectivity.

However, when applying state-of-the-art selectivity estimation techniques for hybrid queries *effectiveness and efficiency issues* (I.1 and I.2) arise:

(I.1) Effectiveness Issues. Queries over RDF data typically comprise a large number of joins. Thus, a data synopsis must capture statistics for multiple (joined) query patterns in order to allow effective estimates. Recent work on selectivity estimation for RDF data captured multiple patterns either via computing statistics for frequent (star/chain) join patterns [10,16], via heuristics [19,20], or by conditional probabilities [23]. These strategies work well for structured query patterns (i.e., class, relation, and attributes), because the number of structured elements (i.e., class, relation, and attributes) is usually *small and independent of the instance data size*. However, in the presence of textual data and hybrid queries, capturing multiple patterns is much harder, since the number of words is oftentimes very large. For instance, the DBLP dataset (used in our evaluation) has 25 million words vs. 56 structure elements.

Example. In Fig. 1-a, there can be many entities of type Person *(i.e., bindings for* ?p a Person*), while only few entities have a* name *"Audrey". So, in order*

---

[1] http://jena.sourceforge.net/ARQ/lucene-arq.html
[2] http://virtuoso.openlinksw.com

to estimate the # bindings for ?p in Fig. 1-b, a synopsis has to capture statistics for any word associated (via name*) with* Person *entities.*

Moreover, the number of words is strongly dependent on the data and text size, respectively. So, with growing data sets, statistics become increasingly complex and space consuming. To address this, all previous works summarized the words via a small synopsis, which is constructed either by hashing [19], heuristics [20], categorization [16], discretization [10], or via string synopses [23]. Unfortunately, such coarse-grained synopses result in an "information loss". That is, oftentimes heuristics must be employed to estimate selectivities of query keywords (e.g., "Audrey"), which leads to severe miss-estimations.

(I.2) Efficiency Issues. All previous works [10,16,19,20,23], aim at constructing a *query-independent* data synopsis at offline time. In fact, previous approaches directly use this offline constructed data synopsis to estimate the query selectivity. Thus, a large synopsis would influence the estimation efficiency. In order to guarantee an efficient selectivity estimation at runtime, existing approaches either construct only *small* synopses [10,16,19,23] or purely rely on heuristics for selectivity estimation [20].

Contributions. (1) In this paper, we propose a novel approach (*TopGuess*), which utilizes relational topic models as data synopsis. Such synopses are well-suited to summarize text data, because they provide statistics for the *complete vocabulary* of words by means of topics. So, no "information loss" can occur due to coarse-grained synopses. Furthermore, correlations between structured query patterns (e.g., ?m ex:starring ?p and ?m rdf:type Movie, see Fig. 1-b) can also be captured. Thus, we have an effective and holistic synopsis for hybrid queries (effectiveness issues, I.1). The TopGuess approach also constructs a query-independent data synopsis at offline time. However, in contrast to previous approaches, we do not directly use this large synopsis at runtime. Instead, we only employ a small and compact synopsis (Bayesian network), which is constructed specifically for the current query (efficiency issues, I.2).

(2) We provide a theoretical analysis: TopGuess achieves a linear space complexity w.r.t. text data size (cf. Thm. 1). Further, TopGuess has an estimation time complexity that is independent of the synopsis size (given the number of topics), cf. Thm. 4.

(3) We conducted experiments on real-world data: TopGuess could improve the effectiveness by up to 88% – without sacrificing runtime performance.

Outline. First, in Sect. 2 we outline preliminaries. We introduce the TopGuess approach in Sect. 3. In Sect. 4, we present evaluation results, before we outline related work in Sect. 5. We conclude with Sect. 6.

2 Preliminaries

Data and Query Model. We use RDF as data model:

Definition 1 (RDF Graph). *Let ℓ_a (ℓ_r) be a set of attribute (relation) labels. A RDF graph is a directed labeled graph $\mathcal{G} = (V, E, \ell_a, \ell_r)$, with nodes $V =$*

$V_E \uplus V_A \uplus V_C$ where V_E are entity nodes, V_A are attribute value nodes, and V_C are class nodes. Edges (so-called triples) $E = E_R \uplus E_A \uplus$ type are a disjoint union of relation edges E_R and attribute edges E_A. Relation edges connect entity nodes: $\langle s, r, o \rangle \in E_R$, with $s, o \in V_E$ and $r \in \ell_r$). Attribute edges connect an entity with an attribute value: $\langle s, a, o \rangle \in E_A$, with $s \in V_E, o \in V_A$ and $a \in \ell_a$. Triple $\langle s, type, o \rangle \in E$ models that entity $s \in V_E$ belongs to class $o \in V_C$.

We conceive an attribute value in V_A as a *bag-of-words*. Further, let a vocabulary W comprise all such words. That is, W is derived from words in attribute values: for each triple $\langle s, p, o \rangle \in E_A$ we add all words in o to W. See also Fig. 1.

Conjunctive queries resemble the basic graph pattern (BGP) feature of SPARQL. In this work, we use hybrid queries:

Definition 2 (Hybrid Query). *A query Q is a directed graph $G_Q = (V_Q, E_Q)$, with $V_Q = V_{Q_V} \uplus V_{Q_C} \uplus V_{Q_K}$, V_{Q_V} as variables, V_{Q_C} as constants, and V_{Q_K} as keywords. Edges E_Q are called predicates: (1) Class predicates $\langle s, type, o \rangle$, with $s \in V_{Q_V}, o \in V_{Q_C}$. (2) Relation predicates $\langle s, r, o \rangle$, with $s \in V_{Q_V}, o \in V_{Q_C} \uplus V_{Q_V}$, and $r \in \ell_r$. (3) String predicates $\langle s, a, o \rangle$, with $s \in V_{Q_V}, o \in V_{Q_K}$, and $a \in \ell_a$.*

Fig. 1-b shows an example query. Query semantics follow those for BGPs. That is, results are subgraphs of the data graph, which match all query predicates. The only difference is due to keyword nodes: a value node $o \in V_A$ matches a keyword $w \in V_{Q_K}$, if the bag-of-words from o contains word w.

We rely on two data synopses: topic models and Bayesian networks (BNs):

Topic Models. Topic models assume that texts are mixtures of "hidden" topics, where a topic is a probability distribution over words. These topics are abstract clusters of words – formed according to word co-occurrences. More formally, a text collection can be represented by k topics $\mathcal{T} = \{t_1, \ldots, t_k\}$, where W is the vocabulary (see above definition) and each topic $t \in \mathcal{T}$ is a multinomial distribution of words in W: $\mathcal{P}(w \mid t) = \beta_{tw}$ and $\sum_{w \in W} \beta_{tw} = 1$.

Example. Three topics are depicted in Fig. 2-c: $\mathcal{T} = \{t_1, t_2, t_3\}$. Every topic t assigns a probability (represented by vector β_t) to each word in the vocabulary. Probabilities in β_t indicate the importance of words within topic t. For instance, "Belgium" is most important for topic t_3 ($\beta_{tw} = 0.014$), cf. Fig. 2-c.

Bayesian Networks. A Bayesian network (BN) is a directed graphical model, which compactly represents a joint probability distribution via its structure and parameters [12]. The structure is a directed acyclic graph, where nodes stand for random variables and edges represent dependencies. Given a node X_i and its parents $\mathbf{Pa}(X_i) = \{X_j, \ldots, X_k\}$, X_i dependents on $\mathbf{Pa}(X_i)$, but is *conditionally independent* of all non-ancestor random variables (given $\mathbf{Pa}(X_i)$).

BN parameters are given by conditional probability distributions (CPDs). That is, each random variable X_i is associated with a CPD capturing the conditional probability $\mathcal{P}(X_i \mid \mathbf{Pa}(X_i))$. The joint distribution $\mathcal{P}(X_1, \ldots, X_n)$ can be estimated via the chain rule [12]: $\mathcal{P}(X_1, \ldots, X_n) \approx \prod_i \mathcal{P}(X_i \mid \mathbf{Pa}(X_i))$.

Example. A BN is shown in Fig. 3. Nodes such as X_m and $X_{holiday}$ stand for random variables. Edges stand for dependencies between those nodes. For instance, the edge $X_m \rightarrow X_{holiday}$ denotes a dependency between the parent,

X_m, and the child, $X_{holiday}$. In fact, given its parent, $X_{holiday}$ is conditionally independent of all non-ancestor variables, e.g., X_p. Every node has a CDP. For example, $X_{holiday}$ has a CDP for $\mathcal{P}(X_{holiday} \mid X_m)$, cf. Fig. 3-b.

Problem. Given a hybrid query Q, we aim at a result size estimation function $\mathcal{F}(Q)$ as [9]: $\mathcal{F}(Q) \approx \mathcal{R}(Q) \cdot \mathcal{P}(Q)$.

Let $\mathcal{R}$ be a function $\mathcal{R} : Q \to \mathbb{N}$ that provides an upper bound cardinality for a result set for query Q. Further, let $\mathcal{P}$ be a *probabilistic component*, which assigns a probability to query Q that models whether Q's result set is non-empty.

$\mathcal{R}(Q)$ can be easily computed as product over "class cardinalities" of Q [9]. That is, for each variable $v \in V_{Q_V}$ we bound the number of its bindings, $R(v)$, as number of entities belonging v's class c: $|\{s|\langle s, type, c\rangle \in E\}|$. If v has no class, we use the number of all entities (i.e., $|V_E|$) as a bound. Finally, $\mathcal{R}(Q) = \prod_v R(v)$.

In the remainder of the paper, we provide an effective (I.1) and efficient (I.2) instantiation of the probabilistic component $\mathcal{P}$.

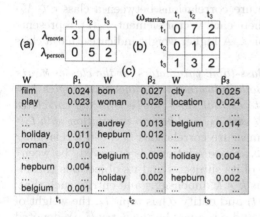

Fig. 2. Synopsis parameters (stored on disk): (a) λ_{movie} and λ_{person} parameter for three topics. (b) ω matrix for **starring** relation and three topics – rows (columns) represent source (target) topics of the relation. (c) Words from the vocabulary W and their corresponding probabilities for each topic, β_t. Note, data is taken from Fig. 1-a/c.

3 TopGuess

Targeting the effectiveness (I.1) and efficiency (I.2) issues of existing works w.r.t. hybrid queries (cf. Sect. 1), we now introduce our novel TopGuess approach.

More precisely, we present an uniform data synopsis based on relational topic models in Sect. 3.1 (I.1), and show in Thm. 1 that this synopsis has a linear space complexity w.r.t. vocabulary W (I.2). Further, we introduce a probabilistic component $\mathcal{P}$ in Sect. 3.2 and 3.3, and show in Thm. 4 selectivity computation complexity to be independent of the synopsis size (I.2).

Note, the topic model (data synopsis) is learned at offline time and may be stored on disk. At runtime, we construct a small BN for each given query – reflecting our data synopsis as well as query characteristics via topic mixtures.

3.1 Relational Topic Models as Data Synopsis

Synopsis Parameters. For an effective synopsis over text-rich RDF data, TopGuess exploits *relational topic models* [2,4,14,25]. These topic models summarize the data by means of one *uniform synopsis* – considering structured and text data. More precisely, our synopsis comprises of two parts:

(1) First, the TopGuess synopsis captures text data in a low-dimensional representation via a set of k topics $\mathcal{T} = \{t_1, \ldots, t_k\}$.

Example. Fig. 2-c groups words from the vocabulary $W = \{$ "Roman", "Holiday", ...$\}$, cf. Fig. 1-c, via three topics, $\mathcal{T} = \{t_1, t_2, t_3\}$. This way, text data in Fig. 1-a, e.g., associated via attribute comment, *is compactly represented.*

The number of topics is dictated by the data characteristics. In particular, previous works allow to learn the optimal number of topics [8]. By means of this compact summary, TopGuess achieves a linear space complexity linear w.r.t. a vocabulary, see Thm. 1.

(2) Second, the TopGuess synopsis captures *correlations between those topics and structured data.* For our query model, we rely on two correlation parameters for selectivity estimation: λ and ω. Note, for other kinds of queries, further types of correlation parameters may be considered.

- Class-Topic Parameter λ. We capture correlations between a class $c \in V_C$ and topics in $\mathcal{T}$ via a vector λ_c, where each vector element, $\lambda_c(t)$, represents the weight between class c and topic t. A higher weight indicates that a class is more correlated with a topic.

  Example. Fig. 2-a shows the two class-topic parameters for the classes Movie *and* Person: λ_{movie} *and* λ_{person}. *Both indicate correlations w.r.t. topics $\mathcal{T} =$ $\{t_1, t_2, t_3\}$. For instance, λ_{movie} states that class* Movie *is highly correlated with topic t_1, has some correlation with t_3, and has no correlation with t_2.*

- Relation-Topic Parameter ω. We measure correlations between a relation r and the topics in $\mathcal{T}$ via a matrix ω_r. Since relation r is observed "between" two entities, say $\langle s, r, o \rangle$, the topic of its subject s and its object o is considered. Given k topics, matrix ω_r has $k \times k$ dimensions and entries such that: if entity s is associated with topic t_i and entity o has topic t_j, the weight of observing a relation r "between" s and o is given by the entry $\langle i, j \rangle$, denoted as $\omega_r(t_i, t_j)$. Note, TopGuess features a matrix ω for each relation.

  Example. Fig. 2-b depicts the relation-topic parameter for the starring *relation:* $\omega_{starring}$. *According to* $\omega_{starring}$, starring *is most often observed (weight 7) if its subject (object) contains words from topic t_1 (t_2).*

Parameter Learning. For training above parameters, we do not restrict TopGuess to a single topic model. Instead, different approaches can be used. For instance, classical topic models such as LDA [3] may be employed to learn the first part, i.e., word/topic probabilities, cf. Fig. 2-c. Then, correlations between those topics and classes/relations must be obtained. For this, topic models have been extended to consider structured data, so-called relational topic models [2,4,14,25]. Most notably, a recent approach, the *Topical Relational Model* (TRM) [2], trains topics as well as class/relation correlations simultaneously from RDF data. We used a TRM as data synopsis in our experiments.

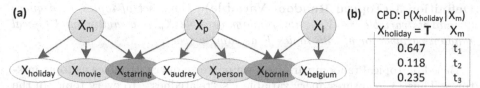

Fig. 3. (a) Query-specific BN for the query in Fig.1-b. It contains three topical variables (color: blue, e.g., X_m), two class predicate variables (color: light gray, e.g., X_{movie}), two relation predicate variables (color: dark gray, e.g., $X_{starring}$), and three string predicate variables (color: white, e.g., $X_{holiday}$). Observed variables (color: white/light gray/dark gray) are independent from each other and only dependent on hidden topical random variables (color: blue) – as dictated by Def. 4. (b) CDP for random variable $X_{holiday}$, cf. parameters in Fig. 2-c.

Discussion. The TopGuess synopsis comes with key advantages: First, in contrast to existing work [23], we do not need separate synopses for structured and text data. This way, we may learn correlations in a uniform manner.

Moreover, TopGuess parameters are not required to be loaded in memory. This is a crucial advantage over state-of-the-art selectivity estimation systems [9,21,23], as memory is commonly a limited resource. So, TopGuess can utilize the *complete vocabulary* W for learning word/topic probabilities β.

Last, as empirically validated by our experiments, correlations between topics and structured data *suffice for an accurate selectivity estimation*. Since even a small number of topics can capture these correlations, our synopsis does not grow exponentially in its vocabulary size.

In fact, we can show that a topic-based data synopsis has linear space complexity w.r.t. its vocabulary:

Theorem 1 (Synopsis Space Complexity). *Given k topics, a vocabulary W, classes V_C, and relations ℓ_r, TopGuess has a storage space complexity in $O(|W| \cdot k + |V_C| \cdot k + |\ell_r| \cdot k^2)$.*

Proof. See our report for a proof [22] ∎

3.2 Probabilistic Component: Query-Specific BN

In this section, we exploit the synopsis parameters for an efficient probabilistic component (I.2, Sect. 1). For this, we first construct a small, query-specific BN and afterwards compute its joint probability in Sect. 3.3. Both steps are done at runtime. In contrast to [9,21,23], all synopsis parameters may be kept on disk, while only the query-specific BN is loaded into memory.

To construct a BN specifically for a query Q, we capture every query predicate in Q via a random variable: For a class predicate, $\langle s, type, c \rangle$, and relation predicate, $\langle s, r, o \rangle$, we create a binary random variable X_c and X_r. Similarly, for a string predicate, $\langle s, a, w \rangle$, we introduce a binary random variable X_w. Most importantly, we assume that each variable v in Q belongs to one or more topics in $\mathcal{T}$. So, we model variable v via a *topical random variable*, X_v. More formally, X_v has a multinomial distribution over the topics:

Definition 3 (Topical Random Variable). *For a set of topics $\mathcal{T}$, a query Q, and its variable $v \in V_{Q_V}$, the random variable X_v is a multinomial topical random variable for v, with topics $\mathcal{T}$ as sample space.*

Based on topical random variables, we perceive query variables as topic mixtures. Thus, X_v captures query variable v's "relatedness" to every topic. In the following, we denote the set of all string, class, relation, and topical random variables for query Q as $\mathbf{X}_w$, $\mathbf{X}_c$, $\mathbf{X}_r$, and $\mathbf{X}_v$.

We create a simple BN structure by means of a fixed structure assumption:

Definition 4 (Topical Dependence Assumption). *Given a class/string predicate $\langle v, *, * \rangle$, the corresponding variable X depends only the topical random variable X_v. Given a relation predicate $\langle v, *, y \rangle$, the corresponding variable X depends only on two topical random variables: X_v and X_y.*

The topical dependence assumption lies at the core of the TopGuess approach. It considers that query predicate probabilities depend on (and are governed by) the topics of their associated topical random variables. Further, the assumption allows us to model the query probability, $\mathcal{P}(Q)$, via a tree-shaped BN.

Example. Fig. 3-a depicts a BN for the query in Fig. 1-b. Adhering to Def. 4, each topical variable (X_m, X_p, and X_l) forms a small tree of dependent random variables. For instance, random variable $X_{holiday}$ is only dependent on its topical variable, X_m. In fact, given X_m, $X_{holiday}$ is conditionally independent of all other variables, e.g., X_{audrey}. This way, topic mixtures of X_m, X_p, and X_l govern the overall query probability, $\mathcal{P}(Q)$.

Last, note that the topical dependence assumption leads to a *valid* BN:

Theorem 2. *A query-specific BN constructed according to Def. 4 is acyclic.*

Proof. See [22] for a proof ∎

3.3   Probabilistic Component: Query Probability Computation

Having formed the BN structure for a given query Q, we may compute the query probability, $\mathcal{P}(Q)$, via the chain rule (CR) [12]:

$$\mathcal{P}(Q) = \mathcal{P}\left(\bigwedge \mathbf{X}_w = \mathbf{T} \quad \bigwedge \mathbf{X}_c = \mathbf{T} \quad \bigwedge \mathbf{X}_r = \mathbf{T} \right) \tag{1a}$$

$$\underset{\text{CR}}{\approx} \prod_{\langle v,a,w \rangle \,\in\, Q} \mathcal{P}(X_w = \mathbf{T} \mid X_v) \cdot \prod_{\langle v,type,c \rangle \,\in\, Q} \mathcal{P}(X_c = \mathbf{T} \mid X_v)$$

$$\cdot \prod_{\langle v,r,y \rangle \,\in\, Q} \mathcal{P}(X_r = \mathbf{T} \mid X_v, X_y) \tag{1b}$$

In order to solve Eq. 1, we require a CPD for each random variable, cf. Fig. 3-b. We rely on TopGuess parameters as well as distributions of topical random variables to approximate these CPDs. As topical variables $\mathbf{X}_v$ are hidden, we learn their distributions from observed random variables ($\mathbf{X}_w$, $\mathbf{X}_c$, $\mathbf{X}_r$).

In the following, we first discuss CPD estimation for observed random variables, given topical random variables (topic distributions). Subsequently, we present learning of topic distributions for hidden topical variables.

Query Predicate Probabilities. Probabilities for query predicates are influenced by their associated topical random variables and their TopGuess parameters. In other words, we may compute the CPDs for $\mathbf{X}_w$, $\mathbf{X}_c$, and $\mathbf{X}_r$ using topic distributions of topical variables and probabilities estimated by the corresponding β, λ, or ω parameter:

(1) Class Predicates. Adhering to the topical dependence assumption, the probability of observing a class, $\mathcal{P}(X_c = \mathbf{T})$, is only dependent on its topical variable X_v. We use the class-topic parameter λ to obtain the weight $\lambda_c(t)$, which indicates the correlation between topic t and class c:

$$\mathcal{P}(X_c = \mathbf{T} \mid X_v, \lambda) = \sum_{t \in \mathcal{T}} \mathcal{P}(X_v = t) \frac{\lambda_c(t)}{\sum_{t' \in \mathcal{T}} \lambda_c(t')}$$

Example. Fig. 3-a shows two random variables, X_{movie} and X_{person}, which dependent on their topical variables X_m and X_p. For computing $\mathcal{P}(X_{movie} = \mathbf{T})$ and $\mathcal{P}(X_{person} = \mathbf{T})$, the parameters λ_{movie} and λ_{person} are used, cf. Fig. 2-a. Assuming $\mathcal{P}(X_m = t_1) = 0.6$, $\mathcal{P}(X_m = t_2) = 0.1$, and $\mathcal{P}(X_m = t_3) = 0.3$, we get: $\mathcal{P}(X_{movie} = \mathbf{T}) = 0.6 \cdot 0.75 + 0.1 \cdot 0 + 0.3 \cdot 0.25 = 0.525$.

(2) Relation Predicates. A relation predicate $\langle v, r, y \rangle$ connects two query variables, which have the two topical variables X_v and X_y. Random variable X_r solely depends on the topics of X_v and X_y. The correlation between relation r and these topics is given by the relation-topic parameter ω_r:

$$\mathcal{P}(X_r = \mathbf{T} \mid X_v, X_y, \omega_r) = \sum_{t,t' \in \mathcal{T}} \frac{\mathcal{P}(X_v = t)\, \omega_r(t,t')\, \mathcal{P}(X_y = t')}{\sum_{t'',t''' \in \mathcal{T}} \omega_r(t'', t''')}$$

Example. In Fig. 3-a, we have the variables $X_{starring}$ and X_{bornIn} – both dependent on two topical variables. For instance, $X_{starring}$ depends on X_m and X_p. $\mathcal{P}(X_{starring} = \mathbf{T})$ is estimated via matrix $\omega_{starring}$, cf. Fig. 2-b.

(3) String Predicates. For each string predicate $\langle v, a, w \rangle$, there is a random variable X_w. The word-topic parameter β_{tw} represents the probability of observing word w given topic t. Thus, $\mathcal{P}(X_w = \mathbf{T})$ is calculated as probability of observing w, given the topics of v's topical variable, X_v:

$$\mathcal{P}(X_w = \mathbf{T} \mid X_v, \beta_{1:K}) = \sum_{t \in \mathcal{T}} \mathcal{P}(X_v = t) \frac{\beta_{tw}}{\sum_{t' \in \mathcal{T}} \beta_{t'w}}$$

Example. Fig. 3-a depicts three random variables for string predicates. Given $\mathcal{P}(X_m)$ as in the above example, the probability for "holiday" is (cf. Fig. 3-b):

$$\mathcal{P}(X_{holiday} = \mathbf{T}) = 0.6 \cdot \frac{0.011}{0.017} + 0.1 \cdot \frac{0.002}{0.017} + 0.3 \cdot \frac{0.004}{0.017} = 0.47$$

Learning Topic Distributions. Finally, we wish to estimate topic distributions for the hidden topical variables based on $\mathbf{X}_w$, $\mathbf{X}_c$, and $\mathbf{X}_r$. We aim at finding a topic distribution for every topical variable, so that the query probability in Eq. 1 is maximized. Thus, this optimal topic distribution directly gives us $\mathcal{P}(Q)$. Let θ_{vt} denote a set of topic parameters for topical random variable X_v. Further, let $\theta = \{\theta_{vt} \mid v \in V_{QV}, t \in \mathcal{T}\}$ be the set of all parameters θ_{vt}. Then, we search for parameter θ that maximizes the log-likelihood of Eq. 1:

$$\arg\max_{\theta} L(\theta : \mathbf{X}_w, \mathbf{X}_c, \mathbf{X}_r) \tag{2}$$

where $L(\theta : \mathbf{X}_w, \mathbf{X}_c, \mathbf{X}_r)$ is the log-likelihood defined as:

$$
\begin{aligned}
L(\theta : \mathbf{X}_w, \mathbf{X}_c, \mathbf{X}_r) &= \mathcal{P}(\mathbf{X}_w, \mathbf{X}_c, \mathbf{X}_r \mid \theta, \beta, \omega, \lambda) \\
&= \sum_{v} \sum_{X_w \in \mathbf{X}_w^v} \log \mathcal{P}(X_w \mid X_v, \beta) + \sum_{v} \sum_{X_c \in \mathbf{X}_c^v} \log \mathcal{P}(X_c \mid X_v, \lambda) \\
&\quad + \sum_{v,y} \sum_{X_r \in \mathbf{X}_r^{v,y}} \log \mathcal{P}(X_r \mid X_v, X_y, \omega)
\end{aligned}
$$

where $\mathbf{X}_w^v$ and $\mathbf{X}_c^v$ is the set of all string/class random variables having X_v as parent. $\mathbf{X}_r^{v,y}$ is the set of all relation random variables with parents X_v and X_y.

We use gradient ascent optimization to learn the parameter θ. First, we parametrize each $\mathcal{P}(X_v = t)$ with θ_{vt} such that

$$\mathcal{P}(X_v = t) = \frac{e^{\theta_{vt}}}{\sum_{t' \in \mathcal{T}} e^{\theta_{vt'}}}$$

to obtain a valid probability distribution over the topics. Obtaining the gradient requires dealing with the log of the sum over the topics of each topical variable. Therefore, we make use of theorem [12]:

Theorem 3. *Given a BN and $\mathcal{D} = \{o[1], \ldots, o[M]\}$ as a partially observed dataset. Let X be a variable in that BN with $\mathbf{Pa}(X)$ as its parents. Then:*

$$\frac{\partial L(\theta : \mathcal{D})}{\partial \mathcal{P}(x \mid \mathbf{pa})} = \frac{1}{\mathcal{P}(x \mid \mathbf{pa})} \sum_{m=1}^{M} \mathcal{P}(x, \mathbf{pa} \mid o[m], \theta),$$

This provides the necessary form of the gradient. Now, the gradient of the log-likelihood w.r.t. parameter θ_{vt} is:

$$\frac{\partial L(\theta : \mathbf{X}_w, \mathbf{X}_c, \mathbf{X}_r)}{\partial \theta_{vt}} = \underbrace{\frac{\partial L(\theta : \mathbf{X}_w, \mathbf{X}_c, \mathbf{X}_r)}{\partial \mathcal{P}(X_v = t)}}_{\text{(i)}} \cdot \underbrace{\frac{\partial \mathcal{P}(X_v = t)}{\partial \theta_{vt}}}_{\text{(ii)}} \tag{3}$$

The (i)-part of the gradient, Eq. 3, may be obtained via Theorem 3:

$$
\begin{aligned}
\frac{\partial L(\theta : \mathbf{X}_w, \mathbf{X}_c, \mathbf{X}_r)}{\partial \mathcal{P}(X_v = t)} &= \frac{1}{\mathcal{P}(X_v = t)} \left(\sum_{X_w \in \mathbf{X}_w^v} \mathcal{P}(X_v = t \mid X_w, \beta) \right. \\
&\quad \left. + \sum_{X_c \in \mathbf{X}_c^v} \mathcal{P}(X_v = t \mid X_c, \lambda) + \sum_{y} \sum_{X_r \in \mathbf{X}_r^{v,y}} \mathcal{P}(X_v = t \mid X_r, X_y, \omega) \right)
\end{aligned}
$$

Using Bayes rule we get:

$$\frac{\partial L(\theta : \mathbf{X}_w, \mathbf{X}_c, \mathbf{X}_r)}{\partial \mathcal{P}(X_v = t)} = \sum_{X_w \in \mathbf{X}_w^v} \frac{\mathcal{P}(X_v = t)\mathcal{P}(X_w \mid \beta, t)}{\sum_{t'} \mathcal{P}(X_v = t')\mathcal{P}(X_w \mid \beta, t')}$$

$$+ \sum_{X_c \in \mathbf{X}_c^v} \frac{\mathcal{P}(X_v = t)\mathcal{P}(X_c \mid \lambda, t)}{\sum_{t'} \mathcal{P}(X_v = t')\mathcal{P}(X_c \mid \lambda, t')}$$

$$+ \sum_{y} \sum_{X_r \in \mathbf{X}_r^{v,y}} \frac{\mathcal{P}(X_v = t)\sum_{t'} \mathcal{P}(X_r \mid X_y, \omega, t')}{\sum_{t''} \mathcal{P}(X_v = t'')\sum_{t'''} \mathcal{P}(X_r \mid X_y, \omega, t''')}$$

Finally, the (ii)-part of the gradient in Eq. 3 is given by:

$$\frac{\partial \mathcal{P}(X_v = t)}{\partial \theta_{tv}} = \frac{e^{\theta_{tv}} \sum_{t'-t} e^{\theta_{t'v}}}{(\sum_{t'} e^{\theta_{t'v}})^2}$$

Time Complexity. Query probability estimation has a complexity bound:

Theorem 4 (Time Complexity for $\mathcal{P}(Q)$ Estimation). *Given k topics and a query Q, the time for computing $\mathcal{P}(Q)$ in Eq. 1 is in $O(\psi \cdot |Q| \cdot k)$, with ψ as number of iterations needed for optimization and $|Q|$ as # predicates in Q.*

Proof. A proof is given in [22]   ∎

Note, ψ is determined by the specific algorithm used for optimization. So, overall complexity for computing $\mathcal{P}(Q)$ is independent of the synopsis size given the topics.

4   Evaluation

We conducted experiments to analyze the effectiveness (I.1) and efficiency (I.2) of TopGuess. Overall, our results are very promising: we achieved up to 88% more accurate selectivity estimates, while runtime was comparable to the baselines. Further, in contrast to the baselines, we noted TopGuess's runtime behavior to be much less influenced by the synopsis size – thereby confirming Thm. 4.

4.1   Evaluation Setting

Systems. We employ two categories of baselines: (1) String predicates are combined with structured predicates via an *independence assumption*: IND baseline. That is, the selectivity of string predicates and structured predicates is estimated using two separate synopses: a string synopsis (explained below) and a synopsis for structured RDF data based on histograms [10]. Obtained probabilities are combined in a greedy fashion while assuming independence. (2) We reuse our previous work on BNs for text-rich data graphs [23]: BN baseline. Here, all query predicates are captured uniformly via a single BN. To handle string predicates, we employ *n-gram string synopses* [24]

A n-gram synopsis summarizes the vocabulary by "omitting" certain n-grams. Thus, a synopsis represents a subset of all possible n-grams occurring in the

Table 1. Data synopsis memory/disk space in MB

	IMDB		DBLP	
	BN/IND	TopGuess	BN/IND	TopGuess
Mem.	$\{2, 4, 20, 40\}$	≤ 0.1	$\{2, 4, 20, 40\}$	≤ 0.1
Disk	0	281.7	0	229.9

data. A simplistic strategy is to choose random n-gram *samples* from the data. Another approach is to construct a *top-k* n-gram synopsis. For this, n-grams are extracted from the data together with their counts. Then, the k most frequent n-grams are included in the synopsis. Further, a *stratified bloom filter* (SBF) synopsis has been proposed [24], which uses bloom filters as a heuristic map that projects n-grams to their counts. Note, we refer to omitted n-grams as "missing". The probability for missing n-grams cannot be estimated with a probabilistic framework, as such strings are not included in a sample space. So, a string predicate featuring a missing n-gram is assumed to be independent from the remainder of the query. Its probability is computed via a heuristic. We employ the *leftbackoff* strategy, which finds the longest known n-gram that is the pre- or postfix of the missing n-gram. Then, the probability of the missing n-gram is approximated based on statistics for its pre-/postfix [24].

Combining string synopses with the two categories of baselines yields six systems: $\text{IND}_{\text{sample}}$, $\text{IND}_{\text{top-k}}$, and IND_{SBF} rely on the independence assumption, while $\text{BN}_{\text{sample}}$, $\text{BN}_{\text{top-k}}$, and BN_{SBF} represent BN approaches.

Data. We employ two real-world RDF datasets: DBLP [15] and IMDB [6]. From both datasets we have large vocabularies: $25,540,172$ (DBLP) and $7,841,347$ (IMDB) words. Note, while DBLP and IMDB feature text-rich attributes, they differ in their overall amount of text. On average an attribute in DBLP contains 2.6 words, with a variance of 2.1 words. In contrast, IMDB attributes contain 5.1 words, with a variance of 95.6 words. Moreover, we observed during learning of the BN baseline that there are more data correlations in IMDB than in DBLP. We expect correlations between query predicates to have a strong influence on the system effectiveness.

Queries. We used IMDB [6] and DBLP [15] keyword search benchmarks: We generated 54 DBLP queries from [15]. Further, we constructed 46 queries for IMDB based on queries in [6]. We omitted 4 queries from [6], as they could not be translated to conjunctive queries. Overall, our load features 100 queries with: 0-4 relation, 1-7 string, 1-4 class predicates, and 2-11 predicates in total. Further query statistics and a complete query listing can be found in [22].

Synopsis Size. We employ baselines with varying synopsis size. For this, we varied # words captured by the string synopsis. The top-k and sample synopsis contained # words $\in \{0.5K, 1K, 5K, 10K\}$. The SBF string synopsis captured $\{2.5K, 5K, 25K, 50K\}$ words for each attribute. Note, SBF systems featured most keywords occurring in our query load. Different string synopsis sizes translated to a memory consumption of baselines $\in \{2, 4, 20, 40\}$ MB. IND and

BN baselines load their synopsis into main memory. In contrast, TopGuess keeps a large topic model at disk and constructs a small, query-specific BN in memory at runtime ($\leq$ 100 KBytes). Table 1 depicts further details.

Implementation and Offline Learning. For IND and BN baselines, we started by constructing their string synopses. Each synopsis was learned in $\leq$ 1h.

Then, we constructed BN systems based on [23]. That is, we capture words and structured data elements using random variables and learn correlations between them, thereby forming a BN structure. For efficient selectivity estimation the network is reduced to a "lightweight" model capturing solely the most important correlations. Then, we calculate model parameters (CPDs) based on frequency counts. For IND systems, we do not need the model structure and merely keep the marginalized BN parameters. Structure and parameter learning combined took up to 3h. To compute query selectivities the BN systems need inferencing strategies. For this, we used a Junction tree algorithm [23].

TopGuess exploits an "off-the-shelf" TRM from [2]. The number of topics is an important factor – determining which correlations are discovered. We experimented with a varying number of topics $\in [10, 100]$. We found 50 topics are sufficient to capture all strong correlations in our datasets. The TopGuess learning took up to 5h and its parameters were stored on hard disk, cf. Table 1. At query time, we employed a greedy gradient ascent algorithm for learning the topic distributions. To avoid local maxima, we used up to 10 random restarts.

We implemented all systems in Java 6. Experiments were run on a Linux server with: 2 Intel Xeon CPUs at 2.33GHz, 16 GB memory assigned to the JVM, and a RAID10 with IBM SAS 10K rpm disks. Before each query execution we cleared OS caches. Presented values are averages over five runs.

4.2 Selectivity Estimation Effectiveness

We employ the multiplicative error metric (me) [7] for measuring effectiveness:

$$me(Q) = \frac{\max\{\mathcal{F}_e(Q), \mathcal{F}_a(Q)\}}{\min\{\mathcal{F}_e(Q), \mathcal{F}_a(Q)\}}$$

with $\mathcal{F}_e(Q)$ and $\mathcal{F}_a(Q)$ as exact and approximated selectivity. Intuitively, $me(Q)$ is the factor to which $\mathcal{F}_a(Q)$ under-/overestimates $\mathcal{F}_e(Q)$.

Overall Results. Figs. 4-a/e (b/f) show the multiplicative error vs. synopsis size (# predicates) for DBLP and IMDB. Baseline system effectiveness strongly varies with their synopsis size. In particular, for small synopses $\leq$ 20 MB IND and BN performed poorly. We explain this with missing words in their string synopses, which led to heuristics being used for probability computation. In simple terms, IND and BN systems traded synopsis space for estimation accuracy.

TopGuess, on the other hand, did not suffer from this issue. All its parameters (cf. Sect. 3.1) could be stored at disk and solely the query-specific BN was loaded at runtime. Thus, TopGuess could exploit very fine-grained probabilities and omitted any kind of heuristic. We observed that TopGuess reduced the error of the best BN system, BN_{SBF}, by 88% (33%) for IMDB (DBLP). Further, we outperformed the best IND system, IND_{SBF}, by 99% (35%) on IMDB (DBLP).

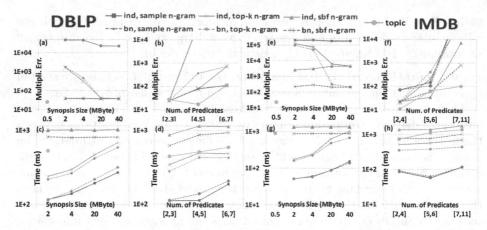

Fig. 4. Effectiveness: (a)+(b) for DBLP and (e)+(f) for IMDB. Efficiency: (c)+(d) for DBLP and (g)+(h) for IMDB. Y-axes are given in logarithmic scale.

Synopsis Size. Figs. 4-a/e show estimation errors w.r.t. in-memory synopsis size. An important observation is that the synopsis size is a key factor for effectiveness. Top-k and sample-based string synopsis systems were strongly affected by their (string) synopsis size. Given a small synopsis ≤ 4 MB, we observed that top-k/sample-based systems performed poorly. Here, many relevant query keywords were missed, leading to inaccurate heuristics being applied. With increasing synopsis size $\in [4, 20]$ MB, the performance of top-k approaches converged to the most accurate baseline (SBF-based systems). For instance given 4 MB space, the BN_{top-k} approach preformed 95% worse than BN_{SBF} on IMDB, but only 33% worse given 20 MB. Further, we noted SBF-based approaches to perform fairly stable. We explain this with SBF systems using bloom filters as an effective summary. Such systems were able to capture most query keywords. Thus, few heuristic-based estimations were necessary. However, SBF-based systems also have a limited memory space and must eventually omit words.

In contrast, we observed TopGuess to use ≤ 0.1 MB memory for IMDB as well DBLP. We explain this extremely compact BN with: (1) TopGuess has a network size, which is bound by the query size. (2) The BN only contains random variables that either are binary or have a sample space, which is bounded by the number of topics. For example, over the DBLP query load TopGuess needed on average 40 KB. Yet, TopGuess resolves the issue of missing words completely: the TopGuess parameters (stored on disk) capture all words in the vocabulary. At runtime, TopGuess retrieves the necessary statistics for a particular query and constructs its query-specific BN. This way, TopGuess achieved up to by 88% (33%) better results on IMDB (DBLP) than the best baselines.

Overall, we can conclude that estimation effectiveness is driven by accurate string predicate probabilities. Thus, there is a strong need for a data synopsis allowing for extensive word/text data statistics.

Correlations. We found system performances to vary for IMDB and DBLP. For the IMDB dataset, BN_{SBF} could reduce errors of the IND_{SBF} approach by up to 93%. On the other hand, for DBLP improvements were much smaller. These differences are due to the varying degree of correlations in our two datasets. While learning the BNs for BN, we observed less correlations in DBLP than in IMDB. For instance, for DBLP queries with string predicates name and label, we noted no significant correlations. Thus, the probabilities obtained from BN systems were almost identical to the ones from IND.

In contrast, even for the less correlated dataset DBLP, TopGuess outperforms the best baselines, IND_{SBF} and BN_{SBF}, by 35% and 33%. We explain this our a fine-grained, query-specific BN. More precisely, we observed that BN approaches exploited data correlations, which were observed in the data graph. However, TopGuess captured even minor correlations via its topic mixtures at query time – learned for each query individually.

Query Size. We depict the multiplicative error vs. # query predicates in Figs. 4-b/f. As expected, estimation errors increase for all systems in # predicates. For our baselines, we explain this behavior with: (1) Given an increasing # predicates, the chances of missing a query keyword increase. (2) When missing a single query keyword, the error is "propagated" throughout the computation.

However, while the TopGuess approach also led to more misestimates for larger queries, the degree of this increase was smaller. For instance, considering IMDB queries with 7-11 predicates, we could observe that TopGuess performs much more stable than BN or IND baselines, cf. Fig. 4-f.

4.3   Selectivity Estimation Efficiency

We now analyze the estimation efficiency vs. synopses size (# query predicates), cf. Figs. 4-c/g (d/h). For TopGuess, the reported times comprise parameter loading, BN construction, and topic learning. For BN and IND, the times represent only selectivity computation, i.e., no model learning or parameter loading.

Overall Results. Considering BN and IND systems, we saw that their string synopsis was a key performance factor. Intuitively, the more words were missed, the "simpler" and the more efficient these systems became. However, such gains came at the expense of effectiveness: the fastest baseline system, IND_{sample}, also computed the least accurate selectivity estimates.

Comparing the two systems with the best effectiveness, TopGuess and BN_{SBF}, TopGuess led to a better performance by up to 45%. Unfortunately, in comparison to top-k systems, TopGuess resulted in a performance decrease of 40%. We explain these drawbacks with the time-consuming disk I/O, which was needed for loading the statistics. However, while BN and IND clearly outperformed TopGuess w.r.t. small synopses $\leq$ 4 MB, TopGuess results are comparable for synopses $\geq$ 20 MB. We expect such effects to be more drastic for "large" BN/IND synopses $\gg$ 100 MB. So, TopGuess guarantees a much more "stable" behavior.

Synopsis Size. Figs. 4-c/g show time vs. synopsis size. For the baselines, we saw a correlation between synopsis size and runtime behavior: While BN and IND reach a high efficiency for synopses $\leq$ 4 MB, their performance decreases rapidly for synopses $\geq$ 20 MB. We explain this effect with the larger CPDs, which led to longer probability estimation times. We observed SBF-based approaches to be less driven by their synopsis size. This is because their computational costs are mainly determined by bloom filters. In contrast, TopGuess did not suffer from this issue at all. That is, for a given query, TopGuess only loads/processes statistics necessary for that query. All others statistics are kept on disk.

Query Size. All systems had increasing estimation times in query size, cf. Figs. 4-d/h. This is because each additional query predicate translated to more probability computations. However, as TopGuess exploits a compact query-specific BN, we expected it's performance to be less influenced by query size. To confirm this, we compared the standard deviation of the estimation time w.r.t. a varying # query predicates. For instance, the standard deviations was 82.48 ms (213.48 ms) for TopGuess (BN). The low deviation for TopGuess indicates that its probability estimation times varied less than those from BN systems.

5   Related Work

For selectivity estimation on *structured data*, existing works exploit various data synopses, e.g., join samples [1], graph synopses [18], or graphical models [9,21,23]. In particular, those synopses have been applied for selectivity estimation of structured SPARQL/BGP queries on RDF data, e.g., [7,10,16,19].

Unfortunately, such synopses can not effectively capture statistics for combinations of words and structured data elements. In order to guarantee a manageable synopsis size, various summarization techniques are commonly applied on words, e.g., hashing [19], heuristics [20], categorization [16], discretization [10], or string synopses [23] (I.1, Sect. 1). Moreover, since the offline constructed data synopsis is directly used for the selectivity estimation at runtime, existing works must either keep the data synopsis small [10,16,19,23] or solely employ heuristics [20] (I.2, Sect. 1). In contrast, our TopGuess approach overcomes both issues (I.1 and I.2) by relying on relational topic models as data synopsis and a query-specific BN for selectivity estimation.

With regard to selectivity estimation on *text data*, language models and other machine learning techniques have been employed [5,11,13,24]. More specifically, some works aim at substring or fuzzy string matching [5,13], while other approaches target "extraction" operators, e.g., dictionary-based operators [24]. However, such works do not consider correlations among multiple string predicates or correlations between string predicates and structured query predicates.

6   Conclusion

We proposed a holistic approach (TopGuess) for selectivity estimation of hybrid queries. We showed space and time complexity bounds for TopGuess. Further, we conducted empirical studies on real-world data and achieved strong effectiveness improvements, while not requiring additional runtime.

As a future work, we plan to extend TopGuess in order to become a more generic selectivity estimation approach for RDF data and BGP queries, respectively. For this, we replace the topic distributions in our data synopsis with different application-specific probability distributions, e.g., a continuous distribution for estimating the selectivity of range queries over numerical data.

References

1. Acharya, S., Gibbons, P., Poosala, V., Ramaswamy, S.: Join synopses for approximate query answering. In: SIGMOD (1999)
2. Bicer, V., Tran, T., Ma, Y., Studer, R.: TRM - Learning Dependencies between Text and Structure with Topical Relational Models. In: Alani, H., et al. (eds.) ISWC 2013, Part I. LNCS, vol. 8218, pp. 1–16. Springer, Heidelberg (2013)
3. Blei, D., Ng, A., Jordan, M.: Latent dirichlet allocation. The Journal of Machine Learning Research 3, 993–1022 (2003)
4. Chang, J., Blei, D.: Relational Topic Models for Document Networks. In: AIStats (2009)
5. Chaudhuri, S., Ganti, V., Gravano, L.: Selectivity Estimation for String Predicates: Overcoming the Underestimation Problem. In: ICDE (2004)
6. Coffman, J., Weaver, A.C.: A framework for evaluating database keyword search strategies. In: CIKM (2010)
7. Deshpande, A., Garofalakis, M.N., Rastogi, R.: Independence is Good: Dependency-Based Histogram Synopses for High-Dimensional Data. In: SIGMOD (2001)
8. Doshi, F., Miller, K., Gael, J.V., Teh, Y.W.: Variational Inference for the Indian Buffet Process. JMLR 5, 137–144 (2009)
9. Getoor, L., Taskar, B., Koller, D.: Selectivity estimation using probabilistic models. In: SIGMOD (2001)
10. Huang, H., Liu, C.: Estimating Selectivity for Joined RDF Triple Patterns. In: CIKM (2011)
11. Jin, L., Li, C.: Selectivity Estimation for Fuzzy String Predicates in Large Data Sets. In: VLDB (2005)
12. Koller, D., Friedman, N.: Probabilistic graphical models. MIT Press (2009)
13. Lee, H., Ng, R.T., Shim, K.: Extending Q-Grams to Estimate Selectivity of String Matching with Low Edit Distance. In: VLDB (2007)
14. Liu, Y., Niculescu-Mizil, A., Gryc, W.: Topic-link LDA: Joint Models of Topic and Author Community. In: ICML (2009)
15. Luo, Y., Wang, W., Lin, X., Zhou, X., Wang, J., Li, K.: SPARK2: Top-k Keyword Query in Relational Databases. TKDE 23(12), 1763–1780 (2011)
16. Neumann, T., Moerkotte, G.: Characteristic sets: Accurate cardinality estimation for RDF queries with multiple joins. In: ICDE (2011)
17. Poosala, V., Haas, P., Ioannidis, Y., Shekita, E.: Improved histograms for selectivity estimation of range predicates. In: SIGMOD (1996)
18. Spiegel, J., Polyzotis, N.: Graph-based synopses for relational selectivity estimation. In: SIGMOD (2006)
19. Stocker, M., Seaborne, A., Bernstein, A., Kiefer, C., Reynolds, D.: SPARQL Basic Graph Pattern Optimization Using Selectivity Estimation. In: WWW (2008)
20. Tsialiamanis, P., Sidirourgos, L., Fundulaki, I., Christophides, V., Boncz, P.: Heuristics-based Query Optimisation for SPARQL. In: EDBT (2012)
21. Tzoumas, K., Deshpande, A., Jensen, C.S.: Lightweight Graphical Models for Selectivity Estimation Without Independence Assumptions. In: PVLDB (2011)
22. Wagner, A., Bicer, V., Tran, D.T.: Topic-based Selectivity Estimation for Text-Rich Data Graphs, http://www.aifb.kit.edu/web/Techreport3039
23. Wagner, A., Bicer, V., Tran, T.D.: Selectivity estimation for hybrid queries over text-rich data graphs. In: EDBT (2013)
24. Wang, D.Z., Wei, L., Li, Y., Reiss, F., Vaithyanathan, S.: Selectivity estimation for extraction operators over text data. In: ICDE (2011)
25. Zhang, L., et al.: Multirelational Topic Models. In: ICDM (2009)

Querying Factorized Probabilistic Triple Databases

Denis Krompaß[1], Maximilian Nickel[2], and Volker Tresp[1,3]

[1] Ludwig Maximilian University, 80538 Munich, Germany
Denis.Krompass@campus.lmu.de
[2] Massachusetts Institute of Technology, Cambridge, MA
and Istituto Italiano di Tecnologia, Genova, Italy
mnick@mit.edu
[3] Siemens AG, Corporate Technology, Munich, Germany
Volker.Tresp@siemens.com

Abstract. An increasing amount of data is becoming available in the
form of large triple stores, with the Semantic Web's linked open data
cloud (LOD) as one of the most prominent examples. Data quality and
completeness are key issues in many community-generated data stores,
like LOD, which motivates probabilistic and statistical approaches to
data representation, reasoning and querying. In this paper we address the
issue from the perspective of probabilistic databases, which account for
uncertainty in the data via a probability distribution over all database
instances. We obtain a highly compressed representation using the recently developed RESCAL approach and demonstrate experimentally
that efficient querying can be obtained by exploiting inherent features of
RESCAL via sub-query approximations of deterministic views.

Keywords: Probabilistic Databases, Tensor Factorization, RESCAL,
Querying, Extensional Query Evaluation.

1 Introduction

The rapidly growing Web of Data, e.g., as presented by the Semantic Web's
linked open data cloud (LOD), is providing an increasing amount of data in
form of large triple databases, also known as triple stores. However, the LOD
cloud includes many sources with varying reliability and to correctly account
for data veracity remains a big challenge. To address this issue, reasoning with
inconsistent and uncertain ontologies has recently emerged as a research field
of its own [6,31,4,9,3,15]. In this paper we approach the veracity issue from the
perspective of probabilistic databases (PDB), which consider multiple possible
occurrences of a database via a possible worlds semantics and account for uncertainty in the data by assigning a probability distribution over all database
instances [27]. As such, querying PDBs has a clear interpretation as generaliza-
tions of deterministic relational database queries.

When applying PDBs to large triple stores various key challenges need to be
addressed. First, consider storage requirements. A common assumption in PDBs

P. Mika et al. (Eds.) ISWC 2014, Part II, LNCS 8797, pp. 114–129, 2014.

is tuple independence, or in our case triple independence, which requires a representation of each triple's uncertainty. Unless default values are used, representing the individual uncertainty levels can lead to huge storage requirements.

Second, there is the question of how the triple uncertainty is quantified and where it is specified. In PDBs one typically assumes that the data uncertainty is specified by the application, e.g., one assumes given measurements of uncertainty. However, in the Web of Data such information is typically not available. Rather the Web of Data is incomplete and contains incorrect information, as triples are missing and existing triples can be false. The third issue concerns probabilistically correct and efficient querying. Although individual triples are assumed to be independent, complex queries introduce dependencies such that correct query answering becomes, in the worst case, intractable.

We address all three issues by exploiting the recently developed RESCAL approach [19], which computes a memory-efficient low-rank tensor representation of a triple store from which probabilities for individual triples can be derived easily without materializing the whole probabilistic representation of the triple store. These probabilities are meaningful in as much as the underlying data generation process (which we explore through the factorization) is sensible for the particular triple store; experimentally it has been shown that this is the case, e.g., for significant parts of the LOD [20]. While the RESCAL model alone allows to query the probability of individual ground triples, more complex queries, which generally might contain complex dependencies between ground triples throughout the complete PDB, remain a major challenge. When restricting the allowed queries to so-called safe queries, extensional query evaluation can provide answers with polynomial time complexity [27]. Unfortunately, polynomial time complexity does not necessarily imply acceptable query time. During query evaluation it might be necessary to materialize sub-queries, which often produce large (dense) views and as such have high computational and high memory complexity. Here, we propose a new method for extensional query evaluation (after factorization) that avoids the expensive materialization of dense database views by exploiting the factorized low-rank representation of a triple store computed by RESCAL. The idea is to first materialize the sub-query in the initial deterministic representation of the triple store (that can be efficiently constructed and is generally sparse) and to then derive a low-rank approximation of that view using fast RESCAL updates, which then produces the probabilistic view.

The paper is organized as follows: In the next section we discuss related work. Section 3 reviews PDBs and Section 4 describes the RESCAL approach. Section 5 contains the main contribution of the paper and addresses the querying of a factorized probabilistic triple databases. Section 6 describes our experimental results and Section 7 contains our conclusions.

2 Related Work

Probabilistic databases (PDB) have gained much interest in recent years and an overview over the state of the art is provided by [27]. Important ongoing research projects include the MayBMS project [10] at Cornell University, the MystiQ project [2] at the University of Washington, the Orion project [26] at the Purdue University, and the Trio project [16] at the Stanford University. The idea of materialized views on PDBs has been developed in [5], where it was proposed to materialize probabilistic views to be used for query answering at runtime.

Uncertainty in Semantic Web ontologies has been addressed in BayesOWL [6] and OntoBayes [31]. Furthermore, PR-OWL [4] is a Bayesian Ontology Language for the Semantic Web. The link between PDBs, Description Logic and Semantic Web data structures has been explored by [9,3,15]. In contrast to these approaches, we start with a deterministic triple store and then derive probabilities via the factorization. Common to all these approaches is the challenge of efficient querying.

In our work we perform a probabilistic ranking of candidate query answers as done by the top-k querying approaches [7,21,25], however without pruning of low-confidence answers. In these top-k querying approaches the computation of exact probabilities for the potential top-k answers are avoided by using lower and upper bounds for the corresponding marginal probabilities. Unfortunately, none of these approaches, apart from [7], can avoid extensive materializations in finding answer candidates [28].

Tensors have been applied to Web analysis in [12] and to ranking predictions in the Semantic Web in [8]. [23] applied tensor models to rating predictions. Using factorization approaches to predict ground atoms was pioneered in [29]; [19], [30], [1], and [11] applied tensor models for this task, where [19] introduced the RESCAL model. [24] applied matrix factorization for relation extraction in universal schemas.

In [20] the YAGO ontology was factorized and meaningful predictions of simple triples in selected subgroups of YAGO were derived through the reconstruction from the low rank representation of the triple store. However, in these papers querying was limited to the evaluation of independent ground triples. Here, we study the significantly more difficult problem of complex queries on predicted triple confidence values (including existentially quantified variables). Thereby we realize extensional query evaluation on safe queries, which can induce complex dependencies between individual predicted triple probabilities throughout the database. In particular, we are concerned with how these queries can be executed efficiently, without the need for extensive materialization of probability tables, by exploiting the factorized representation during querying.

3   Probabilistic Databases

3.1   Semantics

Probabilistic databases (PDB) have been developed to extend database technologies to handle uncertain data. A general overview is provided by [27]. PDBs build on the concept of incomplete databases, i.e. databases that are allowed to be in one of multiple states (worlds): Given an active domain $ADom$ of constants (resources in RDF) each world contains a subset of all possible ground atoms (triples), formed by the elements of $ADom$ and the predicates in the database. A PDB then assigns a probability distribution to all possible worlds $W \in \mathbf{W}$, where $\mathbf{W}$ is the set of all worlds under consideration. More precisely, given an active domain $ADom$ of constants or resources in terms of a RDF framework, each world contains a subset of all possible ground atoms (triples), formed by the elements of $ADom$ and the predicates. A PDB is an incomplete database where, furthermore, a probability distribution is assigned to the possible worlds. In the following, we adopt the common assumption of PDBs that the probabilities for all ground atoms are mutually independent (i.e., tuple independence).

3.2   Querying on Probabilistic Databases

Query evaluation in PDBs remains a major challenge. In particular, scalability to large domains is significantly harder to achieve when compared to deterministic databases.

Of interest here is the *possible answer semantics* which calculates the probability that a given tuple t is a possible answer to a query Q in a world $W \in \mathbf{W}$ of a PDB $\mathbf{D}$. For the marginal probability over all possible worlds, we get

$$P(t \in Q) = \sum_{W \in \mathbf{W}: t \in Q_W} P(W)$$

where Q_W is the query with respect to one possible world of $\mathbf{D}$.

An important concept in query evaluation is the lineage $\Phi_Q^{\mathbf{D}}$ of a possible answer tuple t to Q with respect to $\mathbf{D}$. The lineage of a possible output tuple to a query is a propositional formula over tuple states in the database, which says which input tuples must be present in order for the query to return the particular output. The concept of lineage allows a reduction of the query evaluation problem to the evaluation of propositional formulas. For queries involving many variables the lineage can become very complex but can still be derived in polynomial time (with the size of the database).[1]

In *intensional query evaluation*, probabilistic inference is performed over the lineage of all possible answers to a query Q. Every relational query can be evaluated this way, but the data complexity depends dramatically on the query being evaluated, and can be hard for #P. Thus it is in general advantageous to avoid the evaluation of the lineage.

In contrast, *extensional query evaluation* is concerned with queries where the entire probabilistic inference can be computed in a database engine and thus, can be processed as effectively as the evaluation of standard SQL queries. Relational queries that can be evaluated this way are called *safe queries*. If the extensional query plan does compute the output probabilities correctly for any input database, then it is called a safe query plan.

In this paper we focus on queries that allow an extensional query evaluation, as discussed next.

---

[1] For a more detailed explanation on the concept of lineage we refer to [27, Chp.2].

3.3 Extensional Query Evaluation

Extensional query evaluation is only dependent on the query expression itself and the lineage does not need to be computed. During the evaluation process, several rules are applied to the query in order to divide it into smaller and easier sub-queries until it reduces to ground tuples with elementary probability values. Queries that can be completely simplified to ground tuples with extensional evaluation rules are *safe*, in the sense mentioned above. Extensional query evaluation can be implemented via the application of six rules [27]. In the following we will briefly describe three of those rules relevant throughout this paper.

Consider a query that can be written as a conjunction of two simpler queries

$$Q = Q_1 \wedge Q_2.$$

If one can guarantee that the sub-queries are independent probabilistic events, one can write

$$P(Q_1 \wedge Q_2) = P(Q_1) \cdot P(Q_2). \qquad \text{(independent-join rule)}$$

More formally one needs the condition of a *syntactical independence* between Q_1 and Q_2: Two queries Q_1 and Q_2 are syntactically independent if no two relational atoms unify, which means that it is not possible that exactly the same ground tuples, under any assignments of constants, can occur in both sub-queries. With syntactical independence we also get

$$P(Q_1 \vee Q_2) = 1 - (1 - P(Q_1)) \cdot (1 - P(Q_2)). \qquad \text{(independent-union rule)}$$

Further for queries of the form $\exists x.Q$ we can use the independent-project rule

$$P(\exists x.Q) = 1 - \prod_{b \in ADom} (1 - P(Q[b/x])). \qquad (1)$$

This rule can always be applied if x is a separator variable.[2] As an example, consider that we want to know the probability that Jack is born in Rome and that he likes someone who is a child of Albert Einstein (AE). This query can be written as a conjunction of two sub-queries Q_1 and Q_2,

$$Q_1(x, t) : - \, bornIn(x, t)$$
$$Q_2(x, z) : - \, \exists y.(likes(x, y), childOf(y, z))$$

with $x =$ Jack, $t =$ Rome and $z =$ AE. Q_1 asks if Jack is born in Rome and Q_2 if Jack likes somebody who is a child of Albert Einstein. By exploiting the

---

[2] x is a separator variable if it occurs in all atoms in Q and if in the case that atoms unify, x occurs at a common position. Two atoms unify if they can be made identical by an assignment of constants.

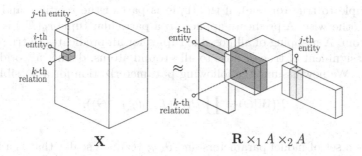

$$\mathbf{X} \qquad\qquad \mathbf{R} \times_1 A \times_2 A$$

Fig. 1. RESCAL model for binary relations

independent join rule on Q_1 and Q_2 and the independent project rule on Q_2 this query can be calculated as,

$$P(Q(x = \mathsf{Jack}, t = \mathsf{Rome}, z = \mathsf{AE}) = P(bornIn(\mathsf{Jack}, \mathsf{Rome}))$$

$$\times \left(1 - \prod_{b \in A\,Dom} [1 - P(likes(\mathsf{Jack}, b)) \cdot P((childOf(b, \mathsf{AE}))] \right).$$

Note that since a person can like many other persons the *likes* atoms in Q_2 are not mutually exclusive what induces a complex expression that is not simply the sum or the product or probabilities.

4   RESCAL

In PDBs one typically assumes that the data uncertainty is specified by the application. Although there are efforts towards uncertainty management for the Web of Data, currently such information not widely available. Rather the Web of Data is incomplete, i.e., many triples are missing, and contains incorrect information, i.e., existing triples are false. To overcome this problem, we employ a probabilistic model of the triple database – i.e. the recently developed RESCAL approach – and derive data uncertainty from the agreement of the data with this model. RESCAL relies on a specific factorization of a third-order adjacency tensor from which triple probabilities can be derived. In addition, RESCAL computes a highly compressed representation of the PDB, reducing the memory footprint dramatically. The latter point is of particular interest, since PDBs can be dense.

4.1   Notation

To describe RESCAL, we need to introduce some notation. We consider a database as a set of M relations $\{r_k\}_{k=1}^{M}$. A relation is a table with attributes as columns and subject-object entity pairs $E_z = (e_i, e_j)$ as rows. If r_k is a relation, then $r_k(\cdot)$ is the corresponding predicate. A predicate is a function that maps a tuple to true (or one), if the tuple is part of the relation, and to false (or zero), otherwise. A predicate applied to a particular tuple $r_k(E_z)$ is called a ground atom. A mapping of all possible tuples for all predicates to true or false, i.e., the assignment of true or false to all ground atoms, defines a world W (see Section 3). We now assume the following parameterization for a possible world,

$$P(W|\Theta) = \prod_{k,z} P(r_k(E_z)|\theta_{k,E_z}(\Theta)). \tag{2}$$

Here, Θ is a set of model parameters and $\theta_{k,E_z}(\Theta)$ is a scalar that is a function of the parameters. As it is common in probabilistic databases, Equation (2) assumes that all ground atoms are independent given the model parameters.

4.2 Parameterization

RESCAL [19] is a latent variable method for learning from multi-relational data where Equation (2) is parametrized as

$$\theta_{k,(e_i,e_j)} = \sum_{l_1=1}^{r} \sum_{l_2=1}^{r} R_{k_{l_1,l_2}} a_{i,l_1} a_{j,l_2} = \boldsymbol{a}_i^T R_k \boldsymbol{a}_j. \tag{3}$$

Thus in RESCAL each entity e_i is assigned a vector of r latent variables $\boldsymbol{a}_i$ and the matrix R_k describes how these latent variables interact for a particular relation.

Note that the parameters $\Theta = \{\{\boldsymbol{a}_i\}_{i=1}^{n}, \{R_k\}_{k=1}^{m}\}$ are coupled via the unique representation of the entities, what permits the global exchange of information across different relations and across subject/object-occurrences of entities. Here, n is the number of entities and m is the number of relation types. This property is also referred to as collective learning.

4.3 Cost Functions

In RESCAL, one uses a least-squares penalty on the parameters (implying a Gaussian prior distribution) and uses the cost function

$$\sum_{k,E_z} \text{loss}_{k,E_z} + \lambda_A \|A\|_F^2 + \lambda_R \sum_k \|R_k\|_F^2$$

where A is the matrix of latent factors with $(A)_{i,j} = a_{i,j}$ and $\lambda_A \geq 0$ and $\lambda_R \geq 0$ are hyperparameters for the regularization. $\|\cdot\|_F$ is the Frobenius norm. For the loss function there are several options. An appropriate choice for the conditional probability in Equation (2) would be a Bernoulli distribution and we would obtain $\text{loss}_{k,E_z} = -r_k(E_z) \log \theta_{k,E_z} - (1 - r_k(E_z))(1 - \theta_{k,E_z})$. After training, we can interpret $\theta_{k,E_z} \approx P(r_k(E_z) = 1|\theta_{k,E_z})$. Alternatively, one can use a least-squared loss

$$\text{loss}_{k,E_z} = (r_k(E_z) - \theta_{k,E_z})^2$$

with the same interpretation of θ_{k,E_z}. A drawback is that we cannot guarantee that predicted values are nonnegative and upper bounded by one. To overcome this issue, we employ a post-processing step of the form,

$$\hat{\theta}_z^B = \text{sig}_\epsilon(\theta_z^G) \tag{4}$$

where θ_z^G is the parameter derived from the Gaussian model and $\hat{\theta}_z^B$ would be an estimate for the corresponding Bernoulli parameter. The precise definition of $\text{sig}_\epsilon(\theta_z^G)$ can be found in the Appendix. Alternatively, a form of Platt scaling can be used to define $\text{sig}_\epsilon(\theta_z^G)$ [22].

In our work we employ the least squares cost function since then the highly efficient alternating least-squares (ALS) updates can be employed that exploit data sparsity [19]. RESCAL has been scaled up to work with several million entities and close to 100 relation types. In contrast, with the Bernoulli cost function it would not be possible to exploit the sparsity of the data efficiently: gradient-based methods for the Bernoulli cost function would require to compute the dense tensor $AR_k A^T$ explicitly, what is both slow and impractical [18] and pattern-based approaches (such as stochastic gradient descent) have not proven to be effective with a Bernoulli cost function.

4.4   Tensor Factorization

Note, that in Equation (3) we need to optimize the latent entity representations a_i and the relation-specific R_k matrices. This can be done by first factorizing an adjacency tensor $\mathbf{X} \in \{0,1\}^{n \times n \times m}$ whose entries x_{ijk} correspond to all possible ground atoms over n entities and m different relation types. In particular, the entries of $\mathbf{X}$ are set to one, if the ground atom $r_k(E_z)$ exists and to zero otherwise. Figure 1 illustrates the tensor factorization.

5   Querying Factorized Probabilistic Databases

We will describe now how complex queries on PDBs can be answered efficiently via the RESCAL model when the queries are restricted to $\exists x.Q$-type safe queries.

A naive approach would be to use the triple probabilities as calculated by the RESCAL model in the extensional query evaluation rules,

$$P(likes(\textsf{Jack}, \textsf{Jane})) = \text{sig}_\epsilon(a_{\textsf{Jack}}^T R_{likes} a_{\textsf{Jane}})$$

where sig_ϵ is defined in Equation (4). However, this would not remove the computational complexity of the evaluation and would computationally be demanding for any reasonably sized triple store. A probabilistic database is not sparse in general: e.g., the evaluation of a query the examples used in Section 3.3 requires on the order of $|ADom|$ evaluations of the RESCAL model. The complexity is mainly introduced by the existentially quantified query variables and their product-aggregation in the independent-project rule (Equation (1)). Assuming further that we are not only interested in the probability with $x = \textsf{Jack}$ but in a probabilistic ranking of all persons in the database, the total costs become already quadratic in $|ADom|$.

The key idea is to *approximate* safe sub-queries of the type $\exists x.Q$ by employing the RESCAL tensor factorization model. Through this approach, we avoid costly evaluations of sub-queries and additionally construct materialized views that have a memory efficient factorized representation. To illustrate the proposed approach, consider the query example from Section 3.3. This query can be subdivided into two parts, $Q(x, t, z) = Q_1(x, t) \wedge Q_2(x, z)$ with

$$Q_1(x, t) : - \; bornIn(x, t)$$
$$Q_2(x, z) : - \; \exists y.(likes(x, y), \; childOf(y, z)).$$

As discussed before, the calculation of Q_2 can become very expensive. To overcome this problem, we approximate the probabilistic answer to Q_2 by a two-step process. First, we create a newly formed compound relation *likesChildOf*, which represents the database view generated by Q_2

$$Q_2(x, z) : -likesChildOf(x, z).$$

To create the compound relation we use the *deterministic* and *sparse* representation of the affected relations from Q_2 and join them into a single relation. This avoids the expensive calculation of the probabilities for each instance of the active domain of y and can be computed efficiently as the deterministic join is not expensive if the (deterministic) domain is sparse. However, the representation of Q_2 would only be based on the available deterministic information so far and would not utilize the probabilistic model of the triple store computed by RESCAL. Hence in a second step we now need to derive probabilities for the triples in the newly formed relation. Fortunately, all that is needed to derive these probabilities under the RESCAL model is to compute a latent representation of the newly created compound relation *likesChildOf*, which can be done very efficiently. In the following, let $X_{(*)}$ denote the newly created compound relation. Furthermore, assume that a meaningful latent representation of the entities has been explored via the factorization of the deterministic triple store. Since the RESCAL model uses a unique representation of entities over *all* relations, all that is needed to derive probabilities for a new relation is to compute its latent representation $R_{(*)}$. The big advantage of the proposed method is that $R_{(*)}$ can now be derived by simply projecting $X_{(*)}$ into the latent space that is spanned by the RESCAL factor matrix A. This can be done very efficiently: Consider the ALS updates derived in [17]. Essentially what is needed is to calculate the latent matrix for the materialized view, i.e., $R_{(*)}$ as

$$R_{(*)} = (Z^T Z + \lambda I)^{-1} Z^T X_{(*)}$$
$$\text{with } Z = A \otimes A.$$

$R_{(*)}$ can be calculated more efficiently by using the following property of the singular value decomposition regarding the Kronecker product [13]

$$A \otimes A = (U \otimes U)(\Sigma \otimes \Sigma)(V^T \otimes V^T)$$

where $A = U\Sigma V^T$. From this property the following update for $R_{(*)}$ can be derived [17],

$$R_{(*)} = V(S \circledast U^T X_{(*)} U)V^T$$

where $\circledast$ represents the Hadamard (element-wise) matrix product and S is defined as

$$[S]_{ij} = \frac{\sigma_i \sigma_j}{\sigma_i^2 \sigma_j^2 + \lambda}$$

where σ_i is the i-th singular value of A. The calculation of $R_{(*)}$ for the newly created relation can now be done in $O(r^3 + nr + pr)$, where p represents the number of nonzero entries in $X_{(*)}$, r represents the rank of the factorization, and where $n \gg r$ represents all entities in the triple database. Please note that the computation of $R_{(*)}$ is now *linear* in all parameters regarding the size of the triple store and cubic only in the number of latent components r that are used to factorize the triple store. As such it can be computed efficiently even for very large triple stores. Furthermore, for each query of the same type the same relational representation can be used, i.e. $R_{(*)}$ only needs to be computed once.

6 Experiments

6.1 Evaluating the Quality of the Approximation

First we conducted experiments on various smaller benchmark datasets. Here, the materialized views (compound relations) can still be computed (and stored) and we can compare the standard approach using materialized views constructed by extensional query evaluation (Section 3.3) with our proposed method that approximates these views. The constructed views that we consider in these experiments range over the join of two relational atoms of the type $\exists y.S(x,y), T(y,z)$. For evaluation, we removed ground tuples only from the deterministic relations S and T and factorized the truncated triple store with RESCAL. From the resulting factorization, we construct the compound relation of S and T by extensional query evaluation or approximated it with our proposed method. For both approaches, we measure the quality of the ranking via the Area Under the Receiver Operating Characteristic Curve (AUC) in two settings: First, we compared the ranking to the full ground truth, i.e. against the ranking constructed from the full triple store(called *all* tuples in the following) including training and test data (evaluation setting all). Second, we compared the ranking to that part of the ground truth that could not have been inferred deterministically from the truncated (training) data, therefore evaluating only the discovery of new tuples (called *unknown* tuples in the following)(evaluation setting unknown). We report the average scores after 10-fold cross-validation. Additionally, we also compared the runtime of both techniques. All experiments were conducted with an Intel(R) Core(TM) i5-3320M CPU @ 2.60GHz.

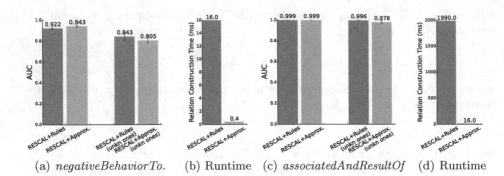

(a) *negativeBehaviorTo.*   (b) Runtime   (c) *associatedAndResultOf*   (d) Runtime

Fig. 2. Results for the two materialized views *negativeBehaviorToAlliedNa-tionOf* (Nations) and *associatedToResultOf* (UMLS): *RESCAL+Rules*(blue) represents the construction solely with the independent-project rule (Section 3.3). *RESCAL+Approx.*(green) represents the approximation of these views with the method proposed in this work (Section 5). (a,c) The left two bars show the performance (AUC) on all tuples of the deterministic version of the corresponding materialized view (evaluation setting all). The right two bars show the performance (AUC) on the tuples that were unknown at factorization and querying time (evaluation setting unknown).(b,d) Show the runtime for constructing the views for each technique (independent-project rule or approximation).

In the experiments, we used the Nations and the UMLS datasets:

Nations. $14 \times 14 \times 56$ multi-relational data that consist of relations between nations (treaties, immigration, etc).

UMLS. $135 \times 135 \times 49$ multi-relational data that consist of biomedical relationships between categorized concepts of the Unified Medical Language System.

For the nations dataset we explored the view : "Does x show negative behavior towards an ally of z?", leading to the query

$$negativeBehaviorToAlliedNationOf(x,z) : -\exists y.negativeBehaviorTo(x,y),$$
$$alliedNationOf(y,z).$$

For the UMLS dataset we materialized the view *associatedToAndResultOf* as

$$associatedToAndResultOf(x,z) : -\exists y.associatedTo(x,y), resultOf(y,z).$$

The results of the experiments are shown in Figure 2. Generally, the results in Figure 2.a and Figure 2.b show that both techniques do a good job when constructing the compound relations. Regarding the ranking of all tuples in these views, very high AUC values could be achieved. In case of the UMLS dataset, the score is almost perfect (0.999). Also the discovery of unknown tuples seems to work quite well (right bars in plots a and c). As would have been expected, in both views the materializations based on the independent-project rule seem to work a little bit better than the ones approximated by our proposed method, but the performance is comparable (0.843/0.805 and 0.996/0.978).

When we are looking at the runtime of the materialization of the views, it can be clearly seen that the approximated compound relations are constructed significantly faster than the ones constructed through the independent-project rule. For the compound relation *negativeBehaviorTo* the rules based approach takes 124 times longer (40 times longer for *negativeBehaviorToAlliedNationOf*). This result was expected since the complexity of the approximation is mostly dependent on the rank of the factorization, where the construction through independent-project is cubic in $|ADom|$.[3]

6.2 Evaluating Queries

In the second set of experiments, we used a larger triple store, i.e., a sample of the DBpedia dataset[4] [14] covering the musical domain and the task was to answer predefined queries. The queries are answered by using both techniques, rules and the sub-query approximation proposed in this work. We measure the quality of the probabilistic ranking of answer tuples to the different predefined queries in AUC. For evaluation we removed ground tuples from those relations that take part in constructing parts of the query where our method is supposed to approximate the sub-query. The resulting truncated triple store is then factorized by RESCAL. We compare the query answers inferred solely through extensional

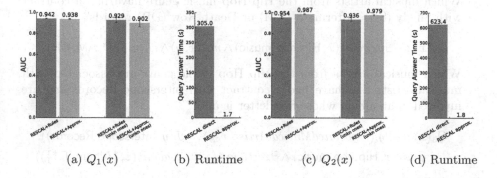

(a) $Q_1(x)$ (b) Runtime   (c) $Q_2(x)$ (d) Runtime

Fig. 3. Results for the queries (a) $Q_1(x)$ and $Q_2(x)$: *RESCAL+Rules*(blue) represents the answering with extensional query evaluation rules (Section 3.3). *RESCAL+Approx.*(green) represents the query answer of a combination of extensional query evaluation rules and the approximation of joined $\exists y.Q$ type relational atoms. (Section 5). (a,c) The left two bars show the quality of the probabilistic ranking (AUC) when compared to all answer tuples returned from the complete deterministic triple store with respect to the corresponding query (evaluation setting all). The right two bars show the ranking quality (AUC) with respect to unknown answer tuples (evaluation setting unknown).(b,d) Shows the runtime for answering the query with each technique (Extensional query evaluation with or without sub-query approximation).

---

[3] $|ADom|$ products have to be computed for each tuple in the compound relation matrix when applying the independent-project rule.

[4] http://wiki.dbpedia.org/Downloads35?v=pb8

query evaluation rules against our method, where sub-queries (compound relations) were approximated instead of applying the independent-project rule. As in the first set of experiments, we compare the ranking of possible answer tuples to the full ground truth, i.e. against the answer tuples inferred from the complete deterministic triple store, including training and test data (called *all* tuples in the following)(evaluation setting all). In addition we compared the ranking to those answer tuples that could not have been inferred deterministically from the truncated (training) data, therefore evaluating only the discovery of new tuples (called *unknown* tuples in the following)(evaluation setting unknown). For the query evaluation process the runtime of both approaches was also compared.

The DBpedia dataset:

DBpedia-Music. $44345 \times 44345 \times 7$ multi-relational data that consists of relations and entities regarding the musical domain. The relations are *Genre*, *RecordLabel* (*rL*), *associatedMusicalArtist*, *associatedBand*, *musicalArtist* (*mA*), *musicalBand*, *album*. We pre-defined the following queries for the experiments:

- What songs or albums from the Pop-Rock genre are from musical artists that have/had a contract with Atlantic Records?

$$Q_1(x) \quad : \quad -\exists y.(genre(x,z) \ \wedge \ mA(x,y) \ \wedge \ rL(y, \mathsf{Atlantic\_Records})).$$

- Which musical artists from the Hip Hop music genre have/had a contract with Shady (SD), Aftermath (AM) or Death Row (DR) records?

$$Q_2(x) : -\exists y.(genre(x, \mathsf{Hip\_hop\_music}) \wedge mA(x,y) \wedge rL(y, \{\mathsf{SD}, \mathsf{AM}, \mathsf{DR}\}))$$

- Which musical artists from the Hip Hop music genre are associated with musical artists that have/had a contract with Interscope Records and are involved in an album whose first letter is a "T"?

$$Q_3(x) : -\exists y.(associatedMusicalArtist(x,y) \wedge rL(y, \mathsf{Interscope\_Records})) \wedge$$
$$genre(x, \mathsf{Hip\_hop\_music}) \wedge \exists z.\exists t.(mA(z,x) \wedge album(z, \{\mathsf{Album\ T.^*}\}))$$

Q_1 and Q_2 are calculated as

$$Q_1(x) = \left[1 - \prod_{z \in \{\mathsf{PopRock}\}} 1 - P(genre(x,z)) \right]$$
$$\times \left[1 - \prod_{b \in ADom} 1 - P(mA(x,b)) \cdot P(rL(b, \mathsf{Atlantic\_record})) \right].$$

$$Q_2(x) = P(genre(x, \mathsf{Hip\_hop\_music}))$$
$$\times \left[1 - \prod_{b \in ADom} 1 - P(mA(x,b)) \left[1 - \prod_{c \in \{\mathsf{SD,AM,DR}\}} 1 - P(rL(b,c)) \right] \right].$$

The computation of Q_3 is omitted, since its structure is a combination of Q_1 and Q_2. For the factorization of the database, a rank of r=100 was used. The results of the experiments for Q_1 and Q_2 are shown in Figure 3. Similar to the previous results, both approaches perform well and comparable in answering the queries. Also the discovery of unknown answer tuples seems to work quite well (above 0.9) for both methods. Regarding the answering time (Figure 3.b,d) it can be clearly seen that the proposed method, which approximates the view on $musicalArtist(x, y) \wedge recordLabel(y, l)$, resulted in a significantly faster response time for both queries, even though the complete join of $musicalArtist$ and $recordLabel$ was not needed when using the independent-project rule. For Q_1, the query was answered 180 times faster and in case of Q_2 this difference is even greater, because we have a nested independent-project in the query (we ask for multiple record labels). The response time of our method is almost the same for both queries, where the runtime of the answer generated solely through the extensional rules doubles for Q_2. In case of Q_3 (results not shown) this becomes even more dramatic, because there are many potential albums that start with T. As expected, the answer generated by the proposed approach doubles its runtime to 3.6 seconds since Q_3 is a combination of Q_1 and Q_2 (AUC 0.997, 0.985 (unknown answer tuples)), but without sub-query approximation the evaluation of Q_3 did not terminate even after 6 hours runtime! In addition, we constructed a factorized representation of the approximated views which can be stored with almost no cost (100×100 entries $\approx$ 80kByte). In comparison, a materialized view constructed with rules would take 44345×44345 entries $\approx$ 15.7GB.

From the results presented in this section, it can be observed that with the technique introduced in Section 5 we are able to join sub-queries of the form $\exists x.Q$ orders of magnitudes faster and that the join is competitive to a probabilistically correct join generated solely through extensional query evaluation rules (independent-project).

7   Conclusions

In this paper we have demonstrated how a factorized model based on the RESCAL approach can lead to a very efficient representation of the probabilistic database and also can be used to derive the probabilities for the ground tuples. Most importantly, we have shown how efficient querying can be achieved within the RESCAL framework by factorizing a deterministic view at query time.

In general, the approach is not restricted to the $\exists x.Q$ type queries but can always be employed when factorized materialized deterministic views can be used to simplify the probabilistic query. Note that after we perform the deterministic joins, we might obtain views with arities larger than two. This is not a serious problem since our approach is not restricted to binary relations.

Acknowledgements. Maximilian Nickel acknowledges support by the Center for Brains, Minds and Machines (CBMM), funded by NSF STC award CCF-1231216

References

1. Bordes, A., Weston, J., Collobert, R., Bengio, Y.: Learning structured embeddings of knowledge bases. In: AAAI (2011)
2. Boulos, J., Dalvi, N.N., Mandhani, B., Mathur, S., Ré, C., Suciu, D.: Mystiq: a system for finding more answers by using probabilities. In: SIGMOD Conference, pp. 891–893 (2005)
3. Calì, A., Lukasiewicz, T., Predoiu, L., Stuckenschmidt, H.: Tightly integrated probabilistic description logic programs for representing ontology mappings. In: Hartmann, S., Kern-Isberner, G. (eds.) FoIKS 2008. LNCS, vol. 4932, pp. 178–198. Springer, Heidelberg (2008)
4. da Costa, P.C.G., Laskey, K.B., Laskey, K.J.: Pr-owl: A bayesian ontology language for the semantic web. In: da Costa, P.C.G., d'Amato, C., Fanizzi, N., Laskey, K.B., Laskey, K.J., Lukasiewicz, T., Nickles, M., Pool, M. (eds.) URSW 2005 - 2007. LNCS (LNAI), vol. 5327, pp. 88–107. Springer, Heidelberg (2008)
5. Dalvi, N.N., Re, C., Suciu, D.: Queries and materialized views on probabilistic databases. J. Comput. Syst. Sci. 77(3), 473–490 (2011)
6. Ding, Z., Peng, Y., Pan, R.: A bayesian approach to uncertainty modelling in owl ontology. In: Proceedings of the International Conference on Advances in Intelligent Systems - Theory and Applications (2004)
7. Dylla, M., Miliaraki, I., Theobald, M.: Top-k query processing in probabilistic databases with non-materialized views. Research Report MPI-I-2012-5-002, Max-Planck-Institut für Informatik, Stuhlsatzenhausweg 85, 66123 Saarbrücken, Germany (June 2012)
8. Franz, T., Schultz, A., Sizov, S., Staab, S.: Triplerank: Ranking semantic web data by tensor decomposition. In: Bernstein, A., Karger, D.R., Heath, T., Feigenbaum, L., Maynard, D., Motta, E., Thirunarayan, K. (eds.) ISWC 2009. LNCS, vol. 5823, pp. 213–228. Springer, Heidelberg (2009)
9. Giugno, R., Lukasiewicz, T.: P-$\mathcal{SHOQ}(\mathbf{D})$: A probabilistic extension of $\mathcal{SHOQ}(\mathbf{D})$ for probabilistic ontologies in the semantic web. In: Flesca, S., Greco, S., Leone, N., Ianni, G. (eds.) JELIA 2002. LNCS (LNAI), vol. 2424, pp. 86–97. Springer, Heidelberg (2002)
10. Huang, J., Antova, L., Koch, C., Olteanu, D.: Maybms: a probabilistic database management system. In: SIGMOD Conference (2009)
11. Jenatton, R., Roux, N.L., Bordes, A., Obozinski, G.: A latent factor model for highly multi-relational data. In: NIPS (2012)
12. Kolda, T.G., Bader, B.W., Kenny, J.P.: Higher-order web link analysis using multilinear algebra. In: ICDM, pp. 242–249 (2005)
13. Laub, A.J.: Matrix analysis - for scientists and engineers. SIAM (2005)
14. Lehmann, J., Isele, R., Jakob, M., Jentzsch, A., Kontokostas, D., Mendes, P.N., Hellmann, S., Morsey, M., van Kleef, P., Auer, S., Bizer, C.: DBpedia - a large-scale, multilingual knowledge base extracted from wikipedia. Semantic Web Journal (2014)
15. Lukasiewicz, T.: Expressive probabilistic description logics. Artif. Intell. 172(6-7), 852–883 (2008)
16. Mutsuzaki, M., Theobald, M., de Keijzer, A., Widom, J., Agrawal, P., Benjelloun, O., Sarma, A.D., Murthy, R., Sugihara, T.: Trio-one: Layering uncertainty and lineage on a conventional dbms (demo). In: CIDR, pp. 269–274 (2007)
17. Nickel, M.: Tensor factorization for relational learning. PhDThesis, p. 48, 49, 74, Ludwig-Maximilian-University of Munich (August 2013)

18. Nickel, M., Tresp, V.: Logistic tensor factorization for multi-relational data. In: Structured Learning: Inferring Graphs from Structured and Unstructured Inputs, ICML WS (2013)
19. Nickel, M., Tresp, V., Kriegel, H.-P.: A three-way model for collective learning on multi-relational data. In: ICML, pp. 809–816 (2011)
20. Nickel, M., Tresp, V., Kriegel, H.-P.: Factorizing yago: scalable machine learning for linked data. In: WWW, pp. 271–280 (2012)
21. Olteanu, D., Wen, H.: Ranking query answers in probabilistic databases: Complexity and efficient algorithms. In: ICDE, pp. 282–293 (2012)
22. Platt, J.C.: Probabilistic outputs for support vector machines and comparisons to regularized likelihood methods. In: Advances in Large Margin Classifiers, pp. 61–74. MIT Press (1999)
23. Rendle, S., Marinho, L.B., Nanopoulos, A., Schmidt-Thieme, L.: Learning optimal ranking with tensor factorization for tag recommendation. In: KDD, pp. 727–736 (2009)
24. Riedel, S., Yao, L., McCallum, A., Marlin, B.M.: Relation extraction with matrix factorization and universal schemas. In: HLT-NAACL, pp. 74–84 (2013)
25. Christopher, R., Dalvi, N., Suciu, D.: Efficient top-k query evaluation on probabilistic data. In: ICDE, pp. 886–895 (2007)
26. Singh, S., Mayfield, C., Mittal, S., Prabhakar, S., Hambrusch, S.E., Shah, R.: Orion 2.0: native support for uncertain data. In: SIGMOD Conference, pp. 1239–1242 (2008)
27. Suciu, D., Olteanu, D., Ré, C., Koch, C.: Probabilistic Databases. Synthesis Lectures on Data Management. Morgan & Claypool Publishers (2011)
28. Theobald, M., De Raedt, L., Dylla, M., Kimmig, A., Miliaraki, I.: 10 years of probabilistic querying - what next? In: Catania, B., Guerrini, G., Pokorný, J. (eds.) ADBIS 2013. LNCS, vol. 8133, pp. 1–13. Springer, Heidelberg (2013)
29. Tresp, V., Huang, Y., Bundschus, M., Rettinger, A.: Materializing and querying learned knowledge. In: First ESWC Workshop on Inductive Reasoning and Machine Learning on the Semantic Web (IRMLeS 2009) (2009)
30. Wermser, H., Rettinger, A., Tresp, V.: Modeling and learning context-aware recommendation scenarios using tensor decomposition. In: ASONAM, pp. 137–144 (2011)
31. Yang, Y., Calmet, J.: Ontobayes: An ontology-driven uncertainty model. In: CIMCA/IAWTIC, pp. 457–463 (2005)

Appendix

The sigmoidal transfer function sig_ϵ is defined as

$$\mathrm{sig}_\epsilon(x) = x \quad \text{if} \quad \epsilon < x < 1 - \epsilon$$

$$\mathrm{sig}_\epsilon(x) = \frac{\epsilon}{\exp(1)} \exp(x/\epsilon) \quad \text{if} \quad x \leq \epsilon$$

$$\mathrm{sig}_\epsilon(x) = 1 - \frac{\epsilon}{\exp(1)} \exp((1-x)/\epsilon) \quad \text{if} \quad x \geq 1 - \epsilon$$

and $0 \leq \epsilon \leq 1/2$.

Hereby, ϵ controls the spreading of the non-probabilistic confidence values in the interval $[0,1]$, and which values are affected by the function. Since sig_ϵ is monotonic, the ordering is maintained. Asymptotically the Gaussian estimate converges to the correct probabilities and we can set $\epsilon \to 0$.

Ontology Search: An Empirical Evaluation

Anila Sahar Butt[1,2], Armin Haller[1], and Lexing Xie[2]

[1] CSIRO CCI, Canberra, Australia
{firstname.lastname}@csiro.au
[2] Australian National University, Canberra, Australia
{firstname.lastname}@anu.edu.au

Abstract. Much of the recent work in Semantic Search is concerned with addressing the challenge of finding entities in the growing Web of Data. However, alongside this growth, there is a significant increase in the availability of ontologies that can be used to describe these entities. Whereas several methods have been proposed in Semantic Search to rank entities based on a keyword query, little work has been published on search and ranking of resources in ontologies. To the best of our knowledge, this work is the first to propose a benchmark suite for ontology search. The benchmark suite, named CBRBench[1], includes a collection of ontologies that was retrieved by crawling a seed set of ontology URIs derived from prefix.cc and a set of queries derived from a real query log from the Linked Open Vocabularies search engine. Further, it includes the results for the ideal ranking of the concepts in the ontology collection for the identified set of query terms which was established based on the opinions of ten ontology engineering experts.

We compared this ideal ranking with the top-k results retrieved by eight state-of-the-art ranking algorithms that we have implemented and calculated the precision at k, the mean average precision and the discounted cumulative gain to determine the best performing ranking model. Our study shows that content-based ranking models outperform graph-based ranking models for most queries on the task of ranking concepts in ontologies. However, as the performance of the ranking models on ontologies is still far inferior to the performance of state-of-the-art algorithms on the ranking of documents based on a keyword query, we put forward four recommendations that we believe can significantly improve the accuracy of these ranking models when searching for resources in ontologies.

1 Introduction

The growth of Linked Data in recent years has given rise to the need to represent knowledge based on ontologies. Prefix.cc[2], a service to register prefixes, counts about ~1250 such ontologies (April 2014) whereby many cover similar domains, e.g. our crawl found the concept *Person* to exist in 379 ontologies. One of the major advantages claimed of ontologies, however, is the potential of "reuse" opposed to creating a new ontology from scratch. Consequently, finding the

---

[1] https://zenodo.org/record/11121
[2] http://prefix.cc

P. Mika et al. (Eds.) ISWC 2014, Part II, LNCS 8797, pp. 130–147, 2014.
© Springer International Publishing Switzerland 2014

right ontology, or more specifically classes and properties within ontologies that match the intended meaning for a specific use case is an important task that is becoming increasingly difficult.

The Linked Open Vocabularies (LOV) search engine[3], initiated in March 2011, is to the best of our knowledge, the only purpose-built ontology search engine available on the Web with an up-to-date index. It uses a ranking algorithm based on the term popularity in Linked Open Data (LOD) and in the LOV ecosystem [22].

There are also some ontology libraries available that facilitate the locating and retrieving of potentially relevant ontology resources [13]. Some of these libraries are domain-specific such as the Open Biological and Biomedical Ontologies library[4] or the BioPortal [14], whereas others are more general such as OntoSearch [20] or the TONES Ontology Repository[5]. However, as discussed by Noy & d'Aquin [13] only few libraries support a keyword search and basic ranking, and only one (Cupboard [2]) supports a ranking of ontologies based on a user query using an information retrieval algorithm (i.e. tf-idf), while no library supports the ranking of resources within the registered ontologies.

Semantic Search engines such as Swoogle [4] (which was initially developed to rank ontologies only), Sindice.com [21], Watson [3], or Yars2 [8] do allow a search of ontology resources through a user query. The ranking in these search engines follows traditional link-based ranking methods [10], in particular adapted versions of the PageRank algorithm [15], where links from one source of information to another are regarded as a 'positive vote' from the former to the latter. Often, these ranking schemes also take the provenance graph of the data into account [9]. Other strategies, mainly based on methods proposed in the information retrieval community, are employed in Semantic Search [5], but what all these methods have in common is that they are targeted to rank entities, but do not work well for ranking classes and properties in ontologies [4,1].

The task of ranking resources defined in ontologies can be based on many different criteria [6], for example, how well an ontology meets the requirements of certain evaluation tests (e.g. [7]) or on methods to evaluate general properties of an ontology based on some requirement (e.g. [11]). However, only limited work has been proposed to rank the returned resources based on a user posed keyword query such that the most relevant results appear higher in the list. Alani et al. [1] propose four measures (i.e. Semantic Similarity, Betweenness, Density and Class Match Measure) to evaluate different representational aspects of the ontology and calculate its ranking.

In the information retrieval community many algorithms, such as the vector space model, the boolean model, BM25, tf-idf, etc. have been proposed to identify and rank a small number of potentially relevant documents through a top-k document retrieval. To the best of our knowledge, no systematic study has been conducted to compare the performance of these state-of-the-art ranking techniques on the task of ranking resources in ontologies. For our study we

---

[3] http://lov.okfn.org
[4] http://www.obofoundry.org/
[5] http://owl.cs.manchester.ac.uk/repository/

have implemented eight ranking algorithms, four of which have been proposed by the information retrieval community whereas the others were adapted for the ranking of ontologies by Alani et al [1]. We defined a set of queries derived from a real query log, and computed the ranking for these queries on a collection of ontology resources that we have crawled with a seed set of ontology URIs derived from prefix.cc. We computed a baseline ranking and established a ground truth by asking ten ontology engineers to manually rank ontologies based on a given search term from the collection of resources obtained by the baseline ranking. We compared the ground truth derived through the human evaluation with the results from each of the ranking algorithms. We calculated the precision at k, the mean average precision and the discounted cumulative gain of the ranking algorithms in comparison to a ground truth to determine the best model for the task of ranking resources/ontologies. The contribution of this paper are:

- a design of a benchmark suite named CBRBench, for Canberra Ontology Ranking Benchmark, including an ontology collection, a set of queries and a ground truth established by human experts for evaluating ontology ranking algorithms,
- a methodology for resource ranking evaluation where we discuss many of the decision that need to be made when designing a search evaluation framework for resources defined in ontologies,
- the evaluation of eight ranking algorithms through these benchmarks, and
- a set of recommendations derived from an analysis of our experiment that we believe can significantly improve the performance of the ranking models.

The remainder of this paper is organised as follows. We begin with a discussion of the ranking algorithms that we have implemented for this experiment in Section 2. In Section 3, we describe the evaluation setup. We then present the results and a result analysis in Section 4. Section 5 discusses some recommendations for the improvement of the ranking models for ontology search, before we conclude in Section 6.

2   Ranking Algorithms

We have chosen eight different ranking models that are commonly used for ranking documents and/or ontologies and applied them on the task of ranking resources/ontologies according to their relevance to a query term. These eight ranking models can be grouped in two different categories.

1. **Content-based Ranking Models**: tf-idf, BM25, Vector Space Model and Class Match Measure.
2. **Graph-based Ranking Models**: PageRank, Density Measure, Semantic Similarity Measure and Betweenness Measure.

Because of the inherit graph structure of ontologies, graph-based ranking models can be used for ranking as such. However, content-based ranking models (e.g. tf-idf, BM25 and Vector Space Model) need to be tailored towards ontologies so that instead of using a word as the basic unit for measuring, we are considering a resource r in an ontology as the measuring unit. Therefore, the relevance of a query word to the ontology is the sum of the relevance of all the resources that match the query term. For tf-idf we compute the relevance score of the resource, all other algorithms generate a cumulative relevance score for the ontology and resources are ranked according to the relevance score of their corresponding ontology. The matched resource set for each term/word is selected from a corpus if a word exists in the value of the 1) `rdfs:label` 2) `rdfs:comment`, or 3) `rdfs:description` property of that resource or if the word is part of the URI of the resource. As most of the existing adaptations of graph ranking models for ontology ranking do not compute a ranking for properties in an ontology we only consider the ranking of classes/concepts in this study. However, it turns out that only 2.6% of all resources in our corpus (cf. Section 3) are properties.

In the following sections we introduce all ranking models, and describe the choices we made to adapt them for the ranking of resources in ontologies. Common notations used in the following sections are shown in Table 2.

Table 1. Notation used

Variable	Description
$\mathbb{O}$	Corpus: The ontology repository
N	Number of ontologies in $\mathbb{O}$
O	An ontology: $O \in \mathbb{O}$
r	A resource uri: $r \in O$ & $r \in URI$
z	Number of resources in O
Q	Query String
q_i	query term i of Q
n	number of keywords in Q
σ_O	set of matched uris for Q in O
$\sigma_O(q_i)$	set of matched uris for q_i in O : $\forall r_i \in \sigma_O$, $r_i \in O$ & r_i matches q_i
m	number of uris in $\sigma_O(q_i)$

2.1   tf-idf

Term frequency inverse document frequency (tf-idf) [18] is an information retrieval statistic that reflects the importance of a word to a document in a collection or corpus. For ranking ontologies we compute the importance of each resource r to an ontology O in a ontology repository, where $r \in R : R = URI$ only (i.e. excluding blank nodes and literals).

$$tf(r,O) = 0.5 + \frac{0.5 * f(r,O)}{max\{f(r_i,O) : r_i \in O\}}$$

$$idf(r,\mathbb{O}) = log\frac{N}{|\{O \in \mathbb{O} : r \in O\}|}$$

$$tf - idf(r,O,\mathbb{O}) = tf(r,O) * idf(r,O) \tag{1}$$

Here $tf(r,O)$ is the term frequency for resource r in O. $tf(r,O)$ is the frequency of r (number of times r appears in O) divided by the maximum frequency of any resource r_i in O. The inverse document frequency $idf(r,\mathbb{O})$ is a measure of commonality of a resource across the corpus. It is obtained by dividing the total number of ontologies in the corpus by the number of documents containing the resource r, and then computing the logarithm of that quotient. The final score of r for this query is the tf-idf value of r.

$$Score(r, Q) = tf - idf(r, O, \mathbb{O}) : \forall r\{\exists q_i \in Q : r \in \sigma(q_i)\} \tag{2}$$

2.2   BM25

BM25 [17] is a ranking function for document retrieval used to rank matching documents according to their relevance to a given search query. Given a query Q, containing keywords $q_1, ..., q_n$, the BM25 score of a document d is computed by:

$$score(d, Q) = \sum_{i=1}^{n} idf(q_i, d) \frac{tf(q_i, d) * k_1 + 1}{tf(q_i, d) + k_1 * (1 - b + b * (\frac{|d|}{avgdl}))} \tag{3}$$

where $tf(q_i, d)$ is the term frequency and $idf(q_i, d)$ is the inverse document frequency of the word q_i. $|d|$ is the length of the document d in words, and $avgdl$ is the average document length in the text collection from which the documents are drawn. k_1 and b are free parameters, usually chosen, in absence of an advanced optimisation, as $k_1 \in [1.2, 2.0]$ and $b = 0.75$.

In order to tailor this statistic for ontology ranking we compute the sum of the score of each $r_j \in \sigma_O(q_i)$ for each query term q_i rather than computing the score for q_i. For the current implementation we used $k_1 = 2.0$, $b = 0.75$ and $|O|$ = total number of terms (i.e. 3 * |axioms|) in the ontology. The final score of the ontology is computed as:

$$score(O, Q) = \sum_{i=1}^{n} \sum_{\forall r_j : r_j \in \sigma_O(q_i)} idf(r_j, O) \frac{tf(r_j, O) * k_1 + 1}{tf(r_j, O) + k_1 * (1 - b + b * (\frac{|O|}{avgol}))} \tag{4}$$

2.3   Vector Space Model (VSM)

The vector space model [19] is based on the assumptions of the document similarities theory where the query and documents are represented as the same kind of vector. The ranking of a document to a query is calculated by comparing the deviation of angles between each document vector and the original query vector. Thus, the similarity of a document to a query is computed as under:

$$sim(d, Q) = \frac{\sum_{i=1}^{n} w(q_i, d) * w(q_i, Q)}{|d| * |Q|} \tag{5}$$

Here $w(q_i, d)$ and $w(q_i, Q)$ are weights of q_i in document d and query Q respectively. $|d|$ is the document norm and $|Q|$ is the query norm. For this implementation, we are considering the *tf-idf* values of a query term as weights. Therefore, the similarity of an ontology to query Q is computed as:

$$sim(O, Q) = \frac{\sum_{i=1}^{n} tf - Idf(q_i, O) * tf - idf(q_i, Q)}{|O| * |Q|}$$

$$tf - idf(q_i, O) = \sum_{j=1}^{m} tf - idf(r_j, O) : r_j \in \sigma_O(q_i)$$

$$tf - idf(q_i, Q) = \frac{f(q_i, Q)}{max\{f(q, Q) : q \in Q\}} * log\frac{N}{|\{O \in \mathbb{O} : r \in O \& r \in \sigma_O(q_i)\}|}$$

$$|O| = \sqrt{\sum_{i=1}^{z}(tf - idf(r_i, O))^2}$$

$$|Q| = \sqrt{\sum_{i=1}^{n}(tf - idf(q_i, O))^2} \tag{6}$$

2.4 Class Match Measure

The Class Match Measure (CMM) [1] evaluates the coverage of an ontology for the given search terms. It looks for classes in each ontology that have matching URIs for a search term either exactly (class label 'identical to' search term) or partially (class label 'contains' the search term). An ontology that covers all search terms will score higher than others, and exact matches are regarded as better than partial matches. The score for an ontology is computed as:

$$score_{CMM}(O, Q) = \alpha score_{EMM}(O, Q) + \beta score_{PMM}(O, Q) \tag{7}$$

where $score_{CMM}(O, Q)$, $score_{EMM}(O, Q)$ and $score_{PMM}(O, Q)$ are the scores for class match measure, exact match measure and partial match measure for the ontology O with respect to query Q, α and β are the exact matching and partial matching weight factors respectively. As exact matching is favoured over partial matching, therefore $\alpha > \beta$. For our experiments, we set $\alpha = 0.6$ and $\beta = 0.4$ (as proposed in the original paper [1]).

$$score_{EMM(O,Q)} = \sum_{i=1}^{n}\sum_{j=1}^{m} \varphi(r_j, q_i) : r_j \in \sigma_O(q_i)$$

$$\varphi(r_j, q_i) = \begin{cases} 1 & \text{if label}(r_j) = q_i \\ 0 & \text{if label}(r_j) \neq q_i \end{cases} \tag{8}$$

$$score_{PMM}(O, Q) = \sum_{i=1}^{n}\sum_{j=1}^{m} \psi(r_j, q_i) : r_j \in \sigma_O(q_i)$$

$$\psi(r_j, q_i) = \begin{cases} 1 & \text{if label}(r_j) \text{ contains } q_i \\ 0 & \text{if label}(r_j) \text{ does not contain } q_i \end{cases} \tag{9}$$

2.5 PageRank (PR)

PageRank [15] is a hyperlink based iterative computation method for document ranking which takes as input a graph consisting of nodes and edges (i.e. ontologies as nodes and `owl:imports` properties as links in this implementation). In each successive iteration the score of ontology O is determined as a summation of the PageRank score in the previous iteration of all the ontologies that link (imports) to ontology O divided by their number of outlinks (owl:imports properties). For the k_{th} iteration the rank of ontology O i.e. ($score_k(O)$) is given as under:

$$score_k(O) = \frac{\sum_{j \in deadlinks(\mathbb{O})} R_{k-1}(j)}{n} + \sum_{i \in ininks(O)} \frac{R_{k-1}(i)}{|outdegree(i)|}$$

$$score_k(O) = d * score_k(O) + \frac{1-d}{n} \tag{10}$$

Here $deadlinks(\mathbb{O})$ are ontologies in corpus $\mathbb{O}$ that have no outlinks, i.e. they never import any other ontology. All nodes are initialised with an equal score (i.e. $\frac{1}{n}$, where n is total number of ontologies in $\mathbb{O}$ before the first iteration. In the experimental evaluation, we set the damping factor d equal to 0.85 (common practise) and we introduced missing `owl:imports` link among ontologies based on reused resources.

2.6 Density Measure

Density Measure (DEM) [1] is intended to approximate the information content of classes and consequently the level of knowledge detail. This includes how well the concept is further specified (i.e. the number of subclasses), the number of properties associated with that concept, number of siblings, etc. Here $score_{DEM}(O, Q)$ is the density measure of ontology O for query Q. $\Theta(r_j, q_i)$ is the density measure for resource r_j and w is a weight factor set for each dimensionality i.e. sub classes = 1, super classes = 0.25, relations = 0.5 and siblings = 0.5 and $k = n * m$ (i.e. number of matched r) for query Q.

$$score_{DEM}(O, Q) = \frac{1}{k} \sum_{i=1}^{n} \sum_{j=1}^{m} \Theta(r_j) : r_j \in \sigma_O(q_i)$$

$$\Theta(r_j) = \sum_{s_k \in S} w_{s_k} |s_k|$$

$$S = \{s_{sub}, s_{sup}, s_{sib}, s_{rel}\}$$

$$w = \{1, 0.25, 0.5, 0.5\} \tag{11}$$

2.7 Semantic Similarity Measure

The Semantic Similarity Measure (SSM) calculates how close the concepts of interest are laid out in the ontology structure. The idea is, if the concepts are positioned relatively far from each other, then it becomes unlikely for those concepts to be represented in a compact manner, rendering their extraction and reuse more difficult. $score_{SSM}(O,Q)$ is the semantic similarity measure score of ontology O for a given query Q. It is a collective measure of the shortest path lengths for all classes that match the query string.

$$score_{SSM}(O,Q) = \frac{1}{z}\sum_{i=1}^{z-1}\sum_{j=i+1}^{z}\Psi(r_i,r_j) : \forall_{q\in Q}((r_i,r_j)\in\sigma_O))$$

$$\Psi(r_i,r_j) = \begin{cases} \dfrac{1}{length(min_{p\in P}\{r_i \xrightarrow{p} r_j\})} & \text{if i} \neq \text{j} \\ 1 & \text{if i} = \text{j} \end{cases}$$

$$z = |(r_i,r_j)| \tag{12}$$

2.8 Betweenness Measure

The Betweenness Measure (BM)[1] is a measure for a class on how many times it occurs on the shortest path between other classes. This measure is rooted on the assumption that if a class has a high betweenness value in an ontology then this class is graphically central to that ontology. The betweenness value of an ontology is the function of the betweenness value of each queried class in the given ontologies. The ontologies where those classes are more central receive a higher BM value.

$score_{BM}(O,Q)$ is the average betweenness value for ontology O and k is the number of matched resources from O for Q. The betweenness measure for resource r_j i.e. $\vartheta(r_j,q_i)$ is computed as:

$$score_{BM}(O,Q) = \frac{1}{k}\sum_{i=1}^{n}\sum_{j=1}^{m}\vartheta(r_j,q_i) : r_j \in \sigma_O(q_i)$$

$$\vartheta(r_j,q_i) = \sum_{r_x\neq r_y\neq r_j}\frac{\lambda(r_x,r_y(r_j))}{\lambda(r_x,r_y)} \tag{13}$$

where $\lambda(r_x,r_y)$ is the number of the shortest path from r_x and r_y and $\lambda(r_x,r_y(r_j))$ is the number of shortest paths from r_x and r_y that passes through r_j.

3 Experiment Setup

To compare and evaluate the implemented ranking models we developed a benchmark suite named CBRBench, for C̲an̲b̲e̲r̲ra Ontology Ranking B̲en̲c̲hmark, which includes a collection of ontologies, a set of benchmark queries and a ground truth established by human experts. The CBRBench suite is available at https://zenodo.org/record/11121.

3.1 Benchmark Ontology Collection

To the best of our knowledge there exists no benchmark ontology collection for ranking of ontologies. To derive at a representative set of ontologies used on the

Web, we used the namespaces registered at prefix.cc[6] as our set of seed ontology URIs. We crawled all registered prefix URIs and for each successfully retrieved ontology (we encountered hundreds of deadlinks and non-ontology namespaces) we also followed its import statements until no new ontologies were found. This resulted in 1022 ontologies that we used as our benchmark collection. In total these ontologies define more than 5.5M triples, including ~280k class definitions and ~7.5k property definitions. We stored each ontology seperately as a named graph in a Virtuoso database.

3.2 Benchmark Query Terms

To test the ranking algorithms on a representative set of query terms we have used the query log[7] of the Linked Open Vocabularies (LOV) search engine [22] as input. We ranked the most popular search terms in the log covering the period between 06/01/2012 and 16/04/2014 based on their popularity. For the most popular query terms we checked through a boolean search if there is a representative sample of relevant resources available in our benchmark ontology collection that at least partially match the query term. We included ten search terms in our corpus where there were at least ten relevant ontology classes in the result set. The chosen search terms and their popularity rank within the Linked Open Vocabularies search log are shown in Table 2. All queries are single word queries – that is for two reasons. First, only about 11% of all queries posed on the LOV search engine use compound search queries and no compound query was among the 200 most used queries and second, for no compound query in the top 1000 query terms did the benchmark collection contain enough relevant resources to derive at a meaningful ranking.

Although shallow evaluation schemes are preferred in web search engine evaluations [16] we opted for a deep evaluation scheme for two reasons. First, there is only a limited set of knowledge domains where there is a sufficient number of ontologies available on the Web, and second, for the domains with a sufficient number of ontologies, many ontologies exist that define or refine similar concepts. This assumption is confirmed by the high number of matching classes for the terms in our query set (see for example Table 3).

3.3 Establishing the Ground Truth

We conducted a user study with ten human experts who were sourced from the Australian National University, Monash University, the University of Queensland and the CSIRO. Eight of the evaluators considered themselves to possess "Expert knowledge" and two considered themselves to have "Strong knowledge" in ontology engineering on a 5-point Likert-Scale from "Expert knowledge" to "No Knowledge". All of the evaluators have developed ontologies before and some are authors of widely cited ontologies. To reduce the number of classes our ten judges had to score for a given query term (for some query terms a naïve string search returns more than 400 results) we asked two experts to pre-select relevant

---

[6] http://www.prefix.cc
[7] See http://lov.okfn.org/dataset/lov/stats/searchLog.csv

Table 2. Query terms   **Table 3.** Ranking of "Person" in ground truth

Search Term	Rank
person	1
name	2
event	3
title	5
location	7
address	8
music	10
organization	15
author	16
time	17

URI	Rank
http://xmlns.com/foaf/0.1/Person	1
http://data.press.net/ontology/stuff/Person	2
http://schema.org/Person	3
http://www.w3.org/ns/person#Person	4
http://www.ontotext.com/proton/protontop#Person	5
http://omv.ontoware.org/2005/05/ontology#Person	6
http://bibframe.org/vocab/Person	7
http://iflastandards.info/ns/fr/frbr/frbrer/C1005	8
http://models.okkam.org/ENS-core-vocabulary.owl#person	9
hhttp://swat.cse.lehigh.edu/onto/univ-bench.owl#Person	9

URIs. The experts were asked to go through all resources that matched a query through a naïve string search and evaluate if the URI is either "Relevant" or "Irrelevant" for the given query term. We asked the two experts to judge URIs as "Relevant" even when they are only vaguely related to the query term, i.e. increasing the false positive ratio.

We developed an evaluation tool which allowed our experts to pose a keyword query for the given term that retrieves all matching ontology classes in the search space. Since keyword queries where the intended meaning of the query is unknown are still the prevalent form of input in Semantic Search [16] and since the meaning of the search terms derived from our real query log was also unknown, we needed to establish the main intention for each of our query terms. We used the main definition from the Oxford dictionary for each term and included it in the questionnaire for our judges. We then asked our ten human experts to rate the relevance of the results to each of the 10 query terms from Table 2 according to their relevance to the definition of the term from the Oxford dictionary. After submitting the keyword query, each evaluator was presented with a randomly ordered list of the matching ontology classes in the search space to eliminate any bias. For each result we showed the evaluator, the URI, the `rdfs:label` and `rdfs:comment`, the properties of the class and its super-classes and sub-classes. A judge could then rate the relevance of the class with radio buttons below each search result on a 5-point Likert scale with values "Extremely Useful", "Useful", "Relevant", "Slightly Relevant" and "Irrelevant". There was no time restriction for the judges to finish the experiment. We assigned values from 0-4 for "Irrelevant"-"Extremely Useful" for each score and performed a hypothesis test on the average scores per evaluator with a H_0 $\mu = 2$ against H_1 μ $<> 0$. This resulted in a p-value of 0.0004, a standard error of mean of 0.144 and a 95% confidence interval for the mean score of (0.83,1.49), indicating there is a strong evidence that the average scores per evaluator are not 2 which would indicate a randomness of the scores. We also asked our ten evaluators to score 62 random response URIs for the ten queries again two months after we performed our initial experiment. The average scores of the ten evaluators for these URIs had a correlation coefficient of 0.93, indicating that in average, the scores of the participants in the second study were highly correlated to the scores in the first study.

Table 3 shows the ideal ranking for the query "Person" as derived from the median relevance scores from our ten experts. For ties we considered the resource with the more consistent relevance scores (i.e. the lower standard deviation) as better ranked. Not all ties could be resolved in this way as can be seen for rank No. 9.

3.4   Evaluation and Performance Measures

We consider three popular metrics from the information retrieval community, precision at k (P@k), mean average precision (MAP), and normalized discounted cumulative gain (NDCG). Since we asked our judges to assign a non-binary value of relevance (on a 5-point Likert scale), we converted these values to a binary value for all those metrics that consider a binary notion of relevance. We chose a resource as being relevant to the query term if the relevance score is equal or higher than the average value on the 5-point Likert scale. Changing this cut off value to the right or to the left of the average changes the overall precision of the result. However, the relative performance of the algorithms remains the same.

Precision@k: We are calculating precision at k (P@k) for a k value of 10. P@k in our experiment is calculated as:

$$p@k = \frac{number\ of\ relevant\ documents\ in\ top\ k\ results}{k}$$

Average Precision: The average precision for the query Q of a ranking model is defined as:

$$AP(Q) = \frac{\sum_{i=1}^{k} rel(r_i) * P@i}{k}$$

where $rel(r_i)$ is 1 if r_i is a relevant resource for the query Q and 0 otherwise, $P@i$ is the precision at i and k is the cut off value (i.e. 10 in our experiment). *MAP* is defined as the mean of *AP* over all queries run in this experiment and is calculated as:

$$MAP = \frac{\sum_{Q \in \mathbb{Q}} AP(Q)}{|\mathbb{Q}|}$$

Normalize Discounted Cumulative Gain (NDCG): NDCG is a standard evaluation measure for ranking tasks with non-binary relevance judgement. NDCG is defined based on a gain vector G, that is, a vector containing the relevance judgements at each rank. Then, the discounted cumulative gain measures the overall gain obtained by reaching rank k, putting more weight at the top of the ranking:

$$DCG(Q) = \sum_{i=1}^{k} \frac{2^{rel_i} - 1}{log_2(1 + i)}$$

To compute the final NDCG, we divide DCG by its optimal value iDCG which puts the most relevant results first. iDCG is calculated by computing the optimal gain vector for an ideal ordering obtained from the median of the user assigned relevance scores.

Table 4. MAP

	Person	Name	Event	Title	Loc.	Addr.	Music	Org.	Author	Time
boolean	0.17	0.00	0.23	0.02	0.00	0.66	0.39	0.02	0.08	0.44
tf-idf	**0.75**	0.44	**0.82**	0.51	**0.73**	0.89	**0.48**	0.70	0.28	0.53
BM25	0.19	**0.74**	0.03	0.40	0.08	0.49	0.18	0.32	**0.62**	0.00
vector-space	0.06	0.00	0.19	0.08	0.00	0.58	0.18	0.00	0.01	0.00
pagerank	0.19	0.38	0.55	**0.70**	0.63	0.18	0.04	0.29	0.49	**0.77**
class-match-measure	0.00	0.00	0.00	0.40	0.00	0.35	0.18	0.00	0.02	0.00
density-measure	0.30	0.00	0.08	0.11	0.00	0.50	0.11	0.00	0.07	0.00
semantic-similarity	0.00	0.00	0.00	0.40	0.00	0.35	0.18	0.00	0.00	0.00
between-measure	0.69	0.23	0.40	0.36	0.55	**0.99**	0.14	**0.80**	0.14	0.66

Table 5. NDCG

	Person	Name	Event	Title	Loc.	Addr.	Music	Org.	Author	Time
boolean	0.06	0.00	0.16	0.11	0.00	0.44	0.22	0.07	0.07	0.15
tf-idf	**0.29**	0.20	**0.46**	**0.27**	**0.32**	0.57	**0.39**	0.32	0.15	**0.30**
BM25	0.07	**0.42**	0.02	0.13	0.07	0.32	0.16	0.19	0.14	0.00
vector-space	0.12	0.00	0.06	0.10	0.00	0.36	0.16	0.00	0.01	0.00
pagerank	0.14	0.18	0.28	0.21	0.15	0.18	0.17	0.22	0.11	0.14
class-match-measure	0.00	0.00	0.00	0.15	0.00	0.17	0.16	0.00	0.05	0.00
density-measure	0.25	0.00	0.07	0.13	0.00	0.27	0.19	0.00	0.04	0.00
semantic-similarity	0.00	0.00	0.00	0.15	0.00	0.17	0.16	0.00	0.03	0.00
between-measure	0.22	0.18	0.17	0.24	0.31	**0.69**	0.15	**0.59**	0.19	0.19

4 Results

Table 4 and 5 show the MAP and the NDCG scores for all ranking models for each query term, whereas Fig. 1 shows the P@10, MAP, DCG, NDCG scores for each of the eight ranking models on all ten queries. For P@10 and MAP, tf-idf is the best performing algorithm with betweenness measure as the second best and PageRank as the third best. In terms of the correct order of top k results, we found again tf-idf as the best performing algorithm, with betweenness measure and PageRank as the second and third best, respectively.

4.1 Results Analysis

From the results of this experiment it can be seen, somehow surprisingly, that content-based models (i.e. tf-idf and BM25) outperform the graph-based ranking models for most queries. Overall, seven out of ten times, the content-based models achieve a better or equal to the highest NDCG for all ranking algorithms.

However, although tf-idf achieved the highest mean average precision value of 0.6 in our experiment, it is still far from an ideal ranking performance. That is, because the philosophy of tf-idf works well for the tf part, but not so for the idf part when ranking resources in ontologies. The intuition behind tf-idf is that if a word appears frequently in a document, it is important for the document and

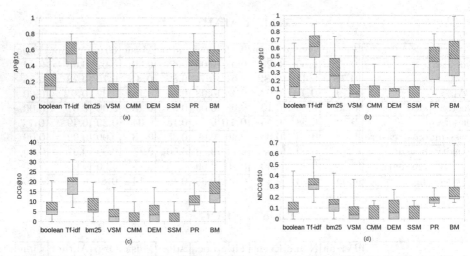

Fig. 1. Effectiveness of Ranking Model

is given a high score (i.e. tf value), but if it appears in many documents, it is not a unique identifier and is given a low score (i.e. idf value). In ontologies, a resource that is reused across many ontologies is a popular and relatively more important resource in the ontology and the corpus. Therefore, in our experiment, tf-idf successfully ranks a resource high in the result set if that resource is the central concept of the ontology (i.e. it is assigned a high tf value). However, if a resource is also popular among the corpus, it is scored down for the idf value. For example, `http://xmlns.com/foaf/0.1/Person` has the highest tf value (i.e. 0.589) of all concepts in the FOAF ontology, but since it is also the most popular concept in our corpus appearing in total in 162 distinct ontologies, it does not appear among the top ten results of tf-idf.

Since BM25 is a cumulative relevance score for an ontology rooted in the tf and idf values of a matched resource, the limitations of tf-idf are implicit in BM25 as well. However, BM25 ranks concept specific ontologies higher in the result set for a query term that matches to that particular concept. The reason is that for a specific ontology, the query term matches to one of the important resource and many of its attached resources. All these matched resources sum up to a higher BM25 score for that ontology. For example, for the "Name" query, BM25 ranks all resources in the GND ontology[8] higher, since this ontology defines different types of Names. All these types of names are important concepts of this ontology and finally leverage the BM25 score for the GND ontology.

The vector space model did not perform well for any query. The main reason is that the vector space model considers tf-idf values of resources as well as query term/s. The idf value for a query term is calculated by considering the idf values of all the resources in the corpus that matched the query term. Therefore, the effect of the wrong assumptions for the idf values doubles for the vector space model.

---

[8] `http://d-nb.info/standards/elementset/gnd#`

PageRank ranks resources according to their popularity, that is why it performs, for example, well in ranking highly the "Person" concept in the FOAF ontology as it is a widely used ontology that is imported by many other ontologies. However, considering popularity in the corpus as the only factor for ranking ontologies sometimes results in poor precision and recall. e.g. http://www.loria.fr/~coulet/ontology/sopharm/version2.0/disease_ontology.owl#DOID_4977 with the label "other road accidents injuring unspecified person" is one of the popular resources in our corpus but not at all relevant for the "Person" concept. Still, PageRank assigns it a higher rank based on its popularity in the corpus. The performance of the PageRank algorithm could be significantly improved if it also takes the data for a given ontology into consideration (as is done in Semantic Search engines). Instead of using only the import statement as the measure of popularity, the links from data will give higher weights to resources in ontologies for which there exists data across multiple domains.

As expected, the class match measures is the least precise algorithm in the experiment. Since the algorithm ranks an ontology only on the basis of the label of the matched resources within that ontology, an ontology with single or zero exact matched labels and many partial match labels gets a higher relevance score than those ontologies where few concepts are relatively more important. Secondly, assigning the same weight to partially matched labels is problematic. For example, for the query "Address" two partially matched resources "Postal address"[9] and "Email address of specimen provider principal investigator"[10] are obviously not equally relevant to the address definition provided in our user study. However, CMM uses equal weights for both of these resources while computing the relevance score of their corresponding ontologies.

The density measure model performs relatively poorly, because it assigns high weights for super-class and sub-class relations. The intention is that the further specified a resource is in an ontology the more important it is. However, in our study the density measure model always favours upper level ontologies or highly layered ontologies, where many subclasses and super classes are defined for a resource (e.g. OBO ontologies), irrespective of its relevance to the query term.

The semantic similarity measure model considers the proximity of matched resources in an ontology. Although this metrics can be useful when considering similarity among the matched resources of two or more query terms of a multi-keyword query, it performs poorly on single word queries. As mentioned earlier, users seem to be not using multi-keyword queries in ontology search yet and thus the semantic similarity measure appears to be not particularly useful for ranking resources in ontologies.

The betweenness measure performs better than all other graph-based ranking models because it calculates the relative importance of the resource to the particular ontology. A resource with a high betweenness value is the central resource of that ontology [1], which means that the resource is well defined and important to the ontology. Further, the betweenness measure performs well even with resources that are irrelevant to the query term if they are not central resources

---

[9] http://purl.obolibrary.org/obo/IAO_0000422
[10] http://purl.obolibrary.org/obo/OBI_0001903

of that ontology, as their score will not contribute greatly to the cumulative relevance score for the ontology. For example, irrelevant resources such as "dislocation" for the query "location" do not appear high in the ranking of the betweenness measure, because all resources with the label including "dislocation" are not central concepts in the ontology where they are defined.

A general observation that can be made is that all ranking models other than tf-idf ignore the relevance and importance of a resources to the query when assigning a weight to a particular ontology for a given query term. This is more prominent for graph-based approaches, where the cumulative ranking score for an ontology is computed based on all the relevant terms of that ontology for this query. An ontology that has more matched URIs to the query term gets a higher weight than an ontology that has few or only a single relevant resource in the ontology. For example, `http://www.ontologydesignpatterns.org/cp/owl/participation.owl#Event` with the label "event" is ranked "Extremely useful" to "Useful" for the query "event" by our human experts. However, since this is the only relevant resource in the ontology and it is a small ontology, none of the graph-based models ranked this URI among the top ten resources.

5   Recommendations

Based on the analysis of our experiment we put forward the following four recommendations that we believe could significantly improve the performance of the different ranking algorithms.

1. **Intended type vs. context resource:** We believe that differentiating the intended type from the context resource of a URI has a positive impact on the performance of all ranking models. For example, for a resource in the GND ontology[11] with the label "Name of the Person", "Name" is the intended type, whereas "Person" is the context resource. This resource URI appears in the search results for both, the "Person" and the "Name" query term in our experiment. The human experts ranked this resource on average from "Extremely useful" to "Useful" for the "Name" query term and only "Slightly useful" for the "Person" query. However, all the ranking algorithms assigned an equal weight to this resource while calculating ranks for either of the two query terms. The performance of the ranking models could be improved if they either only consider those resource URIs whose intended type is matching the queries intended type or if they assign a higher weight to such URIs as compared to the ones where the query terms' intended type matches only the context resource of that URI.

2. **Exact vs. partial matches:** As identified by Alani et al. [1] exact matching should be favoured over partial matching in ranking ontologies. Whereas the class match measure model assigns a value of 0.6 to exact matches and 0.4 to partial matches, all other algorithms consider partial and exact matched resources equally. For example, for the query "Location", results that include "dislocation" as partial matches should not be considered, since the word sense for location and dislocation are different. Instead of assigning static

---

[11] `http://d-nb.info/standards/elementset/gnd#NameOfThePerson`

weight factors, we believe that other means of disambiguation between the actual meaning of the query term and of the resource URI can significantly improve the performance of the algorithms. Wordnet [12] or a disambiguation at the time of entry of the query term could be efficient methods for this purpose.

3. **Relevant relations vs. context relations:** For the graph-based ranking models that calculate the relevance score according to the number of relationships for the resource within that ontology (i.e. density measure and betweenness measure), direct properties, sub-classes and super-classes of a class have to be distinguished from relations (i.e. properties) that are very generic and are inferred from its super-classes. For example, the class "email address"[12] from one of the OBO ontologies has properties like "part of continuant at some time", "geographic focus', "is about", "has subject area", "concretized by at some time", "date/time value" and "keywords". However, not all of these properties are actually relevant to the concept "email address".

4. **Resource relevance vs. ontology relevance:** All ranking models discussed in this study (except tf-idf), rank ontologies for the query term by considering all matched resources from a given ontology against the query term. This results in a global rank for the ontology and all the resources that belong to that ontology share the same ontology relevance score. Therefore, in a result set, many resources hold the same relevance score. While ordering resources with the same relevance score from the ontology, the ranking models lack a mechanism to rank resources within the same ontology. We believe that the tf value of the resource could be a good measure to assign scores to resources within an ontology. Therefore, while ranking all the resources of an ontology, the tf value can be used to further rank resources that belong to the same ontology. Another solution could be to compute individual measures (all measures other than tf-idf) for each resource, independent of how many other matched resources there are in the same ontology.

6   Conclusion

This paper represents, to the best of our knowledge, the first systematic attempt at establishing a benchmark for ontology ranking. We established a ground truth through a user study with ten ontology engineers that we then used to compare eight state-of-the-art ranking models to. When comparing the ranking models to the ideal ranking obtained through the user study we observed that content-based ranking models (i.e. tf-idf and BM25) slightly outperform graph-based models such as betweenness measure. Even though content-based models performed best in this study, the performance is still inferior to the performance of the same models on ranking documents because of the structural differences between documents and ontologies. We put forward four recommendations that we believe can considerably improve the performance of the discussed models for ranking resources in ontologies. In particular:

---

[12] http://purl.obolibrary.org/obo/IAO_0000429

- *Determine the intended type of a resource:* A resource should only match a query if the intended type of the query matches the intended type of the resource.
- *Treat partial matches differently:* Instead of treating partial matches of the query and a resource similar to exact matches or assigning a static weight factor, the models should consider other means of disambiguating the actual meaning of the query when matching it with a resource.
- *Assign higher weight to direct properties:* Instead of considering all relations for a class equally when calculating the centrality score in graph-based models, the models should consider assigning a higher score to relations that describe the class directly.
- *Compute a resource relevance:* Additionally to computing a relevance score for an ontology as a whole, all ranking models should be changed so that they also compute a score for individual resources within the ontology.

In conclusion, we believe that with few modifications several of the tested ranking models can be significantly improved for the task of ranking resources in ontologies. We also believe that the proposed benchmark suite is well-suited for evaluating new ranking models. We plan to maintain, improve and extend this benchmark, in particular by adding further queries and updating the ontology collection as new ontologies become available. We expect that this will motivate others to produce tailor-made and better methods for searching resources within ontologies.

References

1. Alani, H., Brewster, C., Shadbolt, N.R.: Ranking Ontologies with AKTiveRank. In: Cruz, I., Decker, S., Allemang, D., Preist, C., Schwabe, D., Mika, P., Uschold, M., Aroyo, L.M. (eds.) ISWC 2006. LNCS, vol. 4273, pp. 1–15. Springer, Heidelberg (2006)
2. d'Aquin, M., Lewen, H.: Cupboard — A Place to Expose Your Ontologies to Applications and the Community. In: Aroyo, L., et al. (eds.) ESWC 2009. LNCS, vol. 5554, pp. 913–918. Springer, Heidelberg (2009)
3. d'Aquin, M., Motta, E.: Watson, More Than a Semantic Web Search Engine. Semantic Web 2(1), 55–63 (2011)
4. Ding, L., Finin, T., Joshi, A., Pan, R., Cost, R.S., Peng, Y., Reddivari, P., Doshi, V., Sachs, J.: Swoogle: A Search and Metadata Engine for the Semantic Web. In: Proceedings of the 13th ACM International Conference on Information and Knowledge Management, pp. 652–659. ACM, New York (2004)
5. Fernandez, M., Lopez, V., Sabou, M., Uren, V., Vallet, D., Motta, E., Castells, P.: Semantic Search Meets the Web. In: Proceedings of the 2008 IEEE International Conference on Semantic Computing, Washington, DC, USA, pp. 253–260 (2008)
6. Gangemi, A., Catenacci, C., Ciaramita, M., Lehmann, J.: A theoretical framework for ontology evaluation and validation. In: Proceedings of the 2nd Italian Semantic Web Workshop. CEUR Workshop Proceedings, vol. 166. CEUR-WS.org (2005)
7. Guarino, N., Welty, C.: Evaluating ontological decisions with OntoClean. Communications of the ACM 45, 61–65 (2002)
8. Harth, A., Umbrich, J., Hogan, A., Decker, S.: YARS2: A Federated Repository for Querying Graph Structured Data from the Web. In: Aberer, K., et al. (eds.) ISWC/ASWC 2007. LNCS, vol. 4825, pp. 211–224. Springer, Heidelberg (2007)

9. Hogan, A., Harth, A., Decker, S.: Reconrank: A scalable ranking method for semantic web data with context. In: Proceedings of the 2nd Workshop on Scalable Semantic Web Knowledge Base Systems (2006)
10. Hogan, A., Harth, A., Umbrich, J., Kinsella, S., Polleres, A., Decker, S.: Searching and browsing Linked Data with SWSE: The Semantic Web Search Engine. Web Semantics: Science, Services and Agents on the World Wide Web 9(4), 365–401 (2011)
11. Lozano-Tello, A., Gomez-Perez, A.: ONTOMETRIC: A method to choose the appropriate ontology. Journal of Database Management 15(2), 1–18 (2004)
12. Miller, G.A.: WordNet: A Lexical Database for English. Commun. ACM 38(11), 39–41 (1995)
13. Noy, N.F., d'Aquin, M.: Where to Publish and Find Ontologies? A Survey of Ontology Libraries. Web Semantics: Science, Services and Agents on the World Wide Web 11(0) (2012)
14. Noy, N.F., Shah, N.H., Whetzel, P.L., Dai, B., Dorf, M., Griffith, N., Jonquet, C., Rubin, D.L., Storey, M.-A., Chute, C.G., Musen, M.A.: BioPortal: ontologies and integrated data resources at the click of a mouse. Nucleic Acids Research (2009)
15. Page, L., Brin, S., Motwani, R., Winograd, T.: The PageRank citation ranking: Bringing order to the Web. In: Proceedings of the 7th International World Wide Web Conference, Brisbane, Australia, pp. 161–172 (1998)
16. Pound, J., Mika, P., Zaragoza, H.: Ad-hoc Object Retrieval in the Web of Data. In: Proceedings of the 19th International Conference on World Wide Web, pp. 771–780. ACM, New York (2010)
17. Robertson, S.E., Walker, S., Jones, S., Hancock-Beaulieu, M.M., Gatford, M., et al.: Okapi at trec-3. In: NIST Special Publication SP, pp. 109–109 (1995)
18. Salton, G., Buckley, C.: Term-weighting approaches in automatic text retrieval. Information Processing & Management 24(5), 513–523 (1988)
19. Salton, G., Wong, A., Yang, C.-S.: A vector space model for automatic indexing. Communications of the ACM 18(11), 613–620 (1975)
20. Thomas, E., Pan, J.Z., Sleeman, D.: Ontosearch2: Searching ontologies semantically. In: Proceedings of the OWLED 2007 Workshop on OWL: Experiences and Directions. CEUR Workshop Proceedings, vol. 258. CEUR-WS.org (2007)
21. Tummarello, G., Delbru, R., Oren, E.: Sindice.Com: Weaving the Open Linked Data. In: Aberer, K., et al. (eds.) ISWC/ASWC 2007. LNCS, vol. 4825, pp. 552–565. Springer, Heidelberg (2007)
22. Vandenbussche, P.-Y., Vatant, B.: Linked Open Vocabularies. ERCIM News 96, 21–22 (2014)

Pushing the Boundaries
of Tractable Ontology Reasoning

David Carral[1], Cristina Feier[2], Bernardo Cuenca Grau[2],
Pascal Hitzler[1], and Ian Horrocks[2]

[1] Department of Computer Science, Wright State University, Dayton US
[2] Department of Computer Science, University of Oxford, Oxford UK

Abstract. We identify a class of Horn ontologies for which standard reasoning tasks such as instance checking and classification are tractable. The class is general enough to include the OWL 2 EL, QL, and RL profiles. Verifying whether a Horn ontology belongs to the class can be done in polynomial time. We show empirically that the class includes many real-world ontologies that are not included in any OWL 2 profile, and thus that polynomial time reasoning is possible for these ontologies.

1   Introduction

In recent years there has been growing interest in so-called *lightweight* ontology languages, which are based on logics with favourable computational properties. The most prominent examples of lightweight ontology languages are the EL, QL and RL profiles of OWL 2 [23]. Standard reasoning tasks, such as classification and fact entailment, are feasible in polynomial time for all profiles, and many highly scalable profile-specific reasoners have been developed [3,6,8,16,24,26,28].

All the OWL 2 profiles are *Horn* languages: any ontology in a profile can be translated into a set of first-order Horn clauses. However, many Horn OWL 2 ontologies fall outside the profiles, and when reasoning with such ontologies we are forced to resort to a fully-fledged OWL 2 reasoner if a completeness guarantee is required. Indeed, in contrast to the lightweight logics underpinning the profiles, the logics required to capture Horn OWL 2 ontologies are intractable: standard reasoning is ExpTime-complete for the description logic Horn-$\mathcal{SHOIQ}$ and 2-ExpTime-complete for the more expressive Horn-$\mathcal{SROIQ}$ [25].

Our aim is to push the tractability boundaries of lightweight ontology languages, and devise efficiently implementable reasoning algorithms that can be applied to most existing Horn ontologies. In our recent work, we took a first step towards achieving this goal by defining a new class of tractable ontologies based on a role (aka property) safety condition, the idea behind which is to preclude the interactions between language constructs that are ultimately responsible for intractability [9]. We showed that Horn-$\mathcal{SHOIQ}$ ontologies in the QL, RL and EL profiles contain only safe roles,[1] and that for ontologies containing only safe

---

[1] The intersection of the normative profiles and Horn-$\mathcal{SHOIQ}$ excludes certain features such as property chain axioms.

P. Mika et al. (Eds.) ISWC 2014, Part II, LNCS 8797, pp. 148–163, 2014.
© Springer International Publishing Switzerland 2014

roles, standard reasoning tasks are still tractable even if the ontology is not captured by any of the profiles. However, our evaluation revealed that, although this usefully extends the range of ontologies for which tractable reasoning is known to be possible, many real-world Horn ontologies contain (a relatively small number of) unsafe roles, and for these ontologies tractability remains unclear.

In this paper we go a step farther and define a new class of Horn-$\mathcal{SHOIQ}$ ontologies in which unsafe roles are allowed to occur, but only under certain restrictions. Membership in this class can be efficiently checked by first generating a graph from the materialisation of a Datalog program, and then checking whether the generated graph is an oriented forest. We call the ontologies satisfying this condition *role safety acyclic* (RSA), and show that standard reasoning tasks remain tractable for RSA ontologies. To this end, we employ a reasoning algorithm based on a translation from a Horn-$\mathcal{SHOIQ}$ ontology $\mathcal{O}$ into a set $\mathcal{N}_\mathcal{O}$ of first-order Horn rules with function symbols. We show that this transformation preserves standard reasoning outcomes and hence one can reason over $\mathcal{N}_\mathcal{O}$ instead of $\mathcal{O}$. Furthermore, if $\mathcal{O}$ is RSA, then the *Skolem chase* [10,22] terminates in polynomially many steps when applied to $\mathcal{N}_\mathcal{O}$, and yields a Herbrand model of polynomial size from which the relevant reasoning outcomes can be directly retrieved. Finally, we propose a relaxation of the acyclicity condition for which tractability of reasoning is no longer guaranteed, but that still ensures termination of the Skolem chase over $\mathcal{N}_\mathcal{O}$ with a Herbrand model of exponential size. We refer to ontologies satisfying this relaxed condition as weakly RSA (WRSA).

We have tested our acyclicity conditions over two large ontologies repositories. Our results show that a large proportion of out-of-profile ontologies are RSA. Our conditions can thus have immediate practical implications: on the one hand, RSA identifies a large class of ontologies for which reasoning is known to be tractable, and on the other hand, we show that reasoning for both RSA and WRSA ontologies can be implemented using existing Logic Programming engines with support for function symbols, such as DLV [21] and IRIS [5].

Finally, we note that our notion of acyclicity is related to (yet, incomparable with) existing acyclicity notions applicable to existential rules and ontologies [4,10,11,18,22]. Unlike existing notions, our main goal is to ensure tractability of reasoning rather than chase termination. Indeed, even if $\mathcal{O}$ is RSA, the Skolem chase applied to (the clausification of) $\mathcal{O}$ may not terminate.[2]

This paper comes with an extended version with all proofs of our results.[3]

2   Preliminaries

The Logic Horn-$\mathcal{SHOIQ}$. We assume basic familiarity with the logics underpinning standard ontology languages, and refer the reader to the literature for further details [1,13,14]. We next define Horn-$\mathcal{SHOIQ}$ [20,25] and specify its semantics via translation into first-order logic with built-in equality. W.l.o.g. we restrict our attention to ontologies in a normal form close to those in [19,25].

---

[2] We defer a detailed discussion to the Related Work section.

[3] http://www.cs.ox.ac.uk/isg/TR/RSAcheck.pdf

Horn-$\mathcal{SHOIQ}$ axioms α		First-order sentences $\pi(\alpha)$
(R1)	$R_1 \sqsubseteq R_2$	$R_1(x,y) \to R_2(x,y)$
(R2)	$R_1 \sqsubseteq R_2^-$	$R_1(x,y) \to R_2(y,x)$
(R3)	$\mathsf{Tra}(R)$	$R(x,y) \land R(y,z) \to R(x,z)$
(T1)	$A_1 \sqcap \ldots \sqcap A_n \sqsubseteq B$	$A_1(x) \land \ldots \land A_n(x) \to B(x)$
(T2)	$A \sqsubseteq \{a\}$	$A(x) \to x \approx a$
(T3)	$\exists R.A \sqsubseteq B$	$R(x,y) \land A(y) \to B(x)$
(T4)	$A \sqsubseteq\, \leq 1S.B$	$A(x) \land S(x,y) \land B(y) \land S(x,z) \land B(z) \to y \approx z$
(T5)	$A \sqsubseteq \exists R.B$	$A(x) \to \exists y.(R(x,y) \land B(y))$
(T6)	$\mathsf{Ran}(R) = A$	$R(x,y) \to A(y)$
(T7)	$A \sqsubseteq \exists R.\{a\}$	$A(x) \to R(x,a)$
(A1)	$A(a)$	$A(a)$
(A2)	$R(a,b)$	$R(a,b)$

Fig. 1. Horn-$\mathcal{SHOIQ}$ syntax and semantics, where $A_{(i)} \in N_\mathsf{C}$, $B \in N_\mathsf{C}$, $R_{(i)}, S \in N_\mathsf{R}$ with S simple, and $a, b \in N_\mathsf{I}$. Universal quantifiers are omitted. Axioms (T6) and (T7) are redundant, but are useful for defining (resp.) the EL and the RL profiles.

A (DL) signature Σ consists of disjoint countable sets of *concept names* N_C, *role names* N_R and *individuals* N_I, where we additionally assume that $\{\top, \bot\} \subseteq N_\mathsf{C}$. A *role* is an element of $N_\mathsf{R} \cup \{R^- | R \in N_\mathsf{R}\}$. The function $\mathsf{Inv}(\cdot)$ is defined over roles as follows, where $R \in N_\mathsf{R}$: $\mathsf{Inv}(R) = R^-$ and $\mathsf{Inv}(R^-) = R$.

An *RBox* $\mathcal{R}$ is a finite set of axioms (R1)-(R3) in Fig. 1. We denote with $\sqsubseteq_\mathcal{R}$ the minimal relation over roles in $\mathcal{R}$ s.t. $R \sqsubseteq_\mathcal{R} S$ and $\mathsf{Inv}(R) \sqsubseteq_\mathcal{R} \mathsf{Inv}(S)$ hold if $R \sqsubseteq S \in \mathcal{R}$. We define $\sqsubseteq_\mathcal{R}^*$ as the reflexive-transitive closure of $\sqsubseteq_\mathcal{R}$. A role R is *transitive* in $\mathcal{R}$ if there exists S s.t. $S \sqsubseteq_\mathcal{R}^* R$, $R \sqsubseteq_\mathcal{R}^* S$ and either $\mathsf{Tra}(S) \in \mathcal{R}$ or $\mathsf{Tra}(\mathsf{Inv}(S)) \in \mathcal{R}$. A role R is *simple* in $\mathcal{R}$ if no transitive role S exists s.t. $S \sqsubseteq_\mathcal{R}^* R$. A TBox $\mathcal{T}$ is a finite set of axioms (T1)-(T5) in Fig. 1.[4] An ABox $\mathcal{A}$ is a finite, non-empty set of assertions (A1) and (A2) in Fig. 1. An ontology $\mathcal{O} = \mathcal{R} \cup \mathcal{T} \cup \mathcal{A}$ consists of an RBox $\mathcal{R}$, TBox $\mathcal{T}$, and ABox $\mathcal{A}$. The signature of $\mathcal{O}$ is the set of concept names, role names, and individuals occurring in $\mathcal{O}$.

We define the semantics of a Horn-$\mathcal{SHOIQ}$ ontology by means of a mapping π from Horn-$\mathcal{SHOIQ}$ axioms into first-order sentences with equality as specified in Fig. 1. This mapping is extended to map ontologies to first-order knowledge bases in the obvious way. Ontology satisfiability and entailment in first-order logic with built-in equality (written $\models$) are defined as usual.

We sometimes treat $\top$ and $\bot$ as ordinary unary predicates, the meaning of which is axiomatised. For a finite signature Σ, we denote with $\mathcal{F}_\Sigma^{\top\bot}$ the smallest set with a sentence $A(x) \to \top(x)$ for each $A \in N_\mathsf{C}$ and $R(x,y) \to \top(x) \land \top(y)$ for each $R \in N_\mathsf{R}$. This is w.l.o.g. for Horn theories: a Horn-$\mathcal{SHOIQ}$ ontology $\mathcal{O}$ with signature Σ is satisfiable iff $\pi(\mathcal{O}) \cup \mathcal{F}_\Sigma^{\top\bot} \not\models \exists y.\bot(y)$. Furthermore, $\mathcal{O} \models \alpha$ with $\mathcal{O}$ satisfiable and α an axiom over Σ iff $\pi(\mathcal{O}) \cup \mathcal{F}_\Sigma^{\top\bot} \models \pi(\alpha)$.

Similarly, we may treat the equality predicate $\approx$ as ordinary and denote with $\mathcal{F}_\Sigma^\approx$ its axiomatisation as a congruence relation over Σ, and we denote with $\models_\approx$

---

[4] For presentational convenience, we omit axioms $A \sqsubseteq\, \geq n\,R.B$. These can be simulated using axioms $A \sqsubseteq \exists R.B_i$ and $B_i \sqcap B_j \sqsubseteq \bot$ for $1 \leq i < j \leq n$.

the entailment relationship where equality is treated as an ordinary predicate. Axiomatisation of equality preserves entailment: for each set $\mathcal{F}$ of sentences with signature Σ and each sentence α over Σ, we have $\mathcal{F} \models \alpha$ iff $\mathcal{F} \cup \mathcal{F}_{\Sigma}^{\approx} \models_{\approx} \alpha$.

OWL 2 Profiles. The OWL 2 specification defines three normative profiles, EL, QL, and RL, all of which are captured by Horn-$\mathcal{SROIQ}$. In this paper we restrict our attention to the intersection of these profiles with Horn-$\mathcal{SHOIQ}$ (which excludes features such as property chain axioms), as this greatly simplifies the algorithms and proofs. A Horn-$\mathcal{SHOIQ}$ ontology $\mathcal{O}$ is: *(i)* EL if it does not contain axioms of the form (R2) or (T4); *(ii)* RL if it does not contain axioms of the form (T5); and *(iii)* QL if it does not contain axioms of the form (R3), (T2) or (T4), each axiom (T1) satisfies $n = 1$, and each axiom (T3) satisfies $A = \top$.

Horn Rules and Datalog. A Horn rule is a first-order sentence of the form

$$\forall \boldsymbol{x} \forall \boldsymbol{z}. [\varphi(\boldsymbol{x}, \boldsymbol{z}) \rightarrow \psi(\boldsymbol{x})]$$

where tuples of variables $\boldsymbol{x}$, $\boldsymbol{z}$ are disjoint, $\varphi(\boldsymbol{x}, \boldsymbol{z})$ is a conjunction of function-free atoms, and $\psi(\boldsymbol{x})$ is a conjunction of atoms (possibly with function symbols). A fact is a ground, function-free atom. A Horn program $\mathcal{P}$ consists of a finite set of Horn rules and facts. A rule (program) is *Datalog* if it is function-free.[5] Forward-chaining reasoning over Horn programs can be realised by means of the *Skolem chase* [10,22]. We adopt the treatment of the Skolem chase from [10].

A set of ground atoms S' is a *consequence* of a Horn rule r on a set of ground atoms S if a substitution σ exists mapping the variables in r to the terms in S such that $\varphi\sigma \subseteq S$ and $S' \subseteq \psi\sigma$. The result of *applying* r to S, written $r(S)$, is the union of all consequences of r on S. For $\mathcal{H}$ a set of Horn rules, $\mathcal{H}(S) = \bigcup_{r \in \mathcal{H}} r(S)$. Let S be a finite set of ground atoms, let $\mathcal{H}$ be a set of rules, and let Σ be the signature of $\mathcal{H} \cup S$. Let $\mathcal{H}' = \mathcal{H} \cup \mathcal{F}_{\Sigma}^{\approx} \cup \mathcal{F}_{\Sigma}^{\top\perp}$. The *chase sequence* for S and $\mathcal{H}$ is a sequence of sets of ground atoms $S_{\mathcal{H}}^0, S_{\mathcal{H}}^1, \ldots$ where $S_{\mathcal{H}}^0 = S$ and, for each $i > 0 : S_{\mathcal{H}}^i = S_{\mathcal{H}}^{i-1} \cup \mathcal{H}(S_{\mathcal{H}}^{i-1})$.

The *Skolem chase* of the program $\mathcal{P} = \mathcal{H} \cup S$ is defined as the (possibly infinite) Herbrand interpretation $I_{\mathcal{P}}^{\infty} = \bigcup_i S_{\mathcal{H}}^i$. The Skolem chase can be used to determine fact entailment: for each fact α it holds that $\mathcal{P} \models \alpha$ iff $\alpha \in I_{\mathcal{P}}^{\infty}$. The Skolem chase of $\mathcal{P}$ *terminates* if $i \geq 0$ exists such that $S_{\mathcal{H}}^i = S_{\mathcal{H}}^j$ for each $j > i$.

If $\mathcal{P}$ is a Datalog program, then $I_{\mathcal{P}}^{\infty}$ is the finite least Herbrand model of $\mathcal{P}$, which we refer to as the *materialisation* of $\mathcal{P}$. Furthermore, by slight abuse of notation, we sometimes refer to the Skolem chase of a Horn-$\mathcal{SHOIQ}$ ontology $\mathcal{O}$ as the chase for the program obtained from $\pi(\mathcal{O})$ by standard Skolemisation of existentially quantified variables into functional terms.

3   The Notion of Role Safety

In contrast to the logics underpinning the OWL 2 profiles, the logics required to capture existing Horn ontologies are intractable. In particular, satisfiability is

---

[5] We adopt a more liberal definition of Datalog that allows conjunction in rule heads.

EXPTIME-hard already for Horn-$\mathcal{ALCI}$ (the fragment of Horn-$\mathcal{SHOIQ}$ without nominals [15,19] or cardinality restrictions).

A closer look at existing complexity results reveals that the main source of intractability is the phenomenon typically known as *and-branching*: due to the interaction between existential quantifiers over a role R (i.e., axioms of type (T5)) and universal quantifiers over R (encoded by axioms of type (T3) and (R2)), an ontology may only be satisfied in models of exponential size. The same effect can be achieved via the interaction between existential quantifiers and cardinality restrictions (axioms of type (T4)): reasoning in the extension of the EL profile with counting is also known to be EXPTIME-hard [2].

And-branching can be tamed by precluding the harmful interactions between existential quantifiers and universal quantifiers, on the one hand and existential quantifiers and cardinality restrictions, on the other hand. If we disallow existential quantifiers altogether (axioms (T5)), then we obtain the RL profile, and ontologies become equivalent to Datalog programs with equality. Similarly, if we disallow the use of inverse roles and cardinality restrictions, thus precluding both universal quantification over roles and counting, then we obtain the EL profile.

The main idea behind our notion of role safety is to identify a subset of the roles in an ontology over which these potentially harmful interactions between language constructs cannot occur. On the one hand, if a role does not occur existentially quantified in axioms of type (T5), then its "behaviour" is similar to that of a role in an RL ontology, and hence it is *safe*. On the other hand, if a role occurs existentially quantified, but no axioms involving inverse roles or counting apply to any of its super-roles, then the role behaves like a role in an EL ontology, and hence it is also *safe*.

Definition 1. *Let $\mathcal{O} = \mathcal{R} \cup \mathcal{T} \cup \mathcal{A}$ be an ontology. A role R in $\mathcal{O}$ is safe if either it does not occur in axioms of type $A \sqsubseteq \exists R.B$, or the following properties hold for each role S:*

1. *$R \not\sqsubseteq_{\mathcal{R}}^* S$ and $R \not\sqsubseteq_{\mathcal{R}}^* \mathsf{Inv}(S)$ if S occurs in a concept $\leq 1\,S.B$;*
2. *$R \not\sqsubseteq_{\mathcal{R}}^* \mathsf{Inv}(S)$ if S occurs in an axiom of type $\exists R.A \sqsubseteq B$ with $A \neq \top$.*

Example 1. Consider the example ontology $\mathcal{O}_{\mathsf{Ex}}$ in Figure 2, which is not captured by any of the normative profiles. The role Attends is safe: although it occurs existentially quantified in axiom (2), its inverse AttendedBy does not occur in an axiom of type (T3), and the ontology does not contain cardinality restrictions. In contrast, the role AttendedBy is unsafe since it occurs existentially quantified in (5) and its inverse role Attends occurs negatively in (3).   ◇

Note that Definition 1 explains why (Horn-$\mathcal{SHOIQ}$) ontologies captured by any of the normative profiles contain only safe roles: in the case of EL, roles can be existentially quantified, but there are no inverse roles or cardinality restrictions, and hence conditions 1 and 2 in Definition 1 hold trivially; in the case of RL, roles do not occur existentially quantified in axioms of type (T5); and in the case of QL, there are no cardinality restrictions, all axioms of type (T3) satisfy $A = \top$, and hence conditions 1 and 2 also hold.

$$\text{LazySt} \sqsubseteq \text{Student} \tag{1}$$

$$\text{Student} \sqsubseteq \exists\text{Attends.Course} \tag{2}$$

$$\exists\text{Attends.MorningCourse} \sqsubseteq \text{DiligentSt} \tag{3}$$

$$\text{LazySt} \sqcap \text{DiligentSt} \sqsubseteq \bot \tag{4}$$

$$\text{Course} \sqsubseteq \exists\text{AttendedBy.Student} \tag{5}$$

$$\text{Attends}^- \sqsubseteq \text{AttendedBy} \tag{6}$$

$$\text{AttendedBy}^- \sqsubseteq \text{Attends} \tag{7}$$

$$\text{LazySt(David)} \tag{8}$$

Fig. 2. Example ontology $\mathcal{O}_{Ex}$

4 Role Safety Acyclicity

In this section, we propose a novel *role safety acyclicity* (RSA) condition that is applicable to Horn-$\mathcal{SHOIQ}$ ontologies and that does not completely preclude unsafe roles. Instead, our condition restricts the way in which unsafe roles are used so that they cannot lead to the interactions between language constructs that are at the root of EXPTIME-hardness proofs; in particular, *and-branching*.

To check whether an ontology $\mathcal{O}$ is RSA we first generate a directed graph $G_\mathcal{O}$ by means of a Datalog program $\mathcal{P}_\mathcal{O}$. The edges in $G_\mathcal{O}$ are generated from the extension of a fresh "edge" predicate E in the materialisation of $\mathcal{P}_\mathcal{O}$. Intuitively, the relevant facts over E in the materialisation stem from the presence in $\mathcal{O}$ of existential restrictions over unsafe roles. Once the directed graph $G_\mathcal{O}$ has been generated, we check that it is a directed acyclic graph (DAG) and that it does not not contain "diamond-shaped" subgraphs; the former requirement will ensure termination of our reasoning algorithm in Section 5, while the latter is critical for tractability. Furthermore, we define a weaker version of RSA (WRSA) where $G_\mathcal{O}$ is only required to be a DAG. Although this relaxed notion does not ensure tractability of reasoning, it does guarantee termination of our reasoning algorithm, and hence is still of relevance in practice.

Definition 2. *Let $\mathcal{O}$ be an ontology, let Σ be the signature of $\mathcal{O}$, and let π be the mapping defined in Figure 1. Let* PE *and* E *be fresh binary predicates, and let* U *be a fresh unary predicate. Furthermore, for each pair of concepts A, B and each role R from Σ, let $v_{R,B}^A$ be a fresh constant. Let Ξ be the function mapping each axiom α in $\mathcal{O}$ to a datalog rule as given next, and let $\Xi(\mathcal{O}) = \{\Xi(\alpha) \mid \alpha \text{ in } \mathcal{O}\}$:*

$$\Xi(\alpha) = \begin{cases} A(x) \to R(x, v_{R,B}^A) \land B(v_{R,B}^A) \land \text{PE}(x, v_{R,B}^A) & \text{if } \alpha = A \sqsubseteq \exists R.B \\ \pi(\alpha) & \text{Otherwise.} \end{cases}$$

Then, $\mathcal{P}_\mathcal{O}$ is the following datalog program:

$$\mathcal{P}_\mathcal{O} = \Xi(\mathcal{O}) \cup \{\text{U}(x) \land \text{PE}(x, y) \land \text{U}(y) \to \text{E}(x, y)\} \cup \{\text{U}(v_{R,B}^A) \mid R \text{ is unsafe}\}$$

$$\mathsf{LazySt}(x) \to \mathsf{Student}(x)$$
$$\mathsf{Student}(x) \to \mathsf{Attends}(x, v^{St}_{At,Co}) \wedge \mathsf{Course}(v^{St}_{At,Co}) \wedge \mathsf{PE}(x, v^{St}_{At,Co})$$
$$\mathsf{Attends}(x,y) \wedge \mathsf{MorningCourse}(y) \to \mathsf{DiligentSt}(y)$$
$$\mathsf{LazySt}(x) \wedge \mathsf{DiligentSt}(x) \to \perp(x)$$
$$\mathsf{Course}(x) \to \mathsf{AttendedBy}(x, v^{Co}_{la,St}) \wedge \mathsf{Student}(v^{Co}_{la,St}) \wedge \mathsf{PE}(x, v^{Co}_{la,St})$$
$$\mathsf{Attends}(y,x) \to \mathsf{AttendedBy}(x,y)$$
$$\mathsf{AttendedBy}(x,y) \to \mathsf{Attends}(y,x)$$
$$\mathsf{U}(x) \wedge \mathsf{PE}(x,y) \wedge \mathsf{U}(y) \to \mathsf{E}(x,y)$$
$$\mathsf{LazySt}(\mathsf{David})$$
$$\mathsf{U}(v^{Co}_{la,St})$$

Fig. 3. Checking acyclicity of our example ontology $\mathcal{O}_{Ex}$

Let $G_{\mathcal{O}}$ be the smallest directed graph having an edge (c,d) for each fact $\mathsf{E}(c,d)$ s.t. $\mathsf{E}(c,d) \in I^{\infty}_{\mathcal{P}_{\mathcal{O}}}$. Then, $\mathcal{O}$ is Role Safety Acyclic (RSA) if $G_{\mathcal{O}}$ is an oriented forest.[6] Finally, $\mathcal{O}$ is weakly RSA (WRSA) if $G_{\mathcal{O}}$ is a DAG.

The core of the program $\mathcal{P}_{\mathcal{O}}$ is obtained from $\mathcal{O}$ by translating its axioms into first-order logic in the usual way with the single exception of existentially quantified axioms α, which are translated into Datalog by Skolemising the (unique) existential variable in $\pi(\alpha)$ into a constant. The fresh predicate PE is used to track all facts over roles R generated by the application of Skolemised rules, regardless of whether the relevant role R is safe or not. In this way, PE records "possible edges" in the graph. The safety distinction is realised by the unary predicate U, which is populated with all fresh constants introduced by the Skolemisation of existential restrictions over the unsafe roles. Finally, the rule $\mathsf{U}(x) \wedge \mathsf{PE}(x,y) \wedge \mathsf{U}(y) \to \mathsf{E}(x,y)$ ensures that only possible edges between Skolem constants in the extension of U eventually become edges in the graph.

Example 2. Figure 3 depicts the rules in the program $\mathcal{P}_{\mathcal{O}_{Ex}}$ for our example ontology $\mathcal{O}_{Ex}$. The constant $v^{Co}_{la,St}$ is the only fresh constant introduced by the Skolemisation of an existential restriction ($\exists\mathsf{AttendedBy}.\mathsf{Student}$) over an unsafe role (AttendedBy), and hence the predicate U is populated with just $v^{Co}_{la,St}$.

Next consider the application of the Skolem chase on $\mathcal{P}_{\mathcal{O}_{Ex}}$, which applies to the initial facts $S = \{\mathsf{LazySt}(\mathsf{David}), \mathsf{U}(v^{Co}_{la,St})\}$ and rules $\mathcal{H} = \mathcal{P}_{\mathcal{O}_{Ex}} \setminus S$. The chase terminates after the following iterations:

$$S^1_{\mathcal{H}} = S \cup \{\mathsf{Student}(\mathsf{David})\}$$
$$S^2_{\mathcal{H}} = S^1_{\mathcal{H}} \cup \{\mathsf{Attends}(\mathsf{David}, v^{St}_{At,Co}), \mathsf{Course}(v^{St}_{At,Co}), \mathsf{PE}(\mathsf{David}, v^{St}_{At,Co})\}$$
$$S^3_{\mathcal{H}} = S^2_{\mathcal{H}} \cup \{\mathsf{AttendedBy}(v^{St}_{At,Co}, v^{Co}_{la,St}), \mathsf{Student}(v^{Co}_{la,St}), \mathsf{PE}(v^{St}_{At,Co}, v^{Co}_{la,St})\}$$
$$S^4_{\mathcal{H}} = S^3_{\mathcal{H}} \cup \{\mathsf{Attends}(v^{Co}_{la,St}, v^{St}_{At,Co}), \mathsf{PE}(v^{Co}_{la,St}, v^{St}_{At,Co})\}$$

---

[6] An oriented forest is a disjoint union of oriented trees; that is, a DAG whose underlying undirected graph is a forest.

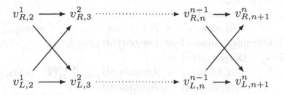

Fig. 4. An acyclic graph which is not an oriented forest

No more atoms are derived in subsequent steps and hence $I^\infty_{P_{O_{Ex}}} = S^4_{\mathcal{H}}$. Note that the graph induced by the auxiliary PE predicate is cyclic; in contrast, the extension of E is empty and $G_{O_{Ex}}$ has no edges. Clearly, O_{Ex} is thus RSA.   ◇

The following example illustrates the difference between RSA and WRSA.

Example 3. Consider the (family of) ontologies O_n consisting of the fact $A_1(a)$ and the following axioms for each $n \geq 1$ and each $1 \leq i \leq n$:

$$A_i \sqsubseteq \exists L.A_{i+1}, \qquad A_i \sqsubseteq \exists R.A_{i+1}$$
$$\top \sqsubseteq\; \leq 1L.\top, \qquad \top \sqsubseteq\; \leq 1R.\top.$$

Clearly, both R and L are unsafe roles since they are defined as functional. The program $\mathcal{P}_{O_n}$ then contains facts $A_1(a)$, $U(v^i_{L,i+1})$, and $U(v^i_{R,i+1})$ for each $1 \leq i \leq n$, as well as the following rules for each $1 \leq i \leq n$:

$$A_i(x) \rightarrow A_{i+1}(v^i_{L,i+1}) \wedge L(x, v^i_{L,i+1}) \wedge PE(x, v^i_{L,i+1})$$
$$A_i(x) \rightarrow A_{i+1}(v^i_{R,i+1}) \wedge L(x, v^i_{R,i+1}) \wedge PE(x, v^i_{R,i+1})$$
$$U(x) \wedge PE(x, y) \wedge U(y) \rightarrow E(x, y)$$

The chase terminates in $n + 1$ steps. The graph G_{O_n} induced by the edge predicate E is given in Figure 4. Note that the graph is always a DAG, but it is a tree only if $n < 3$; hence all ontologies O_n are WRSA, but they are RSA only for $n < 3$.   ◇

The following theorem establishes that checking RSA and WRSA is tractable. Intuitively, the program $\mathcal{P}_O$ is linear in the size of O and each of its rules contains at most three variables regardless of O; as a result, the materialisation (and hence also the resulting graph) is polynomially bounded.

Theorem 1. *Checking whether an ontology O is RSA (resp. WRSA) is feasible in polynomial time in the size of O.*

5   Reasoning over Acyclic Ontologies

In this section, we show that standard reasoning tasks are tractable for RSA ontologies. To this purpose, we propose a translation from a Horn-$\mathcal{SHOIQ}$ ontology O into a set $\mathcal{N}_O$ of first-order Horn rules, which may contain function

$$\text{LazySt}(x) \rightarrow \text{Student}(x)$$
$$\text{Student}(x) \rightarrow \text{Attends}(x, v^{St}_{At,Co}) \wedge \text{Course}(v^{St}_{At,Co})$$
$$\text{Attends}(x,y) \wedge \text{MorningCourse}(y) \rightarrow \text{DiligentSt}(y)$$
$$\text{LazySt}(x) \wedge \text{DiligentSt}(x) \rightarrow \bot(x)$$
$$\text{Course}(x) \rightarrow \text{AttendedBy}(x, f^{Co}_{la,St}(x)) \wedge \text{Student}(f^{Co}_{la,St}(x))$$
$$\text{Attends}(y,x) \rightarrow \text{AttendedBy}(x,y)$$
$$\text{AttendedBy}(x,y) \rightarrow \text{Attends}(y,x)$$
$$\text{LazySt}(\text{David})$$

Fig. 5. Running Example: Reasoning

symbols in the head. Axioms in $\mathcal{O}$ are translated directly into first-order rules as specified in Fig. 1. As can be seen, axioms of type (T5) are translated into rules with existentially quantified variables in the head; such variables are eliminated via Skolemisation into a constant (if the corresponding role is safe) or into a function term (if the corresponding role is unsafe).

Definition 3. *Let $\mathcal{O}$ be an ontology, let Σ be the signature of $\mathcal{O}$, and let π be the mapping defined in Fig. 1. Furthermore, for each pair of concepts A, B and each safe role R from Σ, let $v^A_{R,B}$ be a fresh constant, and for each pair of concepts A, B and each unsafe role R from Σ, let $f^A_{R,B}$ be a fresh unary function symbol. Let Λ be the function mapping each axiom α in $\mathcal{O}$ to a Datalog rule as given next:*

$$\Lambda(\alpha) = \begin{cases} A(x) \rightarrow R(x, v^A_{R,B}) \wedge B(v^A_{R,B}) & \text{if } \alpha = A \sqsubseteq \exists R.B \text{ with } R \text{ safe} \\ A(x) \rightarrow R(x, f^A_{R,B}(x)) \wedge B(f^A_{R,B}(x)) & \text{if } \alpha = A \sqsubseteq \exists R.B \text{ with } R \text{ unsafe} \\ \pi(\alpha) & \text{Otherwise.} \end{cases}$$

Finally, we define the Horn program $\mathcal{N}_\mathcal{O}$ as the set $\{\Lambda(\alpha) \mid \alpha \text{ in } \mathcal{O}\}$.

Example 4. Figure 5 depicts the rules of the Horn program $\mathcal{N}_{\mathcal{O}_{Ex}}$ for our running example $\mathcal{O}_{Ex}$. Let us compare $\mathcal{N}_{\mathcal{O}_{Ex}}$ with the Datalog program $\mathcal{P}_{\mathcal{O}_{Ex}}$ in Fig. 3, which we used for acyclicity checking. In contrast to $\mathcal{P}_{\mathcal{O}_{Ex}}$, the program $\mathcal{N}_{\mathcal{O}_{Ex}}$ contains function terms involving unsafe roles; furthermore, $\mathcal{N}_{\mathcal{O}_{Ex}}$ does not include the auxiliary graph generation predicates from $\mathcal{P}_{\mathcal{O}_{Ex}}$. Next, consider the application of the Skolem chase on $\mathcal{N}_{\mathcal{O}_{Ex}}$, i.e., to the initial fact $S = \{\text{LazySt}(\text{David})\}$ and rules $\mathcal{H} = \mathcal{N}_{\mathcal{O}_{Ex}} \setminus S$. We can check that the chase terminates after four iterations and generates function terms of depth at most one. Furthermore, the only fact that is derived over the individuals from $\mathcal{O}_{Ex}$ is Student(David).   ◇

We next show that this translation preserves satisfiability, subsumption, and instance retrieval reasoning outcomes, regardless of whether the ontology $\mathcal{O}$ is acyclic or not. Thus, we can reason over $\mathcal{N}_\mathcal{O}$ instead of $\mathcal{O}$ without sacrificing correctness. Since $\mathcal{N}_\mathcal{O}$ is a strengthening of $\mathcal{O}$, due to the Skolemisation of some existential quantifiers into constants, completeness is trivial. To show soundness, we propose an embedding of the Skolem chase of $\mathcal{N}_\mathcal{O}$ into the chase of $\mathcal{O}$. This embedding is not a homomorphism, as it does not homomorphically preserve binary facts; however, we can show that unary facts are indeed preserved.

Theorem 2. *The following properties hold for each ontology $\mathcal{O}$, concept names A, B and constants a and b, where Σ is the signature of $\mathcal{O}$ and c is a fresh constant not in Σ:*

1. *$\mathcal{O}$ is satisfiable iff $\mathcal{N}_\mathcal{O}$ is satisfiable iff $I^\infty_{\mathcal{N}_\mathcal{O}}$ contains no fact over $\bot$.*
2. *$\mathcal{O} \models A(a)$ iff $\mathcal{N}_\mathcal{O} \models A(a)$ iff $A(a) \in I^\infty_{\mathcal{N}_\mathcal{O}}$;*
3. *$\mathcal{O} \models A \sqsubseteq B$ iff $\mathcal{N}_\mathcal{O} \cup \{A(c)\} \models B(c)$ iff $B(c) \in I^\infty_{\mathcal{N}_\mathcal{O} \cup \{A(c)\}}$.*

A closer inspection of the proof of the theorem (see our online technical report) reveals that preservation of binary facts can also be ensured if the relevant role satisfies certain properties. The following example illustrates the only situation for which binary facts may not be preserved.

Example 5. Consider the ontology $\mathcal{O}$ consisting of ABox assertions $A(a)$, $A(b)$, TBox axiom $A \sqsubseteq \exists R.B$ and RBox axioms $R \sqsubseteq S$, $R \sqsubseteq S^-$, and $\mathsf{Tra}(S)$. Clearly, R is a safe role, and the fresh individual $v^A_{R,B}$ is introduced by Skolemisation. We can check that $\mathcal{N}_\mathcal{O} \models \{S(a, v^A_{R,B}), S(v^A_{R,B}, b)\}$ and hence $\mathcal{N}_\mathcal{O} \models S(a, b)$ since role S is transitive. Note, however that $\mathcal{O} \not\models S(a, b)$ since $\mathcal{O}$ has a canonical tree model in which a and b are not S-related.   ◇

Proposition 1. *Let $\mathcal{O}$ be an ontology with signature Σ. Furthermore, let $R \in \Sigma$ be a role name satisfying at least one of the following properties: (i) R is simple, (ii) for every axiom of type $A \sqsubseteq \exists S.B$ in $\mathcal{O}$, with S being a safe role $S \not\sqsubseteq^*_\mathcal{R} R$, or (iii) for every axiom of type $A \sqsubseteq \exists S.B$ in $\mathcal{O}$, with S being a safe role $S \not\sqsubseteq^*_\mathcal{R} R^-$. Then, $\mathcal{O} \models R(a, b)$ iff $\mathcal{N}_\mathcal{O} \models R(a, b)$ iff $R(a, b) \in I^\infty_{\mathcal{N}_\mathcal{O}}$.*

Example 6. Coming back to our running example, recall that the only relevant facts contained in the chase of $\mathcal{N}_{\mathcal{O}_{\mathsf{Ex}}}$ are LazySt(David) and Student(David). Thus, we can conclude that $\mathcal{N}_{\mathcal{O}_{\mathsf{Ex}}}$ is satisfiable and does not entail unary facts other than these ones. Furthermore, all roles in $\mathcal{O}_{\mathsf{Ex}}$ are simple and hence we can also conclude that $\mathcal{O}_{\mathsf{Ex}}$ entails no relevant binary facts.   ◇

So far, we have established that we can dispense with the input ontology $\mathcal{O}$ and reason over the Horn program $\mathcal{N}_\mathcal{O}$ instead. The Skolem chase of $\mathcal{N}_\mathcal{O}$, however, may still be infinite. We next show that acyclicity of $\mathcal{O}$ provides a polynomial bound on the size of the Skolem chase of $\mathcal{N}_\mathcal{O}$. Intuitively, every functional term occurring in an atom of the chase of $\mathcal{N}_\mathcal{O}$ corresponds to a single path in $G_\mathcal{O}$, and the size of the graph is polynomial in $\mathcal{O}$. In an oriented forest there is at most one path between any two nodes, which bounds polynomially the number of possible functional terms. In contrast, the latter condition does not hold for DAGs, where only a bound in the length of paths can be guaranteed.

Theorem 3. *Let $\mathcal{O}$ be an RSA ontology with signature Σ. Then, the Skolem chase of $\mathcal{N}_\mathcal{O}$ terminates with a Herbrand model of polynomial size. Furthermore, if $\mathcal{O}$ is WRSA, then the Skolem chase of $\mathcal{N}_\mathcal{O}$ terminates with a Herbrand model of size at most exponential.*

Example 7. As already mentioned, the chase for $\mathcal{N}_{\mathcal{O}_{Ex}}$ terminates and computes only ground atoms of functional depth at most one. Consider, however, the chase for the programs $\mathcal{N}_{\mathcal{O}_n}$ corresponding to the family of ontologies $\mathcal{O}_n$ in Example 3. Program $\mathcal{N}_{\mathcal{O}_n}$ contains the following rules for every $1 \le i \le n$:

$$A_i(x) \to A_{i+1}(f^i_{L,i+1}(x)) \wedge L(x, f^i_{L,i+1}(x))$$
$$A_i(x) \to A_{i+1}(f^i_{R,i+1}(x)) \wedge R(x, f^i_{R,i+1}(x))$$

When initialised with the fact $A_1(a)$, the Skolem chase will generate in each step i the following atoms:

$$A_i(f^{i+1}_{L,i}(t_i)), A_i(f^{i+1}_{R,i}(t_i)), L(t_i, f^{i+1}_{L,i}(t_i)), R(t_i, f^{i+1}_{R,i}(t_i)),$$

where $t_i \in \{g_i(\ldots (g_2(a))\ldots) \mid g_j = f^j_{L,j-1} \text{ or } g_j = f^j_{R,j-1}, 2 \le j \le i\}$. Note that for every i, the number of terms t_i is exponential in i.   ◇

Theorems 2 and 3 suggest a reasoning algorithm for acyclic ontologies $\mathcal{O}$. First, compute the program $\mathcal{N}_{\mathcal{O}}$ as in Definition 3. Then, run the Skolem chase for $\mathcal{N}_{\mathcal{O}}$ and read out the reasoning outcomes from the computed Herbrand model. If $G_{\mathcal{O}}$ is an oriented forest (i.e., $\mathcal{O}$ is RSA) we can implement our algorithm efficiently, which yields the following result as a corollary of the previous theorems.

Theorem 4. *Satisfiability and unary fact entailment is feasible in polynomial time for the class of RSA ontologies.*

In contrast to RSA, our algorithm runs in exponential time for WRSA ontologies. We next show that, indeed, reasoning with WRSA ontologies is intractable under standard complexity-theoretic assumptions.

Theorem 5. *Unary fact entailment is* PSPACE-*hard for WRSA ontologies.*

Finally, note that our reasoning technique can be implemented by reusing existing Logic Programming engines with support for function symbols [21,5].

6   Stronger Notions of Acyclicity

Note that Theorem 4 does not make any claims about the tractability of concept subsumption for RSA ontologies. To check whether $\mathcal{O} \models A \sqsubseteq B$ we need to extend $\mathcal{N}_{\mathcal{O}}$ with an assertion $A(c)$ over a fresh individual c, run the Skolem chase, and check whether $B(c)$ is derived (see Theorem 2). However, as illustrated by the following example, RSA is not robust under addition of ABox assertions.

Example 8. Let $\mathcal{O}$ consist of a fact $B(c)$ and the following axioms:

$$A \sqsubseteq B \quad B \sqsubseteq C \quad A \sqsubseteq \exists R.A \quad \top \sqsubseteq {\le} 1.R.\top$$

Ontology $\mathcal{O}$ is RSA because the rule corresponding to the "dangerous" axiom $A \sqsubseteq \exists R.A$ involving the unsafe role R does not fire during materialisation; as a result, the graph generated by $\mathcal{P}_\mathcal{O}$ is empty. Indeed, the chase terminates on $\mathcal{N}_\mathcal{O}$ and determines satisfiability as well as all the facts entailed by $\mathcal{O}$. In contrast, if we add the fact $A(c)$ to $\mathcal{N}_\mathcal{O}$ to determine the subsumers of A, the chase will no longer terminate because the ontology $\mathcal{O}$ extended with $A(c)$ is now cyclic. ◊

To ensure tractability of subsumption and classification, we therefore propose the following stronger notion of acyclicity.

Definition 4. *Let $\mathcal{O}$ be an ontology with signature Σ. For each concept name $A \in \Sigma$, let c_A be a fresh constant and let $\mathcal{A}_{\mathsf{Cl}} = \{A(c_A) \mid A \in \Sigma\}$. We say that $\mathcal{O}$ is RSA for classification if $\mathcal{O}$ extended with $\mathcal{A}_{\mathsf{Cl}}$ is RSA.*[7]

Tractability of subsumption immediately follows from our results in Section 5.

Proposition 2. *Checking whether $\mathcal{O} \models A \sqsubseteq B$ is feasible in polynomial time for ontologies $\mathcal{O}$ that are acyclic for classification.*

Although this notion is well-suited for TBox reasoning, data-intensive applications where the ABox changes frequently require a further strengthening.

Definition 5. *An ontology $\mathcal{O}$ is* universally RSA *if $\mathcal{O} \cup \mathcal{A}'$ is RSA for every ABox $\mathcal{A}'$.*

Checking whether $\mathcal{O} = \mathcal{R} \cup \mathcal{T} \cup \mathcal{A}$ is universally RSA can be reduced to checking whether the ontology $\mathcal{O}$ extended with a special *critical* ABox $\mathcal{A}_*^\mathcal{O}$ is RSA, where $\mathcal{A}_*^\mathcal{O}$ consists of all facts that can be constructed using concept and role names from $\mathcal{O}$, all individuals occurring in $\mathcal{T}$, and a fresh individual $*$.

Proposition 3. *An ontology $\mathcal{O}$ is* universally RSA *iff $\mathcal{O} \cup \mathcal{A}_*^\mathcal{O}$ is RSA.*

Example 9. The critical ABox for our example ontology $\mathcal{O}_{\mathsf{Ex}}$ consists of all facts $A(*)$ and $R(*, *)$ for A a concept name and R a role name from $\mathcal{O}_{\mathsf{Ex}}$. It can be checked that $\mathcal{O}_{\mathsf{Ex}}$ is universally RSA, and hence also RSA for classification. ◊

Universal RSA is, however, a rather strict condition, especially in the presence of equality. The following example illustrates that, e.g., every ontology with a functional role used in an existential restriction is not universally RSA.

Example 10. Consider $\mathcal{O}$ consisting of axioms $A \sqsubseteq \exists R.B$ and $\top \sqsubseteq\, \leq 1R.\top$. The critical ABox contains facts $A(*)$, $B(*)$, and $R(*, *)$. The corresponding Datalog program entails a fact $R(*, v_{R,B}^A)$ due to axiom $A \sqsubseteq \exists R.B$. Due to the functionality of R, the individuals $*$ and $v_{R,B}^A$ become equal, and hence we have $A(v_{R,B}^A)$ and eventually also $R(v_{R,B}^A, v_{R,B}^A)$. Since R is unsafe, the graph contains a cyclic edge $\mathsf{E}(v_{R,B}^A, v_{R,B}^A)$. Indeed, the chase of both $\mathcal{O}$ and $\mathcal{N}_\mathcal{O}$ is infinite. ◊

It is well-known that the Skolem chase often does not terminate in the presence of equality [10,22]. The standard approach to circumvent this issue is to exploit the so-called *singularisation technique* [22]. Roughly speaking, singularisation

---

[7] Note that ontologies that are RSA for classification are also RSA.

replaces equality $\approx$ in $\mathcal{O}$ with a fresh predicate Eq. The Eq predicate is axiomatised in a similar way to equality, but without the usual replacement rules (i.e., rules of the form $A(x) \wedge \mathsf{Eq}(x,y) \to A(y)$, for each concept name A, are not included in the axiomatisation); instead, the premises of rules in the ontology are modified to compensate for the lack of replacement rules. After application of the singularisation transformation, the ontology is thus equality-free. Singularisation preserves reasoning outcomes in a well-understood way, and it is effective in addressing non-termination problems.

We have exploited this technique by checking acyclicity over a singularisation $\mathcal{O}_s$ of the input ontology $\mathcal{O}$, instead of checking acyclicity over $\mathcal{O}$ itself (see our online TR for further details). If the singularised ontology $\mathcal{O}_s$ is acyclic, then our results in Section 5 ensure that the chase $I^{\infty}_{\mathcal{N}_{\mathcal{O}_s}}$ of $\mathcal{N}_{\mathcal{O}_s}$ is finite and captures reasoning outcomes over $\mathcal{O}_s$. The properties of singularisation then ensure that reasoning outcomes over the original $\mathcal{O}$ are also preserved, and they can be retrieved from $I^{\infty}_{\mathcal{N}_{\mathcal{O}_s}}$. The use of singularisation significantly increased the number of universally acyclic ontologies in our evaluation (see Section 8).

7 Related Work

In recent years the computational properties of Horn Description Logics have been extensively investigated. The logical underpinnings for the EL and QL profiles of OWL 2 are provided by, respectively, the Horn logics $\mathcal{EL}^{++}$ [2] and DL-Lite$_R$ [7], while the RL profile is based on Datalog and its intersection with DLs [12]. Hustadt et al. proposed the expressive logic Horn-$\mathcal{SHIQ}$, and established its complexity [15]. Krötzsch et al. studied the complexity of a wide range of Horn DLs with complexities in-between the tractable logics underpinning the profiles and Horn-$\mathcal{SROIQ}$ [20,19]. Finally, the exact complexity of Horn-$\mathcal{SHOIQ}$ and Horn-$\mathcal{SROIQ}$ was determined by Ortiz et al. [25].

Our techniques in Section 5 extend the so-called combined approach to reasoning in EL [17,27], where ontologies are transformed into Datalog programs by means of Skolemisation of all existentially quantified variables into constants. Skolemisation into constants was also exploited by Zhou et al. [29] to compute upper bounds to query answers.

Finally, in the literature we can find a wide range of acyclicity conditions that are sufficient to ensure chase termination. Weak acyclicity [11] was one of the first such notions, and was subsequently extended to joint acyclicity [18], acyclicity of a graph of rule dependencies [4], and super-weak acyclicity [22], amongst others. The notion of acyclicity closest to ours is model summarising acyclicity (MSA) [10], where acyclicity can also be determined by the materialisation of a Datalog program. Unlike existing acyclicity notions, ours was designed to ensure tractability of reasoning rather than chase termination. In particular, the Skolem chase of our example RSA ontology $\mathcal{O}_{\mathsf{Ex}}$ is infinite and hence $\mathcal{O}_{\mathsf{Ex}}$ cannot be captured by any acyclicity condition designed for chase termination. Instead, our notion ensures termination of the Skolem chase over a particular *transformed* Horn program $\mathcal{N}_{\mathcal{O}}$, which we can use for reasoning over $\mathcal{O}$. Another important

Table 1. Acyclicity evaluation results for ontologies outside the OWL 2 profiles

Repository	Reasoning Task	Total	Safe	RSA no Sing.	RSA Sing.	Cyclic no Sing.	Cyclic Sing.	Time-out no Sing.	Time-out Sing.
Oxford	Satisfiability	126	37	37+43	37+44	46	39	0	6
Ontology	Classification	126	37	37+35	37+35	52	49	2	5
Repository	Universality	126	37	37+2	37+31	87	57	0	1
Ontology	Satisfiability	23	14	14+9	14+9	0	0	0	0
Design	Classification	23	14	14+8	14+8	1	1	0	0
Patterns	Universality	23	14	14+4	14+8	5	1	0	0

difference is that, in contrast to the chase of $\mathcal{O}$, the chase of the transformed program $\mathcal{N}_\mathcal{O}$ is not a universal model of $\mathcal{O}$, and hence it does not preserve answers to general conjunctive queries (but only for satisfiability and fact entailment). Finally, although existing acyclicity conditions guarantee termination of the chase, none of them ensures polynomiality of the computed Herbrand model. Indeed, checking fact entailment over Horn-$\mathcal{SHI}$ ontologies that are weakly acyclic [11] (the most basic acyclicity notion for chase termination) is PSPACE-hard [10].

8   Proof of Concept

We have implemented RSA and WRSA checkers using RDFox [24] as a Datalog reasoner. For testing, we used the ontologies in the Oxford Repository and the Design Patterns repository. The former is a large repository currently containing 761 real-world ontologies; the latter contains a wide range of smaller ontologies that capture design patterns commonly used in ontology modeling (these ontologies are particularly interesting as they highlight common interactions between language constructs). Experiments were performed on a laptop with 16 GB RAM and an Intel Core 2.9 GHz processor running Java v.1.7.0_21, with a timeout of 30 min. The software and data used for testing are available online.[8]

Our results are summarised in Table 1. For each repository, we first selected those ontologies that are Horn-$\mathcal{SHOIQ}$ and are not captured by any of the OWL 2 profiles. We found 126 such ontologies in the Oxford Repository and 23 in the Design Patterns repository. We then tested our acyclicity conditions for satisfiability (Def. 2), classification (Def. 4) and universality (Def. 5) on all these ontologies.[9] We performed tests both with and without singularisation. Interestingly, in both repositories we could not find any ontology that is WRSA but not RSA, and hence the two notions coincided for all our tests.

As we can observe, 37 ontologies in the Oxford Repository contained only safe roles, and hence are RSA. Without singularisation, we found 43 additional ontologies with unsafe roles that are RSA, 35 of which were also RSA for classification and only 2 universally acyclic. When using singularisation the number of

---

[8] https://www.dropbox.com/sh/w1kh3vuhnvindv1/AAD59BK3s5L1D7xCb1Isr1SHa

[9] For classification and universality, we disregarded the ABox part of the ontologies.

additional RSA ontologies increased significantly, and we obtained 29 additional universally RSA ontologies, but unfortunately our tests timed-out for several ontologies. This can be explained by the fact that the use of singularisation leads to more complicated Datalog rules for which RDFox is not optimised.

In the case of the Design Patterns repository, all ontologies are RSA. We only found one ontology that was not universally RSA when using singularisation. Ontologies in this repository are smaller, and we encountered no time-outs.

9   Conclusions and Future Work

We have proposed the new tractable class of RSA ontologies, which is based on the notion of safe roles, and a novel acyclicity condition. Our experiments suggest that a significant proportion of out-of-profile ontologies are RSA; as a result, we can exploit a worst-case optimal algorithm that runs in polynomial time to solve standard reasoning tasks over such ontologies, where only worst-case exponential algorithms were applicable before. This result thus opens the door to further optimisation of ontology reasoning.

So far, our experiments have established that many ontologies satisfy our RSA condition. Our next goal is to develop and optimise our reasoning algorithm as well as our acyclicity checker. We also plan to extend our techniques to apply to Horn-$\mathcal{SROIQ}$ and hence to all Horn OWL 2 ontologies.

Acknowledgements. Work supported by the Royal Society, the EPSRC project Score!, the NSF under award 1017255 "III: Small: TROn: Tractable Reasoning with Ontologies" and "La Caixa" Foundation.

References

1. Baader, F., Calvanese, D., McGuinness, D., Nardi, D., Patel-Schneider, P. (eds.): The Description Logic Handbook: Theory, Implementation, and Applications, 2nd edn. Cambridge University Press (2007)
2. Baader, F., Brandt, S., Lutz, C.: Pushing the $\mathcal{EL}$ envelope. In: Kaelbling, L.P., Saffiotti, A. (eds.) IJCAI, pp. 364–369 (2005)
3. Baader, F., Lutz, C., Suntisrivaraporn, B.: CEL - a polynomial-time reasoner for life science ontologies. In: Furbach, U., Shankar, N. (eds.) IJCAR 2006. LNCS (LNAI), vol. 4130, pp. 287–291. Springer, Heidelberg (2006)
4. Baget, J.-F., Mugnier, M.-L., Thomazo, M.: Towards farsighted dependencies for existential rules. In: Rudolph, S., Gutierrez, C. (eds.) RR 2011. LNCS, vol. 6902, pp. 30–45. Springer, Heidelberg (2011)
5. Bishop, B., Fischer, F.: IRIS - integrated rule inference system. In: ARea (2008)
6. Bishop, B., Kiryakov, A., Ognyanoff, D., Peikov, I., Tashev, Z., Velkov, R.: OWLim: A family of scalable semantic repositories. Semantic Web J. 2(1), 33–42 (2011)
7. Calvanese, D., Giacomo, G.D., Lembo, D., Lenzerini, M., Rosati, R.: Tractable reasoning and efficient query answering in description logics: The DL-Lite family. J. Automated Reasoning (JAR) 39(3), 385–429 (2007)

8. Calvanese, D., De Giacomo, G., Lembo, D., Lenzerini, M., Poggi, A., Rodriguez-Muro, M., Rosati, R., Ruzzi, M., Savo, D.F.: The MASTRO system for ontology-based data access. Semantic Web J. 2(1), 43–53 (2011)
9. Carral, D., Feier, C., Cuenca Grau, B., Hitzler, P., Horrocks, I.: $\mathcal{EL}$-ifying ontologies. In: Demri, S., Kapur, D., Weidenbach, C. (eds.) IJCAR 2014. LNCS, vol. 8562, pp. 464–479. Springer, Heidelberg (2014)
10. Cuenca Grau, B., Horrocks, I., Krötzsch, M., Kupke, C., Magka, D., Motik, B., Wang, Z.: Acyclicity notions for existential rules and their application to query answering in ontologies. JAIR 47, 741–808 (2013)
11. Fagin, R., Kolaitis, P.G., Miller, R.J., Popa, L.: Data exchange: semantics and query answering. Theor. Comput. Sci. 336(1), 89–124 (2005)
12. Grosof, B., Horrocks, I., Volz, R., Decker, S.: Description logic programs: combining logic programs with description logic. In: WWW, pp. 48–57 (2003)
13. Horrocks, I., Kutz, O., Sattler, U.: The even more irresistible $\mathcal{SROIQ}$. In: Doherty, P., Mylopoulos, J., Welty, C. (eds.) Proc. 10th Int. Conf. on Principles of Knowledge Representation and Reasoning (KR 2006), pp. 57–67. AAAI Press (2006)
14. Horrocks, I., Sattler, U.: A tableaux decision procedure for $\mathcal{SHOIQ}$. In: IJCAI, pp. 448–453 (2005)
15. Hustadt, U., Motik, B., Sattler, U.: Data complexity of reasoning in very expressive description logics. In: IJCAI, pp. 466–471 (2005)
16. Kazakov, Y., Krötzsch, M., Simančík, F.: The incredible ELK: From polynomial procedures to efficient reasoning with $\mathcal{EL}$ ontologies. J. Autom. Reas. (JAR) (2013)
17. Kontchakov, R., Lutz, C., Toman, D., Wolter, F., Zakharyaschev, M.: The combined approach to ontology-based data access. In: IJCAI, pp. 2656–2661 (2011)
18. Krötzsch, M., Rudolph, S.: Extending decidable existential rules by joining acyclicity and guardedness. In: IJCAI, pp. 963–968 (2011)
19. Krötzsch, M., Rudolph, S., Hitzler, P.: Complexity boundaries for Horn description logics. In: AAAI, pp. 452–457 (2007)
20. Krötzsch, M., Rudolph, S., Hitzler, P.: Complexities of Horn description logics. ACM Trans. Comp. 14(1), 2:1–2:36 (2013)
21. Leone, N., Pfeifer, G., Faber, W., Eiter, T., Gottlob, G., Perri, S., Scarcello, F.: The DLV system for knowledge representation and reasoning. ACM Trans. Comput. Log. 7(3), 499–562 (2006)
22. Marnette, B.: Generalized schema-mappings: from termination to tractability. In: PODS, pp. 13–22 (2009)
23. Motik, B., Cuenca Grau, B., Horrocks, I., Wu, Z., Fokoue, A., Lutz, C. (eds.): OWL 2 Web Ontology Language: Profiles. W3C Recommendation (October 27, 2009), http://www.w3.org/TR/owl2-profiles/
24. Motik, B., Nenov, Y., Piro, R., Horrocks, I., Olteanu, D.: Parallel materialisation of Datalog programs in centralised, main-memory RDF systems. In: AAAI (2014)
25. Ortiz, M., Rudolph, S., Simkus, M.: Worst-case optimal reasoning for the Horn-DL fragments of OWL 1 and 2. In: KR (2010)
26. Rodriguez-Muro, M., Calvanese, D.: High performance query answering over DL-Lite ontologies. In: KR (2012)
27. Stefanoni, G., Motik, B., Horrocks, I.: Introducing nominals to the combined query answering approaches for $\mathcal{EL}$. In: AAAI (2013)
28. Wu, Z., Eadon, G., Das, S., Chong, E.I., Kolovski, V., Annamalai, M., Srinivasan, J.: Implementing an inference engine for RDFS/OWL constructs and user-defined rules in Oracle. In: ICDE, pp. 1239–1248 (2008)
29. Zhou, Y., Grau, B.C., Horrocks, I., Wu, Z., Banerjee, J.: Making the most of your triple store: Query answering in OWL 2 using an RL reasoner. In: WWW (2013)

Effective Computation of Maximal Sound Approximations of Description Logic Ontologies

Marco Console, Jose Mora, Riccardo Rosati,
Valerio Santarelli, and Domenico Fabio Savo

Dipartimento di Ingegneria Informatica Automatica e Gestionale Antonio Ruberti
Sapienza Università di Roma
{lastname}@dis.uniroma1.it

Abstract. We study the problem of approximating Description Logic (DL) ontologies specified in a source language $\mathcal{L}_S$ in terms of a less expressive target language $\mathcal{L}_T$. This problem is getting very relevant in practice: e.g., approximation is often needed in ontology-based data access systems, which are able to deal with ontology languages of a limited expressiveness. We first provide a general, parametric, and semantically well-founded definition of maximal sound approximation of a DL ontology. Then, we present an algorithm that is able to effectively compute two different notions of maximal sound approximation according to the above parametric semantics when the source ontology language is OWL 2 and the target ontology language is OWL 2 QL. Finally, we experiment the above algorithm by computing the two OWL 2 QL approximations of a large set of existing OWL 2 ontologies. The experimental results allow us both to evaluate the effectiveness of the proposed notions of approximation and to compare the two different notions of approximation in real cases.

1 Introduction

Description Logic (DL) ontologies are the core element of ontology-based data access (OBDA) [15], in which the ontology is utilized as a conceptual view, allowing user access to the underlying data sources. In OBDA, as well as in all the current applications of ontologies requiring automated reasoning, a trade-off between the expressiveness of the ontology specification language and the complexity of reasoning in such a language must be reached. More precisely, most of the current research and development in OBDA is focusing on languages for which reasoning, and in particular query answering, is not only tractable (in data complexity) but also *first-order* rewritable [2,5]. This imposes significant limitations on the set of constructs and axioms allowed in the ontology language.

The limited expressiveness of the current ontology languages adopted in OBDA provides a strong motivation for studying the approximation of ontologies formulated in (very) expressive languages with ontologies in low-complexity languages such as OWL 2 QL. Such a motivation is not only theoretical, but also practical, given the current availability of OBDA systems and the increasing interest in applying the OBDA approach in the real world [1,6,7,16]: for instance, ontology approximation is currently

P. Mika et al. (Eds.) ISWC 2014, Part II, LNCS 8797, pp. 164–179, 2014.

one of the main issues in the generation of ontologies for OBDA within the use cases of the Optique EU project.[1]

Several approaches have recently dealt with the problem of approximating Description Logic ontologies. These can roughly be partitioned in two types: *syntactic* and *semantic*. In the former, only the syntactic form of the axioms of the original ontology is considered, thus those axioms which do not comply with the syntax of the target ontology language are disregarded [17,18]. This approach generally can be performed quickly and through simple algorithms. However, it does not, in general, guarantee soundness, i.e., to infer only correct entailments, or completeness, i.e., all entailments of the original ontology that are also expressible in the target language are preserved [14]. In the latter, the object of the approximation are the entailments of the original ontology, and the goal is to preserve as much as possible of these entailments by means of an ontology in the target language, guaranteeing soundness of the result. On the other hand, this approach often necessitates to perform complex reasoning tasks over the ontology, possibly resulting significantly slower. For these reasons, the semantic approach to ontology approximation poses a more interesting but more complex challenge.

In this paper, we study the problem of approximating DL ontologies specified in a source language $\mathcal{L}_s$ in terms of a less expressive target language $\mathcal{L}_t$. We deal with this problem by first providing a general, parametric, and semantically well-founded definition of maximal sound approximation of a DL ontology. Our semantic definition captures and generalizes previous approaches to ontology approximation [4,8,11,14]. In particular, our approach builds on the preliminary work presented in [8], which proposed a similar, although non-parameterized, notion of maximal sound approximation.

Then, we present an algorithm that is able to effectively compute two different notions of maximal sound approximation according to the above parametric semantics, when the source ontology language is OWL 2 and the target ontology language is OWL 2 QL. In particular, we focus on the *local semantic approximation (LSA)* and the *global semantic approximation (GSA)* of a source ontology. These two notions of approximation correspond to the cases when the parameter of our semantics is set, respectively, to its minimum and to its maximum. Informally, the LSA of an ontology is obtained by considering (and reasoning over) one axiom α of the source ontology at a time, so this technique tries to approximate α independently of the rest of the source ontology. On the contrary, the GSA tries to approximate the source ontology by considering all its axioms (and reasoning over such axioms) at the same time. As a consequence, the GSA is potentially able to "approximate better" than the LSA, while the LSA appears in principle computationally less expensive than the GSA. Notably, in the case of OWL 2 QL, the GSA corresponds to the notion of approximation given in [14], which has been shown to be very well-suited for query answering purposes.

Finally, we experiment the above algorithm by computing the LSA and the GSA in OWL 2 QL of a large set of existing OWL 2 ontologies. The experimental results allow us both to evaluate the effectiveness of the proposed notions of approximation and to compare the two different notions of approximation in real cases. In particular, the main properties pointed out by our experimental results are the following:

---

[1] http://optique-project.eu

1. the computation of the LSA is usually less expensive than computing the GSA of a given source ontology;
2. in many cases, both the LSA and the GSA of an ontology are very good approximations of the ontology, in the sense that the approximated ontologies actually entail a large percentage of the axioms of the source ontology;
3. in many cases, the LSA and the GSA coincide. This and the previous property imply that the computationally less expensive LSA is usually already able to compute a high-quality sound approximation of the source ontology.

The paper is structured in the following way. First, in Section 2 we recall DL ontology languages, in particular OWL 2 and OWL 2 QL. Then, in Section 3 we present our formal, parameterized notion of semantic sound approximation of an ontology, and illustrate some general properties of such a notion. In Section 4 we present the techniques for computing the GSA and the LSA of OWL 2 ontologies in OWL 2 QL. Finally, we present an experimental evaluation of the above techniques in Section 5, and draw some conclusions in Section 6.

2   Preliminaries

Description Logics (DLs) [3] are logics that allow one to represent the domain of interest in terms of *concepts*, denoting sets of objects, *value-domains*, denoting sets of values, *attributes*, denoting binary relations between objects and values, and *roles* denoting binary relations over objects.

In this paper we consider the DL $\mathcal{SROIQ}$ [10], which is the logic underpinning OWL 2, as the "maximal" DL considered in this paper.

Let Σ be a signature of symbols for individual (object and value) constants and predicates, i.e., concepts, value-domains, attributes, and roles. Let Φ be the set of all $\mathcal{SROIQ}$ axioms over Σ.

An *ontology* over Σ is a finite subset of Φ.

A *DL language* over Σ (or simply *language*) $\mathcal{L}$ is a set of ontologies over Σ. We call $\mathcal{L}$-*ontology* any ontology $\mathcal{O}$ such that $\mathcal{O} \in \mathcal{L}$. Moreover, we denote by $\Phi_{\mathcal{L}}$ the set of axioms $\bigcup_{\mathcal{O} \in \mathcal{L}} \mathcal{O}$.

We call a language $\mathcal{L}$ *closed* if $\mathcal{L} = 2^{\Phi_{\mathcal{L}}}$. As we will see in the following, there exist both closed and non-closed DL languages among the standard ones.

The semantics of an ontology is given in terms of first-order (FOL) interpretations (cf. [3]). We denote with $Mod(\mathcal{O})$ the set of models of $\mathcal{O}$, i.e., the set of FOL interpretations that satisfy all the axioms in $\mathcal{O}$ (we recall that every $\mathcal{SROIQ}$ axiom corresponds to a first-order sentence). As usual, an ontology $\mathcal{O}$ is said to be *satisfiable* if it admits at least one model, and $\mathcal{O}$ is said to *entail* a First-Order Logic (FOL) sentence α, denoted $\mathcal{O} \models \alpha$, if $\alpha^{\mathcal{I}} = true$ for all $\mathcal{I} \in Mod(\mathcal{O})$. Moreover, given two ontologies $\mathcal{O}$ and $\mathcal{O}'$, we say that $\mathcal{O}$ and $\mathcal{O}'$ are logically equivalent if $Mod(\mathcal{O}) = Mod(\mathcal{O}')$.

In this work we will mainly focus on two specific languages, which are OWL 2, the official ontology language of the World Wide Web Consortium (W3C) [9], and one of its profiles, OWL 2 QL [12]. Due to the limitation of space, here we do not provide a complete description of OWL 2, and refer the reader to the official W3C specification [13].

We now present the syntax of OWL 2 QL. We use the German notation for describing OWL 2 QL constructs and axioms, and refer the reader to [12] for the OWL functional style syntax.

Expressions in OWL 2 QL are formed according to the following syntax:

$$
\begin{aligned}
B &\longrightarrow A \mid \exists Q \mid \delta_F(U) \mid \top_C \mid \bot_C & E &\longrightarrow \rho(U) \\
C &\longrightarrow B \mid \neg B \mid \exists Q.A & F &\longrightarrow \top_D \mid T_1 \mid \cdots \mid T_n \\
Q &\longrightarrow P \mid P^- \mid \top_P \mid \bot_P & V &\longrightarrow U \mid \top_A \mid \bot_A \\
R &\longrightarrow Q \mid \neg Q & W &\longrightarrow V \mid \neg V
\end{aligned}
$$

where: A, P, and U are symbols denoting respectively an *atomic concept*, an *atomic role*, and an *atomic attribute*; P^- denotes the inverse of P; $\exists Q$, also called *unqualified existential role*, denotes the set of objects related to some object by the role Q; $\delta_F(U)$ denotes the *qualified domain* of U with respect to a value-domain F, i.e., the set of objects that U relates to some value in F; $\rho(U)$ denotes the *range* of U, i.e., the set of values related to objects by U; $T_1, \ldots, T_n$ denote n unbounded value-domains (i.e., datatypes); the concept $\exists Q.A$, or *qualified existential role*, denotes the *qualified domain* of Q with respect to A, i.e., the set of objects that Q relates to some instance of A. $\top_C$, $\top_P$, $\top_A$, and $\top_D$ denote, respectively, the universal concept, role, attribute, and value-domain, while $\bot_C$, $\bot_P$, and $\bot_A$ denote, respectively, the empty concept, role, and attribute.

An OWL 2 QL ontology $\mathcal{O}$ is a finite set of axioms of the form:

$$
\begin{array}{cccccc}
B \sqsubseteq C & Q \sqsubseteq R & U \sqsubseteq V & E \sqsubseteq F & ref(P) & irref(P) \\
& A(a) & P(a,b) & U(a,v) & &
\end{array}
$$

From left to right, the first four above axioms denote subsumptions between concepts, roles, attributes, and value-domains, respectively. The fifth and sixth axioms denote reflexivity and irreflexivity on roles. The last three axioms denote membership of an individual to a concept, membership of a pair of individuals to a role, and membership of a pair constituted by an individual and a value to an attribute.

From the above definition, it immediately follows that OWL 2 QL is a closed language. On the other hand, we recall that OWL 2 is not a closed language. This is due to the fact that OWL 2 imposes syntactic restrictions that concern the simultaneous presence of multiple axioms in the ontology (for instance, there exist restrictions on the usage of role names appearing in role inclusions in the presence of the role chaining constructor).

3 Approximation

In this section, we illustrate our notion of approximation in a target language $\mathcal{L}_T$ of an ontology $\mathcal{O}_S$ in a language $\mathcal{L}_S$.

Typically, when discussing approximation, one of the desirable properties is that of soundness. Roughly speaking, when the object of approximation is a set of models, this property requires that the set of models of the approximation is a superset of those of the original ontology. Another coveted characteristic of the computed ontology is that it be the "best" approximation of the original ontology. In other words, the need of keeping a minimal distance between the original ontology and the ontology resulting from its approximation is commonly perceived.

On the basis of these observations, the following definition of approximation in a target language $\mathcal{L}_T$ of a satisfiable $\mathcal{L}_S$-ontology is very natural.

Definition 1. *Let $\mathcal{O}_S$ be a satisfiable $\mathcal{L}_S$-ontology, and let $\Sigma_{\mathcal{O}_S}$ be the set of predicate and constant symbols occurring in $\mathcal{O}_S$. An $\mathcal{L}_T$-ontology $\mathcal{O}_T$ over $\Sigma_{\mathcal{O}_S}$ is a global semantic approximation (GSA) in $\mathcal{L}_T$ of $\mathcal{O}_S$ if both the following statements hold:*

(i) *$Mod(\mathcal{O}_S) \subseteq Mod(\mathcal{O}_T)$;*
(ii) *there is no $\mathcal{L}_T$-ontology $\mathcal{O}'$ over $\Sigma_{\mathcal{O}_S}$ such that $Mod(\mathcal{O}_S) \subseteq Mod(\mathcal{O}') \subset Mod(\mathcal{O}_T)$.*

We denote with $globalApx(\mathcal{O}_S, \mathcal{L}_T)$ the set of all the GSAs in $\mathcal{L}_T$ of $\mathcal{O}_S$.

In the above definition, statement (i) imposes the soundness of the approximation, while statement (ii) imposes the condition of "closeness" in the choice of the approximation.

We observe that an $\mathcal{L}_T$-ontology which is the GSA in $\mathcal{L}_T$ of $\mathcal{O}_S$ may not exist. This is the case when, for each $\mathcal{L}_T$ ontology $\mathcal{O}'_T$ satisfying statement (i) of Definition 1, there always exists an $\mathcal{L}_T$-ontology $\mathcal{O}''_T$ which satisfies statement (i), but for which we have that $Mod(\mathcal{O}_S) \subseteq Mod(\mathcal{O}''_T) \subset Mod(\mathcal{O}'_T)$.

The following lemma provides a sufficient condition for the existence of the GSA in a language $\mathcal{L}_T$ of an ontology $\mathcal{O}_S$.

Lemma 1. *Given a language $\mathcal{L}_T$ and a finite signature Σ, if the set of non-equivalent axioms in $\Phi_{\mathcal{L}_T}$ that one can generate over Σ is finite, then for any $\mathcal{L}_S$-ontology $\mathcal{O}_S$ $globalApx(\mathcal{O}_S, \mathcal{L}_T) \neq \emptyset$.*

In cases where GSAs exist, i.e., $globalApx(\mathcal{O}_S, \mathcal{L}_T) \neq \emptyset$, given two ontologies $\mathcal{O}'$ and $\mathcal{O}''$ in $globalApx(\mathcal{O}_S, \mathcal{L}_T)$, they may be either logically equivalent or not. The condition of non-equivalence is due to the fact that the language in which the original ontology is approximated is not closed. We have the following lemma.

Lemma 2. *Let $\mathcal{L}_T$ be a closed language, and let $\mathcal{O}_S$ be an ontology. For each $\mathcal{O}'$ and $\mathcal{O}''$ belonging to $globalApx(\mathcal{O}_S, \mathcal{L}_T)$, we have that $\mathcal{O}'$ and $\mathcal{O}''$ are logically equivalent.*

Proof. Towards a contradiction, suppose that $Mod(\mathcal{O}') \neq Mod(\mathcal{O}'')$. From this, and from Definition 1 we have that $Mod(\mathcal{O}') \not\subseteq Mod(\mathcal{O}'')$ and $Mod(\mathcal{O}'') \not\subseteq Mod(\mathcal{O}')$. Hence, there exist axioms α and β in $\Phi_{\mathcal{L}_T}$ such that $\mathcal{O}' \models \alpha$ and $\mathcal{O}'' \not\models \alpha$, and $\mathcal{O}'' \models \beta$ and $\mathcal{O}' \not\models \beta$. Since both $\mathcal{O}'$ and $\mathcal{O}''$ are sound approximations of $\mathcal{O}_S$, $\mathcal{O}_S \models \{\alpha, \beta\}$. Because $\mathcal{L}_T$ is closed, the ontology $\mathcal{O}'_\beta = \mathcal{O}' \cup \{\beta\}$ is an $\mathcal{L}_T$-ontology. From the above considerations it directly follows that $Mod(\mathcal{O}_S) \subseteq Mod(\mathcal{O}'_\beta) \subset Mod(\mathcal{O}')$. This means that $\mathcal{O}'$ does not satisfy condition (ii) of Definition 1, and therefore $\mathcal{O}' \not\in globalApx(\mathcal{O}_S, \mathcal{L}_T)$, which is a contradiction. The same conclusion can be reached analogously for $\mathcal{O}''$. ∎

In other words, if the target language is closed, Lemma 2 guarantees that, up to logical equivalence, the GSA is unique.

Definition 1 is non-constructive, in the sense that it does not provide any hint as to how to compute the approximation in $\mathcal{L}_T$ of an ontology $\mathcal{O}_S$. The following theorem suggests more constructive conditions, equivalent to those in Definition 1, but first we need to introduce the notion of *entailment set* [14] of a satisfiable ontology with respect to a language.

Definition 2. *Let $\Sigma_\mathcal{O}$ be the set of predicate and constant symbols occurring in $\mathcal{O}$, and let $\mathcal{L}'$ be a language. The* entailment set *of $\mathcal{O}$ with respect to $\mathcal{L}'$, denoted as $\mathsf{ES}(\mathcal{O}, \mathcal{L}')$, is the set of axioms from $\Phi_{\mathcal{L}'}$ that only contain predicates and constant symbols from $\Sigma_\mathcal{O}$ and that are entailed by $\mathcal{O}$.*

In other words, we say that an axiom α belongs to the entailment set of an ontology $\mathcal{O}$ with respect to a language $\mathcal{L}'$, if α is an axiom in $\Phi_{\mathcal{L}'}$ built over the signature of $\mathcal{O}$ and for each interpretation $\mathcal{I} \in Mod(\mathcal{O})$ we have that $\mathcal{I} \models \alpha$.

Clearly, given an ontology $\mathcal{O}$ and a language $\mathcal{L}'$, the entailment set of $\mathcal{O}$ with respect to $\mathcal{L}'$ is unique.

Theorem 1. *Let $\mathcal{O}_S$ be a satisfiable $\mathcal{L}_S$-ontology and let $\mathcal{O}_T$ be a satisfiable $\mathcal{L}_T$-ontology. We have that:*

(a) *$Mod(\mathcal{O}_S) \subseteq Mod(\mathcal{O}_T)$ if and only if $\mathsf{ES}(\mathcal{O}_T, \mathcal{L}_T) \subseteq \mathsf{ES}(\mathcal{O}_S, \mathcal{L}_T)$;*
(b) *there is no $\mathcal{L}_T$-ontology $\mathcal{O}'$ such that $Mod(\mathcal{O}_S) \subseteq Mod(\mathcal{O}') \subset Mod(\mathcal{O}_T)$ if and only if there is no $\mathcal{L}_T$-ontology $\mathcal{O}''$ such that $\mathsf{ES}(\mathcal{O}_T, \mathcal{L}_T) \subset \mathsf{ES}(\mathcal{O}'', \mathcal{L}_T) \subseteq \mathsf{ES}(\mathcal{O}_S, \mathcal{L}_T)$.*

Proof. We start by focusing on the first statement. ($\Leftarrow$) Suppose, by way of contradiction, that $\mathsf{ES}(\mathcal{O}_T, \mathcal{L}_T) \subseteq \mathsf{ES}(\mathcal{O}_S, \mathcal{L}_T)$ and that $Mod(\mathcal{O}_S) \not\subseteq Mod(\mathcal{O}_T)$. This means that there exists at least one interpretation that is a model for $\mathcal{O}_S$ but not for $\mathcal{O}_T$. Therefore there exists an axiom $\alpha \in \mathcal{O}_T$ such that $\mathcal{O}_S \not\models \alpha$. Since $\mathcal{O}_T$ is an ontology in $\mathcal{L}_T$, then α is an axiom in $\Phi_{\mathcal{L}_T}$. It follows that $\alpha \in \mathsf{ES}(\mathcal{O}_T, \mathcal{L}_T)$ and that $\alpha \notin \mathsf{ES}(\mathcal{O}_S, \mathcal{L}_T)$, which leads to a contradiction.

($\Rightarrow$) Towards a contradiction, suppose that $Mod(\mathcal{O}_S) \subseteq Mod(\mathcal{O}_T)$, but $\mathsf{ES}(\mathcal{O}_T, \mathcal{L}_T) \not\subseteq \mathsf{ES}(\mathcal{O}_S, \mathcal{L}_T)$. This means that there exists at least one axiom $\alpha \in \mathsf{ES}(\mathcal{O}_T, \mathcal{L}_T)$ such that $\alpha \notin \mathsf{ES}(\mathcal{O}_S, \mathcal{L}_T)$. It follows that $\mathcal{O}_T \models \alpha$ while $\mathcal{O}_S \not\models \alpha$, which immediately implies that $Mod(\mathcal{O}_S) \not\subseteq Mod(\mathcal{O}_T)$. Hence we have a contradiction.

Now we prove the second statement. ($\Leftarrow$) By contradiction, suppose that there exists an $\mathcal{L}_T$-ontology $\mathcal{O}'$ such that $Mod(\mathcal{O}_S) \subseteq Mod(\mathcal{O}') \subset Mod(\mathcal{O}_T)$, and that there does not exist any $\mathcal{L}_T$-ontology $\mathcal{O}''$ such that $\mathsf{ES}(\mathcal{O}_T, \mathcal{L}_T) \subset \mathsf{ES}(\mathcal{O}'', \mathcal{L}_T) \subseteq \mathsf{ES}(\mathcal{O}_S, \mathcal{L}_T)$. From what shown before, we have that $Mod(\mathcal{O}_S) \subseteq Mod(\mathcal{O}') \subseteq Mod(\mathcal{O}_T)$ implies that $\mathsf{ES}(\mathcal{O}_T, \mathcal{L}_T) \subseteq \mathsf{ES}(\mathcal{O}', \mathcal{L}_T) \subseteq \mathsf{ES}(\mathcal{O}_S, \mathcal{L}_T)$. Moreover, since both $\mathcal{O}'$ and $\mathcal{O}_T$ are $\mathcal{L}_T$ ontologies, $Mod(\mathcal{O}') \subset Mod(\mathcal{O}_T)$ implies that $\mathsf{ES}(\mathcal{O}_T, \mathcal{L}_T) \neq \mathsf{ES}(\mathcal{O}', \mathcal{L}_T)$. Hence, $\mathsf{ES}(\mathcal{O}_T, \mathcal{L}_T) \subset \mathsf{ES}(\mathcal{O}', \mathcal{L}_T) \subseteq \mathsf{ES}(\mathcal{O}_S, \mathcal{L}_T)$, which contradicts the hypothesis.

($\Rightarrow$) Suppose, by way of contradiction, that there exists an $\mathcal{L}_T$-ontology $\mathcal{O}''$ such that $\mathsf{ES}(\mathcal{O}_T, \mathcal{L}_T) \subset \mathsf{ES}(\mathcal{O}'', \mathcal{L}_T) \subseteq \mathsf{ES}(\mathcal{O}_S, \mathcal{L}_T)$ and there is no $\mathcal{L}_T$-ontology $\mathcal{O}'$

such that $Mod(\mathcal{O}_S) \subseteq Mod(\mathcal{O}') \subset Mod(\mathcal{O}_T)$. From property (a) we have that $Mod(\mathcal{O}_S) \subseteq Mod(\mathcal{O}'') \subseteq Mod(\mathcal{O}_T)$. Since both $\mathcal{O}''$ and $\mathcal{O}_T$ are $\mathcal{L}_T$ ontologies, then $\mathsf{ES}(\mathcal{O}_T, \mathcal{L}_T) \subset \mathsf{ES}(\mathcal{O}'', \mathcal{L}_T)$ implies that $Mod(\mathcal{O}'') \neq Mod(\mathcal{O}_T)$, which directly leads to a contradiction. ∎

From Theorem 1 it follows that every ontology $\mathcal{O}_T$ which is a GSA in $\mathcal{L}_T$ of an ontology $\mathcal{O}_S$ is also an approximation in $\mathcal{L}_T$ of $\mathcal{O}_S$ according to [8], and, as we shall show in the following section, for some languages, this corresponds to the approximation in [14].

As discussed in [8], the computation of a GSA can be a very challenging task even when approximating into tractable fragments of OWL 2 [12]. This means that even though a GSA is one that best preserves the semantics of the original ontology, it currently suffers from a significant practical setback: the outcome of the computation of the approximation is tightly linked to the capabilities of the currently available reasoners for $\mathcal{L}_S$-ontologies. This may lead, in practice, to the impossibility of computing GSAs of very large or complex ontologies when the source language is very expressive.

We observe that the critical point behind these practical difficulties in computing a GSA of an ontology is that, in current implementations, any reasoner for $\mathcal{L}_S$ must reason over the ontology as a whole. From this observation, the idea for a new notion of approximation, in which we do not reason over the entire ontology but only over portions of it, arises. At the basis of this new notion, which we call *k-approximation*, is the idea of obtaining an approximation of the original ontology by computing the global semantic approximation of each set of k axioms of the original ontology in isolation. Below we give a formal definition of the k-approximation.

In what follows, given an ontology $\mathcal{O}$ and a positive integer k such that $k \leq |\mathcal{O}|$, we denote with $subset_k(\mathcal{O})$ the set of all the sets of cardinality k of axioms of $\mathcal{O}$.

Definition 3. *Let $\mathcal{O}_S$ be a satisfiable $\mathcal{L}_S$-ontology and let $\Sigma_{\mathcal{O}_S}$ be the set of predicate and constant symbols occurring in $\mathcal{O}_S$. Let $\mathcal{U}_k = \{\mathcal{O}_i^j \mid \mathcal{O}_i^j \in globalApx(\mathcal{O}_i, \mathcal{L}_T),$ such that $\mathcal{O}_i \in subset_k(\mathcal{O}_S)\}$. An $\mathcal{L}_T$-ontology $\mathcal{O}_T$ over $\Sigma_{\mathcal{O}_S}$ is a k-approximation in $\mathcal{L}_T$ of $\mathcal{O}_S$ if both the following statements hold:*

- $\bigcap_{\mathcal{O}_i^j \in \mathcal{U}_k} Mod(\mathcal{O}_i^j) \subseteq Mod(\mathcal{O}_T)$;
- *there is no $\mathcal{L}_T$-ontology $\mathcal{O}'$ over $\Sigma_{\mathcal{O}_S}$ such that $\bigcap_{\mathcal{O}_i^j \in \mathcal{U}_k} Mod(\mathcal{O}_i^j) \subseteq Mod(\mathcal{O}') \subset Mod(\mathcal{O}_T)$.*

The following theorem follows from Theorem 1 and provides a constructive condition for the k-approximation.

Theorem 2. *Let $\mathcal{O}_S$ be a satisfiable $\mathcal{L}_S$-ontology and let $\Sigma_{\mathcal{O}_S}$ be the set of predicate and constant symbols occurring in $\mathcal{O}_S$. An $\mathcal{L}_T$-ontology $\mathcal{O}_T$ over $\Sigma_{\mathcal{O}_S}$ is a k-approximation in $\mathcal{L}_T$ of $\mathcal{O}_S$ if and only if:*

(i) $\mathsf{ES}(\mathcal{O}_T, \mathcal{L}_T) \subseteq \mathsf{ES}(\bigcup_{\mathcal{O}_i \in subset_k(\mathcal{O}_S)} \mathsf{ES}(\mathcal{O}_i, \mathcal{L}_T), \mathcal{L}_T)$;
(ii) *there is no $\mathcal{L}_T$-ontology $\mathcal{O}'$ over $\Sigma_{\mathcal{O}_S}$ such that $\mathsf{ES}(\mathcal{O}_T, \mathcal{L}_T) \subset \mathsf{ES}(\mathcal{O}', \mathcal{L}_T) \subseteq$* $\mathsf{ES}(\bigcup_{\mathcal{O}_i \in subset_k(\mathcal{O}_S)} \mathsf{ES}(\mathcal{O}_i, \mathcal{L}_T), \mathcal{L}_T)$.

Proof. (*sketch*) The proof can be easily adapted from the proof of Theorem 1 by observing that in order to prove the theorem one has to show that:

(a) $\bigcap_{\mathcal{O}_i^j \in \mathcal{U}_k} Mod(\mathcal{O}_i^j) \subseteq Mod(\mathcal{O}_T)$ if and only if $\mathsf{ES}(\mathcal{O}_T, \mathcal{L}_T) \subseteq \mathsf{ES}(\bigcup_{\mathcal{O}_i \in subset_k(\mathcal{O}_S)} \mathsf{ES}(\mathcal{O}_i, \mathcal{L}_T), \mathcal{L}_T);$

(b) and that there is no $\mathcal{L}_T$-ontology $\mathcal{O}'$ over $\Sigma_{\mathcal{O}_S}$ such that $\bigcap_{\mathcal{O}_i^j \in \mathcal{U}_k} Mod(\mathcal{O}_i^j) \subseteq Mod(\mathcal{O}') \subset Mod(\mathcal{O}_T)$ if and only if there is no $\mathcal{L}_T$-ontology $\mathcal{O}''$ over $\Sigma_{\mathcal{O}_S}$ such that $\mathsf{ES}(\mathcal{O}_T, \mathcal{L}_T) \subset \mathsf{ES}(\mathcal{O}'', \mathcal{L}_T) \subseteq \mathsf{ES}(\bigcup_{\mathcal{O}_i \in subset_k(\mathcal{O}_S)} \mathsf{ES}(\mathcal{O}_i, \mathcal{L}_T), \mathcal{L}_T).$ ∎

We note that in the case in which $k = |\mathcal{O}_S|$, the k-approximation actually coincides with the GSA. At the other end of the spectrum, we have the case in which $k = 1$. Here we are treating each axiom α in the original ontology in isolation, i.e., we are considering ontologies formed by a single axiom α. We refer to this approximation as *local semantic approximation* (LSA).

We conclude this section with an example highlighting the difference between the GSA and the LSA.

Example 1. Consider the following OWL 2 ontology $\mathcal{O}$.

$$\mathcal{O} = \{\, A \sqsubseteq B \sqcup C \quad B \sqsubseteq D \quad A \sqsubseteq \exists R.D$$
$$B \sqcap C \sqsubseteq F \quad C \sqsubseteq D \quad \exists R.D \sqsubseteq E \,\}.$$

The following ontology is a GSA in OWL 2 QL of $\mathcal{O}$.

$$\mathcal{O}_{GSA} = \{\, A \sqsubseteq D \quad B \sqsubseteq D \quad A \sqsubseteq \exists R \quad A \sqsubseteq \exists R.D$$
$$A \sqsubseteq E \quad C \sqsubseteq D \quad D \sqsubseteq F \,\}.$$

Indeed, it is possible to show that, according to Theorem 1, each axiom entailed by $\mathcal{O}_{GSA}$ is also entailed by $\mathcal{O}$, and that it is impossible to build an OWL 2 QL ontology $\mathcal{O}'$ such that $\mathsf{ES}(\mathcal{O}_{GSA}, OWL\,2\,QL) \subset \mathsf{ES}(\mathcal{O}', OWL\,2\,QL) \subseteq \mathsf{ES}(\mathcal{O}, OWL\,2\,QL)$.

Computing the LSA in OWL 2 QL of $\mathcal{O}$, i.e., its 1-approximation in OWL 2 QL, we obtain the following ontology.

$$\mathcal{O}_{LSA} = \{\, B \sqsubseteq D \quad A \sqsubseteq \exists R$$
$$C \sqsubseteq D \quad A \sqsubseteq \exists R.D \,\}.$$

It is easy to see that $Mod(\mathcal{O}) \subset Mod(\mathcal{O}_{GSA}) \subset Mod(\mathcal{O}_{LSA})$, which means that the ontology $\mathcal{O}_{GSA}$ approximates $\mathcal{O}$ better than $\mathcal{O}_{LSA}$. This expected result is a consequence of the fact that reasoning over each single axiom in $\mathcal{O}$ in isolation does not allow for the extraction all the OWL 2 QL consequences of $\mathcal{O}$.

Moreover, from Lemma 2, it follows that every $\mathcal{O}' \in globalApx(\mathcal{O}_S, OWL\,2\,QL)$ is logically equivalent to $\mathcal{O}_{GSA}$.   □

4   Approximation in OWL 2 QL

In this section we deal with the problem of approximating ontologies in OWL 2 with ontologies in OWL 2 QL.

Based on the characteristics of the OWL 2 QL language, we can give the following theorem.

Algorithm 1. $computeKApx(\mathcal{O}, k)$

Input: a satisfiable OWL 2 ontology $\mathcal{O}$, a positive integer k such that $k \leq |\mathcal{O}|$
Output: an OWL 2 QL ontology $\mathcal{O}_{Apx}$
begin
   $\mathcal{O}_{Apx} \leftarrow \emptyset$;
   foreach ontology $\mathcal{O}_i \in subset_k(\mathcal{O}_S)$
      $\mathcal{O}_{Apx} \leftarrow \mathcal{O}_{Apx} \cup \mathsf{ES}(\mathcal{O}_i, OWL\,2\,QL)$;
   return $\mathcal{O}_{Apx}$;
end

Theorem 3. *Let $\mathcal{O}_S$ be a satisfiable OWL 2 ontology. Then the OWL 2 QL ontology* $\bigcup_{\mathcal{O}_i \in subset_k(\mathcal{O}_S)} \mathsf{ES}(\mathcal{O}_i, OWL\,2\,QL)$ *is the k-approximation in OWL 2 QL of $\mathcal{O}_S$.*

Proof. $(sketch)$ To prove the claim, we observe that Lemma 1 holds for OWL 2 QL ontologies, and this guarantees that for every OWL 2 ontology $\mathcal{O}_S$, there exists at least one OWL 2 QL ontology which is its GSA, i.e., $globalApx(\mathcal{O}_S, OWL\,2\,QL) \neq \emptyset$. Moreover, we have that since OWL 2 QL is closed, for Lemma 2, all ontologies in $\mathsf{ES}(\mathcal{O}_S, OWL\,2\,QL)$ are pairwise logically equivalent. Another consequence of the fact that OWL 2 QL is closed is that, whichever language the original ontology $\mathcal{O}_S$ is expressed in, $\mathsf{ES}(\mathcal{O}_S, OWL\,2\,QL)$ is an OWL 2 QL ontology. Furthermore, given a set of OWL 2 QL ontologies, the union of these ontologies is still an OWL 2 QL ontology. From these observations, it is easy to see that, given an OWL 2 ontology $\mathcal{O}_S$ and an integer $k \leq |\mathcal{O}_S|$, the set $\bigcup_{\mathcal{O}_i \in subset_k(\mathcal{O}_S)} \mathsf{ES}(\mathcal{O}_i, OWL\,2\,QL)$ satisfies conditions (i) and (ii) of Theorem 2. Hence, we have the claim. ∎

Notably, we observe that for $k = |\mathcal{O}_S|$ the k-approximation $\mathcal{O}_T$ in OWL 2 QL of $\mathcal{O}_S$ is unique and coincides with its entailment set in OWL 2 QL. This means that $\mathcal{O}_T$ is also the approximation in OWL 2 QL of $\mathcal{O}_S$ according to the notion of approximation presented in [14]. Therefore, all the properties that hold for the semantics in [14] also hold for the GSA. In particular, the evaluation of a conjunctive query q without non-distinguished variables over $\mathcal{O}_S$ coincides with the evaluation of q over $\mathcal{O}_T$ (Theorem 5 in [14]).

From Theorem 3, one can easily come up with Algorithm 1 for computing the k-approximation of an $\mathcal{L}_S$-ontology $\mathcal{O}_S$ in OWL 2 QL. The algorithm first computes every subset with size k of the original ontology $\mathcal{O}_S$. Then, it computes the ontology which is the result of the k-approximation in OWL 2 QL of the ontology in input as the union of the entailment sets with respect to OWL 2 QL of each such subset. A naive algorithm for computing the entailment set with respect to OWL 2 QL can be easily obtained from the one given in [14] for *DL-Lite* languages. We can summarize it as follows. Let $\mathcal{O}$ be an ontology and let $\Sigma_\mathcal{O}$ be the set of predicate and constant symbols occurring in $\mathcal{O}$. The algorithm first computes the set Γ of axioms in $\Phi_{OWL\,2\,QL}$ which can be built over $\Sigma_\mathcal{O}$, and then, for each axiom $\alpha \in \Gamma$ such that $\mathcal{O} \models \alpha$, adds α to the set $\mathsf{ES}(\mathcal{O}, OWL\,2\,QL)$. In practice, to check if $\mathcal{O} \models \alpha$ one can use an OWL 2 reasoner.

Since each invocation of the OWL 2 reasoner is N2ExpTime, the computation of the entailment set can be very costly [4].

A more efficient technique for its computation is given in [8], where the idea is to limit the number of invocations to the OWL 2 reasoner by exploiting the knowledge acquired through a preliminary exploration of the ontology. To understand the basic idea behind this technique, consider, for example, an ontology $\mathcal{O}$ that entails the inclusions $A_1 \sqsubseteq A_2$ and $P_1 \sqsubseteq P_2$, where A_1 and A_2 are concepts and P_1 and P_2 are roles. Exploiting these inclusions we can deduce the hierarchical structure of the general concepts that can be built on these four predicates. For instance, we know that $\exists P_2.A_2 \sqsubseteq \exists P_2$, that $\exists P_2.A_1 \sqsubseteq \exists P_2.A_2$, that $\exists P_1.A_1 \sqsubseteq \exists P_2.A_1$, and so on. To obtain the entailed inclusion axioms, we begin by invoking the OWL 2 reasoner, asking for the children of the general concepts which are in the highest position in the hierarchy. So we first compute the subsumees of $\exists P_2$ through the OWL 2 reasoner. If there are none, we avoid invoking the reasoner asking for the subsumees of $\exists P_2.A_2$ and so on. Regarding the entailed disjointness axioms, we follow the same approach but starting from the lowest positions in the hierarchy.

The following theorem establishes correctness and termination of algorithm *computeK Apx*.

Theorem 4. *Let $\mathcal{O}_S$ be a satisfiable OWL 2 ontology. computeK Apx($\mathcal{O}_S, k$) terminates and computes the k-approximation in OWL 2 QL of $\mathcal{O}_S$.*

Proof. (*sketch*) Termination of *computeK Apx*($\mathcal{O}_S, k$) directly follows from the fact that $\mathcal{O}_S$ is a finite set of axioms and that, for each $\mathcal{O}_i \in subset_k(\mathcal{O}_S)$, $\mathsf{ES}(\mathcal{O}_i, OWL\ 2\ QL)$ can be computed in finite time. The correctness of the algorithm directly follows from Theorem 3.

5 Experiments

In this section we present the experimental tests that we have performed for the approximation of a suite of OWL 2 ontologies into OWL 2 QL through the two notions of approximation we have introduced earlier.

We notice that by choosing a value for k different from $|\mathcal{O}_S|$, the computation of the entailment set becomes easier. However, observing Algorithm 1, the number of times that this step must be repeated can grow very quickly. In fact, the number of sets of axioms in $subset_k(\mathcal{O}_S)$ is equal to the binomial coefficient of $|\mathcal{O}_S|$ over k, and therefore for large ontologies this number can easily become enormous, and this can be in practice a critical obstacle in the computation of the k-approximation.

For this reason, in these experiments we have focused on comparing the GSA (k-approximation with $k = |\mathcal{O}_S|$) to the LSA (k-approximation with $k = 1$), and we reserve the study of efficient techniques for k-approximation with $1 < k < |\mathcal{O}_S|$ for future works. Furthermore, to provide a standard baseline against which to compare the results of the GSA and LSA, we have compared both our approaches with a syntactic sound approximation approach, consisting in first normalizing the axioms in the ontology and then eliminating the ones that are not syntactically compliant with OWL 2 QL. We will refer to this approach as "SYNT".

Table 1. Characteristics of the ontologies used in the GSA and LSA tests

Ontology	Expressiveness	Axioms	Concepts	Roles	Attributes	OWL2 QL Axioms
Homology	$\mathcal{ALC}$	83	66	0	0	83
Cabro	$\mathcal{ALCHIQ}$	100	59	13	0	99
Basic vertebrate anatomy	$\mathcal{SHIF}$	108	43	14	0	101
Fungal anatomy	$\mathcal{ALEI}+$	115	90	5	0	113
Pmr	$\mathcal{ALU}$	163	137	16	0	159
Ma	$\mathcal{ALE}+$	168	166	8	0	167
General formal Ontology	$\mathcal{SHIQ}$	212	45	41	0	167
Cog analysis	$\mathcal{SHIF(D)}$	224	92	37	9	213
Time event	$\mathcal{ALCROIQ(D)}$	229	104	28	7	170
Spatial	$\mathcal{ALEHI}+$	246	136	49	0	155
Translational medicine	$\mathcal{ALCRIF(D)}$	314	225	18	6	298
Biopax	$\mathcal{SHIN(D)}$	391	69	55	41	240
Vertebrate skeletal anatomy	$\mathcal{ALER}+$	455	314	26	0	434
Image	$\mathcal{S}$	548	624	2	0	524
Protein	$\mathcal{ALCF(D)}$	691	45	50	133	490
Pizza	$\mathcal{SHOIN}$	712	100	8	0	660
Ontology of physics for biology	$\mathcal{ALCHIQ(D)}$	954	679	33	3	847
Plant trait	$\mathcal{ALE}+$	1463	1317	4	0	1461
Dolce	$\mathcal{SHOIN(D)}$	1667	209	313	4	1445
Ont. of athletic events	$\mathcal{ALEH}$	1737	1441	15	1	1722
Neomark	$\mathcal{ALCHQ(D)}$	1755	55	105	488	842
Pato	$\mathcal{SH}$	1979	2378	36	0	1779
Protein Modification	$\mathcal{ALE}+$	1986	1338	8	0	1982
Po anatomy	$\mathcal{ALE}+$	2128	1294	11	0	2064
Lipid	$\mathcal{ALCHIN}$	2375	716	46	0	2076
Plant	$\mathcal{S}$	2615	1644	16	0	2534
Mosquito anatomy	$\mathcal{ALE}+$	2733	1864	5	0	2732
Idomal namespace	$\mathcal{ALER}+$	3467	2597	24	0	3462
Cognitive atlas	$\mathcal{ALC}$	4100	1701	6	0	3999
Genomic	$\mathcal{ALCQ}$	4322	2265	2	0	3224
Mosquito insecticide resistance	$\mathcal{ALE}+$	4413	4362	21	0	4409
Galen-A	$\mathcal{ALEHIF}+$	4979	2748	413	0	3506
Ni gene	$\mathcal{SH}$	8835	4835	8	0	8834
Fyp	$\mathcal{SH}$	15105	4751	69	0	12924
Fly anatomy	$\mathcal{SH}$	20356	8064	72	0	20353
EL-Galen	$\mathcal{ALEH}+$	36547	23136	950	0	25138
Galen full	$\mathcal{ALEHIF}+$	37696	23141	950	0	25613
Pr reasoned	$\mathcal{S}$	46929	35470	14	0	40031
Snomed fragment for FMA	$\mathcal{ALER}$	73543	52635	52	0	35004
Gene	$\mathcal{SH}$	73942	39160	12	0	73940
FMA OBO	$\mathcal{ALE}+$	119560	75139	2	0	119558

The suite of ontologies used during testing contains 41 ontologies and was assembled from the Bioportal ontology repository[2]. The ontologies that compose this suite were selected to test the scalability of our approaches both to larger ontologies and to ontologies formulated in more expressive languages. In Table 1 we present the most relevant metrics of these ontologies.

All tests were performed on a DELL Latitude E6320 notebook with Intel Core i7-2640M 2.8Ghz CPU and 4GB of RAM, running Microsoft Windows 7 Premium operating system, and Java 1.6 with 2GB of heap space. Timeout was set

---

[2] http://bioportal.bioontology.org/

at eight hours, and execution was aborted if the maximum available memory was exhausted. The tool used in the experiments and the suite of ontologies are available at `http://diag.uniroma1.it/~mora/ontology_approximation/iswc2014/`.

As mentioned in Section 4, the computation of the entailment set involves the use of an external OWL 2 reasoner. Therefore, the performance and the results of the computed approximations are greatly effected by the choice of the reasoner. For our tests, we have used the Pellet[3] OWL 2 reasoner (version v.2.3.0.6).

In Table 2 we present the results of the evaluation. An analysis of these results leads to the following observations.

Firstly, we were able to compute the GSA for 26 out of the 41 tested ontologies. For the remaining fifteen, this was not possible, either due to the size of the ontology, in terms of the number of its axioms, e.g., the FMA 2.0 or Gene ontologies, which have more than seventy thousand and one hundred thousand axioms, respectively, or due to its high expressivity, e.g., the Dolce ontology or the General formal ontology. The LSA approach is instead always feasible, it is quicker than the GSA approach for all but one of the tested ontologies, and it is overall very fast: no ontology took more than 250 seconds to approximate with the LSA.

Secondly, it is interesting to observe the comparison between the quality of the approximation that one can obtain through the LSA with respect to that obtained through the GSA. This relationship answers the question of whether the ontology obtained through the LSA (the "LSA ontology") is able to capture a significant portion of the one obtained through the GSA (the "GSA ontology"). Our tests in fact confirm that this is the case: out of the 26 ontologies for which we were able to compute the GSA, in only four cases the LSA ontology entails less than 60 percent of the axioms of the GSA ontology, while in twenty cases it entails more than 90 percent of them. The average percentage of axioms in the original ontologies entailed by the GSA ontologies is roughly 80 percent, and of the axioms of the GSA ontologies entailed by the LSA ontologies is roughly 87 percent.

Furthermore, the LSA provides a good approximation even for those ontologies for which the GSA is not computable. In fact, Table 3 shows the percentage of axioms of the original ontology that are entailed by the LSA ontology. Out of the twelve ontologies for which we were able to obtain this value (the remaining three ontologies caused an "out of memory" error), only in three cases it was less than 60 percent, while in four cases it was higher than 80 percent. These results are particularly interesting with respect to those ontologies for which the GSA approach is not feasible due to their complexity, as is the case for example for the Dolce ontology, for Galen-A, and for the Ontology of physics for biology. Indeed, even though these ontologies are expressed in highly expressive DL languages, the structure of the axioms that compose them is such that reasoning on each of them in isolation does not lead to much worse approximation results than reasoning on the ontology as a whole: for the nine smallest ontologies in Table 3, for which the GSA fails not because of the size of the ontology, the average percentage is 68.6.

---

[3] `http://clarkparsia.com/pellet/`

Table 2. Results of the GSA, LSA, and SYNT. The values represent, from left to right, the number of axioms in the ontology obtained through the GSA, the percentage of axioms of the original ontology that are entailed by the ontology obtained through the GSA, the number of axioms in the ontology obtained through the LSA, the percentage of axioms of the ontology obtained through the GSA that are entailed by the LSA, the number of axioms in the ontology obtained by the SYNT, the percentage of axioms of the ontology obtained through the GSA that are entailed by the ontology obtained through the SYNT, the percentage of axioms of the ontology obtained through the LSA that are entailed by the ontology obtained through the SYNT, and finally the GSA time and the LSA time (both in seconds).

Ontology	GSA axioms	GSA entails original (%)	LSA axioms	LSA entails GSA (%)	SYNT axioms	SYNT entails GSA (%)	SYNT entails LSA (%)	GSA time (s)	LSA time (s)
Homology	83	100	83	100	83	100	100	1	4
Cabro	233	96	121	100	100	100	100	4	2
Basic vertebrate anatomy	192	93	141	97	71	56	67	3	3
Fungal anatomy	318	98	140	69	113	69	100	2	2
Pmr	162	97	159	98	159	98	100	2	2
Ma	411	99	240	95	167	96	100	4	4
General formal ontology	–	–	286	–	177	–	100	–	6
Cog analysis	104407	75	474	46	215	1	82	36	7
Time event	93769	71	662	99	196	1	58	45	11
Spatial	510	63	371	86	155	42	52	9	4
Translational medicine	4089	86	505	99	275	30	64	19	7
Biopax	2182057	–	3217	–	251	–	81	–	11
Vertebrate skeletal anatomy	9488	95	581	92	434	57	99	27	5
Image	1016	95	596	98	571	98	100	178	5
Protein	–	–	10789	–	475	–	88	–	20
Pizza	2587	91	755	92	678	92	99	7	4
Ont. of physics for biology	1789821	–	1505	–	1241	–	100	–	7
Plant trait	2370	99	1496	99	1461	100	100	10	9
Dolce	–	–	2959	–	1555	–	100	–	8
Ontology of athletic events	5073	99	2392	99	1731	92	100	42	9
Neomark	–	–	39807	–	1723	–	63	–	50
Pato	4066	89	2209	100	1976	78	99	99	18
Protein Modification	2195	99	2001	100	1982	100	100	12	19
Po anatomy	11486	96	2783	77	2078	78	100	455	18
Lipid	14659	87	3165	97	2759	89	97	47	10
Plant	18375	96	3512	80	2574	81	100	929	15
Mosquito anatomy	21303	99	4277	43	2732	44	100	214	16
Idomal namespace	67417	99	4259	98	3461	59	100	496	16
Cognitive atlas	7449	97	5324	100	1364	26	30	162	17
Genomic	–	–	86735	–	85037	–	98	–	54
Mosquito insecticide res.	6794	99	4502	100	4409	100	100	86	14
Galen-A	–	–	8568	–	4971	–	90	–	26
Ni gene	46148	99	10415	90	8834	91	100	472	32
Fyp	–	–	19675	–	11800	–	82	–	43
Fly anatomy	460849	99	28436	67	20346	67	100	25499	45
EL-Galen	–	–	70272	–	43804	–	89	–	59
Galen full	–	–	72172	–	44279	–	89	–	61
Pr reasoned	–	–	56085	–	47662	–	100	–	93
Snomed fragment for FMA	–	–	140629	–	101860	–	76	–	250
Gene	–	–	86292	–	73940	–	100	–	178
FMA OBO	–	–	143306	–	119558	–	100	–	113

Finally, both the GSA and LSA compare favorably against the syntactic sound approximation approach. In fact, the average percentage of axioms in the LSA and GSA ontologies that are entailed by the ontologies obtained through the SYNT approach are respectively roughly 90 percent and 72 percent. While the latter result is to be expected, the former is quite significant, even more so when one considers that the LSA is very

Table 3. LSA results for ontologies for which the GSA is not computable

Ontology	Original axioms	LSA axioms	LSA entails original (%)	LSA time (s)
General formal ontology	212	264	67	6
Biopax	391	3204	53	11
Protein	691	10720	47	20
Ontology of physics for biology	954	1074	75	7
Dolce	1667	2914	78	8
Neomark	1755	38966	46	50
Genomic	4322	9844	65	54
Galen-A	4979	8568	70	26
Fyp	15105	19672	85	43
EL-Galen	36547	70272	–	59
Galen full	37696	72172	–	61
Pr reasoned	46929	55391	83	93
SNOMED fragment for FMA	73543	140629	–	250
Gene	73942	86289	99	178
FMA OBO	119560	143306	99	113

fast. Indeed, a "gain" of 10 percent of axiom entailments by the LSA with respect to the SYNT in the case of large ontologies such as Galen and Snomed translates to tens of thousands of preserved axioms in very little computation time.

In conclusion, the results gathered from these tests corroborate the usefulness of both the global semantic approximation and the local semantic approximation approaches. The former provides a maximal sound approximation in the target language of the original approach, and is in practice computable in a reasonable amount of time for the majority of the tested ontologies. The latter instead represents a less optimal but still very effective solution for those ontologies for which the GSA approach goes beyond the capabilities of the currently-available ontology reasoners.

6 Conclusions

In this paper we have addressed the problem of ontology approximation in Description Logics and OWL, presenting (i) a parameterized semantics for computing sound approximations of ontologies, (ii) algorithms for the computation of approximations (the GSA and the LSA) of OWL 2 ontologies in OWL 2 QL, and (iii) an extensive experimental evaluation of the above techniques, which empirically proves the validity of our approach.

The present work can be extended in several ways. First, while we have focused on sound approximations, it would be interesting to also consider complete approximations of ontologies. Also, we would like to study the development of techniques for k-approximations different from GSA and LSA, i.e., for k such that $1 < k < |\mathcal{O}_S|$, as well as to analyze the possibility of integrating ontology module extraction techniques in our approach. Then, this work has not addressed the case when there are differences in the semantic assumptions between the source and the target ontology languages. For instance, differently from OWL 2 and its profiles, some DLs (e.g., $DL\text{-}Lite_A$ [15]) adopt the Unique Name Assumption (UNA). This makes our approach not directly applicable, for instance, if we consider OWL 2 as the source language and $DL\text{-}Lite_A$ as the target language. The reason is that the UNA implies some axioms (inequalities between individuals) that can be expressed in OWL 2 but cannot be expressed in $DL\text{-}Lite_A$. We aim at extending our approach to deal with the presence of such semantic discrepancies in the ontology languages. Finally, we are very interested in generalizing our approach to a full-fledged ontology-based data access scenario [15], in which data sources are connected through declarative mappings to the ontology. In that context, it might be interesting to use both the ontology and the mappings in the target OBDA specification to approximate a given ontology in the source OBDA specification.

Acknowledgments. This research has been partially supported by the EU under FP7 project Optique (grant n. FP7-318338).

References

1. Antonioli, N., Castanø, F., Civili, C., Coletta, S., Grossi, S., Lembo, D., Lenzerini, M., Poggi, A., Savo, D.F., Virardi, E.: Ontology-based data access: the experience at the Italian Department of Treasury. In: Proc. of the Industrial Track of CAiSE 2013. CEUR, vol. 1017, pp. 9–16 (2013), ceur-ws.org
2. Artale, A., Calvanese, D., Kontchakov, R., Zakharyaschev, M.: The DL-Lite family and relations. J. of Artificial Intelligence Research 36, 1–69 (2009)
3. Baader, F., Calvanese, D., McGuinness, D., Nardi, D., Patel-Schneider, P.F. (eds.): The Description Logic Handbook: Theory, Implementation and Applications. Cambridge University Press (2003)
4. Botoeva, E., Calvanese, D., Rodriguez-Muro, M.: Expressive approximations in DL-Lite ontologies. In: Dicheva, D., Dochev, D. (eds.) AIMSA 2010. LNCS (LNAI), vol. 6304, pp. 21–31. Springer, Heidelberg (2010)
5. Calvanese, D., De Giacomo, G., Lembo, D., Lenzerini, M., Rosati, R.: Tractable reasoning and efficient query answering in description logics: The $DL\text{-}Lite$ family. J. of Automated Reasoning 39(3), 385–429 (2007)
6. Calvanese, D., et al.: Optique: OBDA Solution for Big Data. In: Cimiano, P., Fernández, M., Lopez, V., Schlobach, S., Völker, J. (eds.) ESWC 2013. LNCS, vol. 7955, pp. 293–295. Springer, Heidelberg (2013)
7. Civili, C., Console, M., De Giacomo, G., Lembo, D., Lenzerini, M., Lepore, L., Mancini, R., Poggi, A., Rosati, R., Ruzzi, M., Santarelli, V., Savo, D.F.: MASTRO STUDIO: Managing ontology-based data access applications. PVLDB 6, 1314–1317 (2013)
8. Console, M., Santarelli, V., Savo, D.F.: Efficient approximation in DL-Lite of OWL 2 ontologies. In: Proc. of DL 2013. CEUR Workshop Proceedings, vol. 1014, pp. 132–143. ceur-ws.org (2013)
9. Hitzler, P., Krötzsch, M., Parsia, B., Patel-Schneider, P.F., Rudolph, S.: OWL 2 Web Ontology Language: Primer. W3C Recommendation (2012), http://www.w3.org/TR/2012/REC-owl2-primer-20121211/
10. Horrocks, I., Kutz, O., Sattler, U.: The even more irresistible $\mathcal{SROIQ}$. In: Proc. of KR 2006, pp. 57–67 (2006)

11. Lutz, C., Seylan, I., Wolter, F.: An Automata-Theoretic Approach to Uniform Interpolation and Approximation in the Description Logic EL. In: Proc. of KR 2012. AAAI Press (2012)
12. Motik, B., Grau, B.C., Horrocks, I., Wu, Z., Fokoue, A., Lutz, C.: Owl 2 web ontology language: Profiles, 2nd edn. W3C Recommendation (2012), http://www.w3.org/TR/owl2-profiles/
13. Motik, B., Parsia, B., Patel-Schneider, P.F.: OWL 2 Web Ontology Language Structural Specification and Functional-Style Syntax. W3C Recommendation (2012), http://www.w3.org/TR/2012/REC-owl2-syntax-20121211/
14. Pan, J.Z., Thomas, E.: Approximating OWL-DL ontologies. In: Proc. of AAAI 2007, pp. 1434–1439 (2007)
15. Poggi, A., Lembo, D., Calvanese, D., De Giacomo, G., Lenzerini, M., Rosati, R.: Linking data to ontologies. In: Spaccapietra, S. (ed.) Journal on Data Semantics X. LNCS, vol. 4900, pp. 133–173. Springer, Heidelberg (2008)
16. Rodríguez-Muro, M., Kontchakov, R., Zakharyaschev, M.: Ontology-based data access: Ontop of databases. In: Alani, H., et al. (eds.) ISWC 2013, Part I. LNCS, vol. 8218, pp. 558–573. Springer, Heidelberg (2013)
17. Tserendorj, T., Rudolph, S., Krötzsch, M., Hitzler, P.: Approximate OWL-reasoning with Screech. In: Calvanese, D., Lausen, G. (eds.) RR 2008. LNCS, vol. 5341, pp. 165–180. Springer, Heidelberg (2008)
18. Wache, H., Groot, P., Stuckenschmidt, H.: Scalable instance retrieval for the semantic web by approximation. In: Dean, M., Guo, Y., Jun, W., Kaschek, R., Krishnaswamy, S., Pan, Z., Sheng, Q.Z. (eds.) WISE 2005 Workshops. LNCS, vol. 3807, pp. 245–254. Springer, Heidelberg (2005)

Abstraction Refinement for Ontology Materialization

Birte Glimm[1], Yevgeny Kazakov[1], Thorsten Liebig[2],
Trung-Kien Tran[1], and Vincent Vialard[2]

[1] University of Ulm, Ulm, Germany
{firstname.lastname}@uni-ulm.de
[2] derivo GmbH, Ulm, Germany
{lastname}@derivo.de

Abstract. We present a new procedure for ontology materialization (computing all entailed instances of every atomic concept) in which reasoning over a
large ABox is reduced to reasoning over a smaller "abstract" ABox. The abstract
ABox is obtained as the result of a fixed-point computation involving two stages:
1) abstraction: partition the individuals into equivalence classes based on told
information and use one representative individual per equivalence class, and 2)
refinement: iteratively split (refine) the equivalence classes, when new assertions
are derived that distinguish individuals within the same class. We prove that the
method is complete for Horn $\mathcal{ALCHOI}$ ontologies, that is, all entailed instances
will be derived once the fixed-point is reached. We implement the procedure in
a new database-backed reasoning system and evaluate it empirically on existing
ontologies with large ABoxes. We demonstrate that the obtained abstract ABoxes
are significantly smaller than the original ones and can be computed with few refinement steps.

1   Introduction

Ontology based data access (OBDA) is an increasingly popular paradigm in the area
of knowledge representation and information systems. In ODBA, a TBox with background knowledge is used to enrich and integrate large, incomplete, and possibly semi-
structured data, which users can then access via queries. To efficiently handle large data
sets (called ABoxes), OBDA approaches assume that the data is stored in a database
or triple store. Nevertheless, the assumption of complete data that is typically made in
databases does not hold and reasoning is required to compute the (entailed) types of
individuals or answers to queries in general.

Different reasoning approaches have been developed in the OBDA context: (i) Query
rewriting or backward-chaining approaches answer a query, by "compiling" the background knowledge of the TBox into the query [2,12]. The analysis of which languages
are FO rewritable (i.e., which queries can be answered by query rewriting) inspired
the development of DL-Lite [2] and resulted in the OWL QL profile [11] of the Web
Ontology Language OWL 2. (ii) Materialization or forward-chaining techniques take
the opposite approach by pre-computing all entailed information upfront, independent
of the queries [1,14,8]. After extending the ABox with all pre-computed facts, the unmodified queries can be evaluated over the enriched data only (i.e., without considering
the schema). The idea of query answering via materialization is directly present in the

P. Mika et al. (Eds.) ISWC 2014, Part II, LNCS 8797, pp. 180–195, 2014.

OWL RL profile [11], which specifies a suitable set of materialization rules. (iii) Finally, also combined approaches have been proposed, which allow for smaller rewritten queries by materializing some (but not all) entailments [10,9] or for computing the materialization dynamically as required for a given query.

In this paper, we focus on the materialization of entailed facts for large ABoxes that are stored in a (graph)database or triple store and where the schema is expressed in terms of a Horn $\mathcal{ALCHOI}$ ontology. For full OWL RL support, functionality and property chains have to be encoded, but Horn $\mathcal{ALCHOI}$ also goes beyond OWL RL (and OWL QL). For example, existential quantification (*owl:someValuesFrom*) is fully supported, which is a feature that is difficult for standard materialization and rewriting approaches. While the principle of materialization is conceptually simple, it requires considerable computational resources in particular for large ABoxes or expressive TBox languages. Furthermore, reasoners for the language we tackle, are typically main memory and refutation-based, i.e., to show that an individual a is an instance of the concept C, the reasoner tries to derive a contradiction for the ontology (temporarily) extended with $\neg C(a)$ (asserting that a is *not* an instance of C). Consequently, handling large ABoxes directly is infeasible.

Our approach for handling large ABoxes is based on the assumption that individuals with similar asserted types are likely to have the same inferred types. We group such individuals into equivalence classes and compute the types just for one representative individual. For building the initial equivalence classes, we also consider the role (property) assertions in the ABox, but we do not simply merge individuals. Instead, we iteratively compute a so-called *abstraction* that contains one representative individual for each equivalence class plus representative individuals for its direct role successors and predecessors in the ABox. We show how derivations for the latter individuals can be used in the refinement process to split equivalence classes for individuals that no longer have the same assertions. The number of individuals in the abstraction is always bounded exponentially in the number of different concepts and roles and linearly in the size of the original ABox; hence the abstraction is relatively small when the number of individuals is much larger than the number of concepts and roles used in the ontology.

We implement the technique in a database-backed system that interacts with a highly optimized in-memory reasoner that materializes the abstract ABox. The database engine needs to support only simple operations and does not require any knowledge of the TBox. We show that the procedure is sound and it is complete for computing the entailed types of individuals in Horn $\mathcal{ALCHOI}$ ontologies.

The paper is structured as follows: We next introduce directly related approaches. In Section 3, we present some preliminaries and continue with the presentation of the theoretical foundation of our approach in Section 4. In Section 5, we prove completeness of our procedure. In Section 6, we evaluate the procedure on a range of real-world ontologies with large ABoxes, and conclude in Section 7. Full proofs and further details are available in a technical report [5].

2   Related Work

In this section, we focus on work that is closely related to our aim of abstracting the ABox. The SHER approach [4,3] merges similar individuals to obtain a compressed, so-called *summary* ABox, which is then used for (refutation-based) consistency checking. The technique (as well as ours) is based on the observation that individuals with the same asserted types are likely to have the same entailed types. Since merging in SHER is only based on asserted concepts, the resulting summary ABox might be inconsistent even if the original ABox is consistent w.r.t. the TBox. To remedy this, justifications [6] are used to decide which merges caused the inconsistency and to refine the summary accordingly. Justification-based refinements are also needed for query answering since SHER is not a materialization approach and performs reasoning at query time. We avoid justification computation by partitioning individuals of the same type into equivalence classes. Such partitioning guarantees the soundness of derived atomic concept assertions. We also have to perform refinement steps, but the refinement is to incrementally derive more consequences. What is computed before remains sound.

Wandelt and Möller propose a technique for (refutation-based) instance retrieval over $\mathcal{SHI}$ ontologies based on modularization [15,16]. As an optimization and similar to our approach, they group individuals into equivalence classes based on the asserted types of an individual, its successors, predecessors and the asserted types of the successors and predecessors.[1] The assertions that define the equivalence class of an individual are used for finding sound entailments. For checking entailments that cannot be read-off from these assertions, it might be necessary to fall-back to (refutation-based) reasoning over the (possibly large) ABox module for the individual. Instead of falling back to modules of the original ABox, we propose an iterative refinement process for the equivalence classes. The refinement is based on semantic criteria, i.e., only when individuals are semantically distinguishable, we refine the equivalence class, whereas the modules defined by Wandelt and Möller are syntactically defined.

3   Preliminaries

We first define the syntax and semantics of the Description Logic (DL) $\mathcal{ALCHOI}$, which is the main ontology language we consider in this paper.

The syntax of $\mathcal{ALCHOI}$ is defined using a vocabulary (signature) consisting of countably infinite disjoint sets N_C of *concept names*, N_O of *nominals*, N_R of *role names*, and N_I of *individual names*. Note that concepts are called classes and roles are called properties in OWL. Complex *concepts* and *axioms* are defined recursively in Table 1. An *ontology* $\mathcal{O}$ is a finite set of axioms and we often write $\mathcal{O} = \mathcal{A} \cup \mathcal{T}$, where $\mathcal{A}$ is an *ABox* consisting of the concept and role assertions in $\mathcal{O}$ and $\mathcal{T}$ a *TBox* consisting of the concept and role inclusions in $\mathcal{O}$. We use $\mathsf{con}(\mathcal{O})$, $\mathsf{rol}(\mathcal{O})$, $\mathsf{ind}(\mathcal{O})$ for the sets of concept names, role names, and individual names occurring in $\mathcal{O}$, respectively.

An *interpretation* $\mathcal{I} = (\Delta^{\mathcal{I}}, \cdot^{\mathcal{I}})$ consists of a non-empty set $\Delta^{\mathcal{I}}$, the *domain* of $\mathcal{I}$, and an *interpretation function* $\cdot^{\mathcal{I}}$, that assigns to each $A \in N_C$ a subset $A^{\mathcal{I}} \subseteq \Delta^{\mathcal{I}}$, to each $o \in N_O$ a singleton subset $o^{\mathcal{I}} \subseteq \Delta^{\mathcal{I}}$, $\|o^{\mathcal{I}}\| = 1$, to each $R \in N_R$ a binary relation $R^{\mathcal{I}} \subseteq \Delta^{\mathcal{I}} \times \Delta^{\mathcal{I}}$, and to each $a \in N_I$ an element $a^{\mathcal{I}} \in \Delta^{\mathcal{I}}$. This assignment is extended to complex concepts as shown in Table 1. $\mathcal{I}$ *satisfies* an axiom α (written $\mathcal{I} \models \alpha$) if the corresponding condition in Table 1 holds. $\mathcal{I}$ is a *model* of an ontology $\mathcal{O}$ (written $\mathcal{I} \models \mathcal{O}$) if $\mathcal{I}$ satisfies all axioms in $\mathcal{O}$. We say that $\mathcal{O}$ *is consistent* if $\mathcal{O}$ has a model.

---

[1] We ignore the types of successors and predecessors to achieve larger equivalence classes.

Table 1. The syntax and semantics of $\mathcal{ALCHOI}$

	Syntax	Semantics
Roles:		
atomic role	R	$R^{\mathcal{I}} \subseteq \Delta^{\mathcal{I}} \times \Delta^{\mathcal{I}}$ (given by $\mathcal{I}$)
inverse role	R^-	$\{\langle e, d \rangle \mid \langle d, e \rangle \in R^{\mathcal{I}}\}$
Concepts:		
atomic concept	A	$A \subseteq \Delta^{\mathcal{I}}$ (given by $\mathcal{I}$)
nominal	o	$o^{\mathcal{I}} \subseteq \Delta^{\mathcal{I}}, \|o^{\mathcal{I}}\| = 1$ (given by $\mathcal{I}$)
top	$\top$	$\Delta^{\mathcal{I}}$
bottom	$\bot$	$\emptyset$
negation	$\neg C$	$\Delta^{\mathcal{I}} \setminus C^{\mathcal{I}}$
conjunction	$C \sqcap D$	$C^{\mathcal{I}} \cap D^{\mathcal{I}}$
disjunction	$C \sqcup D$	$C^{\mathcal{I}} \cup D^{\mathcal{I}}$
existential restriction	$\exists R.C$	$\{d \mid \exists e \in C^{\mathcal{I}} : \langle d, e \rangle \in R^{\mathcal{I}}\}$
universal restriction	$\forall R.C$	$\{d \mid \forall e \in \Delta^{\mathcal{I}} : \langle d, e \rangle \in R^{\mathcal{I}} \to e \in C^{\mathcal{I}}\}$
Axioms:		
concept inclusion	$C \sqsubseteq D$	$C^{\mathcal{I}} \subseteq D^{\mathcal{I}}$
role inclusion	$R \sqsubseteq S$	$R^{\mathcal{I}} \subseteq S^{\mathcal{I}}$
concept assertion	$C(a)$	$a^{\mathcal{I}} \in C^{\mathcal{I}}$
role assertion	$R(a, b)$	$\langle a^{\mathcal{I}}, b^{\mathcal{I}} \rangle \in R^{\mathcal{I}}$

We say that $\mathcal{O}$ *entails* an axiom α (written $\mathcal{O} \models \alpha$), if every model of $\mathcal{O}$ satisfies α. We say that $\mathcal{O}$ is *concept materialized* if $A(a) \in \mathcal{O}$ whenever $\mathcal{O} \models A(a)$, $A \in \mathsf{con}(\mathcal{O})$ and $a \in \mathsf{ind}(\mathcal{O})$; $\mathcal{O}$ is *role materialized* if $R(a, b) \in \mathcal{O}$ whenever $\mathcal{O} \models R(a, b)$, $R \in \mathsf{rol}(\mathcal{O})$, $a, b \in \mathsf{ind}(\mathcal{O})$; $\mathcal{O}$ is *materialized* if it is both concept and role materialized.

Remark 1. Some definitions do not present nominals as primitive symbols, but use a special *nominal constructor* $\{a\}$ with individual a (in this case, $\{a\}^{\mathcal{I}} = \{a^{\mathcal{I}}\}$). We can easily convert such ontologies to our representation by renaming every nominal $\{a\}$ with the corresponding nominal symbol o_a and adding a concept assertion $o_a(a)$. This transformation is a conservative extension, i.e., it preserves all original entailments.

4 Computing ABox Materialization by Abstraction

The typical OBDA scenario is such that the ABox contains a large number of individuals and its size is significantly larger than the size of the TBox. Hence, the number of different concept names is typically much smaller than the number of different individuals, which also means that many individuals are instances of the same concepts. If we can identify individuals that yield the same consequences, we can compute the materialization by computing entailed consequences only for representative individuals.

4.1 Bi-homomorphic Individuals and Individual Types

In order to (syntactically) characterize individuals that yield the same consequences, we study structure-preserving transformations of ABoxes.

Definition 1. *Let $\mathcal{A}$ and $\mathcal{B}$ be two ABoxes and h: $\text{ind}(\mathcal{A}) \to \text{ind}(\mathcal{B})$ a mapping from the individuals in $\mathcal{A}$ to individuals in $\mathcal{B}$. We extend h to axioms in a straightforward way: $h(C(a)) = C(h(a))$, $h(R(a,b)) = R(h(a), h(b))$, and $h(\alpha) = \alpha$ for other axioms α. We say that h is a* homomorphism *(from $\mathcal{A}$ to $\mathcal{B}$) if $h(\mathcal{A}) \subseteq \mathcal{B}$. An individual a in $\mathcal{A}$ is* homomorphic *to an individual b in $\mathcal{B}$ if there exists a homomorphism h from $\mathcal{A}$ to $\mathcal{B}$ such that $h(a) = b$; in addition, if b is homomorphic to a, then a and b are* bi-homomorphic.

Example 1. Consider the ABox $\mathcal{A} = \{R(a,a), R(a,b), R(b,b)\}$. Then the mappings $h_1 = \{a \mapsto b,\ b \mapsto b\}$ and $h_2 = \{a \mapsto a,\ b \mapsto a\}$ are homomorphisms from $\mathcal{A}$ to $\mathcal{A}$. Since $h_1(a) = b$ and $h_2(b) = a$, the individuals a and b are bi-homomorphic. Note that there is no *isomorphism* h from $\mathcal{A}$ to $\mathcal{A}$ (a bijective homomorphism such that its inverse is also a homomorphism) such that $h(a) = b$ or $h(b) = a$.

It is easy to show that entailed axioms are preserved under homomorphisms between ABoxes. In particular, bi-homomorphic individuals are instances of the same concepts.

Lemma 1. *Let h: $\text{ind}(\mathcal{A}) \to \text{ind}(\mathcal{B})$ be a homomorphism between ABoxes $\mathcal{A}$ and $\mathcal{B}$. Then for every TBox $\mathcal{T}$ and every axiom α, $\mathcal{A} \cup \mathcal{T} \models \alpha$ implies $\mathcal{B} \cup \mathcal{T} \models h(\alpha)$.*

Proof. We show that Lemma 1 even holds for $\mathcal{SROIQ}$ without unique name assumption. Suppose that $\mathcal{A} \cup \mathcal{T} \models \alpha$. Then $h(\mathcal{A} \cup \mathcal{T}) \models h(\alpha)$. Since $h(\mathcal{A} \cup \mathcal{T}) = h(\mathcal{A}) \cup h(\mathcal{T}) = h(\mathcal{A}) \cup \mathcal{T} \subseteq \mathcal{B} \cup \mathcal{T}$, by monotonicity we obtain $\mathcal{B} \cup \mathcal{T} \models h(\alpha)$.   □

Corollary 1. *If individuals a and b in an ABox $\mathcal{A}$ are bi-homomorphic, then for every TBox $\mathcal{T}$ and every concept C, we have $\mathcal{A} \cup \mathcal{T} \models C(a)$ if and only if $\mathcal{A} \cup \mathcal{T} \models C(b)$.*

If an ABox does not have role assertions, the bi-homomorphic individuals are exactly those that have the same concepts in the assertions. Hence, we can identify bi-homomorphic individuals by just looking at their *types*—the set of concepts of which the individual is an (asserted) instance. Clearly, the number of different types, and hence the maximal number of individuals that are not bi-homomorphic to each other is at most exponential in the number of different concepts used in the ABox. With role assertions, however, we cannot decide whether individuals are bi-homomorphic by just looking at their assertions. In fact, the number of non-bi-homomorphic individuals can be arbitrary large even if just one role is used in role assertions and there are no concept assertions.

Example 2. Consider an ABox $\mathcal{A} = \{R(a_{i-1}, a_i) \mid 1 < i \leq n\}$. It can be easily shown that the only homomorphism $h : \text{ind}(\mathcal{A}) \to \text{ind}(\mathcal{A})$ from $\mathcal{A}$ to $\mathcal{A}$ is the identity $h = \{a_i \mapsto a_i \mid 1 \leq i \leq n\}$, i.e., no different individuals in $\mathcal{A}$ are bi-homomorphic to each other. In fact, it is easy to find a TBox $\mathcal{T}$ with which all individuals in $\mathcal{A}$ entail different sets of assertions. Indeed, take $\mathcal{T} = \{\top \sqsubseteq A_1, A_{i-1} \sqsubseteq \forall R.A_i, 1 < i \leq n\}$. Then we have $\mathcal{A} \cup \mathcal{T} \models A_j(a_i)$ if and only if $1 \leq j \leq i \leq n$.

From Example 2 one can see that with many role assertions, an ABox is less likely to have many bi-homomorphic individuals. Note from Corollary 1 that if two individuals are bi-homomorphic, then they entail the same assertions w.r.t. *every* TBox. This property is too strong for our purpose, as we need to deal with just one given TBox. It can be that many (non-bi-homomorphic) individuals are still materialized in the same way. To take this into account, instead of partitioning the individuals in equivalence classes according to the bi-homomorphism relation, we start with an approximation to this relation, which makes more individuals equivalent. As soon as entailed assertions are obtained using a reasoner that distinguish elements within the same equivalence class, we refine our approximation and repeat the process until the fixpoint.

Definition 2. *Let $\mathcal{A}$ be an ABox. The* type *of an individual a (w.r.t. $\mathcal{A}$) is a triple* $\mathrm{tp}(a) = (\mathrm{tp}_\downarrow(a), \mathrm{tp}_\rightarrow(a), \mathrm{tp}_\leftarrow(a))$ *where* $\mathrm{tp}_\downarrow(a) = \{C \mid C(a) \in \mathcal{A}\}$, $\mathrm{tp}_\rightarrow(a) = \{R \mid \exists b : R(a, b) \in \mathcal{A}\}$, *and* $\mathrm{tp}_\leftarrow(a) = \{S \mid \exists c : S(c, a) \in \mathcal{A}\}$.

Intuitively, the type of an individual is obtained by considering all assertions in which this individual occurs in the ABox, and ignoring all other individuals in these assertions. Note that bi-homomorphic individuals have the same types, so the relation between individuals of the same types is an approximation to the bi-homomorphism relation.

4.2 Abstraction of an ABox

If we compress the ABox by simply merging all individuals with the same type into one, we might obtain unexpected entailments, even if all individuals are bi-homomorphic.

Example 3. Consider the following ABox $\mathcal{A} = \{R(a, b), R(b, a)\}$. Clearly, a and b are bi-homomorphic in $\mathcal{A}$. Let $\mathcal{B} = \{R(a, a)\}$ be obtained from $\mathcal{A}$ by replacing individual b with a, and let $\mathcal{T} = \{\top \sqsubseteq B \sqcup C, \exists R.B \sqsubseteq C\}$. It is easy to check that $\mathcal{B} \cup \mathcal{T} \models C(a)$, but $\mathcal{A} \cup \mathcal{T} \not\models C(a)$ (and hence $\mathcal{A} \cup \mathcal{T} \not\models C(b)$).

We could follow the approach in the SHER system and compute justifications for entailed assertions to determine which individuals should not be merged, but our goal is to avoid such computationally expensive operations. Instead of merging all individuals with the same type into one, we realize every individual type in our *abstract ABox*. With abstract ABoxes defined as follows, we can guarantee that assertions that are entailed for the representative individuals also hold for the original individuals.

Definition 3 (ABox Abstraction). *The* abstraction *of an ABox $\mathcal{A}$ is an ABox* $\mathcal{B} = \bigcup_{a \in \mathrm{ind}(\mathcal{A})} \mathcal{B}_{\mathrm{tp}(a)}$, *where for each type* $\mathrm{tp} = (\mathrm{tp}_\downarrow, \mathrm{tp}_\rightarrow, \mathrm{tp}_\leftarrow)$, *we define* $\mathcal{B}_{\mathrm{tp}} = \{C(x_{\mathrm{tp}}) \mid C \in \mathrm{tp}_\downarrow\} \cup \{R(x_{\mathrm{tp}}, y_{\mathrm{tp}}^R) \mid R \in \mathrm{tp}_\rightarrow\} \cup \{S(z_{\mathrm{tp}}^S, x_{\mathrm{tp}}) \mid S \in \mathrm{tp}_\leftarrow\}$, *where x_{tp}, y_{tp}^R, and z_{tp}^S are fresh distinguished abstract individuals.*

Intuitively, the abstraction of an ABox is a disjoint union of small ABoxes witnessing each individual type realized in the ABox.

Example 4. Consider the ABox $\mathcal{A} = \{A(a), A(d), R(a, b), R(a, e), R(b, c), R(b, e), R(c, a), R(d, c), R(e, d)\}$. We have $\mathrm{tp}(b) = \mathrm{tp}(c) = \mathrm{tp}(e) = \mathrm{tp}_1 = (\emptyset, \{R\}, \{R\})$ and $\mathrm{tp}(a) = \mathrm{tp}(d) = \mathrm{tp}_2 = (\{A\}, \{R\}, \{R\})$. The abstraction of $\mathcal{A}$ is $\mathcal{B} = \mathcal{B}_{\mathrm{tp}_1} \cup \mathcal{B}_{\mathrm{tp}_2}$ with $\mathcal{B}_{\mathrm{tp}_1} = \{R(x_{\mathrm{tp}_1}, y_{\mathrm{tp}_1}^R), R(z_{\mathrm{tp}_1}^R, x_{\mathrm{tp}_1})\}$, $\mathcal{B}_{\mathrm{tp}_2} = \{A(x_{\mathrm{tp}_2}), R(x_{\mathrm{tp}_2}, y_{\mathrm{tp}_2}^R), R(z_{\mathrm{tp}_2}^R, x_{\mathrm{tp}_2})\}$.

The following lemma shows the soundness of concept assertions derived from the abstraction.

Lemma 2. *Let $\mathcal{A}$ be an ABox, $\mathcal{B}$ its abstraction, and $\mathcal{T}$ a TBox. Then for every type* $\mathrm{tp} = (\mathrm{tp}_\downarrow, \mathrm{tp}_\rightarrow, \mathrm{tp}_\leftarrow)$, *every $a \in \mathrm{ind}(\mathcal{A})$ with $\mathrm{tp}(a) = \mathrm{tp}$ w.r.t. $\mathcal{A}$, and every concept C:*

(1) $\mathcal{B} \cup \mathcal{T} \models C(x_{\mathrm{tp}})$ implies $\mathcal{A} \cup \mathcal{T} \models C(a)$,
(2) $\mathcal{B} \cup \mathcal{T} \models C(y_{\mathrm{tp}}^R)$ and $R(a, b) \in \mathcal{A}$ implies $\mathcal{A} \cup \mathcal{T} \models C(b)$, and
(3) $\mathcal{B} \cup \mathcal{T} \models C(z_{\mathrm{tp}}^S)$ and $S(c, a) \in \mathcal{A}$ implies $\mathcal{A} \cup \mathcal{T} \models C(c)$.

Proof. Consider all mappings $h : \mathrm{ind}(\mathcal{B}) \to \mathrm{ind}(\mathcal{A})$ such that:

$$h(x_{\mathrm{tp}}) \in \{a \in \mathrm{ind}(\mathcal{A}) \mid \mathrm{tp}(a) = \mathrm{tp}\},$$
$$h(y_{\mathrm{tp}}^R) \in \{b \mid R(h(x_{\mathrm{tp}}), b) \in \mathcal{A}\}, \text{ and}$$
$$h(z_{\mathrm{tp}}^S) \in \{c \mid S(c, h(x_{\mathrm{tp}})) \in \mathcal{A}\}.$$

Clearly, $h(\mathcal{B}) \subseteq \mathcal{A}$ for every such mapping h. Furthermore, for every $a \in \mathrm{ind}(\mathcal{A})$, every $R(a, b) \in \mathcal{A}$ and every $S(c, a) \in \mathcal{A}$, there exists h with $h(x_{\mathrm{tp}}) = a$, $h(y_{\mathrm{tp}}^R) = b$, and $h(z_{\mathrm{tp}}^S) = c$ for $\mathrm{tp} = \mathrm{tp}(a)$. Hence, claims (1)–(3) follow by Lemma 1. $\qquad\square$

4.3   Abstraction Refinement

Note that the individuals from an ABox $\mathcal{A}$ may correspond to several abstract individuals in the ABox abstraction $\mathcal{B}$: Each individual a corresponds to the abstract individual x_{tp} for $\mathrm{tp} = \mathrm{tp}(a)$. In addition, if $R(b, a) \in \mathcal{A}$ or $S(a, b) \in \mathcal{A}$ for some individual b, then a also corresponds to y_{tp}^R and z_{tp}^S respectively for $\mathrm{tp} = \mathrm{tp}(b)$. The additional individuals y_{tp}^R and z_{tp}^S were introduced intentionally to refine the initial abstraction when new assertions of abstract individuals are derived, which in turn, can be used to derive new assertions of individuals in $\mathcal{A}$. Specifically, assume that we have materialized all entailed atomic assertions for the abstract ABox $\mathcal{B}$ w.r.t. the TBox using a reasoner. By Lemma 2, the corresponding assertions must also be entailed in the original ABox $\mathcal{A}$. In particular, by case (1), the new assertions computed for the individual x_{tp}, also hold for every individual a in $\mathcal{A}$ with $\mathrm{tp}(a) = \mathrm{tp}$. If we add all such assertions to the original ABox $\mathcal{A}$, these individuals would still have the same types, so even by building a new abstraction for the extended ABox, we would not derive new assertions for the abstraction. On the other hand, if we add the new assertion according to cases (2) and (3) of Lemma 2, we may obtain different assertions for individuals that previously had the same types. Indeed, if $R(a, b) \in \mathcal{A}$, and we have derived a new assertion $A(b)$ using case (2) of the lemma, then it is not necessary that a similar assertion $A(b')$ will be derived for every b' with $\mathrm{tp}(b') = \mathrm{tp}(b)$, because it is not necessarily the case that there exists $R(a', b') \in \mathcal{A}$ with $\mathrm{tp}(a') = \mathrm{tp}(a)$, for which this case also applies. Hence, adding the newly derived assertions using Lemma 2 may refine the types of the original individuals and, in turn, result in a new abstraction, for which new assertions can be derived once again.

The above suggests the following materialization procedure based on abstraction refinement. Given an ontology $\mathcal{O} = \mathcal{A} \cup \mathcal{T}$ we proceed as follows:

1. Build an initial abstraction $\mathcal{B}$ of $\mathcal{A}$ according to Definition 3.
2. Materialize $\mathcal{B} \cup \mathcal{T}$ using a reasoner.
3. Extend $\mathcal{A}$ with the newly derived assertions according to Lemma 2.
4. Update the types of the individuals in $\mathcal{A}$ and re-compute its abstraction $\mathcal{B}$.
5. Repeat from Step 2 until no new assertions can be added to $\mathcal{A}$.

ABox: $\mathcal{A} =$

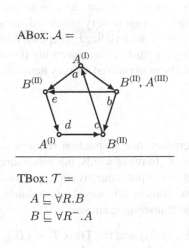

TBox: $\mathcal{T} =$

$A \sqsubseteq \forall R.B$

$B \sqsubseteq \forall R^-.A$

Materialized abstract ABoxes	Abstractions I	II	III
$y_{tp_1}^R$	$\{c,e,a,d\}$		
x_{tp_1}	$\{b,c,e\}$		
$z_{tp_1}^R$	$\{a,b,d\}$		
$+B$ $y_{tp_2}^R$	$\{b,e,c\}$	$\{b,e,c\}$	$\{b,e,c\}$
A x_{tp_2}	$\{a,d\}$	$\{a,d\}$	$\{a,d\}$
$z_{tp_2}^R$	$\{c,e\}$	$\{c,e\}$	$\{c,e\}$
$y_{tp_3}^R$		$\{c,e,a,d\}$	$\{a,d\}$
B x_{tp_3}		$\{b,e,c\}$	$\{c,e\}$
$+A$ $z_{tp_3}^R$		$\{a,b,d\}$	$\{b,d,a\}$
$+B$ $y_{tp_4}^R$			$\{c,e\}$
A,B x_{tp_4}			$\{b\}$
$+A$ $z_{tp_4}^R$			$\{a\}$

Fig. 1. The abstractions I-III produced in Example 5. Each abstraction consists of the ABoxes corresponding to the four individual types. The inferred assertions are indicated with the "+" sign and are added to the corresponding original individuals shown in each column. The materialized assertions in the original ABox are labeled with the first iteration in which they appear.

Example 5 (Example 4 continued). Let $\mathcal{A}_I$ be the ABox $\mathcal{A}$ from Example 4 and $\mathcal{T} = \{A \sqsubseteq \forall R.B, B \sqsubseteq \forall R^-.A\}$ a TBox. Let $\mathcal{B}_I$ be the abstraction $\mathcal{B}$ of $\mathcal{A}_I = \mathcal{A}$ computed in Example 4 (see Figure 1). By materializing $\mathcal{B}_I$ w.r.t. $\mathcal{T}$ we get $B(y_{tp_2}^R)$, from which we obtain $\mathcal{A}_{II} = \mathcal{A}_I \cup \{B(b), B(e), B(c)\}$ using Lemma 2. Recomputing the types of individuals in $\mathcal{A}_{II}$ yields $\mathrm{tp}(b) = \mathrm{tp}(c) = \mathrm{tp}(e) = tp_3 = (\{B\}, \{R\}, \{R\})$, while the types of a and d remain unchanged. The abstraction of $\mathcal{A}_{II}$ is thus $\mathcal{B}_{II} = \mathcal{B}_{tp_2} \cup \mathcal{B}_{tp_3}$, where $\mathcal{B}_{tp_3} = \{B(x_{tp_3}), R(x_{tp_3}, y_{tp_3}^R), R(z_{tp_3}^R, x_{tp_3})\}$. By materializing $\mathcal{B}_{II}$, we get $A(z_{tp_3}^R)$, from which we obtain $\mathcal{A}_{III} = \mathcal{A}_{II} \cup \{A(b)\}$. We again recompute the types of individuals in $\mathcal{A}_{III}$, which gives $\mathrm{tp}(b) = tp_4 = (\{A, B\}, \{R\}, \{R\})$, while the types of the other individuals do not change. The abstraction of $\mathcal{A}_{III}$ is thus $\mathcal{B}_{III} = \mathcal{B}_{tp_2} \cup \mathcal{B}_{tp_3} \cup \mathcal{B}_{tp_4}$, where $\mathcal{B}_{tp_4} = \{A(x_{tp_4}), B(x_{tp_4}), R(x_{tp_4}, y_{tp_4}^R), R(z_{tp_4}^R, x_{tp_4})\}$. Materializing $\mathcal{B}_{III}$ yields $B(y_{tp_4}^R)$ and $A(z_{tp_4}^R)$, which correspond to $B(c)$, $B(e)$, and $A(a)$. However, those assertions already exist in $\mathcal{A}_{III}$, so the procedure terminates.

The abstraction refinement procedure terminates since after every iteration except the last one, new atomic assertions must be added to $\mathcal{A}$, and there is a bounded number of such assertions. Specifically, the number of iterations is at most $\|\mathrm{ind}(\mathcal{O})\| \times \|\mathrm{con}(\mathcal{O})\|$. The number of realized individual types in every ABox $\mathcal{A}$, and hence the size of every abstract ABox $\mathcal{B}$, is at most exponential in the number of different concepts and roles in $\mathcal{O}$. In practice, however, it is likely to be much smaller since not every possible type is realized in real ontologies. Note also that in practice, it is not necessary to add the newly derived assertions explicitly to the original ABox—one can recompute the new types using some simple operations on the sets of individuals (intersection and unions), and keep the derived assertions only once for every new equivalence class. Note also that without nominals, we can exploit that $\mathcal{B}$ is a disjoint union of very simple ABoxes corresponding to the types of individuals, so they can be materialized independently of each other. This is particularly useful for updating the abstraction since only those ABoxes that correspond to newly created types should be materialized at every iteration.

5   Completeness

Lemma 2 guarantees that at every point of the iteration, our abstraction refinement procedure adds only entailed assertions to the ABox $\mathcal{A}$. In other words, our procedure is sound. The main question of this section is, whether our procedure is complete, i.e., whether we always compute all entailed atomic assertions in this way. Unfortunately, this is in general not the case, as demonstrated by the following example.

Example 6. Consider the ABox $\mathcal{A} = \{A(a), R(a, b), B(b)\}$ and the TBox $\mathcal{T} = \{B \sqsubseteq C \sqcup D, \exists R.C \sqsubseteq C, A \sqcap C \sqsubseteq \forall R.D\}$. Note that $\mathcal{A} \cup \mathcal{T} \models D(b)$. Let us compute the materialization using abstraction. We have $\mathrm{tp}(a) = (\{A\}, \{R\}, \emptyset)$ and $\mathrm{tp}(b) = (\{B\}, \emptyset, \{R\})$. Therefore $\mathcal{B} = \mathcal{B}_{\mathrm{tp}(a)} \cup \mathcal{B}_{\mathrm{tp}(b)}$, where $\mathcal{B}_{\mathrm{tp}(a)} = \{A(x_{\mathrm{tp}(a)}), R(x_{\mathrm{tp}(a)}, y^R_{\mathrm{tp}(a)})\}$ and $\mathcal{B}_{\mathrm{tp}(b)} = \{B(x_{\mathrm{tp}(b)}), R(z^R_{\mathrm{tp}(b)}, x_{\mathrm{tp}(b)})\}$. It is easy to see that $\mathcal{B} \cup \mathcal{T}$ does not entail any new atomic concept assertions. Hence, our procedure terminates after the first iteration without producing the entailment $\mathcal{A} \cup \mathcal{T} \models D(b)$.

The primary reason why our method does not work in this example is that our abstraction breaks the ABox into disconnected parts, which cannot communicate the non-deterministic choices, e.g., for the disjunction $C \sqcup D$. The only communication between ABoxes happens through the entailment of new assertions. If the ontology language does not allow such non-deterministic constructors, it is possible to obtain a complete procedure.

5.1   Horn $\mathcal{ALCHOI}$

While the results on the previous sections hold for $\mathcal{ALCHOI}$ in general (and even extensions thereof), we restrict ontologies in this section to a Horn fragment of $\mathcal{ALCHOI}$:

Definition 4 (Horn $\mathcal{ALCHOI}$). *An $\mathcal{ALCHOI}$ ontology $\mathcal{O}$ is Horn if, for every concept assertion $D(a)$ and every axiom $C \sqsubseteq D$, the concepts C and D satisfy, respectively, the following grammar definitions:*

$$C_{(i)} ::= \top \mid \bot \mid A \mid o \mid C_1 \sqcap C_2 \mid C_1 \sqcup C_2 \mid \exists R.C, \tag{1}$$

$$D_{(i)} ::= \top \mid \bot \mid A \mid o \mid D_1 \sqcap D_2 \mid \exists R.D \mid \forall R.D \mid \neg C. \tag{2}$$

Intuitively, negations and universal restrictions should not occur negatively, and disjunctions should not occur positively. We can also allow TBox axioms that are equivalent to Horn axioms. For example, $A \sqcap \neg \forall R.\bot \sqsubseteq \neg \forall S.(B \sqcap C)$ is not Horn according to Definition 4, but is equivalent to the Horn axiom $A \sqcap \exists R.\top \sqsubseteq \exists S.\neg(B \sqcap C)$.

It is a well-known property of Horn languages that every consistent Horn ontology has a so-called *canonical model* that entails exactly the consequences entailed by the ontology. For the purpose of the paper, we require a weaker version of this property that speaks only about entailment of atomic concept assertions.

Theorem 1 (Weak Canonical Model Property for Horn $\mathcal{ALCHOI}$). *Every consistent Horn $\mathcal{ALCHOI}$ ontology $\mathcal{O}$ has a model $\mathcal{I}$ such that $\mathcal{I} \models A(a)$ implies $\mathcal{O} \models A(a)$ for every atomic concept assertion $A(a)$ with $a \in \mathrm{ind}(\mathcal{O})$ and $A \in \mathrm{con}(\mathcal{O})$.*

Theorem 1 can be proved using the property that Horn $\mathcal{ALCHOI}$ models are closed under direct products. Then a canonical model is obtained from the direct product of models refuting (finitely many) atomic non-types.

Before formulating our completeness result, we need to solve one small technical problem illustrated in the following example.

Example 7. Consider $\mathcal{A} = \{A(a), B(b), R(a,b)\}$ and $\mathcal{T} = \{A \sqcap \exists R.B \sqsubseteq C\}$, which consist of Horn axioms. Clearly, $\mathcal{A} \cup \mathcal{T} \models C(a)$. $\mathcal{A}$ realizes two different individual types: $\mathrm{tp}(a) = \mathrm{tp}_1 = (\{A\}, \{R\}, \emptyset)$ and $\mathrm{tp}(b) = \mathrm{tp}_2 = (\{B\}, \emptyset, \{R\})$, so our abstraction $\mathcal{B} = \mathcal{B}_{\mathrm{tp}_1} \cup \mathcal{B}_{\mathrm{tp}_2}$ consist of two ABoxes $\mathcal{B}_{\mathrm{tp}_1} = \{A(x_{\mathrm{tp}_1}), R(x_{\mathrm{tp}_1}, y^R_{\mathrm{tp}_1})\}$, and $\mathcal{B}_{\mathrm{tp}_2} = \{B(x_{\mathrm{tp}_2}), R(z^R_{\mathrm{tp}_2}, x_{\mathrm{tp}_2})\}$. In neither of these ABoxes we obtain a new assertion after materialization, so our procedure terminates without deriving $C(a)$.

In order to see how to fix this problem, note that $\mathcal{B}_{\mathrm{tp}_2} \cup \mathcal{T} \models (\exists R.B)(z^R_{\mathrm{tp}_2})$, so there is an entailed assertion, just not an atomic one. To capture this inference, we introduce a new concept that "defines" $\exists R.B$. Specifically, let $\mathcal{T}' = \{\exists R.B \sqsubseteq X, A \sqcap X \sqsubseteq C\}$ where X is a fresh concept name. Clearly, $\mathcal{T}'$ is a conservative extension of $\mathcal{T}$ (one can extend every model of $\mathcal{T}$ to a model of $\mathcal{T}'$ by interpreting X as $\exists R.B$), so the assertions for A, B, and C entailed by $\mathcal{T}'$ are the same as for $\mathcal{T}$. However, with $\mathcal{T}'$ we can derive a new assertion $\mathcal{B}_{\mathrm{tp}_2} \cup \mathcal{T}' \models X(z^R_{\mathrm{tp}_2})$. If we now add the corresponding assertion $X(a)$ to $\mathcal{A}$ and recompute the abstraction for the updated type $\mathrm{tp}(a) = \mathrm{tp}_3 = (\{A, X\}, \{R\}, \emptyset)$ ($\mathrm{tp}(b)$ does not change), we have $\mathcal{B}_{\mathrm{tp}_3} = \{A(x_{\mathrm{tp}_3}), X(x_{\mathrm{tp}_3}), R(x_{\mathrm{tp}_3}, y^R_{\mathrm{tp}_3})\}$, and obtain $\mathcal{B}_{\mathrm{tp}_3} \cup \mathcal{T}' \models C(x_{\mathrm{tp}_3})$, which gives us the intended result.

Example 7 suggests that to achieve completeness, we need to represent existential restrictions on the left hand side of the axioms using new atomic concepts. Note that $\exists R.B \sqsubseteq X$ is equivalent to $B \sqsubseteq \forall R^-.X$. Thus we can just require that there are no existential restrictions on the left hand side of concept inclusions, and all universal restrictions on the right have only atomic concepts as fillers.

Definition 5 (Normal Form for Horn $\mathcal{ALCHOI}$). *Horn $\mathcal{ALCHOI}$ axioms $D(a)$ and $C \sqsubseteq D$ are in* normal form *if they satisfy the following grammar definitions:*

$$C_{(i)} ::= \top \mid \bot \mid A \mid o \mid C_1 \sqcap C_2 \mid C_1 \sqcup C_2 \tag{3}$$

$$D_{(i)} ::= \top \mid \bot \mid A \mid o \mid D_1 \sqcap D_2 \mid \exists R.D \mid \forall R.A \mid \neg C \tag{4}$$

Intuitively, in addition to the constraints for Horn $\mathcal{ALCHOI}$ ontologies given by (1) and (2) of Definition 4, negative occurrences of existential restrictions are not allowed, and (positive) occurrences of universal restrictions can only have concept names as fillers. It is easy to convert axioms to such a normal form using the well-known structural transformation. Specifically, we can repeatedly replace every existential restriction

$\exists R.C$ in (1) with a fresh concept name X and add a new axiom $C \sqsubseteq \forall R^-.X$. Likewise, we can replace every universal restriction $\forall R.D$ in (2) with $\forall R.Y$ for a fresh concept name Y and add an axiom $Y \sqsubseteq D$. As with Horn axioms, we do not actually need the axioms in the TBox to be syntactically in the normal form. It is sufficient that they are equivalent to axioms in the normal form – the reasoner will still produce the same result. For example, an axiom $\exists R.(A_1 \sqcap A_2) \sqsubseteq B_1 \sqcap B_2$ can be left untouched because it is equivalent to an axiom $A_1 \sqcap A_2 \sqsubseteq \forall R^-.B_1 \sqcap \forall R^-.B_2$ in normal form. Note that the axiom $A \sqcap \exists R.B \sqsubseteq C$ in $\mathcal{T}$ from Example 7 is not equivalent to the pair of axioms $\exists R.B \sqsubseteq X, A \sqcap X \sqsubseteq C$ in $\mathcal{T}'$ because the latter axioms contain a new symbol X. In fact, $A \sqcap \exists R.B \sqsubseteq C$ is not equivalent to any axiom(s) in normal form.

5.2   Completeness Proof

We are now ready to show the following completeness result:

Theorem 2. *Let* $\mathcal{O} = \mathcal{A} \cup \mathcal{T}$ *be a normalized Horn* $\mathcal{ALCHOI}$ *ontology and* $\mathcal{B}$ *the abstraction of* $\mathcal{A}$. $\mathcal{O}$ *is concept materialized if, for every type* tp $= (\text{tp}_\downarrow, \text{tp}_\rightarrow, \text{tp}_\leftarrow)$, *every individual* $a \in \text{ind}(\mathcal{A})$ *with* $\text{tp}(a) = $ tp, *and every atomic concept* A, *we have:*

(1) $\mathcal{B} \cup \mathcal{T} \models A(x_{\text{tp}})$ *implies* $A(a) \in \mathcal{A}$,
(2) $\mathcal{B} \cup \mathcal{T} \models A(y_{\text{tp}}^R)$ *and* $R(a, b) \in \mathcal{A}$ *implies* $A(b) \in \mathcal{A}$, *and*
(3) $\mathcal{B} \cup \mathcal{T} \models A(z_{\text{tp}}^S)$ *and* $S(c, a) \in \mathcal{A}$ *implies* $A(c) \in \mathcal{A}$.

Proof. To prove Theorem 2, we extend the abstraction $\mathcal{B}$ of $\mathcal{A}$ with new role assertions $R(x_{\text{tp}(a)}, x_{\text{tp}(b)})$ for every $R(a, b) \in \mathcal{A}$. Let us denote this extended abstract ABox by $\mathcal{B}'$. Since, for every $C(a) \in \mathcal{A}$, we also have $C \in \text{tp}_\downarrow(a)$ and, thus, $C(x_{\text{tp}(a)}) \in \mathcal{B} \subseteq \mathcal{B}'$, the mapping $h : \text{ind}(\mathcal{A}) \to \text{ind}(\mathcal{B}')$ defined by $h(a) = x_{\text{tp}(a)}$ is a homomorphism from $\mathcal{A}$ to $\mathcal{B}'$. Therefore, by Lemma 1, if $\mathcal{A} \cup \mathcal{T} \models A(a)$, then $\mathcal{B}' \cup \mathcal{T} \models A(x_{\text{tp}(a)})$. The key part of the proof is to demonstrate that in this case we also have $\mathcal{B} \cup \mathcal{T} \models A(x_{\text{tp}(a)})$. That is, the extended abstract ABox $\mathcal{B}'$ does not entail new atomic concept assertions compared to $\mathcal{B}$. It follows then that $A(a) \in \mathcal{A}$ by condition (1) of the theorem. This implies that $\mathcal{O}$ is concept materialized.

To prove that $\mathcal{B}'$ entails the same atomic concept assertions as $\mathcal{B}$, we use the remaining conditions (2) and (3) of Theorem 2 and the canonical model property formulated in Theorem 1. Note that since new role assertions of the form $R(x_{\text{tp}(a)}, x_{\text{tp}(b)})$ are added to $\mathcal{B}'$ only if $R(a, b) \in \mathcal{A}$, we have $R \in \text{tp}_\rightarrow(a)$ and $R \in \text{tp}_\leftarrow(b)$ by Definition 2. Therefore, we already had role assertions $R(x_{\text{tp}(a)}, y_{\text{tp}(a)}^R) \in \mathcal{B}$ and likewise $R(z_{\text{tp}(b)}^R, x_{\text{tp}(b)}) \in \mathcal{B}$ for the same role R. Furthermore, by condition (2) of Theorem 2, if $\mathcal{B} \cup \mathcal{T} \models A(y_{\text{tp}(a)}^R)$, then since $R(a, b) \in \mathcal{A}$, we also have $A(b) \in \mathcal{A}$, and thus $A(x_{\text{tp}(b)}) \in \mathcal{B}$. Likewise, by condition (3), if $\mathcal{B} \cup \mathcal{T} \models A(z_{\text{tp}(b)}^R)$, then $A(x_{\text{tp}(a)}) \in \mathcal{B}$. The following lemma shows that with these properties for $\mathcal{B}$, after adding the new role assertion $R(x_{\text{tp}(a)}, x_{\text{tp}(b)})$ to $\mathcal{B}$, no new atomic concept assertions can be entailed.

Lemma 3 (Four-Individual Lemma). *Let* $\mathcal{O}$ *be a normalized Horn* $\mathcal{ALCHOI}$ *ontology such that* $\{R(x_1, y_1), R(z_2, x_2)\} \subseteq \mathcal{O}$ *for some* x_1, y_1, z_2, x_2, *and* R. *Further, assume that for every concept name* A *we have:*

(1) $\mathcal{O} \models A(y_1)$ *implies* $\mathcal{O} \models A(x_2)$*, and*
(2) $\mathcal{O} \models A(z_2)$ *implies* $\mathcal{O} \models A(x_1)$*.*

Finally, let $\mathcal{O}' = \mathcal{O} \cup \{R(x_1, x_2)\}$*. Then for every concept name A and every individual a, we have* $\mathcal{O}' \models A(a)$ *implies* $\mathcal{O} \models A(a)$*.*

Proof (Sketch). Suppose that $\mathcal{O}' \models A(a)$. We will show that $\mathcal{O} \models A(a)$. If $\mathcal{O}$ is inconsistent then this holds trivially. Otherwise, there exists a model $\mathcal{I}$ of $\mathcal{O}$ satisfying Theorem 1. From $\mathcal{I}$ we construct an interpretation $\mathcal{I}'$ that coincides with $\mathcal{I}$ apart from the interpretation of role names. With the given individuals x_1 and x_2, for every role name S we define

$$
S^{\mathcal{I}'} = S^{\mathcal{I}} \cup \begin{cases} \{(x_1^{\mathcal{I}}, x_2^{\mathcal{I}})\} & \text{if } \mathcal{O} \models R \sqsubseteq S \text{ and } \mathcal{O} \not\models R \sqsubseteq S^- \\ \{(x_2^{\mathcal{I}}, x_1^{\mathcal{I}})\} & \text{if } \mathcal{O} \models R \sqsubseteq S^- \text{ and } \mathcal{O} \not\models R \sqsubseteq S \\ \{(x_1^{\mathcal{I}}, x_2^{\mathcal{I}}), (x_2^{\mathcal{I}}, x_1^{\mathcal{I}})\} & \text{if } \mathcal{O} \models R \sqsubseteq S \text{ and } \mathcal{O} \models R \sqsubseteq S^- \\ \emptyset & \text{otherwise} \end{cases}
$$

We will prove that $\mathcal{I}' \models \mathcal{O}'$, which implies $\mathcal{I}' \models A(a)$ since $\mathcal{O}' \models A(a)$, and thus $\mathcal{I} \models A(a)$ by definition of $\mathcal{I}'$, from which $\mathcal{O} \models A(a)$ follows since $\mathcal{I}$ satisfies Theorem 1.

First, we prove by induction that for each C and D defined respectively by (3) and (4), we have $C^{\mathcal{I}} = C^{\mathcal{I}'}$ and $D^{\mathcal{I}} \subseteq D^{\mathcal{I}'}$. The only non-trivial case is $D = \forall S.A$ with $\mathcal{O} \models R \sqsubseteq S$ and $S \in \text{rol}(\mathcal{O})$ (the case where S is an inverse role can be proved analogously). Take any $d \in D^{\mathcal{I}}$. To show that $d \in D^{\mathcal{I}'}$, we need to prove that $d' \in A^{\mathcal{I}'}$ for every d' with $\langle d, d' \rangle \in S^{\mathcal{I}'}$. If $\langle d, d' \rangle \in S^{\mathcal{I}}$, this is obvious. Otherwise, $\langle d, d' \rangle = \langle x_1^{\mathcal{I}}, x_2^{\mathcal{I}} \rangle$. By assumption, $\mathcal{I} \models R(x_1, y_1)$ and $\mathcal{O} \models R \sqsubseteq S$, hence, $\mathcal{I} \models S(x_1, y_1)$, which, together with $d = x_1^{\mathcal{I}} \in D^{\mathcal{I}}$, implies $y_1^{\mathcal{I}} \in A^{\mathcal{I}}$. Thus $\mathcal{I} \models A(y_1)$. Since $\mathcal{I}$ satisfies Theorem 1, we have $\mathcal{O} \models A(y_1)$. By Condition (1), $\mathcal{O} \models A(x_2)$. Thus $d' = x_2^{\mathcal{I}} \in A^{\mathcal{I}} = A^{\mathcal{I}'}$, and hence, $d = x_1^{\mathcal{I}} \in D^{\mathcal{I}'}$, what was required to show.

It remains to show that $\mathcal{I}' \models \mathcal{O}'$ with $\mathcal{O}' = \mathcal{O} \cup \{R(x_1, x_2)\}$. Since $\mathcal{I} \models \mathcal{O}$, for every $C \sqsubseteq D \in \mathcal{O}$ we have $C^{\mathcal{I}'} = C^{\mathcal{I}} \subseteq D^{\mathcal{I}} \subseteq D^{\mathcal{I}'}$, for every $D(a) \in \mathcal{O}$ we have $a^{\mathcal{I}'} = a^{\mathcal{I}} \in D^{\mathcal{I}} \subseteq D^{\mathcal{I}'}$, and for every $R(a, b) \in \mathcal{O}$ we have $\langle a^{\mathcal{I}'}, b^{\mathcal{I}'} \rangle = \langle a^{\mathcal{I}}, b^{\mathcal{I}} \rangle \in R^{\mathcal{I}} \subseteq R^{\mathcal{I}'}$. Finally, the definition of $\mathcal{I}'$ ensures that for every role inclusion $S \sqsubseteq P \in \mathcal{O}$ we have $S^{\mathcal{I}'} \subseteq P^{\mathcal{I}'}$, and that $\mathcal{I}' \models R(x_1, x_2)$. Thus $\mathcal{I}' \models \mathcal{O}'$. $\square$

By repeatedly applying Lemma 3 for each $x_1 = x_{\text{tp}(a)}$, $y_1 = y^R_{\text{tp}(a)}$, $x_2 = x_{\text{tp}(b)}$, $z_2 = z^R_{\text{tp}(b)}$ and R such that $R(a, b) \in \mathcal{A}$, we obtain that $\mathcal{B}'$ entails only those atomic assertions that are entailed by $\mathcal{B}$, which completes the proof of Theorem 2. $\square$

6   Implementation and Evaluation

To evaluate the feasibility of our approach, we implemented the procedure sketched in Section 4.3 in Java. The system relies on Neo4j 1.9.4[2] to store the ABoxes and uses an external OWL reasoner for materializing the abstractions.

---

[2] http://www.neo4j.org

Table 2. Test suite statistics with the number of atomic concepts in the ontology (#A and #A_N for the normalized ontology), roles (#R), individuals (#I), role (#$R(a, b)$) and concept (#$A(a)$) assertions, and the number of concept assertions inferred by the system

Ontology	#A	#A_N	#R	#I	#$R(a,b)$	#$A(a)$	#$A(a)$ inferred
Gazetteer	710	711	15	516 150	604 164	11 112	538 799
Coburn	719	1 161	109	123 515	237 620	297 002	535 124
LUBM 1	43	49	25	17 174	49 336	18 128	48 326
LUBM 10	43	49	25	207 426	630 753	219 680	593 485
LUBM 50	43	49	25	1 082 818	3 298 813	1 147 136	3 097 722
LUBM 100	43	49	25	2 153 645	6 645 928	2 281 035	6 164 538
LUBM 500	43	49	25	10 189 173	31 073 066	10 793 509	29 169 321
UOBM 1	69	90	35	24 925	153 571	44 680	142 747
UOBM 10	69	90	35	242 549	1 500 628	434 115	1 381 722
UOBM 50	69	90	35	1 227 445	7 594 996	2 197 035	6 991 583
UOBM 100	69	90	35	2 462 012	15 241 909	4 409 891	14 027 772
UOBM 500	69	90	35	12 379 113	76 612 736	22 168 148	72 215 007

The goal of our evaluation is to estimate whether our assumption that in relatively simple ontologies with large ABoxes the number of realized types and, consequently, the size of the abstract ABoxes is small. Furthermore, we analyze whether it is indeed the case that real-world ontologies have relatively simple axioms that do not require many refinement steps, where a refinement step is the process of refining the individual types.

We selected ontologies with large ABoxes that are also used to evaluate other approaches.[3] Table 2 provides relevant metrics for the test ontologies. Gazetteer is from the NCBO BioPortal, Coburn is a large bio ontology from the Phenoscape project, and LUBM (UOBM) refers to the Lehigh University Benchmark[4] (the University Ontology Benchmark).[5] LUBM n (UOBM n) denotes the data set for n universities. Gazetteer is genuinely within Horn $\mathcal{ALEO}$ and the remaining ontologies have been converted to Horn $\mathcal{ALCHOI}$. Note that the increase of normalized concepts (A_N) in comparison to the original concepts (A) in Table 2 is a rough indicator of TBox complexity, which adds extra workload to reasoners.

Tables 3 and 4 show the results of computing and iteratively refining the abstract ABoxes until the fixpoint. The second column in Table 3 shows the number of refinement steps. The third and fourth (fifth and sixth) columns show the number of individuals (assertions) in the first and last abstraction, respectively, while the last four columns show the according relative reduction in percent compared to the original ABoxes. Table 4 shows the type statistics, i.e. the number of types and the average number of individuals, concept names, and property names per type.

In general, the abstract ABoxes are significantly smaller than the original ones and the ontologies can be materialized with few refinement steps. For ontologies with

---

[3] Download and references at http://www.derivo.de/dl14-ontologies/

[4] http://swat.cse.lehigh.edu/projects/lubm

[5] http://www.cs.ox.ac.uk/isg/tools/UOBMGenerator

Table 3. Number of refinement steps, size of the abstract ABoxes, and size of the abstract ABoxes in comparison with the original ABoxes for the first and the last abstraction

Ontology	# of steps	Abstract ABox size				Abstract ABox size (%)			
		# indiv.		# assertions		% indiv.		% assertions	
Gazetteer	1	5 640	5 640	5 142	8 512	1.09	1.09	0.79	1.31
Coburn	2	3 992	4 059	5 569	8 633	3.23	3.29	1.04	2.16
LUBM 1	1	139	139	143	254	0.81	0.81	0.21	0.38
LUBM 10	1	154	154	158	281	0.07	0.07	0.02	0.03
LUBM 50	1	148	148	152	271	0.01	0.01	0.003	0.006
LUBM 100	1	148	148	152	271	0.007	0.007	0.002	0.003
LUBM 500	1	148	148	152	271	0.001	0.001	0.001	0.001
UOBM 1	2	25 378	39 322	31 659	101 324	101.82	157.76	15.97	51.11
UOBM 10	2	98 266	169 579	125 056	448 400	40.51	69.92	6.46	23.18
UOBM 50	2	226 176	395 956	290 652	1 057 854	18.43	32.26	2.97	10.80
UOBM 100	2	311 574	547 361	402 188	1 472 058	12.66	22.23	2.05	7.49
UOBM 500	2	596 135	1 033 685	772 920	2 806 786	4.82	8.35	0.78	2.84

simple TBoxes, which contain mostly atomic concept inclusions, domains and ranges for roles, and conjunctions, only one refinement step is required. This is the case since any concept assertion derived for a successor or predecessor of an abstract individual is also derived for the individual itself. LUBM and UOBM additionally contain universal quantifications, e.g. Department $\sqsubseteq$ $\forall$headOf$^-$.Chair (rewritten from $\exists$headOf.Department $\sqsubseteq$ Chair), but these axioms do not create long propagations of concept Assertions over roles. For LUBM, many individuals have similar types and can be grouped into equivalence classes. This results in an extremely good compression with abstractions of nearly constant size for arbitrarily many LUBM universities. For instance, the final abstractions are just 0.38 % (for LUBM 1) and 0.001 % (for LUBM 500) of the size of the original ABox. This and the fact that only one refinement step is needed also explains that other related approaches like SHER and Wandelt's and Möller's approach show a very good performance for LUBM. UOBM also contains nominals and the individuals are more diverse than in LUBM. Thus, UOBM requires one more refinement step compared to LUBM.

Our qualitative performance evaluation confirms the correlation between the size of abstract ABoxes and the total time for the materialization. We compared the respective materialization times of the original ABox with the sum of materialization times for all abstract ABoxes using the reasoners HermiT and Konclude.[6] For ontologies with small abstract ABoxes such as LUBM, Gazetteer and Coburn, the sum of the reasoning times for all abstract ABoxes is less than a tenth of the reasoning time for the original ABox. While the runtimes for the abstractions of UOBM 1 are still 2 to 4 times that of the original ABox, the runtimes for UOBM 50 are already down by 50%. The original UOBM 100 ontology could neither be processed within eight hours by HermiT nor by Konclude with a 32 GB RAM limit run on Intel Xeon E5-2440 6 cores, but its abstraction can easily be materialized, e.g., within 84 seconds and 8 GB RAM by Konclude. Currently, we re-compute the abstraction after each refinement step. There is certainly

---

[6] See http://www.hermit-reasoner.com and http://www.konclude.com

Table 4. Statistics about individual types for the first and the last abstraction: number of individual types, average number of individuals, concept names, and property names per individual type

Ontology	# Individual types		Individual type statistics					
			# indiv. / type		$\#A_N$ / type		$\#R$ / type	
Gazetteer	1 845	1 845	280	280	0.73	2.56	2.05	2.05
Coburn	1 056	1 072	117	115	2.49	5.27	2.79	2.79
LUBM 1	30	30	572	572	1.13	4.83	3.63	3.63
LUBM 10	29	29	7 153	7 153	1.14	5.38	4.31	4.31
LUBM 50	27	27	40 104	40 104	1.15	5.56	4.48	4.48
LUBM 100	27	27	79 765	79 765	1.15	5.56	4.48	4.48
LUBM 500	27	27	377 377	377 377	1.15	5.56	4.48	4.48
UOBM 1	3 104	4 705	8	5	3.02	14.18	7.18	7.35
UOBM 10	11 453	17 347	21	14	3.34	15.48	7.58	7.86
UOBM 50	25 636	43 283	48	28	3.52	16.29	7.82	8.14
UOBM 100	34 992	59 184	70	42	3.59	16.62	7.91	8.24
UOBM 500	65 148	108 691	190	114	3.71	17.31	8.15	8.51

room for optimizations, e.g. by updating the types and computing the abstractions incrementally.

7   Conclusions and Future Work

We have presented an approach for ontology materialization based on abstraction refinement. The main idea is to represent ABox individuals using several (overlapping) equivalent classes and to use information derived for their abstract representatives to refine the abstraction. Although the approach does not necessarily guarantee that the abstraction is always smaller than the original ABox, the method particularly pays off for ontologies with large ABoxes and relatively small and simple TBoxes.

Currently, our approach is complete for Horn $\mathcal{ALCHOI}$ ontologies due to the property that only (deterministically) derived assertions are used for abstraction refinement. We could potentially extend our approach to non-Horn ontology languages by exploiting additional information about non-deterministically derived instances as provided, for example, by the HermiT reasoner [7]. Some Horn features, on the other hand, could be supported, e.g., it is easy to support transitive roles and role chains by using the well-known encoding of these axioms via concept inclusions [13].

In this paper we mainly focus on concept materialization since role materialization for Horn $\mathcal{ALCHOI}$ can essentially be computed by expanding role hierarchies (special care needs to be taken of nominals though). When ontologies contain role chains and functional roles, however, materialization of role assertions becomes less trivial, e.g. the encoding of role chains is not enough and a naive encoding of functionality is inefficient. We currently investigate how these features can efficiently be supported.

Since the abstraction consists of disjoint parts, these parts can be processed independently of each other (if nominals are taken care of). This can be used in the refinement steps to process only the parts that have really changed or for an efficient support of updates to the ABox. In addition, the abstract ABoxes could serve not only as a generic interface for communication with the reasoner, but also as a compact representation of the materialization. This can be particularly useful when answering instance and conjunctive queries over the materialized ABoxes, where the abstraction can be used to prune the search space.

References

1. Bishop, B., Kiryakov, A., Ognyanoff, D., Peikov, I., Tashev, Z., Velkov, R.: OWLIM: A family of scalable semantic repositories. Semantic Web J. 2(1), 33–42 (2011)
2. Calvanese, D., De Giacomo, G., Lembo, D., Lenzerini, M., Rosati, R.: Tractable reasoning and efficient query answering in description logics: The DL-Lite family. J. of Automated Reasoning 39(3), 385–429 (2007)
3. Dolby, J., Fokoue, A., Kalyanpur, A., Schonberg, E., Srinivas, K.: Scalable highly expressive reasoner (SHER). J. of Web Semantics 7(4), 357–361 (2009)
4. Fokoue, A., Kershenbaum, A., Ma, L., Schonberg, E., Srinivas, K.: The summary ABox: Cutting ontologies down to size. In: Cruz, I., Decker, S., Allemang, D., Preist, C., Schwabe, D., Mika, P., Uschold, M., Aroyo, L.M. (eds.) ISWC 2006. LNCS, vol. 4273, pp. 343–356. Springer, Heidelberg (2006)
5. Glimm, B., Kazakov, Y., Liebig, T., Tran, T.K., Vialard, V.: Abstraction Refinement for Ontology Materialization. Tech. rep., University of Ulm and derivo GmbH (2014), https://www.uni-ulm.de/fileadmin/website_uni_ulm/ iui.inst.090/Publikationen/2014/abstractionrefinementTR.pdf
6. Kalyanpur, A., Parsia, B., Horridge, M., Sirin, E.: Finding all justifications of OWL DL entailments. In: Aberer, K., et al. (eds.) ISWC/ASWC 2007. LNCS, vol. 4825, pp. 267–280. Springer, Heidelberg (2007)
7. Kollia, I., Glimm, B.: Optimizing SPARQL query answering over OWL ontologies. J. of Artificial Intelligence Research (JAIR) 48, 253–303 (2013)
8. Kolovski, V., Wu, Z., Eadon, G.: Optimizing enterprise-scale OWL 2 RL reasoning in a relational database system. In: Patel-Schneider, P.F., Pan, Y., Hitzler, P., Mika, P., Zhang, L., Pan, J.Z., Horrocks, I., Glimm, B. (eds.) ISWC 2010, Part I. LNCS, vol. 6496, pp. 436–452. Springer, Heidelberg (2010)
9. Kontchakov, R., Lutz, C., Toman, D., Wolter, F., Zakharyaschev, M.: The combined approach to query answering in DL-Lite. In: Proc. of the 12th Int. Conf. on the Principles of Knowledge Representation and Reasoning (KR 2010). AAAI Press (2010)
10. Lutz, C., Toman, D., Wolter, F.: Conjunctive query answering in the description logic $\mathcal{EL}$ using a relational database system. In: Proc. of the 21st Int. Joint Conf. on Artificial Intelligence (IJCAI 2009), pp. 2070–2075 (2009)
11. Motik, B., Cuenca Grau, B., Horrocks, I., Wu, Z., Fokoue, A., Lutz, C. (eds.): OWL 2 Web Ontology Language: Profiles, 2nd edn. W3C Recommendation (December 11, 2012), http://www.w3.org/TR/owl2-profiles/
12. Pérez-Urbina, H., Motik, B., Horrocks, I.: Tractable query answering and rewriting under description logic constraints. J. of Applied Logic 8(2), 186–209 (2010)
13. Simančík, F.: Elimination of complex RIAs without automata. In: Proc. of the 25th Int. Workshop on Description Logics (2012)
14. Urbani, J., Kotoulas, S., Maassen, J., van Harmelen, F., Bal, H.: WebPIE: A web-scale parallel inference engine using MapReduce. J. of Web Semantics 10, 59–75 (2012)
15. Wandelt, S.: Efficient instance retrieval over semi-expressive ontologies. Ph.D. thesis, Hamburg University of Technology (2011)
16. Wandelt, S., Möller, R.: Towards ABox modularization of semi-expressive description logics. J. of Applied Ontology 7(2), 133–167 (2012)

Goal-Directed Tracing of Inferences in EL Ontologies

Yevgeny Kazakov and Pavel Klinov

The University of Ulm, Germany
{yevgeny.kazakov,pavel.klinov}@uni-ulm.de

Abstract. $\mathcal{EL}$ is a family of tractable Description Logics (DLs) that is the basis of the OWL 2 EL profile. Unlike for many expressive DLs, reasoning in $\mathcal{EL}$ can be performed by computing a deductively-closed set of logical consequences of some specific form. In some ontology-based applications, e.g., for ontology debugging, knowing the logical consequences of the ontology axioms is often not sufficient. The user also needs to know from which axioms and how the consequences were derived. Although it is possible to record all inference steps during the application of rules, this is usually not done in practice to avoid the overheads. In this paper, we present a goal-directed method that can generate inferences for selected consequences in the deductive closure without re-applying all rules from scratch. We provide an empirical evaluation demonstrating that the method is fast and economical for large $\mathcal{EL}$ ontologies. Although the main benefits are demonstrated for $\mathcal{EL}$ reasoning, the method can be potentially applied to many other procedures based on deductive closure computation using fixed sets of rules.

1 Introduction and Motivation

The majority of existing DL reasoners are based on optimized *(hyper)tableau*-based procedures, which essentially work by trying to construct counter-models for the entailment. If the reasoner could not find a counter-model by trying all alternatives, it declares that the entailment holds. It is not easy to use such procedures to generate an *explanation* for the entailment, or even to determine which axioms are responsible for the entailment—the axioms that were used to construct the models are not necessarily the ones that are causing the clash. Recently another kind of reasoning procedures, which work by deriving logical consequences of ontology axioms directly, became popular. Such *consequence-based* procedures were first introduced for the $\mathcal{EL}$ family of tractable ontology languages [1], and later the same principle has been extended to more expressive (non-tractable) languages such as Horn-$\mathcal{SHIQ}$ and $\mathcal{ALCH}$ [10,19]. The consequence-based procedures work by computing the closure under the rules by forward chaining. The inference rules make sure that the result is *complete*—all entailed conclusions of interest are obtained in the closure.

It is easy to extend any consequence-based procedure so that for each derived conclusion, it also records the inferences that have produced it. This way, one can easily generate proofs for the entailed conclusions. Unfortunately, saving all applied inferences during reasoning is not practical, as each conclusion could be derived in many ways and storing all inferences requires a lot of memory. In practice, one usually does not need to retrieve all inferences, but just inferences for some particular (e.g., unexpected) consequences. In this paper, we demonstrate how these inferences can be traced

P. Mika et al. (Eds.) ISWC 2014, Part II, LNCS 8797, pp. 196–211, 2014.

Table 1. The syntax and semantics of $\mathcal{EL}^+$

	Syntax	Semantics
Roles:		
atomic role	R	$R^{\mathcal{I}}$
Concepts:		
atomic concept	A	$A^{\mathcal{I}}$
top	$\top$	$\Delta^{\mathcal{I}}$
conjunction	$C \sqcap D$	$C^{\mathcal{I}} \cap D^{\mathcal{I}}$
existential restriction	$\exists R.C$	$\{x \mid \exists y \in C^{\mathcal{I}} : \langle x, y \rangle \in R^{\mathcal{I}}\}$
Axioms:		
concept inclusion	$C \sqsubseteq D$	$C^{\mathcal{I}} \subseteq D^{\mathcal{I}}$
role inclusion	$R \sqsubseteq S$	$R^{\mathcal{I}} \subseteq S^{\mathcal{I}}$
role composition	$R_1 \circ R_2 \sqsubseteq S$	$R_1^{\mathcal{I}} \circ R_2^{\mathcal{I}} \subseteq S^{\mathcal{I}}$

back in a goal-directed way using the pre-computed set of conclusions. The main idea, is to split the conclusions on small *partitions* using the properties of the inference system, such that most inferences are applied within each individual partition. It is then possible to re-compute the inferences for conclusions within each partition by forward chaining using conclusions from other partitions as "set of support". A similar idea has been recently used for incremental reasoning in $\mathcal{EL}^+$ [11]. We demonstrate empirically that only a small fraction of inferences is produced when generating proofs for $\mathcal{EL}^+$ consequences and that the inferences can be computed in just a few milliseconds even for ontologies with hundreds thousands of axioms.

2   Tutorial

In this section, we introduce the problem addressed in the paper and present the main ideas of our solution. For simplicity, we focus on reasoning in $\mathcal{EL}^+$ [2]. Later, in Section 3, we generalize the method to arbitrary (deterministic) inference systems.

2.1   The Description Logic $\mathcal{EL}^+$

The syntax of $\mathcal{EL}^+$ is defined using a vocabulary consisting of countably infinite sets of *(atomic) roles* and *atomic concepts*. Complex *concepts* and *axioms* are defined recursively using Table 1. We use letters R, S for roles, C, D, E for concepts, and A, B for atomic concepts. An *ontology* is a finite set of axioms. Given an ontology $\mathcal{O}$, we write $\sqsubseteq_{\mathcal{O}}^*$ for the smallest reflexive transitive binary relation over roles such that $R \sqsubseteq_{\mathcal{O}}^* S$ holds for all $R \sqsubseteq S \in \mathcal{O}$.

An *interpretation* $\mathcal{I} = (\Delta^{\mathcal{I}}, \cdot^{\mathcal{I}})$ consists of a nonempty set $\Delta^{\mathcal{I}}$ called the *domain* of $\mathcal{I}$ and an interpretation function $\cdot^{\mathcal{I}}$ that assigns to each role R a binary relation $R^{\mathcal{I}} \subseteq \Delta^{\mathcal{I}} \times \Delta^{\mathcal{I}}$, and to each atomic concept A a set $A^{\mathcal{I}} \subseteq \Delta^{\mathcal{I}}$. This assignment is extended to complex concepts as shown in Table 1. $\mathcal{I}$ *satisfies* an axiom α (written $\mathcal{I} \models \alpha$) if the corresponding condition in Table 1 holds. $\mathcal{I}$ is a *model* of an ontology $\mathcal{O}$ (written $\mathcal{I} \models \mathcal{O}$) if $\mathcal{I}$ satisfies all axioms in $\mathcal{O}$. We say that $\mathcal{O}$ *entails* an axiom α

$$\mathbf{R_0}\ \frac{}{C \sqsubseteq C} \qquad\qquad \mathbf{R_\sqcap^+}\ \frac{C \sqsubseteq D_1 \quad C \sqsubseteq D_2}{C \sqsubseteq D_1 \sqcap D_2} : D_1 \sqcap D_2 \in G(C)$$

$$\mathbf{R_\top}\ \frac{}{C \sqsubseteq \top} : \top \in G(C) \qquad \mathbf{R_\exists}\ \frac{E \sqsubseteq \exists R.C \quad C \sqsubseteq D}{E \sqsubseteq \exists S.D} : \frac{\exists S.D \in G(E)}{R \sqsubseteq_{\mathcal{O}}^* S}$$

$$\mathbf{R_\sqsubseteq}\ \frac{C \sqsubseteq D}{C \sqsubseteq E} : D \sqsubseteq E \in \mathcal{O} \qquad \mathbf{R_\circ}\ \frac{E \sqsubseteq \exists R_1.C \quad C \sqsubseteq \exists R_2.D}{E \sqsubseteq \exists S.D} : \begin{array}{l} R_1 \sqsubseteq_{\mathcal{O}}^* S_1 \\ R_2 \sqsubseteq_{\mathcal{O}}^* S_2 \\ S_1 \circ S_2 \sqsubseteq S \in \mathcal{O} \end{array}$$

$$\mathbf{R_\sqcap^-}\ \frac{C \sqsubseteq D_1 \sqcap D_2}{C \sqsubseteq D_1 \quad C \sqsubseteq D_2}$$

Fig. 1. The inference rules for reasoning in $\mathcal{EL}^+$

(written $\mathcal{O} \models \alpha$), if every model of $\mathcal{O}$ satisfies α. A concept C is *subsumed* by D w.r.t. $\mathcal{O}$ if $\mathcal{O} \models C \sqsubseteq D$. The *ontology classification task* requires to compute all entailed subsumptions between atomic concepts occurring in $\mathcal{O}$.

2.2 The Reasoning Procedure for $\mathcal{EL}^+$

The $\mathcal{EL}^+$ reasoning procedure works by applying inference rules to derive subsumptions between concepts. In this paper, we use a variant of the rules that does not require normalization of the input ontology [14]. The rules for $\mathcal{EL}^+$ are given in Figure 1, where the premises (if any) are given above the horizontal line, and the conclusions below.

Some inference rules have side conditions given after the colon that restrict the expressions to which the rules are applicable. The side conditions are formulated using the given ontology $\mathcal{O}$ and a mapping that assigns to every concept X the set of *goal subsumers* $G(X)$ consisting of concepts Y (not necessarily occurring in $\mathcal{O}$), subsumptions which should be checked by the procedure. That is, if we want the procedure to check whether the subsumption $X \sqsubseteq Y$ is entailed, we need to add Y to $G(X)$. Intuitively, the mapping $G(X)$ restricts the concepts that should be constructed by the inference rules $\mathbf{R_\top}$, $\mathbf{R_\sqcap^+}$ and $\mathbf{R_\exists}$. For technical reasons, we need to require that each $G(X)$ also contains all concepts occurring in the left-hand sides of concept inclusion axioms of $\mathcal{O}$ (possibly as a sub-concept). Note that the axioms in the ontology $\mathcal{O}$ are only used in side conditions of the rules $\mathbf{R_\sqsubseteq}$, $\mathbf{R_\exists}$, and $\mathbf{R_\circ}$, and never as premises of the rules.

The rules in Figure 1 are complete for deriving all entailed goal subsumptions. That is, if $\mathcal{O} \models X \sqsubseteq Y$ and $Y \in G(X)$ (with X and D not necessarily occurring in $\mathcal{O}$) then $X \sqsubseteq Y$ can be derived using the rules in Figure 1 [14]. The rules can be also applied in a goal-directed way, if the set of concepts X for which subsumptions $X \sqsubseteq Y$ should be derived (with $Y \in G(X)$) is also known in advance.

Theorem 1 (Completeness of the rules in Figure 1 [14]). *Let $\mathcal{O}$ be an $\mathcal{EL}^+$ ontology, F a set of concepts, $G(\cdot)$ a mapping such that for each $X \in F$, and each $C \sqsubseteq D \in \mathcal{O}$, $G(X)$ contains all sub-concepts of C, and S a set of subsumptions such that:*

(i) If $X \in F$ and $X \sqsubseteq Y$ is obtained by a rule in Figure 1 applied to premises in S using $\mathcal{O}$ and $G(\cdot)$ then $X \sqsubseteq Y \in S$,

(ii) If $X \in F$ and $X \sqsubseteq \exists R.Y \in S$ for some R and Y, then $Y \in F$.

Then for every $X \in F$ and $Y \in G(X)$, we have $\mathcal{O} \models X \sqsubseteq Y$ iff $X \sqsubseteq Y \in S$.

$$\stackrel{R_0}{\longmapsto} A \sqsubseteq A \stackrel{R_\sqsubseteq}{\longmapsto} A \sqsubseteq \exists R.B \stackrel{R_\exists}{\longmapsto} A \sqsubseteq \exists H.B \stackrel{R_\sqsubseteq}{\longmapsto} A \sqsubseteq C$$

$$\stackrel{R_0}{\longmapsto} B \sqsubseteq B \stackrel{R_\sqsubseteq}{\longmapsto} B \sqsubseteq \exists S.A \stackrel{R_\exists}{\longmapsto} B \sqsubseteq \exists S.C \stackrel{R_\sqsubseteq}{\longmapsto} B \sqsubseteq C$$

$$\stackrel{R_0}{\longmapsto} C \sqsubseteq C \stackrel{R_\sqsubseteq}{\longmapsto} C \sqsubseteq \exists R.A$$

Fig. 2. The inference diagram for the proof in Example 1

Example 1. Consider the $\mathcal{EL}^+$ ontology $\mathcal{O}$ consisting of the following axioms:

$$A \sqsubseteq \exists R.B, \quad B \sqsubseteq \exists S.A, \quad \exists H.B \sqsubseteq C, \quad \exists S.C \sqsubseteq C, \quad C \sqsubseteq \exists R.A, \quad R \sqsubseteq H.$$

Then the following subsumptions can be derived using the rules in Figure 1 using $G(X) = \{A, B, C, \exists H.B, \exists S.C\}$ for every concept X. We show the premises used in the inferences in parentheses and the matching side conditions after the colon:

$A \sqsubseteq A$	by $R_0()$,	(1)
$B \sqsubseteq B$	by $R_0()$,	(2)
$C \sqsubseteq C$	by $R_0()$,	(3)
$A \sqsubseteq \exists R.B$	by $R_\sqsubseteq(A \sqsubseteq A) : A \sqsubseteq \exists R.B \in \mathcal{O}$,	(4)
$B \sqsubseteq \exists S.A$	by $R_\sqsubseteq(B \sqsubseteq B) : B \sqsubseteq \exists S.A \in \mathcal{O}$,	(5)
$C \sqsubseteq \exists R.A$	by $R_\sqsubseteq(C \sqsubseteq C) : C \sqsubseteq \exists R.A \in \mathcal{O}$,	(6)
$A \sqsubseteq \exists H.B$	by $R_\exists(A \sqsubseteq \exists R.B, B \sqsubseteq B) : \exists H.B \in G(A), R \sqsubseteq_{\mathcal{O}}^* H$,	(7)
$A \sqsubseteq C$	by $R_\sqsubseteq(A \sqsubseteq \exists H.B) : \exists H.B \sqsubseteq C \in \mathcal{O}$,	(8)
$B \sqsubseteq \exists S.C$	by $R_\exists(B \sqsubseteq \exists S.A, A \sqsubseteq C) : \exists S.C \in G(B), R \sqsubseteq_{\mathcal{O}}^* R$,	(9)
$B \sqsubseteq C$	by $R_\sqsubseteq(B \sqsubseteq \exists S.C) : \exists S.C \sqsubseteq C \in \mathcal{O}$.	(10)

The inferences (1)–(10) are shown schematically in Figure 2. Let $F = \{A, B, C\}$. It is easy to see that no new subsumption of the form $X \sqsubseteq Y$ with $X \in F$ and $Y \in G(X)$ can be derived from (1)–(10) using the rules in Figure 1. Furthermore, F satisfies the condition (ii) of Theorem 1 for the set of subsumptions (1)–(10). Hence, by Theorem 1, all subsumptions of the form $X \sqsubseteq Y$ with $X \in F$ and $Y \in G(X)$ that are entailed by $\mathcal{O}$ must occur in (1)–(10). In particular, all entailed subsumptions between atomic concepts A, B, and C that are required for classification of $\mathcal{O}$ are computed.

By Theorem 1, in order to classify an ontology $\mathcal{O}$, it is sufficient to (i) initialize set F with all atomic concepts of $\mathcal{O}$, (ii) assign to every $X \in F$ a set $G(X)$ consisting of all atomic concepts and concepts occurring in the left-hand side of concept inclusion axioms of $\mathcal{O}$, (iii) repeatedly apply the rules in Figure 1 that derive $X \sqsubseteq Y$ with $X \in F$, and (iv) whenever a subsumption of the form $X \sqsubseteq \exists R.Y$ is derived, extend F with Y. By induction, it can be shown that the resulting set S of derived subsumptions satisfies the condition of Theorem 1 and contains only $X \sqsubseteq Y$ for which both X and Y occur in $\mathcal{O}$. Since the number of such subsumptions is at most quadratic in the size of $\mathcal{O}$, the classification procedure terminates in polynomial time.

2.3 Tracing of Inferences

As discussed in the previous section, reasoning in $\mathcal{EL}^+$ is typically performed by computing a set that is *closed* under (restricted) applications of rules in Figure 1, from which all entailed subsumptions of interest (e.g., subsumptions between all atomic concepts for classification) can be obtained using Theorem 1. It is not difficult to use the same procedure to also keep track of how each derived subsumption was obtained. Essentially, for every derived subsumptions, the procedure can store the *inference information* like in (1)–(10). The inference information specifies by which rules the subsumption was obtained, from which premises, and using which side conditions. We refer to a rule application procedure that retains this kind of information as *tracing*.

Tracing of inferences can be used for extracting *proofs* that represent a sequence of inferences producing the given subsumption in the end. Proofs can be reconstructed by simply traversing the inferences backwards: first take the inferences for the given subsumption, then for the subsumptions used in the premises of such inferences, and so on, disregarding cycles. Proofs can be used to automatically check correctness of entailments (proof checking), or to explain how the entailments were produced to the user. The latter is important for *ontology debugging* when the axioms responsible for erroneous conclusions need to be identified. For example, from Figure 2, one can see that the subsumption $A \sqsubseteq C$ was proved in 5 inference steps involving *intermediate subsumptions* $A \sqsubseteq A$, $A \sqsubseteq \exists R.B$, $A \sqsubseteq \exists H.B$, and $B \sqsubseteq B$. From the side conditions of the inferences (4), (7), and (8) used in this derivation, one can see that only axioms $A \sqsubseteq \exists R.B$, $R \sqsubseteq H$, and $\exists H.B \sqsubseteq C$ in $\mathcal{O}$ are responsible for the conclusion $A \sqsubseteq C$.

2.4 Goal-Directed Tracing of Inferences

Keeping information about all inferences in addition to storing the derived subsumptions can be impractical. First, the number of inferences can be significantly larger than the number of the derived conclusions (some conclusions may be derived multiple times by different rules). Second, storing each inference requires more memory than storing just the conclusion of the inference. Finally, inferences may not be required very often. For example, when debugging an ontology, one is usually interested in proofs for only few (unexpected) subsumptions. In applications using large ontologies, such as SNOMED CT, which involve hundreds of thousands of concepts, avoiding storing unnecessary information can make a significant difference in practice.

In this paper, we propose a method for finding the inferences used in the proofs of given subsumptions without performing *full tracing*, i.e., storing all inferences during rule application. The main idea is (i) to over-estimate a subset of subsumptions in the closure from which the given subsumption can be derived (in one inference step), (ii) re-apply the inferences for these subsumptions to find from which premises the subsumption is actually derived, and (iii) repeat the process for these premises.

To illustrate the method, suppose that we have computed the closure (1)–(10) under the rules in Figure 1 (without recording the inference information), and our goal is to identify how subsumption $B \sqsubseteq C$ was derived. By inspecting the conclusions of rules in Figure 1, we can see that every subsumption of the form $X \sqsubseteq Y$ can be either derived by rules $\mathsf{R_0}$ or $\mathsf{R_\top}$, or by other rules using at least one premise of the form $X \sqsubseteq Z$,

$$\vdash^{R_0}_{-\to} A \sqsubseteq A \vdash^{R_\sqsubseteq}_{-\to} A \sqsubseteq \exists R.B \vdash^{R_\exists}_{-\to} A \sqsubseteq \exists H.B \vdash^{R_\sqsubseteq}_{-\to} A \sqsubseteq C$$

$$\xmapsto{\ R_0\ } B \sqsubseteq B \xmapsto{\ R_\sqsubseteq\ } B \sqsubseteq \exists S.A \xmapsto{\ R_\exists\ } B \sqsubseteq \exists S.C \xmapsto{\ R_\sqsubseteq\ } B \sqsubseteq C$$

Fig. 3. The inferences applied for tracing subsumptions of the form $B \sqsubseteq Y$ (solid lines) and of the form $A \sqsubseteq Y$ (dashed lines) in (1)–(10)

i.e., with the same concept X on the left-hand side. Thus, $B \sqsubseteq C$ must have been derived either by R_0 or $R_\top$, or from (2), (5), (9), or (10) using other rules (possibly using other premises from (1)–(10)). It is easy to re-apply all such inferences, this time, with tracing. This way, we reconstruct all inferences producing subsumptions of the form $B \sqsubseteq Y$ in (1)–(10), and, in particular of $B \sqsubseteq C$—see the solid lines in Figure 3.

After we have recorded all inferences producing conclusions of the form $B \sqsubseteq Y$ in (1)–(10), we traverse the computed inferences backwards to see which other premises were involved in the proof for $B \sqsubseteq C$. This way, we arrive at premise $A \sqsubseteq C$, for which no inference was recorded so far. This premise has A on the left-hand side, and similarly as above, we can now compute all inferences deriving subsumptions of the form $A \sqsubseteq Y$ in (1)–(10): see the dashed lines in Figure 3. After we have done this, all inferences used in the proof for $B \sqsubseteq C$ are found.

Our tracing procedure does not guarantee to save only inferences that are used in the proof of the given subsumption. For example, to find the proof for the subsumption $B \sqsubseteq \exists S.A$, we would have similarly saved all inferences for B (solid lines in Figure 3) because at that time, we do not know which of these inferences are used in the proof for $B \sqsubseteq \exists S.A$. Note that producing inferences for A would not be necessary in this case since $A \sqsubseteq C$ is not reachable from $B \sqsubseteq \exists S.A$ when traversing inferences backwards. Similarly, tracing of inferences for B is not necessary when finding proofs for $A \sqsubseteq \exists R.B$, and tracing inferences for neither A nor B is necessary when finding proofs for $C \sqsubseteq \exists R.A$. In our experiments, we will demonstrate that only few inferences need to be re-applied when producing proofs of the entailed subsumptions in existing ontologies.

3   Tracing of Inferences

In this section, we provide a formal description of the goal-directed procedure outlined in the previous section and prove its correctness. The procedure is formulated in a general way and can be used with arbitrary rule systems. In the end of the section we discuss which properties of the inference system are important for efficiency of the method.

3.1   Inferences, Rules, and Closure under the Rules

We start by formalizing the basic notions of inferences and inference rules. Let $\mathbf{E}$ be a fixed countable set of *expressions*. An *inference* over $\mathbf{E}$ is an object *inf* which has a finite set of *premises inf*.Prem $\subseteq \mathbf{E}$ and a *conclusion inf*.concl $\in \mathbf{E}$.[1] When *inf*.Prem $= \emptyset$, we say that *inf* is an *initialization inference*. An *inference rule* R over $\mathbf{E}$ is a countable set

---

[1] We assume that there can be different inferences with the same premises and conclusions.

Algorithm 1. Computing the inference closure by saturation

---

saturation(R):
  input   : R: a set of inferences
  output : S = Clos(R)

1 S, Q ← ∅;
2 **for** *inf* ∈ R **with** *inf*.Prem = ∅ **do**   /* initialize */
3 | Q.add(*inf*.concl);

4 **while** Q ≠ ∅ **do**   /* close */
5 | *exp* ← Q.takeNext();
6 | **if** *exp* ∉ S **then**
7 | | S.add(*exp*);
8 | | **for** *inf* ∈ R **with** *exp* ∈ *inf*.Prem ⊆ S **do**
9 | | | Q.add(*inf*.concl);

10 **return** S;

---

of inferences over **E**; it is an *initialization rule* if all these inferences are initialization inferences. In this paper, we view an *inference system* consisting of several rules as one inference rule R containing all the inferences.

Intuitively, an inference corresponds to an application of a rule to particular premises. For example, the application of $R_\exists$ producing (7) in Example 1 corresponds to an inference *inf* with *inf*.Prem = $\{A \sqsubseteq \exists R.B, B \sqsubseteq B\}$ and *inf*.concl = $(A \sqsubseteq \exists H.B)$. Rule $R_\exists$ in Figure 1 consists of all such inferences in which the premises and conclusions satisfy the side conditions (for the given $G(\cdot)$ and $\mathcal{O}$). Similarly, R_0 is an initialization rule consisting of *inf* with *inf*.Prem = ∅ and *inf*.concl = $(C \sqsubseteq C)$ for all C.

We say that a set of expressions $Exp \subseteq$ **E** is *closed under an inference inf* if *inf*.Prem $\subseteq Exp$ implies *inf*.concl $\in Exp$. *Exp* is *closed under an inference rule* R if *Exp* is closed under every inference *inf* ∈ R. *The closure under* R is the smallest set of expressions Clos(R) that is closed under R. Note that Clos(R) is empty if and only if R does not contain any initialization inferences.

Using the introduced notation, we can now describe the well-known *forward chaining* procedure for computing the closure under the inference rules R. The procedure is formalized in Algorithm 1. Intuitively, the algorithm computes the (expanding) set of expression S, called the *saturation*, by repeatedly matching premises of the rules to S and adding their conclusions back to S until a fixpoint is reached (in contrast, *backward chaining* procedures match the conclusions of rules to the given goals to find the premises). A special care is taken to avoid repeated applications of rules to the same premises. For this purpose, the algorithm uses a queue Q to buffer the conclusions of the inferences. The queue Q is first initialized with conclusions of the initialization inferences (lines 2–3), and then in a cycle (lines 4–9), repeatedly takes the next expression *exp* ∈ Q, and if it does not occur in the saturation S already, inserts it into S and applies all inferences having this expression as one of the premises and other premises from S (line 8). The conclusions of such inferences are then inserted back into Q. Note that every inference *inf* ∈ R with *inf*.Prem ⊆ S is applied by the algorithm exactly once, namely, when the last premise of this inference is added to S.

Algorithm 2. Full tracing of inferences

---

fullTracing(R):

input : R: a set of inferences

output : M: a multimap from expressions to inferences such that M.Keys = Clos(R) and
M(exp) = {$inf \in$ R | inf.Prem $\subseteq$ Clos(R) & inf.concl = exp} ($exp \in$ M.Keys)

1 M, Q ← ∅;

2 **for** $inf \in$ R **with** inf.Prem = ∅ **do**   /* initialize */

3 ⌊ Q.add(inf);

4 **while** Q ≠ ∅ **do**   /* close */

5 │ inf ← Q.takeNext();

6 │ exp ← inf.concl;

7 │ **if** $exp \notin$ M.Keys **then**

8 │ │ M.add($exp \mapsto inf$);

9 │ │ **for** $inf \in$ R **with** $exp \in inf$.Prem $\subseteq$ M.Keys **do**

10 │ │ ⌊ Q.add(inf);

11 │ **else**

12 │ ⌊ M.add($exp \mapsto inf$);

13 **return** M;

3.2 Proofs, Inference Oracle, and Full Tracing

Given the closure S = Clos(R) under the rules R, i.e, the output of Algorithm 1, we are interested in finding proofs for a given expression $exp \in$ S consisting of inferences by which exp was derived in S. Formally, a *proof* (in R) is a sequence of inferences $p = inf_1, \ldots, inf_n$ ($inf_i \in$ R, $1 \le i \le n$) such that inf_j.Prem $\subseteq$ {inf_i.concl | $1 \le i < j$} for each j with $1 \le j \le n$. If $exp = inf_n$.concl then we say p is a *proof for* exp. A proof $p = inf_1, \ldots, inf_n$ for exp is *minimal* if no strict sub-sequence of $inf_1, \ldots, inf_n$ is a proof for exp. Note that in this case inf_i.concl $\neq inf_j$.concl when $i \neq j$ ($1 \le i, j \le n$). For example, the sequence of inferences (1)–(10) in Example 1 is a proof for $A \sqsubseteq C$, but not a minimal proof since there exists a sub-sequence (1), (2), (4), (5), (7)–(10), which is also a proof for $A \sqsubseteq C$ (in fact, a minimal proof for $A \sqsubseteq C$, see Figure 2).

To find minimal proofs, one can use an *inference oracle*, that given $exp \in$ S returns inferences $inf \in$ R such that inf.Prem $\subseteq$ S and inf.concl = exp. Using such an oracle, the proofs can be easily found, e.g., by recursively calling the oracle for the premises of the returned inferences, avoiding repeated requests to ensure minimality of the proofs and termination. If one is interested in retrieving just one proof, it is sufficient to use an inference oracle that returns one inference per expression; if all proofs are required, the oracle should return all inferences producing the given expression from S.

The inference oracle can be implemented by simply precomputing all inferences using a modification of Algorithm 1. This modification is shown in Algorithm 2. We refer to this algorithm as *full tracing*. Instead of collecting the expressions derived by the inferences in S, we collect the inferences themselves and store them in a multimap M: for each applied inference inf, we add a record $exp \mapsto inf$ to M where exp is the conclusion of inf (M is a multimap because several inferences can be stored for the same conclusion). Thus, the *keys* M.Keys of M is the set of all conclusions of inferences in S.

Algorithm 3. Partial tracing of inferences

partialTracing(R, S, *Exp*):
input   : R: a set of inferences, S $\subseteq$ **E**: a subset of expressions,
            Exp $\subseteq$ S $\cap$ Clos({*inf* $\in$ R | *inf*.Prem $\subseteq$ S}): the expressions to trace
output   : M: a multimap from expressions to inferences such that M.Keys = *Exp* and
            M(*exp*) = {*inf* $\in$ R | *inf*.Prem $\subseteq$ S & *inf*.concl = *exp*} (*exp* $\in$ M.Keys)

1 M, Q $\leftarrow$ $\emptyset$;
2 **for** *inf* $\in$ R **with** *inf*.Prem $\subseteq$ S \ *Exp* & *inf*.concl $\in$ *Exp* **do**   /* initialize */
3   $\lfloor$ Q.add(*inf*);

4 **while** Q $\neq$ $\emptyset$ **do**   /* close */
5   $\mid$ *inf* $\leftarrow$ Q.takeNext();
6   $\mid$ *exp* $\leftarrow$ *inf*.concl;
7   $\mid$ **if** *exp* $\notin$ M.Keys **then**
8   $\mid$ $\mid$ M.add(*exp* $\mapsto$ *inf*);
9   $\mid$ $\mid$ **for** *inf* $\in$ R **with** *exp* $\in$ *inf*.Prem $\subseteq$ M.Keys $\cup$ (S \ *Exp*) & *inf*.concl $\in$ *Exp* **do**
10 $\mid$ $\mid$ $\lfloor$ Q.add(*inf*);

11 $\mid$ **else**
12 $\mid$ $\lfloor$ M.add(*exp* $\mapsto$ *inf*);

13 **return** M;

The newly applied inferences are first buffered in the queue Q. When processed, if the conclusion of the inference is new (line 7), we add this inference to M for the conclusion (line 8) and produce all inferences between this conclusion and the previously derived conclusions (lines 9-10). Otherwise, we just store the new inference and do nothing else (line 12). Note that it is easy to modify this algorithm so that only one inference is stored per conclusion. For this, one can just remove line 12 and make M an ordinary map. Similarly to Algorithm 1, Algorithm 2 generates every inference at most once.

Once the multimap is computed, the inference oracle can be easily implemented by performing a lookup in the multimap M for the given expression *exp*.

3.3   Partial Tracing of Inferences and Inference Oracle Based on Partitions

The construction in Algorithm 2 can be further extended to perform *partial tracing*, that is, to compute not all inferences *inf* $\in$ R with *inf*.Prem $\subseteq$ S for S = Clos(R), but only those that produce conclusion in a given set of expressions *Exp*. This idea is realized in Algorithm 3. This algorithm constructs a multimap M that is a restriction of the multimap constructed by Algorithm 2 to the keys from *Exp*. The only difference in this algorithm are lines 2 and 9 where the inferences are applied. First, the algorithm considers only inferences with conclusions in *Exp* (*inf*.concl $\in$ *Exp*). Second, since the algorithm never derives expressions from S \ *Exp*, all premises in S \ *Exp* are considered in each application of the rule. In other words, if to ignore the premises from S \ *Exp* in rule applications, the algorithm would look exactly like Algorithm 2. Note that Algorithm 2 is just an instance of Algorithm 3 when *Exp* = S = Clos(R), in which case S \ *Exp* = $\emptyset$ and the restriction *inf*.concl $\in$ *Exp* can be dropped. In the input of Algorithm 3, we require that *Exp* is a subset of the closure under the inferences *inf* with

$inf.$Prem $\subseteq$ S. This means that every $exp \in Exp$ is derivable by applying $inf \in$ R to only premises in S. This condition holds trivially if $Exp \subseteq$ S = Clos(R).

Theorem 2 (Correctness of Algorithm 3). *Let* R$'$ = $\{inf \in$ R $|$ $inf.$Prem $\subseteq$ S$\}$ *for some set of inferences* R *and a set of expressions* S. *Let* $Exp \subseteq$ S $\cap$ Clos(R$'$), *and* M *the output of Algorithm 3 on* R, S, *and* Exp. *Then* M.Keys = Exp *and* M(exp) = $\{inf \in$ R$'$ $|$ $inf.$concl = $exp\}$ *for each* $exp \in$ M.Keys.

Proof. First, observe that M.Keys $\subseteq Exp$ since only inferences $inf \in$ R with $inf.$concl $\in$ Exp are added to Q. Next we show that M.Keys = Exp. Let Clos$'$ = M.Keys $\cup$ (Clos(R$'$) \ Exp). Note that Clos$'$ $\subseteq$ Clos(R$'$) since M.Keys $\subseteq Exp \subseteq$ Clos(R$'$). We claim that Clos$'$ is closed under R$'$, which implies that Clos$'$ = Clos(R$'$) since Clos(R$'$) is the minimal set closed under R$'$. This proves M.Keys = Exp.

To prove that Clos$'$ is closed under R$'$, take an arbitrary inference $inf \in$ R$'$ such that $inf.$Prem $\subseteq$ Clos$'$. We show that $inf.$concl $\in$ Clos$'$. There are two cases possible:

1. $inf.$concl $\notin Exp$: Since Clos(R$'$) is closed under R$'$, in particular, $inf.$concl $\in$ Clos(R$'$) \ Exp, so $inf.$concl $\in$ Clos$'$.
2. $inf.$concl $\in Exp$: Since $inf.$Prem $\subseteq$ Clos$' \cap$ S, then $inf.$Prem $\subseteq$ M.Keys$\cup$(S \ Exp). Hence inf will be applied either in line 2 if $inf.$Prem $\subseteq$ (S \ Exp), or in line 9 for the last premise $exp \in inf.$Prem $\cap$ M.Keys added to M.Keys. In both cases, inf is added to Q, which means that $inf.$concl $\in$ M.Keys $\subseteq$ Clos$'$.

It remains to prove that M(exp) = $\{inf \in$ R$'$ $|$ $inf.$concl = $exp\}$ for $exp \in$ M.Keys:

($\supseteq$): Take any $exp \in Exp$ and any $inf \in$ R$'$ with $inf.$concl = exp. From Case 2 above, it follows that $inf \in$ M(exp).

($\subseteq$): Take any $exp \in$ M.Keys and any $inf \in$ M(exp). Then from lines 6, 8, and 12 of Algorithm 3 we have $inf.$concl = exp and from lines 2 and 9 we have $inf.$Prem $\subseteq$ M.Keys $\cup$ (S \ Exp). Since M.Keys $\subseteq Exp \subseteq$ S, we obtain that $inf \in$ R$'$.   □

Performance of Algorithm 3 depends on whether it can efficiently enumerate the inferences in lines 2 and 9. Enumerating inferences in line 9 can be simply done by applying all inferences with the given premise exp and other premises from S similarly to Algorithm 2, and disregarding all inferences that do not satisfy the additional conditions (it is reasonable to assume that the number of inference applicable to a given expression exp is already small to start with). Efficient enumeration of inferences in line 2, however, is more problematic and may depend on the particular inference system R and set Exp. As shown in Section 2.4, if we take R to be the $\mathcal{EL}^+$ rules in Figure 1, and Exp the set of subsumptions of the form $X \sqsubseteq Y$ for a fixed concept X, then the inferences $inf \in$ R with $inf.$Prem $\subseteq$ S \ Exp and $inf.$concl $\in Exp$ can be only inferences by $\mathbf{R_0}$ and $\mathbf{R_\top}$ producing $X \sqsubseteq X$ and $X \sqsubseteq \top$ respectively—the other rules cannot derive a subsumption of the form $X \sqsubseteq Z \in Exp$ without a premise of the form $X \sqsubseteq Y \in Exp$.

If all expressions **E** can be partitioned on subsets Exp for which the set of inferences $\{inf \in$ R $|$ $inf.$Prem $\subseteq$ S \ Exp & $inf.$concl $\in Exp\}$ can be efficiently enumerated, then one can implement an inference oracle by (i) identifying the partition Exp to which the given expression exp belongs, (ii) computing the inferences for all expressions in Exp using Algorithm 3, and (iii) returning the inferences for $exp \in Exp$. This approach is more goal-directed compared to the oracle using full tracing, as it only computes and stores the inferences producing conclusions in one partition.

4   Goal-Directed Tracing of Inferences in $\mathcal{EL}^+$

Next we show how to use the approach from Section 3 to implement the tracing procedure for $\mathcal{EL}^+$ described in Section 2.4. We assume that the closure S under the rules R in Figure 1 is computed (for the given parameters $\mathcal{O}$, F, and $G(\cdot)$) and we are given a subsumption $X \sqsubseteq Y \in$ S for which all inferences used in the proofs should be found.

To partition the closure S, we use the partitioning method used for incremental reasoning in $\mathcal{EL}^+$ [11]. Specifically, for a concept X let S$[X]$ be the subset of S consisting of all subsumption $X \sqsubseteq Y \in$ S for all Y. Clearly, S is partitioned on disjoint subsets S$[X]$ for different X. By inspecting the rules in Figure 1, it is easy to see that if the conclusion of the rule belongs to S$[X]$ then either it has a premise that belongs to S$[X]$ as well, or it does not have any premises. Thus, for each $Exp =$ S$[X]$ and each inference inf such that inf.Prem $\in$ S $\setminus Exp$ and inf.concl $\in Exp$, we have inf.Prem $= \emptyset$. Hence, if Algorithm 3 is applied with $Exp =$ S$[X]$, only initialization inferences need to be applied in line 2, which can be done very efficiently.

The inference oracle based on Algorithm 3 can be used to compute the proofs for the derived subsumptions $exp = (X \sqsubseteq Y) \in$ Clos in a goal directed way. For this, we first need to apply Algorithm 3 for the partition $Exp =$ S$[X]$, then, retrieve all inferences inf with conclusion exp from the set of computed inferences, and finally, repeat the process for each premise of the retrieved inferences. This process can be adapted accordingly if only one proof should be generated or proofs are to be explored interactively by the user. Since most inferences by the rules in Figure 1 are applied within individual partitions, this should not result in many calls of Algorithm 3, and since partitions are typically quite small, not many inferences should be saved. We will present empirical evidences confirming these claims in Section 6.

Example 2. Consider the set S consisting of subsumptions (1)–(10) derived in Example 1. These subsumptions are assigned to partitions A, B, and C. To compute the inferences with conclusion $B \sqsubseteq C$, it is sufficient to apply Algorithm 3 for $Exp =$ S$[B]$ using the precomputed closure S. It is easy to see that only inferences for (2), (5), (9), and (10) will be produced by this algorithm (see the solid lines in Figure 3). During initialization (line 2), Algorithm 3 applies only rule R_0 deriving $B \sqsubseteq B$. During closure (line 4), the algorithm applies only inferences to the derived subsumptions in partition S$[B]$, and keeps only inferences that produce subsumptions in the same partition. For example, the inference by $R_\exists$ producing (7) should be ignored, even though it uses a premise $B \sqsubseteq B$ from partition S$[B]$.

Note that knowing S is essential for computing these inferences. E.g., to produce $B \sqsubseteq \exists S.C$ we need to use the premise $A \sqsubseteq C$ from S, which we do not derive during tracing. Thus, the precomputed set S is used in our procedure as a 'set of support'[2] to reach the conclusions of interest as fast as possible.

Now, if we want to traverse the inferences backwards to obtain full proofs for $B \sqsubseteq C$, we need to iterate over the premises that were used to derive $B \sqsubseteq C$ and trace their partitions using Algorithm 3. In our case, $B \sqsubseteq C$ was derived from $B \sqsubseteq \exists S.C$, for which the partition S$[B]$ was already traced, but continuing further to premise $A \sqsubseteq C$ will

---

[2] Analogously to the 'set of support' strategy of resolution, we use premises from S only if at least one other premise comes from the traced partition.

bring us to partition $S[A]$. When tracing partition $S[A]$ using Algorithm 3, we produce the remaining inferences for (1), (4), (7), and (8) used in the proof (see Figure 3). Note that it is not necessary to trace partition $S[A]$ to find the proof for, e.g., $B \sqsubseteq \exists S.A$ because no subsumption in partition $S[A]$ was used to derive $B \sqsubseteq \exists S.A$.

5 Related Work

In the context of ontologies, most research relevant to the issue of explanations has revolved around *justifications*[3]—the minimal subsets of the ontology which entail the result [3,5,8,9,16]. The fact that justifications are minimal subsets is useful to the user but also makes them intractable to compute [16]. Much research has gone into developing optimizations to cope with this complexity in practical cases. The known approaches usually fall into one of the two categories: black-box and glass-box. The former use the underlying reasoning procedure as a black-box and employ generic model-based diagnosis algorithms [17] to find justifications [5,9,8]. Thus, they can work for any (monotonic) logic for which a black-box implementation of a decision procedure is available. On the other hand, such methods cannot use the properties of the reasoning procedure for optimizations and recover the steps used to prove the entailment. Thus, it is still up to the user to understand how to obtain the result from the justifications.

Glass-box methods do use the properties of the underlying reasoning procedure, in particular, for recording how inferences are made. They have been designed for tableau [7], automata [3], and consequence-based procedures [4,18]. The latter methods are similar to what we call full tracing. For example, Sebastiani et. al. [18] encodes every inference performed during $\mathcal{EL}$ classification in propositional Horn logic. E.g., inference (8) in Example 1 would correspond to $s_{[A\sqsubseteq\exists H.B]} \land ax_{[\exists H.B\sqsubseteq C]} \rightarrow s_{[A\sqsubseteq C]}$. Once the entire formula $\phi_\mathcal{O}$ capturing all inferences is built, justifications, e.g., for $A \sqsubseteq C$, can be found by pinpointing conflicts in $\phi_\mathcal{O} \land \neg s_{[A\sqsubseteq C]}$ using the corresponding functionality of SAT solvers.

Any algorithm for computing justifications can be optimized using *ontology modularity* techniques to obtain a goal-directed behaviour (see, e.g., [5]). The so-called *locality-based modules* [6] are well-defined fragments of the ontology which guarantee to contain all justifications for a given entailment. Modules can be often computed efficiently and can limit the search for justifications to a smaller subset of the ontology.

We conclude this section by briefly discussing the relationship between our tracing technique and justifications. From any (minimal) proof obtained by unfolding the inferences computed by Algorithm 3 one can extract the axioms used in the side conditions of inferences ($\mathbf{R}_\sqsubseteq$, $\mathbf{R}_\exists$, and $\mathbf{R}_\circ$ in the $\mathcal{EL}$ case), which represent a subset of the ontology that entails the proved subsumption. This subset, however, might be not a minimal subset for this entailment, but all minimal subsets—that is, *justifications*—can be easily computed from all such sets. Note that this can be done "offline", i.e., the reasoner is not needed after tracing the inferences. Instead of computing the justification by enumerating proofs, one can also simply take the set of all axioms used in the proofs and extract all justifications from this set using any conventional method [4,9,5,8,18]. Our evaluation

---

[3] Not to be confused with justifications in the context of Truth Maintenance Systems.

Table 2. Number of axioms, partitions, conclusions and inferences in test ontologies, running time (in ms.) and memory consumption (in MB) for classification with and without full tracing

Ontology	Num. of axioms	Num. of partitions	Num. of conclusions (max per partition)		Num. of inferences	No tracing time mem.		Full tracing time mem.	
GO	87,492	46,846	2,450,505	(395)	5,715,611	1,877	546	5,004	1,102
GALEN	36,547	25,965	1,922,549	(1,350)	3,944,921	1,326	722	3,786	765
SNOMED	297,327	371,642	19,963,726	(484)	54,553,961	16,968	924	OOM	OOM

shows that these subsets are much smaller than the locality-based modules usually used for this purpose, and computation of justifications from them is much faster.

6   Experimental Evaluation

We implemented algorithms 2 and 3 as well as their recursive extension to obtain full proofs within the $\mathcal{EL}^+$ reasoner ELK[4] (which implements Algorithm 1 as its base procedure). We used three large OWL EL ontologies commonly used in evaluations of $\mathcal{EL}$ reasoners [2,13,15]: a version of the Gene Ontology (GO),[5] an $\mathcal{EL}^+$-restricted version of the GALEN ontology,[6] and the July 2013 release of SNOMED CT.[7] We used a PC with Intel Core i5-2520M 2.50GHz CPU, with Java 1.6 and 4GB RAM available to JVM. The following experiments have been performed:

Full Tracing Overhead: Our first experiment evaluates the overhead of full tracing (Algorithm 2) comparing to pure saturation (Algorithm 1). Each ontology was classified 10 times with and without full tracing and the results were averaged (excluding 5 warm-up runs). The results in Table 2 show that there is roughly x2–x4 time overhead. The memory overhead is also significant which causes the algorithm to run out of memory (OOM) when classifying SNOMED CT with full tracing.[8] In addition, the results show that the maximal number of conclusions per partition is negligible in comparison with the total number of conclusions. Thus the fact that Algorithm 3 saves some inferences not used in proofs of the target expression should not result in a substantial overhead.

Goal-Directed Tracing: Next we evaluate performance of the recursive proof tracing procedure based on goal-directed tracing with partitions (i.e., on Algorithm 3). The experimental setup is as follows: each ontology was classified and then each direct subsumption between concept names was traced with recursive unfolding. Each subsumption was traced independently of others. We separately report results for tracing

---

[4] Version 0.5.0, projected release date Oct 2014, see http://elk.semanticweb.org.

[5] It is a richer version with concept equivalences, role hierarchies and chains. We thank Chris Mungall from the Lawrence Berkley Lab for providing it. It is accessible at:
http://elk.semanticweb.org/ontologies/go_ext.owl.

[6] http://www.co-ode.org/galen/

[7] http://www.ihtsdo.org/snomed-ct/

[8] With the smaller ontologies the difference is less observable because of the relatively high (4GB) memory limit set to JVM; the difference is better observable with lower memory limits.

Table 3. Results for recursive goal-directed tracing partitions on all atomic subsumptions in the ontology when all (resp. the first) inferences for each conclusion are recursively unfolded. All numbers, e.g., the number of traced partitions, are averaged over all traced subsumptions.

Ontology	Total # of traced subsumptions	# of traced partitions	# of traced inferences	# of inferences used in proofs	# of used $\sqsubseteq$ axioms	Time (in ms.)
GO	73,270	3.7 (1.4)	456.2 (244.1)	94.9 (6.4)	18.6 (2.5)	2.0 (1.2)
GALEN	38,527	1.9 (1.5)	414.4 (350.9)	21.7 (10.1)	5.2 (4.4)	1.9 (0.8)
SNOMED	443,402	8.6 (1.6)	788.3 (332.9)	385.9 (12.7)	9.7 (3.7)	10.1 (1.9)

all of the inferences for each conclusion or just of the first inference. The former is useful for generating *all* proofs whereas the latter can be used to produce *one* proof.

The results are presented in Table 3. First, they demonstrate that the proposed method is very fast as it takes just a few milliseconds to find all inferences used in all proofs of a given subsumption. This is the effect of its goal-directed nature: it only traces inferences which belong to the same partitions as inferences actually used in the proofs, and the partitions are relatively small. From Table 2 one can calculate that the biggest partitions do not exceed 0.07% of the total number of derived subsumptions while on average there are only 122, 152, and 146 inferences per partition in GO, GALEN, and SNOMED CT respectively. The performance results thus follow from the low number of traced partitions and traced inferences. Second, the algorithm traces more inferences when all proofs are needed but the difference is not substantial and the running times are usually close. This is because alternative proofs overlap and the algorithm rarely needs to trace new partitions when considering more than one inference per conclusion. Third, the difference between the number of traced and used inferences shows granularity of partitioning in $\mathcal{EL}^+$ (inferences not used in proofs are traced only if they happen to be in one partition with used inferences). Finally, since the results are averaged over all subsumptions, the reader may wonder if the good performance is because most of them can be proved trivially. We present a more detailed evaluation in the technical report [12], where we separately aggregate results over subsumptions that are provable from at least 10 axioms and show that performance stays on the same level.

Tracing and Justifications: In our final experiment, we investigate if it makes sense to use our tracing method to improve the computation of justifications. As discussed in Section 5, the set of axioms used in the side conditions of the inferences in each proof must be a superset of some justification. So it is worth to compare the number of such axioms with the sizes of justifications. Finding all justifications is intractable so we consider only the first proof and the first justification. In addition, we compare the number of axioms used in all proofs of a subsumption with the size of the $(\top\bot)^*$-*module* extracted for this subsumption, and the times needed to extract the first justification from these sets—as discussed, both sets must contain all justifications. We use the OWL API which provides generic methods for extracting modules and finding justifications.

The results are given in Table 4. While we were able to generate the first justifications for all subsumptions in GO, it was not feasible for GALEN and SNOMED CT (with a 10 hours time-out). The problem with GALEN is that modules are large and even the first justification often takes minutes to pinpoint in the corresponding module (but

Table 4. Computing the set of subsumption axioms used in all proofs S_{all} or the first proof S_1 vs. extracting the module M for the signature of the entailment or computing the first justification J_1. Size of M and J_1 is measured as the number of subsumption axioms (concept equivalence axioms in the ontologies are rewritten as two subsumptions). Running times are in milliseconds.

Ontology	Num. of traced subsumptions	S_{all} size (max size)	S_1 size	S_{all} time	S_1 time	J_1^S time	M size	M time	J_1 size	J_1 time
GO	73,270	18.6 (288)	2.5	2.0	1.2	25.1	124.8	164	2.2	85
GALEN	38,527	5.2 (86)	4.4	1.9	0.8	128.1	10,899	195	4.35	N/A
SNOMED CT	10,000 (sample)	9.7 (133)	3.7	10.1	1.9	19.0	38.8	887	1.9	48

not in the results of tracing, as explained below). Thus we focus only on the size of modules and their extraction time. In contrast, modules of SNOMED CT are small but take nearly a second to extract (since the ontology is large). So instead of extracting them for all subsumptions, we took a random uniform sample of 10, 000 subsumptions.

For GO and SNOMED CT it can be seen that on average the number of axioms used in the first proof (S_1) is not much larger than the size of the first justification (J_1) while the number of axioms used in all proofs (S_{all}) is 3–7 times smaller than the module (M). The latter difference is several orders of magnitude for GALEN, which induces very large modules due to cyclic axioms. The time required to extract the first justification from S_{all} (J_1^S time) is also 2.5–3.5 times smaller then the time to extract the first justification from M (J_1 time) for the cases where it was possible.

7 Summary

In this paper we have presented a simple, efficient, and generalizable method for goal-directed tracing of inferences in $\mathcal{EL}^+$. Depending on the application, the inferences can be used offline to produce proofs or compute justifications. The method is goal-directed in the sense that it re-applies only a limited number of inferences using the previously computed conclusions as a set of support. It does not require storing additional indexing information or any sort of bookkeeping during the normal classification.

The method is based on the same *granularity property* of reasoning in $\mathcal{EL}^+$ as was previously used for concurrent and incremental reasoning [13,11]. Specifically, concept subsumers in $\mathcal{EL}^+$ most of the time can be computed independently of each other. This enables efficient partitioning of all derived expressions so that tracing a particular expression requires re-applying inferences only in few partitions, as shown empirically.

It is worth pointing out that our goal-directed procedure does not guarantee to be an improvement over full tracing in worst case: it is easy to construct pathological examples which trigger full tracing. This happens, e.g., for $\mathcal{O} = \{A_i \sqsubseteq A_{i+1} \mid 1 \leq i < n\} \cup \{A_n \sqsubseteq A_1\}$, for which every inference is used in the proof of every entailed subsumption (since all concepts are equivalent), or for $\mathcal{O} = \{A \sqsubseteq B_i \mid 1 \leq i \leq n\}$, for which there is only one partition. Arguably, such examples are not to be often expected in practice as the number of entailed subsumers of each concept is usually relatively small.

References

1. Baader, F., Brandt, S., Lutz, C.: Pushing the $\mathcal{EL}$ envelope. In: Proc. 19th Int. Joint Conf. on Artificial Intelligence (IJCAI 2005), pp. 364–369 (2005)
2. Baader, F., Lutz, C., Suntisrivaraporn, B.: Efficient reasoning in $\mathcal{EL}^+$. In: Proc. 2006 Int. Workshop on Description Logics (DL 2006), vol. 189, CEUR-WS.org (2006)
3. Baader, F., Peñaloza, R.: Automata-based axiom pinpointing. J. of Automated Reasoning 45(2), 91–129 (2010)
4. Baader, F., Peñaloza, R., Suntisrivaraporn, B.: Pinpointing in the description logic $\mathcal{EL}$. In: Proc. 2007 Int. Workshop on Description Logics (DL 2007), vol. 250, CEUR-WS.org (2007)
5. Baader, F., Suntisrivaraporn, B.: Debugging SNOMED CT using axiom pinpointing in the description logic $\mathcal{EL}^+$. In: KR-MED, vol. 410. CEUR-WS.org (2008)
6. Cuenca Grau, B., Horrocks, I., Kazakov, Y., Sattler, U.: Modular reuse of ontologies: Theory and practice. J. of Artificial Intelligence Research 31, 273–318 (2008)
7. Halashek-Wiener, C., Parsia, B., Sirin, E.: Description logic reasoning with syntactic updates. In: Meersman, R., Tari, Z. (eds.) OTM 2006. LNCS, vol. 4275, pp. 722–737. Springer, Heidelberg (2006)
8. Horridge, M., Parsia, B., Sattler, U.: Laconic and precise justifications in OWL. In: Sheth, A.P., Staab, S., Dean, M., Paolucci, M., Maynard, D., Finin, T., Thirunarayan, K. (eds.) ISWC 2008. LNCS, vol. 5318, pp. 323–338. Springer, Heidelberg (2008)
9. Kalyanpur, A., Parsia, B., Horridge, M., Sirin, E.: Finding all justifications of OWL DL entailments. In: Aberer, K., et al. (eds.) ISWC/ASWC 2007. LNCS, vol. 4825, pp. 267–280. Springer, Heidelberg (2007)
10. Kazakov, Y.: Consequence-driven reasoning for Horn $\mathcal{SHIQ}$ ontologies. In: Proc. 21st Int. Joint Conf. on Artificial Intelligence (IJCAI 2009), pp. 2040–2045. IJCAI (2009)
11. Kazakov, Y., Klinov, P.: Incremental reasoning in OWL EL without bookkeeping. In: Alani, H., et al. (eds.) ISWC 2013, Part I. LNCS, vol. 8218, pp. 232–247. Springer, Heidelberg (2013)
12. Kazakov, Y., Klinov, P.: Goal-directed tracing of inferences in $\mathcal{EL}$ ontologies. Tech. rep., University of Ulm (2014), http://elk.semanticweb.org
13. Kazakov, Y., Krötzsch, M., Simančík, F.: Concurrent classification of $\mathcal{EL}$ ontologies. In: Aroyo, L., Welty, C., Alani, H., Taylor, J., Bernstein, A., Kagal, L., Noy, N., Blomqvist, E. (eds.) ISWC 2011, Part I. LNCS, vol. 7031, pp. 305–320. Springer, Heidelberg (2011)
14. Kazakov, Y., Krötzsch, M., Simančík, F.: The incredible ELK: From polynomial procedures to efficient reasoning with $\mathcal{EL}$ ontologies. J. of Automated Reasoning 53(1), 1–61 (2014)
15. Lawley, M.J., Bousquet, C.: Fast classification in Protégé: Snorocket as an OWL 2 EL reasoner. In: Proc. 6th Australasian Ontology Workshop (IAOA 2010), vol. 122, pp. 45–49 (2010)
16. Peñaloza, R., Sertkaya, B.: On the complexity of axiom pinpointing in the $\mathcal{EL}$ family of description logics. In: Proc. 12th Int. Conf. on Principles of Knowledge Representation and Reasoning (KR 2010), pp. 280–289. AAAI Press (2010)
17. Reiter, R.: A theory of diagnosis from first principles. Artificial Intelligence 32(1), 57–95 (1987)
18. Sebastiani, R., Vescovi, M.: Axiom pinpointing in lightweight description logics via Horn-SAT encoding and conflict analysis. In: Schmidt, R.A. (ed.) CADE-22. LNCS (LNAI), vol. 5663, pp. 84–99. Springer, Heidelberg (2009)
19. Simančík, F., Kazakov, Y., Horrocks, I.: Consequence-based reasoning beyond Horn ontologies. In: Proc. 22nd Int. Joint Conf. on Artificial Intelligence (IJCAI 2011), pp. 1093–1098. AAAI Press/IJCAI (2011)

Semantic Web Application Development with LITEQ

Martin Leinberger[1], Stefan Scheglmann[1], Ralf Lämmel[2], Steffen Staab[1],
Matthias Thimm[1], and Evelyne Viegas[3]

[1] Institute for Web Science and Technologies, University of Koblenz-Landau, Germany
[2] The Software Languages Team, University of Koblenz-Landau, Germany
[3] Microsoft Research Redmond, US

Abstract. The Semantic Web is intended as a web of machine readable data where every data source can be the data provider for different kinds of applications. However, due to a lack of support it is still cumbersome to work with RDF data in modern, object-oriented programming languages, in particular if the data source is only available through a SPARQL endpoint without further documentation or published schema information. In this setting, it is desirable to have an integrated tool-chain that helps to understand the data source during development and supports the developer in the creation of persistent data objects. To tackle these issues, we introduce LITEQ, a paradigm for integrating RDF data sources into programming languages and strongly typing the data. Additionally, we report on two use cases and show that compared to existing approaches LITEQ performs competitively according to the Halstead metric.

1 Introduction

RDF has primarily been developed for consumption by applications rather than direct use by humans. However, its design choices, which facilitate the design and publication of data on the Web, complicate the integration of RDF data into applications as its principles do not tie in smoothly with modern concepts in programming languages.

A paradigm that aims to support a developer in integrating RDF data into his application must overcome several challenges. First, accessing an external data source requires knowledge about the structure of the data source and its vocabulary.

Therefore, an approach that provides integration of RDF data sources should include a mechanism for exploring and understanding the RDF data source at development time. Second, it is desirable that an exploration and integration mechanism is well-integrated, easily learnable and useable. The integration should be either on programming language level or at least in the used IDE (*Integrated Development Environment*), as this allows for seamless exploration and integration during application development. Third, there is an impedance mismatch between the way classes or types are used in programming languages compared to how classes are used in RDF data, cf. [8,14,6,3]. For this reason, an approach for integrating RDF data into a programming language must define a clear mapping between these two mismatching paradigms.

To address these challenges, we present LITEQ, a paradigm for querying RDF data, mapping it for use in a host language, and strongly typing[1] it for taking the full benefits

---

[1] By "strongly typed", we refer to languages where it is not possible to have unchecked runtime type errors, e.g., through validating the program by static type checking before execution.

P. Mika et al. (Eds.) ISWC 2014, Part II, LNCS 8797, pp. 212–227, 2014.

of advanced compiler technology. The core of LITEQ is the Node Path Query Language (NPQL), a variable-free schema and data query language, which comprises the following features:

1. various operators for the navigation and exploration of RDF graphs (Section 4.1),
2. an intensional semantics, which defines the retrieval of RDF schema information and enables our implementation of LITEQ to provide persistent code types of RDF entities (Section 4.3),
3. an extensional semantics, which defines the retrieval of RDF resources and enables our implementation of LITEQ to construct persistent objects from the retrieved data (Section 4.3), and
4. an autocompletion semantics, which assigns a formal result set to partially written, i.e. incomplete, queries; this allows an incremental query writing process (Section 4.2).

The fully functional prototype of LITEQ (called $\text{LITEQ}^{F\#}$) is written in F#, a member of Microsoft's .NET family. Up until now, there has been only limited support for RDF in the .NET framework. Our approach $\text{LITEQ}^{F\#}$ is currently being prepared to be added to the FSharp.Data project, a library containing access mechanisms for many different structured data formats. In this in-use paper, we report also on two use cases that show the applicability of LITEQ for practical problems. The prototype is documented at our website[2] and can be downloaded from github[3].

The remainder of the paper is organized as follows. In Section 2, we start with a brief introduction of RDF and F# followed by a general process overview of how a data model based on the Semantic Web is implemented in Section 3. We then describe LITEQs features in Section 4 and its implementation in Section 5 before we show the feasibility of our approach based on two different use cases in Section 6. This is followed by a discussion of related work in Section 7 and a short summary in Section 8.

2   Foundations

The Resource Description Framework[4] is a data model for representing data on the Web. An RDF a data source consist of a graph, which is a set of RDF statements (triples).

Definition 1 (RDF Graph). *Let B (blank nodes), L (literals), and U (URIs) be disjoint sets. An RDF graph G is a set of RDF triples: $G = \{(s\ p\ o)|(s\ p\ o) \in (B \cup U) \times U \times (B \cup L \cup U)\}$. In each RDF triple, s is referred to as subject, p as predicate and o as object.*

In the further course of this paper, we assume that such a graph is enriched with complete RDF schema information such that each predicate between a subject and an object

---

[2] LITEQ Project at WeST
   http://west.uni-koblenz.de/Research/systems/liteq, last visit 12th Mai, 2014.
[3] LITEQ on Github https://github.com/Institute-Web-Science-and-Technologies/Liteq, last visit 12th Mai, 2014.
[4] RDF Primer: http://www.w3.org/TR/rdf-primer last visit January 13th, 2014.

is appropriately typed with a domain class that the subject belongs to and a co-domain class that the object belongs to. In addition, we assume for each property only one single domain class and one single co-domain class exists. If such strict assumptions are not met by the RDF data sources, LITEQ provides configuration possibilities that can make up for not meeting this assumption and which will be explained in Section 4.

The F# language is a statically typed, object-oriented and functional-first programming language based on Microsoft's .NET framework. It has been fully open sourced by the F# Software Foundation and features a cross-platform compiler that allows F# to run on Windows, Linux and OS X. Libraries written in F# can be used in all .NET languages.

3   Process Overview for Implementing a Use Case

Generally, the process of developing an application using an RDF data source can be described by five different tasks that must be addressed during development. First, the developer must design an initial data model based on the requirements of his application (Task 1). He explores the schema of his data set and identifies the RDF classes and properties that are of interest to him (Task 2). To this end, he either has external documentation that he refers to, or has to explore the schema using a series of SPARQL queries. In this step, he will also align his previously created data model to the data source. He can then leave the design phase and enter the coding phase, where he implements a data model prototype in the programming language (Task 3) and designs the queries he needs to access the data (Task 4). Lastly, he has to combine the results of Task 3 and 4. He needs to map the results of his previously written queries onto the code types representing his data model (Task 5). Figure 1 summarizes the process.

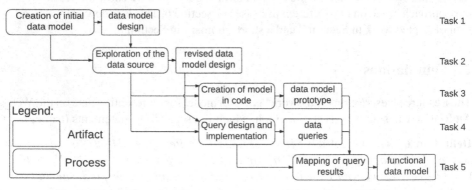

Fig. 1. Process Overview for creating a data model based on a RDF data set

4   Using $LITEQ^{F\#}$ in Practice

The current implementation of LITEQ in F# is IDE-independent and can be used in many F#-IDE like Microsoft's Visual Studio[5], Xamarin Studio[6], or Monodevelop[7].

---

[5] http://www.visualstudio.com/ last visit April 29th, 2014.

[6] https://xamarin.com/studio last visit April 29th, 2014.

[7] http://monodevelop.com/ last visit April 29th, 2014.

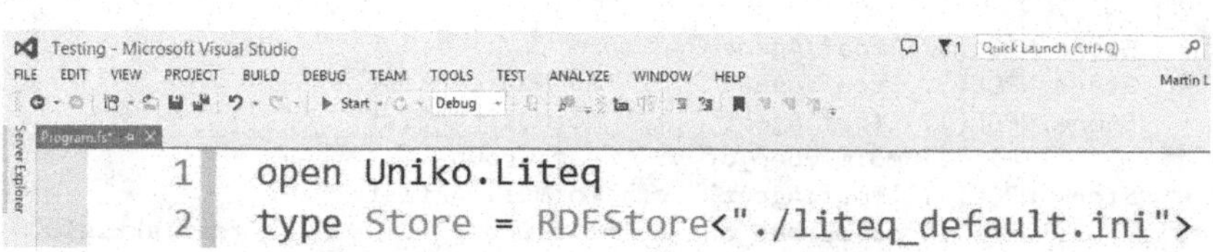

Fig. 2. Setting up LITEQ

As with any other library, LITEQ must be referenced and imported before it can be used. This is shown in Figure 2. The developer imports the LITEQ API, cf. line 1, and sets up a data access object using a specific configuration. Listing 1 shows an example of such a configuration file.

```
serverUri=http ://.../ openrdf−sesame / repositories /Jamendo
isReadOnly=false
prefixfile=prefixes . ini
```

Listing 1. A LITEQ configuration File

The first line of this configuration file defines a SPARQL endpoint that is acting as a data source. The key isReadOnly defines whether the endpoint also accepts SPARQL update queries or not[8]. In the example configuration, it is set to false, meaning that the store can be updated. The prefixfile property points to a file in which RDF vocabulary prefixes are defined. This is optional, as the namespaces and prefixes may not be known beforehand, but improves the readability of expressions as the shortened versions can be used instead of the full URI. As many real world data sources separate the schema from the data and provide the schema only as a separate file, the optional property schemaFile has been introduced. This property can be used to include such an external schema file. If the property is not given, the schema is assumed to be queryable via the given SPARQL endpoint.

The data access object returned by the initialization can then be used to perform the different operations provided by LITEQ, such as exploration, navigation, and data retrieval.

4.1 Node Path Query Language

Core to LITEQ is the Node Path Query Language (NPQL), a schema and data navigation language which supports the developer in navigating and exploring the RDF data source from within his programming environment.

The NPQL method of the data access object mentioned above allows for navigating the schema using NPQL expressions, cf. Figure 3.

Every NPQL expression starts with an URI of the target graph. In case of the example shown in Figure 3, line 10, we start with foaf:Agent as entry point for our NPQL exploration. The different operators of NPQL then allow for traversal of the RDF schema from this entry point on. We provide three different operators in NPQL, which allow for navigating through the schema in different ways.

---

[8] Objects constructed by LITEQ$^{F\#}$ can automatically update the store when assigned new data.

```
 6  Store.NPQL().``foaf:Agent``
 7  Store.NPQL().``foaf:Agent``.v.``mo:MusicArtist``
 8 ⊟Store.NPQL().``foaf:Agent``.v.``mo:MusicArtist``
 9 |     .``->``.``mo:member_of``.``foaf:Group``
10 ⊟Store.NPQL().``foaf:Agent``.v.``mo:MusicArtist``
11 |     .``->``.``mo:member_of``.``foaf:Group``.``<-``.``foaf:skypeID``
```

Fig. 3. Navigating the Schema using NPQL

1. The subtype navigation operator "v" refines the currently selected RDF type to one of its direct subclasses. The expression in Figure 3 line 7, will refine the selected starting point foaf:Agent to mo:MusicArtist.
2. The property navigation operator "->" expects a property that may be reached from the currently selected RDF type. This property is used as an edge to navigate to the next node, which is defined as the range type of that property. So extending the NPQL expression from the Figure 3 lines 8–9, shifts the selection from foaf:Agent to the property and further to its foaf:Group, its range.
3. The property restriction operator "<-" expects a property and uses this property to restrict the extension of the currently selected RDF node. To illustrate this, let us assume a property restriction choosing foaf:skypeID, cf. Figure 3 line 10–11. This will not change the currently selected RDF type but restrict its extension to all URIs of RDF type foaf:Group for which there is also an foaf:skypeID relation.

Using these three operators, the developer can explore the data. Furthermore, he can use the very same expressions to construct data types and objects from the data and schema, as we will demonstrate in Section 4.3.

4.2   Autocompletion Support

LITEQ$^{F\#}$ provides an autocompletion mechanism for NPQL, i.e., at every step of query writing we can formally define the meaning of the partially written query and provide suggestions for completion. This was done in order to support the developer during the exploration of the data source as described in Task 2, Section 3. Figure 4 shows the autocompletion feature when writing an NPQL query in Visual Studio. The developer starts with mo:MusicArtist and decides to perform a property navigation. This evaluates to the list of all properties, that have mo:MusicArtist or one of its supertypes is its domain.

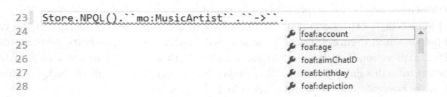

Fig. 4. LITEQs Autocompletion support

In a further step, the developer reduces the results by defining the starting letters of the properties to be "ma", cf. Section 4.1. As shown in Fig. 5, this reduces the results to `foaf:made` and `foaf:maker`.

```
23   Store.NPQL().``mo:MusicArtist``.``->``.foaf:ma
```

Eigenschaft Temporary classes,http://purl.org/ontology/mo/   foaf:made
MusicArtistPropNav.foaf:made: RDFStore.RDFStore<...>.foaf:madeProperty   foaf:maker

Something that was made by this agent.

Fig. 5. Refinement of autocompletion suggestions

4.3 Evaluation of NPQL Expressions

In order to interpret NPQL expressions, LITEQ provides two different functions, (Extension and Intension) that evaluate complete NPQL expressions based on two formal semantics. We only provide an informal overview here, the formal intensional and extensional semantics of NPQL can be found in our technical report published on `https://west.uni-koblenz.de/Research/systems/liteq`

Intension The intensional semantics evaluates an NPQL expression to a code type (the intension). This relates to Task 3 (data model creation) as presented in Section 3. Figure 6 shows the intension of `mo:MusicArtist`, cf. line 11. In the figure, its code type MusicArtist is subsequently used to instantiate a new artist newArtist, cf. line 12. The declared MusicArtist class has property definitions of all properties as they were defined in the RDF schema, e. g., the `foaf:name` property of the new instance which is set to myBandName, cf. line 13.

```
11   type MusicArtist = Store.``mo:MusicArtist``.Intension
12   let newArtist = new MusicArtist("http://.../artist/1234")
13   newArtist.``foaf:name`` <- [ "myBandName" ]
```

Fig. 6. Declaring code types using LITEQ

Extension The extensional semantics evaluates an NPQL expression to its set of RDF objects. The extension could either be a set of URIs (in case of RDF types) or to a set of domain/range tuples (in case of properties). This relates to Task 4 (Query design) as presented in Section 3. However, LITEQ will also automatically type the result of such an extensional evaluation, returning instances of code types as if they were generated through an intensional evaluation. Therefore, extensional evaluation also relates to Task 5 (Mapping of query results). Figure 7 shows such a extensionally evaluated NPQL expression, cf. line 15. This statement returns a sequence of all `mo:MusicArtist` to allArtists. This sequence is subsequently iterated in order to print the music records of all artists, cf. lines 16-17.

```
17  let allArtists = Store.NPQL().``mo:MusicArtist``.Extension
18  for artist in allArtists do
19    printfn "Artist %A made the following records: %A" artist artist.``foaf:made``
```

Fig. 7. Querying for all artists and iterating through the result

In $LITEQ^{F\#}$, both, the intensional and extensional evaluation is implemented by transforming the expressions into SPARQL queries which are then executed against a SPARQL endpoint.

5   Implementation of LITEQ$^{F\#}$

$LITEQ^{F\#}$ is based on the type provider[9] framework. This framework allows us to generate code types based on the available schema information.

Figure 8 shows a class diagram of the current implementation. It is centered around the LITEQ type provider, which serves as an entry point. It is also responsible for building the navigational classes for NPQL. All code necessary for the mapping from RDF types to actual programming language types is contained in the TypeMapper class. Both need access to the triples and schema information, which can currently either be a generic SPARQL endpoint via the SPARQL HTTP interface or a dump of the schema.

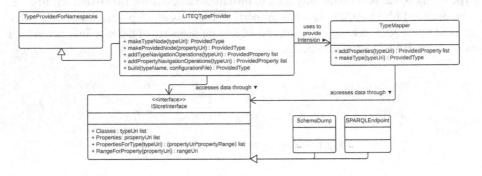

Fig. 8. Simplified (for brevity) class diagram of the implementation

Figure 9 shows the runtime behavior of the system. At some point, the library is called via the *build* method. This will trigger the creation of all necessary classes for NPQL queries and usage in the language. However, they newly created classes do not yet contain any properties as this turned out to be to slow in practice. Properties are only added once the IDE asks the object for its properties. The objects contain callbacks to the methods of the LITEQ type provider or type mapper that will return all properties for the specific object. This step finalizes the object.

---

[9] http://msdn.microsoft.com/en-us/library/hh156509.aspx

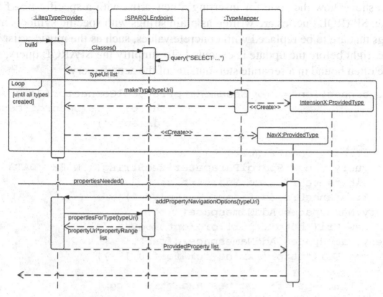

Fig. 9. Sequence diagram of behavior during usage

6 Use Cases

In order to show the feasibility of $LITEQ^{F\#}$, we have chosen to implement two tasks using a traditional framework such as dotNetRDF and the $LITEQ^{F\#}$ approach. We then compare the implementations using the Halstead metric [5] to determine the difficulty and effort of the implementations.

6.1 Use Case: Creating a New Artist Object and Listing All Tracks

An RDF data source in a programming language should be easily queryable but also modifiable. Therefore, our first simple use case is about inserting new data and iterating over a subset:

R1 The program shall create a new instance of type music artist and assign a name to that instance.

R2 The program shall iterate over all instances of type music artist and print the music records associated with them.

The data that serves as the input for this task comes from the Jamendo data set[10].

6.1.1 Implementation Using the dotNetRDF Framework

A SPARQL implementation of this task relies on the SPARQL Update functionality. This type of SPARQL queries allow the insertion of new triples into the triple store.

---

[10] http://moustaki.org/resources/jamendo-rdf.tar.gz, last accessed on 08.05.14.

Listing 3 shows how the code for inserting a new artist with a specific foaf:name looks like. SPARQL queries are written as plain strings with specific symbols marking substrings that are to be replaced with concrete values, such as the music artist URI or the name, right before the update is executed. To simplify the SPARQL query, namespaces are often bound in a separate step outside of the actual query.

```
let connection = new SesameHttpProtocolConnector(
                                "http://.../openrdf-sesame",
                                "Jamendo")

// Defining Update query
let query = new SparqlParameterizedString("INSERT DATA {
    @instanceUri a mo:MusicArtist .
    @instanceUri foaf:name @name . }")
query.Namespaces.AddNamespace("mo",
    new Uri("http://purl.org/ontology/mo/"))
query.Namespaces.AddNamespace("foaf",
    new Uri("http://xmlns.com/foaf/0.1/"))

// Setting specific values and executing
query.SetUri("instanceUri",
    new Uri("http://artist/1234"))
query.SetLiteral("name", "myBandName")
connection.Update( query.ToString() )
```

Listing 2. Inserting a new MusicArtist with a specific name

Iterating over the music artists is similar. Listing 3 shows how it can be implemented. Again, the query is defined as a string with the namespaces being bound separately. In this specific query, the expected result contains always the artist URI and the record URI that was made by this artist. The result of this query is initially a result set, which can be grouped by artists by piping[11] it to the *group by* function and specifying a projection function. The computation will result in tuples containing the specific artist and a list of result sets that contain the query results about the artist. These result sets associated with the different artists can then be mapped to a list containing only the record URIs. The resulting tuple containing artist and the list of records they made can then be printed to the console.

```
let query' = new SparqlParameterizedString("SELECT
    ?artist ?record WHERE {
    ?artist a mo:MusicArtist .
    ?artist foaf:made ?record .
}")
query'.Namespaces.AddNamespace("foaf",
    new Uri("http://xmlns.com/foaf/0.1/"))
query'.Namespaces.AddNamespace("mo",
    new Uri("http://purl.org/ontology/mo/"))
```

---

[11] The pipe operator f | > g is used to pass the result of one computation to the next one. An equal statement has the form g(f()).

```
let results =
    connection.Query(query'.ToString()):?>SparqlResultSet
    |> Seq.groupBy( fun res ->
        res.Value("artist").ToString() )
    |> Seq.map( fun (artist, results) ->
        artist, results |> Seq.map(fun res ->
            res.Value("record").ToString())
    )
for (artist, records) in results do
    printfn "Artist %A made the following records: %A"
```

Listing 3. Iterating over artists and printing records

6.1.2 Implementation Using LITEQ

The LITEQ implementation has already been used as an example. Creating a new music artist is an intensional evaluation of the mo:MusicArtist URI. The resulting type can afterwards be instantiated and assigned data via setter methods as displayed in Fig. 6.

Iterating over the music artists in the data source is an extensional evaluation of mo:MusicArtist—this returns a sequence of music artists that is iterable as done in Fig. 7.

6.1.3 Comparison

In order to evaluate the two different approaches, we chose to apply the Halstead metric. According to Halstead, a program can be seen as a collection of tokens that are classified as operators and operands. Halstead [5] then defines:

Definition 2 (Halsteads complexity measure). *Let n_1 be the number of distinct operators, N_1 the total number of operators, n_2 the number of distinct operands, and N_2 the total number of operands. Then one has:*

Program vocabulary $n = n_1 + n_2$
Program length $N = N_1 + N_2$
Volume $V = N \times log_2 n$
Difficulty $D = \frac{n_1}{2} \times \frac{N_2}{n_2}$
Effort $E = D \times V$
Necessary time $T = \frac{E}{18} seconds$

Of special interest to us is the difficulty of a program, which expresses how hard it is to understand it a code review, and the theoretical time that is needed to code such a program. When applying the metric, we defined that all language constructs, such as "let .. =", "type .. =" or "for .. in .. do" and access operators were to be counted as operations. The same holds for static parameters[12] and "," creating tuples in mappings[13].

---

[12] <> indicate a static parameter.

[13] We omitted them when they were used as separators for method parameters due to language differences between F#, for which LITEQ is optimized and C#, which dotNetRDF was written in.

The remaining type and method names were counted as operands. The same holds for strings, except for those representing SPARQL queries. SPARQL queries were counted as one operator for the general construct (INSERT DATA .. or SELECT .. WHERE ..), one operation to form a specific triple pattern and three operands per triple. In LITEQ namespaces are defined in an separate file, so we did not count the code necessary to add namespace definitions, as shown in Listing 3, By applying this metric to the Use Case, we get the results shown in Table 2[14]

Table 1. Halsteads complexity applied to Use Case 1

	dotNetRDF	LITEQ
No. of distinct operators (n_1)	12	7
No. of distinct operands (n_2)	39	18
Total no. of operators (N_1)	36	15
Total no. of operands (N_2)	63	25
Program Vocabulary	51	25
Program length	99	40
Program Volume	561,57	185,75
Difficulty	9,69	4,86
Effort	5442,91	902,97
Time needed	302s	50s

6.2   Use Case: Analyzing Number of EU Seats for Countries

RDF data sets, especially governmental data, are often used for analysis and visualization. Therefore, the second use case visualizes the number of EU seats hold by different countries:

R1 The program shall select all countries that hold at least one EU seat
R2 The program shall then transform this data into a suitable structure and visualize it

The data set used for this task was a dump of the DBpedia data set[15].

6.2.1   Implementation Using the dotNetRDF Framework
Using the dotNetRDF framework, a developer needs to open the connection to the SPARQL endpoint and can then write a query receiving the name of the country and its number of seats. He then needs to map the result from the result set to a tuple containing a string representing the name of the country and the number of EU seats. The visualization is then only a function call. Listing 4 shows the the necessary code to do so in F#.

---

[14] The full source code with annotations that describe what we counted as operand and operator or omitted(e.g. brackets) can be found under
http://www.uni-koblenz-landau.de/campus-koblenz/fb4/west/
Research/systems/liteq
[15] Available under http://wiki.dbpedia.org/Downloads39, last accessed on 06.05.14

```
let connection = new SparqlRemoteEndpoint(
        new Uri("http://dbpedia.west.uni-koblenz.de:8890/sparql"))
let data =
    connection.QueryWithResultSet("""SELECT ?countryName
    ?numberOfSeats WHERE {
        ?country <http://dbpedia.org/property/euseats>
            ?numberOfSeats .
        ?country <http://xmlns.com/foaf/0.1/name> ?countryName .
        }""")
    |> Seq.map ( fun resultSet ->
        resultSet.Value("countryName").ToString(),
        int(resultSet.Value("numberOfSeats").ToString()
        .Replace("^^http://www.w3.org/2001/XMLSchema#integer",
            "")))
    )

data
|> Chart.Pie
```

Listing 4. Calculating percentage of EU seats

6.2.2 Implementation Using LITEQ

All countries holding an EU seat can be selected using an NPQL expression. The expressions returns a sequence of `Country` objects as if created through the intension, the name and number of EU seats can be accessed as in an object model. While they return proper types (strings for the name and ints for the number of EU seats), they return lists of these types as the schema did not specify the cardinality. In order to visualize the countries are mapped to a sequence of tuples containing name and number of EU seats by accessing the corresponding members and taking the first element out of the result list. Listing 5 shows the necessary code to do so.

```
type Store = RDFStore<".\liteq_default.ini">

let euCountries =
    Store.NPQL().``dbpedia:Country``.``<-``.``dbpediapr:euseats``
    .Extension

euCountries
|> Seq.map( fun country ->
    country.``foaf:name``.[0],
        country.``dbpediapr:euseats``.[0] )
|> Chart.Pie
```

Listing 5. Calculating percentage of EU seats using SPARQL

However, as the DBPedia ontology did not specify any range or domain for the number of EU seats a country holds, we had to extend the schema, in the local schema file, with the specific values to enable this implementation.

6.2.3   Implementation Using a Custom Object Model

Apart from comparing the implementations in LITEQ and plain SPARQL, we also want to compare to an custom implementation. Such an implementation bases on a object model which incorporates schematic information that exceeds the information currently available in RDFS such as information about cardinalities of properties.

As such object models usually do not incorporate query languages, all countries have to be selected in this scenario. The resulting sequence can then be filtered to contain only countries that hold at least one EU seat. To visualize the data, the same approach as with LITEQ can be used — mapping the sequence of countries to a sequence of tuples containing name and number of seats for the country and passing this to the visualization function. Listing 6 displays such code.

```
connectToStore "http://.../openrdf-sesame/Jamendo"

let euCountries =
    Country.findAllInstances
    |> Seq.filter( fun country -> country.EuSeats > 0 )

euCountries
|> Seq.map( fun country -> country.Name, country.EuSeats )
|> Chart.Pie
```

Listing 6. Calculating percentage of EU seats with an object model

6.2.4   Comparison

To evaluate the three different approaches, we again apply the Halstead metric as defined in Def. 2.

Table 2. Halsteads complexity applied to Use Case 2

	dotNetRDF	LITEQ	Custom Object Model
No. of distinct operators (n_1)	9	7	6
No. of distinct operands (n_2)	25	16	13
Total no. of operators (N_1)	19	18	13
Total no. of operands (N_2)	34	22	20
Program Vocabulary	34	23	19
Program length	53	40	33
Program Volume	269,64	180,94	140,20
Difficulty	6,12	4,81	4,62
Effort	1650,17	870,79	646,99
Time needed	92s	49s	36s

Again, the version using dotNetRDF and SPARQL is the most difficult to understand and slowest to code. LITEQ improves on this while a custom object model can improve on LITEQ.

6.3   Evaluation of the Results

The Halstead metric supports our assumption—in both use cases, it is much easier to understand the code implementing such a scenario with LITEQ than using SPARQL queries. The same holds for the time necessary to write the code, which is, in all cases less for LITEQ than a implementation using dotNetRDF.

When comparing LITEQ to a custom object model, it can be seen that there is still room for improvement. A better mapping from RDF types to code types manifests itself in less difficulty and less effort. However, if such a better mapping exists, we can incorporate it into LITEQ and get similar results.

7 Related Work

LITEQ is generally related to three different research directions: query languages for RDF, the integration of data access into a host languages in particular mappings of RDF into the object oriented paradigm, and exploration tools for unknown RDF data sources.

Considering query languages, a number of different languages are available for RDF. In general, we can distinguish two different ways of querying graph data as RDF. The first one considers querying as a graph matching problem, matching subgraphs descriptions against the data, like in SPARQL queries. The second way is by using a graph traversal language, like Gremlin[16] or Cypher[17] or the languages mentioned in [16]. Examples of graph traversal languages for RDF data are nSPARQL [13], a language with focus on navigation through RDF data, or GuLP [4], which can include preferential attachment into its queries. However, there are two major differences between these two, exemplary chosen, languages and LITEQ. While nSPARQL and GuLP both use their own evaluation implementations, LITEQ exploits the widely spread SPARQL support by mapping its queries to SPARQL. The second difference lies in the type generation provided by LITEQ.

NPQL queries and Description Logics (DL) expressions share some similarities. A DL expressions always describes a concept, its place in the concept lattice and the extension of the concept. Similarly, NPQL expressions can be evaluated extensionally to a set of entities or intensionally to a type description including its place in the type hierarchy. The intensional evaluation of NPQL expressions also consists information about the attributes of the type, in contrast to DL concepts which only contain information about constrains over attributes.

The problem of accessing and integrating RDF data in programming environments has already been recognized as a challenge in various work. Most approaches focus on ontology driven code generation in order to realize RDF access in the programming environment. Frameworks like ActiveRDF [9], AliBaba[18], OWL2Java [8], Jastor[19], RDFReactor[20], OntologyBeanGenerator[21], and Àgogo [12] were developed in the past.

---

[16] Gremlin graph traversal language
   https://github.com/tinkerpop/gremlin/wiki last visit January 13th, 2014.
[17] Cypher graph traversal language in Neo4J
   http://docs.neo4j.org/chunked/stable/cypher-query-lang.html last visit January 13th, 2014.
[18] http://www.openrdf.org/alibaba.jsp last visit January 13th, 2014.
[19] http://jastor.sourceforge.net/ last visit January 13th, 2014.
[20] http://semanticweb.org/wiki/RDFReactor last visit January 13th, 2014.
[21] http://protege.cim3.net/cgi-bin/wiki.pl?OntologyBeanGenerator
   last visit January 13th, 2014.

An overview can be found at Tripresso[22], a project web site on mapping RDF to the object-oriented world. The common goal for all these frameworks is to translate the concepts of the ontology into an object-oriented representation. While the previous examples are targeted at specific languages, some concepts which are language-agnostic language exist. Àgogo [12] and OntoMDE [15] are programming-language independent model driven approaches for automatically generating ontology APIs. They introduce intermediate steps in order to capture domain concepts necessary to map ontologies to object-oriented representations. All the aforementioned approaches rely on external exploration of the data, dedicated type declarations, and code generation steps in order to provide the desired data representations in a programming language.

The basic mapping principles of RDF triples to objects common to the previously presented approaches [10] and programming language extensions to integrate RDF or OWL constructs [11] have already been explored. LITEQ also uses these principles. However, there are two main differences that sets LITEQ apart. For one, LITEQ has build-in type generation support, that can automatically generate such types. Another examples that also features this is [11]. This is a language extension for C# that offers features to represent OWL constructs in C# and that is able to create the types at compile time. In contrast to LITEQ however, there is no means for querying and navigating unknown data sources. The developer must be fully aware of the structure of the ontology ahead of development time.

Other research work has a dedicated focus on exploration and visualization of Web data sources. The main motivation of this work is to allow users without SPARQL experiences an easy means to get information from RDF data sources. tFacet [1] and gFacet [7] are tools for faceted exploration of RDF data sources via SPARQL endpoints. fFacet provides a tree view for navigation, while gFacet has a graph view for browsing. The navigation of RDF data for the purpose of visualizing parts of the data source is studied in [2], but with the focus on visualization aspects like optimization of the displayed graph area. In contrast to LITEQ, these approaches do not consider any kind of integration aspects like code generation and typing. Furthermore, the navigation is rather restricted to a simple hierarchical top-down navigation.

8   Summary

This paper presented the fully functional prototype of LITEQ$^{F\#}$ targeted for release as part of FSharp.Data library. The implementation features a new paradigm to access and integrate representations for RDF data into typed programming languages. We also showed the feasibility of our approach. The documentation of the current LITEQ$^{F\#}$ library, including a video showing LITEQ in use, can be found on our website[23], while the source code is available at Github[24]. In the near future, we plan to improve performance

---

[22] http://semanticweb.org/wiki/Tripresso last visit January 13th, 2014.

[23] http://west.uni-koblenz.de/Research/systems/liteq, last visit 12th Mai, 2014.

[24] https://github.com/Institute-Web-Science-and-Technologies/Liteq, last visit 12th Mai, 2014.

and stability of the system, before shifting focus and ensuring a smooth integration into FSharp.Data.

Acknowledgments. This work has been supported by Microsoft.

References

1. Brunk, S., Heim, P.: tFacet: Hierarchical Faceted Exploration of Semantic Data Using Well-Known Interaction Concepts. In: DCI 2011. CEUR-WS.org, vol. 817, pp. 31–36 (2011)
2. Dokulil, J., Katreniaková, J.: Navigation in RDF Data. In: iV 2008, pp. 26–31. IEEE Computer Society (2008)
3. Eisenberg, V., Kanza, Y.: Ruby on semantic web. In: Abiteboul, S., Böhm, K., Koch, C., Tan, K.-L. (eds.) ICDE 2011, pp. 1324–1327. IEEE Computer Society (2011)
4. Fionda, V., Pirrò, G.: Querying graphs with preferences. In: CIKM 2013, pp. 929–938 (2013)
5. Halstead, M.H.: Elements of Software Science (Operating and Programming Systems Series). Elsevier Science Inc., New York (1977)
6. Hart, L., Emery, P.: OWL Full and UML 2.0 Compared (2004), http://uk.builder.com/whitepapers/0and39026692and60093347p-39001028qand00.htm
7. Heim, P., Ziegler, J., Lohmann, S.: gFacet: A Browser for the Web of Data. In: IMC-SSW 2008. CEUR-WS, vol. 417, pp. 49–58 (2008)
8. Kalyanpur, A., Pastor, D.J., Battle, S., Padget, J.A.: Automatic Mapping of OWL Ontologies into Java. In: SEKE 2004 (2004)
9. Oren, E., Delbru, R., Gerke, S., Haller, A., Decker, S.: Activerdf: object-oriented semantic web programming. In: WWW 2007, pp. 817–824. ACM (2007)
10. Oren, E., Heitmann, B., Decker, S.: ActiveRDF: Embedding Semantic Web Data into Object-oriented Languages. J. Web Sem., 191–202 (2008)
11. Paar, A., Vrandečić, D.: Zhi# - OWL Aware Compilation. In: Antoniou, G., Grobelnik, M., Simperl, E., Parsia, B., Plexousakis, D., De Leenheer, P., Pan, J. (eds.) ESWC 2011, Part II. LNCS, vol. 6644, pp. 315–329. Springer, Heidelberg (2011)
12. Parreiras, F.S., Saathoff, C., Walter, T., Franz, T., Staab, S.: 'a gogo: Automatic Generation of Ontology APIs. In: ICSC 2009. IEEE Press (2009)
13. Pérez, J., Arenas, M., Gutierrez, C.: nsparql: A navigational language for rdf. J. Web Sem. 8(4), 255–270 (2010)
14. Rahmani, T., Oberle, D., Dahms, M.: An adjustable transformation from owl to ecore. In: Petriu, D.C., Rouquette, N., Haugen, Ø. (eds.) MODELS 2010, Part II. LNCS, vol. 6395, pp. 243–257. Springer, Heidelberg (2010)
15. Scheglmann, S., Scherp, A., Staab, S.: Declarative representation of programming access to ontologies. In: Simperl, E., Cimiano, P., Polleres, A., Corcho, O., Presutti, V. (eds.) ESWC 2012. LNCS, vol. 7295, pp. 659–673. Springer, Heidelberg (2012)
16. Wood, P.T.: Query languages for graph databases. SIGMOD Record 2012 41(1), 50–60 (2012)

Semantic-Based Process Analysis[*]

Chiara Di Francescomarino[1], Francesco Corcoglioniti[1], Mauro Dragoni[1],
Piergiorgio Bertoli[2], Roberto Tiella[1], Chiara Ghidini[1], Michele Nori[2],
and Marco Pistore[2]

[1] FBK—IRST, Trento, Italy
{dfmchiara,corcoglio,dragoni,tiella,ghidini}@fbk.eu
[2] SayService, Trento, Italy
{bertoli,nori,pistore}@sayservice.it

Abstract. The widespread adoption of Information Technology systems and
their capability to trace data about process executions has made available Information Technology data for the analysis of process executions. Meanwhile,
at business level, static and procedural knowledge, which can be exploited to
analyze and reason on data, is often available. In this paper we aim at providing an approach that, combining static and procedural aspects, business and data
levels and exploiting semantic-based techniques allows business analysts to infer knowledge and use it to analyze system executions. The proposed solution
has been implemented using current scalable Semantic Web technologies, that
offer the possibility to keep the advantages of semantic-based reasoning with
non-trivial quantities of data.

1 Introduction

The last decades have witnessed a rapid and widespread adoption of Information Technology (IT) to support business activities in all phases, governing the execution of business processes and the processing and storage of related documents. This, together with
knowledge at the business level, gives the potential to leverage IT techniques to analyze
business procedures, thus bringing several remarkable advantages, as for example to allow business analysts to observe and analyze process executions; to identify bottlenecks
and opportunities of improvement of processes; to identify discrepancies between the
way processes have been designed, and the way they are really executed.

In fact, a variety of Business Intelligence tools have been proposed, even by major
vendors, that aim at supporting Business Activity Monitoring (BAM), and hence the
activities above, to different extent; examples are Engineering's eBAM,[1] Microsoft's
BAM suite in BizTalk,[2] Oracle's BAM.[3] However, all these approaches mainly focus,
besides data, on the only procedural knowledge. The knowledge related to the static

---

[*] This work is supported by "ProMo - A Collaborative Agile Approach to Model and Monitor
Service-Based Business Processes", funded by the Operational Programme "Fondo Europeo
di Sviluppo Regionale (FESR) 2007-2013 of the Province of Trento, Italy.

[1] http://www.eclipse.org/ebam

[2] https://www.microsoft.com/biztalk/en/us/business-activity-
monitoring.aspx

[3] http://www.oracle.com/technetwork/middleware/bam/
overview/index.html

P. Mika et al. (Eds.) ISWC 2014, Part II, LNCS 8797, pp. 228–243, 2014.

aspects of the domain (e.g., concerning documental or organizational aspects), generally representable as domain ontologies, is not taken into account, thus precluding the capability to reason on and analyze execution data from a business domain perspective.

On the contrary, existing approaches for the semantic monitoring and analysis of processes usually separately focus on model or execution aspects. Several works, including [1,2,3,4,5,6,7], enrich process models with semantic knowledge either for specifying the execution semantics of models or for denoting the meaning of their elements. Only few attempts have been made to combine the static and the procedural model at the business layer with execution data (e.g., [8]). In these works, however, business knowledge is mainly exploited to provide domain-independent solutions to automate the reconciliation between the business and data layers, rather than to support analysis. In this paper we focus on enabling business analysts to perform useful analysis on process execution data, covering both static and procedural dimensions as well as business and data levels. Our contribution is twofold: (i) by extending our previous work [6,9] combining static and procedural dimensions, we define a semantic model for combining static, procedural and data knowledge, which enables semantic reasoning and allows analysts to query asserted and inferred knowledge to bring execution data analysis at business level; and (ii) we propose an implementation of the approach on top of current Semantic Web technologies – namely triplestores – that aims at coping with the large quantities of data and the high data rates typical of real application scenarios.

The paper is organized as follows. In Section 2 we present the problem through an example scenario, which is then used, in Section 3, to introduce the orthogonal dimensions we tackle and the high level idea of the proposed approach. In Section 4 we describe the integrated model and its components from a conceptual point of view, while Section 5 and Section 6 report about implementation and evaluation on a project use case, respectively. Finally, Section 7 presents related works and Section 8 concludes.

2 Scenario

In this section we present an application scenario for the proposed approach. It will be used throughout the paper to clarify the concepts and the motivation behind the work. The example has been taken from an industrial case study related to the Public Administration field in the context of the *ProMo* project for the collaborative modeling, monitoring and analysis of business processes. Figure 1 shows the process model (represented in the BPMN [10] notation) describing the Italian birth management procedure, that aims at recording citizens' birth data. Data have to be stored both in the municipality registry and in the central national registry (SAIA) – since newborns are Italian citizens who live in a given municipality – as well as in the national welfare system repository (APSS) – as newborns are users of the welfare system. For instance, the newborn can be first registered in the welfare repository and then in the registry systems or viceversa, according to the parents' choice. This, in turn, requires the coordination of several actors, as well as the generation of some crucial data that will become part of the personal data of the newborn – e.g. his/her ID, the Fiscal Code (FC).

In scenarios like this one, which are applied on a large scale and with high public costs, it is important to be able to analyze the actual executions of the procedures or to

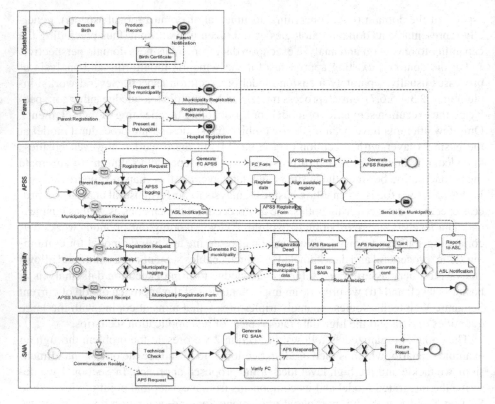

Fig. 1. Birth Management Process

realize what-if analyses for maintenance purposes. This means understanding how procedures perform; how many, when and where failures and bottlenecks occur; whether executions deviate from the model. Examples of queries related to the birth management procedure that business analysts could be interested to answer are:

Q.1 the average time per process execution spent by the municipality of Trento;
Q.2 the total number of Registration Request documents filled from January, 1st, 2014;
Q.3 the percentage of times in which the flow followed is the one which passes first through the APSS pool and then through the Municipality one;
Q.4 the number of cases and the average time spent by each public office involved in the birth management procedure for executing optional activities (i.e., activities which, taken a path on the model, can be either executed or not);

Finding an answer to this kind of questions poses three interesting challenges.

Challenge 1. Combining Three Different Dimensions. Scenarios in which a procedure is carried out in a specific domain, as the one described above, are very common in practice. They are usually characterized by three main dimensions that need to be taken into account per se and in combination in order to be able to analyse the scenario: a *procedural dimension*, a dimension describing the specific *domain of interest* and an *execution dimension*. The *procedural dimension* is defined by the process model describing the carried out procedure. For example, such a dimension is required for detecting in Q.3

whether the execution flow passes first through the APSS pool and then through the municipality pool or viceversa. Knowledge about the *domain of interest*, i.e., the domain in which the procedure is carried out, makes it possible, for example, to identify in Q.2 what are Registration Request documents. Finally, the *execution dimension*, i.e., the actual execution data both in terms of the procedural execution trace and of produced data is required for example for retrieving in Q.1 the actual execution time.

Challenge 2. Semantic Reasoning. In many cases and especially in complex scenarios, data explicitly asserted in collected execution traces and in process and domain models represent only part of the information that is globally available about a process. In these cases, semantic reasoning enabled on top of the three orthogonal components makes it possible to query not only asserted but also inferrable information. For example, in query Q.4 semantic reasoning allows both making explicit the semantics of public offices, as well as reasoning about paths in the process model to detect optional activities (which are situated on alternative paths between two directly connected gateways).

Challenge 3. Scalability. Scenarios characterizing complex organizations, as, for example, Public Administrations (PAs), tend to deal with massive data. PAs usually have huge and complicated procedures with several variants and exceptions, which relate to as much huge and structured domains (e.g., in all PA domains the document classification is usually very intricate). In this kind of scenarios a huge quantity of data is usually produced at a very high rate. For example, in Italy there are about 500000 newborns per year with, on average, a birth per minute.[4] It means that, at least 500000 (one per minute) execution traces of the birth management procedure are produced per year and have to be readily managed and analyzed. This demands for a scalable system able to manage this huge quantity of data in a reasonable time, so as to (i) process and store execution data with a high throughput; and (ii) provide a prompt answer, which also takes into account procedures not yet completed, to queries involving this data.

3 An Integrated View

Analysts dealing with situations like those characterizing complex organizations usually need to face the problem of combining and reconciling knowledge and information related to different orthogonal dimensions, the business and the data as well as the static and the dynamic one. Figure 2 depicts these layers and dimensions:

- At **business level**, knowledge describes the domain of interest (e.g., the company's documents, organization and procedures) and pertains to two dimensions:
  D.1 the *procedural* knowledge (**P**), usually represented using business process models that offer a view on the steps carried out to realize specific objectives;
  D.2 the (static) *domain* knowledge (**K**), which describes aspects of the domain such as the organization structure (e.g., role hierarchy), the data structures (e.g., document organization) and the relations among these and other domain entities; these aspects are usually described in terms of ontological knowledge.
- At **data level**, the data stored by information systems provide information on the actual *execution*s of business procedures, leading to our third dimension:

---

[4] Data by the Italian statistical office for year 2011
(http://www.istat.it/it/archivio/74300).

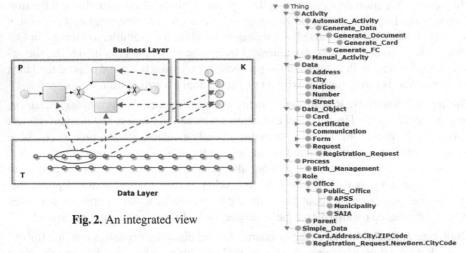

Fig. 2. An integrated view

Fig. 3. Extract of domain ontology

D.3 the IT data, i.e., the execution traces (**T**) collected by IT systems that describe the sequence of events and the data related to a process execution.

Concerning IT data, we focus on knowledge integration and exploitation assuming that heterogeneous data have already been reconciled and collected into execution traces. A preprocessing step to collect IT data into execution traces (e.g., [11]) and to align traces with the business layer (e.g., semantic-based [8] or structural approaches [12]) can be realized by exploiting existing approaches in the literature.

In order to improve on state-of-the-art approaches, which do not allow analysts to investigate these three dimensions together, we propose to combine the knowledge related to the domain described at business level K, the one related to the procedural aspects P and the data captured by IT systems T, into a semantic solution and take advantage of it for inferencing and querying purposes.

The first step towards the integration is combining the two types of business knowledge: the static (K) and the procedural (P) one. Intuitively, combining K and P, means enriching the process diagram components with the semantic knowledge [6,9] and viceversa, i.e., adding a procedural view to the static knowledge. For instance, in the example of the birth management procedure, a role APSS, semantically characterized as a Public Office role by the taxonomy of roles shown in the excerpt of domain ontology of Figure 3, can be associated to the APSS pool of the process in Figure 1.

The second step consists of combining the business and the data layers, i.e., K and P with T. Assuming to have (i) an execution trace that collects all the events and the associated data and performers related to a single execution , and (ii) an alignment of these components with the business knowledge, combining the business and the data layers intuitively means instantiating the business level components with the corresponding set of execution data. For example, an event "Fiscal Code Generation" in an execution trace, according to the alignment between data and business, could be an instance of the activity labeled with "Generate FC Municipality" enriched with its domain semantics.

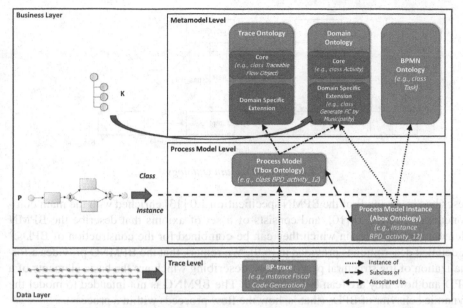

Fig. 4. Integrated Ontological Model. For each component of the model, a class or instance example is provided (among parenthesis).

4 A Comprehensive Model for Process Execution Analysis

To be exploited for query purposes, the three types of knowledge (K, P and T) described in Section 2 need to be expressed in a unique language and plugged into an integrated system. In this section we present the conceptual model used for the integration. To this purpose, three ontologies were formalized – a *BPMN Ontology*, a *Domain Ontology* and a *Trace Ontology* – and a three-level *architectural model* was built on top of them. Purpose of the *Domain Ontology* is to provide a formal description of the static aspects of the domain (K), while the *BPMN Ontology* and the *Trace Ontology* provide a formalization of a metamodel of the procedural (P) and data (T) aspects, respectively.

Figure 4 shows how the three ontologies are used to formalize and combine the three starting ingredients (P, K and T) along with the three levels. Specifically, at the *Metamodel* level, which deals with all types of knowledge encompassing process model scenarios (i.e., the core parts of the *Trace Ontology*, *Domain Ontology* and *BPMN Ontology*), K is formalized as an extension of the core *Domain Ontology*. At the *Process Model* level, which deals with knowledge specific to a process model, the integration of P and K is formalized. Finally, at the *Trace* level, focusing on the execution traces, T and its relationships with P and K are formalized.

In the following we discuss in more details each of the three ontologies (Section 4.1) and then describe their integration into the three-level architectural model (Section 4.2).

4.1 Component Description

BPMN Ontology. The *BPMN Ontology* (BPMNO) formalizes the structure of a business process model diagram (BPD). It is a formalization of the BPMN standard as

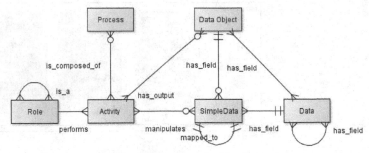

Fig. 5. *Core Domain Ontology*

described in Annex B of the BPMN specification 1.0 [13] enriched with the main components of BPMN2.0 [10], and consists of a set of axioms that describe the BPMN elements and the way in which they can be combined for the construction of BPDs.[5] A detailed description is provided in [6,9]. We remark that the BPMNO provides a formalization of the structural part of BPDs, describing which are the basic elements of a BPD and how they are (can be) connected. The BPMNO is not intended to model the dynamic behavior of BPDs (that is, how the flow proceeds within a process).

Domain Ontology. The *Domain Ontology*, which is in charge of providing a formalization of the static aspects of the domain of interest, is composed of an upper-level part – the *Core Domain Ontology* – that describes the high level concepts and is independent from the specific domain, and, for each domain, of a domain-dependent extension.

Goal of the *Core Domain Ontology* (reported in Figure 5) is offering a framework for the definition of the key entities and relationships characterizing the domain of a business process. Its central entity is the *activity*, which can constitute the building block of a *process*, i.e., a process *is composed of* a non-empty set of activities. An activity is usually performed by an executor with a specific *role*, which, in turn, can be classified in a hierarchy of roles (e.g., in the case of complex organizations) and can produce in output *data objects* (e.g., a document), which are collections of *data*. Data in data objects are organized in data structures, which, in turn, can be further structured in other data structures and so on, so that, only at the end of the chain, a value can be associated to a *simple data* (e.g., a non-decomposable field of a document).

The *domain-dependent extension* specializes classes and properties of the *Core Domain Ontology* for a specific domain of interest, as shown in Figure 3 for the birth management scenario. In this example, the activity of type `Generate_card` performed by the `Municipality` role could have as output a `Card` data object. The `Address` is one of the data reported in the data object. However, `Address` could be, in turn, a data structure organized in `Street`, `Number`, `City`, `Nation`. Also `City` can be further structured (e.g., in terms of `CityName` and `ZIPCode`) and so on up to reach simple data.

It is worth pointing out that the *Core Domain Ontology* defines and emphasizes the relationship between activities and simple data, i.e., how an activity *manipulates* (cre-

---

[5] The BPMN 1.0 ontology enriched with some of the new main elements of BPMN2.0 can be found at `https://shell-static.fbk.eu/resources/ontologies/bpmn2_ontology.owl`

ates, updates, displays) a simple data. To this end, a unique semantics is associated to each simple data nested in a specific chain of data structures and on each manipulation property defined between manipulating activities and data fields. For example, `Card.Address.City.ZIPCode` is a simple data on which it is possible to explicitly define the activity manipulations. Moreover, simple data of different data objects can be mapped one to another (via property *mapped_to*, see Figure 5) to indicate that they hold the same value, thus providing useful knowledge to perform reasoning. For example, the data on the card emitted by the municipality corresponds to the data reported by the citizen on the registration request module, thus `RegistrationRequest.NewBorn.CityCode` and `Card.Address.City.ZIPCode` are mapped one to another.

Trace Ontology. The *Trace Ontology* ontology has finally been designed to specifically address the aspects related to the execution, providing a metamodel representation of the knowledge that can be collected and traced by IT systems (i.e., knowledge in terms of instances) and stored in execution traces. It also has a core part – the *Core Trace Ontology* – whose key entity is the *Trace*. A trace is composed of *Traceable Process Elements*, which can be either *Traceable Flow Objects* and *Traceable Data Objects*. The first are (instances of) events traced by IT systems that can have both a start and an end time intervals and an actual *Performer*. The latter are (instances of) data structures collecting sets of data. The core part of the *Trace Ontology* (the *Core Trace Ontology*) can then be enriched and structured according to the specific types of information collected by IT systems and analyzed in a particular scenario. For example, properties defining the provenance of data or events of the execution trace (e.g., the IT system they come from), could need to be stored, and hence the *Trace Ontology* extended accordingly.

4.2   A Three-Level Architectural Model

Starting from the components previously described, a three-level architectural model has been built to combine the three dimensions K, P and T. Figure 4 depicts such a model, which extends our previous work [6,9] that only accounts for K and P.

The first level (*Metamodel* level) contains the three ontologies mentioned in the previous subsection, i.e., the initial building blocks of the integrated model: the *BPMN Ontology*, the *Domain Ontology*, representing an ontological formalization of the domain knowledge, and the *Trace Ontology*. Referring to the examples shown (within parenthesis) in Figure 4, classes `Task`, `Activity` and `Traceable_Flow_Object` are representative of the contents of the *BPMN Ontology*, *Domain Ontology* and *Trace Ontology* respectively, and all of them lie in the Metamodel level.

The second level (*Process Model* level) contains an integrated description of a single process model diagram in terms of domain and procedural aspects. Such an integrated model can be looked in two different ways. On one side (and similarly to the approach in [6,9]), a process diagram and the elements it contains are *instances* of the corresponding semantic classes in the *Domain Ontology* and *BPMN Ontology*. On the other side (and differently from [6,9]), a process model diagram and its elements are model components which, though still inheriting their domain semantics from a *Domain Ontology*, act as *classes* that are instantiated by process execution traces. In this view, a more agile and specific semantics than the heavy one given by the BPMN notation, can be provided by these classes to the execution traces (e.g., there is no need to constraint the event corresponding to an activity execution to have at most an outgoing sequence flow). For example, in the birth management process, the BPMN activity labeled with "Generate FC Municipality" (e.g., the diagram element with id "BPD_activity_12") is an instance of the *Domain Ontology* class `Generate_FC_by_Municipality` and of the *BPMN Ontology* class `Task` (see the examples in Figure 4). However, the same element is also a class instantiated by the actual executions (in the trace level) of the "Generate FC Municipality" activity, that, by exploiting subsumption relations, inherits the characteristics of `Traceable_Flow_Object` from the *Trace Ontology* and of `Generate_FC_by_Municipality` in the *Domain Ontology*. To represent these two perspectives on process model elements, we decided to model them both as individuals of an *Abox Ontology* (as modelling is at instance level) that instantiates the *Domain Ontology* and the *BPMN Ontology*, and as classes of a *Tbox Ontology* (as modelling is at the terminological level) that specializes the *Domain Ontology* and the *Trace Ontology*; a special *associated_to* relation links corresponding elements in the two ontologies.[6]

Finally, a third level (*Trace* level) is devoted to store the execution traces. An execution trace is actually an instance of the process model diagram class of the *Tbox Ontology* that is, as described above, a subclass of the *Domain Ontology* class specifying the process domain semantics and of the `Trace` class of the *Trace Ontology*. For example, an execution trace of the birth management process will be an instance of the *Tbox Ontology* class inheriting from the *Domain Ontology* `Birth_Management` class and the *Trace Ontology* `Trace` class, the latter related to properties typical of execution traces. Events and data structures in the execution trace are managed similarly.

By looking at the examples in Figure 4 we can get an overall clarifying view of the three levels and their relationships. For instance, the trace event "Fiscal Code Generation" is represented as an instance of the *Tbox Ontology* class corresponding to the BPMN diagram element "BPD_activity_12". This class, which extends the *Trace Ontology* class `Traceable_Flow_Object` and the *Domain Ontology* class `Generate_FC_by_Municipality`, is *associated_to* the corresponding instance ("BPD_activity_12") in the *Abox Ontology*. The latter, in turn, is an instance of classes `Task` of the *BPMN Ontology* and `Generate_FC_by_Municipality` of the *Domain Ontology*.

5 Architectural Solution

In this section we propose an architecture for the runtime collection of information at the various dimensions (P, K, T), its integration according to the comprehensive model of Section 4 and its unified querying to support business analysts needs.

The two major challenges at the architectural level are to cope with the huge quantity of collected trace data and their fast rate of arrival on the one hand, and to allow analysts to query also for implicit knowledge in collected data on the other hand, which requires some kind of reasoning support in the system (respectively, challenges 3 and 2 of Section 2). To address these challenges, we investigate the use of Semantic Web technologies in the form of *triplestores*. Triplestores are repositories for RDF data, possibly

---

[6] Despite the described scenario and the technological solution adopted would allow the use of punning, i.e., treating classes as instances of meta-classes, we chose to have separate entities for classes and instances, in order to keep the solution in line with the traditional conceptual distinction between classes and instances.

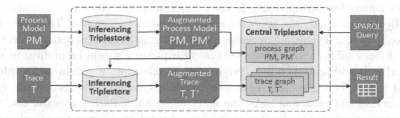

Fig. 6. Architecture. PM and T denote asserted triples, PM' and T' inferred triples.

organized into *named graphs*, with support for reasoning with different semantics (e.g., RDFS, OWL 2 RL and OWL 2 QL) and querying via the standard SPARQL query language and protocol [14]. Triplestore solutions have been widely investigated in recent years as a means to manage huge quantities of data, and several triplestore implementations have become mature products (e.g., OWLIM[7] and Virtuoso[8], to name a few), so they represent a natural choice for implementing our model.

In the rest of the section we detail, referring to Figure 6 for a general overview, how data is organized, populated and queried in our architecture using triplestores, while in the next section we present some results pointing out the potential of the solution.

5.1 Data Organization

The most efficient way to support SPARQL querying is to place all data in a *central triplestore*, materializing all the inferrable triples so that no reasoning has to be done at query time. We thus exclude federated queries over multiple triplestores as well as backward-chaining reasoning approaches (e.g., based on query rewriting), as they both introduce additional delay that is unacceptable for complex analytical queries.

The central triplestore has to store the process model data (the *Tbox Ontology* and *Abox Ontology* of Figure 4, which in turn encompasses both the procedural knowledge P and the static knowledge K) and all the completed/running execution traces collected so far (the IT data T). To better organize this information we store it in different named graphs: one for the process model and one for each trace (see Figure 6). This solution allows for the use of SPARQL constructs related to named graphs (FROM and USING clauses and graph management operations) to more easily select and manipulate traces.

5.2 Data Population

Process model data is produced at design time and can be stored once per all, while a *trace update* operation must occur every time a new piece of information about a running process is captured. Each trace update operation requires either the creation or the modification of the named graph of the trace. While these modifications are often monotonic (i.e., only new data is added), for the sake of generality we consider them as non-monotonic. In particular, non-monotonicity may arise when only a subset of process activities are observed and recorded in a trace (e.g., only e-mail exchanges are

---

[7] http://www.ontotext.com/owlim
[8] http://virtuoso.openlinksw.com/

recorded among human activities). In these cases, missing information could be automatically reconstructed in an approximate way based on known data. This could imply the possibility of a revisitation of reconstructed information as new data is observed.

An obvious solution to populate the central triplestore would be to directly access and modify it with collected data, relying on its reasoning capabilities for inferring implicit triples. This approach is however inefficient, as it overloads a single system with querying and reasoning tasks, the latter being particularly expensive due to the need to retract inferred triples that are no longer valid after a non-monotonic update. A better solution can be devised by considering that traces are largely independent one to each other, as they describe different and unrelated instances of documents, process activities and other execution events. This means that no meaningful knowledge can be inferred by combining two different traces,[9] and thus inference over traces can be computed by processing each trace in isolation (together with the process model) and merging all the inferred triples that have been separately computed.

The trace independence assumption leads naturally to the processing scheme shown in Figure 6. When the system is first started, the process model (PM) is read and the inference machinery of a temporary *inferencing triplestore* is employed to augment it with inferred triples (PM'), producing an *augmented process model* that is stored once per all in the *central triplestore*. Whenever a trace update operation is triggered, the trace data (T) is fed into another temporary *inferencing triplestore* together with the TBox definitions of the augmented process model, producing an *augmented trace* containing inferred triples (T'). The augmented trace is then extracted from the inferencing triplestore, filtered to remove triples of the augmented process model (as already stored) and triples that are not needed by queries[10] (for efficiency reasons), and finally stored in a trace-specific named graph in the central triplestore.

A first benefit of the described scheme is a clear separation of reasoning and querying through the use of separate triplestores, which can be chosen and optimized based on each particular task. To that respect, in our implementation we use OWLIM-Lite for both tasks, configuring OWL 2 RL inference and no persistence when used as an inferencing triplestore, and disabling inference and increasing index sizes when using it as the central triplestore. A second and more important benefit, however, is the possibility to parallelize trace update operations using multiple worker threads and/or machines, thus enabling massive scalability. The only 'bottleneck' is represented by the storage of processed data in the central triplestore, but this operation is very efficient as it does not involve any reasoning or inference retraction.

5.3 Data Querying

As shown in Figure 6, SPARQL queries by business analysts are targeted at the central repository, where they are evaluated against the integrated knowledge base built and

---

[9] We refer here to inference at the ABox level (the trace data) based on the OWL 2 semantics. The limited overlapping in terms of instances (e.g., documents) among traces means that little or nothing about an instance in a trace can be inferred in OWL 2 exploiting knowledge about unrelated instances in other traces. This does not exclude, however, the possibility to 'infer' useful knowledge by comparing or aggregating trace data in a non-OWL setting, a task supported by the querying facilities of our approach.

[10] In detail, we drop unnecessary `x owl:sameAs x` and `x rdf:type owl_restriction_bnode` triples.

augmented with inferred triples as previously described. As an example, Listing 1 reports the formulation in SPARQL of query Q.4, whose results are shown in Table 1. In general, we found analytical queries to greatly benefit from SPARQL 1.1 aggregates, but SPARQL support for managing dates and other temporal information (e.g., for computing time differences) resulted quite inadequate. We addressed this problem by defining a suite of user-defined SPARQL functions that can be used by analysts, leveraging the extension mechanisms provided by Sesame,[11] though this solution is generally not portable across different triplestore implementations.

```
PREFIX bpmn:    <http://dkm.fbk.eu/index.php/BPMN_Ontology#>
PREFIX domain:  <https://dkm.fbk.eu/#>
PREFIX trace:   <http://dkm.fbk.eu/Trace_Ontology#>
PREFIX ttrace:  <http://dkm.fbk.eu/TTrace_Ontology#>
PREFIX fn:      <http://shell.fbk.eu/custom_functions/>

SELECT ?office_name ?activity_name (COUNT(?t) AS ?executions) (AVG(?t) AS ?time)
WHERE {
   [] a bpmn:business_process_diagram , domain:Birth_Management;   # retrieve process
     bpmn:has_business_process_diagram_pools [                     # and public office
       bpmn:has_pool_participant_ref [                             # participants for
         a domain:Public_Office ;                                 # each pool of the
         bpmn:has_participant_name ?office_name ];                # birth management
       bpmn:has_pool_process_ref ?process ].                      # process diagram

   ?gateway1 a bpmn:gateway .                                      # require the
   ?gateway2 a bpmn:gateway .                                      # presence of two
   ?activity a bpmn:activity .                                     # gateways and
                                                                   # an activity in
   ?process bpmn:has_process_graphical_elements                    # the participant
     ?gateway1 , ?gateway2 , ?activity .                           # process

   ?gateway1                                                       # require two paths
     bpmn:is_directly_connected_via_sequence_flow ?gateway2;       # between gateways:
     bpmn:is_connected_via_sequence_flow ?activity .               # - a direct path
                                                                   # - an indirect
   ?activity ttrace:associated_to ?Activity ;                      # path passing
     bpmn:has_flow_object_name ?activity_name;                     # through the
     bpmn:is_connected_via_sequence_flow ?gateway2 .               # activity

   OPTIONAL {                                                      # if the activity
     ?activity_execution a ?Activity;                              # was performed ,
     trace:initial_start_dateTime ?start;                          # get its execution
     trace:final_end_dateTime ?end.                                # time using the
     BIND ((fn:timestamp(?end) − fn:timestamp(?start)) AS ?t)     # custom function
   }                                                               # fn:timestamp
}
GROUP BY ?office_name ?activity_name
```

Listing 1. SPARQL formulation of query Q.4: "Number of cases and avg. time spent for optional activities by public offices involved in the birth management procedure".

Table 1. Query results

office_name	activity_name	executions	time
"SAIA"	"Verifica CF"	86	501.097 s
"SAIA"	"Genera CF SAIA"	15009	270.122 s
"Comune"	"Genera CF Comune"	21000	485.541 s
"APSS"	"Genera CF APSS"	8315	418.327 s

---

[11] http://www.openrdf.org/

6 Evaluation

In this section we report on the evaluation of the proposed model and architecture on a real case study – the birth management scenario –investigated in the scope of the *ProMo* project, with the goal to assess the usefulness and scalability of the approach.

In the above mentioned scenario:

- P is a BPMN process model (see Figure 1) containing 4 pools, 19 activities, 11 domain objects, 19 events, 14 gateways, 54 sequence flows and 6 message flows;
- K is a domain ontology (an extract is shown in Figure 3) containing 5 properties and 379 classes covering 28 activities and 12 data objects such that, on average, each data object contains 25 simple data fields organized in a 4 levels-depth structure;
- T is a set of execution traces automatically generated based on the aforementioned P and K and a few samples of real traces (that we can not directly use as containing sensitive personal data); on average each trace covers 10 events with associated data objects, and is encoded with 2040 triples from which 1260 triples can be inferred.

In order to assess the approach in real contexts, we selected and analyzed 8 queries among those that business analysts involved in the *ProMo* project were interested to investigate, with the selection driven by our perception about their importance for business analysts as well as by the goal to cover as much variety as possible (e.g., type of query result, multiple VS single trace analysis) so to increase their representativeness. Queries and their analysis are reported in Table 2. For each query, the columns corresponding to the component(s) (P, K or T) involved by the query, are marked. Similarly, the inference column (Inf.) is marked when the query demands for reasoning support. The table suggests that all the three dimensions explored by the proposed approach, as well as the inference support, are indeed needed to answer business analysts' queries, thus suggesting the usefulness of the proposed approach in real business scenarios.

Concerning scalability, we mainly focus on the storing and querying aspects. Assuming the data rates of the Italian birth management scenario at national level (Section 2), we investigated a one day, one week and one month loads (respectively $\sim$1500, $\sim$10500 and $\sim$42000 traces). Table 3 shows the corresponding performance figures, measured on a quad-core Intel Core I7 860 workstation with 16 GB of memory. For each load, we

Table 2. Query analysis

Query	Description	P	K	T	Inf.
Q.1	Average time per process execution spent by the municipality of Trento			X	
Q.2	Total number of Registration Request documents filled from Jan 1st, 2014		X	X	
Q.3	Percentage of times in which the flow followed is the one which passes first through the APSS pool and then through the municipality one	X		X	
Q.4	Number of cases and average time spent by each public office involved in the birth management procedure for executing optional activities	X	X	X	X
Q.5	Number of times the municipality sends to SAIA a request without FC	X	X	X	X
Q.6	Last event of trace TRACEID			X	
Q.7	Average time spent by trace TRACEID			X	
Q.8	Does trace TRACEID go through activity labeled "Present at the hospital"?	X		X	

Table 3. Scalability Results

Traces	Stored triples			Storing		Querying	
	Asserted	Inferred	Total	Throughput	Total time	Time Q.4	Time Q.8
1500	3062349	1895471	4957820	37.89 trace/min	2426.88 s	324 ms	41.4 ms
10500	21910269	13057464	34967773	37.41 trace/min	16851.21 s	881.4 ms	26.2 ms
42000	87503538	52045200	139548738	37.34 trace/min	67537.95 s	4510.0 ms	105.0 ms

report the number of stored triples (asserted, inferred, total), the storing time (throughput in traces per minute and total population time) and the average evaluation times for queries Q.4 and Q.8 (from Table 2), which are representative, respectively, of analytical and non-selective queries and of very specific and selective queries.

Overall, the system is able to manage a throughput of about 37 traces per minute, which is perfectly adequate with the Italian scenario (a newbirth per minute). More significantly, the throughput is largely independent of the load, demonstrating how the choice to decouple inference for each trace allows to efficiently cope with increasingly large amounts of data. Finally, the time required for performing a query as complex as Q.4, which involves all the dimensions and exploits inferred knowledge (e.g., for identifying public offices and determining whether an activity is optional), is still acceptable for the specific context and for an online analysis of data. Of course, the more the repository grows, the slower the answer is. Nevertheless, queries concerning the whole set of data collected in a month, can be managed in times of the order of seconds.

7 Related Works

Approaches adding formal semantics to process models (also defined in the BPMN notation) are not new in the literature [1,2,3,4,5,6]. We can divide the existing proposals into two groups: (1) those adding semantics to specify the dynamic behavior exhibited by a business process [1,2,3], and (2) those adding semantics to specify the meaning of the entities of a Business Process Diagram (BPD) in order to improve the automation of business process management [4,5,6]. The latter are more relevant in our context, as they focus on models, rather than the execution semantics of the processes.

Thomas and Fellmann [5] consider the problem of augmenting EPC process models with semantic annotations. They propose a framework which joins process model and ontology through properties (such as the "semantic type" of a process element). This enrichment associates annotation properties to the process instances. In the SUPER project [4], the SUPER ontology is used for the creation of semantic annotations of both BPMN and EPC process models in order to support automated composition, mediation and execution. In [1], semantic annotations are introduced for validation purposes, i.e. to verify constraints about the process execution semantics.

In our previous work [6,9], we enrich process models with semantic knowledge and establish a set of subsumption (aka subclass) relations between the classes of two ontologies: one formalizing the notation used (the BPMN meta-model) and another describing the specific domain of the process model. This way we provide an ontology integration scheme, based on hierarchical ontology merge, that supports automated verification of semantic constraints defining the correctness of semantic process annotations as well as of structural constraints [6].

Only few works (e.g., [15,8,16]) in the context of the SUPER project have tried to combine static and procedural business level aspects (very close to the ones we consider) with the execution data. Nevertheless either they try to provide a comprehensive Semantic Business Process Management framework (e.g., [15]) or, when explicitly dealing with process monitoring and analysis [8], they mainly focus on the usage of semantic technologies to provide domain-independent solutions to process monitoring, which, instantiated by concrete organizations in their specific domain, aims at automate the reconciliation between the business and the data level. In this work, semantic technologies are exploited to integrate the three investigated dimensions, thus supporting process analysis by means of inference and querying.

Finally, there exist works dealing with the formalization of abstract frameworks for describing process executions. For instance, the standardized PROV-O [17] ontology, whose aim is providing a formalization for representing and interchanging provenance information generated in different systems, provides a set of classes (and relationships and axioms) to be instantiated with activity executions and artefacts, similarly to the *Trace Ontology*. Through the opportune mapping between PROV-O and *Trace Ontology* classes (e.g., the PROV-O `activity` and the *Trace Ontology* `Traceable_Flow_Object`), it would be possible to align the proposed model to PROV-O and thus allow the consumption of *Trace Ontology* data by PROV-O aware applications.

The problem of exploiting the advantages deriving from semantic-based approaches with large amounts of data has been widely investigated in the last years. One of the most known and used solutions is the Ontology Based Data Access [18] (OBDA). OBDA aims at providing access to data stored in relational heterogeneous data sources through the mediation of a semantic layer in the form of an ontology, that provides a high level conceptual view of the domain of interest [19]. Among the available efficient query answering reasoners we can find MASTRO-i [18] and the most recent Quest [20].

Triplestore solutions like Virtuoso, Owlim, Bigdata and others provide similar query answering functionalities though a different mechanism. Among the available Semantic Web technologies we chose to use a semantic triplestore solution. Indeed, besides allowing us to address the semantic as well as the big data requirements, it also allows us to update the model structure in a lightweight way. Being based on triples, it does not strongly constraint the meta-level, thus leaving the flexibility to change the model in an agile way, without loosing the data already stored.

8 Conclusion

In this paper we show how to combine different orthogonal dimensions and exploit reasoning services in order to expose interesting analysis on organizations' execution data in business terms. In detail, static domain knowledge, procedural domain knowledge and execution data have been plugged into a semantic solution and Semantic Web technologies have been exploited to cope with large quantities of data. The approach has been applied to an industrial case study investigated in the context of the *ProMo* project for the modeling, monitoring and analysis of Italian Public Administration procedures. In the future we plan to further investigate the reasoning capabilities that semantic technologies can offer, also in terms of user-defined rule-sets.

References

1. Weber, I., Hoffmann, J., Mendling, J.: Semantic business process validation. In: Proc. of Semantic Business Process and Product Lifecycle Management workshop (SBPM) (2008)
2. Wong, P.Y., Gibbons, J.: A relative timed semantics for BPMN. Electronic Notes in Theoretical Computer Science 229(2), 59–75 (2009); Proc. of 7th Int. Workshop on the Foundations of Coordination Languages and Software Architectures (FOCLASA 2008)
3. Koschmider, A., Oberweis, A.: Ontology based business process description. In: Proceedings of the CAiSE 2005 Workshops. LNCS, pp. 321–333. Springer (2005)
4. Dimitrov, M., Simov, A., Stein, S., Konstantinov, M.: A BPMO based semantic business process modelling environment. In: Proc. of SBPLM at ESWC. CEUR-WS (2007)
5. Thomas, O., Fellmann, M.: Semantic EPC: Enhancing process modeling using ontology languages. In: Proc. of Semantic Business Process and Product Lifecycle Management workshop (SBPM), pp. 64–75 (2007)
6. Di Francescomarino, C., Ghidini, C., Rospocher, M., Serafini, L., Tonella, P.: Reasoning on semantically annotated processes. In: Bouguettaya, A., Krueger, I., Margaria, T. (eds.) ICSOC 2008. LNCS, vol. 5364, pp. 132–146. Springer, Heidelberg (2008)
7. Tomasi, A., Marchetto, A., Di Francescomarino, C., Susi, A.: reBPMN: Recovering and reducing business processes. In: ICSM, pp. 666–669 (2012)
8. Pedrinaci, C., Lambert, D., Wetzstein, B., van Lessen, T., Cekov, L., Dimitrov, M.: SENTINEL: A semantic business process monitoring tool. In: Proc. of Ontology-supported Business Intelligence (OBI), pp. 1:1–1:12. ACM (2008)
9. Di Francescomarino, C., Ghidini, C., Rospocher, M., Serafini, L., Tonella, P.: Semantically-aided business process modeling. In: Bernstein, A., Karger, D.R., Heath, T., Feigenbaum, L., Maynard, D., Motta, E., Thirunarayan, K. (eds.) ISWC 2009. LNCS, vol. 5823, pp. 114–129. Springer, Heidelberg (2009)
10. Object Management Group (OMG): Business process model and notation (BPMN) version 2.0. Standard (2011)
11. Bertoli, P., Kazhamiakin, R., Nori, M., Pistore, M.: SMART: Modeling and monitoring support for business process coordination in dynamic environments. In: Abramowicz, W., Domingue, J., Węcel, K. (eds.) BIS Workshops 2012. LNBIP, vol. 127, pp. 243–254. Springer, Heidelberg (2012)
12. de Leoni, M., Maggi, F.M., van der Aalst, W.M.P.: Aligning event logs and declarative process models for conformance checking. In: Barros, A., Gal, A., Kindler, E. (eds.) BPM 2012. LNCS, vol. 7481, pp. 82–97. Springer, Heidelberg (2012)
13. Business Process Management Initiative (BPMI): Business process modeling notation: Specification (2006), http://www.bpmn.org
14. Seaborne, A., Harris, S.: SPARQL 1.1 Query Language. Recommendation, W3C (2013)
15. Hepp, M., Roman, D.: An ontology framework for semantic business process management. In: Wirtschaftsinformatik (1), Universitaetsverlag Karlsruhe, pp. 423–440 (2007)
16. Pedrinaci, C., Domingue, J., Alves de Medeiros, A.K.: A core ontology for business process analysis. In: Bechhofer, S., Hauswirth, M., Hoffmann, J., Koubarakis, M. (eds.) ESWC 2008. LNCS, vol. 5021, pp. 49–64. Springer, Heidelberg (2008)
17. Sahoo, S., Lebo, T., McGuinness, D.: PROV-O: The PROV ontology. Recommendation, W3C (2013)
18. Calvanese, D., De Giacomo, G., Lembo, D., Lenzerini, M., Poggi, A., Rodriguez-Muro, M., Rosati, R., Ruzzi, M., Savo, D.F.: The MASTRO system for ontology-based data access. Semant. Web 2(1), 43–53 (2011)
19. Calvanese, D., De Giacomo, G., Lembo, D., Lenzerini, M., Rosati, R.: Conceptual modeling for data integration. In: Borgida, A.T., Chaudhri, V.K., Giorgini, P., Yu, E.S. (eds.) Mylopoulos Festschrift. LNCS, vol. 5600, pp. 173–197. Springer, Heidelberg (2009)
20. Rodriguez-Muro, M., Calvanese, D.: Quest, an OWL 2 QL reasoner for ontology-based data access. In: OWLED, vol. 849. CEUR-WS.org (2012)

Efficient RDF Interchange (ERI) Format for RDF Data Streams

Javier D. Fernández, Alejandro Llaves, and Oscar Corcho

Ontology Engineering Group (OEG), Univ. Politécnica de Madrid, Spain
{jdfernandez,allaves,ocorcho}@fi.upm.es

Abstract. RDF streams are sequences of timestamped RDF statements or graphs, which can be generated by several types of data sources (sensors, social networks, etc.). They may provide data at high volumes and rates, and be consumed by applications that require real-time responses. Hence it is important to publish and interchange them efficiently. In this paper, we exploit a key feature of RDF data streams, which is the regularity of their structure and data values, proposing a compressed, efficient RDF interchange (ERI) format, which can reduce the amount of data transmitted when processing RDF streams. Our experimental evaluation shows that our format produces state-of-the-art streaming compression, remaining efficient in performance.

1 Introduction

Most of the largest RDF datasets available so far (*e.g.* Bio2RDF,[1] LinkedGeoData,[2] DBpedia[3]) are released as static snapshots of data coming from one or several data sources, generated with some ETL (Extract-Transform-Load) processes according to scheduled periodical releases. That is, data are mostly static, even when they contain temporal references (*e.g.* the Linked Sensor Data dataset, which contains an historical archive of data measured by environmental sensors). Typical applications that make use of such datasets include those performing simulations or those training numerical models.

In contrast, some applications only require access to the most recent data, or combine real-time and historical data for different purposes. In these cases a different approach has to be followed for RDF data management, and RDF streams come into play. RDF streams are defined as potentially unbounded sequences of time varying RDF statements or graphs, which may be generated from any type of data stream, from social networks to environmental sensors.

Several research areas have emerged around RDF streams, *e.g.* temporal representation in RDF [12,6,11], or RDF stream query languages and processing engines (C-SPARQL [2], SPARQLStream and morph-streams [4], CQELS Cloud [15], Ztreamy [1]). The recently-created W3C community group on RDF Stream

---

[1] http://bio2rdf.org/.
[2] http://linkedgeodata.org/.
[3] http://www.dbpedia.org/.

P. Mika et al. (Eds.) ISWC 2014, Part II, LNCS 8797, pp. 244–259, 2014.

Processing is working on the provision of "a common model for producing, transmitting and continuously querying RDF Streams".[4]

In this paper, we focus on the efficient transmission of RDF streams, a necessary step to ensure higher throughput for RDF Stream processors. Previous work on RDF compression [9,14] shows important size reductions of large RDF datasets, hence enabling an efficient RDF exchange. However, these solutions consider static RDF datasets, and need to read the whole dataset to take advantage of data regularities. A recent proposal, RDSZ [10], shows the benefits of applying the general-purpose stream compressor Zlib [8] to RDF streams, and provides a compression algorithm based on the difference of subject groups (provided in Turtle [17]), with some gains in compression (up to 31% *w.r.t.* Zlib).

Our work sets on the basis of RDSZ and exploits the fact that in most RDF streams the structural information is well-known by the data provider, and the number of variations in the structure are limited. For instance, the information provided by a sensor network is restricted to the number of different measured properties, and in an RDF context the SSN ontology [5] will be probably used for representing such data. Furthermore, given that "regularities" are also present in very structured static datasets (*e.g.* statistical data using the RDF Data Cube Vocabulary [7]), our approach may be also applicable to those datasets. Thus, our **preliminary hypothesis** states that our proposed RDF interchange format can optimize the space and time required for representing, exchanging, and parsing RDF data streams and regularly-structured static RDF datasets.

In this paper, we propose a complete efficient RDF interchange (ERI) format for RDF streams. ERI considers an RDF stream as a continuous flow of blocks (with predefined maximum size) of triples. Each block is modularized into two main sets of channels to achieve large spatial savings:

- Structural channels: They encode the subjects in each block and, for each one, the structural properties of the related triples, using a dynamic dictionary of structures.
- Value channels: They encode the concrete data values held by each predicate in the block in a compact fashion.

We also provide a first practical implementation with some decisions regarding the specific compression used in each channel. An empirical evaluation over a heterogeneous corpora of RDF streaming datasets shows that ERI produces state-of-the-art compression, remaining competitive in processing time. Similar conclusions can be drawn for very regular datasets (such as statistical data) and general datasets in which the information is strongly structured.

Our main **contributions** are: (i) the design of an efficient RDF interchange (ERI) format as a flexible, modular and extensible representation of RDF streams; (ii) a practical implementation for ERI which can be tuned to cope with specific dataset regularities; and (iii) an evaluation that shows our gains in compactness *w.r.t.* current compressors, with low processing overheads.

The rest of the paper is organized as follows. Section 2 reviews basic foundations of RDF streaming and compression. Our approach for efficient RDF

---

[4] http://www.w3.org/community/rsp/.

interchange (ERI) is presented in Section 3, as well as a practical deployment for ERI encoding and decoding. Section 4 provides an empirical evaluation analyzing compactness and processing efficiency. Finally, Section 5 concludes and devises future work and application scenarios.

2   Background and Related Work

A key challenge for stream processing systems is the ability to consume large volumes of data with varying and potentially large input rates. Distributed stream processing systems are a possible architectural solution. In these systems, the circulation of data between nodes takes an amount of time that depends on parameters like data size, network bandwidth, or network usage, among others. Hence it is crucial to minimize data transmission time among processing nodes.

To reach this goal, our work focuses on RDF stream compression techniques. RDF compression is an alternative to standard compression such as gzip. It leverages the skewed structure of RDF graphs to get large spatial savings. The most prominent approach is HDT [9], a binary format that splits and succinctly represents an RDF dataset with two main components: the *Dictionary* assigns an identifier (ID) to all terms in the RDF graph with high levels of compression, and the *Triples* uses the previous mapping and encodes the pure structure of the underlying RDF graph. HDT achieves good compression figures while providing retrieving features to the compressed data [9]. However, these are at the cost of processing the complete dataset and spending non-negligible processing time. The same applies to other recent RDF compression approaches based on inferring a grammar generating the data [14] or providing other dictionary-based compression on top of MapReduce [19].

Streaming HDT [13] is a deviation from HDT that simplifies the associated metadata and restricts the range of available dictionary IDs. Thus, the scheme is a simple dictionary-based replacement which does not compete in compression but allows operating in constrained devices. RDSZ [10] is the first specific approach for RDF streaming compression. RDSZ takes advantage of the fact that items in an RDF stream usually follow a common schema and, thus, have structural similarities. Hence it uses differential encoding to take advantage of these similarities, and the results of this process are compressed with Zlib to exploit additional redundancies. Experiments show that RDSZ produces gains in compression (17% on average) at the cost of increasing the processing time.

The increasing interest on RDF compression over streaming data has also been recently highlighted by RDF stream processing systems such as CQELS Cloud [15] and Ztreamy [1]. The first one uses a basic dictionary-based approach to process and move fixed-size integers between nodes. The latter exploits the Zlib compressor with similar purposes. In addition, it is also relevant to detect trends in data, extract statistics, or compare historic data with current data to identify anomalies, although historical data management is not considered in most of stream processing systems [16]. A potential use case of RDF compression may be the integration of historical data and real-time data streams.

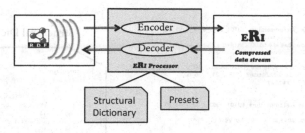

Fig. 1. ERI processing model

3 Efficient RDF Interchange (ERI) Format

The ERI format is a compact RDF representation designed to leverage the inherent structural and data redundancy in RDF streams. In the following, we introduce the basic concepts behind the ERI format, and we present a practical implementation for encoding and decoding RDF data.

3.1 Basic Concepts

In ERI, we consider the generic processing model depicted in Figure 1. In this scheme, RDF data, potentially in the form of a data stream, is encoded or decoded to ERI, resulting in a compressed data stream. We refer to an **ERI processor** as any application able to encode such RDF data to ERI or to decode the ERI compressed stream (defined below) to make the RDF data accessible. A processor mainly leverages on two information sets to improve compactness: (i) the Structural Dictionary and (ii) the Presets, defined as follows.

The **Structural Dictionary** holds a dynamic catalog of all different structural patterns found for a given set of triples called **Molecules**.

Definition 1 (RDF (general) molecule). *Given an RDF graph G, an RDF molecule $M \subseteq G$ is a set of triples $\{t_1, t_2, \cdots, t_n\}$.*

Molecules are the unit elements for encoding; each molecule will be codified as its corresponding identifier (ID) in the dictionary of structures and the concrete data values held by each predicate.

The most basic (but inefficient) kind of grouping is at the level of triples (one group per triple), *i.e.* having as many molecules as the total number of triples in the RDF data. In this case, the Structural Dictionary will assign an ID to each structure which is just the predicate in the triple. Trying to set up larger groups sharing regularities is much more appropriate.

A straightforward approach is to consider the list of all triples with the same subject (similar to abbreviated triple groups in Turtle [17]). We take this grouping as the method by default, then managing RDF subject-molecules:

Definition 2 (RDF subject-molecule). *Given an RDF graph G, an RDF subject-molecule $M \subseteq G$ is a set of triples $\{t_1, t_2, \cdots, t_n\}$ in which $subject(t_1) = subject(t_2) = \cdots = subject(t_n)$.*

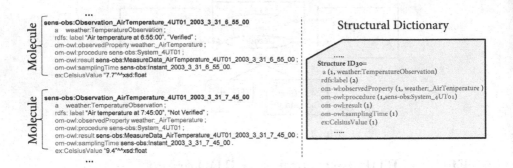

Fig. 2. Example of molecules and their Structural Dictionary

Note that an RDF stream can be seen as a sequence of (potentially not disjoint) RDF subject-molecules[5]. Figure 2 illustrates two molecules in a sequence of weather sensor data and their entry in the Structural Dictionary. This data excerpt (inspired by the data examples in SRBench [20]) represents temperature measures of a sensor at two sampling times. As can be seen, the lists of predicates is exactly the same for both molecules. In addition, we can observe regularities in certain property values (in different color). In particular, the values for *rdf:type*, *om-owl:observedProperty* and *om-owl:procedure* are exactly the same, and will be repeated throughout the data stream for all the air temperature observations of the same sensor. We call this type of predicates producing massive data repetitions, **discrete predicates**. Thus, we avoid these repetitions and save space codifying the concrete values for discrete predicates as part of the structural patterns, as shown in Figure 2 (right). In this example, the structure in the dictionary is encoded as the list of related predicates and, for each one, it counts the number of objects for the predicate and the aforementioned fixed property value if the predicate is discrete.

We assume that discrete predicates can be easily identified by streaming data providers and set up before encoding, or they can be statistically detected at run time. In any case, this kind of information that must be shared between encoders and decoders, is kept in the information set called **Presets**. Presets include all the configuration and compression-oriented metadata supplied by the data provider or inferred at run time. We distinguish between (a) mandatory features in Presets, which include the aforementioned set of discrete predicates and the selected policy for grouping triples into molecules, and (b) application-specific configurations. The latter opens up the format for extensions as long as the concrete application clearly states the decisions and available configurations. For instance, specific features could include common prefixes, suffixes or infixes in URIs and BNodes, or a set of common datatypes in some concrete predicates.

---

[5] For simplicity, we will use the term molecules hereinafter, assuming that they are subject-molecules by default.

3.2   ERI Streams

At a high level, an **ERI Stream** is a sequence of contiguous blocks of molecules, as depicted in Figure 3. That is, ERI first splits the incoming RDF data into contiguous blocks of a maximum predefined *blockSize*, measured in number of triples and set up in the encoder. Then, the molecules (groups) within each block are identified according to the established grouping policy. Note that the grouping by default could slightly alter the original order of triples once it groups triples by subject. Other grouping policies may be established for those scenarios with specific ordering needs.

ERI follows an encoding procedure similar to that of the Efficient XML Interchange (EXI) format [18]: each molecule is multiplexed into **channels**:

Definition 3 ((general) Channel). *A channel is a list of lower entropy items (similar values), which is well suited for standard compression algorithms.*

The idea is to maintain a channel per different type of information, so that a standard compressor can be used in each channel, leveraging its data regularities to produce better compression results. In ERI we distinguish between two types of channels: (i) *structural channels* and (ii) *value channels*.

Structural channels hold the information of the structure of the molecules in the block and keep the Structural Dictionary updated. We define the following high-level minimum channels:
- *Main Terms of molecules*: In the grouping by default, it states the subject of the grouping. Other kinds of groupings may assign different values.
- *ID-Structures*: It lists the ID of the structure of each molecule in the block. The ID points to the associated structural entry in the Structural Dictionary.
- *New Structures*: It includes new entries in the Structural Dictionary.

Value channels organize the concrete values in the molecules of the block for each non-discrete predicate. In short, ERI mainly considers one channel per different predicate, listing all objects with occurrences in the molecules related to it. Having property values of a predicate grouped together may help parsers to directly retrieve information corresponding to specific predicates.

The complete ERI stream consists of an ERI header followed by an ERI body, as shown in Figure 3 (bottom). The ERI header includes the identification of the stream and the initial Presets, as previously described. The ERI body carries the content of the streaming representing each block as (i) a set of metadata identifying the block and updating potential changes in Presets, and (ii) its compressed channels, using standard compression for each specific channel.

The decoding process is the exact opposite: the stream body is decompressed by channels, and demultiplexed into blocks containing the molecules.

3.3   Practical ERI Encoding and Decoding

Now we describe our current deployment for ERI encoding and decoding. For simplicity, we obviate citing the representation of metadata as it is relatively easy to define a key set of keywords, and we focus on channel representations.

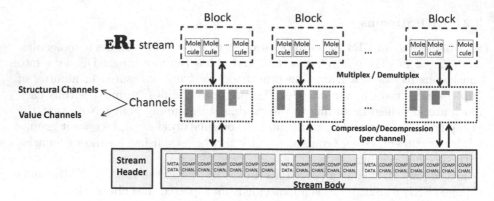

Fig. 3. Overview of the ERI format

Figure 4 illustrates our practical decisions over the previous example in Figure 2. The figure represents the structural and value channels of the data excerpt, as well as the potential standard compression that could be used to produce each compressed channel. Regarding structural channels, we first follow a straightforward approach for *Main Terms of Molecules* and list main terms (subjects) in plain. Advanced representations could consider the usage of an additional dictionary mapping terms to identifiers, and using the corresponding identifier to refer to a main term previously seen in the input streaming data. However, our experience with streaming data suggests that main terms are rarely repeated because they refer to a certain timestamp.

The *ID-Structures* channel lists integer IDs representing the entry in the Structural Dictionary. New entries are identified by means of an additional channel called *New Structure Marker*. This channel has a bit for each ID in the *ID-Structures* channel: a 0-bit states that the corresponding ID is already in the Structural Dictionary, whereas a 1-bit shows that the ID points to a new entry that is retrieved in the *New Structures* channel. In Figure 4, the first molecule is related to the structure having the ID-30, which is marked as new. Then, the concrete structure can be found in *New Structures*. Similarly to the example in Figure 2, we codify each dictionary entry as the predicates in the structure, the number of objects for each predicate and the concrete property values for discrete predicates. To improve compactness in the representation we use a dictionary of predicates, hence the predicate in the structure is not a term but an ID pointing to the predicate entry in this dictionary. If there is a new predicate never seen before in a block, it is listed in an additional *New Predicates* channel, as shown in Figure 4.

The decoder will maintain a pointer to the next entry to be read in *New Structures* (and increment it after reading), and to hold and update the dictionary of structures and predicates. Given that the number of predicates is relatively low in RDF datasets, we consider a consecutive list of IDs in the predicate dictionary for the encoder and decoder. For the dictionary of structures, we use a *Least Recently Used* (LRU) policy for the dictionary in the encoder. That is, whenever the maximum capacity is reached, the LRU entry is erased and the

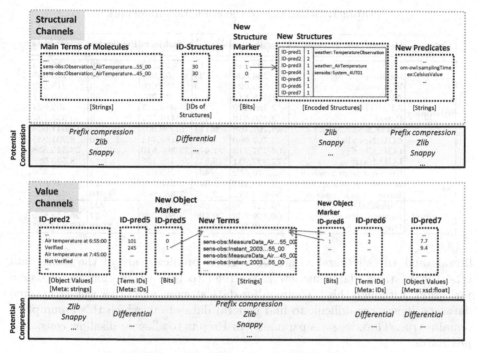

Fig. 4. Example of ERI channels

ID is available to encode the next entry, which must be marked as new in the *New Structure Marker* channel. Therefore, the decoder can make use of simple hashing for the dictionary, as it always knows if the entry is new.

Regarding value channels, Figure 4 illustrates several options. The channel *ID-pred2* storing the values of the second predicate (*rdfs:label*) simply lists all the values. In contrast, *ID-pred5* and *ID-pred6* make use of a dictionary of objects. This case is similar to the dictionary of structures: the channels hold the ID of the entry, and an associated list of bits (*New Object Marker ID-pred5* and *New Object Marker ID-pred6*, respectively) describes if this corresponds to a new entry in the dictionary. The ERI processor maintains an object dictionary per predicate. This decision produces shorter IDs per predicate *w.r.t.* maintaining one general dictionary of objects. In contrast, the processor manages more dictionaries, although the number of different predicates always remains proportionally low, and so the number of dictionaries. In our implementation we maintain one channel (*New Terms*) with all the new terms in the dictionaries. As this list is coordinated with the IDs, there are no overlaps; the decoder must keep a pointer to the next entry to be decoded when a 1-bit in a marker indicates that there is a new term.

Finally, *ID-pred7* also holds the object values directly, as in *ID-pred2*. However, as shown in the figure, it extracts the datatype of all values (*xsd:float*). We assume that all property values for a given predicate are of the same kind. In practice, this means that (i) every channel holds whether URIs/BNodes or

Table 1. Description of the evaluation framework

Category	Dataset	Triples	Nt Size (MB)	Subjects	Predicates	Objects
Streaming	Mix	93,048	12	17,153	89	36,279
	Identica	234,000	25	56,967	12	116,065
	Wikipedia	359,028	33	119,676	3	215,382
	AEMET-1	1,018,815	133	33,095	59	5,812
	AEMET-2	2,788,429	494	398,347	7	403,824
	Petrol	3,356,616	485	419,577	8	355,122
	Flickr_Event_Media	49,107,168	6,714	5,490,007	23	15,041,664
	LOD_Nevada	36,767,060	7,494.5	8,188,411	10	8,201,935
	LOD_Charley	104,737,213	21,470	23,306,816	10	23,325,858
	LOD_Katrina	172,997,931	35,548	38,479,105	10	38,503,088
Statistics	Eurostat_migr_reschange	2,570,652	467	285,629	16	2,376
	Eurostat_tour_cap_nuts3	2,849,187	519	316,576	17	47,473
	Eurostat_avia_paexac	66,023,172	12,785	7,335,909	16	235,253
General	LinkedMDB	6,147,996	850	694,400	222	2,052,959
	Faceted DBLP	60,139,734	9,799	3,591,091	27	25,154,979
	Dbpedia 3-8	431,440,396	63,053	24,791,728	57,986	108,927,201

literals and (ii) all literal values of a given predicate are of the same data type (float, string, dateTime, etc.). We refer to this assumption as *consistent predicates*. Although this is common for data streams and other well-structured datasets, it is more difficult to find general datasets in which this assumption remains true. Thus, we set a parameter in Presets to allow or disallow *consistent predicates*.

Regarding potential channel compressions, Figure 4 includes some standard compression techniques and tools for each type of data. In practice, to simplify the following evaluation, our ERI processor uses Zlib whenever textual information is present, *i.e.* in the main terms of molecules, new structures, new predicates and new terms channels. As for those channels managing IDs, each ID is encoded with $log(n)$ bits, n being the maximum ID in the current channel.

4   Evaluation

We implemented a first prototype of an ERI processor in Java, following the aforementioned practical decisions. We used some tools provided by the HDT-Java library 1.1.2[6], and the default Deflater compressor provided by Zlib. Tests were performed on a computer with an Intel Xeon X5675 processor at 3.07 GHz and 48 GB of RAM, running Ubuntu/Precise 12.04.2 LTS. The network is regarded as an ideal communication channel for a fair comparison.

4.1   Datasets

Table 1 lists our experimental datasets[7], reporting: number of triples, size in N-Triples (Nt herinafter) format, and the different number of subjects, predicates

---

[6] https://code.google.com/p/hdt-java.

[7] We have set a Research Object with all the datasets as well as the prototype source code at http://purl.org/net/ro-eri-ISWC14.

and objects. We choose representative datasets based on the number of triples, topic coverage, availability and, if possible, previous uses in benchmarking.

We define three different categories of datasets: *streaming* (10), *statistics* (3) and *general* (3). Obviously, **Streaming datasets** are our main application focus; the first six datasets in Table 1 have been already used in the evaluation of RDSZ [10] and correspond to RDF messages in the public streamline of a microblogging site (*Identica*), Wikipedia edition monitoring (*Wikipedia*), information from weather stations in Spain (*AEMET-1* and *AEMET-2*), credit card transactions in petrol stations (*Petrol*) and a random mix of these datasets (*Mix*). We complete the corpora with information of media events (*e.g.* concerts and other performances) in Flickr (*Flickr_Event_Media*), and weather measurements of a blizzard (*LOD_Nevada*) and two hurricanes (*LOD_Charley* and *LOD_Katrina*) extracted from the Linked Observation Data dataset which is the core of SRBench [20].

Statistical datasets are the prototypical case of other (non-streaming) data presenting clear regularities that ERI can take advantage of. We consider three datasets[8] (*Eurostat_migr-reschange*, *Eurostat_tour_cap_nuts3* and *Eurostat_avia_paexac*) using the RDF Data Cube Vocabulary [7], providing population, tourism and transport statistics respectively.

Finally, we experiment with **general static datasets**, without prior assumptions on data regularities. We use well-known datasets in the domains of films (*LinkedMDB*) and bibliography (*Faceted DBLP*), as well as *Dbpedia 3-8*.

4.2 Compactness Results

ERI allows multiple configurations for encoding, providing different space/time tradeoffs for different scenarios. In this section we focus on evaluating three different configurations: ERI-1K (blocksize - 1024), ERI-4k (blocksize - 4096) and ERI-4k-Nodict (blocksize - 4096). ERI-1K and ERI-4K include a LRU dictionary for each value channel whereas ERI-4k-Nodict does not. We allow the *consistent predicates* option (*i.e.* we save datatype tag repetitions) in all datasets except for the *mix* dataset and all the *general* category in which the aforementioned assumption is not satisfied. In turn, we manually define a set of common discrete predicates in Presets. Finally, according to previous experiences [10], the *blockSize* selection introduces a tradeoff between space and delays: the bigger the blocks, the more regular structures can be found. This implies better compression results, but with longer waiting times in the decoder. Based on this, we select two configurations, 1K and 4K triples providing different tradeoffs.

We compare our proposal with diverse streaming compression techniques. Table 2 analyzes the compression performance providing compression ratios as $\frac{Compressed\_size}{Original\_size}$, taking Nt as the *Original size*. First, we test standard deflate over Nt (*Nt Deflate-4K*), flushing the compression internal buffer each 4096 triples, and over the Turtle (*TTL Deflate*) serialization[9] in the best scenario of compressing the complete dataset at once. We also test the RDSZ approach,

---

[8] Taken from Eurostat-Linked Data, http://eurostat.linked-statistics.org/.

[9] For the conversion process we use Any23 0.9.0, http://any23.apache.org/.

Table 2. Compression results on the different datasets

Dataset	Compression Ratio						
	Nt Deflate-4K	TTL Deflate	ERI-4k	ERI-4k-Nodict	RDSZ	HDT-4K	HDT
Mix	8.2%	5.1%	5.2%	**5.1%**	**4.9%**	10.6%	7.6%
Identica	11.0%	8.5%	8.4%	**8.0%**	8.7%	16.4%	13.6%
Wikipedia	10.5%	7.5%	7.5%	7.7%	**7.2%**	13.4%	10.9%
AEMET-1	4.1%	1.5%	1.2%	**0.8%**	1.3%	4.4%	2.9%
AEMET-2	2.8%	**1.1%**	**1.1%**	1.1%	1.1%	3.8%	3.8%
Petrol	6.5%	3.8%	2.9%	**2.6%**	3.9%	9.9%	5.2%
Flickr_Event_Media	9.0%	6.9%	6.6%	**6.3%**	6.6%	14.4%	7.2%
LOD_Nevada	3.2%	1.3%	1.5%	1.3%	**1.2%**	4.9%	3.2%
LOD_Charley	3.1%	1.3%	1.4%	**1.2%**	**1.2%**	4.9%	3.2%
LOD_Katrina	3.1%	1.3%	1.4%	**1.2%**	**1.2%**	5.0%	3.2%
Eurostat_migr.	2.1%	**0.5%**	**0.5%**	0.5%	-	2.6%	2.5%
Eurostat_tour.	2.2%	0.6%	**0.5%**	0.6%	-	2.6%	2.5%
Eurostat_avia_paexac	2.2%	**0.6%**	**0.6%**	0.6%	-	3.2%	2.6%
LinkedMDB	4.7%	2.9%	3.1%	**2.6%**	-	9.5%	5.9%
Faceted DBLP	5.4%	3.7%	4.0%	**3.5%**	-	11.3%	9.2%
Dbpedia 3-8	8.0%	**6.4%**	8.0%	7.5%	-	16.0%	8.0%

which is focused on compressing streams of RDF graphs, whereas ERI considers continuous flows of RDF triples. Thus, the evaluation with RDSZ is limited to streaming datasets (the first category in the table), for which we can configure the RDSZ input as a set of Turtle graphs merged together (the input expected by the RDSZ prototype), one per original graph in the dataset. The results of RDSZ depend on two configuration parameters: we use batchSize=5 and cacheSize=100, the default configuration in [10]. For a fair comparison, we consider the original size in Nt in the reported RDSZ compression results. To complete the comparison, we evaluate the HDT serialization, although it works on complete datasets. Thus, we also analyze HDT on partitions of 4096 triples (HDT-4k).

The results show the varied compression ratio between categories and different datasets. The considered statistical datasets are much more compressive than the rest. Besides structural repetitions, they are highly compressible because they include few objects (see Table 1) repeated throughout the dataset.

As can be seen, ERI excels in space for streaming and statistical datasets. As expected, it clearly outperforms Nt compression (up to 5 times) thanks to the molecule grouping. This grouping is somehow also exploited by Turtle, which natively groups items with the same subject. Thus, the deflate compression over Turtle can also take advantage of datasets in which predicates and values are repeated within the same compression context. In turn, ERI clearly outperforms Turtle compression (up to 1.9 times) in those datasets in which the repetitions in structures and values are distributed across the stream (*e.g. Petrol* and *Identica*).

Similar reasoning can be made for the slightly different results reported by ERI-4k and ERI-4k-Nodict. As can be seen, the presence of the object dictionary can overload the representation, although it always obtains comparable compression ratios. Note that, since ERI groups the objects by predicate within each block, ERI-4k-Nodict using Zlib can already take advantage of the redundancies in objects whenever these repetitions are present in the same block. In turn, ERI-4k slightly improves ERI-4k-Nodict in those cases (such as statistical datasets) in which the object repetitions are distributed across different blocks.

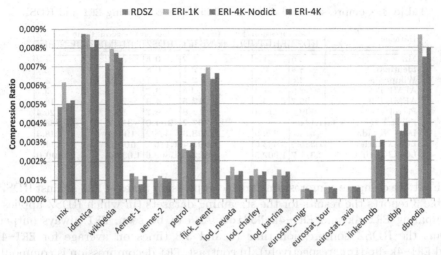

Fig. 5. Analysis of compression results of the considered ERI configurations

RDSZ remains comparable to our approach. ERI outperforms RDSZ in those datasets in which the division in graphs of the input fails to group redundancies in compression contexts. In contrast, the RDSZ compression slightly outperforms ERI in two particular cases of interest: *Mix*, where the information is randomly distributed, and the simple *Wikipedia* dataset, where only 3 predicates are present. In such cases, ERI pays the cost of having several compression channels and thus flushing the metadata of several compressors (in contrast to one compressor in RDSZ). An alternative, which is not exploited in the present proposal, is to group channels and use one compressor per group of channels. This kind of decision has also been taken by EXI [18].

As for general data, *LinkedMDB* and *Faceted DBLP* datasets provide well-structured information and thus ERI can also take advantage of repetitive structures of predicates, obtaining the best compression as well. As expected, ERI losses efficiency in a dataset with very diverse information and structures such as *Dbpedia*. Nonetheless, Turtle compression is the only competitor in this case.

As expected, HDT is built for a different type of scenario and the results are not competitive *w.r.t.* ERI. Although the compression of the full dataset with HDT improves the compression by blocks (HDT-4k), it remains far from ERI efficiency.

Figure 5 compares the compression ratio of the three ERI configurations that have been considered. As expected, a smaller buffer in ERI-1k slightly affects the efficiency; the more blocks, the more additional control information and smaller regularities can be obtained and compressed. The comparison between ERI-4k and ERI-4k-Nodict corresponds with the results in Table 2 and the aforementioned analysis denoting the object dictionary overhead.

4.3   Processing Efficiency Results

In this section we measure the processing time of ERI, reporting elapsed times (in seconds) for all experiments, averaging five independent executions.

Table 3. Compression and decompression times comparing ERI and RDSZ

Dataset	Compression Time (sec.)			Decompression Time (sec.)		
	RDSZ	ERI-4k	ERI-4k-Nodict	RDSZ	ERI-4k	ERI-4k-Nodict
Mix	2.5	1.8	**1.2**	**0.5**	1.4	1.2
Identica	8.4	3.1	**2.1**	**0.8**	2.9	2.1
Wikipedia	3.8	2.8	**2.2**	**2.7**	3.2	**2.7**
AEMET-1	17.9	**4.3**	4.6	**3.7**	6.3	5.1
AEMET-2	95.7	15.7	**12.5**	**4.8**	20.3	16.8
Petrol	149.9	13.4	**11.8**	**6.7**	16.8	20.4
Flickr_Event_Media	1,141.8	262.4	**207.2**	204.0	311.7	388.2
LOD_Nevada	534.7	329.9	**208.3**	428.2	**191.8**	218.3
LOD_Charley	1,388.9	663.6	**501.4**	1,115.7	**600.6**	611.1
LOD_Katrina	2,315.7	1,002.5	**822.0**	1,869.6	1,038.0	**890.0**

First, we compare compression and decompression times of ERI against RDSZ. Table 3 reports the results for the streaming datasets (in which RDSZ applies), comparing ERI-4k and ERI-4k-Nodict. As can be seen, ERI always outperforms the RDSZ compression time (3 and 3.8 times on average for ERI-4k and ERI-4k-Nodict, respectively). In contrast, ERI decompression is commonly slower (1.4 times on average in both ERI configurations). Note again that RDSZ processes and outputs streams of graphs, whereas ERI manages a stream of triples. Thus, RDSZ compression can be affected by the fact that it has to potentially process large graphs with many triples (as is the case of the LOD datasets), hence the differential encoding process takes a longer time. In contrast, ERI compresses blocks of the same size. In turn, ERI decompression is generally slower as it decompresses several channels and outputs all triples in the block. In those datasets in which the number of value channels is very small (*Wikipedia* with three predicates and LOD datasets with many discrete predicates), ERI decompression is comparable or even slightly better than RDSZ.

As expected, the object dictionary in ERI-4k deteriorates the performance against ERI-4k-Nodict, once the dictionary has to be created in compression and continuously updated in decompression. The decompression is faster in ERI-4k when there are series of triples in which the dictionary does not change.

Then, we test an application managing ERI for compression, exchange and consumption processes. We assume hereinafter an average unicast transmission speed of 1MByte/s. Although applications could work on faster channels, we assume that there is a wide range of scenarios, such as sensor networks, where the transmission is much poorer, limited, or costly. In the following, we only focus on streams of RDF triples. Thus, we obviate RDSZ (managing streams of graphs) and Turtle (grouping human-readable triples by default), and we establish compressed Nt as the baseline for a fair comparison.

We first focus on transmission and decompression, without considering at this stage the compression process as many scenarios allow the information to be compressed beforehand. Thus, we measure the **parsing throughput** provided to the client of the transmission, *i.e.* the number of triples parsed per time unit. In turn, the total time includes the exchange time of the considered network, the decompression time and the parsing process to obtain the components (subject, predicate and object) of each triple. Figure 6 reports the average results over the corpora, in triples per second, comparing ERI-4k and ERI-4k-Nodict against the

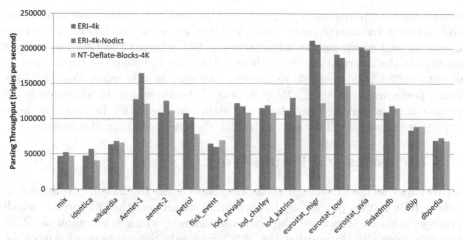

Fig. 6. Analysis of Parsing (Exchange+Decompressing) throughput

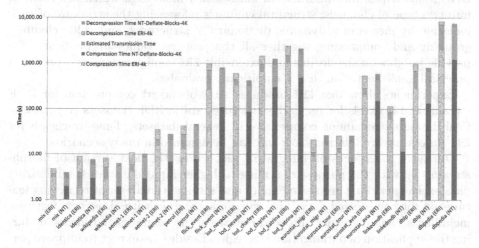

Fig. 7. Comparison of processing performance, *ERI-4K* against *NT-Deflate-Blocks-4k*

baseline *NT-Deflate-Blocks-4K*. As can be seen, both `ERI-4k` and `ERI-4k-Nodict` outperform the baseline in most cases except for those datasets with less regularities in the structure or the data values, which is in line with the previous results for compression. This is the case of *general datasets* as well as two streaming datasets (*Wikipedia* and *Flickr_Event_Media* in which most objects are unrepeated (as can be seen in Table 1). On average, the gains in parsing throughput for both `ERI` configurations are 110.64% and 142.36% for streaming and statistical datasets respectively, whereas they only decrease to 99.65% for general datasets.

Finally, we address a scenario where compression is subsequently followed by transmission and decompression (including parsing the final output to obtain each triple). Figure 7 compares the resulting times (in logarithmic scale) of *ERI-4k* against the baseline *NT-Deflate-Blocks-4K*. We choose *ERI-4k* over *ERI-4k-Nodict* because the first one produces bigger sizes and worse parsing throughput, hence we are comparing our worst case over the baseline. Under these conditions, *ERI-4k* suffers an expected overhead, given that we are always including the time to process and compress the information in ERI whereas the baseline directly compresses the information. Nevertheless, the time in which the client receives all data in ERI is comparable to the baseline even in this worst case (*ERI-4k-Nodict* performs better than *ERI-4k* as stated above), which the aforementioned improvement in parsing throughput (as shown in Figure 6). In turn, the huge savings in the statistical dataset make ERI slightly faster than the baseline.

5   Conclusions and Future Work

In this paper we have focused on compression as a way to minimize transmission costs in RDF stream processing. In particular, we propose the ERI format, which leverages inherent structural and data redundancy, which is common on RDF streams, especially those using the W3C Semantic Sensor Network Ontology. ERI groups triples into information units called molecules, which are encoded into two type of channels: structural channels referencing the structure of each molecule by means of a dynamic dictionary of structures, and value channels grouping and compressing together all the property values by predicate. We provide insights on the flexible and extensible ERI configurations and present a practical implementation that is empirically evaluated.

Experiments show that ERI produces state-of-the-art compression for RDF streams and it excels for regularly-structured static RDF datasets (*e.g.*, statistical datasets), remaining competitive in general datasets. Time overheads for ERI processing are relatively low and can be assumed in many scenarios.

Our next plans focus on integrating ERI within the next version of morph-streams [3], with the purpose of scaling to higher input data rates, minimizing data exchange among processing nodes and serving a small set of retrieving features on the compressed data. This will come together with other new features, including an adaptive query processor aware of the compression dimension during the application of optimization strategies. Besides, we expect to improve performance of ERI management by exploring parallel compression/decompression and the use of caches and other fast compressors besides Zlib.

Acknowledgments. This research has been funded by the European Commission under the grant PlanetData (FP7-257641) and by Ministerio de Economía y Competitividad (Spain) under the project "4V: Volumen, Velocidad, Variedad y Validez en la Gestión Innovadora de Datos" (TIN2013-46238-C4-2-R). We are thankful for discussions with authors of the RDSZ approach, specially with Norberto Fernández.

References

1. Arias, J., Fernandez, N., Sanchez, L., Fuentes-Lorenzo, D.: Ztreamy: A middleware for publishing semantic streams on the Web. Web Semantics: Science, Services and Agents on the World Wide Web 25, 16–23 (2014)

2. Barbieri, D.F., Braga, D., Ceri, S., Grossniklaus, M.: An execution environment for C-SPARQL queries. In: Proc. of the International Conference on Extending Database Technology (EDBT), pp. 441–452. ACM (2010)
3. Calbimonte, J.P., Jeung, H., Corcho, O., Aberer, K.: Enabling query technologies for the semantic sensor web. International Journal on Semantic Web and Information Systems 8(1), 43–63 (2012)
4. Calbimonte, J.-P., Corcho, O., Gray, A.J.G.: Enabling ontology-based access to streaming data sources. In: Patel-Schneider, P.F., Pan, Y., Hitzler, P., Mika, P., Zhang, L., Pan, J.Z., Horrocks, I., Glimm, B. (eds.) ISWC 2010, Part I. LNCS, vol. 6496, pp. 96–111. Springer, Heidelberg (2010)
5. Compton, M., Barnaghi, P., Bermudez, L., et al.: The SSN Ontology of the W3C Semantic Sensor Network Incubator Group. Web Semantics: Science, Services and Agents on the World Wide Web 17 (2012)
6. Correndo, G., Salvadores, M., Millard, I., Shadbolt, N.: Linked Timelines: Temporal Representation and Management in Linked Data. In: Proc. of Workshop on Consuming Linked Data (COLD). CEUR-WS, vol. 665, paper 7 (2010)
7. Cyganiak, R., Reynolds, D., Tennison, J.: The RDF Data Cube Vocabulary. W3C Recommendation (January 16, 2014)
8. Deutsch, P., Gailly, J.-L.: Zlib compressed data format specification version 3.3. Internet RFC (1950) (May 1996)
9. Fernández, J.D., Martínez-Prieto, M.A., Gutiérrez, C., Polleres, A., Arias, M.: Binary RDF Representation for Publication and Exchange. Journal of Web Semantics 19, 22–41 (2013)
10. Fernández, N., Arias, J., Sánchez, L., Fuentes-Lorenzo, D., Corcho, Ó.: RDSZ: An approach for lossless RDF stream compression. In: Presutti, V., d'Amato, C., Gandon, F., d'Aquin, M., Staab, S., Tordai, A. (eds.) ESWC 2014. LNCS, vol. 8465, pp. 52–67. Springer, Heidelberg (2014)
11. Grandi, F.: Introducing an Annotated Bibliography on Temporal and Evolution Aspects in the Semantic Web. SIGMOD Rec. 41, 18–21 (2013)
12. Gutierrez, C., Hurtado, C.A., Vaisman, A.A.: Temporal rdf. In: Gómez-Pérez, A., Euzenat, J. (eds.) ESWC 2005. LNCS, vol. 3532, pp. 93–107. Springer, Heidelberg (2005)
13. Hasemann, H., Kroller, A., Pagel, M.: RDF Provisioning for the Internet of Things. In: Proc. of the International Conference on the Internet of Things (IOT), pp. 143–150. IEEE (2012)
14. Joshi, A.K., Hitzler, P., Dong, G.: Logical Linked Data Compression. In: Cimiano, P., Corcho, O., Presutti, V., Hollink, L., Rudolph, S. (eds.) ESWC 2013. LNCS, vol. 7882, pp. 170–184. Springer, Heidelberg (2013)
15. Le-Phuoc, D., Nguyen Mau Quoc, H., Le Van, C., Hauswirth, M.: Elastic and Scalable Processing of Linked Stream Data in the Cloud. In: Alani, H., et al. (eds.) ISWC 2013, Part I. LNCS, vol. 8218, pp. 280–297. Springer, Heidelberg (2013)
16. Margara, A., Urbani, J., Harmelen, F., Bal, H.: Streaming the Web: Reasoning over Dynamic Data. Web Semantics 25 (2014)
17. Prud'hommeaux, E., Carothers: RDF 1.1 Turtle-Terse RDF Triple Language. W3C Recommendation (February 25, 2014)
18. Schneider, J., Kamiya, T., Peintner, D., Kyusakov, R.: Efficient XML Interchange (EXI) Format 1.0, 2nd edn. W3C Recommendation (February 11, 2014)
19. Urbani, J., Maassen, J., Drost, N., Seinstra, F., Bal, H.: Scalable RDF data compression with MapReduce. Concurrency and Computation: Practice and Experience 25(1), 24–39 (2013)
20. Zhang, Y., Duc, P.M., Corcho, O., Calbimonte, J.-P.: SRBench: a streaming RDF/SPARQL benchmark. In: Cudré-Mauroux, P., et al. (eds.) ISWC 2012, Part I. LNCS, vol. 7649, pp. 641–657. Springer, Heidelberg (2012)

Knowledge-Driven Activity Recognition and Segmentation Using Context Connections

Georgios Meditskos, Efstratios Kontopoulos, and Ioannis Kompatsiaris

Information Technologies Institute
Centre for Research & Technology - Hellas
6th km Xarilaou - Thermi, 57001, Thessaloniki, Greece
{gmeditsk,skontopo,ikom}@iti.gr

Abstract. We propose a knowledge-driven activity recognition and segmentation framework introducing the notion of context connections. Given an RDF dataset of primitive observations, our aim is to identify, link and classify meaningful contexts that signify the presence of complex activities, coupling background knowledge pertinent to generic contextual dependencies among activities. To this end, we use the Situation concept of the DOLCE+DnS Ultralite (DUL) ontology to formally capture the context of high-level activities. Moreover, we use context similarity measures to handle the intrinsic characteristics of pervasive environments in real-world conditions, such as missing information, temporal inaccuracies or activities that can be performed in several ways. We illustrate the performance of the proposed framework through its deployment in a hospital for monitoring activities of Alzheimer's disease patients.

Keywords: ontologies, activity recognition, segmentation, context.

1 Introduction

In recent years, the demand for intelligent, customized user task support has proliferated across a multitude of application domains, ranging from smart spaces and healthcare [30] to transportation and energy control [10]. The key challenge in such applications is to abstract and fuse the captured *context* in order to elicit a higher level understanding of the situation. Towards this direction, a growing body of research has been investigating ontology-based (knowledge-driven) frameworks for modelling and reasoning about context [4], [5], [7]. The idea is to map low-level information (e.g. objects used, postures, location) and activity models onto ontologies, enabling the inference of high-level activities using domain knowledge and ontology reasoning. In many cases, activity recognition is further augmented with rules [12] for representing richer relationships not supported by the standard ontology semantics, like e.g. structured (composite) activities [19].

A significant challenge in activity recognition is the ability to identify and recognise the context signifying the presence of complex activities. Time windows [21], [9] and slices [24], [20], background knowledge about the order [27], [23]

P. Mika et al. (Eds.) ISWC 2014, Part II, LNCS 8797, pp. 260–275, 2014.

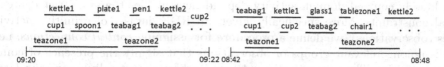

Fig. 1. Example observations detected during tea preparation

or duration [32] of activities constitute commonly used approaches in knowledge-driven activity recognition. Such approaches, however, define strict contextual dependencies, e.g. start/end activities or maximum activity duration, assuming that all the information is available. Thus, they fail to capture many intrinsic characteristics of pervasive environments in real-world conditions, such as imperfect information, noise or inaccurate temporal correlations.

An important factor to take into consideration is that contextual information is typically collected by multiple sensors and complementary sensing modalities. Each modality generates information from a different perspective, but by combining them together we are in a position to infer far more about a person's activities than by any sensor alone. Thus, a further challenge is to effectively fuse multiple sources of heterogeneous, noisy and potentially inconsistent information in a way that provides accurate and useful outputs.

In order to better highlight the challenges, consider the two example time-lines in Fig. 1 that contain information regarding the location and the objects that a person interacts with when preparing hot tea. These are subsets of real-world data obtained by monitoring Alzheimer's disease patients in the FP7 project Dem@Care[1]. As illustrated in the figure:

- The duration of activities usually varies, even when they are performed by the same person. The use of time windows, slices or background knowledge regarding activity duration fails to capture this characteristic, or, at least, the segmentation task becomes too complex.
- Many activities are carried out differently even by the same person. Thus, the use of strictly structured background knowledge relevant to the order of activities or their temporal boundaries is not always practical and flexible.
- The information integrated from heterogeneous sources is intrinsically noisy, incomplete, with inaccurate temporal correlations. For example, the cup2 and teabag2 observations in the second time-line in Fig. 1 do not coincide with information regarding the location of the person. Such information cannot be processed by patterns that, e.g., explicitly enumerate the sub-activities and temporal relations involved in a complex behaviour.

Towards addressing these intrinsic challenges of pervasive applications, this paper presents a practical ontology-based activity recognition framework. The framework detects complex activities in multi-sensor fusion environments based

---

[1] Dementia Ambient Care: Multi-Sensing Monitoring for Intelligent Remote Management and Decision Support, http://http://www.demcare.eu/

on loosely coupled domain activity dependencies rather than on strict contextual constraints. More specifically, given an RDF dataset of primitive activities (observations), we define a procedure for assigning *context connections*, i.e. links among relevant groups of observations that signify the presence of complex activities. The connections are determined by semantically comparing *local contexts*, i.e. the type and number of neighbouring observations, against *context descriptors*, i.e. background knowledge about domain activity dependencies. We formalise these descriptors by capitalising on the Situation concept of the DnS pattern [13] of the DOLCE+DnS Ultralite (DUL) [11] ontology, exploiting the OWL 2 meta-modelling capabilities (punning [15]) for defining generic relations among classes. As a result, this paper features the following contributions:

- We deliver a flexible and reusable framework for recognising complex activities that is applicable to a wide range of activity recognition scenarios.
- We propose a simple and reusable ontology pattern for capturing common sense background knowledge regarding domain activity dependencies.
- We present a context-aware activity recognition and segmentation algorithm that incorporates the level of relaxation needed during context classification.

In this work we consider non-interleaving human activities, i.e. only one activity can be performed each time. Moreover, we focus on offline activity recognition. We consider the support of interleaved and concurrent activities, as well as, the real-time continuous activity recognition as very important research directions of our ongoing work. On the other hand, we believe our approach is quite suitable for further research purposes, e.g. towards extracting behaviour patterns and detecting behaviour changes, including the manner in which activities are performed, idiosyncratic and habitual knowledge, as well as recurrent routines. We further elaborate on this direction in Section 5.

The rest of the paper is structured as follows: Section 2 reviews relevant ontology-based activity recognition frameworks. Section 3 describes the ontology pattern we use to associate high-level activities with generic context descriptors, whereas the algorithms for segmentation and activity recognition are described in Section 4. Section 5 presents the results of the evaluation of our approach on real-world data. Conclusions and future directions are presented in Section 6.

2   Related Work

Ontologies have been gaining increasing attention as a means for modelling and reasoning over contextual information and, particularly, human activities. Under this paradigm, OWL is used for describing the elements of interest (e.g. events, activities, location), their pertinent logical associations, as well as the background knowledge required to infer additional information. For example, a tea preparation activity in the kitchen that is inferred on the basis of heating water and using a tea bag and a cup could be modelled in OWL (TBox) as:

$$MakeTea \equiv Activity \text{ and } (actor \text{ only } (Person \text{ and } (uses \text{ some } TeaBag)$$
$$\text{and } (uses \text{ some } Cup) \text{ and } (uses \text{ some } Kettle) \text{ and } (in \text{ some } Kitchen)))$$

In such cases, the data (ABox) needs to be segmented into chunks of activities to allow complex activities to be derived using standard OWL reasoning. However, the issue of data segmentation in ontology-based activity recognition has received little attention. For instance, in [8] and [26], situations correspond to OWL individuals, while DL reasoning [2] is used for determining which contextual concepts a specific situation falls into. However, no details are provided with respect to the method used for segmenting the data. In [25] statistical inferencing is used for segmenting the data and for predicting the most probable activities, whereas symbolic DL reasoning is applied for further refining the results.

The most common approach for ontology-based activity segmentation involves the use of time windows and slices. In [9] and [21] dynamically sliding time windows are used for activity recognition. The activities are specified as sequences of user-object interactions, whereas subsumption reasoning is used for inferring the ongoing activity. In [20], time slices are used for grouping activities and inferring complex situations. In [24], one-minute fixed time slices are used for activity recognition, using notions such as *recently used* and *second last activity*. In most cases, though, such approaches require prior domain knowledge, such as maximum duration of activities or window length, which results in inflexible and difficult to implement approaches, even if they can be dynamically adjusted.

In [32], an approach is presented for the recognition of multi-user concurrent activities where each activity is constrained by necessary conditions, e.g. activity "prepare breakfast" should occur in the morning and activity "bath" should last more than 5 minutes. In [23], an ontology is used for capturing atomic and compound events and for defining operators among event sets (e.g. sequence, concurrency). In addition, many approaches combine ontologies with rules [20], [31], [33], CEP patterns [18], [28] and SPARQL queries [29], [1], [3], [17]. The main limitation of these approaches is that they encapsulate strict activity patterns that cannot provide enough flexibility for handling the imprecise and ambiguous nature of real-world events in multi-sensor fusion environments.

The authors in [27] conceive activity recognition as a plan recognition problem. An activity plan consists of a partially ordered sequence of temporal constraints and actions that must be carried out in order to achieve the activity's goals. Though relevant to environments where the order of observations is accurate, plans fall short when more intricate activity patterns are involved, e.g. when fusing multi-sensor data with inherent temporal incoherences.

Our work has been mainly inspired by [22] and [14]. In [22], a data-driven approach is described for human activity recognition based on the order of object usage. The authors use web mining for extracting the objects most relevant to specific activities and each activity is then associated with a key object. The limitation is that each activity in the list is assumed to have a unique key object. Moreover, the proposed algorithms handle only sequential traces without overlaps. In our work, we follow a more formal and flexible approach, defining the activities relevant to high-level situations in terms of an ontology, without needing to specify key objects. Moreover, the recognition algorithms take into account the type and number of overlapped activities.

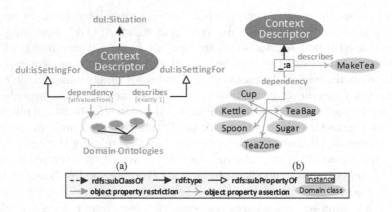

Fig. 2. (a) The `ContextDescriptor` class, (b) Example annotation of the `MakeTea` domain activity

In [14] a similarity-based segmentation approach is proposed. Generic activity models are built that are specific to the deployment environment and contain sensor activation sets for each complex activity. The segmentation and recognition are based on similarity measures for comparing timely ordered sensor sequences and sensor models of activities. The key difference of our work is that we use an ontology for modelling common sense high-level knowledge about activity dependencies, which also allows us to incorporate hierarchical relationships in context classification. Moreover, similarly to [22], instead of using window thresholds for analysing input data, we examine neighbouring events.

3   Domain Context Descriptors

In order to describe the context pertinent to each high-level activity in an abstract yet formal way, we reuse the *Situation* concept of the Descriptions and Situations (DnS) [13] pattern of DOLCE+DnS Ultralite (DUL) [11]. The aim is to provide the conceptual model for annotating domain activity classes with lower-level observation types. Fig. 2 (a) shows the specialisation of the *Situation* class, along with two sub-properties of the *isSettingFor* upper-level property.

Our aim is to define relations among classes, therefore, the proposed ontology treats classes as instances, allowing property assertions to be made among domain concepts. Intuitively, the ontology can be thought of as a conceptual (meta) layer that can be placed on top of any domain activity ontology. This way, instances of the *ContextDescriptor* are used to link domain activities (*describes* property) with one or more lower-level conceptualisations through *dependency* property assertions. Fig. 2 (b) presents an example of annotating class *MakeTea* with class types relevant to objects (e.g *Cup*) and location (e.g. *TeaZone*).

The model also allows annotated classes to inherit the context dependencies of the superclasses through the following property chain axiom:

$$describes \circ subClassOf \circ isDescribedBy \circ dependency \sqsubseteq dependency$$

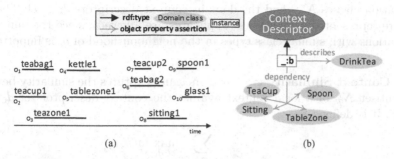

Fig. 3. (a) Example observations relevant to making and drinking tea, (b) The context descriptor of $DrinkTea$

In the rest of the paper, we use the term "context descriptor" to refer to the set of classes, denoted as d_C, that a domain activity C has been annotated with. For example, the context descriptor of $MakeTea$ is denoted as $d_{MakeTea}$ and is equal to the set $\{Cup, Kettle, Spoon, TeaZone, Sugar, TeaBag\}$.

4   Segmentation and Activity Recognition

Given a set $O = \{o_1, o_2, ..., o_n\}$ with RDF instances representing low-level observations, e.g. objects, locations, postures, etc., and a set of domain context descriptors $D = \{d_{C_1}, d_{C_2}, ..., d_{C_k}\}$, we describe in this section the steps involved in identifying meaningful contexts in O for recognizing higher level activities. We use Fig. 3 (a) as a running example that involves observations relevant to making and drinking tea, while the corresponding context descriptors are depicted in Fig. 2 (b) and Fig. 3 (b), respectively.

4.1   Local Contexts

The first step of the segmentation algorithm is to define the *local contexts* for each observation $o_i \in O$ that capture information relevant to the neighbouring observations of o_i and the most plausible activities that o_i can be part of. More specifically, let N_i^r be the set of observations o_j in the neighbourhood of o_i that either overlap with o_i ($o_i \circ o_j$) or are the r-nearest to o_i ($n(o_i, o_j) \leq r$), based on their temporal ordering. Moreover, let $T(o_i)$ be the most specific class of o_i, D the set of domain context descriptors and φ a local context similarity function.

Definition 1. *A local context l_i of an observation $o_i \in O$ is defined as the tuple $\langle o_i, N_i^r, C \rangle$, where $N_i^r = \{o_j \mid \forall o_j \in O, o_i \circ o_j \vee n(o_i, o_j) \leq r\}$ and C is the high-level class of the most plausible classification of l_i, such that $\nexists d_A \in D : \varphi(N_{i,T}^r, d_A) > \varphi(N_{i,T}^r, d_C)$, where $d_C \in D, d_C \neq d_A$ and $N_{i,T}^r = \{t \mid \forall o_j \in N_i^r, t = T(o_j)\}$.*

The class C denotes the most plausible domain activity classification of l_i, derived by computing the φ similarity between the set with the most specific observation classes $N_{i,T}^r$ and the domain context descriptors $d_k \in D$. The sets $N_{i,T}^r$ are represented as multisets (duplicates are allowed), since the number of observations with similar class types in the neighbourhood of o_i is important.

Local Context Similarity φ. The φ measure captures the similarity between the multiset N_T^r of a local context against the context descriptor set d_C of a class C. It is defined as

$$\varphi(N_T^r, d_C) = \frac{\sum_{\forall n \in N_T^r} \max_{\forall c \in d_C} [\delta(n, c)]}{|N_T^r|} \tag{1}$$

where N_T^r is the multiset with neighbouring observation class types and d_C is the context descriptor of C. φ is computed as the mean value of the maximum δ similarities for each concept $n \in N_T^r$, since each n may have more than one relevant concepts in d_C. Intuitively, φ captures the local plausibility of an observation o_i to be part of a complex activity C. If $\varphi = 1$, then all the classes in N_T^r appear in d_C and, therefore, it is very likely that the corresponding local context is part of the complex activity C.

Equation (1) uses the δ function that computes the similarity of a neighbouring observation class $n \in N_T^r$ against a context descriptor class $c \in d_C$ as

$$\delta(n, c) = \begin{cases} 1, & \text{if } n \sqsubseteq c \text{ (includes } n \equiv c) \\ \frac{|U(n) \cap U(c)|}{|U(n)|}, & \text{if } c \sqsubseteq n \\ 0, & \text{otherwise} \end{cases} \tag{2}$$

where $U(C)$ is the set of the superclasses of C, excluding the $Thing$ concept, such that $U(C) = \{A \mid C \sqsubseteq A, A \neq \top\}$. Intuitively, an observation class n in the neighbourhood of o_i exactly matches a class c in the context descriptor set d_C, if it is equivalent to or a subclass of c. In this case, n is subsumed by c and, thus, fully satisfies the contextual dependency imposed by d_C that there should be at least one observation of type c. On the other hand, if c is subsumed by n ($c \sqsubseteq n$), then n is a more general concept than the one required by the context descriptor and the similarity is computed based on the rate of the superclasses of n that are also superclasses of c. For example, if $Spoon$ is a direct subclass of $Cutlery$ ($Spoon \sqsubseteq Cutlery$), $n = Spoon$ and $c = Cutlery$, then $\delta(Spoon, Cutlery) = 1$, since $Spoon$ is subsumed by $Cutlery$. If $n = Cutlery$ and $c = Spoon$, then $\delta(Cutlery, Spoon) < 1$, depending on their superclasses.

Creating Local Contexts. Algorithm 1 describes the procedure for creating set L with the most plausible local contexts for each $o_i \in O$. The algorithm begins by defining set N_i^r with the neighbour observations of o_i (line 3). Then, the partial context set P_i is created as the multiset of the most specific class types of the observations in N_i^r (line 4). The algorithm then computes the φ similarity S_k of P_i against each context descriptor d_{C_k}, creating the set G_i with tuples

---

Algorithm 1. Creating local contexts

Data: Observations: $O = \{o_1, o_2, ..., o_i\}$, Domain context descriptors:
$D = \{d_{C_1}, d_{C_2}, ..., d_{C_k}\}$, Nearest observations threshold: r.

Result: The set L with the most plausible local contexts.

1 $L \leftarrow \emptyset$;

2 **foreach** $o_i \in O$ **do**

3 $\quad N_i^r = \{o_j \mid \forall o_j \in O, o_i \circ o_j \vee n(o_i, o_j) \leq r\}$;

4 $\quad P_i \leftarrow \{t \mid \forall o_j \in N_i^r, t = T(o_j)\}$;

5 $\quad G_i \leftarrow \emptyset$;

6 $\quad$ **foreach** $d_{C_k} \in D$ **do**

7 $\quad\quad$ **if** $\exists A \in d_{C_k}, T(o_i) \sqsubseteq A$ **then** $\;G_i \leftarrow G_i \cup \{\langle C_k, \varphi(P_i, d_{C_k}) \rangle\}, \varphi \neq 0$

8 $\quad$ **forall the** $\langle C_k, S_k \rangle \in G_i$ *with the max* S_k **do**

9 $\quad\quad$ $L \leftarrow L \cup \{\langle o_i, N_i^r, C_k \rangle\}$;

---

of the form $\langle C_k, S_k \rangle$ (lines 5 to 7). If the class type of o_i does not semantically belong to class descriptor d_{C_k}, then the corresponding similarity tuple is omitted (line 7), ignoring noisy observations. Finally, a tuple $\langle o_i, N_i^r, C_k \rangle$ is created for all $\langle C_k, S_k \rangle$ with the maximum similarity in G_i and inserted into L. Note that G_i may contain more than one $\langle C_k, S_k \rangle$ tuples with the maximum similarity, and, therefore, more than one local contexts can be generated for o_i.

Example. We describe the definition of the local context for $teacup2$ (o_7) in Fig. 3 (a), using $r = 1$. Observations o_5, o_6 and o_8 overlap with o_7, whereas o_9 and o_4 are the 1-nearest to o_7. Thus, $N_7^1 = \{o_7, o_5, o_6, o_8, o_9, o_4\}$ (line 3) and $P_7 = \{TeaCup, TableZone, TeaBag, Sitting, Spoon, Kettle\}$ (line 4). According to Figs. 2 (b) and 3 (b), the context descriptor set is $D = \{d_{MakeTea}, d_{DrinkTea}\}$, where $d_{MakeTea} = \{TeaCup, Kettle, Spoon, TeaZone, Sugar, TeaBag\}$ and $d_{DrinkTea} = \{TeaCup, Sitting, TableZone, Spoon\}$. The class type for o_7 is $TeaCup$ that exists in both context descriptors, therefore φ will be computed for both of them. According to (1), $\varphi(P_7, d_{MakeTea}) = \frac{1+0+1+0+1+1}{6} = 0.66$ and $\varphi(P_7, d_{DrinkTea}) = \frac{1+1+0+1+1+0}{6} = 0.66$ (assuming that there are no hierarchical relationships among the domain class types). Thus, there are two local contexts for o_7 with maximum plausibility 0.66: $l_7 = \langle o_7, N_7^1, MakeTea \rangle$ and $l_7' = \langle o_7, N_7^1, DrinkTea \rangle$. Similarly, we have the following local contexts (φ similarity is also depicted for completeness): $l_1 = \langle o_1, N_1^1, MakeTea \rangle^{1.0}$, $l_2 = \langle o_2, N_2^1, MakeTea \rangle^{1.0}$, $l_3 = \langle o_3, N_3^1, MakeTea \rangle^{0.83}$, $l_4 = \langle o_4, N_4^1, MakeTea \rangle^{0.75}$, $l_5 = \langle o_5, N_5^1, DrinkTea \rangle^{0.5}$, $l_6 = \langle o_6, N_6^1, MakeTea \rangle^{0.66}$, $l_8 = \langle o_8, N_8^1, Drink$-$Tea \rangle^{0.57}$, $l_9 = \langle o_9, N_9^1, MakeTea \rangle^{0.5}$, $l_9' = \langle o_9, N_9^1, DrinkTea \rangle^{0.5}$, $l_{10} = $ -.

4.2   Context Connections

Based on the local contexts obtained in the previous section, the next step is to define *context connections*, that is, links among relevant local contexts that will be used to create the final segments for activity recognition.

Algorithm 2. Creating context connections

Data: Local contexts: $L = \{l_1, l_2, ..., l_j\}$, where $l_j = \langle o_j, N_j^r, C_k \rangle$.
Result: Set C_{set} with context connections.

1 $C_{set} \leftarrow \emptyset$;
2 **foreach** $l_i = \langle o_i, N_i^r, C_m \rangle \in L$ **do**
3 $\quad$ **foreach** $l_j = \langle o_j, N_j^r, C_n \rangle \in L$, *where* $o_i \neq o_2$, $C_m \equiv C_n$ *and* $o_i \in N_j^r$ **do**
4 $\quad\quad$ $C_{set} \leftarrow C_{set} \cup \{l_i \xmapsto{C_m} l_j\}$

Definition 2. *Two local contexts* $l_i = \langle o_i, N_i^r, C_m \rangle$ *and* $l_j = \langle o_j, N_j^r, C_n \rangle$ *are linked with a context connection, denoted as* $l_i \xmapsto{C_m} l_j$, *if* $o_i \in N_j^r$ *and* $C_m \equiv C_n$.

Intuitively, a context connection captures the contextual dependency between two neighbouring observations o_i and o_j with respect to a common high-level classification activity C_m ($C_m \equiv C_n$). Note that symmetry and transitivity do not hold. For example, in Fig. 3 (a), *spoon1* (o_9) belongs to the neighbourhood set N_5^1 of *table.zone1* (o_5) ($N_5^1 = \{o_1, o_3, o_4, o_5, o_6, o_7, o_8, o_9\}$), but *table.zone1* does not belong to the neighbourhood set N_9^1 of *spoon1* ($N_9^1 = \{o_6, o_8, o_9, o_{10}\}$).

Algorithm 2 describes the process for creating the set of context connections C_{set}. Two local contexts $l_i = \langle o_i, N_i^r, C_m \rangle$ and $l_j = \langle o_j, N_j^r, C_n \rangle$ are retrieved from L, such that o_i belongs to the neighbourhood of o_j ($o_i \in N_j^r$) and $C_m \equiv C_n$ (lines 2 and 3), and the context connection $l_i \xmapsto{C_m} l_j$ is added to C_{set} (line 4).

Example. Algorithm 2 creates 29 context connections among the local contexts described in Section 4.1 for the running example in Fig. 3 (a). For example, o_7 belongs to the neighbourhood of the local contexts l_5, l_6 and l_8, i.e. $o_7 \in N_5^1, o_7 \in N_6^1$ and $o_7 \in N_8^1$. As described in Section 4.1, the classification class of l_5 and l_8 is $DrinkTea$ (DT), whereas the classification class of l_6 is $MakeTea$ (MT). Moreover, o_7 has two local contexts: l_7 with classification class $MakeTea$ and l_7' with classification class $DrinkTea$. Therefore, $l_7 \xmapsto{MT} l_6$ and $l_7' \xmapsto{DT} l_5$, $l_7' \xmapsto{DT} l_8$. The other context connections that are generated are: $l_1 \xmapsto{MT} l_2$, $l_1 \xmapsto{MT} l_3$, $l_1 \xmapsto{MT} l_4$, $l_2 \xmapsto{MT} l_1$, $l_2 \xmapsto{MT} l_3$, $l_3 \xmapsto{MT} l_1$, $l_3 \xmapsto{MT} l_2$, $l_3 \xmapsto{MT} l_4$, $l_4 \xmapsto{MT} l_1$, $l_4 \xmapsto{MT} l_2$, $l_4 \xmapsto{MT} l_3$, $l_4 \xmapsto{MT} l_6$, $l_4 \xmapsto{MT} l_7$, $l_6 \xmapsto{MT} l_3$, $l_6 \xmapsto{MT} l_7$, $l_6 \xmapsto{MT} l_9$, $l_9 \xmapsto{MT} l_6$, $l_9 \xmapsto{MT} l_7$, $l_5 \xmapsto{DT} l_7$, $l_5 \xmapsto{DT} l_8$, $l_8 \xmapsto{DT} l_5$, $l_8 \xmapsto{DT} l_7$, $l_8 \xmapsto{DT} l_9$, $l_9 \xmapsto{DT} l_5$, $l_9 \xmapsto{DT} l_7$, $l_9 \xmapsto{DT} l_8$.

4.3 Activity Situations and Recognition

The last step is to create *activity situations*, i.e. subsets of the initial set of observations O, and to compute the similarity σ to the context descriptor d_C.

Definition 3. *An activity situation S is defined as the tuple* $\langle Obs, C, V \rangle$, *where* $Obs \subseteq O$ *is the set of the observations that belong to the activity situation and V denotes the similarity of S to the context descriptor d_C, such that $V = \sigma(d_C, Obs_T)$, where $d_C \in D$ and $Obs_T = \{t \mid \forall o_i \in Obs, t = T(o_i)\}$.*

Situation Similarity σ. The σ measure captures the similarity between the domain context descriptor of class C, namely d_C, and set Obs_T with the most specific classes of the observations in a situation.

$$\sigma(d_C, Obs_T) = \frac{\sum\limits_{\forall n \in d_C} \max\limits_{\forall c \in Obs_T} [\delta(c, n)]}{|d_C|} \tag{3}$$

Similarly to φ in (1), σ denotes the similarity of two sets of concepts. However, φ aims to capture the local (partial) similarity of neighbourhood class types (N_T^r) against the context descriptor d_C. In contrast, σ captures the similarity of the context descriptor d_C against the set of situation observation class types (Obs_T), in order to derive the final plausibility for the corresponding situation. If $\sigma = 1$, then all the classes in d_C appear in Obs_T, meaning that the situation can be considered identical to the context descriptor d_C, and, therefore, to class C.

Creating Activity Situations. An activity situation is derived by simply traversing the path defined by context connections $l_a \xmapsto{C_m} l_b \xmapsto{C_m} \dots \xmapsto{C_m} l_e$, collecting the observations o_i of the local contexts l_i found in the path. The collected observations constitute set Obs of a situation $S = \langle Obs, C_m, V \rangle$.

Algorithm 3 describes the aforementioned procedure. It begins by selecting a context connection $l_i \xmapsto{C_m} l_j$, which has not been visited yet (line 2), as the root of the current path, adding it to the $Expand$ set (line 4). In each iteration, a context connection $l_k \xmapsto{C_m} l_l$ is selected from the $Expand$ set and: (a) the observations of the pertinent local contexts are added to Obs (line 7), (b) the current context connection is added to the $Visited$ set (line 8), and (c) the context connections $l_p \xmapsto{C_m} l_q$ are retrieved from C_{set} and added to the $Expand$ set, such that $l_p = l_l$ (lines 9, 10). An empty $Expand$ set denotes that there are no other context connections in the current path. In this case, the context descriptor of C_m (d_{C_m}) is compared against the set Obs_T with the most specific types of observations in Obs to compute the σ similarity of S (line 11).

Example. By applying Algorithm 3 over the context connections presented in Section 4.2, two situations are generated: $S_1 = \langle Obs_1, MakeTea, 0.833 \rangle$ and $S_2 = \langle Obs_2, DrinkTea, 1.0 \rangle$, where $Obs_1 = \{o_1, o_2, o_3, o_4, o_6, o_7, o_9\}$ and $Obs_2 = \{o_5, o_7, o_8, o_9\}$. It is worth noting that despite the overlapping and noisy nature of the observations in the example (e.g. the location-related observations o_3 and o_5 overlap), the algorithm is able to discriminate the two situations of making and drinking tea by also connecting the relevant observations.

Moreover, the nearest observations threshold r in the running example was set to 1, meaning that, apart from overlapping observations, the 1-nearest observations were also taken into account to define neighbourhood relations. If we instead use $r = 0$, then we get the following situations: $S_1' = \langle Obs_1', MakeTea, 0.666 \rangle$ and $S_2' = \langle Obs_2', DrinkTea, 1.0 \rangle$, where $Obs_1' = \{o_1, o_2, o_3, o_4\}$ and $Obs_2' = \{o_5, o_7, o_8, o_9\}$. In this case, o_6 ($teabag2$) is not connected with observations

---

Algorithm 3. Creating activity situations

Data: Context connections: $C_{set} = \{l_a \xmapsto{C_k} l_b, l_e \xmapsto{C_l} l_f, ..., l_i \xmapsto{C_m} l_j\}$.
Result: The set S_{set} with activity situations S.

1   $S_{set}, Visited \leftarrow \emptyset$;

2   **foreach** $l_i \xmapsto{C_m} l_j \in C_{set} \wedge l_i \xmapsto{C_m} l_j \notin Visited$ **do**

3      $Obs \leftarrow \emptyset$;

4      $Expand \leftarrow \{l_i \xmapsto{C_m} l_j\}$;

5   **while** $Expand \neq \emptyset$ **do**

6         $l_k \xmapsto{C_m} l_l \leftarrow Expand.pop$;

7         $Obs \leftarrow Obs \cup \{o_k, o_l\}$;

8         $Visited \leftarrow Visited \cup \{l_k \xmapsto{C_m} l_l\}$;

9         $Cons \leftarrow \{l_p \xmapsto{C_m} l_q \mid l_p = l_l, \forall l_p \xmapsto{C_m} l_q \in C_{set}, l_p \xmapsto{C_m} l_q \notin Visited\}$;

10        $Expand \leftarrow Expand \cup Cons$;

11      $S_{set} \leftarrow S_{set} \cup \{S\}$, where $S \leftarrow \langle Obs, C_m, \sigma(d_{C_m}, Obs_T) \rangle$ and
      $Obs_T = \{t \mid \forall o \in Obs, t = T(o)\}$;

---

relevant to the *MakeTea* activity, and is considered as noise, breaking also the connection of o_7 and o_9 with the *MakeTea* activity. Despite the fact that the *MakeTea* activity is detected with a lower plausibility when $r = 0$, it could be argued that the resulted situations are more meaningful for further analysis. Intuitively, r allows to control the amount of contextual information taken into account during the definition of the neighbourhood sets and local contexts of observations. Currently, r is defined manually based on domain knowledge regarding the quality and temporal characteristics of the data used.

5   Deployment, Results and Discussion

We have implemented our approach on top of OWLIM [6], following an ontology-based representation of local contexts, context connections and situations and using SPARQL queries (rules) for implementing the algorithms (SPARQL Inferencing Notation - SPIN [16]). Fig. 4 presents a sample SPARQL query that implements Algorithm 2 for creating context connections.

Our framework is part of a real-world deployment for monitoring Alzheimer's disease patients in a hospital[2]. The aim is to help clinicians assess the patients' condition through a goal-directed protocol of 10 Instrumental Activities of Daily Living (IADL), e.g. preparing the drug box (Fig. 5). Based on primitive observations, high-level activities are recognised that inform the clinicians, who are not present during the protocol, about activities with too long duration or activities that have been missed or repeated. The setting involves wearable and ambient video and audio sensors, accelerometers and physiological sensors. Table 1 presents the context descriptors used for the detection of the 10 activities.

---

[2] The system has been installed in the Memory Resource and Research Centre (CMRR) of the University Hospital in Nice (CHUN), under Dem@Care FP7 Project.

```
CONSTRUCT {
  [] a :ContextConnection; :li ?li; :lj ?lj; :classification ?Cm.
}
WHERE {
  ?li a :LocalContext; :obs ?oi; :classification ?Cm.
  ?lj a :LocalContext; :obs ?oj; :classification ?Cm; :neighbour ?oi.
  FILTER (?oi != ?oj).
  NOT EXISTS {[] a :ContextConnection; :li ?li; :lj ?lj; :classification ?Cm.}.
}
```

Fig. 4. SPARQL-based implementation of Algorithm 2

Table 1. The context descriptor dependencies of the high-level activities

IADL	Context Descriptor Classes
Establish account balance	Sitting, Accounts, Table, TableZone, Pen
Prepare drug box	Pillbox, Basket, MedicationZone
Prepare hot tea	Kettle, TeaZone, TeaBag, Cup, Sugar, TeaBox
Search for bus line	Map, MapZone, RouteInstructions
Make a phone call	Phone, PhoneZone, PickUpPhone, Talk
Watch TV	Remote, TV, TVZone, Sitting
Water the plant	WateringCan, PlantZone, Bending, Plant
Write a check	Sitting, Pen, Check, TableZone, Table
Read an article	Sitting, TableZone, Newspaper, Table
Enter/Leave the room	DoorOpen, EmptyRoom

Table 2 summarises the performance on a dataset of 25 participants, where True Positives (TP) is the number of IADLs correctly recognised, False Positives (FP) is the number of IADLs incorrectly recognised as performed and False Negatives (FN) is the number of IADLs that have not been recognised. The True Positive Rate (TPR) and Positive Predicted Value (PPV) measures denote the recall and precision, respectively, and are defined as:

$$TPR = \frac{TP}{TP+FN}, \quad PPV = \frac{TP}{TP+FP}$$

We used $r = 0$, since the dataset contains highly overlapping observations, and we set a minimum threshold on σ (≥ 0.65), so as to ignore activities with low plausibility. To demonstrate the effect of a higher r value in our experiments, we also present the performance using $r = 5$. By increasing the r value, the number of neighbours for each observation also increases. This way, more local contexts are generated, affecting precision and recall. As explained, the optimal r value depends on the data quality and temporal characteristics and, in principle, datasets with highly overlapping and incoherent observations need small r values.

Our approach achieves the best accuracy for activities "Prepare hot tea", "Make a phone call", "Watch TV" and "Water the plant", whose context descriptors encapsulate richer domain contextual information, compared to "Prepare drug box" and "Search for bus line". On the other hand, the recall of these

Table 2. Activity recognition performance

| | | | | $r = 0$ | | $r = 5$ | |
IADL	TP	FP	FN	TPR%	PPV%	TPR%	PPV%
Establish account balance	30	10	4	88.24	75.00	85.71	73.17
Prepare drug box	23	3	2	92.00	88.46	85.19	82.14
Prepare hot tea	23	1	6	79.31	95.83	76.67	88.46
Search for bus line	24	4	1	96.30	86.67	92.86	83.87
Make a phone call	24	1	3	89.29	96.15	86.21	92.59
Watch TV	21	1	4	84.00	95.45	80.77	91.30
Water the plant	20	1	5	80.00	95.24	80.00	86.96
Write a check	28	8	4	87.50	77.78	87.50	75.68
Read an article	23	4	1	95.83	85.19	92.00	85.19
Enter/Leave the room	49	0	1	98.00	100	98.00	98.00

(a) Writing a check   (b) Preparing the drug box

Fig. 5. Example IADL activities of the protocol (wearable and ambient camera)

activities is relatively low, since they are more susceptible to false negatives, requiring richer contextual dependencies to be present.

Another interesting finding involves activities "Establish account balance", "Write a check" and "Read an article". The context descriptors of these activities have many members in common; e.g. "Accounts" and "Checks" are the only discriminating contextual objects between "Establish account balance" and "Write a check". This way, our approach detects both activities when the corresponding observations are missing, resulting in low accuracy. Finally, the "Enter/Leave the room" activities share exactly the same context descriptors; however, we distinguish them (in an ad hoc manner) by the order in which they take place.

As already mentioned, our approach is currently used in an offline mode, where each participant's data is collected and processed after the execution of the protocol; therefore, the processing time is not a critical requirement in the current setting. However, Fig. 6 gives a gist about the required time for processing different sets of observations using a Dell Optiplex 7010 PC configuration (i7-3770 Processor, Quad Core, 3.40GHz). In each protocol execution, approx. 500 to 800 observations are generated, depending on the participant's performance.

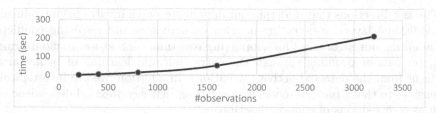

Fig. 6. Activity recognition time in relation to the number of observations

Discussion. Our framework achieves an average TPR and PPV close to 90%, demonstrating the feasibility of our approach in real-world settings. However, there are still certain limitations, which we consider as very important research directions for future work. First, our approach cannot handle interleaved activities, nor can it resolve conflicts after the recognition process, as argued for the "Establishing account balance" and "Write check" activities. We are investigating the use of defeasible reasoning on top of the framework for further enhancing the activity recognition capabilities. Second, our next step is to deploy the framework in homes for providing context-aware real-time assistance to Alzheimer's patients. To this end, we are currently investigating adaptations of our algorithms to allow the dynamic and incremental generation of local contexts and context connections for real-time activity segmentation and recognition.

In addition, one of the most challenging tasks in pervasive healthcare is patient profiling, which can provide the behaviour interpretation and feedback services with knowledge-driven personalisation capabilities and adaptive support services. To this end, we are exploring methods for extracting behaviour patterns and detecting behaviour changes from activity situations that are generated based on the abstract context descriptors presented here. Regarding the representation of these patterns, our objective is to take full advantage of the DnS pattern, associating each Situation to one or more behavioural Description instantiations pertinent to patients' idiosyncratic and habitual information.

6 Conclusions

We propose a knowledge-driven framework towards activity recognition and segmentation, coupling ontology models of abstract domain activity dependencies with a context-aware approach for multi-sensor fusion and monitoring. We formalise activity dependencies, capitalising upon the *Situation* conceptualisation of the DnS ontology pattern in DUL for defining generic context descriptors, whereas activity segmentation and recognition is reduced in linking and classifying meaningful contextual segments. We elaborated on the obtained results from the evaluation of our approach in a real-world deployment, monitoring activities of elderly people during the execution of a clinical protocol for assessing Alzheimer's disease. The use of generic context descriptors in representing activity models achieves very promising results, leading to handling the intrinsically noisy and imperfect information in multi sensory environments, beyond strict activity patterns and background knowledge (e.g. max activity duration).

The key directions that underpin our ongoing research involve (a) introducing an additional layer for detecting interleaved activities and resolving conflicts, (b) adapting our algorithms for supporting real-time context-aware monitoring, and, (c) patient profiling through the extraction and learning of behavioural patterns from the detected activity situations. In addition, we are investigating extensions to the *Situation* model for capturing richer contextual dependencies, such as compositions of context descriptors.

Acknowledgments. This work has been supported by the EU FP7 project Dem@Care: Dementia Ambient Care – Multi-Sensing Monitoring for Intelligent Remote Management and Decision Support under contract No. 288199.

References

1. Anicic, D., Fodor, P., Rudolph, S., Stojanovic, N.: Ep-sparql: a unified language for event processing and stream reasoning. In: Proceedings of the 20th International Conference on World Wide Web, pp. 635–644. ACM (2011)
2. Baader, F., Calvanese, D., McGuinness, D.L., Nardi, D., Patel-Schneider, P.F. (eds.): The Description Logic Handbook: Theory, Implementation, and Applications. Cambridge University Press (2003)
3. Barbieri, D., Braga, D., Ceri, S., Della Valle, E., Grossniklaus, M.: C-SPARQL: A Continuous Query Language for RDF Data Streams. International Journal of Semantic Computing (IJSC) 4(1) (2010)
4. Bettini, C., Brdiczka, O., Henricksen, K., Indulska, J., Nicklas, D., Ranganathan, A., Riboni, D.: A survey of context modelling and reasoning techniques. Pervasive Mob. Comput. 6(2), 161–180 (2010)
5. Bikakis, A., Antoniou, G., Hasapis, P.: Strategies for contextual reasoning with conflicts in ambient intelligence. Knowl. and Infor. Systems 27(1), 45–84 (2011)
6. Bishop, B., Kiryakov, A., Ognyanoff, D., Peikov, I., Tashev, Z., Velkov, R.: OWLIM: A family of scalable semantic repositories. Sem. Web 2(1), 33–42 (2011)
7. Chen, L., Khalil, I.: Activity recognition: Approaches, practices and trends. In: Activity Recognition in Pervasive Intelligent Environments, vol. 4, pp. 1–31 (2011)
8. Chen, L., Nugent, C.D.: Ontology-based activity recognition in intelligent pervasive environments. Int. Journal of Web Information Systems 5(4), 410–430 (2009)
9. Chen, L., Nugent, C.D., Wang, H.: A knowledge-driven approach to activity recognition in smart homes. IEEE Trans. Knowl. and Data Engin. 24(6), 961–974 (2012)
10. Cook, D.J., Augusto, J.C., Jakkula, V.R.: Ambient intelligence: Technologies, applications, and opportunities. Perv. and Mobile Computing 5(4), 277–298 (2009)
11. DOLCE Ultralite ontology, http://www.loa.istc.cnr.it/ontologies/DUL.owl
12. Eiter, T., Ianni, G., Krennwallner, T., Polleres, A.: Rules and ontologies for the semantic web. In: Baroglio, C., Bonatti, P.A., Małuszyński, J., Marchiori, M., Polleres, A., Schaffert, S. (eds.) Reasoning Web. LNCS, vol. 5224, pp. 1–53. Springer, Heidelberg (2008)
13. Gangemi, A., Mika, P.: Understanding the semantic web through descriptions and situations. In: Meersman, R., Schmidt, D.C. (eds.) CoopIS/DOA/ODBASE 2003. LNCS, vol. 2888, pp. 689–706. Springer, Heidelberg (2003)
14. Hong, X., Nugent, C.D., Mulvenna, M.D., Martin, S., Devlin, S., Wallace, J.G.: Dynamic similarity-based activity detection and recognition within smart homes. Int. J. Pervasive Computing and Communications 8(3), 264–278 (2012)
15. Jekjantuk, N., Gröner, G., Pan, J.Z.: Modelling and reasoning in metamodelling enabled ontologies. In: Bi, Y., Williams, M.-A. (eds.) KSEM 2010. LNCS (LNAI), vol. 6291, pp. 51–62. Springer, Heidelberg (2010)

16. Knublauch, H., Hendler, J.A., Idehen, K.: SPIN - overview and motivation. W3C member submission, World Wide Web Consortium (February 2011)
17. Meditskos, G., Dasiopoulou, S., Efstathiou, V., Kompatsiaris, I.: Sp-act: A hybrid framework for complex activity recognition combining owl and sparql rules. In: PerCom Workshops, pp. 25–30 (2013)
18. Moser, T., Roth, H., Rozsnyai, S., Mordinyi, R., Biffl, S.: Semantic event correlation using ontologies. In: Meersman, R., Dillon, T., Herrero, P. (eds.) OTM 2009, Part II. LNCS, vol. 5871, pp. 1087–1094. Springer, Heidelberg (2009)
19. Motik, B., Cuenca Grau, B., Sattler, U.: Structured objects in OWL: representation and reasoning. In: World Wide Web, pp. 555–564 (2008)
20. Okeyo, G., Chen, L., Hui, W., Sterritt, R.: A hybrid ontological and temporal approach for composite activity modelling. In: TrustCom, pp. 1763–1770 (2012)
21. Okeyo, G., Chen, L., Wang, H., Sterritt, R.: Dynamic sensor data segmentation for real-time knowledge-driven activity recognition. Pervasive and Mobile Computing 10(Pt. B), 155–172 (2014)
22. Palmes, P., Pung, H.K., Gu, T., Xue, W., Chen, S.: Object relevance weight pattern mining for activity recognition and segmentation. Perv. Mob. Comput. 6(1), 43–57 (2010)
23. Patkos, T., Chrysakis, I., Bikakis, A., Plexousakis, D., Antoniou, G.: A reasoning framework for ambient intelligence. In: Konstantopoulos, S., Perantonis, S., Karkaletsis, V., Spyropoulos, C.D., Vouros, G. (eds.) SETN 2010. LNCS (LNAI), vol. 6040, pp. 213–222. Springer, Heidelberg (2010)
24. Riboni, D., Pareschi, L., Radaelli, L., Bettini, C.: Is ontology-based activity recognition really effective? In: Perv. Comp. and Commun., pp. 427–431 (2011)
25. Riboni, D., Bettini, C.: COSAR: hybrid reasoning for context-aware activity recognition. Personal Ubiquitous Comput. 15(3), 271–289 (2011)
26. Riboni, D., Bettini, C.: OWL 2 modeling and reasoning with complex human activities. Pervasive and Mobile Computing 7(3), 379–395 (2011)
27. Roy, P., Giroux, S., Bouchard, B., Bouzouane, A., Phua, C., Tolstikov, A., Biswas, J.: A possibilistic approach for activity recognition in smart homes for cognitive assistance to alzheimers patients. In: Activity Recognition in Pervasive Intelligent Environments, Atlantis Ambient and Pervasive Intelligence, vol. 4, pp. 33–58 (2011)
28. Teymourian, K., Paschke, A.: Semantic rule-based complex event processing. In: Governatori, G., Hall, J., Paschke, A. (eds.) RuleML 2009. LNCS, vol. 5858, pp. 82–92. Springer, Heidelberg (2009)
29. Teymourian, K., Rohde, M., Paschke, A.: Fusion of background knowledge and streams of events. In: Proceedings of the 6th ACM International Conference on Distributed Event-Based Systems, New York, NY, USA, pp. 302–313 (2012)
30. Tiberghien, T., Mokhtari, M., Aloulou, H., Biswas, J.: Semantic reasoning in context-aware assistive environments to support ageing with dementia. In: Cudré-Mauroux, P., et al. (eds.) ISWC 2012, Part II. LNCS, vol. 7650, pp. 212–227. Springer, Heidelberg (2012)
31. Wessel, M., Luther, M., Wagner, M.: The difference a day makes - recognizing important events in daily context logs. In: C&O:RR (2007)
32. Ye, J., Stevenson, G.: Semantics-driven multi-user concurrent activity recognition. In: Augusto, J.C., Wichert, R., Collier, R., Keyson, D., Salah, A.A., Tan, A.-H. (eds.) AmI 2013. LNCS, vol. 8309, pp. 204–219. Springer, Heidelberg (2013)
33. Zhang, S., McCullagh, P., Nugent, C., Zheng, H.: An ontology-based context-aware approach for behaviour analysis. In: Activity Recognition in Pervasive Intelligent Environments, vol. 4, pp. 127–148. Atlantis Press (2011)

A Use Case in Semantic Modelling and Ranking for the Sensor Web

Liliana Cabral[1], Michael Compton[2], and Heiko Müller[1]

[1] Digital Productivity and Services Flagship, CSIRO, Hobart, Australia
{liliana.silvacabral,heiko.mueller}@csiro.au
[2] Digital Productivity and Services Flagship, CSIRO, Canberra, Australia
michael.compton@csiro.au

Abstract. Agricultural decision support systems are an important application of real-time sensing and environmental monitoring. With the continuing increase in the number of sensors deployed, selecting sensors that are fit for purpose is a growing challenge. Ontologies that represent sensors and observations can form the basis for semantic sensor data infrastructures. Such ontologies may help to cope with the problems of sensor discovery, data integration, and re-use, but need to be used in conjunction with algorithms for sensor selection and ranking. This paper describes a method for selecting and ranking sensors based on the requirements of predictive models. It discusses a Viticulture use case that demonstrates the complexity of semantic modelling and reasoning for the automated ranking of sensors according to the requirements on environmental variables as input to predictive analytical models. The quality of the ranking is validated against the quality of outputs of a predictive model using different sensors.

Keywords: Semantic sensor data, Sensor ranking, Sensor Cloud Ontology, Viticulture, Predictive analytical models.

1 Introduction

Real-time sensing for agricultural environmental monitoring has been an intense area of research (e. g., [6], [13]). Farmers and crop managers monitor crop growth and health continuously to make decisions based on their local knowledge and experience. Decision making is supported by environmental data as provided by automatic weather stations and by analytical tools that make predictions based on this data, e. g., predicting the risk of frost or plant disease.

In viticulture, for example, *botrytis bunch rot*, or *botrytis*, causes ripening bunches to rot on the vine [2]. Botrytis can develop during the ripening period and bunches may have to be harvested early at low sugar, having negative impact on wine quality. Wet weather is one of the factors that promotes the development of botrytis. To assist farmers, analytical models have been developed that simulate the effects of risk factors and control options on the development of botrytis epidemics. These models use weather information and crop management inputs to predict the risk that a major botrytis epidemic will occur at harvest.

P. Mika et al. (Eds.) ISWC 2014, Part II, LNCS 8797, pp. 276–291, 2014.
© Springer International Publishing Switzerland 2014

The proliferation of sensing devices deployed in our environment benefits farmers in terms of enhanced situational awareness. There are, however, remaining challenges related to the deployment of sensors [5], the usability of decision support systems [16], as well as the discovery of sensors and re-use of data from different sensing devices. The latter is the focus of our work. Models that predict the risk of botrytis require specific sensor data as part of their input (e. g., air temperature, wind speed, and leaf wetness) and are sensitive to the quality of the input data. For a model to produce reliable results it is of great importance to run the model with input data that is fit for purpose.

Our contribution is the development of a generic method for analysing sensors based on their capabilities, observed phenomena, calibration history, previous measurements, and current state to find sensors that meet the requirements of a particular model. Ontologies that represent sensors and observations may help to cope with the problems of sensor discovery, data integration, and re-use, but need to be used in conjunction with algorithms for sensor selection and ranking. We present an algorithm that ranks available sensors based on their suitability as input for a given model. Model-specific requirements towards input data are expressed using a set of fitness functions. Our algorithm runs queries over the semantically annotated resources to evaluate these functions. The result is an ordered list of sensors that satisfy model requirements.

In addition, we discuss our experience in using ontologies to model knowledge about sensing data and sensing devices in the context described above. We build on the SSN Ontology [4] and ontologies derived from OGC's Semantic Web Enablement data models to provide an umbrella ontology, named Sensor Cloud Ontology (SCO), for our Sensor Web infrastructure. We discuss a number of use cases, in which we applied SCO.The design goal of SCO was to refine the semantic models provided by the imported ontologies according to the data and metadata captured by our infrastructure.

We evaluate our modelling and ranking based on requirements of a Viticulture use case that demonstrates the complexity of semantic modelling and reasoning for automated ranking of sensors according to the requirements on input data by predictive analytical models. The quality of the ranking is validated against the quality and sensitivity of the predictive model regarding different inputs.

The remainder of this paper is structured as follows. Section 2 describes our semantic sensor infrastructure and SCO. Section 3 gives details about application requirements through use cases. The semantic modelling to address the use cases in discussed in Section 4. Section 5 presents our ranking algorithm. We evaluate the results of our algorithm in Section 6. Section 7 concludes the paper by discussing related work and giving a brief outlook into future work.

2   The Semantic Sensor Cloud

The Commonwealth Scientific and Industrial Research Organisation (CSIRO) collects and archives data from a large number of terrestrial and marine sensors. Parts of the data are made available via an in-house sensor data infrastructure, referred to as *Sensor Cloud*. An overview of the architecture is given in [14].

Within the Sensor Cloud, sensor data is structured following the hierarchy of $Network \to Platform \to Sensor \to Phenomenon \to Observation$. This structure resembles the deployment of sensors in the physical world, i.e., a sensor network consists of platforms, each platform has one or more sensors attached, and each sensor observes one or more phenomena. Besides observations, information such as sensor device characteristics and calibration history can also be accessed through the Sensor Cloud.

2.1   The Sensor Cloud Ontology

To semantically describe sensor data from the Sensor Cloud we created the *Sensor Cloud Ontology* (SCO)[1]. Figure 1 shows the main classes and properties of SCO. The principle behind its design is to use and extend existing ontologies, meanwhile aligning with the Sensor Cloud terminologies. Accordingly, classes and properties are created and mapped to the ones in existing ontologies. We reuse several ontologies, including the Semantic Sensor Network ontology (SSN)[2], the DOLCE ontology (DUL)[12], the OGC's Observation and Measurements (OM) ontology[3], and the GEO location (WGS84) vocabulary[4]. The advantages of reusing and extending existing ontologies are that sensor data can be queried according to the original terminologies while their consistency can be checked against SCO. We create SCO instances (RDF) from data in the Sensor Cloud using a system called SERAW, as described in [14].

SSN was designed to describe sensors: what is observed, how observations are made and the qualities of the sensors and observations [4]. SSN is built around a central pattern that describes the relationship between `ssn:Sensors`, the `ssn:Property` measured, the real-world `ssn:Stimulus` that 'triggers' the sensor and the resultant `ssn:Observation` [9] . The ontology expands on this to describe the `ssn:MeasurementCapability` (`ssn:Accuracy`, `ssn:Frequency`, etc.) of the sensor as well as to provide a skeleton structure for describing `ssn:Platforms` and `ssn:Deployments`.

Concepts that aggregate multiple sensors into larger units, such as sensor networks or sensors grouped by properties, are required by our applications. SSN provides `ssn:System` and `ssn:hasSubSystem` for describing multi-instrument units of technology. In SCO, such aggregations become `sco:Networks`, which can be used for wireless sensor networks, organisational networks, geographically related networks or mission oriented networks. These aggregations enable ranking and organisation of sensing resources: from `sco:Sensor` through `sco:Network` up to `sco:SensorCloud`. Such aggregations further enable the propagation of quality and trust estimates both up and down the hierarchy. For example, tending to increase the quality estimates of observations on a sensor because it is associated with networks of a known high-quality provider, or decreasing the trust on a provider because their sensors are not regularly maintained and calibrated.

---

[1] http://www.sense-t.csiro.au/sensorcloud/ontology
[2] http://purl.oclc.org/NET/ssnx/ssn
[3] http://def.seegrid.csiro.au/isotc211/iso19156/2011/observation
[4] http://www.w3.org/2003/01/geo/wgs84_pos

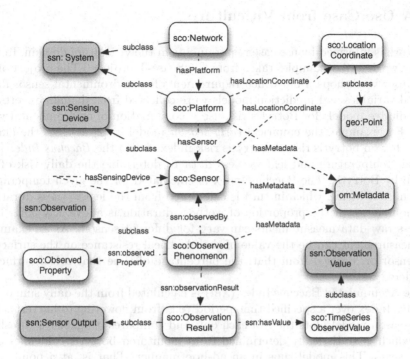

Fig. 1. Main Concepts in the Sensor Cloud Ontology

To describe sensor observations in SCO, we introduced the four concepts sco:ObservedPhenomenon, sco:ObservedProperty, sco:ObservationResult and sco:TimeSeriesObservedValue as subclasses of concepts ssn:Observation, ssn:Property, ssn:SensorOutput, and ssn:ObservationValue, respectively. SSN leaves open the representation of time — fixing time only as a dul:Region — and does not include a definition of time series. We model time series as observation results of time-value pairs, by setting sco:TimeSeriesObservedValue ⊑ sco:ObservationValue, and with the sco:TimeSeriesObservedValues having sco:hasTimeValuePair relations to sco:TimeValuePairs. In Section 4, we give more details of sco:ObservedPhenomenon and sco:ObservedProperty.

To be compatible with GEO and OM, we introduce sco:LocationCoordinate as a type of geo:Point, and use om:Metadata to describe metadata of several classes (e.g. sco:Sensor). In doing so, we are then able to use standardised (ISO) vocabularies for coordinates, deployment, and quality that are left open in SSN. Furthermore, we introduce some properties that are specific to the Sensor Cloud, e. g., those describing the number of time-value pairs of time series, and the first or last observation time.

3   A Use Case from Viticulture

Our work is informed by use case requirements in the viticulture domain. In this section we describe examples taken from the Sense-T project[5]. The project organized user workshops, from which requirements for environmental sensor data, derived variables and prediction models were collected from domain experts.

Predictive models for Botrytis risk use a combination of environmental variables. For example, the empirical *early-season* model in [2] assesses the effects of weather on botrytis risk. A botrytis risk index, called the *Bacchus Index* [10], uses air temperature and leaf wetness data to determine the daily risk of infection by Botrytis. The Bacchus Index is calculated for the given temperature at each "wet hour", which in turn is calculated from the leaf wetness duration. The hour is wet if the proportion of wetness duration is above, say 50%. Leaf wetness raw data measurements can vary for different sensors. As an example, the measurement can be the value of the electrical resistance on the surface of the sensor or, derived from that, the percentage of time that a leaf surface is considered wet[6].

The Accumulated Bacchus Index (ABI) is calculated from the daily sum of the Bacchus Index over a specified time period (e.g. from flowering to harvest). The early-season model plots the ABI each day and compares it against a threshold line, which is statistically determined from monitored botrytis epidemics over many years. This model runs in an ad-hoc manner. That is, at a point prior to the harvesting period the farmer decides to run the ABI. At this point, the challenge is to discover suitable sensors from a network of available sensors. We may find automatic weather stations or low-cost sensors deployed in a vineyard or in surrounding areas. In many cases suitable sensors may be deployed and operational, but if sensors are malfunctioning or not well maintained, data needs to be gathered from other suitable sensors. The choice of sensors can be based on their location as well as on their maintenance status and their current behaviour, for instance excluding sensors that have not been calibrated recently as well as sensors that show "unexpected" readings , for example, from interference to the sensing mechanism.

Although we have given the example of a predictive model, the same considerations apply to derived variables for the purpose of situational awareness. These include derived variables such as *Growing Degree Days*, *Evapotranspiration* or the *hourly Bacchus Index* (see for example [13]). From the user or application perspective, environmental variables derived from automatic weather stations sensor data streams are usually summarized in expressions like "Average daily temperature", "Total daily rainfall", "Maximum monthly discharge", "9am Relative Humidity", or "Average 10m wind speed (m/s)".

For the purpose of finding or reusing sensors, representing the meaning of these expressions can make the search or querying process much more efficient and precise. Say we are looking at measurements recorded as time series, these

---

[5] http://www.sense-t.org.au/projects/viticulture
[6] http://www.campbellsci.com.au/237-1

expressions constitute a combination of a functional (statistical) aggregation operator (e.g. average) and a temporal aggregator (e.g. daily) for an environmental property (e.g. temperature) with a unit of measure (e.g. degree Celsius). Composing properties with modifiers in a structured way can facilitate the reuse of sensor measurements that usually incur in very expensive computations. Usually these computations are necessary for the visualisation of time series, but they are equally important when used as input for predictive models.

Predictive models not only require observation data of a certain type, but also, in many cases, models have further (weak) constraints that define desired properties for the input data. One of the main constraints affecting the quality of the observation is the location of the sensors. For example, the sensors chosen for measuring temperature for the risk of frost in a vineyard should be the ones as close as possible to the frost event location. Another example of importance is proper sensor calibration. Data from poorly calibrated sensors can have a negative impact on forecast performance.

There might also be additional quality constraints that may require to examine values in time series e.g., no gaps longer than 6 hours, accuracy of all observations ≥ 0.95. In addition, we may want to propagate quality information along the hierarchy of Network, Platform, Sensor, and ObservedPhenomenon, for example a platform with many poorly calibrated sensors is considered low quality; if a network is considered poorly maintained the observations from the sensors are not reliable. Thus, in order to improve quality and reduce uncertainty in models, the discovery of sensors can involve finding information about sensor capability, deployment, calibration as well as measuring or ranking the quality of these factors so that they fit the requirements. Having knowledge of quality information for model input may also be used to estimate the uncertainty associated with the model output.

4   Semantic Modelling

In the following we describe the required semantic modelling and the solution given by the SCO and SSN ontologies according to the use case described in the last section. We look at environmental variables from two perspectives. First, as observed phenomena, where the observed property and the features of its measurement are represented. Then from the perspective of the sensor device and its influence on the quality of the measurement.

We use sco:observedPhenomenon to describe the context of the measurement for an environmental variable. This is aligned with the representation of ssn:Observation as a dul:Situation. As partially shown in the example below, this context includes a temporal modifier (e.g. daily), a functional modifier (e.g. total), the unit of measure (e.g. degree Celsius) and the sensor height (sco classes and properties accordingly). This is in addition to the inherited ssn class properties, which relate the observation to its observed property and result, among others. The sco:ObservedProperty is independent of an observation. It may be decomposed into parts using sco:hasPropertyPart, which is a sub-property of dul:hasPart. This aligns with dul:Quality and thus sub concept ssn:Property being decomposable with dul:hasPart. We use dul:UnitOfMeasure as the super-class for units of measure from MUO[7]. Property sco:hasUnitPart can be used to decompose units of measure into parts.

```
<sco:ObservedPhenomenon rdf:ID="daily-sum-of-Bacchus-index">
    <sco:hasFunctionalModifer rdf:resource="#total"/>
    <sco:hasTemporalModifier rdf:resource="#daily"/>
    <ssn:observedProperty rdf:resource="#bacchus-index"/>
</sco:ObservedPhenomenon>

<sco:ObservedProperty rdf:ID="bacchus-index">
    <sco:hasPropertyPart rdf:resource="#leaf-wetness"/>
    <sco:hasPropertyPart rdf:resource="http://purl.oclc.org/NET/ssnx/
                          cf/cf-property#air_temperature"/>
</sco:ObservedProperty>
```

The decomposition of observed properties and units into smaller parts enables finding variables that are related to the derived variables in the user query. For example, a query for "daily temperature" can closely match any temperature that has a unit of measure equal to the "day" unit of measure or any of the "day"'s unit parts (e.g. minute, second). Similarly, a query for "degree days" can match related variables that are equal to "degree days's" property parts.

Regarding the quality of sensors, SSN has no capacity for describing calibration or maintenance, both of which often change a deployed sensor's properties (the properties described by ssn:MeasurementCapability). Calibration is adjusting a single device's output based on comparison against reference devices. Manufacturer specifications may describe the full accuracy range of a sensing device, but the actual performance of the device within this range depends on its particular calibration and the time and conditions since calibration. SSN does provide ssn:Drift as a way of describing the degradation of accuracy over time. But the interaction of calibration, time since calibration, expected drift, and dependence on calibration method, are subtle properties of a sensor that are important in some applications.

Our solution for this issue, as shown below, is to use ssn:inCondition to specify a time range for which the particular capability is valid. More specifically, we model sco:CalibrationEvent as a condition, in effect stating, for example, that the accuracy holds for the given calibration period. This approach is powerful because the combination of SSN capabilities and conditions can express many properties of sensors and the conditions under which they are true. Further, such a method is invariant to the passage of time and consequent changes in the world: to make a fixed specification, such as classifying a sensor as having accuracy 2.9% or classifying it into a concept such as HighAccuracy, means that any changes require retracting the assertion as well as any derived consequences and making new assertions. In our system, where changes in time affect our choices of the best sensors, and where we may need to revisit the history of a sensor (e.g. find the sensors that have always been well maintained), retraction and reassertion would be awkward and wouldn't give the required functionality.

---

[7] http://purl.oclc.org/NET/muo

```
<sco:Sensor rdf:ID="RIMCO_Rainfall">

 <ssn:hasMeasurementCapability rdf:resource="#calibration-capability-12-06-13"/>
 <ssn:hasMeasurementCapability rdf:resource="#calibration-capability-20-01-14"/>
 ...
</sco:Sensor>

<ssn:MeasurementCapability rdf:ID="calibration-capability-20-01-14">
  <ssn:inCondition rdf:resource="#calibrationEvent_20-01-14"/>
  <ssn:forProperty rdf:resource="http://purl.oclc.org/NET/ssnx/cf/
                                  cf-feature#rainfall"/>
  <ssn:hasMeasurementProperty rdf:resource="#RIMCO_Low_Rainfall_Accuracy"/>
</ssn:MeasurementCapability>

<ssn:Accuracy rdf:ID="RIMCO_Low_Rainfall_Accuracy">
  <sco:hasMaxValue rdf:resource="#max_low_rainfall_mm_s"/>
  <sco:hasMinValue rdf:resource="#min_low_rainfall_mm_s"/>
</ssn:Accuracy>

<sco:MaximumAmount rdf:ID="max_low_rainfall_mm_s">
  <dul:hasDataValue rdf:datatype="http://www.w3.org/2001/XMLSchema#string"
                                 >0.3</dul:hasDataValue>
  <dul:isClassifiedBy rdf:resource="#uom_mm_s"/>
</sco:MaximumAmount>

<sco:CalibrationEvent rdf:ID="calibrationEvent_20-01-14">
  <ssn:endTime rdf:resource="#calibration_date_20-01-14"/>
</sco:CalibrationEvent>

<dul:TimeInterval rdf:ID="calibration_date_20-01-14">
  <sco:hasIntervalDateTime rdf:datatype="http://www.w3.org/2001/
  XMLSchema#dateTime">2014-01-20T00:00:00</sco:hasIntervalDateTime>
</dul:TimeInterval>
```

Further to this issue, SSN gives no guidance on how to describe the measurement capabilities of an installed sensor instance versus the full range of potential properties defined for the device. For example, it is typical to describe properties of types of sensors using TBox assertions and properties of instances of such sensors as ABox assertions; if the TBox asserts that the device may have an accuracy of ±2–4%, and the ABox asserts that a particular instance of the device has accuracy ±2–2.9% (due to calibration), both are still asserted (using ssn:hasMeasurementCapability) for the instance because the TBox assertion is still inferred. Some method of distinguishing between general (possible) properties of sensors and actual properties of deployed and calibrated instances of such sensors is required. Our solution using instances (ABox assertions) according to SCO modelling is shown in the example above.

Attaching assertions, such as a sensor's accuracy or an assessment of its suitability as input to a model, to time points is in line with the fluents approach [18] and the modelling of the passage of time in DOLCE. The approach allows objects, such as sensors, to keep a fixed URI, but still show the variance of the object over time. As in the example below, it is easy to SPARQL for the latest accuracy assertion or all the quality assessments made on a sensor.

```
SELECT ?s (MAX(?time) AS ?lastCalibration)
  WHERE {
    ?s ssn:hasMeasurementCapability ?mc .
    ?mc ssn:inCondition ?c .
    ?c a sco:CalibrationEvent .
    ?c ssn:endTime ?ti .
    ?ti sco:hasIntervalDateTime ?time .
  } GROUP BY ?s
```

5   Ranking of Sensors Based on Fitness for Purpose

In this section we describe a ranking algorithm for selecting sensors that provide suitable input for a predictive model or to compute a derived variable. Our algorithm is based on the semantic modelling described in Section 4. It takes a description of model requirements for sensor data as input and returns a list of suitable sensors together with their observations. Results are ranked based on their fitness for purpose. In the following we describe the design of our ranking algorithm based on the definitions of fitness functions and fitness queries.

5.1   Fitness Functions and Fitness Queries

In our queries we distinguish *required properties* and *desired properties* for sensor data. Required properties (RPs) define data properties that are essential in order to run a model. A typical example is the observed property. If a model requires air temperature as input it does not make sense to use rainfall observations instead. We consider SCO classes and properties associated with `sco:observedPhenomenon` to define RPs, e. g., temporal modifier, functional modifier, and unit of measure. The temporal modifier defines the interval between observed values (e. g., hour). The functional modifier describes how observed values within the interval are aggregated (e. g., average). In addition, most models expect observations to be represented in a specific measurement unit (e. g., Fahrenheit).

Desired properties (DPs) describe preferences that models have towards the input data in order to ensure high quality results. A common example is sensor location. When running a predictive model we are interested in finding sensors that are in close proximity to the location for which the prediction is made (e. g., a vineyard). Other examples include calibration history (e. g., we prefer sensors that are calibrated regularly), age of the sensing device (e. g., newer devices are preferred over older ones), or state of the time series of observation (e. g., number of missing observations). In our ranking algorithm DPs are used to further restrict the set of sensors suitable to run a model as well as to rank results based on how they satisfy the DPs.

From our examples it becomes clear that there is a wide variety of DPs. To account for this variety we model DPs using *fitness functions*. We assume a set of fitness functions $F = \{f_1, \ldots, f_n\}$. Each function $f(G, op, KV)$ takes as input a knowledge base in the form of a RDF graph G, an observed phenomenon op, and a set of function-specific key-value pairs KV. Each function returns a value in an ordered domain D or a special null value $\bot$. A typical example is a spatial distance function. The function takes latitude and longitude information as additional parameters. It retrieves the latitude and longitude of the sensor that observed the given phenomenon and returns the Euclidean distance between that sensor and the given location. If latitude and longitude information does not exist for the given sensor the function returns $\bot$.

Fitness functions may also access external data sources. This is particularly important for functions that operate on time series. Currently we exclude the actual observed time-value pairs from our knowledge base. The two main reasons for this decision are that (1) the data changes frequently and we would need to continuously update the knowledge base, and (2) RDF is not well suited to represent time series data potentially leading to increased query execution times. Observed time-value pairs can be stored using different architectures (e. g., the Sensor Cloud), instead. Our knowledge base contains a reference (URL) to the data. Using these references a fitness function can retrieve the time series from the external source and compute a value over the data (e. g., the maximal time gap between consecutive observations).

Formally, a query for sensors suitable to run a given model, referred to as *fitness query*, is a pair (Q, FFS). Q is a SPARQL query for observed phenomena that satisfy the RPs of a model. Note that we focus on observed phenomena instead of sensors since each sensor can observe multiple phenomena. We later retrieve the sensor that made the observations for our final result. *FFS* is a set of *fitness function statements*. Each fitness query contains a non-empty set of fitness functions $FFS = \{(f_1, \omega_1, c_1, KV_1), \ldots, (f_n, \omega_n, c_n, KV_n)\}$. With each function we associate a weight ω to reflect the importance given to that particular property. For example, a model may give higher importance to the distance of a sensor to a given location than to calibration status. Although fitness functions represent desired properties (or weak constraints), models can have thresholds on fitness values, e. g., only consider sensors that have been calibrated within the last 12 months. We associate a Boolean function c with each fitness function to represent such strong constraints. Function c returns *true* if the value returned by f satisfies the constraint and *false* otherwise.

5.2   Ranking Algorithm

Our ranking algorithm, which executes fitness queries, is shown in Figure 2. Information about sensors and their properties is maintained in a knowledge base in RDF format. The algorithm takes the RDF graph G, a SPARQL query Q, and fitness function statements *FFS* as input. It returns a ranked list of (sensor, observed phenomenon)-pairs. There are three main steps in our algorithm: (1) retrieve observed phenomena that satisfy the RPs, (2) compute a ranking of returned phenomena for each fitness function in *FFS*, and (3) compute an aggregate ranking of phenomena from the individual rankings.

The first step in the algorithm returns observed phenomena in G that satisfy the RPs by executing the SPARQL query Q. The only constraint towards Q is that it returns a list of URIs for `sco:ObservedPhenomenon`. An example query is shown below. The query retrieves all observed phenomena for the observed property `cf:air_temperature`, which have been measured hourly and classified according to http://purl.oclc.org/NET/muo/ucum/unit/time/hour.

```
SELECT DISTINCT ?observation
WHERE {
    ?observation a sco:ObservedPhenomenon .
    ?observation ssn:observedProperty cf:air_temperature .
    ?observation sco:hasTemporalModifier ?tempMod .
    ?tempMod dul:isClassifiedBy <http://purl.oclc.org/NET/muo/ucum/unit/time/hour>
}
```

Input: G, Q, FFS
Output: List of (sensor, observed phenomenon)-pairs and their overall ranking score

```
CANDIDATES ← SPARQL(G, Q);        /* Step 1 */
RANKINGS ← ∅;                     /* Step 2 */
for all (f, ω, c, KV) ∈ FFS do
    RANK ← ∅;
    for all op ∈ CANDIDATES do
        val ← f(G, op, KV);
        if c(val) then
            RANK ← RANK ∪ {(op, val)};
        else
            CANDIDATES ← CANDIDATES \ op;
        end if
    end for
    RANKINGS ← RANKINGS ∪ sort_f(RANK);
end for
RESULT ← ∅;                       /* Step 3 */
for all op ∈ CANDIDATES do
    score ← 0;
    for all (f, ω, c, KV) ∈ FFS do
        score ← score + (ω × get-rank-position(op, RANKINGS, f));
    end for
    RESULT ← RESULT ∪ {((op, get-sensor-for(op)), score)};
end for
sort_ASC(RESULT);
return RESULT;
```

Fig. 2. Pseudo-code for ranking algorithm

The second step in the algorithm ranks candidate phenomena for each fitness function f individually. Should a candidate fail the respective strong constraint c associated with f it is removed from the set of candidates. For those candidates that satisfy the constraint we maintain the URI of the phenomenon and the returned function value. We then rank all candidates that have not been pruned. We assume the existence of a ranking function $sort_f$ that returns a list of URI-value pairs such that the pair with the best value (according to function f) is ranked first, the second-best value second, and so on. For a spatial distance function, for example, the pairs are sorted in ascending order of distance values.

The last step of the algorithm computes an aggregate ranking for candidates based on the individual rankings and the weights given to the respective fitness functions. We maintain a list of rankings ($RANKINGS$). The problem of combining ranking results has been studied extensively in social choice theory and web search (e. g., [7], [1]). Dwork et al. show that the problem of computing an optimal solution can by NP-hard (for certain distance measures) given four or more input rankings [7] and propose several heuristic algorithms for rank aggregation. Our current implementation is based on Borda's positional method [3] that can be computed in linear time. Borda's method assigns a score to each candidate corresponding to the position at which it appears in each individual ranking. The function $get\text{-}rank\text{-}position(op, RANKINGS, f)$ returns the rank position of the candidate identified by op in the ranking computed for fitness function f. We multiply the result by the weight assigned to f. Function $get\text{-}sensor\text{-}for(op)$ retrieves the URI of the sensor that observed phenomenon op. For our result we sort all (sensor, observed phenomenon)-pairs in ascending order of their accumulated score. Note that we can use other rank aggregation methods, e. g., using Markov chains as proposed in [7]. The main purpose of this section, however, is to present a method for discovering sensors that are fit for purpose based on the semantic modelling in Section 4. We consider the problem of evaluating the effectiveness of different ranking methods as future work.

Table 1 gives examples of fitness functions that we have implemented. The functions use SPARQL queries to retrieve information such as sensor location, most recent calibration event, or the URL that provides access to the time series of observed values. The spatial distance function expects coordinates for a point of interest (PoI). It computes the Euclidean distance between the PoI and the retrieved coordinates. The gap count function looks at the time intervals between consecutive values in a time series. If the interval between two values is larger than the maximum interval it increments the gap count by the quotient of the actual interval and the expected interval.

To give an example for fitness function statements consider a model like the accumulated Bacchus index that requires leaf wetness data. The DPs are (i) close proximity to a PoI, and (ii) calibrated recently. We use the following statements to express the DPs for location (f: Spatial Distance, ω: 0.8, $c(val)$: $val \leq 10$ km, KV: $\{lat : -42.15, lon : 147.45\}$) and calibration ($f$: Calibration, ω: 0.2, $c(val)$: $val \leq 6$ months, KV: $\{\}$). We exclude sensors that are more than 10 km away from the PoI or that have not been calibrated in the last 6 months. We also put higher importance on the distance of the leaf wetness sensor to PoI than on the calibration date, e. g., due to the model being more sensitive to location.

Table 1. Three examples of fitness functions for spatial distance, last calibration date, and number of gaps in a time series of observed values

	Steps	Parameter
Spatial Distance	1) SPARQL for location of measuring sensor	Latitude for PoI
	2) Calculate Euclidean distance	Longitude for PoI
Calibration	1) SPARQL as shown on page 283	
Gap Count	1) SPARQL for URL to access data	Expected Time Interval
	2) Retrieve time series of observed values	Max. Time Interval
	3) Count number of gaps	

6 Implementation and Evaluation

We implemented a number of derived variables from our Viticulture use case. We used the Kepler [11] workflow engine to compute the variables, having the Sensor Cloud infrastructure as the source of raw data.

We use the Accumulated Bacchus Index (ABI) (see Section 3) to evaluate our modelling and fitness for purpose ranking algorithm. The ABI requires hourly air temperature and leaf wetness observations as input. Our evaluation consists of the following steps. We first compute a baseline ABI graph for a fixed period (Jan. 2014) using a pair of well maintained sensors for air temperature and leaf wetness, i. e., our gold standard. We then fix the leaf wetness sensor and re-run the ABI with different temperature sensors from a set of candidates. That is, we assume that we need to find a replacement for the gold standard temperature sensor. We plot the different ABI outputs in Figure 3. From these results we derive the optimal ranking of candidates based on how good they resemble the baseline result. We then show that our ranking algorithm produces the optimal ranking according to the user criteria.

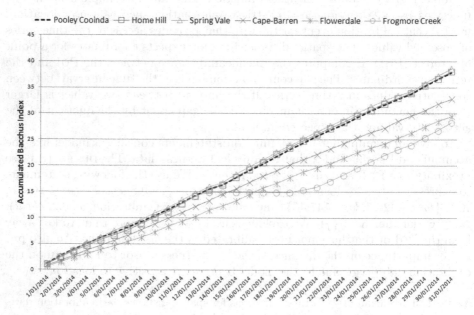

Fig. 3. ABI computed for Jan. 2014 using a fixed leaf wetness sensor (at *Pooley Cooinda*) and six different air temperature sensors

Our baseline is obtained using sensors at *Pooley Cooinda*. Our set of candidates contains five air temperature sensors that are in close proximity to *Pooley Cooinda*. Figure 3 shows that the sensor at *Home Hill* results in an ABI that almost exactly resembles the baseline result. The sensor at *Spring Vale* gives a less accurate but still acceptable result. Using the sensor at *Frogmore Creek* produces the worst result. This is mainly due to the fact that the sensor has a large gap (approximately seven days) with missing data. Based on Figure 3 we define an optimal ranking for candidates in order of increasing mean squared error (MSE) with the baseline (shown in brackets): *Home Hill* (0.008), *Spring Vale* (0.015), *Cape-Barren* (0.068), *Flowerdale* (0.110), *Frogmore Creek* (0.371).

We now show that our ranking algorithm can produce the optimal ranking based on user criteria expressed using fitness function statements. To do so, we use two different fitness functions: one for spatial distance and one for missing data (as shown in Section 5). For the latter we count the number of missing observed values considering that the ABI requires input on an hourly basis.

Table 2 shows rankings of candidate sensors using different fitness function statements. The ranking using the spatial distance fitness function solely uses distance from the leaf wetness sensor at *Pooley Cooinda* to rank the temperature sensors. According to this ranking the sensor at *Frogmore Creek* is the best replacement sensor and the sensor at *Cape-Barren* is the worst replacement sensor. The result clearly contradicts the optimal ranking. When ranked by increasing number of gaps, *Home Hill* is the best choice and *Frogmore Creek* the worst. This ranking exactly reflects the optimal ranking and highlights that the quality of data is of higher importance to the ABI than the distance of the sensor. The aggregated rankings are weighted over distance and gap count. When giving a higher importance to distance (Aggreg. (0.8, 0.2)), the sensor at *Frogmore Creek* is still ranked as one of the preferred replacements. The situation changes when giving higher importance to gap count instead.

Table 2. Rankings of candidate sensors for different fitness functions

Rank	Spatial Distance	Gap Count	Aggreg. (0.8, 0.2)	Aggreg. (0.2, 0.8)
1	Frogmore Creek	Home Hill	Home Hill	Home Hill
2	Home Hill	Spring Vale	Frogmore Creek	Spring Vale
3	Spring Vale	Cape-Barren	Spring Vale	Cape-Barren
4	Flowerdale	Flowerdale	Flowerdale	Flowerdale
5	Cape-Barren	Frogmore Creek	Cape-Barren	Frogmore Creek

We repeat the experiment for Apr. 2014 where none of the candidate sensors has gaps (graph not shown). The optimal ranking (based on MSE) is: *Frogmore Creek* (0.001), *Home Hill* (0.004), *Spring Vale* (0.011), *Flowerdale* (0.022), *Cape-Barren* (0.075). This ranking equals the ranking based on spatial distance (as shown in Figure 2). A ranking on gaps, on the other hand, will rank all sensors the same. Thus, for the different time periods different fitness functions produce the optimal result, i. e., gap count for Jan. 2014 and distance for Apr. 2014. For both time periods the aggregated ranking that gives higher importance to gaps always produces the optimal result. This clearly shows the benefit of combining fitness function statements to receive optimal results for different situations.

The evaluation shows that our algorithm is able to produce optimal rankings. The quality of ranking, however, depends on the user supplied fitness function statements. If the statements correctly capture the fact that the ABI has high sensitivity to gap count, our algorithm correctly ranks the replacement candidates. Should the user decide to give higher weight to the distance, on the other hand, the results could be non-optimal. In general, the choice of functions and their weights requires knowledge about the sensitivity of the model. We envision that developers of a model will specify these fitness requirements. The user then only specifies user dependent properties such as the location of their vineyard.

7 Conclusions

In this paper we propose an ontology-based framework for finding observation data that is fit for purpose as input to predictive models. In particular, we focus on the modelling methodology and approaches to handling the difficulties of describing sensors and evaluating them in a dynamic environment.

Within this framework, we further present a generic approach to ranking sensor data based on fitness for purpose. Our framework allows to rank sensors against criteria such as location, most recent calibration event, administered by an organisation that maintains sensors regularly, and data quality over a period of time (e. g., number of gaps). Ranking makes use of the accumulated metadata and semantics in the ontology for long term analysis and semantic analysis of the sensors. Since the quality of sensor measurements is not fixed over time our semantic model accounts for this changing behaviour.

Our work presents a first approach to exploit sensor properties for ranking based on fitness for a particular purpose. Existing approaches rank sensors based on the probability that they have a certain output state at a given time [8] or based on the similarity of their observed values [17]. The work in [15] goes into a similar direction as ours, however, our work has a strong focus on semantic modelling. Furthermore, the fitness functions that we consider allow for more complex expressions of fitness for purpose.

In future work, we consider automating the search for compatible sensors. For example, when a model requires maximum hourly air temperature, sensors that observe air temperature on a minutely basis are candidates because the data can convert through aggregation. Performance of evaluating fitness functions is another area of future work. Here, our particular focus is on caching the results of functions that incur high cost, e. g., computing values over time series data from external data sources.

Acknowledgements. This work was conducted as part of the Sense-T Program, and was jointly funded by the Australian Government, Tasmanian Government, the University of Tasmania, through the Tasmanian Institute of Agriculture, and the CSIRO Digital Productivity and Services Flagship. We would like to thank K. Evans, C. Peters, J. Forbes, D. Peel, S. Foster, D. Biggins and C. Sharman.

References

1. Ailon, N.: Aggregation of partial rankings, p-ratings and top-m lists. In: Proc. ACM-SIAM Symposium on Discrete Algorithms, SODA 2007, pp. 415–424 (2007)
2. Beresford, R., Evans, K., Hill, G.: Botrytis decision support: online tools for predicting seasonal risk of botrytis bunch rot. Wine and Viticulture Journal 27, 46–52 (2012)

3. Borda, J.C.: Memoire sur les elections au scrutin. Histoire de l'Academie Royale des Sciences (1781)
4. Compton, M., et al.: The SSN ontology of the W3C semantic sensor network incubator group. Web Semantics: Science, Services and Agents on the World Wide Web 17, 25–32 (2012)
5. Corke, P., Wark, T., Jurdak, R., Hu, W., Valencia, P., Moore, D.: Environmental wireless sensor networks. Proceedings of the IEEE 98(11) (December 2010)
6. De Wolf, E.D., Isard, S.A.: Disease cycle approach to plant disease prediction. Annual Review of Phytopathology 45, 203–220 (2007)
7. Dwork, C., Kumar, R., Naor, M., Sivakumar, D.: Rank aggregation methods for the web. In: Proceedings of the 10th International Conference on World Wide Web, WWW 2001, pp. 613–622. ACM (2001)
8. Elahi, B.M., Romer, K., Ostermaier, B., Fahrmair, M., Kellerer, W.: Sensor ranking: A primitive for efficient content-based sensor search. In: Proceedings of the International Conference on Information Processing in Sensor Networks, IPSN 2009, pp. 217–228. IEEE Computer Society (2009)
9. Janowicz, K., Compton, M.: The Stimulus-Sensor-Observation Ontology Design Pattern and its Integration into the Semantic Sensor Network Ontology. In: Proc. Int'l. Workshop on Semantic Sensor Networks, vol. 668. CEUR-WS (2010)
10. Kim, K., Beresford, R., Henshall, W.: Prediction of disease risk using site-specific estimates of weather variables. New Zealand Plant Protection 60, 128–132 (2007)
11. Ludäscher, B., et al.: Scientific workflow management and the kepler system: Research articles. Concurr. Comput.: Pract. Exper. 18(10), 1039–1065 (2006)
12. Masolo, C., Borgo, S., Gangemi, A., Guarino, N., Oltramari, A.: WonderWeb deliverable D18 ontology library (final). Tech. rep., IST Project 2001-33052 WonderWeb: Ontology Infrastructure for the Semantic Web (2003)
13. Matese, A., Gennaro, S.D., Zaldei, A., Genesio, L., Vaccari, F.: A wireless sensor network for precision viticulture: The NAV system. Computers and Electronics in Agriculture 69, 51–58 (2009)
14. Mueller, H., Cabral, L., Morshed, A., Shu, Y.: From RESTful to SPARQL: A Case Study on Generating Semantic Sensor Data. In: 6th International Workshop on Semantic Sensor Networks in Conjunction with ISWC 2013 (2013)
15. Perera, C., Zaslavsky, A., Christen, P., Compton, M., Georgakopoulos, D.: Context-aware sensor search, selection and ranking model for internet of things middleware. In: Intl. Conf. on Mobile Data Management, MDM 2013, pp. 314–322. IEEE Computer Society (2013)
16. Shtienberg, D.: Will decision-support systems be widely used for the management of plant diseases? Annual Review of Phytopathology 51, 1–16 (2013)
17. Truong, C., Romer, K., Chen, K.: Sensor similarity search in the web of things. In: IEEE Symp. on a World of Wireless, Mobile and Multimedia Networks (WoWMoM), pp. 1–6 (2012)
18. Welty, C., Fikes, R.: A reusable ontology for fluents in OWL. In: Proc. Intl. Conf. on Formal Ontology in Information Systems (FOIS) (2006)

Semantic Traffic Diagnosis with STAR-CITY: Architecture and Lessons Learned from Deployment in Dublin, Bologna, Miami and Rio*

Freddy Lécué[1], Robert Tucker[1], Simone Tallevi-Diotallevi[1], Rahul Nair[1],
Yiannis Gkoufas[1], Giuseppe Liguori[2], Mauro Borioni[2], Alexandre Rademaker[3],
and Luciano Barbosa[3]

[1] IBM Dublin Research Centre, Ireland
[2] SRM - Reti e Mobilita, Bologna, Italy
[3] IBM Rio Research Centre, Brazil

Abstract. IBM **STAR-CITY** is a system supporting **S**emantic road **T**raffic **A**nalytics and **R**easoning for **CITY**. The system has ben designed (i) to provide insight on historical and real-time traffic conditions, and (ii) to support efficient urban planning by integrating (human and machine-based) sensor data using variety of formats, velocities and volumes. Initially deployed and experimented in Dublin City (Ireland), the system and its architecture have been strongly limited by its flexibility and scalability to other cities. This paper describes its limitations and presents the "*any-city*" architecture of STAR-CITY together with its semantic configuration for flexible and scalable deployment in any city. This paper also strongly focuses on lessons learnt from its deployment and experimentation in Dublin (Ireland), Bologna (Italy), Miami (USA) and Rio (Brazil).

1 Introduction

Entering 2014, the transportation system has matured in all major cities in the world; it only expands its infrastructure by a fraction of a percentage each year [1]. However, as projections indicate that more than half the world's population will be living in cities by 2030, congestion will continue to grow at an alarming rate, adversely impacting our quality of life and increasing the potential for accidents, long delays and other indirect consequences such as bus bunching. These are expected to escalate, calling for IT professionals to increase the functionalities, scalability, integration and productivity of existing transportation systems through the use of operational improvements.

There are several traffic analysis tools available, and some open, for use; however, they rarely encompass mechanisms for handling data heterogeneity, variety and integration. Therefore very few traffic systems are easily really portable from one city to another one. Most of the existing modern traffic systems[1] such as US TrafficView [2], TrafficInfo, French Sytadin or Italian 5T mainly focus on monitoring traffic status in cities using pre-determined and dedicated sensors (e.g., loop indiction detectors), all exposing numerical data. Others, more citizen-centric such as the traffic layer of Google

---

* The research leading to these results has received funding from the European Union's Seventh Framework Programme (FP7/2007-2013) under grant agreement ID 318201 (SIMPLI-CITY).

[1] Traffic Systems: `trafficview.org`, `trafficinfo.lacity.org`, `www.sytadin.fr`, `www.5t.torino.it/5t`

P. Mika et al. (Eds.) ISWC 2014, Part II, LNCS 8797, pp. 292–307, 2014.

Maps or [3], provide real-time traffic conditions and estimation but do not deliver insight to interpret historical and real-time traffic conditions. For instance the diagnosis of traffic condition [4] or the problem of explaining traffic condition is not addressed by state-of-the-art traffic systems. Basic in-depth but semantics-less state-of-the-art analytics are employed, limiting also large scale real-time data interpretation and integration. Thus, context-aware computing together with reusability of the underlying data and flexible deployment of traffic systems are limited. The reasoning functionalities are also very limited and reduced to basic analytics such as traffic monitoring or prediction.

STAR-CITY[2,3] (Semantic **T**raffic **A**nalytics and **R**easoning for **CITY**) [5], as a daily-used system which integrates heterogeneous data in terms of format variety (structured and unstructured data), velocity (static and dynamic data) and volume (large amount of historical data), has been mainly designed to provide such insights on historical and real-time traffic conditions. STAR-CITY completely relies on the W3C semantic Web stack e.g., OWL 2 (Web Ontology Language) and RDF (Resource Description Framework) for representing semantics of information and delivering inference outcomes. The strength of STAR-CITY lies in the ability of the system to perform various types of semantic inferences i.e., spatio-temporal analysis, diagnosis, exploration and prediction of traffic condition and congestion (cf. [5] for an high level presentation). These inferences are all elaborated through a combination of various types of reasoning i.e., (i) semantic based i.e., distributed ontology classification-based subsumption [6], (ii) rules-based i.e., pattern association [7], (iii) machine learning-based i.e., entities search [8] and (iv) sensor dynamic-based i.e., correlation [7].

Initially deployed and experimented in Dublin City (Ireland), the system, its architecture and its semantic-related components have shown limitations regarding their flexibility and scalability to other cities. This paper describes their scenarios and their limitations. We also present the "*any-city*" architecture of STAR-CITY together with its semantic configuration for flexible and scalable deployment in any city. The paper also strongly focuses on lessons learnt from the deployment and experimentation of the new architecture in Dublin (Ireland), Bologna (Italy), Miami (USA) and Rio (Brazil), which is completely novel with respect to past presented work [4] (STAR-CITY diagnosis in Dublin), [9] (STAR-CITY prediction in Dublin) and [5] (STAR-CITY in Dublin). To the best of our knowledge there is no single traffic system which (i) supports advanced traffic analysis functionalities as STAR-CITY does, and (ii) scales up to major cities.

The paper is organized as follows: Section 2 presents the contexts and scenarios associated to Bologna, Miami, Rio and their main differentiators with Dublin. Section 3 describes the new flexible system architecture and configuration for "*any city*". Section 4 reports some experimental results regarding scalability, flexibility and semantic expressivity. Section 5 reports on lessons learned from deploying STAR-CITY in major cities. Section 6 draws some conclusions and talks about possible future directions.

2   Diagnosing Anomalies in Dublin, Bologna, Miami and Rio

As highlighted in Section 1 the STAR-CITY system has been designed for analyzing, diagnosing, exploring and predicting traffic condition in cities. We focus on the

---

[2] Video (.avi, .mov, m4v format) available: http://goo.gl/TuwNyL
[3] Live system: http://dublinked.ie/sandbox/star-city/

Table 1. (Raw) Data Sources for STAR-CITY in Dublin, Bologna, Miami and Rio

Source Type	Data Source	Description	Dublin (Ireland)	Bologna (Italy)	Miami (USA)	Rio (Brazil)
Traffic Anomaly	Journey travel times across the city	Traffic Department's TRIPS system[a]	CSV format (47 routes, 732 sensors) 0.1 GB per day[b]	✗ (not available)		
Traffic Anomaly	Dublin Bus Dynamics	Vehicle activity (GPS location, line number, delay, stop flag)	✗ (not used)	SIRI: XML format[c] (596 buses, 80KB per update 11GB per day[d])	CSV format (893 buses, 225 KB per update 43 GB per day[e])	CSV format (1, 349 buses, 181 KB per update 14 GB per day[f])
Traffic Diagnosis	Social-Media Related Feeds	Reputable sources of road traffic conditions in Dublin City	"Tweet" format - Accessed through Twitter streaming API[g]			
Traffic Diagnosis	Social-Media Related Feeds	Reputable sources of road traffic conditions in Dublin City	Approx. 150 tweets per day[h] (approx. 0.001 GB)	✗ (not available)	Approx. 500 tweets per day[i] (approx. 0.003 GB)	✗ (not available)
Traffic Diagnosis	Road Works and Maintenance		PDF format (approx. 0.003 GB per day[j])	XML format (approx. 0.001 GB per day[k])	HTML format (approx. 0.001 GB per day[l])	✗ (not available)
Traffic Diagnosis	Social events e.g., music event, political event	Planned events with small attendance	XML format - Accessed once a day through Eventbrite[m]APIs			
Traffic Diagnosis	Social events e.g., music event, political event	Planned events with small attendance	Approx. 85 events per day (0.001 GB)	Approx. 35 events per day (0.001 GB)	Approx. 285 events per day (0.005 GB)	Approx. 232 events per day (0.01 GB)
Traffic Diagnosis	Social events e.g., music event, political event	Planned events with large attendance	XML format - Accessed once a day through Eventful[m]APIs			
Traffic Diagnosis	Social events e.g., music event, political event	Planned events with large attendance	Approx. 180 events per day (0.05 GB)	Approx. 110 events per day (0.04 GB)	Approx. 425 events per day (0.1 GB)	Approx. 310 events per day (0.08 GB)
Traffic Diagnosis	Bus Passenger Loading / Unloading (information related to number of passenger getting in / out)		✗ (not available)	✗ (not available)	CSV format (approx. 0.8 GB per day[e])	CSV format (approx. 0.1 GB per day[e])

[a] Travel-time Reporting Integrated Performance System - http://www.advantechdesign.com.au/trips
[b] http://dublinked.ie/datastore/datasets/dataset-215.php (live)
[c] Service Interface for Real Time Information - http://siri.org.uk
[d] http://82.187.83.50/GoogleServlet/ElaboratedDataPublication (live)
[e] Private Data - No Open data
[f] http://data.rio.rj.gov.br/dataset/gps-de-onibus/resource/cfeb367c-c1c3-4fa7-b742-65c2c99d8d90 (live)
[g] https://sitestream.twitter.com/1.1/site.json?follow=ID
[h] https://twitter.com/LiveDrive - https://twitter.com/aaroadwatch - https://twitter.com/GardaTraffic
[i] https://twitter.com/fl511_southeast
[j] http://www.dublincity.ie/RoadsandTraffic/ScheduledDisruptions/Documents/TrafficNews.pdf
[k] http://82.187.83.50/TMC_DATEX/
[l] http://www.fl511.com/events.aspx
[m] https://www.eventbrite.com/api - http://api.eventful.com

diagnosis-based reasoning scenarios of Bologna, Miami and Rio as they are the most representative and exposed in terms of semantic Web technologies. In particular we differentiate the latter three innovative in-use scenarios with the one from Dublin, which has already been implemented, tested and experimented [4]. Table 1 synthesizes the main important details of the data sets we have considered for this reasoning task.

We report major in-use challenges for each scenario where concrete solutions are presented (Section 3) and experimentation conducted (Section 4) for validation.

2.1   Diagnosing Traffic Congestion in Dublin City (*Reminder* of [4])

• *Description*: The diagnosis task in Dublin consists in explaining why the road traffic is congested. Anomalies are captured by the Dublin journey travel time data set in Table 1 (cf. traffic anomaly row). There are a number of specific circumstances which cause or aggravate congestion. However capturing an accurate explanation of the reasons of congestion is a challenging problem. Traffic accidents, road works and social events (e.g., music, political events) are considered as potential sources of explanation in the Dublin context (cf. traffic diagnosis related rows).

• *Motivation*: Traffic congestion has a number of negative effects, which strongly affects cities, their citizens and operators. For instance it reduces economic health because of the (i) non-productive activity of people stuck in their vehicles, (ii) wasted fuel, among others. Capturing the explanation of traffic congestion will support the city and transportation operators to act upon changing scenarios in real-time. For instance, given accurate explanations of congestion, the city traffic manager could be pro-active by (i) taking corrective actions on incoming traffic flow by changing the traffic strategies of close traffic lights, (ii) alerting the appropriate emergency services, (iii) re-routing traffic, (iv) better planning events in the city and more importantly (iv) informing its citizen in real-time

• **Challenge**: Diagnosing traffic condition is a challenging research problem of interest for the semantic Web community because (i) relevant data sets (e.g., road works, social events, incidents), (ii) their correlation (e.g., road works and social events connected to the same city area) and (iii) historical traffic conditions (e.g., road works and congestion in Canal street on May 9th, 2014) are not fully integrated, linked and jointly exploited. Recent progress in the area [4] demonstrated the applicability of semantic Web technologies in solving this challenge.

2.2 Diagnosing Bus Congestion in Bologna

• **Description**: The diagnosis task in Bologna consists in explaining why buses are congested. Contrary to the Dublin scenario, bus data is considered, providing more sparse data (because of the moving bus-related sensors) and a different data format i.e., SIRI XML instead of CSV. In addition the amount of data used for diagnosis (cf. traffic diagnosis row) is not as significative as in the Dublin scenario in terms of (i) size and (ii) number of data sets e.g., no report of traffic incident in Bologna. Finally the road works are exposed in Italian and digitalized in a different format.

• **Motivation**: cf. Motivation of Section 2.1 with a focus on bus congestion in Bologna.

• **Challenges and STAR-CITY Limitations**: Conceptually, diagnosing bus congestion relies in a similar reasoning task of the one described in Section 2.1. However from an in-use perspective diagnosing bus congestion in Bologna requires to address the following technical challenges:

C_1 Traffic anomalies are identified and represented differently.
   How to capture a semantic, core representation of anomalies in any city?
C_2 The sources of diagnosis and their size are not similar e.g., social media is missing.
   How accuracy of diagnosis is impacted by its sources? Are they still representative?
C_3 The sources of diagnosis are heterogeneous from one city to another one.
   How to configure STAR-CITY in a way that is scalable and flexible to any city?
C_4 Data exposed in Bologna is real-time information but with a very low throughput.
   Could the architecture of STAR-CITY be decoupled from its streaming components?
C_5 The schema of some data sources is in Italian cf. road works in Table 1.
   How to make use of cross languages data sources?

2.3 Diagnosing Bus Bunching in Miami

• **Description**: The diagnosis task in Miami consists in explaining why buses bunched. Fig.1 illustrates STAR-CITY in Miami. In public transport, bus bunching refers to a group of two or more buses, which were scheduled to be evenly spaced running along

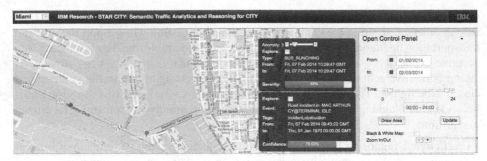

Fig. 1. STAR-CITY In Miami. (color).

the same route, instead running in the same location at the same time. This occurs when at least one of the vehicles is unable to keep to its schedule and therefore ends up in the same location as one or more other vehicles of the same route at the same time. Contrary to Dublin but similarly to Bologna scenario, bus data is considered but with a much higher throughput, which may raise some questions regarding scalability of STAR-CITY in Miami. Contrary to Dublin and Bologna scenarios, much more data sources (i.e., passengers-related data) with larger size are considered. Again the format of data slightly changed across cities.

• *Motivation*: The end result can be unreliable service and longer effective wait times for some passengers on routes that had nominally shorter scheduled intervals. Another unfortunate result can be overcrowded vehicles followed closely by near-empty ones.

• *Challenges and STAR-CITY Limitations*: In addition to challenges C_1, C_2 and C_3 in Section 2.2 which are also valid in this context, diagnosing bus bunching in Miami requires to address the following technical challenge:

C_6 The number of diagnosis sources is larger e.g., bus passenger loading set is added. *How accuracy of diagnosis is impacted by new external sources? (dual to (b)).*

2.4 Diagnosing Low On-Time Performance of Buses in Rio

• *Description*: The diagnosis task in Rio consists in explaining the low on-time performance of buses i.e., buses which are heavily delayed. The reasons can range from traffic incidents, accidents, bus bunching, detour, or unrealistic scheduling. Contrary to the Dublin and Miami scenarios the amount of data sets of potential use for diagnosis is very low i.e., only events and information about passengers loading are available. In addition the schema of the latter data set is different and in Portuguese.

• *Motivation*: Such problems can result in unreliable bus services for Rio, which could turn in complex problems such as bus bunching, and even more critical problems such as emphasized in motivation of Section 2.1.

• *Challenges and STAR-CITY Limitations*: In addition to challenges C_1, C_2, C_3, C_5 and C_6 in Sections 2.2 and 2.3 which are also valid in this context, diagnosing bus delays in Rio requires to address the following technical challenges:

C_7 The historic of information is 480 days while it is more than 3 years for other cities. *How accurate is the diagnosis in a context of limited historical information?*

This section described the problems which have not been foreseen by the initial architecture of STAR-CITY, but which have strong impacts and limitations for flexible and scalable deployment in Bologna, Miami and Rio. All challenges C_1, C_3-C_5 are problems where semantic web technologies have been strongly considered in the innovative and deployed architecture of STAR-CITY in Bologna, Rio and Miami (cf. Section 3) while challenges C_2, C_6 and C_7 are related to data characteristics (availability, relevance, accuracy) and their fit-for-purpose (cf. Section 4).

3 Flexible System Architecture and Semantic Configuration

The high-level architecture of STAR-CITY (both Dublin and Bologna, Miami, Rio versions) in Fig.2 consists of four main components: (i) semantic application configuration, (ii) semantic application server, (iii) data layer and (iv) user interface. In this section we explain how we adapted the initial version of STAR-CITY (running for Dublin) and its underlying technologies (i) to address the aforementioned challenges C_1, C_3-C_5 of Section 2, and then (i) to be flexible for deployment in other major cities in the world.

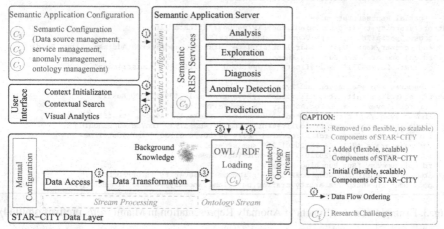

Fig. 2. High-Level System Architecture of STAR-CITY with References to (a) **Challenges** C_i of Section 2, and (b) **Initial**, **Removed**, **Added** Components of Dublin STAR-CITY to Support Flexible Deployment in Bologna, Miami and Rio. (color).

3.1 Semantic Application Configuration

The *semantic application management and configuration* component is the main component of STAR-CITY which enables flexible and scalable deployment of the system to other cities. Initially deployed and experimented in Dublin city, STAR-CITY did not address the challenges C_1, C_3 and C_5.

• *Challenge C_1 "Anomaly Identification"*: The identification of anomalies in the initial version of STAR-CITY is pre-determined by some very simple fixed encoded rules, for instance (1) encoding the rule *"if travel time between sensorID$_{203}$ and sensorID$_2$ is less than 183 seconds then trigger diagnosis service"*.

$$TriggerDiagnosis(s_1, s_2, time) \leftarrow Sensor(s_1) \wedge Sensor(s_2) \wedge travelTime(s_1, s_2, time, value)$$
$$\wedge\ equalTo(s_1, 203) \wedge equalTo(s_2, 2)$$
$$\wedge\ lessThan(value, 183)\ \%\ with\ "183"\ is\ the\ min.\ threshold \qquad (1)$$

Obviously such an approach is not scalable to other domains and even other cities. Indeed, one would need to redefine the rules at every new deployment phase from scratch. We address this problem by following [10], which provides semantics for capturing anomalies at semantic level. The approach consists in supervising the end-user in annotating values ranges of sensors with predefined concepts *"Anomaly"* and *"Normal"* from our domain ontology $\mathcal{O_D}$. This ontology, represented as a RDF-S taxonomy, is simply used for defining the domain e.g., Dublin Travel Time and its anomalies. Further domains can be easily added e.g., Bologna, Miami and Rio Bus domain. The appropriate rules are then encoded semantically using SWRL rules[4], which connect the logical rules to the domain of application. Following this semantic extension of STAR-CITY, end-user can easily extend $\mathcal{O_D}$, and then encode any anomaly identification rules.

```
@prefix geo: <http://www.w3.org/2003/01/geo/wgs84_pos#> .
@prefix dbpr: <http://dbpedia.org/resource/> .
@prefix addr: <http://schemas.talis.com/2005/address/schema#> .
@prefix rdfcal: <http://www.w3.org/2002/12/cal/icaltzd#> .
@prefix ibmVoc: <http://www.ibm.com/smartercities/cityfabric/voc#> .
@prefix busVoc: <http://www.ibm.com/SCTC/ontology/BusOntology.owl#> .
@prefix xmls: <http://www.w3.org/2001/XMLSchema#> .

<!-- Spatial Representation -->
<http://starcity.traffic.bus.miami.anomaly/venues/AltonRoad_10>
    a geo:SpatialThing ; dbpr:Country_Code <dbpr#ISO_3166-1:US> ;
    addr:countryName "USA" ; addr:localityName "Miami" ; addr:streetAddress "Alton Road" ;
    rdfcal:summary "Bus Bunching Anomaly" ;
    geo:lat "25.788371^^<xmls#float>" ; geo:long "-80.141280^^<xmls#float>" .

<!-- Temporal Representation and Type -->
<http://starcity.traffic.bus.miami.anomaly/event/Anomaly_1398032000_Bus113>
    a rdfcal:Vevent ; a ibmVoc:Anomaly ; a ibmVoc:Traffic ;
    ibmVoc:eventTag "flow" , "speed", "bunching", "delay", "road", "traffic" ;
    ibmVoc:hasEventCategory rdfcal:Vevent , ibmVoc:Anomaly , ibmVoc:BusBunching ;
    rdfcal:tzname "GMT" ; rdfcal:created "2014-04-20T20:01:20^^<xmls#dateTime>" ;
    rdfcal:dtstart "2014-04-20T20:01:20^^<xmls#dateTime>" ;
    rdfcal:dtend "2014-04-20T20:13:20^^<xmls#dateTime>" ;
    rdfcal:summary "Bus Bunching Anomaly" ;
    ibmVoc:hasSensingBUS <busVoc#Bus113> ; ibmVoc:hasSeverity "STOPPEDFLOW" ;
    geo:location <http://starcity.traffic.bus.miami.anomaly/venues/AltonRoad_10> .
```

Fig. 3. Example of a Bus Bunching Anomaly Representation in Miami (rdf/s prefixes omitted)

• *Challenge* C_1 *"Anomaly Representation" (Fig.3)*: The initial representation of anomalies did not require any semantics has only one type of anomaly was diagnosed in the Dublin scenario. In larger cities, traffic anomalies could be of different types, which need to be captured. The new representation of anomalies in STAR-CITY follows a strict and simplistic (on purpose) representation of anomalies i.e., spatial, temporal representations, types and associated key tags e.g., Miami bus 113 bunching in Fig.3. Such a semantic representation is specifically important in the context of bus-related diagnosis since different types of bus anomalies may occur in one city e.g., delay, congestion, bunching. Capturing and representing their types is very important to (i) understand how anomalies and their types are correlated to their diagnoses, (ii) easily search among anomalies which are captured by different systems e.g., bus congestion by a TRIPS system, bus delays by a bus operator related system (cf. Dublin case where bus delay and travel time could be provided by two different systems).

• *Challenge* C_3 *"Semantic Inter-City Configuration"*: The semantic inter-city configuration challenge C_3 is complimentary addressed by the semantic application config-

---

[4] http://www.w3.org/Submission/SWRL/

```
@prefix ibmVoc: <http://www.ibm.com/smartercities/cityfabric/voc#> .

<!-- Configuration Settings for Bus Congestion Diagnosis in Bologna -->
<http://starcity.traffic.bus.bologna/reasoning/diagnosis>
    <!-- Configuration of inputs to be considered for diagnosis reasoning -->
  <Class ibmVoc:Input> <Type ibmVoc:RoadWork> <Source "BolognaRoadWorkComplete">
      <Property geo:lat> <Property geo:long> <!-- Spatial Constraints -->
      <Property rdfcal:dtstart> <Property rdfcal:dtend> <!-- Temporal Constraints -->
      <Property ibmVoc:description> <Property ibmVoc:areaOfWork> <!-- RoadWork Features -->
  <Class ibmVoc:Input> <Type ibmVoc:MajorEvent> <Source "Eventful"> <!-- Property omitted -->
  <Class ibmVoc:Input> <Type ibmVoc:MinorEvent> <Source "Eventbrite"> <!-- Property omitted -->

<!-- Configuration Settings for Bus Bunching Diagnosis in Miami -->
<http://starcity.traffic.bus.miami/reasoning/diagnosis>
  <Class ibmVoc:Input> <Type ibmVoc:RoadWork> <Source "BolognaRoadWorkComplete">
      <Property geo:lat> <Property geo:long> <!-- Spatial Constraints -->
      <Property ibmVoc:description> <Property ibmVoc:areaOfWork> <!-- RoadWork Features -->
      <Property rdfcal:dtstart> <Property rdfcal:dtend> <!-- Temporal Constraints -->
      <Property ibmVoc:impact>
  <Class ibmVoc:Input> <Type ibmVoc:MajorEvent> <Source "Eventful"> <!-- Property omitted -->
  <Class ibmVoc:Input> <Type ibmVoc:MinorEvent> <Source "Eventbrite"> <!-- Property omitted -->
  <Class ibmVoc:Input> <Type ibmVoc:Incident> <Source "Twitter"> <!-- Property omitted -->
  <Class ibmVoc:Input> <Type ibmVoc:BusLoading> <Source "BusTransit"> <!-- Property omitted -->
```

Fig. 4. Semantic Configuration for Bologna and Miami Diagnosis Reasoning

uration (i.e., configuration-layer in this section), server (services-side in Section 3.2) and data layer (data-side Section 3.3) in STAR-CITY. In the initial version of STAR-CITY for Dublin, each and every dimension of our data sets has been represented in OWL / RDF, reaching to a very detailed contextual information but also to (i) a very tight model which is not flexible to other cities, and (ii) a time-consuming mapping process (i.e., mapping from raw to RDF data cf. Section 3.3). The migration of STAR-CITY from one city to another one requires major customization and many steps of configuration. For instance the traffic impact of a road work event is defined in Dublin and Miami, not Bologna; its area of work (e.g., secondary, pavement) is defined in Miami and Bologna, not in Dublin. Similarly traffic accidents (through social media) are captured in the Dublin and Miami scenarios, but not for Bologna and Rio. Since the diagnosis is highly coupled to the level and categories of representation of events, it is very important that the inputs of diagnosis (i.e., traffic diagnosis row of Table 1) are pre-configurable. To this end we let the (admin) users define the relevant raw data and associated concepts to be considered for diagnosis. For instance, the diagnosis application of Bologna and Miami could be defined as in Fig.4. In such a configuration, the diagnosis reasoning can be configured with respect to its inputs (e.g., input of diagnosis for diagnosing bus congestion in Bologna), their types (e.g., RoadWork defined in the ibmVoc ontology) and raw data sources (e.g., BolognaRoadWorkComplete) and respective properties (e.g., latitude, longitude, area of work).

The new configuration settings of STAR-CITY, defined through the IBM Rational family of software configuration management solutions and extended with semantics, is flexible, easy to be exported to any city. Instead of directly interacting with the REST APIs (cf. Fig.2), the semantic configuration is used to automatically adapt the APIs with the appropriate settings. The city-wide customization is then driven by (the semantics of) the vocabulary used for defining the inputs, their types, sources, properties.

• *Challenge C_5 "Multi-Lingual System"*: STAR-CITY has been designed for running with english vocabularies such as IBM ibmVoc. Such vocabularies, which strongly drive the reasoning engine, do not offer multi-lingual features and very few connections to open vocabularies. This strongly limits the entry of non-english speakers to the

STAR-CITY configuration, which turns to be the case for Bologna (Italian language) and Rio (Portuguese language) administrators. Therefore the interpretation and customization of inputs (e.g., configuration in Fig.4), results (e.g., diagnosis schema-related such as their types cf. Fig.5) are rather difficult, and even impossible in some cases. We address this problem by simply manually adding extra links (i.e., Linked Open Data resources [11]) to all concepts of our IBM vocabulary.

(a) Diagnosis in Dublin (English)   (b) Diagnosis in Bologna (Italian)

Fig. 5. Semantics-driven Multi-Lingual STAR-CITY (color). Diagnosis results are automatically provided in preferred language by using language-related links of DBpedia. (Hyperlinks are provided for describing specific terms e.g., cantiere - construction - not displayed for sake of readability).

By adding LOD links to our vocabulary we also give the possibility for non expert users to get extra and detailed information related to non self-explanatory events such as construction, obstruction, drainage (by simply follow new hyperlinks in STAR-CITY). Fig.6 illustrates a simple extension of our vocabulary, where associated Italian[5] and Portuguese[6] transcriptions of Traffic collision are used in the appropriate context.

```
<http://www.ibm.com/smartercities/cityfabric/voc#TrafficIncident>
  a http://www.ibm.com/smartercities/cityfabric/voc#Event
  owl:sameAs <http://dbpedia.org/resource/Traffic_collision"> <!-- [A] -->
  <!-- owl:sameAs <http://it.dbpedia.org/resource/Incidente_stradale> through ref. to [A] -->
  <!-- owl:sameAs http://pt.dbpedia.org/resource/Acidente_rodovirio> through ref. to [A] -->
```

Fig. 6. Sample of a Simple LOD Extension of IBM STAR-CITY Vocabulary

3.2 Semantic Application Server

• *Challenge C_3 "Semantic Inter-City Configuration"*: As reported in Fig.2 and Fig.7, web-facing services use a set of SA-REST services[7]. These services are implemented on a custom application running on IBM WebSphere Application Server. REST-related technologies have been considered in STAR-CITY because of its lightweight protocol. Extended with a semantic layer, SA-REST was the most appropriate solution to accommodate our semantic configuration (cf. Challenge C_3 in Section 3.1). In details the semantic configuration is combined with the skeleton of each STAR-CITY APIs to

---

[5] Italian http://it.dbpedia.org/resource/Incidente_stradale for English Traffic Collision.

[6] Portuguese http://pt.dbpedia.org/resource/Acidente_rodovirio for English Traffic Collision.

[7] http://www.w3.org/Submission/SA-REST/

provide customized SA-REST analysis, exploration, diagnosis and prediction services e.g., diagnosing bus bunching in Miami with road works and accidents, or both. The description of the low-level implementation of the services is described in the APIs registry (e.g., how technically diagnosis reasoning is interacting with input data sources) while the semantic and high-level representation of the expected services are described in the semantic configuration (e.g., Figure 4 for configuring STAR-CITY Bologna and Miami). Such an architecture, which discharges the manual and syntactic configuration of services, ensures flexible deployment of customized STAR-CITY functionalities in the context of any city.

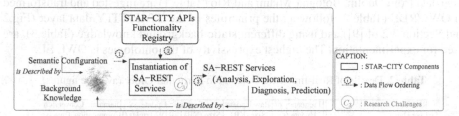

Fig. 7. Semantic Instantiation and Implementation of STAR-CITY SA-REST Services. (color).

3.3 Data Layer

Contrary to the semantic application server, a step of manual configuration is required in the data layer. It is mainly in charge of defining the data access points (e.g., URL of TRIPS data[b] in Table 1), protocols (e.g., HTTP for TRIPS), frequency (e.g., every minute for TRIPS) and various basic raw data parsing (e.g., adding timestamp to data collected for TRIPS). The Perl programming language, its standard modules together with CRON jobs are used for this purpose. We also manually define the mapping procedure from raw data source to semantic representation. The mapping procedure, completely described in Section 3.2 of [9], consists of a set of mapping files which describes how raw data is transformed in semantic representations associated to our domain ontology. Basic XSLT (for XML) and custom tabular transformation procedures (for CSV) are applied.

• **Challenge C_4 "Semantic Stream Agnostic Architecture"**: Initially designed in a streaming infrastructure, the data access and transformation of STAR-CITY is now stream-agnostic. Ontology streams are not generated anymore from the data layer. The main reasons of this architecture shift are: (i) low throughput of STAR-CITY-related sensors in our city test cases, (ii) cost of streaming platform deployment, (iii) cost of configuration, and (iv) weak flexibility (regarding the on-the-fly integration of new data). Instead data transformation and aggregation is performed independently in a traditional manner (i.e., using pre-defined java routines and Perl scripts). The output of the transformation is a semantic and temporal representation. Therefore, conceptually, the output is similar to the initial version i.e., OWL statements are stored in jena TDB, where some temporal indexes have been added.

4 Experimental Results

This section focuses on challenges C_2, C_6 and C_7 by comparing and analyzing the scalability and accuracy of the reasoning component of STAR-CITY in Dublin, Bologna,

Miami and Rio. In particular we aim at (i) analyzing how our approach reacts to the size (C_2), number (C_6) and historic (C_7) of data sources (cf. Sections 4.2 and 4.3) within our city context (cf. Section 4.1), and (ii) studying the impact of semantic expressivity by adjusting the underlying ontologies (cf. Section 4.4). Requested by traffic controllers, scalability and accuracy of the system have been extensively tested to validate the relevance, usefulness and (agreed) deployment of STAR-CITY. The experiments have been conducted on a server of 6 Intel(R) Xeon(R) X5650, 3.46GHz cores, and 6GB RAM.

4.1   Context

Live data from Dublin, Bologna, Miami and Rio (Table 1) are ingested and transformed in OWL/RDF (Table 2) following the principles of the STAR-CITY data layer (Fig.2 and Section 3.2 of [9]) and using different static background knowledge (Table 3), are used for experimentation. The highest expressivity of the ontologies is OWL EL.

Table 2. Details of Real-time Live Data in No Particular Order (average figures)

Real Time, Live Data	City	Frequency of Update (s)	Raw Update Size (KB)	Semantic Update Size (KB)	#RDF Triples	Semantic Conversion Computation Time (s)
[a] Journey Times	Dublin	60	20.2	6, 102	63, 000	0.61
[b] Bus	Bologna	120	31.8	1, 166	4, 550	0.295
	Miami	40	66.8	1, 766	11, 000	0.415
	Rio	60	96.8	2, 366	16, 145	0.595
[c] Incident	Dublin	600	0.2	1.0	7	0.002
	Miami	180	0.2	1.0	9	0.002
[d] Road Works	Dublin	once a week	146.6	77.9	820	3.988
	Bologna	once a day	78.9	133.2	1, 100	0.988
	Miami	3600	102.6	103.6	912	1.388
[e] City Events	Dublin	once a day	240.7	297	612	1.018
	Bologna		111.2	149	450	0.434
	Miami		637.2	789	1, 190	1.876
	Rio		585.3	650	950	1.633
[f] Bus Loading	Miami	40	833	2, 500	4, 500	0.390
	Rio	60	69.7	650	1, 230	0.147

The objective is to diagnose traffic anomalies in the different test cities i.e., traffic congestion in Dublin, bus congestion in Bologna, bus bunching in Miami, low on-time performance of buses in Rio. The evaluation is achieved on a different data sets combinations since our test cities have access to different data sets. From the most to the least complete case we have: [b,c,d,e,f] for Miami, [a,c,d,e] for Dublin, and [b,e,f] for Rio,[b,d,e] for Bologna (cf. Table 2 for data set {a,b,c,d,e,f} reference). Specifically we evaluate the impact of the data sets combination on scalability and accuracy.

Table 3. Static Background Knowledge for Semantic Encoding

Ontology	Size (KB)	#Concepts	#Object Properties	#Data Properties	#Individuals	Imported Ontologies	Data Sets Covered
IBM Travel Time	4, 194	41	49	22	1, 429	Time	[a]
IBM SIRI-BUS [4]	41.9	21	17	18	-	Geo	[b]
LODE[a] (initial)	12	14	16	-	-		[e]
(extended)	56	87	68	31	-	Time, Geo	[c-f]
W3C Time[b]	25.2	12	24	17	14	-	[a-f]
W3C Geo[c]	7.8	2	4	-	-	-	[a-f]
DBpedia	Only a subset is used for annotation i.e., 28 concepts, 9 data properties						[c-e]

[a] http://linkedevents.org/ontology/2010-10-07/rdfxml/
[b] http://www.w3.org/TR/owl-time/
[c] http://www.w3.org/2003/01/geo/

4.2   Scalability Experimentation and Results

Fig.8 reports the scalability of our diagnosis reasoning and core components (i.e., data transformation, OWL / RDF loading in Jena TDB, anomaly detection) of STAR-CITY by comparing their computation time in different cities and contexts. Similarly to data transformation and OWL / RDF loading, the anomaly detection and diagnosis reasoning have been performed over one day of traffic.

• *Challenges C_2, C_6 "Impact of Data Sources (and their combination)"*: The number and size of data sets have strong negative impact on the overall STAR-CITY. Indeed the more data sets the more overhead on transformation, loading, and reasoning. For instance STAR-CITY performs better in Bologna (data sets [b,d,e]) than in Miami (data sets [b,c,d,e,f]), although the latter results remain scalable.

• *Challenges C_7 "Impact of Historic Data"*: As expected the computation performance (of one day) of raw data transformation is not impacted by the size of historical information (cf. secondary vertical x axis) while the computation of the OWL / RDF loading slightly increases accordingly. The latter is caused by the overhead of RDF triples loading on the TDB store, which requires some non negligible time times for re-indexing e.g. 100 minutes of indexing over one complete day of RDF storage in Rio. More interestingly the more historical information the more computation time, specifically for diagnosis reasoning e.g., a factor of 5.3 from an historic of 10 days to 480 days in Miami. This is caused by the intensive event similarity search over historical events performed by the diagnosis [4].

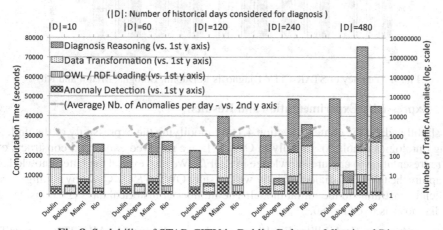

Fig. 8. Scalability of STAR-CITY in Dublin, Bologna, Miami and Rio

4.3   Accuracy Experimentation and Results

Fig.9 reports the impact of historical information (challenges C_2, C_6) and size and number of data sets (challenge C_7) on accuracy of diagnosis results in Dublin, Bologna, Miami and Rio. The accuracy has been evaluated by comparing our explanation results against those estimated by transportation experts (used as ground truth) in their respective cities. A basis of one complete day of experimentation has been used i.e., 2,800, 240, 1190 and 3,100 traffic anomalies for respectively Dublin, Bologna, Miami and Rio. Fig.9 reports the average accuracy of diagnosis results.

• **Challenges C_2, C_6 "Impact of Data Sources (and their combination)"**: The more data sources the more accurate the diagnosis results. For instance the accuracy of diagnosis is the highest in the context of Miami (with the largest number of datasets i.e., [b,c,d,e,f]) while the accuracy is the lowest for Bologna (with the smallest number of datasets i.e., [c,d,e]) for all historical configurations. Interestingly, we learned that the *bus passenger loading* dataset has a stronger positive impact on diagnosis accuracy than the *traffic incident* dataset in all historical configurations $|D| = 10, 60, 120, 240$ and 480 cf. Bologna context vs. Miami context.

• **Challenges C_7 "Impact of Historic Data"**: Reducing the number of historical events decreases accuracy of diagnosis. The more similar historical events the higher the probability to catch accurate diagnosis. For instance the accuracy of diagnosis results is improved by a factor of 1.5 by multiplying the number of historical days by a factor 8 (from 60 to 480 days).

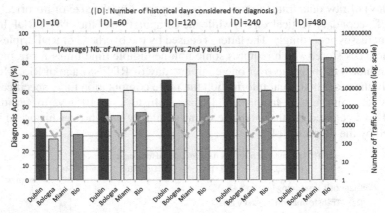

Fig. 9. Accuracy of STAR-CITY Diagnosis in Dublin, Bologna, Miami and Rio

4.4 Expressivity Experimentation and Results

We slightly adjust the context (Section 4.1) by modifying the expressivity of the underlying ontologies (Table 3). Initially in OWL EL, we removed existential constructs of the representation to capture knowledge in RDF/S. We also extend the latter knowledge to capture the OWL RL dialect. Finally we consider OWL $\mathcal{SROIQ(D)}$ by adding extra artificial constraints to the initial model. The number of historical days $|D|$ considered for diagnosis is fixed to 480.

• **Expressivity vs. Scalability**: Fig.10 reports the scalability of STAR-CITY using different levels of representation. Unsurprisingly the RDF/S configuration is the most scalable while the $\mathcal{SROIQ(D)}$ is the most time consuming in all contexts. The diagnosis reasoning is the most impacted components i.e., (on average) +750% from RDF/S to $\mathcal{SROIQ(D)}$. The computation time of anomaly detection (+410%) is also altered while the OWL / RDF loading (+1.5%) and data transformation (+1.1%) are less impacted. The diagnosis reasoning is based on consistency checking and semantic matching functionalities[8], which are constrained by the expressivity of the model.

---

[8] Diagnosis reasoning is achieved by semantically comparing events and their characteristics over time.

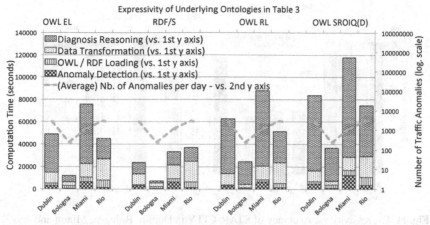

Fig. 10. Expressivity vs. Scalability of STAR-CITY in Dublin, Bologna, Miami and Rio

Similarly the more expressive the model the more time consuming is the anomaly detection, following results from [10]. These claims are demonstrated by results of Fig.10.

• **Expressivity vs. Accuracy**: Fig.11 reports the accuracy of STAR-CITY using different levels of representation. Interestingly the RDF/S version of STAR-CITY is over performed by the OWL EL (+186%), OWL RL (+174%) and OWL $\mathcal{SROIQ(D)}$ (+190%) versions. By reducing the expressivity of the model (i.e., RDF/S) we tend to light and loose the semantic representation of events in Table 3, which in turn largely reduces the accuracy of the semantic matching functions (crucial during the diagnosis phase). In other words downgrading the model to RDF/S largely impacts the accuracy of diagnosis since all discriminating elements of the events cannot be considered by the matching procedure, which ends up with a large portion of similar (and more critically non-discriminable) events. Upgrading the models to OWL EL, RL or $\mathcal{SROIQ(D)}$ adds extra semantic features to events which can be used for semantic matching and comparison, hence a better semantic events discrimination and diagnosis accuracy.

The OWL EL, RL and $\mathcal{SROIQ(D)}$ configurations reach roughly similar accuracy results, although the OWL $\mathcal{SROIQ(D)}$ version is slightly better than the OWL EL (+0.97%) and RL (+0.91%) versions. The differences are not significative since the OWL RL and $\mathcal{SROIQ(D)}$ versions do not differentiate events descriptions much further than OWL EL. They actually simply support a refinement of the matching scores.

5   Lessons Learned

Deploying STAR-CITY and its semantics-aware architecture in more than one city raised new challenges C_1-C_7 which we addressed in the new version of the deployed system. The universal anomaly identification, representation (C_1) and configuration (C_3) were the most critical challenges from a flexible, scalable deployment inter-city. We extensively use semantic technologies for addressing these issues i.e., (i) semantic model for C_1, (ii) semantic configuration and SA-REST services for C_3. Even so some manual tasks are required to be achieved e.g., identification of anomalies ranges, definition of OWL / RDF mapping process (for data transformation). The OWL / RDF (concept) linking (alignment) process has also been performed manually to address C_5,

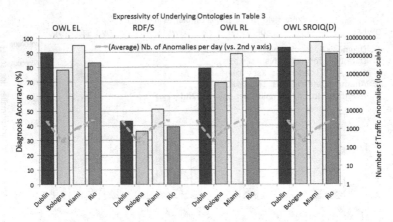

Fig. 11. Expressivity vs. Accuracy of STAR-CITY in Dublin, Bologna, Miami and Rio

but only once. However the latter needs to be replicated for each new data source and mapping presented to STAR-CITY. The automation of this process is a complex task as it required to align descriptions from very expressive vocabularies with concepts from unexpressive models such as DBpedia.

The semantic stream conversion was not beneficial to the overall architecture as it adds overhead on costs, deployment, configuration, systems interactions. Since the throughput of sensors in the four cities was considerably low we shifted the semantic transformation to a more traditional architecture. Shifting architectures did not impact the performance of the system (experimentation not reported in this paper). Even if higher throughput sensors could be an issue, we did not face it in our city contexts.

As experimented in Fig.10, expressive representation models means scalability issues. Even if the accuracy of the reasoning results is correlated to the expressivity of the semantic model, we noted differences in scale and impact cf. OWL EL vs. RDF/S configurations in Fig.11, cf. OWL EL vs. $\mathcal{SROIQ}(\mathcal{D})$ configurations in Fig.11. Therefore defining the appropriate level of representation is not a trivial task, and need to be driven by the application needs while ensuring scalable and accurate processing.

Data from sensors evolve over time. We considered a subset of the W3C Time ontology to represent the starting date/time and a simple temporal extension of TDB. However more complex time feature could have been used for compacting semantic information e.g., temporal intervals. We did not address this problem but a complex temporal-aware representation mode would support more complex reasoning e.g., over time intervals. STAR-CITY uses basic methods to evaluate loose temporal similarity. However research challenges, already tackled by [12], would need to be considered for more accurate temporal joints.

From a pure STAR-CITY perspective, reducing the number of historical events (together with the number and size of sources for diagnosis) increases scalability, but also decreases accuracy. Therefore the more source the better for STAR-CITY. However the scalability of the ingestion, transformation and loading of semantic representation is strongly altered by these dimensions (cf. indexing issues raised by challenge C_7 in Section 4.2). The latter raises requirements towards scalable (big) semantic data structure.

Applying STAR-CITY to other cities raise also challenges regarding the well-known problem of data interpretation in general. Before adding any semantics, we were facing the problem of making sense of schema-less data, specifically when data was described in Italian and Portuguese. For instance most content of *bus passengers loading* data set is not really necessary and does not need semantic transformation.

6 Conclusion

IBM **STAR-CITY** is a system supporting Semantic (road) **T**raffic **A**nalytics and **R**eason-ing for **CITY**. Initially deployed and experimented in Dublin City (Ireland), the system, its architecture and its semantic-related components have shown limitations regarding their flexibility and scalability to other cities. This paper, focusing on the diagnosis reasoning component of STAR-CITY, described (i) its semantics-related limitations in the context of Bologna (Italy), Miami (USA), Rio (Brazil), and (ii) the innovative "*any-city*" architecture of STAR-CITY together with its semantic configuration for flexible and scalable deployment in any city. The paper also reported experimentations of STAR-CITY in Bologna, Miami and Rio, which have validated the architecture, design and specifications of new deployed system.

As emphasized in Section 5 the challenges related to automated semantic data linking and loading are immediate in-use problems to be addressed, while the issues related to temporal compact representation are longer-term challenges.

References

1. Alexiadis, V., Jeannotte, K., Chandra, A.: Traffic analysis toolbox volume i: Traffic analysis tools primer. Technical report (2004)
2. Nadeem, T., Dashtinezhad, S., Liao, C., Iftode, L.: Trafficview: traffic data dissemination using car-to-car communication. ACM SIGMOBILE Mobile Computing and Communications Review 8(3), 6–19 (2004)
3. Valle, E.D., Celino, I., Dell'Aglio, D., Grothmann, R., Steinke, F., Tresp, V.: Semantic traffic-aware routing using the larkc platform. IEEE Internet Computing 15(6), 15–23 (2011)
4. Lécué, F., Schumann, A., Sbodio, M.L.: Applying semantic web technologies for diagnosing road traffic congestions. In: Cudré-Mauroux, P., et al. (eds.) ISWC 2012, Part II. LNCS, vol. 7650, pp. 114–130. Springer, Heidelberg (2012)
5. Lécué, F., Tallevi-Diotallevi, S., Hayes, J., Tucker, R., Bicer, V., Sbodio, M.L., Tommasi, P.: Star-city: semantic traffic analytics and reasoning for city. In: IUI, pp. 179–188 (2014)
6. Mutharaju, R.: Very large scale owl reasoning through distributed computation. In: Cudré-Mauroux, P., et al. (eds.) ISWC 2012, Part II. LNCS, vol. 7650, pp. 407–414. Springer, Heidelberg (2012)
7. Lécué, F., Pan, J.Z.: Predicting knowledge in an ontology stream. In: IJCAI (2013)
8. Bicer, V., Tran, T., Abecker, A., Nedkov, R.: Koios: Utilizing semantic search for easy-access and visualization of structured environmental data. In: Aroyo, L., Welty, C., Alani, H., Taylor, J., Bernstein, A., Kagal, L., Noy, N., Blomqvist, E. (eds.) ISWC 2011, Part II. LNCS, vol. 7032, pp. 1–16. Springer, Heidelberg (2011)
9. Lécué, F., Tucker, R., Bicer, V., Tommasi, P., Tallevi-Diotallevi, S., Sbodio, M.: Predicting severity of road traffic congestion using semantic web technologies. In: Presutti, V., d'Amato, C., Gandon, F., d'Aquin, M., Staab, S., Tordai, A. (eds.) ESWC 2014. LNCS, vol. 8465, pp. 611–627. Springer, Heidelberg (2014)
10. Lécué, F.: Towards scalable exploration of diagnoses in an ontology stream. In: AAAI (2014)
11. Bizer, C., Heath, T., Berners-Lee, T.: Linked data - the story so far. Int. J. Semantic Web Inf. Syst. 5(3), 1–22 (2009)
12. Lutz, C.: Interval-based temporal reasoning with general tboxes. In: IJCAI, pp. 89–96 (2001)

Adapting Semantic Sensor Networks
for Smart Building Diagnosis

Joern Ploennigs, Anika Schumann, and Freddy Lécué

IBM Research

Abstract. The Internet of Things is one of the next big changes in which devices, objects, and sensors are getting linked to the semantic web. However, the increasing availability of generated data leads to new integration problems. In this paper we present an architecture and approach that illustrates how semantic sensor networks, semantic web technologies, and reasoning can help in real-world applications to automatically derive complex models for analytics tasks such as prediction and diagnostics. We demonstrate our approach for buildings and their numerous connected sensors and show how our semantic framework allows us to detect and diagnose abnormal building behavior. This can lead to not only an increase of occupant well-being but also to a reduction of energy use. Given that buildings consume 40 % of the world's energy use we therefore also make a contribution towards global sustainability. The experimental evaluation shows the benefits of our approach for buildings at IBM's Technology Campus in Dublin.

1 Introduction

With the development of embedded cyber physical systems and large computational resources in the cloud, the availability of sensor information continuously increases towards the Internet of Things. Semantic Sensor Networks (SSN) play an important role in this development as they provide a homogeneous semantic layer for sensor information and simplify the detection and retrieval of data [1,2]. This is key for connecting cloud-based analytic tasks that process this data. However, advanced analytics need also knowledge of the system's internal processes. Diagnostics, for example, require hypotheses of the cause-effect relationships between sensors. SSN do not provide ways to model such aspects and it is often necessary to add this information manually [3,4]. However, this can turn into a very tedious task and prevent the exploitation of SSN for large scale analytic applications.

Building automation systems (BAS) are one established example of large scale sensor and control networks that contain thousands of devices in newer buildings. Analyzing the data allows to improve the building's energy consumption with large environmental impact as buildings consume about 40 % of the energy in industrialized countries and are responsible for 36 % of their CO_2 emissions [5]. For large companies building energy management is done at enterprise scale that enables them to monitor, analyze, report and reduce energy consumption

P. Mika et al. (Eds.) ISWC 2014, Part II, LNCS 8797, pp. 308–323, 2014.

across their building portfolio, including retail and office properties. However, the integration of thousands of sensors of buildings in different locations, with different systems and technologies is a challenging task.

This paper presents the architecture and approach of IBM's Semantic Smart Building Diagnoser. It allows to automatically derive complex analytic tasks in buildings from a semantic sensor network model. With some small extensions to the SSN ontology we are able to derive large models of the physical processes within the building using solely semantics techniques such as SPARQL update.

The following section reviews the state of the art. Section 3 explains the architecture of our approach that is detailed in Section 4. We present the evaluation of our approach at IBM's Technology Campus in Dublin in Section 5. The paper concludes with remarks on the lessons we learned.

2   State of the Art

The building automation domain has a long history with interoperability problems due to the diversity of systems and technologies [6]. The trend is to use semantic web technologies to describe sensors and the observed context as states and events [3,6,7]. Similar capabilities are provided by the domain independent W3C Semantic Sensor Network (SSN) ontology [2], which will be explained in Sec. 4.1. The benefit of these ontologies is that they provide a homogeneous semantic model of sensors to backend systems that then can be agnostic of the underlying technology. However, the approaches model sensors only as interfaces of the system and do not describe the processes within the system. This information is important for many in-depth analytic tasks such as diagnosis.

An estimated 15 % to 30 % of energy in buildings could be saved if faults in the BAS system and its operation could be detected in a timely manner [8]. Katipamula and Brambley [9] provide an extensive review of the common approaches. They classified them in three categories: physical model based approaches, data driven approaches, and rule-based approaches. The first require physical models of the building components like boilers or chillers. These approaches can diagnose faults precisely. However, the model development requires time and expertise and the models are difficult to adapt to different buildings. Data driven approaches like [10] are solely based on the building's sensor data. While this makes them easily adaptable to different buildings their diagnostic capability is limited to the detection of faults rather than their identification. Therefore, rule-based approaches are most established and also used by IBM's TRIRIGA Environmental and Energy Management Software. The rules capture domain knowledge of conditions for anomalies and their cause-effect relationships [11]. It was shown in [3,4] that the rules can also be executed directly on the semantic model. This leads to a more integrated approach that simplifies the deployment. However, it still requires data modeling engineers to create the diagnostic model. Herein also lies its biggest limitation: as rules can detect predefined situations only, they need to be manually adapted to each system by people with in-depth knowledge of all potential cause-effect relationships.

Our approach combines the benefits of these three concepts to overcome their disadvantages: it models high level physical processes in the systems to derive diagnosis rules; it parameterizes the rules using data analytics and applies them effectively during runtime. The strength of a semantic approach is that we can use reasoning and semantic web techniques to automate this process for the large scale sensor networks found in buildings such that the human modeling and calibration effort is minimal.

3   Architecture

Figure 1 shows the architecture of the Semantic Smart Building Diagnoser. It is designed to allow energy management of a global portfolio of buildings. The individual building's BAS are integrated via REST services that are usually available and allow retrieving time series information and non-semantic text labels for sensors. This data is enriched with additional semantic information in different steps such that we can autonomously run different analytic processes on the top layers that are agnostic of the underlying BAS. The process is divided into an initialization phase, that creates the semantic model once, and a runtime phase, that uses the semantic model to efficiently process online stream data.

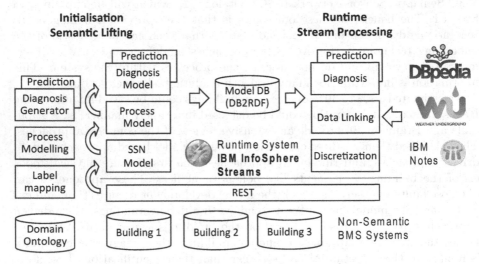

Fig. 1. Architecture of the approach

During the *initialization* phase we lift the usually non-semantic data to a semantic representation in a domain ontology that specifies common semantic types and physical processes in buildings as extension of the W3C SSN ontology (Sec. 4.1). The lifting is composed of three steps. First, we create a *SSN model* that describes the available sensors. The step is semi-automated by an internal label mapping tool that maps the non-semantic BAS text labels to their semantic equivalents in the domain ontology and asks a human for validation [12].

From this homogeneous semantic representation we then automatically derive a *physical process model* that expands the relationships between sensors (Sec. 4.2). It allows us to automate individual analytic tasks based on sensor data from the building by extending specific semantic information. For example, the diagnosis model generator extends cause-effect relationships between sensors (Sec. 4.3). The different semantic models are stored in a DB2RDF database for efficient access during runtime.

The *runtime* environment is using the semantic version of IBM InfoSphere Streams [13], which handles mixed time series and RDF data based stream processing/reasoning in real-time. This hybrid setup is important as not all time series data can be rendered in RDF for scalability reasons (Sec. 4.4). We enrich the dataset with external information by linking, for example, additional explanations of semantic types to DBpedia. Historical weather data and forecasts from wunderground are used for diagnosis and energy predictions [14]. Room booking information from IBM Notes is used to estimate and predict room occupancy. We use this semantically-enriched dataset for the different analytic tasks (Sec. 4.4). The individual steps of our approach are detailed in the following section.

4   Approach

We start by introducing a necessary extension to the SSN ontology that will enable us to automatically derive the physical process model and a diagnostic model.

4.1   Extended SSN Ontology

In the first step, we create a SSN representation for each BAS using an internal label mapping tool [12]. The tool semi-automatically assigns the corresponding semantic sensor type in our domain ontology to each BAS label using common structure, acronyms, and units in the textual descriptions (e. g. we extract "Temperature Sensor in Room R1" from the label "R1_Tmp").

The resulting model is an extension of the Semantic Sensor Network (SSN) skeleton ontology defined by the W3C incubator group [2]. SSN consolidates concepts from various sensor network ontologies and was chosen because it provides differentiated views on the aspects of sensing beyond the building domain. In particular it uses the Stimulus-Sensor-Observation ontology design pattern [15]. The pattern separates the concepts of *ssn:Sensor* for physical devices taking measurements in form of *ssn:Observation* and the actual changes that happen in the environment, which is the *ssn:Stimulus* of the measurement. This separation is important as it recognizes that: 1) stimuli occur in the environment independently of the number and kind of sensors that observe them and 2) observations made by a sensor are not identical to stimuli as measurements can be incorrect due to measurement noise, outliers, or sensor failures. We use the following classes from the skeleton ontology:

- *ssn:FeatureOfInterest*: The monitored (diagnosed) system is defined as a FeatureOfInterest. In the following we will use the shorter feature as synonym.

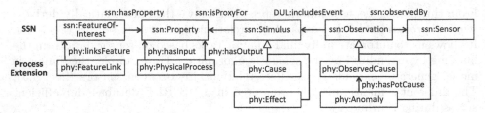

Fig. 2. Extension to the SSN ontology

- *ssn:Property*: Properties are qualities of a Feature. They can be observed like the air temperature of a room. In extension to the SSN, we define that properties may also be unobservable. Unobservable properties are often relevant to correctly understand the physical processes within features. One example is the inner energy of the room. The inner energy is the heat stored in the air in the room. It is related to the air temperature, but not measurable.
- *ssn:Sensor*: A time series provided by a physical device or computational method observing a property.
- *ssn:Observation*: Observations describe discrete states that are derived from the sensor time series data. An observation state may be that an air temperature is above 20 °C.
- *ssn:Stimulus*: A stimulus is an event or state of a property. A stimulus is not identical with the observation made by a sensor, as the sensor itself may fail.

The SSN ontology provides no means to model physical and cause-effect relationships between sensors. Therefore, we have extended the SSN ontology in [16] using the namespace *phy* by the concepts[1] shown in Figure 2:

- *phy:PhysicalProcess*[2]: The properties of many real world features are related by physical processes. A *phy:PhysicalProcess* models this as directed relationship of a source property (*phy:hasInput*) that influences a target property (*phy:hasOutput*). We differentiate different process types that relate to common models used in control theory[3]. In the paper we will only use positive and negative correlated properties. The influence is a *phy:PosCorrProc* if a factor increases with its influence and it is a *phy:NegCorrProc* if it decreases with an increase of the influence. The temperature we feel, for example, is influenced by the inner energy in a room via a positive correlation process, as it feels warmer when we increase the energy. The cooling system uses a negative correlation process as it removes heat from this energy.
- *phy:FeatureLink*: Physical processes occur not only between properties within the same feature, but, also between related features. A FeatureLink denotes such a relationship between features that are defined by the object

---

[1] A complete version of the provided example and an extended one is available at *https: // www. dropbox. com/ s/ z369tzmm00f1jv9/ demopackage. zip*.

[2] Not to be confused with *ssn:Process* or *dul:Process* from DOLCE subset used by SSN. The first describes the sensing process and the second an event in transition.

[3] We use classes of linear time-invariant systems such as proportional, integral, derivative, or delay processes. This is similar to data flow models such as Matlab/Simulink.

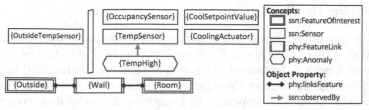

Fig. 3. Example input of the approach

property *phy:linksFeature*. They are, for instance, used to model spatial relationships between two adjacent rooms connected by a wall.

- *phy:Cause*, *phy:Effect*: are subconcepts of *ssn:Stimulus* and describe the not necessarily observed stimulus of a cause and the resulting effect.
- *phy:Anomaly*: is a subconcept of *ssn:Observation* that is used to describe abnormal observations that should be diagnosed. An anomaly may be for example a high room temperature.
- *phy:ObservedCause*: is another subconcept of *ssn:Observation* describing the observable discrete states of potential causes of an anomaly. A cause for a high temperature in a room may be an inactive cooling system.

We will later introduce additional object and annotation properties to model the generic process knowledge in a domain ontology. In the following example we use the namespace *sb* for this smart building domain ontology.

Example 1 *(Semantic Input)*
We illustrate the approach with the running example of a single office room {*Room*}[4] shown in Figure 3. It is separated from to the outside by a wall. The room contain sensors for air temperature {*TempSensor*} and occupancy {*OccupancySensor*}. A virtual sensor {*OutsideTempSensor*} links to the outside temperature retrieved from wunderground.com The room also contains a cooling system with actuator {*CoolingActuator*} and setpoint {*CoolingSetpointValue*}. The setpoint value is automatically decreased if the room is occupied to save cooling energy if it is unoccupied.

We map the sensors in the example from Figure 3 to our domain ontology. It contains concepts for the sensors *sb:TemperatureSensor*, *sb:OccupancySensor*, *sb:CoolingActuatorValue*, and *sb:CoolingSetpointValue* $\sqsubseteq$ *ssn:Sensor*. The sensors observe the corresponding room properties *sb:Temperature*, *sb:Occupancy*, *sb:Cooling*, *sb:CoolingSetpoint* $\sqsubseteq$ *ssn:Property*. In addition we define *sb:Energy* $\sqsubseteq$ *ssn:Property* for the unobservable property of a rooms inner energy. The rooms are instances of *sb:Room* and the environment of *sb:Outside* which are both features, thus *sb:Room*, *sb:Outside* $\sqsubseteq$ *ssn:FeatureOfInterest*.The locations are connected by *sb:Wall* $\sqsubseteq$ *ssn:FeatureLink*.

Our aim is to determine which of the sensors, related to the room or its surrounding, can localize the cause of an abnormally high temperature {*TempHigh*}. Here we consider any sensor value abnormal that deviates by more than two degrees from the cooling set point of that room.

---

[4] We denote by {*c*} $\sqsubseteq$ *C* an instance *c*, internalized as a concept {*c*} which is a specialization of *C*.

4.2   Deriving the Process Model

The SSN is automatically extended by the properties and processes within the system. We do this in two steps. First, we create property instances for all feature instances, even if they are not observed as they may be involved in physical processes. Second, we connect these property instances by processes. The necessary knowledge about the properties and processes is modeled on concept level in the domain ontology using annotation properties. As the same domain ontology is used by all buildings, this modeling effort needs to be done only once. For example, our smart building ontology contains concepts for 62 sensor and 18 properties as well as 53 process annotations (see footnote 1). This will enable us in Sec. 5.1 to create several thousand property and process instances for the IBM Technology Campus Dublin.

We differentiate mandatory and optional properties. Mandatory properties are characteristic physical properties of a FeatureOfInterest and need to be created for each feature instance. Optional properties are not explicitly required by a feature and are only created if they are observed by a sensor. We define these relationships on concept level of the domain ontology using annotation properties. For example, we may not find a temperature sensor in each room, but, each room has a temperature. Thus, we annotate the *sb:Room* class using the annotation *phy:requiresProperty* to link to *sb:Temperature* as a mandatory property. The cooling actuator on the other hand is not mandatory to a room as not all rooms have a cooling unit. We annotate the sensor subclass *sb:CoolingActuator* using the annotation *phy:defaultObserved* referring to the *sb:Cooling* property. It specifies that a room only possesses a Cooling property if it also has a CoolingActuator as sensor.

We use these annotation properties to create the property instances using SPARQL 1.1 update (SPARUL). SPARUL is an extension of SPARQL that does not only allow the search for specific RDF patterns, but also allows modifying and extending the RDF graph around such patterns. Figure 4 shows on the top left and top right two SPARUL queries that create mandatory and optional properties, respectively. The SPARUL blocks consist of a modification pattern (INSERT) that is executed for each match of a search pattern (WHERE). With the top left query #1 we search for instances of a feature class annotated by *phy:requiresProperty* that refers to a mandatory property. For each instance found we create an instance of the property using an unique URI that is computed by the function $UURI$[5]. The SPARUL query #2 for optional properties works similarly and creates properties for these features that have a sensor of a class with the *phy:defaultObserved* annotation.

In the second step, we connect the created properties by process instances. We use again annotation properties to model the generic relationships on concept level of the domain ontology and then use SPARUL to extend the specific SSN instances. Please note, that physical processes may exist between properties of the same feature (e. g. cooling reduces internal energy) as well as between prop-

---

[5] The function $UURI$ needs to compute the same unique URI for identical inputs such that mandatory and optional properties extend each other.

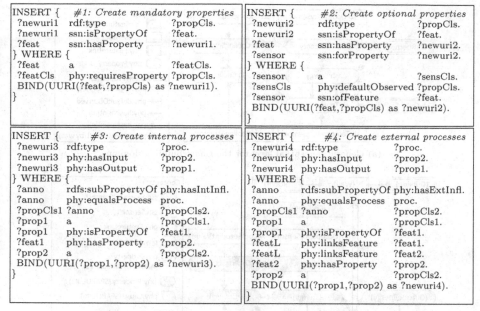

INSERT {	#1: Create mandatory properties
?newuri1	rdf:type	?propCls.
?newuri1	ssn:isPropertyOf	?feat.
?feat	ssn:hasProperty	?newuri1.
} WHERE {		
?feat	a	?featCls.
?featCls	phy:requiresProperty ?propCls.
BIND(UURI(?feat,?propCls) as ?newuri1).
}

INSERT {	#2: Create optional properties
?newuri2	rdf:type	?propCls.
?newuri2	ssn:isPropertyOf	?feat.
?feat	ssn:hasProperty	?newuri2.
?sensor	ssn:forProperty	?newuri2.
} WHERE {		
?sensor	a	?sensCls.
?sensCls	phy:defaultObserved ?propCls.
?sensor	ssn:ofFeature	?feat.
BIND(UURI(?feat,?propCls) as ?newuri2).
}

INSERT {	#3: Create internal processes
?newuri3	rdf:type	?proc.
?newuri3	phy:hasInput	?prop2.
?newuri3	phy:hasOutput	?prop1.
} WHERE {		
?anno	rdfs:subPropertyOf phy:hasIntInfl.
?anno	phy:equalsProcess	proc.
?propCls1	?anno	?propCls2.
?prop1	a	?propCls1.
?prop1	phy:isPropertyOf	?feat1.
?feat1	phy:hasProperty	?prop2.
?prop2	a	?propCls2.
BIND(UURI(?prop1,?prop2) as ?newuri3).
}

INSERT {	#4: Create external processes
?newuri4	rdf:type	?proc.
?newuri4	phy:hasInput	?prop2.
?newuri4	phy:hasOutput	?prop1.
} WHERE {		
?anno	rdfs:subPropertyOf phy:hasExtInfl.
?anno	phy:equalsProcess	proc.
?propCls1	?anno	?propCls2.
?prop1	a	?propCls1.
?prop1	phy:isPropertyOf	?feat1.
?featL	phy:linksFeature	?feat1.
?featL	phy:linksFeature	?feat2.
?feat2	phy:hasProperty	?prop2.
?prop2	a	?propCls2.
BIND(UURI(?prop1,?prop2) as ?newuri4).
}

Fig. 4. SPARUL code to create the process model

erties of different features (e. g. two adjacent rooms exchange energy). Therefore, we use two different annotation patterns to: i) describe internal process relationships of properties within the same feature and ii) external process relationships connecting properties of linked features. An internal process relationship is detected by the SPARUL query #3 in Figure 4. It searches for two properties of the same feature, whose classes are linked by an annotation property *?anno* that is a subproperty of *phy:hasIntInfl*. For each match it creates a physical process of type *?proc*. The type is specified by a property *phy:equalsProcess* of the annotation *?anno*. The SPARUL query #4 in Figure 4 uses a similar pattern, but, searches for *phy:hasExtInfl* annotations as well as for properties of different features that are linked by the *phy:linksFeature* property of a feature link.

Example 2 *(Process Model Creation)*
Let us consider that the following triples are defined in our domain ontology

sb:Room	phy:requiresProperty	sb:Energy.
sb:CoolingActuator	phy:defaultObserved	sb:Cooling.
phy:hasNegIntInfl	rdfs:subPropertyOf	sb:hasIntInfl.
phy:hasNegIntInfl	phy:equalsProcess	phy:PosCorrProc.
sb:Energy	phy:hasNegIntInfl	sb:Cooling.

and the following part from the SSN ontology of example 1 in RDF N3 syntax

:Room	a	sb:Room.
:CoolingActuator	a	sb:CoolingActuator.
:CoolingActuator	ssn:ofFeature	:Room.

The left top SPARUL query #1 in Figure 4 matches the room as *?feat =* :Room that instantiates class *?featCls = sb:Room* and requires the property class *?propCls = sb:Energy*. A new unique URI *?newuri1* is computed for this

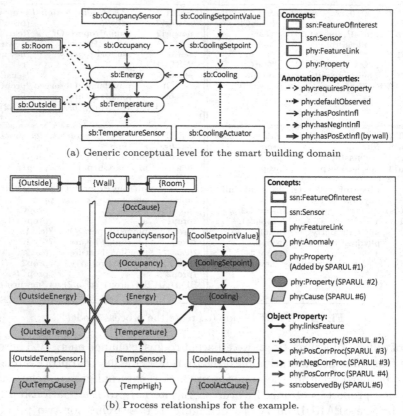

(a) Generic conceptual level for the smart building domain

(b) Process relationships for the example.

Fig. 5. Conceptual level and process model for the example

match. The insert part then adds a new instance $\{?newuri1\} \sqsubseteq sb{:}Energy$ and links it to :*Room* as *ssn:isPropertyOf* and *ssn:hasProperty* vice versa.

The top right SPARUL query #2 will match $?sensor = {:}CoolingActuator$ of class $?sensCls = sb{:}CoolingActuator$ that links to $?propCls = sb{:}Cooling$ and create a new instance of *sb:Cooling* under the URI *?newuri2*.

The bottom left query #3 in Figure 4 matches these newly created properties with $?prop1 = ?newuri1$ and $?prop2 = ?newuri2$ as their classes $?propCls1 = sb{:}Energy$ and $?propCls2 = sb{:}CoolingActuator$ are linked by *phy:hasNegIntInfl*. The query creates a new *phy:hasNegIntInfl* instance connecting the properties as the annotation property links to the class via *phy:equalsProcess*.

In a similar way the relationships between all properties can be described. We illustrate this in Figure 5a for the case of smart buildings. The generic domain knowledge was extracted from physical models such as [17]. The figure shows that occupancy, temperature and energy are defined as mandatory properties for a room by *phy:requiresProperty* annotation properties. For the outside only energy and temperature are mandatory as occupancy has a negligible influence on the temperature outside. The sensors define occupancy, temperature, cooling setpoint and cooling as optional via the *phy:defaultObserved* annotation.

The *phy:hasPosIntInfl* and *phy:hasNegIntInfl* annotations define the positive and negative correlation processes within a room. The temperature in the room is positively influenced by the internal energy. The energy is increased by people in the rooms and decreased by an active cooling system. The cooling system actuates based on the room temperature and setpoint. A room also exchanges energy with the outside and neighboring rooms depending on the temperature difference at the wall. This is defined by a *phy:hasPosExtInfl* annotation property between temperature and energy.

Applying this knowledge to our example in Figure 3 using the SPARUL queries in Figure 4 results in the processes shown in Figure 5b. The added mandatory properties by SPARUL query #1 are light gray. The optional properties and the links between sensors and properties added by query #2 are dark gray. The adaptation of the model is visible for the *Outside* feature, which does not have properties for the cooling actuator, setpoint or occupancy as they were not defined as mandatory. The internal processes added by query #3 are identical to Figure 5a. To keep readability we replaced the process classes by solid and dashed arrows representing positively and negatively correlated processes, respectively. The external processes added by query #4 are highlighted by a double line. After these four simple queries the SSN contains a semantic physical model that describes the relationships between sensors in the whole building.

4.3 Generating the Diagnosis Model

The physical process model can be used for automating analytics. We illustrate this for the task of extracting a diagnosis model for an anomaly of a sensor. The diagnosis model defines hypotheses of potential causes for each anomaly. The physical processes can be used to trace these cause-effect-relationships. We consider sensors as potentially observing the cause of an anomaly, if the properties they observe are either linked directly by a physical process to the anomaly or via a sequence of unobserved properties linked by processes in the direction of effect.

Example 3 *(Potential Causes of an Effect)*
Consider the generation of diagnosis rules for the anomaly $\{TempHigh\} \sqsubseteq phy:Anomaly$ that is observed by the room temperature sensor $\{TempSensor\}$ in our example. By tracing back the physical processes plotted in Figure 5b the following potential causes can be identified:

- Observation $\{OccCause\} \sqsubseteq phy:ObservedCause$ of the $\{OccupancySensor\}$ is a potential cause since $\{Occupancy\}$, $\{Energy\}$, $\{Temperature\}$ is a chain of properties linked by physical processes in Figure 5b with $\{Occupancy\}$ and $\{Temperature\}$ being the only properties observed by a sensor,
- $\{OutTempCause\}$ observed by $\{OutsideTempSensor\}$ is a *phy:ObservedCause* since $\{OutsideTemp\}$, $\{Energy\}$, $\{Temperature\}$ is a chain without other observable properties,
- $\{CoolActCause\} \sqsubseteq phy:ObservedCause$ is observed by $\{CoolingActuator\}$ and a potential cause via the chain $\{Cooling\}$, $\{Energy\}$, $\{Temperature\}$.

There is no potential cause at the cooling setpoint value as $\{CoolingSetpoint\}$ is only connected through the already observed $\{Cooling\}$ property.

To implement the detection of process chains in SPARUL, we iteratively combine a chain of two successive physical process instances by adding a new direct process instance. We preserve the type of the process correlation as it is relevant for the diagnosis. The occupancy sensor for example influences the energy by a positive correlation process and the energy influences the temperature also positively. From these two successive positive correlation processes it follows that the occupancy influences also the temperature by a positive correlation via the energy. Thus, we can add a new positive process that connects the occupancy to the temperature. In a similar way, we can combine any successive positive and negative correlation process by a negative one and two negative ones neutralize each other to one positive correlation process. The SPARUL code #5 of Figure 6 shows an example for a process chain with positive and negative correlation. It filters observable properties. Three similar SPARUL queries replace other combinations of positive and negative correlation processes.

```
INSERT {        #5: Combine process chains
?newuri5 rdf:type        phy:NegCorrProc.
?newuri5 phy:hasInput    ?prop1.
?newuri5 phy:hasOutput   ?prop3.
} WHERE {
?proc1   a               phy:PosCorrProc.
?proc2   a               phy:NegCorrProc.
?proc1   phy:hasInput    ?prop1.
?proc1   phy:hasOutput   ?prop2.
?proc2   phy:hasInput    ?prop2.
?proc2   phy:hasOutput   ?prop3.
FILTER NOT EXISTS
         {?prop2 ssn:forProperty ?anyDP}
BIND(UURI(?prop1,?prop3) as ?newuri5).
}
```

```
INSERT {          #6: Create potential causes
?newuri6 rdf:type        phy:ObservedCause.
?abnom   phy:hasPotCause ?newuri6.
?newuri6 ssn:observedBy  ?sensor2.
} WHERE {
?abnom   a               phy:Anomaly.
?abnom   ssn:observedBy  ?sensor1.
?sensor1 ssn:forProperty ?prop1.
?proc1   phy:hasOutput   ?prop1.
?proc1   a               phy:PhysicalProcess.
?proc1   phy:hasInput    ?prop2.
?sensor2 ssn:forProperty ?prop2.
BIND(UURI(?sensor2) as ?newuri6).
}
```

Fig. 6. SPARUL code to create diagnosis rules

Example 4 *(Process Chains)*
From example 3, we can combine the process chain {*Occupancy*}, {*Energy*}, {*Temperature*} of only positive correlation processes by a direct positive correlation process linking {*Occupancy*} to {*Temperature*}. The chain {*OutsideTemp*}, {*Energy*}, {*Temperature*} also contains only positive correlation processes and can be combined into a new positive correlation process between {*OutsideTemp*} and {*Temperature*}. The chain {*Cooling*}, {*Energy*}, {*Temperature*} contains one negative and one positive correlation process that can be combined into one negative correlation process between {*Cooling*} and {*Temperature*}.

The above approach creates direct process links between the influencing properties. This enables us to directly link potential causes of an anomaly with the SPARUL code #6 in Figure 6. The query first looks for anomalies defined in the ontology. It then identifies the property of the sensor that observed the anomaly. For each observable property that is connected by a physical process to the former property, a potential cause observation is created for the observing sensor. This cause state is then assigned to the anomaly as potential cause.

We utilize the semantic type of processes to narrow down the nature of the potential cause. For example, if the anomaly is characterized by a *sb:High* state, then a cause that is connected by a positive correlation process is probably also *sb:High*. If the cause is connected by a negative correlation process it is probably *sb:Low*. This is implemented by modifying query #6 for the different cases.

Example 5 *(Cause Classification)*
The anomaly {*TempHigh*} is defined as *sb:High* in our input SSN. Using the semantic information of the direct link processes in example 4 it can be derived that {*OccCause*} and {*OutTempCause*} should also be instance of *sb:High* as the linking processes are positively correlated. Only {*CoolActCause*} is an instances of *sb:Low* as it is linked by a negative correlation process.

4.4 Discretisation and Diagnosis

To use our diagnosis model it is necessary to discretize the sensor time series values. For scalability reason, we only extract abnormal observations. An anomaly is detected if predefined rules are violated. These rules define a normal operation range and we classify observations as *sb:High* if they are above this range and *sb:Low* if they are below it. For example, all room temperatures higher 22 °C are assigned to the observation instance *sb:TempHigh* by adding the property *ssn:observationSamplingTime* with the current time. The same applies to potential causes, which are assigned to corresponding *sb:High* or *sb:Low* observation instances if the current sensor value is above or below an upper and lower threshold. These limits are determined from historical data using a statistical model [14]. The model learns from historical anomaly-free time series data what the data range is under normal circumstances. It bases on the intuition that a cause of an anomaly is also characterized by abnormal values in comparison to the anomaly-free data. The discretization allows for a fast diagnosis using SPARQL query #7 in Figure 7.

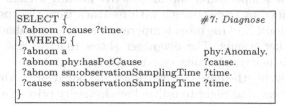

```
SELECT {                                        #7: Diagnose
  ?abnom ?cause ?time.
} WHERE {
  ?abnom a                                      phy:Anomaly.
  ?abnom phy:hasPotCause                        ?cause.
  ?abnom ssn:observationSamplingTime ?time.
  ?cause ssn:observationSamplingTime ?time.
}
```

Fig. 7. SPARQL code to query diagnosis results

5 Experiments

We tested the accuracy and scalability of our approach using real-world and synthetic examples. All examples are described using the domain ontology in Fig. 5a that we extended by more subconcepts to model BAS components and related properties and processes (see footnote 1).

5.1 Results at IBM's Technology Campus in Dublin

Our system is in-use for the IBM Technology Campus in Dublin. The site consists of six buildings from different IBM divisions and operated by an external

Table 1. Diagnosis results for different examples with: TP - true positives, TN - true negatives, FP - false positives, FN - false negatives in % of anomalies

(a) Real office building.

	TP	TN	FP	FN
Heating Issues	67.95	32.05	0.00	0.00
Bad Isolation	89.58	1.62	0.10	8.70

(b) Running example.

	TP	TN	FP	FN
CoolFault	94.90	0.00	5.10	0.00
CoolFault (sem)	94.90	5.10	0.00	0.00
Occupancy	86.77	0.84	12.40	0.00
Occupancy (sem)	86.77	8.93	4.30	0.00
WindOpen	89.69	0.00	10.31	0.00
WindOpen (sem)	89.69	0.00	10.31	0.00

contractor. The buildings provide more than 3,500 sensors. Mapping sensors to the SSN representation and defining the features took more than a day in a first manual approach. We now use an internal label mapping tool that does this in a few minutes. Afterwards the Smart Building Diagnoser is initialized automatically as described above. A big benefit of our approach is the coverage of the resulting diagnostic rules that allows detecting and diagnosing many new anomalies. The campus was formerly managed by the IBM TRIRIGA Environmental and Energy Management Software that monitored 194 sensors with 300 rules. Our test system covers 2,411 sensors, with 1,446 effects and 47,284 potential cause observations linked via 10,029 processes.

We investigated deeper into a $3,500\,m^2$ office building on the campus to evaluate the diagnostic accuracy of the approach. The building contains 271 sensors including temperature sensors and a heating system in most of the 100 rooms. We defined as abnormal if the temperature falls two degrees below the setpoint. The potential causes for the anomaly are a low outside temperature, neighboring rooms with a low temperature, and an inactive heating system. We compared the causes identified by our approach with feedback from the operator.

In the simulation 4 % of the room temperature samples are abnormal. Table 1a summarizes further results. The diagnoser shows that 67.95 % of these cases are related to an inactive heating system. All cases could be validated by the operator by analyzing the data. He explained the behavior by the fact that the building is only heated at night to utilize low electricity prices. In 89.58 % of the abnormal cases the diagnoser relates the outside temperature which the operator largely confirmed to be the case. Only 8.7 % of the cases that he identified could not be retrieved by our approach. Most relevant for the operator was, that our approach revealed that most of these cases occurred in 11 rooms with severe isolation problems which were using an estimated 50 % of the buildings heating energy.

5.2 Benefits of a Semantic Diagnosis Model

We use a commercial building simulator [17] to evaluate the diagnostic accuracy of the approach for the running example of a room with a cooling system. The anomaly *TempHot* is detected if the room temperature rises above 22 °C. We first run experiments testing the situation in the room without faults where the cooling system controlled the room temperature without anomalies. We then defined temporarily break downs of the cooling system, high room occupancy, or an air exchange through an open window. We simulated the room behavior for a full year for a building in Athens to have a constantly high outside temperature and applyed the introduced semantic diagnoser as well as a non-semantic diagnoser. This non-semantic diagnoser has no information whether the cause could be tracked back to a too high or to a too low sensor reading.

Table 1b illustrates the results. In case of the *cooling system break down* the room heats slowly to the higher outside temperature. The approach correctly detects 94.9 % of the cases when the anomaly $TempHot$ occurs together with a cooling break down. The non-semantic approach has a high false positive rate of 5.1 % as it assigns also cases when the cooling actuator is active. The semantic diagnoser knows that the actuator value has to be low and correctly refuses other cases. In the scenario of a high *occupancy*, the room temperature increases due to a large group of people. 86.77 % of the cases are correctly identified by both approaches. However, the non-semantic diagnosis approach has again a higher false positive rate: 12.4 % compared to 4.3 % of the semantic approach. It avoids assigning situations with low room occupancy. If the *window is open* the room temperature quickly adjusts to the outside temperature. In this scenario both approaches have the same true positive rate of 89.69 % and the same false positive rate of 10.31 %. The latter cases occur when the effect of a high room temperature still persists for a while after the window was closed.

These results demonstrate that the semantic diagnosis approach is not only capable of correctly diagnosing different fault scenarios. The cooling fault and occupancy scenario also shows that the semantic model provides additional information and can exclude illegitimate causes. Further improvements are expected by considering more specific types of processes including delays to further reduce the false positive rate of delayed effects such as the already closed window. This simple example illustrates already that semantic information benefits diagnosis.

5.3   Scalability

Finally, we investigated in the scalability of the approach using synthetic examples. For this we evaluated the performance of the approach for examples of different size and reasoner configurations. We evaluated examples with up to 10 storeys with 100 rooms each arranged north and south of a long corridor. All rooms are equipped with heating, cooling, lighting and ventilation systems.

For the example the number of created processes, observations, and triples scales linearly with the number of sensors. It starts with 78 thousand triples for 55 sensors and reaches 20 million triples for the large example with 15 thousand sensors. The small example contains 92 processes and 99 observations and the large example has 70 thousand processes and 80 thousand observations.

Figure 8 shows the mean computational time on a PC with an Intel Xeon X5690 processor for different reasoner configurations of the Jena framework. The performance strongly depends on the reasoning capabilities of the model. The micro OWL rules inference engine takes in mean 130 minutes to apply the SPARUL queries #1 to #7 to the large example with 15 thousand sensors. The RDFS inferencer applies the same SPARUL rules in 85 minutes. An OWL model

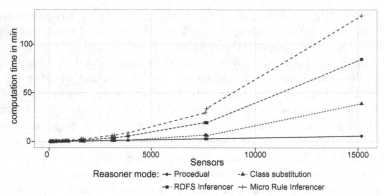

Fig. 8. Computation times for the diagnosis model generation and diagnosis

with no additional entailment reasoning computes in 38 minutes including the required preprocessing of the necessary class subsumption by two additional SPARUL queries. The reasoner spend in total 37 % of the time for the combination of process chains with query #5 and 58 % for identifying the potential causes with query #6 in Figure 6. This is primarily related to the generality of query #5, which creates many physical processes unneeded for the diagnosis purpose. This significantly increases the search space for query #6. The best computation time performance shows a procedural implementation of the SPARUL queries #1 to #6 in Java. It benefits from a depth-first search in the graph model of only the processes connected to an anomaly. Note that, the IBM campus model computes in 55 s with the procedural implementation.

Please note that queries #1 to #6 are only executed once during the initialization phase of the system. During runtime only the discretizer and query #7 are executed. They compute in less than a second for the IBM Campus.

6 Conclusion

We have shown that semantic techniques can be used for automating analytic tasks in complex systems such as buildings. Specifically we have presented IBM's Semantic Smart Building Diagnoser which is the first of its kind that can automatically derive diagnosis rules from the sensor network definition and behaviour of a specific building. This allows not only for the diagnosis of smart building problems that existing techniques cannot diagnose but also for easier adaptability to other buildings.

Our approach was realized by using semantic techniques for: (i) integrating heterogeneous data from different buildings, (ii) extending SSN for automating the creation and configuration of physical models, and by (iii) automatically deriving the diagnosis rules from the latter. The addition and extension of new sensor types and processes is also straightforward given the annotation patterns of our domain ontology.

Our experiments have shown that we can indeed efficiently identify the causes of anomalies for real buildings. They also revealed that semantic information can even be used to improve the accuracy of the diagnosis result. Our approach currently runs on IBM's Technology Campus in Dublin and has provided several insights for improving energy performance. Future deployments on further sites are planned.

References

1. Pfisterer, D., Romer, K., Bimschas, D., et al.: SPITFIRE: Toward a semantic web of things. IEEE Commun. Mag. 49(11), 40–48 (2011)
2. Compton, M., Barnaghi, P., Bermudez, L., et al.: The SSN ontology of the W3C semantic sensor network incubator group. Web Semantics 17, 25–32 (2012)
3. Han, J., Jeong, Y.K., Lee, I.: Efficient building energy management system based on ontology, inference rules, and simulation. In: Int. Conf. on Int. Building and Mgmt., pp. 295–299 (2011)
4. Lécué, F., Schumann, A., Sbodio, M.L.: Applying semantic web technologies for diagnosing road traffic congestions. In: Cudré-Mauroux, P., et al. (eds.) ISWC 2012, Part II. LNCS, vol. 7650, pp. 114–130. Springer, Heidelberg (2012)
5. International Energy Agency: World energy outlook 2012 (2012)
6. Ploennigs, J., Hensel, B., Dibowski, H., Kabitzsch, K.: BASont - a modular, adaptive building automation system ontology. In: IEEE IECON, pp. 4827–4833 (2012)
7. Bonino, D., Corno, F.: DogOnt-ontology modeling for intelligent domotic environments. In: Sheth, A.P., Staab, S., Dean, M., Paolucci, M., Maynard, D., Finin, T., Thirunarayan, K. (eds.) ISWC 2008. LNCS, vol. 5318, pp. 790–803. Springer, Heidelberg (2008)
8. Zhou, Q., Wang, S., Ma, Z.: A model-based fault detection and diagnosis strategy for HVAC systems. Int. J. Energ. Res. 33(10), 903–918 (2009)
9. Katipamula, S., Brambley, M.: Methods for fault detection, diagnostics, and prognostics for building systems - a review. HVAC&R Research 11(1), 3–25 (2005)
10. Jacoba, D., Dietza, S., Komharda, S., Neumanna, C., Herkela, S.: Black-box models for fault detection and performance monitoring of buildings. J. Build. Perf. Sim. 3(1), 53–62 (2010)
11. Schein, J., Bushby, S.T.: A hierarchical rule-based fault detection and diagnostic method for HVAC systems. HVAC&R Research 1(1), 111–125 (2006)
12. Brady, N., Lecue F., Schumann, A., Verscheure, O.: Configuring Building Energy Management Systems Using Knowledge Encoded in Building Management System Points Lists. US20140163750 A1 (2012)
13. Tallevi-Diotallevi, S., Kotoulas, S., Foschini, L., Lécué, F., Corradi, A.: Real-time urban monitoring in Dublin using semantic and stream technologies. In: Alani, H., et al. (eds.) ISWC 2013, Part II. LNCS, vol. 8219, pp. 178–194. Springer, Heidelberg (2013)
14. Ploennigs, J., Chen, B., Schumann, A., Brady, N.: Exploiting generalized additive models for diagnosing abnormal energy use in buildings. In: BuildSys - 5th ACM Workshop on Embedded Systems for Energy-Efficient Buildings, pp. 1–8 (2013)
15. Janowicz, K., Compton, M.: The stimulus-sensor-observation ontology design pattern and its integration into the semantic sensor network ontology. In: Int. Workshop on Semantic Sensor Networks, pp. 7–11 (2010)
16. Ploennigs, J., Schumann, A., Lecue, F.: Extending semantic sensor networks for automatically tackling smart building problems. In: ECAI - PAIS (2014)
17. Sahlin, P., Eriksson, L., Grozman, P., Johnsson, H., Shapovalov, A., Vuolle, M.: Whole-building simulation with symbolic DAE equations and general purpose solvers. Building and Environment 39(8), 949–958 (2004)

Semantic Patterns for Sentiment Analysis of Twitter

Hassan Saif[1], Yulan He[2], Miriam Fernandez[1], and Harith Alani[1]

[1] Knowledge Media Institute, The Open University, United Kingdom
{h.saif,m.fernandez,h.alani}@open.ac.uk
[2] School of Engineering and Applied Science, Aston University, United Kingdom
y.he@cantab.net

Abstract. Most existing approaches to Twitter sentiment analysis assume that sentiment is explicitly expressed through affective words. Nevertheless, sentiment is often implicitly expressed via latent semantic relations, patterns and dependencies among words in tweets. In this paper, we propose a novel approach that automatically captures patterns of words of similar contextual semantics and sentiment in tweets. Unlike previous work on sentiment pattern extraction, our proposed approach does not rely on external and fixed sets of syntactical templates/patterns, nor requires deep analyses of the syntactic structure of sentences in tweets. We evaluate our approach with tweet- and entity-level sentiment analysis tasks by using the extracted semantic patterns as classification features in both tasks. We use 9 Twitter datasets in our evaluation and compare the performance of our patterns against 6 state-of-the-art baselines. Results show that our patterns consistently outperform all other baselines on all datasets by 2.19% at the tweet-level and 7.5% at the entity-level in average F-measure.

Keywords: Sentiment Analysis, Semantic Patterns, Twitter.

1 Introduction

Sentiment analysis on Twitter has established itself in the past few years as a solid research area, providing organisations and businesses with efficient tools and solutions for monitoring their reputation and tracking the public opinion on their brands and products.

Statistical methods to Twitter sentiment analysis rely often on machine learning classifiers trained from syntactical and linguistic features such as word and letter n-grams, part-of-speech tags, prior sentiment of words, microblogging features, etc [2,5,13]. However, merely relying on the aforementioned features may not lead to satisfactory sentiment detection results since sentiment is often context-dependent. Also, people tend to convey sentiment in more subtle linguistic structures or patterns [16]. Such patterns are usually derived from the syntactic [16] or semantic relations [6] between words in text. For example, the adjective word "mean" when preceded by a verb, constitutes a pattern of negative sentiment as in: "she said mean things". Also, the word "destroy" formulates a positive pattern when occurs with the concept "invading germs".

Both syntactic and semantic approaches to extracting sentiment patterns have proven successful when applied to documents of formal language and well-structured sentences [16,8]. However, applying either approach to Twitter data faces several challenges. Firstly, tweets data are often composed of sentences of poor grammatical and syntactical structures due to the the extensive use of abbreviations and irregular expressions in tweets [20].

P. Mika et al. (Eds.) ISWC 2014, Part II, LNCS 8797, pp. 324–340, 2014.

Secondly, both approaches function with external knowledge sources. Most syntactic approaches rely on fixed and pre-defined sets of syntactic templates for pattern extraction. On the other hand, semantic approaches rely on external ontologies and common sense knowledge bases. Such resources, although useful, tend to have fixed domains and coverages, which is especially problematic when processing general Twitter streams, with their rapid semiotic evolution and language deformations [19].

In this paper, we propose a novel approach for automatically extracting semantic sentiment patterns of words on Twitter. We refer to these patterns from now on as *SS-Patterns*. Unlike most other approaches, our proposed approach does not rely on the syntactic structure of tweets, nor requires pre-defined syntactic templates. Instead, it extracts patterns from the contextual semantic and sentiment similarities between words in a given tweet corpus [19]. Contextual semantics (aka statistical semantics) are based on the proposition that meaning can be extracted from words co-occurrences [28,26].

We apply our approach to 9 different Twitter datasets, and validate the extracted patterns by using them as classification features in two sentiment analysis tasks: (i) tweet-level sentiment classification, which identifies the overall sentiment of individual tweets, and (ii) entity-level sentiment classification, which detects sentiment towards a particular entity (e.g., Obama, Cancer, iPad). To this end, we train several supervised classifiers from SS-Patterns and compare the sentiment classification performance against models trained from 6 state-of-the-art sets of features derived from both the syntactic and semantic representations of words.

Our results show that our SS-Patterns consistently outperform all our baseline feature sets, on all 9 datasets, in both tweet-level and entity-level sentiment classification tasks. At the tweet level, SS-Patterns improve the classification performance by 1.94% in accuracy and 2.19% in F-measure on average. Also, at the entity level, our patterns produce 6.31% and 7.5% higher accuracy and F-measure than all other features respectively.

We also conduct quantitative and qualitative analyses on a sample of the patterns extracted by our approach and show that the effectiveness of using SS-Patterns as additional features for classifier training is attribute to their ability in capturing words with similar contextual semantics and sentiment. We also show that our extraction approach is able to detect patterns of controversial sentiment (strong opposing sentiment) expressed by people towards certain entities.

The main contributions of this paper can be summarised as follows:

- Propose a novel approach that automatically extracts patterns from the contextual semantic and sentiment similarities of words in tweets.
- Use patterns as features in tweet- and entity-level sentiment classification tasks, and compare the classification performance against 6 state-of-the-art baselines on 9 Twitter datasets in order to avoid the bias that any single dataset or baseline may introduce.
- Perform a cross comparison between the syntactic and semantic baseline feature sets used in our work and show the effectiveness of the latter for tweet-level sentiment classification over the former.
- Conduct quantitative and qualitative analyses on a sample of our extracted semantic sentiment patterns and show the potential of our approach for finding patterns of entities of controversial sentiment in tweets.

The remainder of this paper is structured as follows. Related work is discussed in Section 2. The proposed approach to extracting semantic sentiment patterns is presented in Section 3. Experimental setup and results are presented in Sections 4 and 5 respectively. Our pattern analysis study is described in Section 6. Discussion and future work are covered in Section 7. Finally, we conclude our work in Section 8.

2   Related Work

Much work on Twitter sentiment analysis follows the statistical machine learning approach by training supervised classifiers (e.g., Naïve Bayes, Maximum Entropy and Support Vector Machines) from features extracted from tweets such as word and letter n-grams [9,15,2], lexicon features (i.e., prior sentiment of words in sentiment lexicons) [5], microblogging features [10], POS tags [1] and several combinations of them [13]. Classifiers trained from these types of features have produced relatively high performance on various Twitter datasets with accuracies ranging between 80% and 86%. However, it has been argued that sentiment in text is not always associated with individual words, but instead, through relations and dependencies between words, which often formulate sentiment [16].

In previous work, these relations are usually complied as a set of syntactic patterns (i.e., Part-of-Speech patterns) [25,16,24], common sense concepts [6], semantic concepts [21,8], or statistical topics [20,11].

For example, Riloff et al. [16] proposed extracting sentiment patterns from the syntactic relations between words in sentences. To this end, they used a fixed set of pre-defined POS templates, e.g., `<subject> passive-verb` which maps to the opinionated sentence "`<customer> was satisfied`" and `<subject> active-verb` that maps to "`<she> complained`". The extracted patterns were then incorporated into high-precision classifiers (HP-Subj and HP-Obj) in order to increase their recall.

One limitation of the syntactic extraction methods is that they are usually limited to the number of the syntactic templates they use. Moreover, these methods are often semantically weak, that is, they do not consider the semantics of individual words in their patterns. This may constitute a problem when trying, for example, to identify context-sensitive sentiment (e.g., `<beer> is cold` and `<weather> is cold`).

Conceptual semantic sentiment methods, on the other hand, utilize both syntactic and semantic processing techniques in order to capture the latent conceptual semantic relations in text that implicitly convey sentiment. For example, Cambria and Hussain [6] proposed *Sentic Computing*, a sentiment analysis paradigm, in which common sense concepts (e.g., "`happy birthday`", "`simple life`") are extracted from texts and assigned to their sentiment orientations using semantic parsing and affective common sense knowledge sources. Gangemi et al. [8] further investigated the syntactic structure of sentences in order to detect more fine grained relations between the different semantic parts within it. For example, their approach is able to detect not only the sentiment in text, but also the opinionated topics, subtopics, the opinion holders and their sentiment.

The semantic methods, therefore, are more sensitive to the latent semantic relations between words in texts than syntactic methods. Nevertheless, in the above works, neither syntactic nor semantic methods are tailored to Twitter due to the lack of language formality and well structured sentences in tweets. Moreover, Semantic methods are usually limited to the scope of their underlying knowledge bases, which is especially problematic when processing general Twitter streams, with their rapid semiotic evolution and language deformations.

Contextual or statistical semantic methods extract patterns of semantically similar words by looking at the words' co-occurrence patterns in a given corpus [28,26]. LDA is a state-of-the-art method that have been widely used to this end [4].[1] For example, Lin et al. [11] propose JST, a topic generative model based on LDA. JST extracts, not only the patterns (topics) of words in text, but also their associated sentiment. The topics along with their associated sentiment have been evaluated in our previous work [20] and proven valuable for sentiment analysis on Twitter. However, these methods usually rely on the bag-of-words representation, and therefore are often unable to handle negations and other patterns that strongly influence sentiment.

In order to overcome the aforementioned limitations of the above methods, we design our sentiment pattern extraction approach in a way that captures patterns based on the contextual semantic and sentiment similarities between words in a Twitter corpus. Our approach does not rely on the syntactic structures in tweets, nor requires using predefined syntactic template sets or external semantic knowledge sources.

3   Semantic Sentiment Patterns of Words

Semantic sentiment patterns, by definition, are clusters of words which have similar contextual semantics and sentiment in text. Based on this definition, the problem of capturing these patterns in tweets data breaks down into three phases as illustrated in Figure 1. In the first phase, tweets in a given data collection are syntactically processed in order to reduce the amount of noise and language informality in them. In the second phase we apply the SentiCircle representation model [19] on the processed tweets to capture the contextual semantics and sentiment of words in the tweets. In the third step, the semantic sentiment patterns are formed by clustering words that share similar semantics and sentiment (i.e., similar SentiCircles).

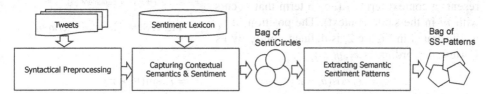

Fig. 1. The systematic workflow of capturing semantic sentiment patterns from Twitter data

In the subsequent sections we further describe each of the aforementioned phases in some more details:

3.1   Syntactical Preprocessing

Tweets are usually composed of incomplete, noisy and poorly structured sentences due to the frequent presence of abbreviations, irregular expressions, ill-formed words and

---

[1] Patterns extracted by LDA are usually called Topics.

non-dictionary terms. Such noisy nature of tweets has been shown to indirectly affect the sentiment classification performance [20]. This phase therefore, aims at reducing the amount of noise in the tweets by applying a series of pre-processing steps as follows:

- All URL links in the corpus are replaced with the term "URL"
- Remove all non-ASCII and non-English characters
- Revert words that contain repeated letters to their original English form. For example, the word "maaadddd" will be converted to "mad" after processing.
- Process contraction and possessive forms. For example, change "he's" and "friend's" to "he" and "friend"

Note that we do not remove stopwords from the data since they tend to carry sentiment information as shown in [18].

3.2 Capturing Contextual Semantics and Sentiment of Words

SS-patterns are formed from the contextual semantic similarities among words. Therefore, a key step in our pipeline is to capture the words' contextual semantics in tweets. To this end, we use our previously proposed semantic representation model, SentiCircle [19].

Briefly speaking, the SentiCircle model extracts the contextual semantics of a word from its co-occurrences with other words in a given tweet corpus. These co-occurrences are then represented as a geometric circle which is subsequently used to compute the contextual sentiment of the word by applying simple trigonometric identities on it. In particular, for each unique term m in a tweet collection, we build a two-dimensional geometric circle, where the term m is situated in the centre of the circle, and each point around it represents a context term c_i (i.e., a term that occurs with m in the same context). The position of c_i, as illustrated in Figure 2, is defined jointly by its Cartesian coordinates x_i, y_i as:

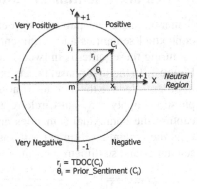

Fig. 2. SentiCircle of a term m

$$x_i = r_i \cos(\theta_i * \pi) \qquad\qquad y_i = r_i \sin(\theta_i * \pi)$$

Where θ_i is the polar angle of the context term c_i and its value equals to the prior sentiment of c_i in a sentiment lexicon before adaptation, r_i is the radius of c_i and its value represents the degree of correlation (tdoc) between c_i and m, and can be computed as:

$$r_i = tdoc(m, c_i) = f(c_i, m) \times \log \frac{N}{N_{c_i}}$$

where $f(c_i, m)$ is the number of times c_i occurs with m in tweets, N is the total number of terms, and N_{c_i} is the total number of terms that occur with c_i. Note that all terms' radii in the SentiCircle are normalised. Also, all angles' values are in radian.

The rational behind using this circular representation shape is to benefit from the trigonometric properties it offers for encoding the contextual semantics of a term as *sentiment orientation* and *sentiment strength*. Y-axis defines the sentiment of the term, i.e., a positive y value denotes a positive sentiment and vice versa. The X-axis defines the sentiment strength of the term. The smaller the x value, the stronger the sentiment.[2] This, in turn, divides the circle into four sentiment quadrants. Terms in the two upper quadrants have a positive sentiment ($\sin \theta > 0$), with upper left quadrant representing stronger positive sentiment since it has larger angle values than those in the top right quadrant. Similarly, terms in the two lower quadrants have negative sentiment values ($\sin \theta < 0$). Moreover, a small region called the *"Neutral Region"* can be defined. This region, as shown in Figure 2, is located very close to X-axis in the *"Positive"* and the *"Negative"* quadrants only, where terms lie in this region have very weak sentiment (i.e, $|\theta| \approx 0$).

The Sentiment Median of SentiCircle. In summary, the SentiCircle of any term m is composed by the set of (x, y) Cartesian coordinates of all the context terms of m. An effective way to compute the overall sentiment of m is by calculating the geometric median of all the points in its SentiCircle. Formally, for a given set of n points $(p_1, p_2, ..., p_n)$ in a SentiCirlce Ω, the 2D geometric median g is defined as: $g = \arg\min_{g \in \mathbb{R}^2} \sum_{i=1}^{n} \|p_i - g\|_2$. The boundaries of the neutral region can be computed by measuring the density distribution of terms in the SentiCircle along the Y-axis. In this paper we use similar boundary values to the ones in [19] as we use the same evaluation datasets. We call the geometric median g the **SentiMedian** as its position in the SentiCircle determines the total contextual-sentiment orientation and strength of m.

3.3 Extracting Patterns from SentiCircles

At this stage all the unique words in the tweet collection have their contextual semantics and sentiment extracted and represented by means of their SentiCircles. It is very likely to find words in text which share similar contextual semantics and sentiment. In other words, finding words with similar SentiCircles. Therefore, this phase seeks to find such potential semantic similarities in tweets by building clusters of similar SentiCircles. The output of this phase is a set of clusters of words, which we refer to as the *semantic sentiment patterns of words (SS-Patterns)*.

SentiCircles Clustering. We can capture patterns that emerge from the similarity of word's sentiment and contextual semantics by clustering the SentiCircles of those words. In particular, we perform a clustering task fed by dimensions that are provided by SentiCircles; *density, dispersion*, and *geometry*. Density and dispersion usually characterise terms and entities that receive controversial sentiment in tweets as will be further explained and validated in Section 6. Geometry, on the other hand, preserves the contextual sentiment orientation and strength of terms. Once we extract the vectors that represent these three dimensions from all the terms' SentiCircles, we feed them into a common clustering method; k-means.

---

[2] This is because $\cos \theta < 0$ for large angles.

In the following, we describe the three dimensions we extract from each term's Senti-Circle Ω along with the components they consist of:

- *Geometry*: includes the X- and Y-component of the SentiMedian $g(x_g, y_g) \in \Omega$
- *Density*: includes the total density of points in the SentiCircle Ω and its computed as: $density(\Omega) = N/M$, where N is the total number of points in the SentiCircle and M is the total number of points in the SentiCircles of all terms.

  We also compute five density components, representing the density of each sentiment quadrant in the SentiCircle (i.e., positive, very positive, negative and very negative quadrants) along with the density of its neutral region. Each of these components is computed as $density(Q) = P/N$ where P is the total number of points in the sentiment quadrant Q.

- *Dispersion*: the total dispersion of a SentiCircle refers to how scattered or condensed the points (context terms) in the circle. To calculate the value of this component, we use the *median absolute deviation measure (MAD)*, which computes the dispersion of Ω as the median of the absolute deviations from the SentiCircle's median point (i.e., the SentiMedian g_m) as:

$$mad(\Omega) = (\sum_{i=1}^{n} |p_i - g_m|)/N$$

  Similarly, using the above equation, we calculate the dispersion of each sentiment quadrant and the neutral region in the SentiCircle. We also calculate the dispersion of the active region in SentiCircle (i.e., The SentiCircle after excluding points in the neutral region)

The last step in our pipeline is to apply k-means on all SentiCircles' dimensions' vectors. This results in a set of clusters $\mathcal{K} = (k_1, k_2, ..., k_c)$ where each cluster consists of words that have similar contextual semantics and sentiment. We call $\mathcal{K}$ as the pattern set and and $k_i \in \mathcal{K}$ the *semantic sentiment pattern*.

In the subsequent section we describe how to determine the number of patterns (clusters) in the data and how to validate the extracted patterns by using them as features in two sentiment classification tasks.

4   Experimental Setup

Our proposed approach, as shown in the previous section, extracts patterns of words of similar contextual semantics and sentiment. We evaluate the extracted SS-patterns by using them as classification features to train supervised classifiers for two sentiment analysis tasks, tweet- and entity-level sentiment classification. To this end, we use 9 publicly and widely used datasets in Twitter sentiment analysis literature [17]. Nine of them will be used for tweet-level evaluation and one for entity-level evaluation. As for evaluation baselines, we use 6 types of classification features and compare the performance of classifiers trained from our SS-patterns against those trained from these baseline features.

4.1   Tweet-Level Evaluation Setup

The first validation test we conduct on our SS-patterns is to measure their effectiveness as features for binary sentiment analysis of tweets, i.e., classifying the individual tweets as positive or negative. To this end, we use SS-patterns extracted from a given Twitter dataset to train two supervised classifiers popularly used for tweet-level sentiment analysis, Maximum Entropy (MaxEnt) and Naïve Bayes (NB) from Mallet.[3] We use 9 different Twitter datasets in our validation in order to avoid any bias that a single dataset can introduce. Numbers of positive and negative tweets within these datasets are summarised in Table 1, and detailed in the references added in the table.

Table 1. Twitter datasets used for tweet-level sentiment analysis evaluation. Instructions on how to obtain these datasets are provided in [17].

Dataset	Tweets	#Negative	#Positive	#Unigrams
Stanford Twitter Test Set (STS-Test) [9]	359	177	182	1562
Sanders Dataset (Sanders) [17]	1224	654	570	3201
Obama McCain Debate (OMD) [7]	1906	1196	710	3964
Health Care Reform (HCR) [22]	1922	1381	541	5140
Stanford Gold Standard (STS-Gold) [17]	2034	632	1402	4694
Sentiment Strength Twitter Dataset (SSTD) [23]	2289	1037	1252	6849
The Dialogue Earth Weather Dataset (WAB) [3]	5495	2580	2915	7485
The Dialogue Earth Gas Prices Dataset (GASP) [3]	6285	5235	1050	8128
Semeval Dataset (Semeval) [14]	7535	2186	5349	15851

4.2 Entity-Level Evaluation Setup

In the second validation test, we evaluate the usefulness of SS-Patterns as features for entity-level sentiment analysis, i.e., detecting sentiment towards a particular entity. To this end, we perform a 3-way sentiment classification (negative, positive, neutral) on a dataset of 58 named entities extracted from the STS-Gold dataset and manually labelled with their sentiment class. Numbers of negative, positive and neutral entities in this dataset are listed in Table 2 along with five examples of entities under each sentiment class. Details of the extraction and the annotation of these entities can be found in [17].

Table 2. Numbers of negative, positive and neutral entities in the STS-Gold Entity dataset along with examples of 5 entities under each sentiment class

	Negative Entities	Positive Entities	Neutral Entities
Total Number	13	29	16
	Cancer	Lakers	Obama
	Lebron James	Katy Perry	Sydney
Examples	Flu	Omaha	iPhone
	Wii	Taylor Swift	Youtube
	Dominique Wilkins	Jasmine Tea	Vegas

The entity sentiment classifier we use in our evaluation is based on maximum likelihood estimation (MLE). Specifically, we use tweets in the STS-Gold dataset to estimate the conditional probability $P(c|e)$ of an entity e assigned with a sentiment class $c \in \{Positive, Negative\}$ as: as $P(c|e) = N(e,c)/N(e)$ where $N(e,c)$ is the frequency of an entity e in tweets assigned with a sentiment class c and $N(e)$ is the frequency of the entity e in the whole corpus.

---

[3] http://mallet.cs.umass.edu/

We incorporate our SS-Pattern features and other baseline features (Section 4.3) into the sentiment class estimation of e by using the following back-off strategy:

$$\hat{c} = \begin{cases} P(c|e) & \text{if } N(e,c) \neq 0 \\ P(c|f) & \text{if } N(e,c) = 0 \end{cases} \quad (1)$$

where f is the incorporated feature (e.g., the SS-Pattern of e) and $P(c|f)$ is the conditional probability of the feature f assigned with a sentiment class c and it can be also estimated using MLE. The rationale behind the above back-off strategy is that some entities might not occur in tweets of certain sentiment class, leading therefore, to zero probabilities. In such cases we resort to the sentiment of the latent features associated with these entities in the dataset.

The final sentiment of e can be derived from the ratio $R_e = P(c = Positive|e)/P(c = Negative|e)$. In particular, the sentiment is *neutral* if R_e is less than a threshold γ, otherwise the sentiment is *negative* if $R_e < 1$ or *positive* if $R_e > 1$.

We determine the value of γ by plotting the ratio R_e for all the 58 entities and check where the plot converges. In our case, the ratio plot converged with $\gamma = 0.3$.

4.3 Evaluation Baselines

The baseline model in our evaluation is a sentiment classifier trained from word unigram features. Table 1 shows the number of unique unigram features extracted from our datasets.

In addition to unigrams, we propose comparing our SS-Pattern features against the below described five state-of-the-art types of features in sentiment analysis. Amongst them, two sets of features are derived from the syntactical characteristics of words in tweets (POS features, and Twitter features), one is based on the prior sentiment orientation of words (Lexicon features) and two are obtained from the semantic representation of words in tweets (Semantic Concept features and LDA-Topic features):

1. Twitter Features: refer to tokens and characters that are popularly used in tweet messages such as hashtags (e.g., "#smartphone"), user mentions (e.g, "@obama"), the tweet reply token ("RT") and emoticons (e.g., ":) :D <3 o_0").

2. Part-of-Speech Features: refer to the part-of-speech tags of words in tweets (e.g., verbs, adjectives, adverbs, etc). We extract these features using the TweetNLP POS tagger.[4]

3. Lexicon Features: these features are formed from the opinionated words in tweets along with their prior sentiment labels (e.g., "good_positive", "bad_negative", "nice_positive", etc.). We assign words with their prior sentiments using both Thelwall [23] and MPQA [27] sentiment lexicons.

4. Semantic Concept Features: This type of features refers to the semantic concepts (e.g., "person", "company", "city") that represent entities (e.g., "Obama", "Motorola", "Vegas") appearing in tweets. To extract the entities and their associated concepts in our datasets we use AlchemyAPI,[5] which we have previously evaluated its semantic extraction performance on Twitter data [21]. The number of extracted concepts in each dataset is listed in Table 3.

---

[4] http://www.ark.cs.cmu.edu/TweetNLP/
[5] http://www.alchemyapi.com

Table 3. Numbers of the semantic concepts extracted from all datasets

Dataset	STS-Test	Sanders	OMD	HCR	STS-Gold	SSTD	WAB	GASP	Semeval
No. of Concepts	299	1407	2191	1626	1490	699	1497	3614	6875

5. LDA-Topic Features: These features denote the latent topics extracted from tweets using the probabilistic generative model, LDA [4]. LDA assumes that a document is a mixture of topics and each topic is a mixture of probabilities of words that are more likely to co-occur together under the topic. For example the topic "iPhone" is more likely to generate words like "display" and "battery". Therefore, LDA-Topics represent groups of words that are semantically related. To extract these latent topics from our datasets we use an implementation of LDA provided by Mallet. LDA requires defining the number of topics to extract before applying it on the data. To this end, we ran LDA with different choices of numbers of topics (e.g., 1 topic, 10 topics, 20 topics, 30 topics, etc). Among all choices, 10 topics was the opitmal number that gave the highest sentiment classification performance when the topics were incorporated as additional features into the feature space.

Note that all the above sets of features are combined with the original unigram features when training the baseline sentiment classifiers for both entity- and tweet-levels.

4.4 Number of SS-Patterns in Data

As described earlier, extracting SS-patterns is a clustering problem that requires determining beforehand the number of clusters (patterns) to extract. To this end, we run k-means for multiple times with k varying between 1 and 100. We then plot the within-cluster sum of squares for all the outputs generated by k-means. The optimum number of clusters is found where an "*elbow*" appears in the plot [12]. For example, Figure 4 shows that the optimum number of clusters for the GASP dataset is 17, which in other words, represents the number of SS-Patterns features that our sentiment classifiers should be trained from. Table 4 shows the number of SS-Patterns extracted by our model for each dataset.

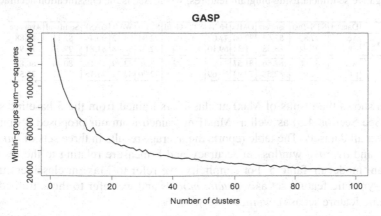

Fig. 3. Within-cluster sum of squares for different numbers of clusters (SS-Patterns) in the GASP dataset

Table 4. Numbers of SS-Patterns extracted from all datasets

Dataset	STS-Test	Sanders	OMD	HCR	STS-Gold	SSTD	WAB	GASP	Semeval
No. of SS-Patterns	18	20	23	22	26	24	17	17	19

5   Evaluation Results

In this section, we report the results from using our proposed SS-Patterns as features for tweet- and entity-level sentiment classification tasks and compare against the baselines described in Section 4.3. All experiments in both evaluation tasks are done using 10-fold cross validation.

5.1   Sentiment Patterns for Tweet-Level Sentiment Classification

The first task in our evaluation aims to asses the usefulness of SS-Patterns as features for binary sentiment classification of tweets (positive vs. negative).[6] We use NB and MaxEnt classifiers trained from word unigrams as the starting baseline models (aka, unigram models). We then compare the performance of classifiers trained from other types of features against these unigram models.

Table 5 shows the results in accuracy and average F1 measure of both unigram models across all datasets. The highest accuracy is achieved on the GASP dataset using MaxEnt with 90.49%, while the highest average F-measure of 84.08% is obtained on the WAB dataset. On the other hand, the lowest performance in accuracy is obtained using NB on the SSTD dataset with 72.36%. Also, NB produces the lowest F1 of 66.69% on the HCR dataset. On average, MaxEnt outperforms NB by 1.04% and 1.35% in accuracy and F1 respectively. Hence, we use MaxEnt only to continue our evaluation in this task.

Table 5. Accuracy and the average harmonic mean (F1 measure) obtained from identifying positive and negative sentiment using unigram features, where *Acc* is the classification accuracy

	Dataset	STS-Test	Sanders	OMD	HCR	STS-Gold	SSTD	WAB	GASP	SemEval	Average
MaxEnt	Acc	77.82	83.62	82.90	77.02	86.02	72.84	84.12	90.49	82.11	**81.88**
	F1	77.94	83.58	81.34	69.10	83.10	72.27	84.08	81.81	77.03	**78.91**
NB	Acc	81.06	82.66	81.57	74.27	84.22	72.36	82.79	88.16	80.44	**80.84**
	F1	81.07	82.52	79.93	66.69	80.46	72.20	82.74	78.15	74.35	**77.57**

Table 6 shows the results of MaxEnt classifiers trained from the 5 baseline sets of features (See Section 4.3) as well as MaxtEnt trained from our proposed SS-patterns, applied over all datasets. The table reports the average results in three sets of *minimum*, *maximum*, and *average* win/loss in accuracy and F-measure relating to the results of the unigram model in Table 5. For simplicity, we refer to MaxEnt classifiers trained from any syntactic feature set as *syntactic models* and we refer to those trained from any semantic feature set as *semantic models*.

---

[6] Unlike entity-level, we do not perform 3-way classification (positive, negative, netrual) in this task since not all the 9 datasets contain tweets of neutral sentiment.

It can be observed from these results in Table 6 that all syntactic and semantic models outperform on average the unigram model in both accuracy and F-measure. However, MaxEnt trained from our SS-Patterns significantly outperforms those models trained from any other set of features. In particular, our SS-Patterns produce on average 3.05% and 3.76 % higher accuracy and F1 than the unigram model. This is 2% higher performance than the average performance gain of all syntactic and semantic models. Moreover, we get a maximum improvement in accuracy and F-measure of 9.87% and 9.78% respectively over the unigram model when using our SS-Patterns for training. This is at least 3.54% and 3.61% higher than any other model. It is also worth noting that on the GASP dataset, where the minimum performance gain is obtained, MaxEnt trained from SS-Patterns gives a minimum improvement of 0.70%, while all other models suffer a performance loss of -0.45% averagely.

Table 6. Win/Loss in Accuracy and F-measure of using different features for sentiment classification on all nine datasets

Features		MaxEnt Classifier					
		Accuracy			F-Measure		
		Minimum	Maximum	Average	Minimum	Maximum	Average
Syntactic	Twitter Features	-0.23	3.91	1.24	-0.25	4.53	1.62
	POS	-0.89	2.92	0.79	-0.91	5.67	1.25
	Lexicon	-0.44	4.23	1.30	-0.38	5.81	1.83
	Average	-0.52	3.69	1.11	-0.52	5.33	1.57
Semantic	Concepts	-0.22	2.76	1.20	-0.40	4.80	1.51
	LDA-Topics	-0.47	3.37	1.20	-0.68	6.05	1.68
	SS-Patterns	**0.70**	**9.87**	**3.05**	**1.23**	**9.78**	**3.76**
	Average	0.00	5.33	1.82	0.05	6.88	2.32

Finally, we notice that syntactic features, and more specifically the lexicon ones are highly competitive features to the semantic type of features. For example, lexicon features slightly outperform concept and LDA-Topic features. However, from the average performance in Table 6 of both types of features, we can see that semantic models are still bypassing syntactic models in both accuracy and F-measure by 0.71% and 0.75% on average respectively.

5.2   Results of Entity-Level Sentiment Classification

In this section, we report the evaluation results of using our SS-Patterns for entity-level sentiment classification on the STS-Gold Entity dataset using the entity sentiment classifier described in Section 4.2. Note that STS-Gold is the only dataset among the other 9 that provides named entities manually annotated with their sentiment labels (positive, negative, neutral). Therefore, our evaluation in this task is done using the STS-Gold dataset only.

Table 7 reports the results in accuracy, precision (P), recall (R) and F1 measure of positive, negative and neutral sentiment classification performances from using unigrams, semantic concepts, LDA-Topics and SS-Patterns features. Generally, our SS-Patterns outperform all other features including word unigrams in all measures. In particular,

Table 7. Accuracy and averages of Precision, Recall, and F measures of entity-level sentiment classification using different features

Features	Accuracy	Positive Sentiment			Negative Sentiment			Neutral Sentiment			Average		
		P	R	F1	P	R	F1	P	R	F1	P	R	F1
Unigrams	48.28	92	79.31	85.19	6.67	7.69	7.14	22.22	25	23.53	40.3	37.33	38.62
LDA-Topics	58.62	92	79.31	85.19	31.82	53.85	40	36.36	25	29.63	53.39	52.72	51.6
Semantic Concepts	55.17	92	79.31	85.19	25	38.46	30.3	30.77	25	27.59	49.26	47.59	47.69
SS-Patterns	**60.34**	92	79.31	85.19	34.78	61.54	44.44	40	25	30.77	55.59	55.28	53.47

merely using word unigrams for classification gives the lowest performance of 48.24% and 38.62% in accuracy and average F1. However, augmenting the feature space with SS-Patterns improves the performance significantly by 12.06% in accuracy and 14.85% in average F1. Our SS-Patterns also outperform LDA-Topics and semantic concepts features by at least 1.72% and 1.87% in accuracy and average F1.

As for per-class sentiment classification performance, we observe that all features produce high and similar performances on detecting positive entities. This is because classifiers trained from either feature set fail in detecting the sentiment of the same entities. Moreover, it seems that detecting negative and neutral entities are much more difficult tasks than detecting positive ones. For example, unigrams perform very poorly in detecting negative entities with a F1 less then 8%. Although the performance improves a lot by using SS-Patterns, it is still much lower than the positive classification performance. For neutral sentiment classification the performance is the lowest with unigrams (F1 = 23.53%) while it is the highest with SS-Patterns (F1 = 30.77%). Such varying performance might be due to the uneven sentiment class distribution in the entity dataset. As can be noted from Table 2, positive entities constitute 50% of the total number of entities while the neutral and negative entities form together the other 50%.

6   Within-Pattern Sentiment Consistency

Our approach, by definition, seeks to find SS-Patterns of terms of similar contextual semantics and sentiment. Therefore, SS-Patterns are best when they are consistent with the sentiment of their terms, that is, they consist mostly of terms of similar contextual sentiment orientations. In this section, we further study the sentiment consistency of our patterns on a set of 14 SS-Patterns extracted from the 58 annotated entities in the STS-Gold dataset. These number of patterns was determined based on the elbow method as explained in Section 4.4.

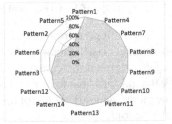

Table 8 shows four of the extracted patterns along with the top 5 entities within them and the entities' gold-standard sentiment. Patterns 3, 12 and 11 are strongly consistent since all entities within them have the same sentiment. On the other hand, Pattern 5 has low sentiment consistency as it contains entities of mixed sentiment orientations. We systematically calculate the sentiment consistency of a given SS-Pattern k_i as:

Fig. 4. Within-Cluster sentiment consistencies in the STS-Gold Entity dataset

$$consistency(k_i) = \arg\max_{s \in \mathcal{S}} \frac{E_s}{E'} \qquad (2)$$

where $s \in \mathcal{S} = \{Positive, Negative, Neutral\}$ is the sentiment label, E_s is the number of entities of sentiment s and E' is the total number of entities within K_i.

Figure 4 depicts the sentiment consistency of the 14 SS-Patterns. 9 patterns out of 14 are perfectly consistent with the sentiment of their entities while two patterns have a consistency higher than 77%. Only patterns 2,5 and 6 have a consistency lower than 70%. Overall, the average consistency value across the 14 patterns reaches 88%.

Table 8. Example of three strongly consistent SS-Patterns (Patterns 3, 11, and 12) and one inconsistent SS-Pattern (Pattern 5), extracted from the STS-Gold Entity dataset

Pattern.3 (Neutral)		Pattern.12 (Positive)		Pattern.5 (Mixed)		Pattern.11 (Positive)	
Entity	True Sentiment	Entity	True Sentiment	Entity	True Sentiment	Entity	True Sentiment
Brazil	Neutral	Kardashian	Positive	Cancer	Negative	Amy Adams	Positive
Facebook	Neutral	Katy Perry	Positive	Fever	Negative	Dallas	Positive
Oprah	Neutral	Beatles	Positive	Headache	Negative	Riyadh	Positive
Sydney	Neutral	Usher	Positive	McDonald	Neutral	Sam	Positive
Seattle	Neutral	Pandora	Positive	Xbox	Neutral	Miley Cyrus	Positive

Sentiment Consistency vs. Sentiment Dispersion. From the above, we observed that patterns 2,5 and 6 have low sentiment consistency. Looking at characteristics of entities in these patterns, we notice that the average dispersion of their SentiCircles is 0.18 on average. This is twice higher than the dispersion of the entities within the other 11 strongly consistent patterns. Overall, we found a negative correlation of -0.42 between the sentiment consistency of SS-Patterns and the dispersion of their entities' SentiCircles. This indicates that SS-Patterns that contain entities of high dispersed SentiCircles are more likely to have low sentiment consistency. Based on the SentiCircle model (Section 3), these high dispersed entities either occur very infrequently or occur in different contexts of different sentiment in the tweet corpus.

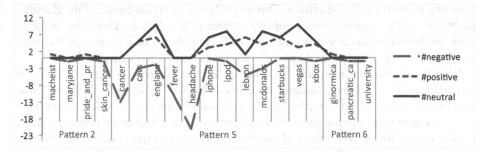

Fig. 5. Number of times that entities in Pattern 2, 5 and 6 receive negative, positive and neutral sentiment

To validate our above observation, we analyse the human sentiment votes on the 58 entities in STS-Gold dataset.[7] Figure 5 shows entities under patterns 2,5 and 6 along

---

[7] Human votes on each entity are available to download with the STS-Gold dataset under http://tweenator.com.

with number of times they receive negative, positive and neutral sentiment in tweets according to the three human coders. We observe that entities in patterns 2 and 6 occur very infrequently in tweets, yet with consistent sentiment. On the other hand, most entities in Pattern 5 occur more frequently in tweets. However, they receive strong and controversial sentiment (i.e., opposite sentiment). For example, the entity "McDonald's" occurs 3, 4 and 8 times with negative, positive and neutral sentiment respectively.

The above analysis shows the potential of our approach for generating patterns of entities that indicate sentiment disagreement or controversy in tweets.

7 Discussion and Future Work

We showed the value of our proposed approach in extracting semantic sentiment patterns of words and exploiting them for sentiment classification of tweets and entities. Our patterns, by definition, are based on words' similarities in a given context in tweets, which make them relevant to that specific context. This means that they might need updating more frequently than context-independent patterns, i.e., patterns derived based on pre-defined syntactic templates [16] or common-sense knowledge bases [6]. Hence, potential gain in performance may be obtained by combining context-independent patterns with our patterns, which constitutes a future task to this work.

For tweet-level sentiment classification, SS-Patterns were evaluated on 9 Twitter datasets with different results. For example, our SS-Patterns produced the highest performance improvement on the STS-Test dataset (+9.78% over the baseline) while the lowest improvement was obtained on the GASP dataset (+1.23%). Different factors might be behind such variance. For example our datasets differ in their sizes, sparsity degrees and sentiment classification distributions. We plan to further study the impact of these factors on (i) the quality of the extracted patterns and (ii) the sentiment classification performance.

For entity sentiment classification, evaluation was performed on one dataset and by using a single classifier. We noticed that detecting positive entities was much easier than detecting neutral or negative entities. This might be due to (i) the choice of the classifier we use or (ii) the large number of positive entities in this dataset. Therefore, as future work, we intend to continue experimenting with our patterns on multiple and balanced entity datasets and using several and more advanced entity sentiment classifiers.

We showed that our approach was able to discover patterns of terms and entities that could indicate sentiment disagreement, instability, or controversy in tweets. Those patterns have also shown low consistency with the sentiment of entities within them. Thus, one may expect terms under these patterns to have low contribution to the sentiment classification performance, and therefore, remove them from the feature space for sentiment classification. We are currently investigating this issue and its impact on the classification performance.

8 Conclusions

We proposed a novel approach for extracting patterns of words of similar contextual semantics and sentiment on Twitter. Our approach does not rely on the syntactical structure of tweets, nor uses external syntactic templates for pattern extraction.

We applied our approach on 9 Twitter datasets and validated the extracted patterns by incorporating them as classification features for sentiment classification of both tweets and entities. For tweet level sentiment classification, we used two supervised classifiers, NB and MaxEnt while for entity level we proposed a sentiment classifier based on Maximum Likelihood Estimation.

In both sentiment classification tasks and on all datasets, classifiers trained from our SS-Patterns showed a consistent and superior performance over classifiers trained from other 4 syntactical and 2 semantic sets of features.

We conducted an analysis of our SS-Patterns and showed that our patterns are strongly consistent with the sentiment of the terms within them. Also, the analysis showed that our approach was able to derive patterns of entities of controversial sentiment in tweets.

Acknowledgment. This work was supported by the EU-FP7 project SENSE4US (grant no. 611242).

We thank Grégoire Burel and Carlos Pedrinaci for the helpful discussions.

References

1. Agarwal, A., Xie, B., Vovsha, I., Rambow, O., Passonneau, R.: Sentiment analysis of twitter data. In: Proc. ACL 2011 Workshop on Languages in Social Media, Portland, Oregon (2011)
2. Aisopos, F., Papadakis, G., Varvarigou, T.: Sentiment analysis of social media content using n-gram graphs. In: Proc. the 3rd ACM International Workshop on Social Media (2011)
3. Asiaee, T.A., Tepper, M., Banerjee, A., Sapiro, G.: If you are happy and you know it... tweet. In: Proc. the 21st ACM Conference on Information and Knowledge Management (2012)
4. Blei, D.M., Ng, A.Y., Jordan, M.I.: Latent dirichlet allocation. The Journal of Machine Learning Research 3, 993–1022 (2003)
5. Bravo-Marquez, F., Mendoza, M., Poblete, B.: Combining strengths, emotions and polarities for boosting twitter sentiment analysis. In: Proc. the Second International Workshop on Issues of Sentiment Discovery and Opinion Mining (2013)
6. Cambria, E., Hussain, A.: Sentic computing: Techniques, tools, and applications, vol. 2. Springer (2012)
7. Diakopoulos, N., Shamma, D.: Characterizing debate performance via aggregated twitter sentiment. In: Proc. 28th Int. Conf. on Human Factors in Computing Systems. ACM (2010)
8. Gangemi, A., Presutti, V., Reforgiato Recupero, D.: Frame-based detection of opinion holders and topics: A model and a tool. IEEE Computational Intelligence Magazine (2014)
9. Go, A., Bhayani, R., Huang, L.: Twitter sentiment classification using distant supervision. CS224N Project Report, Stanford (2009)
10. Kouloumpis, E., Wilson, T., Moore, J.: Twitter sentiment analysis: The good the bad and the omg! In: Proceedings of the ICWSM, Barcelona, Spain (2011)
11. Lin, C., He, Y., Everson, R., Ruger, S.: Weakly supervised joint sentiment-topic detection from text. IEEE Transactions on Knowledge and Data Engineering 24(6), 1134–1145 (2012)
12. Milligan, G.W., Cooper, M.C.: An examination of procedures for determining the number of clusters in a data set. Psychometrika 50(2), 159–179 (1985)
13. Mohammad, S.M., Kiritchenko, S., Zhu, X.: Nrc-canada: Building the state-of-the-art in sentiment analysis of tweets. arXiv preprint arXiv:1308.6242 (2013)

14. Nakov, P., Rosenthal, S., Kozareva, Z., Stoyanov, V., Ritter, A., Wilson, T.: Semeval-2013 task 2: Sentiment analysis in twitter. In: Proc. the 7th ACL International Workshop on Semantic Evaluation (2013)
15. Pak, A., Paroubek, P.: Twitter as a corpus for sentiment analysis and opinion mining. In: Proceedings of LREC 2010, Valletta, Malta (2010)
16. Riloff, E., Wiebe, J.: Learning extraction patterns for subjective expressions. In: Proc. The 2003 Conference on Empirical Methods in Natural Language Processing (2003)
17. Saif, H., Fernandez, M., He, Y., Alani, H.: Evaluation datasets for twitter sentiment analysis a survey and a new dataset, the sts-gold. In: Proceedings, 1st ESSEM Workshop, Turin, Italy (2013)
18. Saif, H., Fernandez, M., He, Y., Alani, H.: On Stopwords, Filtering and Data Sparsity for Sentiment Analysis of Twitter. In: Proc. 9th Language Resources and Evaluation Conference (LREC), Reykjavik, Iceland (2014)
19. Saif, H., Fernandez, M., He, Y., Alani, H.: Senticircles for contextual and conceptual semantic sentiment analysis of twitter. In: Proc. 11th Extended Semantic Web Conf. (ESWC), Crete, Greece (2014)
20. Saif, H., He, Y., Alani, H.: Alleviating data sparsity for twitter sentiment analysis. In: Proc. Workshop on Making Sense of Microposts (#MSM2012) in WWW 2012, Lyon, France (2012)
21. Saif, H., He, Y., Alani, H.: Semantic sentiment analysis of twitter. In: Proc. 11th Int. Semantic Web Conf. (ISWC), Boston, MA (2012)
22. Speriosu, M., Sudan, N., Upadhyay, S., Baldridge, J.: Twitter polarity classification with label propagation over lexical links and the follower graph. In: Proceedings of the EMNLP First workshop on Unsupervised Learning in NLP, Edinburgh, Scotland (2011)
23. Thelwall, M., Buckley, K., Paltoglou, G.: Sentiment strength detection for the social web. J. American Society for Information Science and Technology 63(1), 163–173 (2012)
24. Thet, T.T., Na, J.C., Khoo, C.S., Shakthikumar, S.: Sentiment analysis of movie reviews on discussion boards using a linguistic approach. In: Proc. the 1st International CIKM Workshop on Topic-sentiment Analysis for Mass Opinion (2009)
25. Turney, P.: Thumbs up or thumbs down? semantic orientation applied to unsupervised classification of reviews. In: Proceedings of the 40th Annual Meeting of the Association for Computational Linguistics (ACL 2002), Philadelphia, Pennsylvania (2002)
26. Turney, P.D., Pantel, P., et al.: From frequency to meaning: Vector space models of semantics. Journal of artificial Intelligence Research 37(1), 141–188 (2010)
27. Wilson, T., Wiebe, J., Hoffmann, P.: Recognizing contextual polarity in phrase-level sentiment analysis. In: Proceedings of the conference on Human Language Technology and Empirical Methods in Natural Language Processing, Vancouver, British Columbia, Canada (2005)
28. Wittgenstein, L.: Philosophical Investigations. Blackwell, London (2001)

Stretching the Life of Twitter Classifiers
with Time-Stamped Semantic Graphs

Amparo Elizabeth Cano[1], Yulan He[2], and Harith Alani[1]

[1] Knowledge Media Institute, Open University, UK
ampaeli@gmail.com, h.alani@open.ac.uk
[2] School of Engineering and Applied Science, Aston University, UK
y.he@cantab.net

Abstract. Social media has become an effective channel for communicating both trends and public opinion on current events. However the automatic topic classification of social media content pose various challenges. Topic classification is a common technique used for automatically capturing themes that emerge from social media streams. However, such techniques are sensitive to the evolution of topics when new event-dependent vocabularies start to emerge (e.g., Crimea becoming relevant to War_Conflict during the Ukraine crisis in 2014). Therefore, traditional supervised classification methods which rely on labelled data could rapidly become outdated. In this paper we propose a novel transfer learning approach to address the classification task of new data when the only available labelled data belong to a previous epoch. This approach relies on the incorporation of knowledge from DBpedia graphs. Our findings show promising results in understanding how features age, and how semantic features can support the evolution of topic classifiers.

Keywords: social media, topic detection, DBpedia, concept drift, feature relevance decay.

1 Introduction

Microbloging platforms such as Twitter, has proven to be powerful tools for sharing opinions and spreading the word on trends and current events. Understanding what is being discussed on social media has been the focus of much research and development, to monitor opinion and sentiment [21,11], to detect emerging events [27,8], to track topics [5,12], etc. One persistent challenge often faced by such works is the task of assigning topic labels to microposts; a core step in classifier training. The continuous change in topics and vocabulary on social media raises the need for retraining such classifiers with fresh topic-label annotations, which are often time consuming and costly to acquire. Topic classification of microposts is also challenged by the inherent characteristics of social media content, which often consists of ill-formed language, abbreviations, and hashtags.

In an event-dependent topic, not only new lexical features could potentially recharacterise the topic, but also previous features could fade out and become irrelevant for this topic. Because of the progressive feature drifts of topics in dynamic environments the expectation that training data and future data to be in the same feature space is not

P. Mika et al. (Eds.) ISWC 2014, Part II, LNCS 8797, pp. 341–357, 2014.

normally met. One such topic is Violence in Social Media and microposts, whose language model is continuously reshaping based on current violence-related events. For example, the word Crimea might not have been relevant to the topic Violence two years ago, but has become increasingly relevant in recent months. Similarly, the term Jan25, which was characteristic of violence behaviour during the Egyptian revolution, is now less representative of violence in current microblogs.

Such concept drifts [9][16] introduce new challenges to the topic classification of tweets. These linguistic and topic evolutions contribute to the progressive reshaping of the language model that characterises a topic, which renders existing topic classification models less and less efficient. To maintain the adequacy of our models, it is necessary to regularly retune them to fit current social media content. Relearning the models would enable us to incorporate new relevant features, and to reuse the weight of features which have become outdated or less relevant to the topic.

Particularly on a topic classification of tweets at a current epoch, it is common to only have sufficient training data from previous epochs. An extensive area of research which addresses this problem is Transfer Learning [18], which aims to apply knowledge learned in the past to solve new problems.

In this paper we propose a transfer learning approach to the epoch-based topic classification of tweets, where no label data is available on a current epoch but label data from past epochs is available. This approach relies on the incorporation of semantic features derived from temporal topic graphs extracted from a structured knowledge source. DBpedia has become one of the major sources of structured knowledge extracted from Wikipedia. Such structures gradually re-shape the representation of Topics as new events relevant to such topics emerge. The incorporation of new event-data to a topic representation leads to a linguistic evolution of a topic, but also to a change on its semantic structure. To the best of our knowledge, none of the existing approaches for topic classification using semantic features [10][3][26], has focused on the epoch-based transfer learning task. In this work we present a comparison of lexical and semantic features on epoch-based transfer learning tasks. The main contributions of this paper can be summarised as follows:

(1) we generate a cross-epoch dataset consisting of 12,000 annotated tweets over three different years and three topics;
(2) we enrich our classification models with 4 types of semantic features extracted from our Twitter content using different DBpedia dumps (3.6 to 3.9) to simulate epoch-based settings;
(3) we propose a novel weighting strategies for epoch-based transfer learning which relies on topic-based semantic graphs at a given point in time. Our findings show that the proposed strategies improve performance upon our baseline while outperforming F-measure upon lexical features; and
(4) we compare the performance of lexical feature-based models against semantic features. Our findings demonstrate that class-based (rdf:type) features alone can achieve on average a gain in F of 12% over lexical features on cross-epoch settings.

2 Related Work

Topic classification of tweets consists of the task of labelling a tweet as being either *topic-related* or *non-topic-related*. Various works have made use of lexical and profile based features to approach this task [19,24]. Other approaches have incorporated the use of external knowledge sources (KS) to enrich Twitter content. Some of them relying only on KS [10,23,17]; others incorporating semantic features derived from semantic meta graphs [26,3] on supervised settings; and others incorporating DBpedia lexical features on unsupervised classification tasks [2]. However to the best of our knowledge, none of these approaches focused on the epoch-based transfer learning task. In contrast to previous work, rather than focusing on how semantic features perform against lexical features within the same epoch datasets, we focus on analysing the change in performance on cross-epoch settings. In these settings, models are trained on data from an epoch t, and tested on data for which no training data is available yet.

Transfer learning was proposed over a decade ago [25,4]. However, its use in natural language processing is relatively new[18]. [1] introduced a structural correspondence learning method for domain adaptation applied to part-of-speech tagging. [7] introduced the feature augmentation strategy for domain adaptation. [15] studied cross-domain classification by applying word similarities using semantic nets. However, their setting is not cross-epoch dependent but rather cross-domain. Previous work on sentiment analysis [12] studied the simultaneous sentiment and topic detection on a dynamic setting based on an unsupervised approach. As opposed to previous work which rely on the use of lexical features, we propose the incorporation of semantic features in the cross-epoch learning task. To the best of our knowledge no existing work has been formally studied for the topic classification of tweets as a cross-epoch transfer learning task on a supervised setting.

3 Characterising Topic Changes with DBpedia

DBpedia is periodically updated to incorporate any additions and modification in Wikipedia. This enables us to track how specific resources evolve over time, by comparing these resources over subsequent DBpedia editions.

For example, changes to the semantic graph for the concept Barack_Obama can be derived from snapshots of this resource's semantic graph from different DBpedia dumps.[1] Consider Figure 1, although some of the triples remain unchanged in consecutive dumps, (e.g. [dbp:Barack_Obama, dbo:birthPlace, dbpedia:Hawaii]) new triples provide further information on the resource: i) current contexts (e.g. DBpedia 3.7 [dbp:Barack_Obama, skos:subject, dbp:Al-Qaeda]); ii) future contexts (e.g. DBpedia 3.7 [dbp:Barack_Obama, dbo:wikiPageWikiLink, dbp:Uni-ted_States_presidential_candidates,_2012]) and iii) past context (e.g. DBpedia 3.8 [dbp:Barack_Obama, dbo:wikiPageWikiLink, dbp:Budget_Control_Act_of_2011]). Changes regarding a resource are exposed

---

[1] The DBpedia dumps correspond to Wikipedia articles at different time periods as follows: DBpedia 3.6 generated on 2010-10-11; DBpedia 3.7 on 2011-07-22, DBpedia 3.8 on 2012-06-01, DBpedia 3.9 on late April. DBpedia have them available to download at DBpedia http://wiki.dbpedia.org/Downloads39

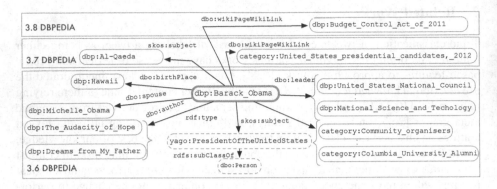

Fig. 1. Triples of the Barack_Obama resource extracted from different DBpedia dumps (3.6 to 3.8). Each DBpedia dump presents a snapshot in time of factual information of a resource.

both through new semantic features (i.e triples) and new lexical features –appearing on changes in a resource's abstract–.

DBpedia therefore covers a wealth of structured resources exhibiting both lexical and semantic information. Moreover, these resources are commonly characterised with a Topic via the `skos:subject` property, which links a DBpedia resource with a `skos:Concept`. Hence in DBpedia each particular topic (e.g. `cat:War`[2]) is broadly represented through its associations with a large number of resources (e.g. `dbp:War_-profiteering`). This resource-concept relationship yields to a broad set of resources characterising a topic. A topic can be therefore represented by a collection of resources belonging to both the main topic (e.g. `cat:War`) and resources (e.g `dbp:Combat_assess-ment`) belonging to subcategories (e.g. `cat:Military_operations`) of the main Topic.

Using multiple DBpedia dumps, we are able to characterise topics during different time periods. This paper proposes a novel approach which makes use of time-based semantic graph changes for characterising the relevance of a feature to a given Topic. The following section introduces our framework for extracting a time-dependent DBpedia-based representations of tweets. It also presents a set of feature weighting strategies which aim to overcome the drop in classification performance when classifiers are applied to previously unseen datasets.

4   Framework for Twitter Topic Classification with DBpedia

Since the changes on the lexical and semantic representation of a topic are time-dependent, we propose to make use of temporal features in the form of semantic-graphs snapshots. In this paper we aim to understand how the relevance of features for classifying a topic changes once the characterisation of that topic changes over time. To this end, we perform an analysis based on the lexical and semantic feature expansion of tweets using DBpedia[3]. This involves investigating how the availability of resources

---

[2] Where cat is the qname for `http://dbpedia.org/resource/Category:`

[3] Analysis of joint KSs is future work.

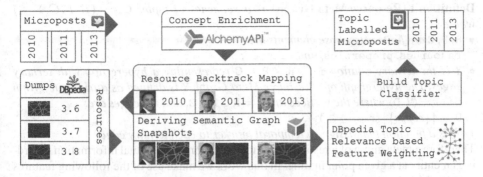

Fig. 2. Architecture for backtrack mapping of resources to DBpedia dumps and deriving topic-relevance based features for epoch-dependent topic classification

overtime can impact the classification performance on previously unseen data. As depicted in Figure 2, our framework makes use of different DBpedia dumps for the topic classification of tweets. The main stages of this framework are: 1) Extraction of lexical and semantic features from tweets; 2) Time-dependent content modelling; 3) Strategy for weighting topic-relevant features with DBpedia; and 4) Construction of time-dependent topic classifiers based on lexical, semantic and joint features . These stages are described in the following subsections.

4.1 Lexical and Semantic Feature Extraction

We focus on two main feature types: lexical and semantic features. The lexical feature representation of a tweet consists of a bag of words approach using a TF-IDF weighting strategy [13]. To generate a semantic feature representation of a tweet, we make use of DBpedia information for all entities appearing on this content. The semantic feature generation consists of three stages: 1) entity extraction; 2) entity linking to DBpedia resources, and 3) generation of semantic features. We first extract entities from a tweet content using the AlchemyAPI entity extraction and Linked Data service.[4] This service takes a piece of text as an input, and returns a collection of annotated entities appearing in the given text. Each entity annotation provides both the entity type and a set of disambiguated links for this entity. An entity's disambiguated links include links pointing to DBpedia, Freebase,[5] and Yago[6] resources. In this analysis we only kept entities disambiguated to DBpedia resources. The following section describes the generation of time-based semantic features.

4.2 Time-Based Content Modeling

A *Resource Meta Graph* is an aggregation of all resources, properties and classes related to a resource [3]. Here we extend this definition by assigning a temporal marker to this graph:

---

[4] AlchemyAPI, http://www.alchemyapi.com/
[5] http://freebase.com
[6] http://www.mpi-inf.mpg.de/yago-naga/yago/

Definition 1 (Resource Meta Graph) *is a sequence of tuples* $\texttt{G} := (R, P, C, Y, f_t)$ *where*

- $\texttt{R, P, C}$ *are finite sets whose elements are* $\texttt{resources, properties,}$ *and* $\texttt{classes;}$
- $\texttt{Y}$ *is the ternary relation* $\texttt{Y} \subseteq \texttt{R} \times \texttt{P} \times \texttt{C}$ *representing a hypergraph with ternary edges. The hypergraph of a Resource Meta Graph* $\texttt{Y}$ *is defined as a tripartite graph* $\texttt{H}(\texttt{Y}) = \langle \texttt{V}, \texttt{D} \rangle$ *where the vertices are* $\texttt{V} = \texttt{R} \cup \texttt{P} \cup \texttt{C}$, *and the edges are:* $\texttt{D} = \{\{r, p, c\} \mid (r, p, c) \in Y\}$.
- f_t *is a function that assigns a temporal marker to each ternary edge.*

Therefore a meta graph of a resource provides additional contextual information regarding an entity at a given point in time. In this work we make use of the following features extracted from a resource meta graph:

- **Resource feature** (*Res*)**:** Consisting of the resource for which the semantic meta graph is derived. For example for the dbp:Barack_Obama resource.
- **Class Type features** (*Cls*)**:** Consisting of all classes appearing in the semantic meta graph of a resource that we derive from DBpedia. For example for the dbp:Barack-
  _Obama resource these features include dbo:OfficeHolder.
- **Category features** (*Cat*)**:** Consisting of all resources of type skos:Concept appearing in the DBpedia semantic meta graph of an entity. For example for the dbp:Barack_Obama resource these features include cat:Obama_family.
- **Property features** (*Prop*)**:** Consisting of all properties appearing on the DBpedia-derived semantic meta graph of an entity. For example for the dbp:Barack_Obama resource these features include foaf:givenName and dbo:writer.

Therefore a document can be represented by the semantic features derived from the entities it contains. One approach to weight the semantic feature vector of a document is to use a frequentist approach, like the Semantic Feature Frequency (SFF)[3] weighting strategy which computes the frequency of a feature on a document applying a Laplace smoothing. This SFF will be our baseline for comparing the set of weighting strategies introduced in the following subsection.

4.3 Topic-Relevance Strategy for Weighting Features with DBpedia

Rather than characterising the relevance of a feature on a resource's graph (as in [3] [26]), here we aim to characterise the global relevance of a semantic feature to a given topic in DBpedia at a given point in time. For this we propose a novel set of semantic feature weighting strategies which rely on the semantic representation of a topic derived from DBpedia. As discussed in Section 3, a topic such as War can be represented by the collection of resources belonging to the cat:War category, and resources from its subcategories. This collection of resources build a topic-based graph structure that characterises this topic and evolves as new resources are added to the DBpedia graph.

The following strategies make use of a time-stamped DBpedia Topic graph to derive a feature's relative importance to this topic at a given time. When analysing the children to parent category relations we set the number of traversing steps to 2. In order to capture the relative importance of a feature to a given topic, we propose the following weighting strategies:

- **Class-based Topic Relevance** (Cls_W): Weights a type-feature f as the ratio of the number of distinct resources whose rdf:type is f and are labeled with categories appearing on the Topic graph, and the number of resources of rdf:type f derived from a DBpedia graph at time t (DB_t). For example to weight the type dbo:OfficeHolder[7] in the context of the Topic War we compute this weight as depicted in Figure 3.

Fig. 3. Class Feature Weighting Strategy (Cls_W)

where DB_t[8] represents the DBpedia graph at time t. A higher weight means that the type feature f appears more often on resources derived from cat:War, therefore is more relevant to this Topic.

- **Property-based Topic Relevance** ($Prop_W$): Weights a property-feature f as the ratio of the number of distinct resources whose property is f and are labeled with categories appearing on the Topic graph; and the number of resources of type f derived from a DBpedia graph at time t (DB_t). For example to weigh the property dbProp:currency[9] in the context of the Topic War we compute this weight as depicted in Figure 4.

Fig. 4. Property Feature Weighting Strategy ($Prop_W$)

- **Category-based Topic Relevance** (Cat_W): Weighs a category-feature f based on the number of resources appearing on sibling categories, which are also descendants of the main Topic category; divided by the number of resources belonging to the category and subcategories of the main Topic category derived from a DBpedia graph at time t (DB_t). For example to weight the type cat:Conflict in the context of the Topic War we compute this weight as described in Figure 5:
- **Resource Relevance** (Res_W): This weighting strategy does not make use of the topic graph, but rather characterises the relevance of a resource by comparing it to other resources. It is defined as the ratio of the number of resources which share this resource's categories and the number of resources in DBpedia labelled by a category derived from a DBpedia graph at time t (DB_t). For example to weight the resource dbp:Barack_Obama[10] we compute this weight as described in Figure 6:

---

[7] dbo, qname for http://dbpedia.org/ontology/
[8] DBpedia graph snapshots are based on different DBpedia dumps described in section 5.
[9] dbProp, qname for http://dbpedia.org/property/
[10] dbp, qname for http://dbpedia.org/resource/

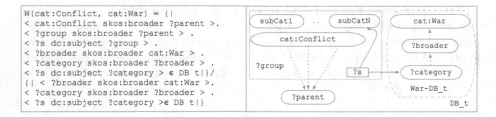

```
W(cat:Conflict, cat:War) = {|
< cat:Conflict skos:broader ?parent >.
< ?group skos:broader ?parent > .
< ?s dc:subject ?group > .
< ?broader skos:broader cat:War > .
< ?category skos:broader ?broader > .
< ?s dc:subject ?category > ∈ DB t|}/
{| < ?broader skos:broader cat:War >.
< ?category skos:broader ?broader > .
< ?s dc:subject ?category >∈ DB t|}
```

Fig. 5. Category Feature Weighting Strategy (Cat_W)

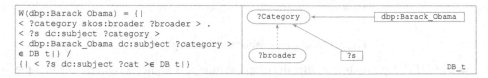

```
W(dbp:Barack Obama) = {|
< ?category skos:broader ?broader > .
< ?s dc:subject ?category >
< dbp:Barack_Obama dc:subject ?category >
∈ DB t|} /
{| < ?s dc:subject ?cat >∈ DB t|}
```

Fig. 6. Resource Feature Weighting Strategy (Res_W)

Once the semantic feature space of a corpus has been weighted based on the above weighting strategies, we integrate these weights into the feature representation of a tweet post by multiplying the number of times the feature appears on the document by the feature weight derived from the DBpedia graph ($\mathcal{DB}\_t$). Therefore the semantic feature f in a document x is weighted based on the frequency of a semantic feature f in a document x with Laplace smoothing and the topic-relevance of the feature in the $\mathcal{DB}\_t$ graph:

$$W_x(f)_{\mathcal{DB}\_t} = [\frac{[N_x(f)_{\mathcal{DB}\_t} + 1}{|F| + \sum_{f' \in F} N_x(f')_{\mathcal{DB}\_t}}] * (W_{\mathcal{DB}\_t}(f))^{1/2} \tag{1}$$

where $N_x(f)$ is the number of times feature f appears in all the semantic meta-graphs associated with document x derived from the $\mathcal{DB}\_t$ graph ; F is the semantic features' vocabulary of the semantic feature type and $W_{\mathcal{DB}\_t}(f)$ is the weighting function corresponding to the semantic feature type computed based on the $\mathcal{DB}\_t$ graph.[11] This weighting function captures the relative importance of a document's semantic features against the rest of the corpus and incorporates the topic-relative importance of these features in the $\mathcal{DB}\_t$ graph.

4.4 Construction of Time-Dependent Topic Classifiers

To characterise the time-dependent impact on the decay in performance of a topic classifier we focus on the binary topic classification task in cross-epoch-based scenarios. In these scenarios the classifier that we train on a corpus from epoch $t - 1$, is tested on a corpus on epoch t. We use our semantic graphs to characterise the two corpora, to verify our hypothesis that, as opposed to lexical features which are situation-dependent and can change progressively in time, semantic structures – including ontological classes and properties – can provide a more stable representation of a Topic in cross-epoch settings.

---

[11] Notice that the square root on the proposed weight aids to emphasize this value, since the order of magnitude of this weight tends to be low.

Following the weighting strategies in the previous section, the semantic feature representations of the $t - 1$ corpus and the t corpus, are both generated from the DBpedia graph available at $t - 1$. For example when applying a classifier trained on data from 2010, the feature space of a target test set from 2011 is computed based on the DBpedia version used for training the 2010-based classifier. This is in order to simulate the availability of resources in a DBpedia graph at a given time.[12]

5 Experimental Setup

In this section we introduce our datasets and present the experimental setting for evaluating the effectiveness of the proposed weighting strategies on a cross-epoch transfer learning task.

5.1 Dataset Description

Our datasets comprise two main collections: DBpedia and Twitter datasets. The DBpedia collection is comprised of four DBpedia dumps (3.6 to 3.9).[13] These dumps were installed on a Virtuoso server using separate named-graphs for each dump to facilitates dump-specific SPARQL queries. The DBpedia dumps allow us to extract semantic features for resources contained on a tweet, based on a specific DBpedia graph available at a particular epoch.

The Twitter datasets consist of a collection of Violence-related topics: Disaster_Accident, Law_Crime and War_Conflict. Each of these datasets comprises three epoch-based collections of tweets, corresponding to 2010, 2011, and 2013. The 2010 collection was gathered during November 2010 and December 2010 comprising over 1 million tweets. The 2011 collection was gathered during August 2011 also comprising over 1 million tweets. Finally the 2013 collection was sampled during September of 2013 also comprising of over 1 million tweets. To generate our gold standard we first labelled these tweets using the topic labelling service from OpenCalais[14] which classifies a tweet into 18 different categories.[15] Then for each year we retrieved those tweets with labels corresponding to "Disaster & Accident", "Law & Crime" and "War & Conflict".

Based on a random selection of 10,000 tweets for each year of each Topic we used the AlchemyAPI service to extract entities. Then we performed a manual annotation based only on those tweets which contained at least one resource. We stop the manual annotation of a randomly sorted sample for each Topic for each year when reaching 1,000 tweets per topic per year, giving us a total of 9,000 tweets. In order to generate a negative set for each year, we used a 10,000 sample of the OpenCalais annotated set with tweets annotated with categories other than these three. We also pre-filtered tweets which contained at least one entity. Since in this work our aim is topic characterisation rather than violence detection we decided to keep balanced sets. Therefore for each

---

[12] The comparison based on progressive availability of resources is future work.

[13] General statistics of these dumps are available at
http://wiki.dbpedia.org/Downloads39

[14] OpenCalais, http://www.opencalais.com

[15] Full list of OpenCalais categories, http://www.opencalais.com/documentation/calais-web-service-api/api-metadata/document-categorization

year we kept a manual annotation of 1,000 tweets which are not related to any of these three topics. Based on the manual re-annotation of two annotators (computer science researchers) we achieved an averaged inter-annotator Kappa score of 73.5%. The final Twitter dataset therefore contained 12,000 annotated tweets.

In order to derive the lexical features, these datasets were preprocessed by first removing punctuation, numbers, non-alphabet characters, stop words, and links. We then performed Porter stemming [20] in order to reduce the vocabulary size. To generate the semantic features we used the disambiguated DBpedia links provided by AlchemyAPI. However since Alchemy is based on the most recent DBpedia dump, we resolved each disambiguated DBpedia resource to the DBpedia dump available at the time in which the tweet was created. Therefore for each document we only kept those entities which existed on the DBpedia dump available at the time in which the tweet was created.

The general statistics of these datasets including semantic features is summarised in Table 1. In this work we follow a frequency-based weighting strategy, which is a common approach in Information Retrieval. However here we report that only 26% of the lexical features in our Twitter dataset have frequency greater than 1 on a document. For the semantic feature spaces we have the following distributions: Cat-11%,Prop-94.7%,Res-1%,Cls-29%[16]. Notice that for each cross-time setting scenario presented in Section 6 where a classifier at time t is tested on a dataset at $t + 1$, we recalculated the semantic features of the $t + 1$ dataset to point back to the DBpedia graph available at time t.

Table 1. Statistics of the lexical and semantic features extracted for the Disaster_Accident (D & A), Law_Crime (L & C), War_Conflict (W & C), and Negative (Neg) tweet collections. The reported statistics for Unigrams is after preprocessing.

		Unigram	Category	Properties	Resource	Class	tweets
D & A	2010	1,361	1,224	1,862	218	60	1,000
	2011	1,118	711	1,533	111	66	1,000
	2013	1,380	1,615	2,260	220	63	1,000
L & C	2010	1,427	1,577	1,795	213	65	1,000
	2011	1,012	870	1,698	111	70	1,000
	2013	1,288	1,530	2,202	208	104	1,000
W & C	2010	1,300	1,196	1,440	182	46	1,000
	2011	1,038	601	1,245	95	58	1,000
	2013	1,263	1,515	2,105	202	98	1,000
Neg	2010	1,634	2,044	2,167	229	86	1,000
	2011	1,244	1,562	2,080	160	101	1,000
	2013	1,194	1,896	2,048	162	114	1,000

Table 2, presents the top three lexical and semantic features ranked based on the SFF baseline strategy and based on our weighting strategies for the 2010 Law_Crime topic. The left column present the top semantic features ranked using our baseline (SFF) while the right column presents top features ranked using our semantic weighting strategies (SFG). Notice that while the frequency based strategy (SFF) seem to provide a representation specific to the current-situation modelling the Topic; the proposed SFG seem to provide a broader representation of the Topic based on the information derived from the DBpedia graph.

---

[16] Averaged for the three topics and three years.

Table 2. An extract of the feature space of the Law_Crime Topic of 2010. We also present the top three features for unigram. The qualified names used in this table are mapped as follows: [dbp, http://dbpedia.org/ontology], [dbc, http://dbpedia.org/resource/Category/], [dbpr, http://dbpedia.org/resource/], [dbpProp, http://dbpedia.org/property/], [gml, http://www.opengis.net/gml/], [skos, http://www.w3.org/2004/02/skos/core#], [foaf, http://xmlns.com/foaf/0.1/], [dc, http://purl.org/dc/terms/subject].

		2010-SFF		2010-SW	
Law_Crime	Lex	wikileak, arrest, law		wikileak, arrest, law	
	Cat	cat:Living_People, cat:G20_nations	cat:Liberal_democracies,	cat:Living_People, cat:Commercial_crimes	cat:Theft,
	$Prop$	dc:subject, foaf:name, dbpProp:leaderName		foaf:page, rdf:label, dbpProp:name	
	Res	dbpr:United_States, dbpr:Wikileaks	dbpr:Julian_Assange,	dbpr:Marc_Emery, dbpr:Reggie_Bush	dbpr:Erik_Bornmann,
	Cls	dbp:Place, gml:_Feature, dbp:PopulatedPlace		dbp:Work, dbp:Criminal, dbp:Person	

5.2 Experimental Setting

To assess the features temporal impact on a classification task we use as a baseline the performance of a topic classifier trained and tested on an epoch t. In this case we assess performance differences when a classifier is tested on future epochs as we described in Section 4.4. We use the standard weighting strategies as a baseline (i.e., TF-IDF for BoW and SFF for semantic features[17]) to compare against the weighting ones introduced in section 4.2.

To test whether semantic features can aid on this cross-epoch transfer learning task, we performed the following series of experiments. For each topic we built supervised topic classifiers using the independent feature types (i.e., bag of words features [BoW], semantic features –class [Cls], property [Prop], category [Cat], resource [Res]–) and the merged features (i.e., joint-semantic features, [Sem], and the BoW + semantic features [All]). In this collection of classifiers features were weighted based on our baseline weighting strageties: TF-IDF for the BoW features and SFF for the semantic features ($\_SFF$). We also generated the same set of classifiers but this time using the SFG weighting strategies ($\_SFG$) introduced in Section 4. We also generated merged settings, here Sem_{SFF} and Sem_{SFG} correspond to classifiers trained on joint semantic features weighted with SFF and SFG respectively. Sem_{joint} refers to classifiers using all semantic features weighted with the $SFF+SFG$ setting. The All classifiers are based on the semantic + BoW settings; the subscript indicates the weighting scheme.

6 Experimental Results

In this section we address the following questions: *Do semantic features built from DBpedia Graphs aid on a cross-epoch transfer learning task for the topic classification of Tweets? if so, to what extent can these semantic features help the classification task?* In our experiments we used Support Vector Machine (SVM) [6] with polynomial kernel classifiers. All the experiments reported here were conducted using a 10-fold cross validation setting [22][14].

---

[17] We used the SSF weighting strategy in order to have a one to one comparison based on semantic feature types. This is the reason why we did not include the class-property co-occurrence frequency [3] strategy in our baseline.

Table 3. Performance of the classifiers trained and tested on the same epoch. The classifiers where applied on testsets weighted based on the classifier weighting scheme. The values highlighted in bold correspond to the best results obtained in F measure for each topic and each year. A $\star$ denotes that the P-measure of a given weighted feature significantly outperforms the corresponding SFF baseline. Significance levels: p-value < 0.01.

	Dissaster_Acc			Law_Crime			War_Conflict		
	P	R	$F1$	P	R	$F1$	P	R	$F1$
BoW	0.855	0.809	**0.831**	0.776	0.756	**0.765**	0.868	0.821	**0.844**
Cat_{SFF}	0.740	0.661	0.697	0.639	0.663	0.650	0.781	0.712	0.744
Cat_{SFG}	0.744	0.546	0.629	0.731	0.458	0.562	0.797	0.698	0.743
Cat_{joint}	0.769	0.608	0.678	0.716	0.508	0.594	0.793	0.686	0.735
$Props_{SFF}$	0.720	0.646	0.680	0.612	0.671	0.639	0.749	0.694	0.720
$Props_{SFG}$	0.711	0.618	0.659	0.584	0.697	0.635	0.735	0.678	0.705
$Prop_{joint}$	0.734	0.623	0.673	0.588	0.685	0.632	0.759	0.679	0.716
Res_{SFF}	0.773	0.627	0.692	0.724	0.569	0.637	0.812	0.720	0.762
Res_{SFG}	0.776	0.567	0.654	0.749	0.499	0.599	0.812	0.656	0.725
Res_{joint}	0.775	0.600	0.675	0.751	0.510	0.607	0.821	0.677	0.741
Cls_{SFF}	0.637	0.631	0.633	0.552	0.629	0.583	0.688	0.595	0.637
Cls_{SFG}	0.632	0.608	0.619	0.582	0.486	0.527	0.666	0.573	0.614
Cls_{joint}	0.635	0.606	0.619	0.583	0.510	0.542	0.684	0.584	0.628
Sem_{SFF}	0.746	0.700	0.720	0.639	0.683	0.659	0.782	0.740	0.760
Sem_{SFG}	0.685	0.773	0.725	0.629	0.738	0.678	0.757	0.740	0.748
Sem_{joint}	0.777$\star$	0.652	0.708	0.716$\star$	0.553	0.623	0.795$\star$	0.715	0.752
All_{SFF}	0.817	0.791	0.803	0.761	0.766	0.763	0.851	0.830	0.840
All_{SFG}	0.807	0.814	0.809	0.764	0.789	0.776	0.847	0.837	0.841
All_{joint}	0.829	0.769	0.797	0.782	0.726	0.752	0.860	0.814	0.836
BoW	0.899	0.853	**0.875**	0.868	0.808	**0.836**	0.905	0.860	**0.882**
Cat_{SFF}	0.841	0.735	0.784	0.830	0.697	0.756	0.881	0.817	0.847
Cat_{SFG}	0.848	0.698	0.765	0.849	0.681	0.755	0.881	0.798	0.837
Cat_{joint}	0.852	0.724	0.782	0.842	0.683	0.753	0.879	0.806	0.840
$Props_{SFF}$	0.815	0.722	0.765	0.763	0.661	0.706	0.856	0.806	0.830
$Props_{SFG}$	0.812	0.714	0.759	0.780	0.652	0.709	0.872	0.797	0.832
$Prop_{joint}$	0.825	0.716	0.766	0.778	0.656	0.711	0.856	0.797	0.824
Res_{SFF}	0.856	0.736	0.791	0.849	0.706	0.770	0.886	0.810	0.846
Res_{SFG}	0.882	0.702	0.781	0.871	0.655	0.746	0.896	0.779	0.832
Res_{joint}	0.880	0.699	0.779	0.865	0.679	0.760	0.893	0.788	0.837
Cls_{SFF}	0.714	0.712	0.712	0.700	0.616	0.653	0.824	0.773	0.797
Cls_{SFG}	0.716	0.710	0.712	0.705	0.584	0.636	0.814	0.761	0.786
Cls_{joint}	0.714	0.709	0.711	0.697	0.613	0.650	0.811	0.761	0.784
Sem_{SFF}	0.814	0.761	0.786	0.805	0.729	0.764	0.861	0.824	0.841
Sem_{SFG}	0.807	0.767	0.786	0.774	0.727	0.748	0.855	0.823	0.838
Sem_{joint}	0.831$\star$	0.744	0.784	0.824$\star$	0.714	0.764	0.871$\star$	0.809	0.838
All_{SFF}	0.876	0.846	0.861	0.843	0.804	0.822	0.882	0.844	0.862
All_{SFG}	0.884	0.858	0.870	0.846	0.814	0.829	0.884	0.853	0.868
All_{joint}	0.878	0.844	0.860	0.856	0.787	0.819	0.887	0.836	0.860
BoW	0.862	0.806	**0.833**	0.875	0.832	**0.852**	0.870	0.808	**0.838**
Cat_{SFF}	0.774	0.687	0.727	0.798	0.682	0.734	0.756	0.657	0.701
Cat_{SFG}	0.807	0.625	0.704	0.817	0.634	0.713	0.780	0.606	0.681
Cat_{joint}	0.791	0.658	0.717	0.826	0.644	0.723	0.788	0.622	0.694
$Props_{SFF}$	0.762	0.680	0.718	0.771	0.682	0.723	0.742	0.657	0.696
$Props_{SFG}$	0.748	0.657	0.699	0.772	0.680	0.722	0.753	0.665	0.705
$Prop_{joint}$	0.768	0.672	0.716	0.777	0.673	0.720	0.765	0.665	0.711
Res_{SFF}	0.788	0.660	0.718	0.821	0.663	0.733	0.787	0.611	0.687
Res_{SFG}	0.800	0.623	0.700	0.836	0.634	0.720	0.804	0.606	0.690
Res_{joint}	0.806	0.614	0.696	0.836	0.632	0.719	0.813	0.578	0.673
Cls_{SFF}	0.707	0.659	0.680	0.745	0.657	0.697	0.694	0.653	0.671
Cls_{SFG}	0.717	0.609	0.657	0.750	0.647	0.693	0.704	0.649	0.672
Cls_{joint}	0.716	0.634	0.671	0.748	0.658	0.699	0.702	0.674	0.686
Sem_{SFF}	0.767	0.719	0.741	0.772	0.725	0.747	0.751	0.706	0.728
Sem_{SFG}	0.741	0.762	0.751	0.754	0.755	0.754	0.736	0.743	0.739
Sem_{joint}	0.778$\star$	0.694	0.733	0.803$\star$	0.681	0.736	0.770$\star$	0.656	0.708
All_{SFF}	0.832	0.799	0.814	0.844	0.800	0.821	0.836	0.804	0.819
All_{SFG}	0.837	0.824	0.830	0.845	0.821	0.832	0.835	0.819	0.827
All_{joint}	0.844	0.781	0.811	0.854	0.779	0.814	0.840	0.764	0.799

The three blocks correspond to the years 2010, 2011, and 2013 respectively.

6.1 Evaluation of Semantic Features on Same-Epoch Scenarios

In order to assess the benefit of using semantic features in topic classification, we start by studying their role when a topic classifier is trained and tested on the same epoch.

Table 3 shows the results of topic classifiers trained and tested on the same years and datasets, using (1) BoW features (i.e., lexical features); (2) baseline semantic features weighted based on SFF (Section 4.2); (3) semantic features with our graph-based weighting strategies (SFG, Section 4.3); (4) using joint semantic features (Sem); and (5) using the joint BoW and semantic features (All).

Results show that in same-epoch scenarios, BoW features outperform all semantic features in topic classification. They also show that while results with SFF are better than with SFG in almost all cases, their joint use outperform the SFF baseline in P. These are interesting, but unsurprising results. This is because the training and classification are done on the same dataset and epoch, and hence the current data content should be more representative of the topic. However this set of same-year results become our baseline against cross-epoch settings (where these classifiers are tested on future epochs).

6.2 Evaluation of Semantic Features on Cross-Epoch Scenarios

Now we study the performance of our BoW and semantic features when the training is done on one epoch and the classification is applied to another. This will help us understand how these features decay across epochs.

Table 4 presents results for three cross-epoch scenarios for the Disaster_Accident (Dis_Acc) topic. Each X-Y column refers to the performance of a classifier trained on epoch X and tested on epoch Y. The last column presents the average results of this topic across these cross-epoch scenarios. Comparing the performance of the Dis_Acc 2010 classifier (Table 3) with the 2010-2011, and 2010-2013 results (Table 4) we observe a consistent drop in F measure when this Dis_Acc 2010 TC is applied using BoW features. The same occurs when comparing performance of Dis_Acc 2011 when applied to 2013. Moreover we observe that for this Topic all individual semantic features types -weighted with SFF, SFG and SFF+SFG (Joint)–, consistently outperform the BoW baseline in F-measure. When analysing the overall contribution of semantic features we observe that in average all semantic features weighted with SFG (Sem_{SFG}) significantly improve P when compared to the SFF baseline (Sem_{SFF}) (t-test with $\alpha < 0.01$), while consistently improve F-measure when compared to the averaged BoW features (t-test with $\alpha < 0.01$).

To compare the benefit of the proposed weighting strategies across all topics we computed the averaged P, R, F1 across epochs for each Topic. These averages, presented in Table 5, show that in average the merged SFG $(Sem_{SFG}$ features significantly outperforms the merged SFF (Sem_{SFF}) features (t-test with $\alpha < 0.01$) classifiers by 4.3%. These results also show that on cross-epoch scenarios, on average, some individual semantic features-based classifiers outperform the BoW classifier in F-measure obtaining a maximum increment of 16.37% (t-test with $\alpha < 0.01$) when using the Cls_{joint} weighted feature. Moreover Class semantic features(Cls) alone (ClsSFF, ClsSFG, ClsJoint) in average consistently outperform BoW in F with a gain of 12.5% for all cross-epoch scenarios for all three topics. This demostrates that the use of Cls semantic features alone compared to lexical features is benefitial in characterising a topic in time.

Table 4. Presents results for the cross-epoch scenarios for the Disaster_Accident topic. A ⋆ denotes that the P-measure of the shaded cell significantly outperforms their corresponding SFF baseline. A † denotes that the F-measure of a weighted feature outperforms the BoW baseline. Significance levels: p-value < 0.01.

		2010-2011			2010-2013			2011-2013			Average	
		P	R	F1	P	R	F1	P	R	F1	P	R	F1
	BoW	0.807	0.526	0.634	0.773	0.350	0.481	0.857	0.155	0.261	0.812	0.343	0.458
	Cat_{SFF}	0.721	0.650	0.683	0.696	0.443	0.539	0.808	0.389	0.524	0.741	0.494	0.582
	Cat_{SFG}	0.766	0.613	0.677	0.766	0.483	0.592	0.809	0.468	0.592	0.780	0.521	0.620
	Cat_{Joint}	0.798	0.645	0.713	0.734	0.310	0.434	0.818	0.381	0.518	0.783	0.445	0.555
	$Props_{SFF}$	0.708	0.631	0.665	0.656	0.486	0.557	0.718	0.387	0.502	0.694	0.501	0.574
	$Props_{SFG}$	0.689	0.676	0.681	0.668	0.489	0.564	0.750	0.453	0.564	0.702	0.539	0.603
Disaster_Acc	$Prop_{Joint}$	0.724	0.652	0.686	0.686	0.480	0.564	0.717	0.352	0.470	0.709	0.494	0.573
	Res_{SFF}	0.794	0.756	0.774	0.723	0.438	0.544	0.770	0.317	0.445	0.762	0.503	0.587
	Res_{SFG}	0.818	0.752	0.783	0.791	0.486	0.599	0.786	0.299	0.423	0.798	0.512	0.601
	Res_{Joint}	0.806	0.754	0.779	0.765	0.477	0.586	0.788	0.284	0.409	0.786	0.505	0.591
	Cls_{SFF}	0.684	0.701	0.691	0.666	0.667	0.665	0.705	0.638	0.669	0.685	0.668	0.675
	Cls_{SFG}	0.679	0.700	0.689	0.663	0.657	0.660	0.700	0.644	0.670	0.680	0.667	0.673
	Cls_{Joint}	0.688	0.704	0.695	0.668	0.656	0.661	0.699	0.640	0.667	0.685	0.666	0.674
	Sem_{SFF}	0.720	0.683	0.700	0.699	0.493	0.578	0.814	0.411	0.545	0.744	0.529	0.607
	Sem_{SFG}	0.755⋆	0.599	0.668†	0.776⋆	0.371	0.501†	0.816⋆	0.333	0.472†	0.782⋆	0.434	0.547†
	Sem_{Joint}	0.781⋆	0.623	0.693†	0.720⋆	0.402	0.515†	0.815†	0.313	0.451†	0.772⋆	0.446	0.553†
	All_{SFF}	0.768	0.555	0.642	0.771	0.428	0.549	0.845	0.205	0.330	0.565	0.396	0.457
	All_{SFG}	0.791⋆	0.546	0.644†	0.724⋆	0.388	0.505†	0.850⋆	0.210	0.335†	0.788⋆	0.381	0.494†
	All_{Joint}	0.798⋆	0.527	0.632	0.791⋆	0.372	0.504†	0.844⋆	0.168	0.279†	0.811⋆	0.355	0.471†

We also observe that when incorporating BoW to the semantic feature space – extended feature representation of a document, where a tweet is represented using its lexical+semantic features – we consistently outperform the BoW baseline for the three joint settings (All_{SFG}, All_{SFG}, All_{joint}) with the highest F-measure achieved by the All_{SFG} classifier. This setting significantly outperforms the BoW classifier in F-measure by 1.6% (t-test with $\alpha < 0.01$) while providing the best precision across semantic features. This positive increment indicates that the incorporation of external knowledge (DBpedia-graph) in the cross-epoch transfer learning task is beneficial when applied jointly with document derived weighting strategies.

We analyse the relevance decay of features based on performance gain on the cross-epoch scenarios. These is calculated by comparing the cross-scenario performance of each classifier against the performance of the corresponding classifier on the same-year scenario (e.g. 2010-2011 compared against 2010). The heatmap to the left in Figure 7 presents our results for all features. The heatmap to the right in Figure 7 presents the averaged gain on BoW for three cross-epochs for each Topic. The heatmap to the left presents average gain on F-measure on a cross-scenario compared against its corresponding same-year scenario classifier. A higher value indicates that the feature adapts better (i.e. lower decay) in a cross-epoch setting, while a lower value indicates that on average the feature is less relevant for a topic on a cross-epoch setting. The heatmap to the right presents the average gain on BoW F-measure on a cross-scenario compared against its corresponding BoW gain on a same-year scenario classifier. Here a higher value indicates that a feature adapts better than the BoW on a cross-epoch setting, while a lower value indicate otherwise. Here we observe that on a cross-epoch setting the Cls semantic features are highly relevant for the cross-epoch learning task. Moreover based on these results, these semantic feature appears to provide more stable (i.e. lower decay)

Table 5. Average results for the cross-epoch scenarios for each topic. The last column present the average results of all three topics. A $\star$ denotes that the P-measure of the shaded cell significantly outperforms their corresponding SFF baseline. A † denotes that the F-measure of a weighted feature outperforms the BoW baseline. Significance levels: p-value < 0.01.

	Disaster_Acc			Law_Crime			War_Conflict			Average		
	P	R	$F1$	P	R	$F1$	P	R	$F1$	P	R	$F1$
BoW	0.812	0.343	0.458	0.739	0.549	0.620	0.873	0.394	0.531	0.808	0.429	0.536
Cat_{SFF}	0.741	0.494	0.582	0.641	0.479	0.537	0.774	0.325	0.453	0.719	0.433	0.524
Cat_{SFG}	0.780	0.521	0.620	0.769	0.432	0.549	0.803	0.350	0.480	0.784	0.434	0.55
Cat_{Joint}	0.783	0.445	0.555	0.766	0.426	0.542	0.777	0.280	0.406	0.775	0.383	0.501
$Props_{SFF}$	0.694	0.501	0.574	0.604	0.445	0.504	0.755	0.411	0.506	0.684	0.452	0.528
$Props_{SFG}$	0.702	0.539	0.603	0.596	0.468	0.509	0.731	0.391	0.460	0.676	0.460	0.524
$Prop_{Joint}$	0.709	0.494	0.573	0.618	0.462	0.518	0.767	0.383	0.487	0.698	0.446	0.526
Res_{SFF}	0.762	0.503	0.587	0.756	0.473	0.578	0.773	0.338	0.466	0.764	0.438	0.544
Res_{SFG}	0.798	0.512	0.601	0.757	0.428	0.539	0.771	0.337	0.448	0.775	0.426	0.529
Res_{Joint}	0.786	0.505	0.591	0.761	0.413	0.528	0.786	0.307	0.432	0.777	0.408	0.517
Cls_{SFF}	0.685	0.668	0.675	0.626	0.679	0.647	0.764	0.599	0.660	0.692	0.649	0.660
Cls_{SFG}	0.680	0.667	0.673	0.668	0.617	0.640	0.724	0.632	0.661	0.691	0.638	0.658
Cls_{Joint}	0.685	0.666	0.674	0.669	0.645	0.656	0.761	0.608	0.664	0.705	0.640	0.665
Sem_{SFF}	0.744	0.529	0.607	0.603	0.457	0.509	0.778	0.329	0.459	0.708	0.438	0.525
Sem_{SFG}	0.782	0.434	0.547	0.710	0.384	0.494	0.762	0.302	0.431	0.751	0.373	0.490
Sem_{Joint}	0.772	0.446	0.553	0.734	0.397	0.512	0.743	0.369	0.490	0.75	0.404	0.518
All_{SFF}	0.565	0.396	0.507	0.709	0.507	0.586	0.819	0.387	0.520	0.774	0.43	0.537
All_{SFG}	0.788$\star$	0.381	0.494	0.756$\star$	0.523	0.613	0.859$\star$	0.411	0.550	0.801$\star$	0.438	0.552†
All_{Joint}	0.811	0.355	0.471	0.762	0.471	0.578	0.795	0.449	0.571	0.789$\star$	0.425	0.540†

information than the one provided by the BoW. In this case the Cls_{joint} exhibits a gain which exceeds on over 7% the BoW one.

Finally to analyse the gain over BoW on the cross-epochs, we computed gain differences on the BoW F-measure obtained by each feature, and compared it with the one of the same-year scenarios. These results indicate that on average the Cls features exhibit a lower decay when compared to the BoW providing a more stable F-measure on the cross-epoch scenarios.

Dis_Acc	Law_Crime	War_Conf		Dis_Acc	Law_Crime	War_Conf	
0.041	-0.046	-0.088	AllJoint	0.013	-0.042	0.039	AllJoint
0.038	-0.059	-0.046	AllSFF	0.0483	-0.034	-0.011	AllSFF
0.022	-0.038	-0.035	AllSFG	0.036	-0.006	0.018	AllSFG
0.022	-0.007	0.009	BoW	0.096	-0.078	-0.125	CatJoint
0.018	0.006	-0.098	CatJoint	0.123	-0.083	-0.078	CatSFF
0.029	-0.023	-0.071	CatSFF	0.161	-0.0706	-0.051	CatSFG
0.081	0.025	-0.023	CatSFG	0.215	0.035	0.133	ClsJoint
0.054	0.04	0.141	ClsJoint	0.216	0.027	0.128	ClsSFF
0.044	0.013	0.138	ClsSFF	0.214	0.019	0.13	ClsSFG
0.051	0.036	0.147	ClsSFG	0.114	-0.102	-0.044	PropJoint
0.066	-0.02	0.053	PropJoint	0.089	-0.067	0.0733	PropSFF
0.041	-0.051	0.066	PropSFF	0.144	-0.111	-0.071	PropSFG
0.04	0.032	0.148	PropSFG	0.132	-0.091	-0.099	ResJoint
0.128	0.038	-0.036	ResJoint	0.129	-0.042	-0.065	ResSFF
0.093	0.035	-0.069	ResSFF	0.143	-0.081	-0.083	ResSFG
0.144	0.037	0.028	ResSFG	0.149	-0.111	-0.0726	SemFF
0.026	-0.055	-0.065	SemFF	0.094	-0.107	-0.0416	SemJoint
0.041	-0.018	-0.087	SemJoint	0.088	-0.126	-0.1	SemSFG
0.011	-0.051	-0.075	SemSFG				
Dis_Acc	Law_Crime	War_Conf		Dis_Acc	Law_Crime	War_Conf	

Fig. 7. Averaged gain on BoW for three cross-epochs for each Topic

7   Discussion

In this paper we introduce a novel approach to the cross-epoch transfer learning task. This approach proposes the use of semantic features as a more stable representation of a topic over time. While the proposed set of weighting strategies is based on heuristics, other weighting strategies could be studied in future work. Such strategies could be enhanced with methods and results from work on ontology and linked data searching, ranking, and summarisation. Also other lexical features (e.g. part-of-speech) and structure information (e.g. WordNet)[18] could be used along with semantic features to improve performance.

The limited availability of annotated datasets spanning across longer periods of time made us focus only on a range of three different epochs. This work could be further expanded by considering longer periods of time, and by experimenting with different type of topics. So far we have demostrated that for the violence-related topics the Cls feature exhibited the lowest relevance decay on the transfer learning task. For these topics some individual features were less performing that others. However further research is necessary to understand what makes a semantic feature a good option for the cross-epoch modeling task depending on the type of topic.

8   Conclusions and Future Work

In this paper we proposed the use of semantic features to approach the cross-epoch transfer learning task for topic classification of tweets. Moreover we introduced a framework which proposes to enrich semantic features by incorporating information derived from an external knowledge source. The framework introduced a set of weighting strategies which calculates the relevance of features from time-stamped topic graphs extracted from DBpedia. Our results showed that semantic features are much slower to decay than other features, and that they can improve performance upon traditional BoW-based classifiers in cross-epoch scenarios. Furthermore, results showed that the proposed strategies improve performance upon our baseline while outperforming F-measure upon BoW features. These results demonstrate the feasibility of the use of semantic features in epoch-based transfer learning tasks. This opens new possibilities for the research of concept drift tracking for transfer learning based on existing Linked Data sources. Future work includes the comparison of semantic feature based transfer learning with other state of the art transfer learning approaches based on lexical features.

Acknowledgements. This work was partially supported by European Project Sense4us (611242).

References

1. Blitzer, J., McDonald, R., Pereira, F.: Domain adaptation with structural correspondence learning. In: Proc. Conf. on EMNLP (2006)
2. Cano, E., He, Y., Liu, K., Zhao, J.: A weakly supervised bayesian model for violence detection in social media. In: Proc. 6th IJCNLP 2013 (2013)

---

[18] WordNet, http://wordnet.princeton.edu/

3. Cano, A.E., Varga, A., Rowe, M., Ciravegna, F., He, Y.: Harnessing linked knowledge source for topic classification in social media. In: Proc. 24th ACM Conf. on Hypertext and Social Media, Paris, France (2013)

4. Caruana, R.: Multitask learning. 28(1), 41–75 (1997)

5. Chen, G.H., Nikolov, S., Shah, D.: A latent source model for nonparametric time series classification. In: Advances in Neural Information Processing Systems (2013)

6. Cristianini, N., Shawe-Taylor, J.: An Introduction to Support Vector Machines: And Other Kernel-Based Learning Methods. Cambridge University Press (2000)

7. Daumé, I.: Frustratingly easy domain adaptation. In: Proceedings of the 2007 ACL (2007)

8. Diao, Q., Jiang, J., Zhu, F., Lim, E.-P.: Finding bursty topics from microblogs. In: Proc. 50th Annual Meeting of the ACL, Jeju Island, Korea (2012)

9. Dries, A., Rückert, U.: Adaptive concept drift detection. Stat. Anal. Data Min. 2(56) (2009)

10. Genc, Y., Sakamoto, Y., Nickerson, J.V.: Discovering context: Classifying tweets through a semantic transform based on wikipedia. In: Schmorrow, D.D., Fidopiastis, C.M. (eds.) FAC 2011. LNCS, vol. 6780, pp. 484–492. Springer, Heidelberg (2011)

11. He, Y.: Incorporating sentiment prior knowledge for weakly supervised sentiment analysis. ACM Transactions on Asian Language Information Processing 11(2), 4:1–4:19 (2012)

12. He, Y., Lin, C., Gao, W., Wong, K.-F.: Tracking sentiment and topic dynamics from social media. In: Proc. of the Sixth Int. Conf. on Weblogs and Social Media, Dublin, Ireland (2012)

13. Jones, K.S., Walker, S., Robertson, S.E.: A probabilistic model of information retrieval: Development and comparative experiments. Inf. Process. Manage. 36(6), 779–808 (2000)

14. Kohavi, R.: A study of cross-validation and bootstrap for accuracy estimation and model selection. In: Proc. 14th IJCAI, vol. 2 (1995)

15. Lv, W., Xu, W., Guo, J.: Transfer learning in classification based on semantic analysis. In: 2nd Int. Conf. on ICCSNT (2012)

16. Milikic, N., Jovanovic, J., Stankovic, M.: Discovering the dynamics of terms semantic relatedness through twitter. In: Proceedings, 1st Workshop on #MSM 2011 (2011)

17. Muñoz García, O., García-Silva, A., Corcho, O., de la Higuera Hernández, M., Navarro, C.: Identifying Topics in Social Media Posts using DBpedia. In: Proc. of the NEM Summit (2011)

18. Pan, S.J., Yang, Q.: A survey on transfer learning. IEEE Trans. on Knowl. and Data Eng. 22(10), 1345–1359 (2010)

19. Phan, X.-H., Nguyen, L.-M., Horiguchi, S.: Learning to classify short and sparse text & web with hidden topics from large-scale data collections. In: Proc. 17th Int. Conf. on World Wide Web, WWW 2008, Beijing, China (2008)

20. Porter, M.: An algorithm for suffix stripping. Program 14(3) (1980)

21. Saif, H., Fernandez, M., He, Y., Alani, H.: Senticircles for contextual and conceptual semantic sentiment analysis of twitter. In: Presutti, V., d'Amato, C., Gandon, F., d'Aquin, M., Staab, S., Tordai, A. (eds.) ESWC 2014. LNCS, vol. 8465, pp. 83–98. Springer, Heidelberg (2014)

22. Salzberg, S.L., Fayyad, U.: On comparing classifiers: Pitfalls to avoid and a recommended approach. In: Data Mining and Knowledge Discovery, pp. 317–328 (1997)

23. Song, Y., Wang, H., Wang, Z., Li, H., Chen, W.: Short text conceptualization using a probabilistic knowledgebase. In: Int. Joint. Conf. of AI (IJCAI). IJCAI/AAAI (2011)

24. Sriram, B., Fuhry, D., Demir, E., Ferhatosmanoglu, H., Demirbas, M.: Short text classification in twitter to improve information filtering. In: Proc. of the Int. ACM SIGIR (2010)

25. Thrun, S.: Is learning the n-th thing any easier than learning the first? In: Advances in Neural Information Processing Systems (1996)

26. Varga, A., Cano, A., Rowe, M., Ciravegna, F., He, Y.: Linked knowledge sources for topic classification of microposts: A semantic graph-based approach. In: JWS: Science, Services and Agents on the WWW (2014)

27. Zhao, X., Shu, B., Jiang, J., Song, Y., Yan, H., Li, X.: Identifying event-related bursts via social media activities. In: Proc. of the Joint Conference on EMNLP, Jeju Island, Korea (2012)

Linked Open Data Driven Game Generation

Rob Warren[1] and Erik Champion[2]

[1] Big Data Institute,
Dalhousie University,
Halifax, Canada
rhwarren@dal.ca
[2] School of Media, Culture and Creative Arts,
Curtin University,
WA, Australia
erik.champion@curtin.edu.au

Abstract. Linked Open Data provides a means of unified access to large and complex interconnected data sets that concern themselves with a surprising breath and depth of topics. This unified access in turn allows for the consumption of this data for modelling cultural heritage sites, historical events or creating serious games. In the following paper we present our work on simulating the terrain of a Great War battle using data from multiple Linked Open Data projects.

Keywords: Simulations, Consuming Linked Open Data, Serious Games.

1 Introduction

Linked Open Data (LOD, [1]) has created new avenues for content publishers to distribute their data while providing detailed linkages and annotations. We report here on a prototype method for automated Linked Open Data driven procedural game generation. This was a part of an interdisciplinary partnership between The Games Institute at the University of Waterloo, The Big Data Institute at Dalhousie University and the School of Media, Culture & Arts at Curtin University. The collaboration is the result of discussions on the generalizability and implementations of approaches such as Distant Reading [2], operational history and virtual heritage [3] using Big Data and Linked Open Data.

1.1 Simulation as an Information Retrieval Interface

The amount of information available digitally is increasing and the use of Linked Open Data approaches have made it a) available through standardized interfaces within structures that are self-documenting and b) these structures and their definitions can be linked across to different data sets.

These two items are most relevant in that they allow the retrieval of the information through a standardized interface while ensuring it relevancy through complex querying. Simulations, visualizations and games[1] have long been known

---

[1] In the course of this paper, we will use 3D simulation, visualization and game as interchangeable terms.

P. Mika et al. (Eds.) ISWC 2014, Part II, LNCS 8797, pp. 358–373, 2014.

to be effective means of communicating information. However their design and construction is a crafting process that is multidisciplinary, intuitive and does not lend itself easily to mass customization.

Because of the linkability and the built-in ontological support of linked open data, we believe the data-integration cost significantly lowered and that generalized information retrieval through simulation is now possible. As an example, the queries that unite Linked Geo Data, DBPedia and Muninn data to generate flora information in Section 4.2 can be hard-coded using conventional SQL and/or XML databases. However, the use of public facing SPARQL interfaces and OWL ontological constructs allow us to retrieve the data without requiring special access to the databases like conventional databases would.

Google Earth is a analogous example of a standardized visualization engine that represents data from multiple concurrent sources each with its own API, data definitions and administrative process. The ongoing data reach of Google Earth is only possible through the large ecosystem supported by Google that ensures the ongoing maintenance of the data-source specific translation mechanisms.

The objective of this research direction is not to replace the simulation designer, but rather automate a number of processes that are fundamentally sophisticated information retrieval and processing. This automation has already occurred with areas such as game physics which are now mostly handled by the game engine instead of the game designer. This is the next logical step as we move from one-off game designs to game engines, to manual content generation, to the current procedural game generation and then to this proposed linked open data-driven game generation.

This paper reviews our initial attempt at creating a generalizable engine capable of making use of Linked Open Data to construct a simulation. We also state that these simulations as realistic not because of the visual accuracy of the rendering, but in that the events, places and things that occur within the simulation are based on documented facts.

The organisation of the paper is as follows: we first discuss previous work and the benefits of using LOD for simulations, followed by a description of a prototype based on the events of the Great War using data from the Muninn Project, a LOD project focused on the Great War. We then review some of the lessons learned from the exercise and we close with a discussion of ongoing work on the methodologies needed to consume data in context.

2 Previous Work

Data driven simulations are not new and in common use with Building Information Management [4], Cultural Heritage [5] and even recreational game development. Concurrently, Linked Open Data has been used extensively for describing archival [6] and bibliographic [7] material and as well as GIS data [8]. A renewed interest in the ideas of the Venice Charter is driving the markup and storage of Cultural Heritage data using LOD formats owing to its ability to record data in a long lasting description format.

Linked Open Data is seen as a desirable technology for Digital Humanities especially those focused on the Galleries, Libraries, Archives and Museums (GLAM) industries. LOD for cultural heritage allows updateable information, closer collaboration with archival institutes and more responsive design for different platforms while being aligned with some of ideas of the London Charter on cultural heritage visualization.

Using LOD to procedurally create content directly from a live database on a as-needed basis is the next logical step that builds on previous works on procedural content generation and the Semantic Virtual Environment [9]. From the game generation perspective, a taxonomy of possible methods is reviewed by Togelius et al. [10] with some early work on [11,12] Procedural Content Generation (PCG). Kallman and Thalman [13] proposed the precursor of current "prefabricated" objects within games by having an event model where different objects could interact with one another. Müller et al. [14] and Andrés et al. [15] also using combined photogrammetric and procedural modelling to build models of a city in a automatable fashion.

Tutenel et al. [16] primarily saw the semantics problem of the data as a means of tracking the contents within games and keeping track of the physical constraints at design time. Vanacken et al. [17] used a similar approach using Ontology Web Language (OWL) to track objects within the virtual world and their properties. The Semantic Virtual Environment (SVE) was proposed by Otto [9] where the minutia of the virtual environment was linked to a semantic web database holding the properties and hierarchy of the environment. The intent was to have a higher level knowledge system of the items within the virtual environment using inheritance of properties between object classes. Fuhrmann et al. [18] designed an ontology to record the appearance and organisation of clothing within a virtual environment so that it could be procedurally generated while Gutiérrez et al. [19] human beings ontology where a person's motions were related to ensure realistic motion. Games With A Purpose (GWAP) have also been proposed [20] as a means of acquiring ontological or annotation data. Most recently Fribeger and Togelius [21] made use of LOD to create a Monopoly-like board game customized to a locality. Reitmayr et al. [22] used a similar concept with augmented reality to relate objects within the world to external data sources, such as web pages. Grimaldo et al. [23] saw the semantics and ontological aspects primarily as a means of negotiating relationships and behaviours between objects within the virtual world.

A large part of procedural game design was the simulation and creation of "game level" as outlined by Tutenel et al. in 2008 [24]. While the procedural generation of game terrain through the detailed simulation of an ecosystem, as described by Dussel et al. [25] can be simulated from scratch, the trade-off between random simulation and data-driven parameter simulation is based on the data available for the simulation. In a similar vein, Lu et al. [26] reviewed simulation of weathering, rusting and cracking of paint based on both computation simulations of the break of the material and the emulation of the visual aspect of the cracking.

Trinh et al. [27] wrote about the use of the semantic web for the representation of orientation, direction and attitude within a a virtual world. Coyne et al. [28] had a similar approach that was used to translate contextual descriptions of a world into a virtual materialization based on the use of constraints to disambiguate the world objects and their positions.

To the best of our knowledge the use of Linked Open Data to automated the creation of data-driven procedurally generated 3D simulations of historical and current locations is a novel contribution. Previous contributions were primarily tools supporting the designer in creating an environment that would then be statically used within a game. A secondary contribution is the creation of culturally sensitive prefabricated assets within a simulation environment that taken on the content appropriate to the both location and time.

3   Theoretical Framework

A significant amount of data exists encoded in Resource Description Framework (RDF) and Ontology Web Language (OWL) formats on the web about topics ranging from geography to linguistics. Unlike previous approaches to data markup and storage, the detail contained within LOD has reached sufficient complexity that it is now difficult for a human to enumerate, let alone query, LOD.

Creating a generalizable data-driven simulation implies the following two types of queries:

a) Well defined, structured queries that return deterministic results based on known parameters. These include spatial and temporal information to which a number of other events and objects are tied to, such as the sun, the moon, terrain, etc. Some uncertainty may be contained within this process but the actual query process itself remains deterministic.

b) Poorly defined, serendipitous queries whose goals are ancillary to the era or the story telling aspect of the simulation and that create the minor details that are relevant to its realism. This can include "litter" on the ground, posters, titles of books on shelves and so on.

The use of ontologies and databases is ideal for this purpose in that the ontological description of a thing enables the simulation engine to determine what properties should be located to materialize an instance. A more generalizable approach is the use of a simulation; the detailed minutia of information lends itself well to automated querying of the information necessary to answering a hypothesis.

A secondary benefit is that the ontology can also be used to determine what details can be omitted from a materialized instance and which can be estimated. It also gives guidance to the simulation engine as to how to query the database in order to estimate a missing property. As an example, a military trench on a battlefield has been dug into the ground at a depth and width. In many cases geometry information or archival information will reveal the dimension of a specific trench and it can be rendered. When the dimensions of the trench are not known, they can be replaced by the statistical average width and depth of trenches within the area.

4   Simulating the Great War

Given the centenary of the Great War and the primary author's ongoing work in this era, an area of Western France in late 1914 was chosen as case study to simulate[2]. Later on in 1917, this would be the site of the Battle of Vimy Ridge, which would see the Canadian Corps fight as a single entity for the first time. This location is ideal as a test case for a number of reasons including the presence of two distinct areas (Entente trenches versus Central trenches) with different cultures and features changing over time.

Fig. 1. A modern topographical map of Vimy Ridge (OpenTopomap)

Fig. 2. Vimy Ridge on September 16, 1914 at about 50.366N, 2.796E

An example use case for this methodology would be an historian attempting to determine who had the advantage of the terrain shown in Figure 1. Given this map, an experienced historian or geographer could make an educated evaluation based on his interpretation of a two dimensional document. If the contents of the map are digitized into a GIS data structure and merged with other information, a programmer could design a one-off algorithm to try and determine terrain advantage. No doubt, this would require extensive consultation with the historian and a significant amount of time wrestling with deep methodological questions.

Within a simulated environment based on the actual digital terrain elevation and trench data, a historian can simply walk around in the virtual world and have direct understanding of the advantages of terrain. The argumentation and narrative proof of the conclusion conducted by the researcher has not changed from previous methodologies but the ease of access and interpretation of a highly described information source is dramatically improved. Linked Open Data also allows us to promote the convergence of multiple consumption and analysis strategies.

We review here four aspects of the simulation generator based on the issues that they identify: the layout of the trenches on the battlefield, the elements of the vegetation estimation, the use of culturally attuned prefabricated objects and the crediting of work and data sources within the simulation. The simulation was

---

[2] http://rdf.muninn-project.org/demo

implemented with the Unity game engine drawing data from LOD databases. The approach is meant to use multiple concurrent SPARQL servers, however given Unity's lack of Cross Origin Request Security (CORS) support, we use a intermediary SPARQL server that proxies the retrieval of data from multiple LOD servers.

4.1   Trenches

The First World War in Western Europe was a war of attrition fought in trenches that were often within earshot of the enemy. In this section we review the creation of the terrain through geometries that are obtained through the Muninn project. The geometries and features are derived from British Trench Maps in a Linked Geo[8] format that also support access using the Ordered List Ontology, further details have been previously published in [29]. Figure 2 is a screenshot of the simulated trenches. The information used to generate the trenches includes both depth and width, however additional information about the state of the trench (abandoned, occupied) is also available and effects how the trench is represented.

The state of an object, or its serviceability can be recorded in one of two ways: a state property or the use of a class hierarchy as Linked Geo Data does. An example is RailwayThing which is the superclass for Rail, LightRail and AbandonedRailway. Muninn makes use of the graves:hasState property that allows us to record the state of the feature as reported on the original British Trench Maps. The reason for this decision was that while the state of a real world object changes over time, its fundamental identity does not and the use of sub-classes to encode state results in an unmanageable number of classes.

This state is what the simulation engine uses to make decisions on how the LOD is translated into the visuals, materials and terrain. In the case of the trenches, 'abandoned' trenches will be filled with debris and the width and depth of the trenches will be reduced by a small, randomly changing percentage to simulate neglect.

This process of simulating a trench is executed by depressing the terrain in the median line of the trench as reported by the LOD. Width is set according to each position node within the LOD stream and the textures of the trench bottom, walls and fields set according to generic Unity textures.

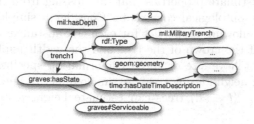

Fig. 3. Basic ontological view of trench data

4.2   Vegetation

We review here the generation of vegetation as recorded in archival and GIS information sources. Different data sources report information on vegetation at different levels of granularity over time. Trees and forested areas are created based on the basis of available and the processes described in this section are applicable to shrubs, bushes, hedges and plantation fields.

When inserting new vegetation in the simulation, select 3D assets or textures that fit the particular class of vegetation is not difficult given the availability of 3D assets. The difficulty lies in managing under-specified vegetation instances or aggregates of vegetation instances such as a forest. In some cases, an area may be a tree plantation of a very specific species, in others an old-growth forest and in some cases, individual trees.

What species of tree, tree size, height and any seasonal effects on appearance will dictate appearance and modification of generic assets. Furthermore, in the case of historical data the vegetation information may only be available for certain points in time and any visualisation in between these points has to estimate the state of the information by interpolation or other means.

Within our prototype simulation, trees are programmatically generated based on reported flora information from British Trench Maps. These maps provide an interesting challenge as in this era they were printed using a generic base plate from one date while coloured overlays were added with the most up-to-date information. Both layers represent information at different points in time where not all features are up to date.

The state of the features is an interesting problem: it is obvious that trees within a battlefield would be heavily scarred by projectiles and shrubbery would have been destroyed by the movement of personnel and pack animals. Additional statistical simulations driven from external event data, such as battles, could be used to infer the amount of damage that would occur. In this case we chose not to implement such a non-trivial process but note that there may be some opportunities for ontologically inferring the state of a feature based on the presence of a second feature: that a ground track has been indicated on a map implies that it can be visually differentiated from the ground next to it and thus the state of the general area can also be determined.

As with the previous section on Trenches, an ontological approach to data management has some advantages under uncertainty. The ontology can be reused to locate or estimate properties that are missing from the source data or derived from other ontological constructs. Consider a simple tree ontology T that presents the following properties for each tree instance: h height from the ground, c height of the crown of the tree and the width w of the crown[3]. If a single tree does not have size or species information specified, it can be estimated by querying neighbouring trees. A simple query of neighbouring $G_{Avg(h)}$ $\rho_{Dist(Lat,Lot)<Radius}$ $(t \in T)$ trees can estimate height h or use a frequency

---

[3] These measurements were chosen because of their simplicity and their direct use in classifying trees using LIDAR data [30].

approach for a species s for a value or $\pi_{s_i}\ G_{Max(Count(s))}\ \rho_{Dist(Lat,Lot)<Radius}$ ($t \in T$) to select a species instance s_i of the species class S.

Another means of estimating foliage data is to infer its properties based on other data-sets. Given the coordinates of the tree and the month of the year, one should be able to find LOD about foliage properties and the regions in which they thrive. DBpedia presented a ready made collection of information against which queries could be run to answer the basic question: *at a certain time and place, if a tree were to exists, what would it be and how would it look like?*. The triple pattern in Figure 4 represents the graph required to locate the tree species probable in the area being simulated.

dbpedia:Flora_by_country   skos:broader   ?f .
?f   dcterms:subject ?tree .
Category:Ornamental_trees dcterms:subject ?tree .
Category:Trees   skos:broader   Category:Ornamental_trees .

Fig. 4. Finding the right species of ?tree based on a regional category ?f

Binding ?f should be Category:Flora_of_France for the right set of ?tree's to be retrieved. However there exists no term that links country or regional terms to these categories, limiting the generalization of the approach: in an ideal case, we should be able to translate coordinates to a country or region to a tree category.

A similar experience occurred when querying ontologies and data-sets dedicated to flora and forestry. Designed and authored by domain specialists, these data-sets are deeply integrated into the biology application ecosystems and descend directly from human readable, portal published databases. Tightly coupled to their primary objectives and have no connections to generalizable concepts that would frame their data to solve other problems.

For example, the Plant Ontology data-set has for mandate to be a "controlled, structured vocabulary (ontology) of terms to describe plant anatomy, morphology and the stages of plant development". Its contents are effectively a taxonomy for biological classification using Binomial nomenclature. As per accepted ontology best practices, it lacks a generalizable object that would relate its terms to dbpedia:Tree or dbpedia:Plant as this would be a "lazy concept" [31]. While appropriate in the pure theoretical ontological view, these design decisions make ontological discovery and matching impossible. Thus, in our experimental implementation we chose to use dbpedia as a data source for our fauna information.

Figure 5 is a screenshot of what occurs when a user clicks on a specific tree in the simulation. The information about the tree is reported as well as the provenance of its information and the decision mechanism that was used for its placement, shape and species.

4.3 Culturally Aware Prefabricated Game Assets

Realistic simulations can contain 3D assets that represent everyday objects. These are not directly relevant to the simulation or information need but help

Fig. 5. Objects such as individual trees are created based on actual data. The simulation provides both the individual tree instance and tree class information.

Fig. 6. A culturally aware phonograph in the Canadian trenches. It's placement is purely demonstrative, but the content played is relevant to the locality.

create a comfortable aesthetic. Within the framework of Section 3, these queries are poorly defined as their objective is to be sensical without necessarily being relevant to the initial query.

Designers usually make these assets to be simple image placeholders that carry no information beyond appearing realistic. With a LOD approach, the creation of these assets can be mechanized through the retrieval of contents from Linked Open databases relevant to the time or place. We note that projects, such as CARARE [32] are working on creating repositories of 3D objects that could be expanded with these specific behaviours.

In our simulation, we chose to focus on documents and media that are described in period texts as littering the trenches of a battlefields such as discarded newspapers or postcards. Dugouts are similarly documented as containing creature comforts such as books, posters, paperwork or maps.

Fig. 7. A discarded *Figaro* newspaper in the *Entente* trenches.

Fig. 8. A discarded *Gumbinner Kreisblatt* newspaper in the *Central* trenches.

Figures 7 and 8 are screen shots of discarded newspapers that move in the wind across a battlefield. The newspaper is a prefabricated asset ("prefab") that can be instantiated anywhere on the battlefield but which displays a random page from a newspaper that is appropriate to the location or nationalities nearby on a date that is weeks beforehand the simulations. This is made possible by partial LOD made available by the French and German National Libraries of their holdings.

The same can be done with books whose contents and covering images are available from LOD data-sets such as Project Gutenberg or Archive.org. Another interesting prefabricated asset that was developed for this project was that of a phonograph, an item which would be commonly available in some of the rear areas of the battlefield to entertain the troops. The phonograph 3D asset of Figure 6 is one that is freely available, through behaviour has been added which is similar to that of the newspaper 3D asset: songs and airs related to nearby locations or nationalities are chosen from the appropriate era. As with the example of Figure 5, clicking on the phonograph reveals the LOD resources used by the 3D asset. These types of 3D assets supported by LOD data sets are desirable because they add realism relevant to the era without requiring further localisation work.

4.4   Credit Generation

Lastly, the use of Linked Open Data entails that some measure of provenance is available to tell us about every single term retrieved from servers. This opens up the interesting possibility of creating a bibliography, citation list or credit listing for both the creators and sources that were involved (in)directly in the simulation. The traditional notion of authorship is now challenged as the increase in the complexity of creative works [33] makes assigning credit and authorship non-trivial.

In this case, our simulation creates a new LOD document that links to all of the URL's retrieved to create the simulation. This document is then parsed when the simulation is exited and used to create a rolling credits scene that outlines all data sources used by the simulation. Individual roles played in its construction can be recovered from a series of statements attached to the consumed LOD. The question then becomes how much detail should be shown in the credits: should every contributor to a Wikipedia page be credited for the use of a DBPedia term? Should the order of the credits be based on the relative importance of each contribution or on its chronological use within the simulation?

The current generation of credit sequence is driven by the number of terms used from each source, with the intuition being that the data-set used most often is the most important. As an added aesthetic touch, the media assets (images and music) can be randomly played in the background while credits move up. This serves to remind the audience that the individual assets used by the simulation were retrieved from several sources and were not statically chosen.

5   Experimental Results

In this section the performance of our experimental implementation is reviewed and conclusions drawn from our use of Linked Open Data.

5.1   Performance Evaluation

One of the concerns with online procedural content generation was the speed with which scenes could be generated from Linked Open Data. This is a valid concern given the amount of information needed to generate an ad-hoc scene and the use of the SPARQL query language which is often criticised as being unresponsive.

In practice, the retrieval time of information from different LOD databases is not a concern, even with consumer grade internet connections. A disproportionate amount of wall-clock time is spent in creating the virtual world within the simulation engine. The amount of detail that linked open data driven procedural generation entails is high and for a few LOD entities, several dozen operations on a specific area of the virtual world need to be performed and prefabricated objects instantiated.

Procedural content generation has traditionally been a design tool used to create a terrain or world that is then statically stored for use. In this case, the LOD is retrieved directly from the endpoint and a new terrain is generated from the most up-to-date data available at run time.

The use of SPARQL servers over that of APIs was a necessity in that they provide standardized access to information using a generalizable query language. In some cases, the retrieval of content could only be done through other APIs or by parsing the HTML code of web portals. This situation should be remediated as it limits the ability of the content consumers to search multiple information sources without significant investment for each additional source. The Museum API[4] Page lists over 50 different APIs of historical interest. The diversity of methods, formats and specifications becomes a hindrance to a generalizable method as each new data source must be integrated and maintained individually.

Accuracy is a thorny problem which remains an open area of research. Domain expert and layman interpretation of the same visualization can be different as well as their requirements. For example, in our demonstration simulation we randomly place discarded newspapers as described in Section 4.3. While first hand accounts of the war tell us that discarded newspapers were common and the date and instance of the newspaper respects locality, its placement is random and only for aesthetic purposes. Depending on the audience, one can argue that this is needed for communicative purposes or deliberately misleading to the audience.

In our prototype, every prefabricated object placed within the environment can be selected and a pop-up window will report on its provenance, instance and class, as in Figure 5. This type of reporting is an effective means of providing justification or explanation on the asset placement and has been previously been used by Pauwels et al. [34] in documenting engineering drawings.

This works well for discrete objects such as basic shapes like individual trees but poorly for complex structures such as buildings or terrain surfaces where the object of interest is hard to select. Interestingly, from the perspective of creating a simulation, there is no difference between a historical simulation and a current-world simulation as the uncertainty that is represented within the LOD is dealt with in the same way. While not done here for lack of space, we can change the location and time of the simulation for a current day metropolitan city and display a simulation without problem.

---

[4] http://museum-api.pbworks.com/Museum%C2%A0APIs

5.2   Insufficient Provenance Information

An element in historical reconstruction and building information management is the tracking of the provenance of information both in terms of information provider and creation process. Currently, semantic web terms can be related to their home URI through the rdfs:isDefinedBy, a data-set description void:inDataset, a "source" dc:source or to detailed provenance information with the PROV ontology.

In attempting to locate data sources for this project, few data-sets were found that had detailed provenance, as confirmed independently by Buil-Aranda et al [35]. The underlying assumption is that the data-set is already known and explicitly queried by a particular user or his agent. There is anecdotal evidence that suggests the reason for this is that the ontology or data-set is created with a specific community in mind and no outside use was foreseen.

This lack of overall description is a concern in that this makes the automated discovery of additional data in ways similar to that of Akar et al. [36] impossible. This prevents tracking the authorship or ownership of data that would make citation straightforwards and credit sharing possible. But foremost, it prevents the sharing of quality, precision and process information that should apply to all terms of the data-set, such as the date of issue or validity. This information is especially necessary when dealing historical data as the data set description may be the only means of assigning temporal information to the remaining terms.

As an example, DBPedia has attempted to document its processes and the raw source used to created a dbpedia term through the use of the dc:source term linked to the original Wikipedia page. It is not possible to gleam publication date for the resource without parsing the HTML source or already knowing the location of the data set description since no void:inDataset is provided to link back to it.

When using LOD that moves beyond small, known data sets the necessity of including rdfs:isDefinedBy and void:inDataset terms with every resource becomes evident. The reason for this is that the necessary use of aggregating and triple search services obfuscates the original provenance of the information, including by changing the base of the URL. We did notice a bias in data-set authorship in that having one's data linked to (cited) is valuable, while linking to (citing) another data-set less so. Some of the most linked to data-sets, are also the least likely to link to other data-sets. Part of this is due to the concern that their data might be tainted with inaccuracies. Of course, linking (citing) requires effort on the part of the data-set author while the effort of being linked to is externalized to others. This classic agency theory problem remains to be solved within LOD systems.

5.3   Semantic Versus Appearance

The semantic web is meant to provide semantic information to a thing as opposed to the World Wide Web which provides appearance information to a thing. It therefore comes as a concerns that a number of practices meant to support human consumption of the data are hindering machine consumption of the data. An example of this is the use of basic descriptive terms that contain content which are mapped directly from text fields from a catalogue entry. This is due to data providers using a "mapping approach" to creating LOD from existing databases. This is a problem in that the fields in these initial systems were meant to be human readable, but are of little use to a machine.

This has primarily to do with the fact that most archival LOD is being generated through a "mapping" approach to creating LOD that does not necessarily translate classifications as linkages and simply copies strings. In many cases a search for a certain type of publication, such as a newspaper, is not possible unless the correct human-readable string is used. Some cataloguing implementations use the the original description strings to record publication types, such as <dc:type>czasopismo</dc:type>, requiring a prior knowledge of the national language before the data can be queried. This shows a deep-seated assumption that content is still retrieved by keywords or that the RDF properties contents are only meant as displayable content.

The above case makes locating newspapers impossible unless searching for every translation of the string "newspaper" in use within the data-set. The concern is that the considerable efforts that have been made in using standardized cataloguing processes are being wasted by simply "mapping" the string values into LOD terms without appropriate pre-processing. Another example of the problems created by direct mapping occurs when using audio recording data from the PCDHN data-set. Here recordings are represented by LOD structures that represent a concept, its manifestations and the actual recordings at items. However, it is impossible to programmatically determine what language the songs are actually interpreted in, and whether the materialization of the concept is the whole record or a single track. This materialized expression has the property<dc:subject xml:lang="fr">Chansons française</dc:subject>, which is ambiguous as to whether the song is culturally French or performed in French. Lastly, the two items linked to the manifestation are in two different binary formats which require either parsing the extension type or connecting to the web server until an acceptable encoding is found, requiring extra exemption handling on the part of the client. The problematic structure of the LOD is due to an archival view of the data where the approach of LinkedBrains / MusicBrains to representing audio recordings may be preferable.

The same concerns about mapping human readable data apply to Library of Congress (LOC) headings and terms, where *chansons françaises* makes no differentiation between the cultural origins, the localization or the specific interpretation of the works. In trying to locate content that is localised both linguistically and culturally these are important concerns. The problem is compounded by the use of strings, which need to be both culturally localised and transliterated.

The aggressive use of SKOS vocabularies, without supporting OWL statements, makes the discovery of additional resources and their query difficult in that the taxonomy must be known before the SPARQL query is written. Worse, authoritative vocabularies such as the LOC Subject Headings have traditionally had multiple top-level concepts that have intermingling hierarchies. This means that concept Tree has skos:broader concepts Nursery stock, Woody plants and skos:narrower concepts Bark peeling and Fruit trees. Primarily meant for human consumption, subject headings were never meant as a hierarchy of concepts and the implicit change in conceptSchemes prevents it from being used for automated querying, even in a non-transitive context. This same model of "multiple trees" is used by DBPedia to translate Wikipedia category data into LOD and highlights some of the hurdles in transforming human generated data to machine readable data.

5.4   Separation of Meta-data and Data

One of the early users of LOD has been the GLAM communities that see a flexible means of distributing data to their clients and amongst themselves. One of the challenges of consuming this data is the underlying assumption that LOD is meant as a meta-data framework, separate from the document.

This reflects the strong cataloguing tradition of these institution in a pre-digitization environment where interacting with the document (eg: a book) was a separate act from its discovery in a catalogue. In some cases online LOD sources have the document available in digital format but it is segregated in a separate system that is neither machine readable nor linked to by the LOD catalogue.

It would be preferable if both data and meta-data were represented in the LOD set as this would enable not only seamless access but opportunities for supporting data mining projects. Furthermore we note that HTTP content negotiation as it is currently used to support different LOD representations (See [37]) can also be applied to media formats. As an example, the Project Gutenberg RDF catalogue makes extensive use of dc:hasFormat term to link a document to the different file formats it is available under. It is desirable, especially for human consumption, to have different URL's that allow a client to explicitly specify a format. But given the sophistication that is expected from a LOD client, and indeed that is already present in the average Web browser, offloading media type negotiation to the HTTP transport layer seems reasonable.

The Muninn Project currently makes use of content negotiation to not only select the appropriate LOD serialization but also serve images in the format requested or accepted by the browser. Similarly, the Stanford IIIF JSON-LD API also uses the same approach in its image content negotiations. The unification and simplification in the number of APIs and endpoints needed to reach the content needed is desirable from both an efficiency point of vue and to lower the cost of development.

6   Conclusions

In this paper we presented a novel, generalizable way of consuming LOD within a game engine to create on-the-fly digital simulations of historical or present day places. We also presented the novel contribution of culturally adaptable 3D prefabricated assets that can take on the content or appearance appropriate to time and location.

The following issues were noted in consuming LOD for 3D virtual worlds: a) LOD is being published under the assumption that it will be consumed by humans, sometimes making machine consumption impossible, b) data-set authors are neglecting to provide provenance and data-set information that would allow proper data-set discovery and c) some LOD publishers still see publication as a meta-data search mechanism for other services which requires unnecessary retrieval steps on the client's part.

In future work, we will focus on scenario and story generation using detailed event data found within Linked Open Data databases as well as generalizing the extraction of behaviours from generic objects within the virtual world.

References

1. Bizer, C., Heath, T., Berners-Lee, T.: Linked data-the story so far. International Journal on Semantic Web and Information Systems 5, 1–22 (2009)
2. Moretti, F.: Distant Reading. Verso (2013)
3. Gaitatzes, A., et al.: Reviving the past: Cultural heritage meets virtual reality. In: Conf. Virtual Reality, Archeology, and Cultural Heritage, pp. 103–110 (2001)
4. Fai, S., Graham, K., Duckworth, T., et al.: Building information modelling and heritage documentation. In: CIPA International Symposium, vol. 47 (2011)
5. Anderson, E., McLoughlin, L., et al.: Developing serious games for cultural heritage: a state-of-the-art review. Virtual Reality 14, 255–275 (2010)
6. Mazzini, S., Ricci, F.: EAC-CPF ontology and linked archival data. In: Workshop on Semantic Digital Archives, pp. 72–81 (2011)
7. Ford, K.: Lc's bibliographic framework initiative and the attractiveness of linked data. Information Standards Quarterly 24, 46–50 (2012)
8. Stadler, C., Lehmann, J., Höffner, K., Auer, S.: Linkedgeodata: A core for a web of spatial open data. Semantic Web Journal 3, 333–354 (2012)
9. Otto, K.A.: The semantics of multi-user virtual environments. In: Workshop Towards Semantic Virtual Environments, pp. 35–39 (2005)
10. Togelius, J., Yannakakis, G.N., Stanley, K.O., Browne, C.: Search-based procedural content generation. In: Di Chio, C., et al. (eds.) EvoApplicatons 2010, Part I. LNCS, vol. 6024, pp. 141–150. Springer, Heidelberg (2010)
11. Togelius, J., Preuss, M., et al.: Towards multiobjective procedural map generation. In: Workshop on Procedural Content Generation in Games, p. 3 (2010)
12. Hartsook, K., et al.: Toward supporting stories with procedurally generated game worlds. In: Computational Intelligence and Games, pp. 297–304 (2011)
13. Kallmann, M., Thalmann, D.: Modeling objects for interaction tasks. In: Proc. Eurographics Workshop on Animation and Simulation, pp. 73–86 (1998)
14. Arisona, S., et al.: Increasing detail of 3d models through combined photogrammetric and procedural modelling. GIS 16, 45–53 (2013)
15. Andrés, A.N., Pozuelo, F.B., et al.: Generation of virtual models of cultural heritage. Journal of Cultural Heritage 13, 103–106 (2012)
16. Tutenel, T., Smelik, R.M., et al.: Using semantics to improve the design of game worlds. In: Artificial Intelligence for Interactive Digital Entertainment (2009)
17. Vanacken, L., et al.: Semantic information during conceptual modelling of interaction for virt. env. In: Multimodal Intf. in Semantic Interaction, pp. 17–24 (2007)

18. Fuhrmann, A., Groß, C., Weber, A.: Ontologies for virtual garments. In: Workshop towards Semantic Virtual Environments, pp. 101–109 (2005)
19. Gutiérrez, M., García-Rojas, A., et al.: An ontology of virtual humans: Incorporating semantics into human shapes. Visual Computer 23, 207–218 (2007)
20. von Ahn, L., Dabbish, L.: Labeling images with a computer game. In: SIGCHI Conference on Human Factors in Computing Systems, pp. 319–326 (2004)
21. Friberger, M.G., Togelius, J.: Generating game content from open data. In: Conference on the Foundations of Digital Games, pp. 290–291 (2012)
22. Reitmayr, G., Schmalstieg, D.: Semantic world models for ubiquitous augmented reality. In: Workshop towards Semantic Virtual Environments (2005)
23. Grimaldo, F., Barber, F., et al.: Semantic virtual environments for interactive planning agents. In: International Digital Games Conference, vol. 17 (2006)
24. Tutenel, T., Bidarra, R., Smelik, R.M., et al.: The role of semantics in games and simulations. Computers in Entertainment 6, 57 (2008)
25. Deussen, O., et al.: Realistic modeling and rendering of plant ecosystems. In: Conference on Computer Graphics and Interactive Techniques, pp. 275–286 (1998)
26. Lu, J., Georghiades, A.S., Glaser, A., Wu, H., Wei, L.Y., Guo, B., Dorsey, J., Rushmeier, H.: Context-aware textures. ACM Trans. Graph. 26 (2007)
27. Trinh, T.H., et al.: Integrating semantic directional relationships into virt. environments. In: Virt. Env. & 3rd Joint Virt. Reality, pp. 67–74 (2011)
28. Coyne, B., Sproat, R.: Wordseye: an automatic text-to-scene conversion system. In: Computer Graphics and Interactive Techniques, pp. 487–496 (2001)
29. Warren, R.H., Evans, D.: From the trenches - API issues in linked geo data. In: Linking Geospatial Data Workshop, W3C (2014)
30. Ko, C., Sohn, G., et al.: Tree genera classification with geometric features from high-density airborne lidar. Cdn. Jour. of Remote Sensing 39, S73–S85 (2013)
31. Gherasim, T., Berio, G., Harzallah, M., Kuntz, P., et al.: Problems impacting the quality of automatically built ontologies. In: Proceedings of KESE, vol. 949 (2012)
32. D'Andrea, A., Niccolucci, F., Fernie, K.: Carare 2.0: a metadata schema for 3d cultural objects. In: Digital Heritage 2013. IEEE (2013)
33. Horton, R., Smith, R.: Time to redefine authorship: A conference to do so. BMJ: British Medical Journal 312, 723 (1996)
34. Pauwels, P., et al.: Linking a game engine environment to architectural information on the semantic web. Journal of Civil Eng. and Arch. 5, 787–798 (2011)
35. Buil-Aranda, C., Hogan, A., Umbrich, J., Vandenbussche, P.-Y.: Sparql web-querying infrastructure: Ready for action? In: Alani, H., et al. (eds.) ISWC 2013, Part II. LNCS, vol. 8219, pp. 277–293. Springer, Heidelberg (2013)
36. Akar, Z., Halaç, T.G., Ekinci, E.E., Dikenelli, O.: Querying the web of interlinked datasets using void descriptions. In: Linked Data on the Web (2012)
37. Heath, T., Bizer, C.: Linked data: Evolving the web into a global data space. Synthesis Lectures on the Semantic Web: Theory and Technology 1, 1–126 (2011)

On the Semantics of SPARQL Queries with Optional Matching under Entailment Regimes

Egor V. Kostylev and Bernardo Cuenca Grau

Department of Computer Science, University of Oxford

Abstract. We study the semantics of SPARQL queries with optional matching features under entailment regimes. We argue that the normative semantics may lead to answers that are in conflict with the intuitive meaning of optional matching, where unbound variables naturally represent unknown information. We propose an extension of the SPARQL algebra that addresses these issues and is compatible with any entailment regime satisfying the minimal requirements given in the normative specification. We then study the complexity of query evaluation and show that our extension comes at no cost for regimes with an entailment relation of reasonable complexity. Finally, we show that our semantics preserves the known properties of optional matching that are commonly exploited for static analysis and optimisation.

1 Introduction

SPARQL became the standard language for querying RDF in 2008 [1]. Since then, the theoretical properties of SPARQL have been the subject of intensive research efforts and are by now relatively well-understood [2,3,4,5,6,7]. At the same time, SPARQL has become a core technology in practice, and most RDF-based applications rely on SPARQL endpoints for query formulation and processing.

The functionality of many such applications is enhanced by OWL 2 ontologies [8], which are used to provide background knowledge about the application domain, and to enrich query answers with implicit information. A new version of SPARQL, called SPARQL 1.1, was released in 2013 [9]. This new version captures the capabilities of OWL 2 by means of the so-called *entailment regimes* [10]: a flexible mechanism for extending SPARQL query answering to the W3C standards layered on top of RDF. A regime specifies which RDF graphs and SPARQL queries are legal (i.e., admissible) for the regime, as well as an entailment relation that unambiguously defines query answers for all legal queries and graphs.

The semantics of SPARQL under entailment regimes is specified for the conjunctive fragment, where queries are represented as *basic graph patterns* (i.e., sets of RDF triples with variables) and query answers are directly provided by the entailment relation of the regime. Roughly speaking, to check whether a mapping from variables of the query to nodes in the RDF graph is an answer to the query, one first transforms the query itself into an RDF graph by substituting each variable with the corresponding value, and then checks whether this graph is entailed in the regime by the original data graph [10,11].

P. Mika et al. (Eds.) ISWC 2014, Part II, LNCS 8797, pp. 374–389, 2014.

When one goes beyond the basic fragment of SPARQL the language becomes considerably more complicated, but the effect of entailment regimes on the query semantics remains circumscribed to basic graph patterns. Thus, to evaluate a query one must first evaluate its component basic patterns using the relevant regime, and then compose the results by means of the SPARQL algebra operations.

Of particular interest from both a theoretical and a practical perspective is the extension of the basic fragment of SPARQL with the *optional matching feature*, which is realised in the language by means of the OPTIONAL operator (abbreviated by OPT in this paper). This feature allows the optional information to be added to query answers only when the information is available in the RDF data graph: if the optional part of the query does not match the data, then the relevant variables are left unbounded in query answers.

One of the main motivations behind optional matching in SPARQL was to deal with the "lack of regular, complete structures in RDF graphs" (see [9] Section 6) and hence with the inherent incompleteness of information in RDF data sources where only partial information about the relevant Web resources is typically available. In this setting, an unbound variable in an answer mapping is naturally interpreted as a "null" value, meaning that there might exist a binding for this variable if we consider other information elsewhere on the Web, but none is currently available in the RDF graph at hand. An additional (and slightly different) motivation for optional matching was to introduce a mechanism for "not rejecting solutions because some part of the query pattern does not match" [1]; in this sense, one would naturally expect optional matching to either extend solutions with the optional information, or to leave solutions unchanged.

Both readings of optional matching coincide if we focus just on RDF, and they are faithfully captured by the normative semantics. In this paper, however, we argue that they naturally diverge once we consider more sophisticated entailment regimes. Furthermore, the differences that arise, even if subtle, can have a major impact on expected answers.

To make this discussion concrete, let us briefly discuss a simple example of an RDF graph representing the direct train lines between UK cities as well as ferry boat transfers from UK cities to international destinations. Let this graph be exhaustive in its description of rail connections, but much less so in what concerns ferry transfers. We may exploit optional matching to retrieve all direct train connections between cities X and Y, extended with ferry transfers from Y to other cities Z whenever possible. Under the normative semantics of SPARQL we may obtain answers (*London, Oxford,* −) and (*London, Holyhead,* −) provided the graph has information about direct train lines from *London* to both *Oxford* and *Holyhead*, but no matching can be found in the graph for ferry connections starting from *Oxford* or *Holyhead* to other cities. Suppose next that the data graph is extended to a graph corresponding to an OWL 2 ontology in which it is stated that inland cities do not have ferry connections, and that *Oxford* is an inland city. The ontology establishes a clear distinction between *Oxford* and *Holyhead*: whereas the former is inland and cannot have ferry connections, the latter may still well be (and indeed is) a coastal city offering a number of transfers to international destinations. The normative OWL 2 direct semantics entailment regime, however, does not distinguish between the case of *Holyhead* (where the information about ferry connections is still unknown) and *Oxford* (where the information is certain), and both answers would be returned. In this way, the normative semantics adopts the reading of optional matching where the optional information is used to complete (but never discard) query answers. In contrast, under the reading of unbounded variables as placeholders for unknown information, one would naturally expect the answer on *Oxford* to be ruled out. Indeed, if our goal were to find rail to ferry transfers starting from *London* and terminating in *Dublin* by first querying this graph and then looking for the missing information elsewhere on the Web, discarding cities like *Oxford* on the first stage would significantly facilitate our task.

In this paper, we propose an alternative semantics for the OPT operator which adopts the aforementioned reading of optional matching as an incomplete "null". We call our semantics *strict*, which reflects the fact that it rules out those answers in which unbound variables in the optional part cannot be matched to *any* consistent extension of the input graph. Our semantics is given as an extension of the SPARQL algebra and hence satisfies the expected compositionality properties of algebraic query languages. Furthermore, it is backwards-compatible with the normative semantics for regimes in which all legal graphs are consistent, such as the RDF regime [10]. We also study the complexity of query evaluation and show that our extension comes at no cost for regimes in which entailment is not harder than query evaluation under normative semantics for the RDF regime. Finally, we show that our semantics preserves the known properties of optional matching that are commonly exploited for static analysis and optimisation.

2   SPARQL 1.1 under Entailment Regimes

In this section, we formalise the syntax and normative semantics of a core fragment of SPARQL 1.1 with optional matching under entailment regimes. Our formalisation is based on the normative specification documents [9,10,11] and builds on the well-known foundational works on SPARQL [2,3,6].

2.1   Syntax

Let $\mathbf{I}$, $\mathbf{L}$, and $\mathbf{B}$ be countably infinite sets of *IRIs*, *literals*, and *blank nodes*, respectively. The set of *RDF terms* $\mathbf{T}$ is $\mathbf{I} \cup \mathbf{L} \cup \mathbf{B}$. An *RDF triple* is a triple $(s\ p\ o)$ from $\mathbf{T} \times \mathbf{I} \times \mathbf{T}$, where s is called *subject*, p *predicate*, and o *object*. An *(RDF) graph* is a finite set of RDF triples.

Assume additionally the existence of a countably infinite set $\mathbf{V}$ of variables disjoint from $\mathbf{T}$. A *triple pattern* is a tuple from $(\mathbf{T} \cup \mathbf{V}) \times (\mathbf{I} \cup \mathbf{V}) \times (\mathbf{T} \cup \mathbf{V})$. A *basic graph pattern (BGP)* is a finite set of triple patterns. *Built-in conditions* are inductively defined as follows:

1. if $?X, ?Y \in \mathbf{V}$ and $c \in \mathbf{T}$ then *bound*$(?X)$, $?X = c$, and $?X = ?Y$ are built-in conditions; and

2. if R_1 and R_2 are built-in conditions then $\neg R_1$, $R_1 \wedge R_2$ and $R_1 \vee R_2$ are built-in conditions.

Complex graph patterns are constructed from BGPs using a wide range of available operators that are applicable to graph patterns and built-in conditions. We focus on the AND-OPT-FILTER fragment (i.e., we consider neither union nor projection), which is widely accepted to be the fundamental core of SPARQL [2]. In this setting, *graph patterns* are inductively defined as follows (e.g., see [11]):

1. every BGP is a graph pattern;
2. if P_1 and P_2 are graph patterns that share no blank nodes then $(P_1 \text{ AND } P_2)$ and $(P_1 \text{ OPT } P_2)$ are graph patterns (called AND and OPT patterns); and
3. if P is a graph pattern and R is a built-in condition, then $(P \text{ FILTER } R)$ is a graph pattern (called FILTER pattern).

We denote vars(P) (resp. with triples(P)) all the variables from **V** (resp. all triple patterns) which appear in a graph pattern P.

We conclude with the definition of a special class of graph patterns with intuitive behaviour [2]. A graph pattern is *well-designed* iff (a) for each of its FILTER sub-patterns $(P \text{ FILTER } R)$ all the variables of R are in vars(P), and (b) for each of its OPT sub-patterns $(P_1 \text{ OPT } P_2)$ the pattern P_1 mentions all the variables of P_2 which appear outside this sub-pattern. Note that all graph patterns in the examples of this paper are well-designed.

2.2   Semantics of BGPs under Entailment Regimes

The semantics of graph patterns is defined in terms of *mappings*; that is, partial functions from variables **V** to terms **T**. The *domain* dom(μ) of a mapping μ is the set of variables on which μ is defined. For a BGP P we denote with $\mu(P)$ the BGP obtained by applying μ to all variables in P from dom(μ).

Two mappings μ_1 and μ_2 are *compatible* (written as $\mu_1 \sim \mu_2$) if $\mu_1(?X) = \mu_2(?X)$ for all variables $?X$ which are in both dom(μ_1) and dom(μ_2). If $\mu_1 \sim \mu_2$, then we write $\mu_1 \cup \mu_2$ for the mapping obtained by extending μ_1 with μ_2 on variables undefined in μ_1. A mapping μ_1 is *subsumed* by a mapping μ_2 (written $\mu_1 \sqsubseteq \mu_2$) iff $\mu_1 \sim \mu_2$ and dom$(\mu_1) \subseteq$ dom(μ_2). Finally, a set of mappings Ω_1 is *subsumed* by a set of mappings Ω_2 (written $\Omega_1 \sqsubseteq \Omega_2$) iff for each $\mu_1 \in \Omega_1$ there exists $\mu_2 \in \Omega_2$ such that $\mu_1 \sqsubseteq \mu_2$.

Based on [10], an *entailment regime* $\mathfrak{R}$ (or simply a *regime*) can be formalised as a tuple $(\mathbf{R}, \mathcal{G}, \mathcal{P}, \mathcal{C}, \llbracket \cdot \rrbracket)$, where

1. $\mathbf{R}$ is a set of *reserved* IRIs from **I**;
2. $\mathcal{G}$ is the set of *legal* graphs;
3. $\mathcal{P}$ is the set of *legal* BGPs;
4. $\mathcal{C}$ is the set of *consistent* graphs, such that $\mathcal{C} \subseteq \mathcal{G}$; and
5. $\llbracket \cdot \rrbracket$ is the *query answering* function, that takes a graph G from $\mathcal{G}$ and a BGP P from $\mathcal{P}$ and returns either a set $\llbracket P \rrbracket_G$ of mappings μ such that dom$(\mu) = $ vars(P), if $P \in \mathcal{C}$; or *Err*, otherwise.

As in most theoretical works on SPARQL [2,3,6,12], we assume that the query answering function returns a set of mappings, rather than a multiset. In the normative specification [10] the value of $\llbracket \cdot \rrbracket$ for inconsistent graphs is explicitly undefined, and the only thing which is guaranteed is that the answer is finite. However, an assumed behaviour is to at least issue a warning for inconsistent graphs. Moreover, in some regimes such as the OWL 2 Direct Semantics Regime issuing an error is mandatory. A regime must also satisfy certain basic additional conditions, which are immaterial to our results (see [10] Section 1.3).

The definitions of query answering and consistency in a regime are based on an entailment relation [10], which is also specified as part of the regime. We do not model the entailment relation explicitly, but assume two conditions that capture the effects of any reasonable entailment relation on legality and consistency. All regimes mentioned in the normative specification satisfy these properties and in this paper we consider only regimes that do so.

(C1) If graphs G, G_1 and G_2 are legal and there is $h : \mathbf{T} \to \mathbf{T}$, preserving $\mathbf{R}$, such that $h(G_1 \cup G_2) \subseteq G$ then $G_1 \cup G_2$ is legal; if, in addition, G is in $\mathcal{C}$ then $G_1 \cup G_2$ is also in $\mathcal{C}$.

(C2) If a BGP P is in $\mathcal{P}$ then $\mu(P)$ is in $\mathcal{G}$ for any (total) $\mu : \mathbf{V} \to (\mathbf{T} \setminus \mathbf{R})$, such that $\mu(P)$ is a graph; if also $\mu(P)$ is in $\mathcal{C}$ then $\mu \in \llbracket P \rrbracket_{\mu(P)}$.

Condition (C1) formalises (a weak form of) the monotonicity of legality and consistency: an illegal graph that is a union of legal ones cannot be made legal by identifying and renaming of non-reserved terms or adding triples to it; moreover, a similar property holds for consistency. Condition (C2) guarantees, that "freezing" variables of a legal BGP to non-reserved terms gives us a legal graph, and, moreover, if such a graph is consistent, then the answer of the BGP on this graph contains the mapping corresponding to the "freezing".

The notions introduced in the remainder of this paper are parameterised with a regime $\mathfrak{R}$, which is not mentioned explicitly for brevity.

2.3   Normative Semantics under Entailment Regimes

Following [2], now we show how the query answering function $\llbracket \cdot \rrbracket$ extends to complex graph patterns (we refer to [2] for details). A mapping μ *satisfies* a built-in condition R, denoted $\mu \models R$, if one of the following holds:

1. R is $bound(?X)$ and $?X \in \mathrm{dom}(\mu)$; or
2. R is $?X = c$, $?X \in \mathrm{dom}(\mu)$ and $\mu(?X) = c$; or
3. R is $?X = ?Y$, $?X \in \mathrm{dom}(\mu)$, $?Y \in \mathrm{dom}(\mu)$ and $\mu(?X) = \mu(?Y)$; or
4. R is an evaluating to true Boolean combination of other built-in conditions.

Given two sets of mappings Ω_1 and Ω_2, the *join*, *union* and *difference* operations are defined as follows:

$$\Omega_1 \bowtie \Omega_2 = \{\mu_1 \cup \mu_2 \mid \mu_1 \in \Omega_1 \text{ and } \mu_2 \in \Omega_2 \text{ such that } \mu_1 \sim \mu_2\},$$
$$\Omega_1 \cup \Omega_2 = \{\mu \mid \mu \in \Omega_1 \text{ or } \mu \in \Omega_2\},$$
$$\Omega_1 \setminus \Omega_2 = \{\mu_1 \mid \mu_1 \in \Omega_1, \text{ there is no } \mu_2 \in \Omega_2 \text{ such that } \mu_1 \sim \mu_2\}.$$

Based on these, the *left outer join* operation is defined as follows:

$$\Omega_1 \bowtie\!\!\!\!\!\!\!\!\!\!\!\!{}_{\_} \; \Omega_2 = (\Omega_1 \bowtie \Omega_2) \cup (\Omega_1 \setminus \Omega_2).$$

A graph pattern is *legal* for a regime $\mathfrak{R}$ if all the BGPs it contains are legal. The *normative query answering* function $[\![\cdot]\!]^n$ is inductively defined for all legal graph patterns P on the base of $[\![\cdot]\!]$ as follows. For graphs G from $\mathcal{C}$ we have:

1. if P is a BGP then $[\![P]\!]^n_G = [\![P]\!]_G$;
2. if P is P_1 AND P_2 then $[\![P]\!]^n_G = [\![P_1]\!]^n_G \bowtie [\![P_2]\!]^n_G$;
3. if P is P_1 OPT P_2 then $[\![P]\!]^n_G = [\![P_1]\!]^n_G \bowtie\!\!\!\!\!\!\!\!\!\!\!\!{}_{\_} \; [\![P_2]\!]^n_G$; and
4. if P is P' FILTER R then $[\![P]\!]^n_G = \{\mu \mid \mu \in [\![P']\!]^n_G$ and $\mu \models R\}$.

If $G \notin \mathcal{C}$ then $[\![P]\!]^n_G = Err$ for any graph pattern P (which again coincides with $[\![P]\!]_G$ when P is a BGP). Note, that by these definitions $\mu \in [\![P]\!]^n_G$ implies that $\mathrm{dom}(\mu) \subseteq \mathrm{vars}(P)$, but this inclusion may be strict if P contains OPT operator.

Having the semantics defined, we say that two legal patterns P_1 and P_2 are *equivalent (under normative semantics)* with respect to a regime $\mathfrak{R}$, denoted by $P_1 \equiv^n P_2$, if $[\![P_1]\!]^n_G = [\![P_2]\!]^n_G$ for every RDF graph $G \in \mathcal{G}$.

3   On Optional Matching under the Normative Semantics

One of the main motivations for optional matching in SPARQL was to deal with the "lack of regular, complete structures in RDF graphs" [9]. In contrast to relational databases, RDF data is loosely structured and hence in many applications it is not satisfactory to reject an answer if some relevant information is missing. For example, if we are interested in retrieving the names, emails, and websites of employees, we may not want to discard a partial answer involving the name and email address of a particular employee merely because the information on the employee's website is not available in the graph.

The normative semantics was designed to deal with such situations: the optional information is included in query answers only when the information is available; otherwise, the relevant variables are left unbounded. An unbound variable in an answer is thus a manifestation of inherent incompleteness of RDF data sources, and the missing information is interpreted as unknown.

This natural interpretation of query results, however, no longer holds if the query is evaluated under certain entailment regimes, as we illustrate next by means of examples. In these and all other examples given later on, we focus on the OWL 2 direct semantics regime. In order for an RDF graph to be legal for this regime, it must correspond to an OWL 2 ontology; similarly, legal BGPs must correspond to an extended ontology in which variables are allowed [10]. Thus, in the examples we express RDF graphs and BGPs in (extended) OWL 2 functional syntax, and use words "ontology" and "graph" interchangeably.[1]

---

[1] Declaration axioms are omitted in ontologies and BGPs. Also, we use shortened names for some constructs, i.e., PropertyDomain instead of ObjectPropertyDomain.

Example 1. Consider the OWL 2 ontology $\mathcal{O}_1$ consisting of the following axioms:

ClassAssertion(*InlandCity Oxford*),   PropertyAssertion(*train London Oxford*),

ClassAssertion(*CoastalCity Holyhead*), PropertyAssertion(*train London Holyhead*),

PropertyDomain(*ferry CoastalCity*),   DisjointClasses(*CoastalCity InlandCity*).

Consider also the following graph pattern P_1, which we wish to evaluate over $\mathcal{O}_1$:

PropertyAssertion(*train ?X ?Y*) OPT PropertyAssertion(*ferry ?Y ?Z*).

Intuitively, solutions to P_1 provide direct train lines from city X to city Y as well as, optionally, the ferry transfers from Y to other cities Z. Under the normative semantics, the BGPs in P_1 are evaluated separately. In particular, the optional BGP is evaluated to the empty set, and $[\![P_1]\!]^n_{\mathcal{O}_1} = \{\mu_1, \mu_2\}$, where

$$\mu_1 = \{?X \mapsto London, ?Y \mapsto Oxford\}, \text{ and}$$
$$\mu_2 = \{?X \mapsto London, ?Y \mapsto Holyhead\}.$$

In both answers, variable $?Z$ is unbounded and hence we conclude that $\mathcal{O}_1$ contains no relevant information about ferry connections starting from *Oxford* or *Holyhead*. However, the nature of the lack of such information is fundamentally different. On the one hand, the connections from *Holyhead* (e.g., to *Dublin*) are missing from $\mathcal{O}_1$ just by the incompleteness of the information in the graph, which is usual in (and also a feature of) Semantic Web applications. On the other hand, *Oxford* cannot have a ferry connection because it is a landlocked city, and hence the information about its (lack of) ferry connections is certain. Thus, the normative semantics cannot distinguish between unknown and non-existent ferry connections. However, if we adhere to the reading of unbounded variables as incomplete information or "nulls", then μ_1 should not be returned as an answer.

The issues described in this example become even more apparent in cases where the optional part alone cannot be satisfied, as it is incompatible with the information in the graph, as illustrated by the following example.

Example 2. Consider the ontology $\mathcal{O}_2$ with the following axioms:

ClassAssertion(*Person Peter*),   DisjointProperties(*hasFather hasMother*).

Furthermore, consider the following pattern P_2:

ClassAssertion(*Person ?X*) OPT ({

PropertyAssertion(*hasFather ?X ?Y*),

PropertyAssertion(*hasMother ?X ?Y*)}).

The optional BGP is evaluated to the empty mapping and hence under the normative semantics we have the mapping $\{?X \mapsto Peter\}$ forming the answer set $[\![P_2]\!]^n_{\mathcal{O}_2}$. Note, however, that the optional BGP in P_2 is in contradiction with the disjointness axiom: under the OWL 2 regime, no solution to P_2 can exist for any ontology containing that axiom.

As these examples suggest, if we interpret unbound variables in answers to queries with optional parts as an indication of unknown information in the data graph, then the normative semantics may yield counter-intuitive answers.

At the core of this issue is the inability of the normative semantics to distinguish between answers in which it is possible to assign values to the missing optional part (a natural reflection of incompleteness in the data), and those where this is impossible (a reflection that the missing information is fundamentally incompatible with the answer). This distinction is immaterial for regimes in which all legal graphs are consistent, but it quickly becomes apparent in more sophisticated regimes, such as those based on OWL 2.

4 Semantics of Strict Optional Matching

In this section, we propose our novel semantics for optional matching under regimes. In a nutshell, our semantics addresses the issues described in Section 3 by ruling out those answer mappings where unbound variables in the optional part cannot be matched to any consistent extension of the input graph. Our semantics is therefore *strict* , in the sense that only answers in which unbound variables are genuine manifestations of incompleteness in the data are returned.

4.1 Definition of Strict Semantics

We start by introducing the notion of a frozen RDF graph for a pattern P and a mapping μ. Roughly speaking, this graph is obtained by taking all the triple patterns in P and transforming them into RDF triples by applying the extension of μ where unbounded variables are "frozen" to arbitrary fresh constants.

Definition 1. *Let* $\mathfrak{R} = (\mathbf{R}, \mathcal{G}, \mathcal{P}, \mathcal{C}, \llbracket \cdot \rrbracket)$ *be an entailment regime. Let P be a legal graph pattern, and let μ be a mapping from variables $\mathbf{V}$ to RDF terms $\mathbf{T}$. Then, the* freezing G_μ^P *of P under μ is the RDF graph $\bar{\mu}(\mathsf{triples}(P))$, where $\bar{\mu}$ is the mapping that extends μ by assigning each variable in $\mathsf{vars}(P)$, which is not in $\mathsf{dom}(\mu)$, to a globally fresh IRI from $\mathbf{I}$ (not belonging to $\mathbf{R}$).*

The freezing G_μ^P depends only on the candidate mapping μ and the triple patterns occurring in P; thus, it does not depend either on the specific operators used in P, or on the RDF graph over which the query pattern is to be evaluated.

Example 3. For the pattern P_1 and mappings μ_1 and μ_2 from Example 1 we have the following freezings in functional-style syntax:

$$G_{\mu_1}^{P_1} = \{\mathsf{PropertyAssertion}(\textit{train London Oxford}),$$
$$\mathsf{PropertyAssertion}(\textit{ferry Oxford } w_1)\};$$
$$G_{\mu_2}^{P_1} = \{\mathsf{PropertyAssertion}(\textit{train London Holyhead}),$$
$$\mathsf{PropertyAssertion}(\textit{ferry Holyhead } w_2)\};$$

where w_1 and w_2 are freshly introduced IRIs.

Intuitively, the freezing represents the simplest, most general, RDF graph over which all the undefined variables in a given solution mapping could be bounded to concrete values. Thus, if G_μ^P together with the input graph G is not a consistent graph for the relevant regime, we can conclude, using condition (C1) of the regime, that the undefined variables in μ will never be matched to concrete values in any consistent extension of G and hence μ should be ruled out as an answer. On the other hand, if $G \cup G_\mu^P$ is consistent, then such an extension exists and, by condition (C2), the undefined variables can be mapped in this extension.

Definition 2. *Let $\mathfrak{R} = (\mathbf{R}, \mathcal{G}, \mathcal{P}, \mathcal{C}, \llbracket \cdot \rrbracket)$ be an entailment regime. A mapping μ is $\mathfrak{R}$-admissible for a graph $G \in \mathcal{C}$ and legal graph pattern P if $G \cup G_\mu^P$ is a graph belonging to $\mathcal{C}$. The set of all $\mathfrak{R}$-admissible mappings for a consistent graph G and a legal graph pattern P is denoted as $Adm(G, P)$.*

Example 4. Clearly, $\mathcal{O}_1 \cup G_{\mu_1}^{P_1}$ is inconsistent since ferries only depart from coastal cities, but Oxford is an inland city. In contrast, $\mathcal{O}_1 \cup G_{\mu_2}^{P_1}$ is consistent. Thus, we have $\mu_1 \notin Adm(\mathcal{O}_1, P)$, but $\mu_2 \in Adm(\mathcal{O}_1, P)$.

We are now ready to formalise our semantics.

Definition 3. *Let $\mathfrak{R} = (\mathbf{R}, \mathcal{G}, \mathcal{P}, \mathcal{C}, \llbracket \cdot \rrbracket)$ be an entailment regime. The* strict *query answering function $\llbracket \cdot \rrbracket^s$ is inductively defined for all legal graph patterns P on the base of $\llbracket \cdot \rrbracket$ as follows. For graphs G from $\mathcal{C}$ we have:*

1. *if P is a BGP then $\llbracket P \rrbracket_G^s = \llbracket P \rrbracket_G$;*
2. *if P is P_1 AND P_2 then $\llbracket P \rrbracket_G^s = (\llbracket P_1 \rrbracket_G^s \bowtie \llbracket P_2 \rrbracket_G^s) \cap Adm(G, P)$;*
3. *if P is P_1 OPT P_2 then $\llbracket P \rrbracket_G^s = (\llbracket P_1 \rrbracket_G^s \bowtie\!\!\!\!\!\rule[0.5ex]{1.2ex}{0.1pt} \llbracket P_2 \rrbracket_G^s) \cap Adm(G, P)$; and*
4. *if P is P' FILTER R then $\llbracket P \rrbracket_G^s = \{\mu \mid \mu \in \llbracket P' \rrbracket_G^s \text{ and } \mu \models R\}$,*

where $\cap$ denotes the standard set-theoretic intersection. If $G \notin \mathcal{C}$ then $\llbracket P \rrbracket_G^s = Err$ for any graph pattern P. Finally, legal patterns P_1 and P_2 are equivalent (under strict semantics), written $P_1 \equiv^s P_2$, if $\llbracket P_1 \rrbracket_G^s = \llbracket P_2 \rrbracket_G^s$ for any legal G.

Example 5. The strict semantics behaves as expected for our running examples. For $\mathcal{O}_1$ and P_1 from Example 1 we have that $\llbracket P_1 \rrbracket_{\mathcal{O}_1}^s = \{\mu_1\}$, whereas for $\mathcal{O}_2$ and P_2 from Example 2 we have $\llbracket P_2 \rrbracket_{\mathcal{O}_2}^s = \emptyset$.

The strict and normative semantics coincide in two limit cases. First, if the entailment regime does not allow for inconsistent graphs (i.e., if $\mathcal{C} = \mathcal{G}$) as is the case for the RDF regime [10], then $\llbracket P \rrbracket_G^s = \llbracket P \rrbracket_G^n$ for every legal pattern P and graph G. Second, if the relevant pattern P is OPT-free then the freezing for every candidate answer mapping contains no fresh IRIs and is $\mathfrak{R}$-entailed by G; thus, we again have $\llbracket P \rrbracket_G^s = \llbracket P \rrbracket_G^n$ for every legal graph G.

Thus, the difference between the normative semantics $\llbracket \cdot \rrbracket^n$ and strict semantics $\llbracket \cdot \rrbracket^s$ manifests only for regimes that admit inconsistency, and is circumscribed to the presence of OPT in graph patterns, where non-admissible mappings are excluded in the case of the strict semantics. Note, however, that even if a mapping

μ_1 (resp. μ_2) is admissible for a sub-pattern P_1 (resp. P_2) containing OPT, it is possible for $\mu_1 \cup \mu_2$ not to be admissible for the joined pattern $P = P_1$ AND P_2. Thus, the admissibility restriction is also explicitly reflected in the semantics of AND given in Definition 3. This is illustrated in the example given next.

Example 6. Consider ontology $\mathcal{O}_3$, consisting of the following axioms:

> SubClassOf(
>> IntersectionOf(SomeValuesFrom(*husband* Thing)
>>> SomeValuesFrom(*wife* Thing))
>
>> Nothing),
>> ClassAssertion(*Person Mary*).

The first axiom establishes that a person cannot have both a husband and a wife. Consider also the following well-designed graph pattern P_3:

(ClassAssertion(*Person* ?X) OPT (PropertyAssertion(*husband* ?X ?Y))) AND

(ClassAssertion(*Person* ?X) OPT (PropertyAssertion(*wife* ?X ?Z))).

Clearly, $\mu = \{?X \mapsto Mary\}$ belongs to the strict answer to each of the OPT sub-patterns of P_3 since each of them independently can match to a consistent extension of $\mathcal{O}_3$. However, μ is not admissible for P_3 since *Mary* has both a husband and a wife in $G_\mu^{P_3}$, and hence $\mathcal{O}_3 \cup G_\mu^{P_3}$ is inconsistent. Thus, $[\![P_3]\!]_{\mathcal{O}_3}^s = \emptyset$.

4.2 Comparing the Normative and Strict Semantics

Our previous examples support the expected behaviour of our semantics, namely that its effect is circumscribed to filtering out problematic answers returned under the normative semantics. We next formally show that our semantics behaves as expected *in general*, provided that we restrict ourselves to well-designed patterns and negation-free FILTER expressions (which are rather mild restrictions).

It is known that patterns which are not well-designed easily lead to unexpected answers, even under the normative semantics (we refer to [2] for a detailed discussion). Therefore, it comes at no surprise that the intuitive behaviour of our semantics is only guaranteed under this assumption.

But before stating our main result in this section, we establish first a useful lemma that is applicable to well-designed patterns under both semantics.

Lemma 1. *Let $\mathfrak{R} = (\mathbf{R}, \mathcal{G}, \mathcal{P}, \mathcal{C}, [\![\cdot]\!])$ be an entailment regime, and let P be a sub-pattern of a well-designed graph pattern. If a variable appears both inside and outside P, then it is defined in each mapping from $[\![P]\!]_G^n$ for any consistent G as well as in each mapping from $[\![P]\!]_G^s$.*

Proof. For the sake of contradiction, let ?X be a variable which appears both inside and outside P, but is undefined in some mapping $\mu \in [\![P]\!]_G^n \cup [\![P]\!]_G^s$. Since ?X is undefined, it appears in the optional (i.e., right) part of an OPT-sub-pattern of P. The overall graph pattern is well-designed, so ?X must appear in the mandatory (i.e., left) part of the OPT-sub-pattern of P. If this sub-pattern is not in the optional part of another higher-level sub-pattern, then $?X$ must be defined in μ, which contradicts the original assumption. Otherwise, we can apply the same argument and show that $?X$ is in the mandatory part of the higher-level sub-pattern. Such reasoning would eventually lead to a contradiction.   □

Theorem 1. *Let* $\mathfrak{R} = (\mathbf{R}, \mathcal{G}, \mathcal{P}, \mathcal{C}, \llbracket \cdot \rrbracket)$ *be an entailment regime. The inclusion* $\llbracket P \rrbracket_G^s \sqsubseteq \llbracket P \rrbracket_G^n$ *holds for any graph* G *from* $\mathcal{C}$ *and any legal well-designed graph pattern* P *which does not use negation* $\neg$ *in* FILTER *expressions.*

Proof. The proof is by induction on the structure of the graph pattern P.

1. Let P be a BGP. Then $\llbracket P \rrbracket_G^s = \llbracket P \rrbracket_G^n = \llbracket P \rrbracket_G$ by definition of the semantics.
2. Let P be P_1 AND P_2, $\llbracket P_1 \rrbracket_G^s \sqsubseteq \llbracket P_1 \rrbracket_G^n$, $\llbracket P_2 \rrbracket_G^s \sqsubseteq \llbracket P_2 \rrbracket_G^n$, and μ be a mapping from $\llbracket P \rrbracket_G^s$. By the definition of the semantics of AND patterns we have that $\llbracket P \rrbracket_G^s = (\llbracket P_1 \rrbracket_G^s \bowtie \llbracket P_2 \rrbracket_G^s) \cap Adm(G, P)$, that is there exist compatible $\mu_1 \in \llbracket P_1 \rrbracket_G^s$ and $\mu_2 \in \llbracket P_1 \rrbracket_G^s$ such that $\mu = \mu_1 \cup \mu_2$. By the inductive assumption, there exist $\mu_1' \in \llbracket P_1 \rrbracket_G^n$ and $\mu_2' \in \llbracket P_1 \rrbracket_G^n$ such that $\mu_1 \sqsubseteq \mu_1'$ and $\mu_2 \sqsubseteq \mu_2'$. By Lemma 1, μ_1' and μ_2' are compatible. Indeed, if a variable is defined in both of them, it occurs in P_1 and P_2, so, by the lemma, it is defined in both μ_1 and μ_2 which are compatible; hence the values of this variable in all μ_1, μ_2, μ_1' and μ_2' coincide, which implies that the last two are compatible. So, $\mu_1' \cup \mu_2'$ is in $\llbracket P_1 \rrbracket_G^n \bowtie \llbracket P_2 \rrbracket_G^n = \llbracket P \rrbracket_G^n$ as required.
3. Let P be P_1 OPT P_2, $\llbracket P_1 \rrbracket_G^s \sqsubseteq \llbracket P_1 \rrbracket_G^n$, $\llbracket P_2 \rrbracket_G^s \sqsubseteq \llbracket P_2 \rrbracket_G^n$, and μ be a mapping from $\llbracket P \rrbracket_G^s$. By the definition of the semantics of OPT patterns we have that $\llbracket P \rrbracket_G^s = (\llbracket P_1 \rrbracket_G^s \bowtie \llbracket P_2 \rrbracket_G^s) \cap Adm(G, P)$, that is, we have two options.
   (a) Let $\mu \in \llbracket P_1 \rrbracket_G^s \bowtie \llbracket P_2 \rrbracket_G^s$ and $\mu \in Adm(G, P)$. In this case the rest of the proof goes the same lines as the case when P is an AND graph pattern.
   (b) Let $\mu \in \llbracket P_1 \rrbracket_G^s \setminus \llbracket P_2 \rrbracket_G^s$ and $\mu \in Adm(G, P)$. Hence, in particular, $\mu \in \llbracket P_1 \rrbracket_G^s$. By the inductive assumption, there exists a mapping μ_1' in $\llbracket P_1 \rrbracket_G^n$ such that $\mu \sqsubseteq \mu_1'$. Hence, as required, there exists a mapping μ' in $\llbracket P \rrbracket_G^n$ (which is either $\mu_1' \cup \mu_2'$ for some $\mu_2' \in \llbracket P_2 \rrbracket_G^n$ compatible with μ_1', or μ_1' itself, if such a μ_2' does not exist), such that $\mu \sqsubseteq \mu'$.
4. Let P be P' FILTER R, $\llbracket P' \rrbracket_G^s \sqsubseteq \llbracket P' \rrbracket_G^n$, R be a built-in condition not using $\neg$, and $\mu \in \llbracket P \rrbracket_G^s$. By the definition of semantics of FILTER patterns, $\mu \in \llbracket P' \rrbracket_G^s$. Hence, by the inductive assumption, there exists $\mu' \in \llbracket P' \rrbracket_G^n$ such that $\mu \sqsubseteq \mu'$. Since R does not use $\neg$, $\mu' \models R$. So, $\mu' \in \llbracket P \rrbracket_G^n$, as required.   □

Note that Theorem 1 is formulated in terms of subsumption, instead of set-theoretic containment. The rationale behind this formulation is clarified next.

Example 7. Consider the ontology $\mathcal{O}_1'$, which is obtained from $\mathcal{O}_1$ in Example 1 by removing all axioms involving *Holyhead*, and adding the following axiom:

$$\text{PropertyAssertion}(bus\ Canterbury\ London).$$

Consider also the following graph pattern P_1':

PropertyAssertion(bus $?U$ $?X$) OPT

        (PropertyAssertion($train$ $?X$ $?Y$) OPT

                PropertyAssertion($ferry$ $?Y$ $?Z$)).

The following mapping μ is returned by the normative semantics:

$$\{?U \mapsto Canterbury, ?X \mapsto London, ?Y \mapsto Oxford\}.$$

As already discussed, Oxford is an inland city and hence cannot have ferry connections; thus, μ is not returned under strict semantics. However, it may be possible to reach a ferry connection from London (although none is given), and hence the following answer μ' is returned instead of μ under strict semantics.

$$\{?U \mapsto Canterbury, ?X \mapsto London\}.$$

Clearly, μ' is not returned under normative semantics and hence $[\![P_1']\!]_{\mathcal{O}_1'}^s \not\subseteq [\![P_1']\!]_{\mathcal{O}_1'}^n$; however, $\mu' \sqsubseteq \mu$ and $[\![P_1']\!]_{\mathcal{O}_1'}^s \sqsubseteq [\![P_1']\!]_{\mathcal{O}_1'}^n$.

5 Computational Properties and Static Optimisation

In this section, we first study the computational properties of our semantics. We show that the complexity of graph pattern evaluation under strict and normative semantics coincide, provided that consistency checking is feasible in PSPACE for the regime at hand. Then we focus on static query analysis, and in particular on pattern equivalence. We show that the key equivalence-preserving transformation rules that have been proposed for static optimisation of SPARQL queries continue to hold if we consider equivalence under strict semantics.

5.1 Complexity of Strict Graph Pattern Evaluation

Recall that the graph pattern evaluation is the key reasoning problem in SPARQL. In the context of entailment regimes, it is defined as given next, where x is either n or s, depending of the semantics.

GRAPH PATTERN EVALUATION
Input: Regime $\mathfrak{R}$, legal graph G, legal graph pattern P, and mapping μ.   *Question:* Is $\mu \in [\![P]\!]_G^x$ under the regime $\mathfrak{R}$?

Here, when we say that regime $\mathfrak{R}$ is a part of the input, we mean that it includes two oracle functions checking consistency of legal graphs and evaluating legal BGPs over legal graphs, respectively. In what follows, we refer to the problem as NORMATIVE if $x = n$, and as STRICT if $x = s$.

It is known that the normative graph pattern evaluation problem is in PSPACE for the RDF regime [2]. We next argue that membership in PSPACE holds in general for any regime satisfying the basic properties discussed in Section 2 and for both normative and strict versions of the problem, provided that the complexity of both oracles of the regime is in PSPACE.

Theorem 2. NORMATIVE *and* STRICT GRAPH PATTERN EVALUATION *problems are in* PSPACE, *provided the oracles associated to input regimes are in* PSPACE.

Proof. We start with the normative semantics. If the regime $\mathfrak{R}$ allows for inconsistent graphs, then the regime may require to first check the input graph for consistency, which is feasible in PSPACE by the assumptions of the theorem. Then, the same recursive procedure $Eval(\mu, P, G)$ for a mapping μ, graph pattern P and graph G described in [2] for the RDF regime is applicable to evaluate queries under $\mathfrak{R}$. The procedure is in PSPACE because each BGP in the input pattern can be evaluated by the second oracle in PSPACE by the assumptions.

The situation is analogous for the strict semantics: consistency checking may be required upfront by the regime and the recursive PSPACE procedure $Eval(\mu, P, G)$ can be designed by a straightforward implementation of the definition of strict semantics. The only difference with the normative case is that in each step we need to check for admissibility, which is possible in PSPACE given our assumptions about the oracles of the regime. For example, if P is a pattern of the form P_1 OPT P_2, then $Eval$ first checks whether $Eval(\mu, P_1$ AND $P_2, G)$ holds, or $Eval(\mu, P_1, G)$ with not $Eval(\mu', P_2, G)$ for any mapping μ', dom$(\mu') \subseteq$ vars(P_2), holds; and then checks, by means of the oracle function, whether $\mu \in Adm(G, P)$. If both of the checks are positive, then the answer is true, otherwise, it is false.   □

Consequently, the use of our strict semantics does not increase the computational complexity for reasonable regimes. In particular, it follows directly from Theorem 2 that the evaluation problem is in PSPACE under both semantics for the tractable entailment regimes associated to the OWL 2 profiles [13].

It is also well-known that graph pattern evaluation under normative semantics is PSPACE-hard for the RDF regime [2]. To formulate a general hardness result that holds for *any* regime we would need to require additional properties for a regime to qualify as "reasonable". In order not to unnecessarily complicate the presentation, we simply point out that PSPACE-hardness holds for all the regimes mentioned in the specification under both normative and strict semantics [10]. This is immediate for the normative semantics. The hardness for the strict semantics can be proved by reduction from quantified boolean formula validity as it is done in [2]. This reduction encodes a formula in the query pattern, and relies on a fixed RDF dataset, which corresponds to a set of first-order facts. Thus, the extension of such fixed graph with the freezing of a sub-pattern of the query pattern is always consistent under all the regimes in the specification.

5.2   Static Analysis and Optimisation

Static analysis and optimisation of SPARQL queries has received significant attention in recent years [4,6,14,15,16]. A key ingredient for query optimisation is the availability of a comprehensive catalog of equivalence-preserving transformation rules for SPARQL patterns. Schmidt et al. [4] and Perez et al. [2] provide a rich set of such equivalences, which holds under normative semantics for RDF regime. Some of these equivalences, such as idempotence, commutativity, and associativity of the AND operator, hold without any restrictions (for our core fragment of SPARQL) and are quite easy to prove. However, those that involve OPT are more intricate and hold only for well-designed patterns.

The claim of this section is that these equivalences continue to hold for any entailment regime, under both normative and strict semantics. For brevity, we concentrate only on strict semantics and the equivalences with OPT, leaving the proofs for the rest out of the scope of this paper. But before doing so we state the following auxiliary lemma, which proof is straightforward application of conditions (C1)–(C2) on regimes and omitted for brevity.

Lemma 2. *Let* $\mathfrak{R} = (\mathbf{R}, \mathcal{G}, \mathcal{P}, \mathcal{C}, \llbracket \cdot \rrbracket)$ *be an entailment regime. If* $\mu \in Adm(G, P)$ *for a mapping* μ, *graph* $G \in \mathcal{C}$ *and legal graph pattern* P, *then* $\mu' \in Adm(G, P')$ *for any mapping* $\mu' \sqsubseteq \mu$ *and legal graph pattern* P' *such that* triples$(P') \subseteq$ triples(P).

The following theorem establishes that the known equivalences involving OPT in well-designed patterns hold for any entailment regime under strict semantics.

Theorem 3. *Let* $\mathfrak{R}$ *be an entailment regime. The following equivalences hold, provided the graph patterns on both sides are legal and well-designed:*

$$(P_1 \text{ OPT } P_2) \text{ FILTER } R \equiv^s (P_1 \text{ FILTER } R) \text{ OPT } P_2, \tag{1}$$

$$P_1 \text{ AND } (P_2 \text{ OPT } P_3) \equiv^s (P_1 \text{ AND } P_2) \text{ OPT } P_3, \tag{2}$$

$$(P_1 \text{ OPT } P_2) \text{ AND } P_3 \equiv^s (P_1 \text{ AND } P_3) \text{ OPT } P_2, \tag{3}$$

$$(P_1 \text{ OPT } P_2) \text{ OPT } P_3 \equiv^s (P_1 \text{ OPT } P_3) \text{ OPT } P_2. \tag{4}$$

Proof. Equivalence (1). For brevity we give a proof only for the fact that for every graph each mapping in the semantics of the pattern on the left is in the semantics of the pattern on the right, and the other direction is similar. Let $\mu \in \llbracket (P_1 \text{ OPT } P_2) \text{ FILTER } R \rrbracket_G^s$ for a consistent graph G, built-in condition R and legal graph patterns P_1 and P_2, such that the both sides of the equivalence are well-designed. By the definition of strict semantics there are two possibilities.
Case 1: $\mu = \mu_1 \cup \mu_2$ for $\mu_i \in \llbracket P_i \rrbracket_G^s$, such that $\mu \in Adm(G, P_1 \text{ OPT } P_2)$ and $\mu \models R$. To show that $\mu \in \llbracket (P_1 \text{ FILTER } R) \text{ OPT } P_2 \rrbracket_G^s$ the only thing we need to prove is that $\mu_1 \models R$, and we do it by showing that for every $?X$ which appears in R the values of μ and μ_1 on $?X$ are either the same or both undefined. Indeed, if such $?X$ is in P_2 then, since $(P_1 \text{ OPT } P_2) \text{ FILTER } R$ is well-designed, it appears in P_1, and hence, by Lemma 1, $?X \in \text{dom}(\mu_1)$, which means that $\mu(?X) = \mu_1(?X)$. On the other hand, if $?X$ is not in P_2, then $?X \notin \text{dom}(\mu_2)$, that is either the value of μ on $?X$ coincides with the value of μ_1 or both of them are undefined.
Case 2: $\mu \in \llbracket P_1 \rrbracket_G^s$, such that $\mu \in Adm(G, P_1 \text{ OPT } P_2)$, $\mu \models R$, and there is no $\mu_2 \in \llbracket P_2 \rrbracket_G^s$ such that $\mu \sim \mu_2$. Immediately we have that $\mu \in \llbracket (P_1 \text{ FILTER } R) \text{ OPT } P_2 \rrbracket_G^s$.

Equivalence (2). For brevity, we show the more involved direction that shows containment from right to left. Let $\mu \in \llbracket (P_1 \text{ AND } P_2) \text{ OPT } P_3 \rrbracket_G^s$ for a consistent G, and legal patterns P_1, P_2 and P_3, such that the both sides of the equivalence are well-designed. We have the following cases by the definition of strict semantics.
Case 1: $\mu = \mu_1 \cup \mu_2 \cup \mu_3$ for $\mu_i \in \llbracket P_i \rrbracket_G^s$, such that $\mu_1 \cup \mu_2 \in Adm(G, P_1 \text{ AND } P_2)$ and $\mu \in Adm(G, (P_1 \text{ AND } P_2) \text{ OPT } P_3)$. By Lemma 2 the last inclusion implies

the first. Moreover, it implies that $\mu_2 \cup \mu_3 \in Adm(G, P_2 \,\mathsf{OPT}\, P_3)$, which, together with the fact that $Adm(G, (P_1 \,\mathsf{AND}\, P_2) \,\mathsf{OPT}\, P_3) = Adm(G, P_1 \,\mathsf{AND}\, (P_2 \,\mathsf{OPT}\, P_3))$ guarantees that $\mu \in [\![P_1 \,\mathsf{AND}\, (P_2 \,\mathsf{OPT}\, P_3)]\!]_G^s$ as required.

Case 2: $\mu = \mu_1 \cup \mu_2$ for $\mu_i \in [\![P_i]\!]_G^s$, such that $\mu \in Adm(G, P_1 \,\mathsf{AND}\, P_2)$, $\mu \in Adm(G, (P_1 \,\mathsf{AND}\, P_2) \,\mathsf{OPT}\, P_3)$, and there is no $\mu_3 \in [\![P_3]\!]_G^s$ such that $\mu \sim \mu_3$. By Lemma 2 $\mu_2 \in Adm(G, P_2 \,\mathsf{OPT}\, P_3)$ holds. Also, since $P_1 \,\mathsf{AND}\, (P_2 \,\mathsf{OPT}\, P_3)$ is well-designed, there is no $\mu_3' \in [\![P_3]\!]_G^s$ such that $\mu_2 \sim \mu_3'$; otherwise there would be a variable $?X \in \mathsf{dom}(\mu_1) \cap \mathsf{dom}(\mu_3)$, but $?X \notin \mathsf{dom}(\mu_2)$, with $\mu_1(?X) \neq \mu_3(?X)$, which by the fact that the pattern is well-designed would imply that $?X$ appears in P_2 and by Lemma 1 would lead to a contradiction. Putting the facts above together with the equality $Adm(G, (P_1 \,\mathsf{AND}\, P_2) \,\mathsf{OPT}\, P_3) = Adm(G, P_1 \,\mathsf{AND}\, (P_2 \,\mathsf{OPT}\, P_3))$ we obtain that $\mu \in [\![(P_1 \,\mathsf{AND}\, P_2) \,\mathsf{OPT}\, P_3]\!]_G^s$ as required.

Equivalence (3) follows from (2) and commutativity of AND.

Equivalence (4). We concentrate again on forward direction. Let $\mu \in [\![(P_1 \,\mathsf{OPT}\, P_2) \,\mathsf{OPT}\, P_3]\!]_G^s$ for a consistent graph G, and legal patterns P_1, P_2 and P_3 such that the both sides of the equivalence are well-designed. We have four possibilities. We prove the first two, omitting the very similar proofs for other two for brevity.

Case 1: $\mu = \mu_1 \cup \mu_2 \cup \mu_3$ for $\mu_i \in [\![P_i]\!]_G^s$, such that $\mu_1 \cup \mu_2 \in Adm(G, P_1 \,\mathsf{OPT}\, P_2)$ and $\mu \in Adm(G, (P_1 \,\mathsf{OPT}\, P_2) \,\mathsf{OPT}\, P_3)$. By Lemma 2 the last inclusion implies $\mu_1 \cup \mu_3 \in Adm(G, P_1 \,\mathsf{OPT}\, P_3)$, which, together with $Adm(G, (P_1 \,\mathsf{OPT}\, P_2) \,\mathsf{OPT}\, P_3) = Adm(G, (P_1 \,\mathsf{OPT}\, P_3) \,\mathsf{OPT}\, P_2)$ guarantees $\mu \in [\![(P_1 \,\mathsf{OPT}\, P_3) \,\mathsf{OPT}\, P_2]\!]_G^s$.

Case 2: $\mu = \mu_1 \cup \mu_2$ for $\mu_i \in [\![P_i]\!]_G^s$, where $\mu \in Adm(G, P_1 \,\mathsf{OPT}\, P_2)$, $\mu \in Adm(G, (P_1 \,\mathsf{OPT}\, P_2) \,\mathsf{OPT}\, P_3)$, and there is no $\mu_3 \in [\![P_3]\!]_G^s$ with $\mu \sim \mu_3$. By Lemma 2 we have $\mu_1 \in Adm(G, P_1 \,\mathsf{OPT}\, P_3)$. Similar to Case 2 in the proof of (2), since $(P_1 \,\mathsf{OPT}\, P_2) \,\mathsf{OPT}\, P_3$ is well-designed, by Lemma 1 there is no $\mu_3' \in [\![P_3]\!]_G^s$ such that $\mu_1 \sim \mu_3'$. But then, since $Adm(G, (P_1 \,\mathsf{OPT}\, P_2) \,\mathsf{OPT}\, P_3) = Adm(G, (P_1 \,\mathsf{OPT}\, P_3) \,\mathsf{OPT}\, P_2)$ we have $\mu \in [\![(P_1 \,\mathsf{OPT}\, P_3) \,\mathsf{OPT}\, P_1]\!]_G^s$ as required.

Case 3: $\mu = \mu_1 \cup \mu_3$ for $\mu_i \in [\![P_i]\!]_G^s$, such that $\mu_1 \in Adm(G, P_1 \,\mathsf{OPT}\, P_2)$, $\mu \in Adm(G, (P_1 \,\mathsf{OPT}\, P_2) \,\mathsf{OPT}\, P_3)$, and there is no $\mu_2 \in [\![P_2]\!]_G^s$ such that $\mu_1 \sim \mu_2$.

Case 4: $\mu \in [\![P_1]\!]_G^s$, $\mu \in Adm(G, P_1 \,\mathsf{OPT}\, P_2)$, $\mu \in Adm(G, (P_1 \,\mathsf{OPT}\, P_2) \,\mathsf{OPT}\, P_3)$, and neither $\mu_2 \in [\![P_2]\!]_G^s$ such that $\mu \sim \mu_2$, nor $\mu_3 \in [\![P_3]\!]_G^s$ such that $\mu \sim \mu_3$. $\square$

6   Conclusion

In this paper, we have proposed a novel semantics for optional matching in SPARQL under entailment regimes where unbound variables in answer mappings are naturally interpreted as "null" values. Our *strict* semantics has been designed to deal in a faithful way with the "lack of regular, complete structures in RDF graphs" and hence with the fundamental incompleteness of information on the Semantic Web [1]. We believe that both strict and normative semantics are valid, but one may be more appropriate than the other in certain applications. Both semantics are compatible at a fundamental level and it would be possible to exploit them in the same application by letting users commit to one or the other explicitly when posing queries. Integrating them in a clean way from a syntactic point of view is more tricky, and it is something we leave for future investigation.

Acknowledgements. This work was supported by the Royal Society, and the EPSRC projects Score!, Exoda, and MaSI³.

References

1. Prud'hommeaux, E., Seaborne, A.: SPARQL query language for RDF. W3C Recommendation (2008), http://www.w3.org/TR/rdf-sparql-query/
2. Pérez, J., Arenas, M., Gutierrez, C.: Semantics and complexity of SPARQL. ACM Trans. Database Syst. 34(3) (2009)
3. Angles, R., Gutierrez, C.: The expressive power of SPARQL. In: Sheth, A.P., Staab, S., Dean, M., Paolucci, M., Maynard, D., Finin, T., Thirunarayan, K. (eds.) ISWC 2008. LNCS, vol. 5318, pp. 114–129. Springer, Heidelberg (2008)
4. Schmidt, M., Meier, M., Lausen, G.: Foundations of SPARQL query optimization. In: ICDT, pp. 4–33 (2010)
5. Arenas, M., Pérez, J.: Querying semantic web data with SPARQL. In: PODS, pp. 305–316 (2011)
6. Letelier, A., Pérez, J., Pichler, R., Skritek, S.: Static analysis and optimization of semantic web queries. ACM Trans. Database Syst. 38(4), 25 (2013)
7. Polleres, A.: From SPARQL to rules (and back). In: WWW, pp. 787–796 (2007)
8. Motik, B., Patel-Schneider, P.F., Parsia, B.: OWL 2 Web Ontology Language Structural Specification and Functional-style Syntax. W3C Recommendation (2012), http://www.w3.org/TR/owl2-syntax/
9. W3C SPARQL Working Group: SPARQL 1.1 Query language. W3C Recommendation (2013), http://www.w3.org/TR/sparql11-query/
10. Glimm, B., Ogbuji, C.: SPARQL 1.1 Entailment Regimes. W3C Recommendation (2013), http://www.w3.org/TR/sparql11-entailment/
11. Glimm, B., Krötzsch, M.: SPARQL beyond subgraph matching. In: Patel-Schneider, P.F., Pan, Y., Hitzler, P., Mika, P., Zhang, L., Pan, J.Z., Horrocks, I., Glimm, B. (eds.) ISWC 2010, Part I. LNCS, vol. 6496, pp. 241–256. Springer, Heidelberg (2010)
12. Pérez, J., Arenas, M., Gutierrez, C.: Semantics and complexity of SPARQL. In: Cruz, I., Decker, S., Allemang, D., Preist, C., Schwabe, D., Mika, P., Uschold, M., Aroyo, L.M. (eds.) ISWC 2006. LNCS, vol. 4273, pp. 30–43. Springer, Heidelberg (2006)
13. Motik, B., Cuenca Grau, B., Horrocks, I., Wu, Z., Fokoue, A., Lutz, C.: OWL 2 Web Ontology Language: Profiles (October 27, 2009), http://www.w3.org/TR/owl2-profiles/
14. Chekol, M.W., Euzenat, J., Genevès, P., Layaïda, N.: SPARQL query containment under RDFS entailment regime. In: Gramlich, B., Miller, D., Sattler, U. (eds.) IJCAR 2012. LNCS, vol. 7364, pp. 134–148. Springer, Heidelberg (2012)
15. Chekol, M.W., Euzenat, J., Genevès, P., Layaïda, N.: SPARQL query containment under $\mathcal{SHI}$ axioms. In: AAAI (2012)
16. Wudage Chekol, M., Euzenat, J., Genevès, P., Layaïda, N.: Evaluating and benchmarking SPARQL query containment solvers. In: Alani, H., et al. (eds.) ISWC 2013, Part II. LNCS, vol. 8219, pp. 408–423. Springer, Heidelberg (2013)

Strategies for Executing Federated Queries in SPARQL1.1

Carlos Buil-Aranda[1,*], Axel Polleres[2,**], and Jürgen Umbrich[2]

[1] Department of Computer Science, Pontificia Universidad Católica, Chile
cbuil@ing.puc.cl
[2] Vienna University of Economy and Business (WU)
{first.last}@wu.ac.at

Abstract A common way for exposing RDF data on the Web is by means of SPARQL endpoints which allow end users and applications to query just the RDF data they want. However, servers hosting SPARQL endpoints often restrict access to the data by limiting the amount of results returned per query or the amount of queries per time that a client may issue. As this may affect query completeness when using SPARQL1.1's federated query extension, we analysed different strategies to implement federated queries with the goal to circumvent endpoint limits. We show that some seemingly intuitive methods for decomposing federated queries provide unsound results in the general case, and provide fixes or discuss under which restrictions these recipes are still applicable. Finally, we evaluate the proposed strategies for checking their feasibility in practice.

1 Introduction

The Linked Open Data initiative promotes the publication and linkage of RDF data on the Web. Under this initiative many organisations (either public or private) expose billions of statements using the RDF data model and also provide links to other RDF datasets. A common way for accessing such RDF datasets is by means of SPARQL endpoints. These endpoints are Web services that implement the SPARQL protocol and then allow end users and applications to query just the RDF data they want. However, servers hosting SPARQL endpoints often restrict the access to the data by limiting the server resources available per received query and client. These physical resource limitations most commonly include restrictions of the size of result set returned to the end users (e.g., a 10.000 result limit for each query) or simply generating errors such as time outs on queries that spend too many resources. Such imposed limitations are necessary due to too many resource limits [2] when serving queries concurrently to many clients.

However, in practice, particularly in the context of using SPARQL1.1's Federated Query Extension [9], these limitations prevent users from obtaining complete answers to their SPARQL queries. The result set size limitation is particularly relevant when a user wants to federate SPARQL queries over a number of SPARQL endpoints.

---

* Supported by the Millennium Nucleus Center for Semantic Web Research under Grant NC120004 and CONICYT/FONDECYT project 3130617.
** Supported by the Vienna Science and Technology Fund (WWTF) project ICT12-015.

P. Mika et al. (Eds.) ISWC 2014, Part II, LNCS 8797, pp. 390–405, 2014.

Using different combinations of SPARQL patterns is possible to overcome the servers' result size limits and obtain complete result sets for SERVICE queries. A common pattern that can be used for that purpose is using the VALUES operator from the new SPARQL 1.1 Recommendation. This operator allows to "ship" the results from a local query to be joined with a remote pattern along with the service query. However this operator is still not widely implemented in currently deployed endpoints [2] and thus alternative options might have to be considered. After some preliminaries (§2) this paper presents a study of several alternative strategies (§3), allowing users to obtain sound and complete answers to SPARQL queries; for instance, we show that using naive nested loops or combinations of the UNION and FILTER operators for constraining remote queries may return unsound results; we further discuss how to fix these naive approaches to obtain correct results. Finally in §4+5 we evaluate different settings, depending on the data, the local SPARQL engine and the engine running at the involved remote endpoints in a federated query, before we conclude in § 6.

2 Preliminaries

We first describe the basics of the SPARQL syntax we will use thorough the paper followed by the semantics of the most relevant SPARQL operators used.[1]

Syntax. The official syntax of SPARQL1.1 [3] considers operators OPTIONAL, UNION, FILTER, SELECT, concatenation via a point symbol (.), { } to group patterns, as well as keywords (new in SPARQL 1.1) SERVICE to delegate parts of a query to a remote endpoint, and VALUES to define sets of variable bindings.

We follow [1,8] for defining the SPARQL syntax operators including the VALUES and SERVICE operators. We use letter B,I,L,V for denoting the (infinite) sets of blank nodes, IRIs, RDF literals, and variables as usual.[2]

(1) A triple $(I \cup L \cup V) \times (I \cup V) \times (I \cup L \cup V)$ is a graph pattern (a triple pattern).
(2) If P_1 and P_2 are graph patterns, then expressions $(P_1$ AND $P_2)$, $(P_1$ OPT $P_2)$, and $(P_1$ UNION $P_2)$ are graph patterns.[3]
(3) If P is a graph pattern and R is a *SPARQL built-in* condition, then the expression $(P$ FILTER $R)$ is a graph pattern.
(4) If P is a graph pattern, then SELECT W P ORDER BY V LIMIT l OFFSET o is a graph pattern (subquery), where ORDER BY, LIMIT, and OFFSET clauses (aka *solution modifiers*) are optional, W, V are sets of variables, and $l, o \in \mathbb{N}$.[4]
(5) If P is a graph pattern and $a \in (I \cup V)$, then (SERVICE a P) is a graph pattern.

---

[1] Note that we assume a set-based semantics as in [8] here, i.e. implicitly we assume DISTINCT queries. We also used DISTINCT queries in our experiments.

[2] In SPARQL patterns, blank nodes and variables can be used interchangeably, which is why we ignore blank nodes in SPARQL patterns.

[3] AND is syntactically written as either a sequence of '{ }'-delimited group graph patterns, or a sequence of '.'-separated triple patterns.

[4] We simplify here, as general ORDER BY clauses in SPARQL allow arbitratry expressions.

(6) VALUES WA is a graph pattern where $W = [?X_1, \ldots, ?X_n]$ is a sequence of pairwise distinct variables, and

$$A = \begin{bmatrix} a_{1,1}, & \cdots, & a_{1,n} \\ a_{2,1}, & \cdots, & a_{2,n} \\ & \vdots & \\ a_{m,1}, & \cdots, & a_{m,n} \end{bmatrix}$$

is a matrix of values where $a_{i,j} \in (I \cup L \cup \{UNBOUND\})$.

For the exposition of this paper, we leave out further more complex graph patterns such as GRAPH graph patterns, or new SPARQL 1.1 [3] like aggregates and property paths. We will use the notion of FILTER expressions as defined in [8]. We also use unary predicates like *bound*, *isBlank*, and the binary equality predicate '=', which herein we consider as synonym for $sameTerm(\cdot, \cdot)$ from [3].[5]

Let P be a graph pattern; in what follows, we use $var(P)$ to denote the set of variables occurring in P. In particular, if t is a triple pattern, then $var(t)$ denotes the set of variables occurring in the components of t. Similarly, for a built-in condition R, we use $var(R)$ to denote the set of variables occurring in R.

Semantics. As in [8], we consider a set-based semantics (which can always be achieved in SPARQL using the keyword DISTINCT), since conjunctive query containment is already undecidable for bag-semantics [4].

We use terminology defined in [8] for compatibility between solution mappings, written $\mu_1 \sim \mu_2$. Let Ω_1 and Ω_2 be sets of mappings; the join, union, difference, and left outer-join operations for Ω_1 and Ω_2 are defined as follows:

$$\Omega_1 \bowtie \Omega_2 = \{\mu_1 \cup \mu_2 \mid \mu_1 \in \Omega_1,$$
$$\mu_2 \in \Omega_2 \text{ and } \mu_1 \sim \mu_2\},$$
$$\Omega_1 \cup \Omega_2 = \{\mu \mid \mu \in \Omega_1 \text{ or } \mu \in \Omega_2\},$$
$$\Omega_1 \smallsetminus \Omega_2 = \{\mu \in \Omega_1 \mid \forall \mu' \in \Omega_2 : \mu \not\sim \mu'\},$$
$$\Omega_1 \bowtie\!\!\!\!\!\!\!\!{} \Omega_2 = (\Omega_1 \bowtie \Omega_2) \cup (\Omega_1 \smallsetminus \Omega_2).$$

As usual, we use $dom(\mu)$ for denoting the variables bound within – i.e. the domain of – a SPARQL solution mapping μ. The evaluation semantics of SPARQL patterns with respect to an RDF graph G is defined in Fig. 1.

The evaluation of a FILTER expression R wrt. solution mapping μ relies on a three-valued logic $(\top, \bot, \varepsilon)$, cf. [3, §17.2], where
$\mu(R) = \top$, if:

- R is *bound*($?X$) and $?X \in dom(\mu)$;
- R is *isBlank*($?X$), $?X \in dom(\mu)$ and $\mu(?X) \in B$;
- R is *isIRI*($?X$), $?X \in dom(\mu)$ and $\mu(?X) \in I$;
- R is *isLiteral*($?X$), $?X \in dom(\mu)$ and $\mu(?X) \in L$;

---

[5] Note that '=' would otherwise also involve certain datatype inferences, e.g. `"1.0"^^xsd:decimal="1"^^xsd:integer` in SPARQL, whereas $sameTerm($`"1.0"^^xsd:decimal`, `"1"^^xsd:integer`$) = false$.

- R is $?X = c, ?X \in dom(\mu)$ and $sameTerm(\mu(?X), c)$;
- R is $?X =?Y, ?X \in dom(\mu), ?Y \in dom(\mu)$ and $sameTerm(\mu(?X), \mu(?Y))$;
- R is $\neg R_1$ with $\mu(R_1) = \bot$;
- R is $(R_1 \vee R_2)$, and $\mu(R_1) = \top \vee \mu(R_2) = \top$;
- R is $(R_1 \wedge R_2)$, and $\mu(R_1) = \top \wedge \mu(R_2) = \top$

$\mu(R) = \varepsilon$, if:
- R is $isBlank(?X), R = isIRI(?X)$, or $R = isLiteral(?X)$ and $?X \notin dom(\mu)$;
- R is $?X = c$ or $?X =?Y$ with $?X \notin dom(\mu)$ or, in the latter case $?Y \notin dom(\mu)$;
- R is $\neg R_1$ with $\mu(R_1) = \varepsilon$;
- R is $(R_1 \vee R_2)$, and $\mu(R_1) = \varepsilon \wedge \mu(R_2) = \varepsilon$;
- R is $(R_1 \wedge R_2)$, and $\mu(R_1) = \varepsilon \vee \mu(R_2) = \varepsilon$

$\mu(R) = \bot$, otherwise.

---

(1) If P is a triple pattern t, then $[\![P]\!]_G = \{\mu \mid dom(\mu) = var(t)$ and $\mu(t) \in G\}$.

(2) If P is $(P_1 \text{ AND } P_2)$, then $[\![P]\!]_G = [\![P_1]\!]_G \bowtie [\![P_2]\!]_G$.

(3) If P is $(P_1 \text{ OPT } P_2)$, then $[\![P]\!]_G = [\![P_1]\!]_G \bowtie\!\!\!\!\!\!\!{\scriptstyle\sqsubset}\ [\![P_2]\!]_G$.

(4) If P is $(P_1 \text{ UNION } P_2)$, then $[\![P]\!]_G = [\![P_1]\!]_G \cup [\![P_2]\!]_G$.

(5) If P is $(P_1 \text{ FILTER } R)$, then $[\![P]\!]_G = \{\mu \in [\![P_1]\!]_G \mid \mu(R)\}$.

(6) If P is $(\text{SERVICE } c\ P_1)$ with $c \in I \cup V$, then

$$[\![P]\!]_G = \begin{cases} [\![P_1]\!]_{ep(c)} & \text{if } c \in dom(ep) \\ \{\mu_\emptyset\} & \text{if } c \in I \setminus dom(ep) \\ \left\{\mu \cup [c \rightarrow s] \mid \exists s \in dom(ep), \mu \in [\![P_1]\!]_{ep(s))} \wedge [c \rightarrow s] \sim \mu\right\} & \text{if } c \in V \end{cases}$$

(7) If $P = \text{VALUES } \boldsymbol{W} \ \boldsymbol{A}$ then

$$[\![P]\!]_G = \{\mu_j | 1 \leq j \leq m, dom(\mu_j) = \{?X_i \in \boldsymbol{W} \mid a_{i,j} \neq \text{UNBOUND}\}, \mu_j(?X_i) = a_{i,j}\}$$

(8) If P is $\text{SELECT } \boldsymbol{W} \ P_1 \text{ ORDER BY } \boldsymbol{V} \text{ LIMIT } l \text{ OFFSET } o$, then
$[\![P]\!]_G = \Pi_{\boldsymbol{W}}(\text{lmt}(\text{order}([\![P_1]\!]_G, \boldsymbol{V}), l, o))$, where $\Pi_{\boldsymbol{W}}$ is projection as in Rel. Alg., and
$\text{order}(\Omega, \boldsymbol{V}) = L$ the sequence of $\mu \in \Omega$ obtained from ordering $\mu(\boldsymbol{V})$ as per [3, §15.1].
$\text{lmt}(L, l, o) = L'$ obtained from L by removing all $L[i]$ with $i \leq o$ or $o + l < i$

Fig. 1. Definition of $[\![P]\!]_G$ for a graph pattern P using FILTER and VALUES operators.

Note in Fig. 1, that the semantics of SELECT queries is actually non-deterministic, in the sense that a compliant implementation can give different results, as illustrated by the following example.

Example 1. Let us assume the default graph $G_1 = \{(a, b, 1), (a, b, 2)\}$. and the pattern $P_1 = \text{SELECT } ?X(a, b, ?X) \text{ LIMIT } 1$ then obviously both $\{[?X \rightarrow 1]\}$ and $\{[?X \rightarrow 2]\}$ would be allowed results, since there is no order prescribed among the results of $[\![(a, b, ?X)]\!]_G$. Likewise, $P_2 = \text{SELECT } ?X(a, b, ?X) \text{ LIMIT } 1 \text{ OFFSET } 1$ could have the same two possible results, indeed a compliant SPARQL engine could – according to the specification return the same result for both P_1 and P_2.

Note that even an ORDER BY does not necessarily remedy such ambiguities in all cases, since, according to the ordering rules in [3, §15.1], not all RDF terms are ordered; particularly, no order is specified for instance for blank nodes. To illustrate this, assume the default graph $G_1 = \{(a, b, \_:b1), (a, b, \_:b2)\}$ such that $\_:b1, \_:b2 \in B$. Then, similarly, both $\{[?X \rightarrow \_:b1]\}$ and $\{[?X \rightarrow \_:b2]\}$ would be allowed results for either P_3 = SELECT $?X(a, b, ?X)$ ORDER BY $?X$ LIMIT 1 or P_4 = SELECT $?X(a, b, ?X)$ ORDER BY $?X$ LIMIT 1 OFFSET 1.

3   Evaluation Strategies for SPARQL SERVICE Patterns

In this section we outline several potential evaluation strategies for queries to a remote SPARQL endpoint using SERVICE patterns of the form $P = P_1$ AND (SERVICE $c\,P_2$).

Symmetrical Hash Join (SYMHASH). A classical alternative to implement SERVICE patterns is to use a symmetrical hash join, a type of hash join commonly used in data streams. We evaluate both query parts P_1 and P_2 separately and locally join the results ($[\![P]\!]_G = [\![P_1]\!]_G \bowtie [\![P_2]\!]_{G_c}$) using two hash tables (one for each sub query). Depending on the interim result sizes of P_1 and P_2, this join algorithm can be a very efficient solution due to its possible parallelisation. However, the symmetrical hash join is expensive if the interim result sets are much larger then the join result size, plus, particularly, if the remote endpoint c imposes a result size limit of n being smaller than the size of $[\![P_2]\!]_{G_c}$, then join results may be lost.

Pagination with ORDERBY and LIMIT (SYMHASHP). An alternative to circumvent the problems of a local symmetric hash join would be to use "pagination". Here, by "pagination" we mean issuing queries of the form P_1 AND (SERVICE c (SELECT * $\{P_2\}$ ORDER BY $inScopeVars(P_2)$) LIMIT n OFFSET o) where $o = n * i$ with increasing $i \in \mathbb{N}$ until less than n results are returned from service c. Each batch of remote results can again be joined with the local results of P_1 using a hash join.

However, Ex. 1 above already shows that there is no simple work-around for circumventing result size limits when querying remote SPARQL endpoints in terms of "pagination": that is, let us assume $P = P_1$ AND (SERVICE $c\,P_2$) be a SPARQL pattern, where service c limits result size to delivering at most n results. Then, as a consequence of the Ex. 1, one cannot simply use "pagination" of the results of the remote endpoint.

Getting back to the ordering rules in [3, §15.1], we note that there are still cases where we can safely use pagination, namely, (1) if the total result size of the remote endpoint query is below the remote result size limit n, then there are no problems. This can be easily checked by issuing a query ASK { SERVICE c { SELECT * { P_2 } LIMIT n }} to the remote endpoint. In case this delivers less than n results, we do not need pagination anyway. Otherwise, we have to check whether we can safely order the results to guarantee that we can get all available results by "pagination". To this end, we need to be sure that all bindings to "output variables" (i.e., variables that are "in-scope" [6]) in the service pattern P_2 are either unbound or can be ordered by the "<" operator according to [3, §15.1]: *the "<" operator (see [3, §17.3.1] Operator Extensibility) defines the relative order of pairs of numerics, simple literals, xsd:strings,*

---

[6] These are just the variables that would be included in a SELECT *,
cf. http://www.w3.org/TR/sparql11-query/#ins

xsd:booleans and xsd:dateTimes. Pairs of IRIs are ordered by comparing them as simple literals. In fact, we can check this "orderability" condition — which would allow us to impose a total order on the in-scope variables of the service pattern by using ORDER BY — by another ASK query:[7]

```
ASK { SERVICE c { P2  FILTER (  ! (
        ∧ for each variable ?v ∈ inScopeVars(P2)
          ( !bound(?v) ∨
            isNumeric(?v) ∨
            datatype(?v) = xsd:boolean ∨
            datatype(?v) = xsd:dateTime ∨
            datatype(?v) = xsd:string ) ) ) } }
```

If this query returns false, the remote results can be indeed ordered, and we can proceed with "pagination". However, while this approach is feasible, it is not applicable in general, plus executing several consecutive ORDER BY queries might actually be quite expensive on the remote side and trigger resource limits nonetheless. We thus look for other, more feasible alternatives, that allow to "push" the results from the local side into the remote query, which we will describe in the following.

Nested Loop Join (NESTED). A straightforward method to alternatively evaluate a query of the form $P = P_1$ SERVICE c P_2 – with the particular advantage to keep the intermediate size of results shipped from the remote endpoint low, and thus potentially circumventing result size limits – is to use a nested loop join. Here, we first evaluate P_1, iterate over the solution bindings $\mu \in [\![P_1]\!]_G$, execute $\mu(P_2)$ remotely and extend μ with the additionally obtained variable bindings.

One potential problem of this approach is that we issue one request for each binding of P_1; this can lead to denial of service attacks if there is no appropriate wait time between two requests for large interim result sets.

Even worse, when done naively, this method fails in relatively simple queries as shown in the following example.

Example 2. Assume $P_1 = (?X, c, d)$ and $P_2 = ((?Y, ?Z, ?T)$ UNION $(?X, ?Y, b))$ FILTER $(?X = ?Y)$. With the local default graph $G_1 = \{(a, c, d)\}$ and the remote service's default graph $G_2 = \{(a, a, b), (e, c, d)\}$, we obtain: $[\![P_1]\!]_{G_1} = \{\mu\}$, with $\mu = \{[?X \rightarrow a]$, whereas $[\![P_2]\!]_{G_2} = \{[?X \rightarrow a, ?Y \rightarrow a]\}$. However, if we proceed as suggested above, then $\mu(P_2) = ((?Y, ?Z, ?T)$ UNION $(a, ?Y, b))$ FILTER $(a = ?Y)$ which yields an additional solution $[?Y \rightarrow a, ?Z \rightarrow a, ?T \rightarrow b]$ that was not admissible in the original P_2 but is also compatible with $\{[?X \rightarrow a]\}$.

Another problem is with blank nodes. Assume $P_1 = P_2 = (?X, c, d)$ with $G_1 = \{(\_ : b, c, d)\}$ and $G_2 = \{(a, c, d)\}$. Here, as replacement would yield $\mu(P_2) = (\_ : b, c, d)$ and since SPARQL engines treat blank nodes in patterns as variables, again a non-admissible solution would arise.

Thus, applying a nested loop join with naive replacement in a federation scenario, would potentially obtain inconsistent results.

---

[7] Note that the datatype(·) function also returns xsd:string on simple literals.

SPARQL 1.1 VALUES **Operator** (VALUES). As a further alternative, the new VALUES operator in SPARQL 1.1 can be used for "shipping" the local result bindings from $[\![P_1]\!]_G$ along with the remote query that is sent using the SERVICE operator as follows: let again $P = P_1$ AND (SERVICE c P_2). If we pre-evaluate the solution bindings for P_1, written $[\![P_1]\!]_G$, the SERVICE operator could then be equivalently evaluated by replacing pattern P_2 with

$$P_2^{\text{VALUES}_{P_1}} = P_2 \text{ VALUES } \boldsymbol{W} \boldsymbol{A}$$

where $\boldsymbol{W} = [var(P_1) \cap var(P_2)]$ and $\boldsymbol{A} = [\![P_1]\!]_G$ to endpoint c, i.e. if G_c is the default graph of service c

$$[\![P]\!]_G = [\![P_1]\!]_G \bowtie [\![P_2^{\text{VALUES}_{P_1}}]\!]_{G_c}$$

However, a potential problem with this approach is that the VALUES operator is not yet widely deployed in existing endpoints [2] and other operators have to be used in order to simulate the desired behaviour.

SPARQL FILTER (FILTER). As an alternative to the usage of VALUES one may consider using FILTERs to "inject" the results of P_1 into P_2, namely, by replacing P_2 with

$$P_2^{\text{FILTER}_{P_1}} = \{P_2 \text{ FILTER} \bigvee_{\mu \in [\![P_1]\!]_G} (\bigwedge_{v \in dom(\mu) \cap vars(P_2)} v = \mu(v))\}$$

The FILTER expression here makes sure that only those solution bindings of P_2 survive that join with some solution binding of of P_2.

SPARQL UNION (UNION). Yet another alternative is the use of the UNION operator in combination with FILTERs. Here, the idea is to use the results of P_1 to create a large UNION query, where in each branch of the UNION the bindings of one solution for P_1 are 'injected" by means of a FILTER, instead of one large FILTER. I.e., for $[\![P_1]\!]_G = \{\mu_1, \ldots, \mu_n\}$ we replace P_2 by

$$P_2^{\text{UNION}_{P_1}} = \{(\mu_1^{\text{FILTER}}(P_2)) \text{ UNION} \ldots \text{UNION}(\mu_n^{\text{FILTER}}(P_2))\}$$

Here, $\mu^{\text{FILTER}}(P_2) = P_2 \text{ FILTER}(\bigwedge_{v \in dom(\mu) \cap vars(P_2)} v = \mu(v))$.

However, there are problems with unbound variables in both $P_2^{\text{FILTER}_{P_1}}$ and $P_2^{\text{UNION}_{P_1}}$, as shown in the following example.

Example 3. Assume $P_1 = (?X, b, c)$, $c = I$ and $P_2 = ((?Y,d,e) \text{ UNION } (?X,d,e))$. With the local default graph $G_1 = \{(a, b, c)\}$ and the remote service' default graph $G_2 = \{(a, d, e)\}$, we obtain: $[\![P_1]\!]_{G_1} = \{[?X \rightarrow a]\}$ and $[\![P_2]\!]_{G_2} = \{[?X \rightarrow a], [?Y \rightarrow a]\}$; here, the second solution for $[\![P_2]\!]_{G_2}$, i.e. $\mu_2 = [?Y \rightarrow a]$ is compatible with the single solution for $[\![P_1]\!]_{G_1}$, i.e., $\mu_1 = [?Y \rightarrow a]$ yielding overall $\mu = [?X \rightarrow a, ?Y \rightarrow a]$. However, $P_2^{\text{FILTER}_{P_1}} = P_2^{\text{UNION}_{P_1}} = \{ \{(?Y,d,e) \text{ UNION } (?X,d,e)\} \text{ FILTER}(?X = a)\}$ which would not yield μ as a solution.

So, while the use of nested loops may yield incorrect additional results, the version using FILTER and UNIONs seem to miss some results,. In the next subsection we discuss refined versions of these three alternatives, that solve these issues.

3.1   Two Equivalence Theorems for SPARQL Federated Queries

As we have seen, some queries may return unexpected result mappings when substituting a variable for a specific value in nested loops. Thus, we aim at finding out a restricted class of SPARQL remote queries for which we obtain correct results. It turns out that one class of queries which avoid the above-mentioned problems is the class of queries where all join variables are *strongly bound*[1]: strong boundedness ensures, by the following syntactic restrictions, that a variable $?X$ in a SPARQL pattern P will be bound to a value in each solution binding, independent of the underlying data.

Definition 1   (Strong boundedness (from [1]). *Let P be a SPARQL pattern; the set of strongly bound variables in P, denoted by* $\mathrm{SB}(P)$, *is recursively defined as follows:*
- *if $P = t$, where t is a triple pattern, then* $\mathrm{SB}(P) = var(t)$;
- *if $P = (P_1$ AND $P_2)$, then* $\mathrm{SB}(P) = \mathrm{SB}(P_1) \cup \mathrm{SB}(P_2)$;
- *if $P = (P_1$ UNION $P_2)$, then* $\mathrm{SB}(P) = \mathrm{SB}(P_1) \cap \mathrm{SB}(P_2)$;
- *if $P = (P_1$ OPT $P_2)$ or $P = (P_1$ FILTER $R)$, then* $\mathrm{SB}(P) = \mathrm{SB}(P_1)$;
- *if $P = (P_1$ FILTER $R)$, then* $\mathrm{SB}(P) = \mathrm{SB}(P_1)$;
- *if $P = (\text{SERVICE } c\ P_1)$, with $c \in I$, or $P = (\text{SERVICE } ?X\ P_1)$, with $?X \in V$, then* $\mathrm{SB}(P) = \emptyset$;
- *if $P = (P_1$ VALUES $S\ \{A_1, \ldots, A_n\})$, then* $\mathrm{SB}(P) = \mathrm{SB}(P_1) \cup \{?X \mid$ *$?X$ is in S and for every $i \in \{1, \ldots, n\}$, it holds that $?X \in dom(\mu_{S,A_i})\}$.*
- *if $P = (\text{SELECT } W\ P_1)$, then* $\mathrm{SB}(P) = (W \cap \mathrm{SB}(P_1))$.

Indeed, one source of problems in Ex. 2 was the query results containing the empty result mapping. That empty result mapping combined with other operators generates result sets different to the original one (aside of being unexpected) since the empty result mapping is not *null rejecting*.

The following Lemma essentially states that replacing strongly bound variables with IRIs or literals in a pattern will not yield additional results for P.

Lemma 1. *Given a SPARQL pattern P with $v \in SB(P)$, let $\mu_e = [v \to e]$ for an $e \in I \cup L$, then $[\![\mu_e(P)]\!]_G \bowtie \mu_e = \{\mu \in [\![P]\!]_G | v \in dom(\mu) \wedge \mu(v) = e\}$.*

Indeed, we can remedy the aforementioned issue of blank nodes if we replace $\mu(P_2)$ with $\mu^B(P_2) = \{\mu(P_2)\ \text{FILTER}(\neg(\bigvee_{v \in dom(\mu) \cap vars(P_2)} isBlank(\mu(v))))\}$ within the nested loop, i.e. the problematic solutions containing blank nodes are filtered out.

Indeed, we confirm that nested loop replacement with this modification works for remote patterns with only strongly bound variables; plus, it turns out that remote queries with only strongly bound join variables also are evaluated correctly using the $FILTER$ and $UNION$ approaches:

Theorem 1. *Let $P = P_1$ AND $(\text{SERVICE } c\ P_2)$ such that $(vars(P_2) \cap vars(P_1)) \subseteq$ $\mathrm{SB}(P_2)$, i.e. all variables that participate in a join are strongly bound in the pattern appearing on the service side, and let G_c be the default graph of service c and let $P_2^{UNION_{P_1}}$ and $P_2^{FILTER_{P_1}}$ be as defined above, then*
  (i) $[\![P]\!]_G = \bigcup_{\mu \in [\![P_1]\!]_G} (\mu \bowtie [\![\mu^B(P_2)]\!]_{G_c})$
  (ii) $[\![P]\!]_G = [\![P_1]\!]_G \bowtie [\![P_2^{UNION_{P_1}}]\!]_{G_c} = [\![P_1]\!]_G \bowtie [\![P_2^{FILTER_{P_1}}]\!]_{G_c}$

We note that if the local graph G does not contain any blank nodes[8], then Theorem 1(i) would also hold using the original replacement $\mu(P_2)$. Moreover, it turns out that we can generalise the result in Theorem 1(ii) to also work in the general case with potentially unbound variables in the service pattern. To this end, in both $P_2^{\text{FILTER}_{P_1}}$ and $P_2^{\text{UNION}_{P_1}}$ expressions we replace $v = \mu(v)$ by $v = \mu(v) \vee \neg bound(v)$, obtaining $P_2^{\text{FILTER}'_{P_1}}$ and $P_2^{\text{UNION}'_{P_1}}$, resp.

The trick to only filter for variables bound within P_2 fixes the problem from Ex. 3 above, as stated in the following theorem.

Theorem 2. *Let* $P = P_1$ AND (SERVICE c P_2) *and* G_c *be the default graph of service* c *then*

$$[\![P]\!]_G = [\![P_1]\!]_G \bowtie [\![P_2^{\text{FILTER}'_{P_1}}]\!]_{G_c} = [\![P_1]\!]_G \bowtie [\![P_2^{\text{UNION}'_{P_1}}]\!]_{G_c}$$

4   Evaluation

In total, we have 6 alternative evaluation strategies for a $P = P_1$ SERVICE P_2 query, as listed in the overview given in Table 1. The goal of our evaluation is to study how systems implement the SERVICE keyword and how the alternative evaluation strategies behave for different queries.

Table 1. Overview of evaluation strategies as detailed in §3

ID	Description
SERVICE	Baseline evaluation strategy
VALUES	Evaluation as described in §3
SYMHASH	A symmetrical hash join without pagination
SYMHASHP	A symmetrical hash join with pagination of the remote results
NESTED	A naive nested loop evaluation strategy
UNION	Evaluation as described in Theorem 1
FILTER	Evaluation as described in Theorem 2

All of our evaluation strategies are implemented in Java7 using the Jena ARQ library (version 2.9.4)[9]. The three systems under test are 1) Jena Fuseki 0.2.7 with on disk index (TDB), 2) Sesame workbench 2.7.11 and 3) Virtuoso Open Source Edition 7.10.

We did not pose any result limit to the systems and followed the official documentation for the installation.

---

[8] Existence of blank nodes in a dataset could be easily tested with a query such as ASK {?S ?P ?O FILTER isBlank(?S) ∨ isBlank(?O)) }.

[9] The implementation and all queries are online at
https://github.com/cbuil/sparql_strategies

4.1 Methodology

The methodology followed in our evaluation consists in two parts: first we evaluate the correctness of our strategies by using the data and queries presented in §3.1 and next we evaluate the strategies using real data from the Bio2RDF project[10].

SERVICE Implementation Test
First, we test the implementation of the selected SPARQL HTTP servers and how they deal with the problems addressed in this work. We created two small datasets that contain the RDF data in the examples before. Next we evaluate each of the strategies presented using these datasets to check the correctness of our approach and the engines serving SPARQL.

Compare Alternative Strategies
Next, we verify that all strategies can produce the right results if 1) the queries do not involve unbound join variables and 2) if the queries contain variables that may be unbound. We remove the result set size limit that the servers usually impose to the query execution. We also use this test to measure the performance differences of the strategies depending on the query characteristics and we also test how the symmetrical hash joins perform with and without pagination. We measured for each configuration of query and join implementation result size, and query times.

4.2 Data and Queries

SERVICE Evaluation: we use the data and queries from Examples 2 and 3 to test the SERVICE implementation of the different stores. These two queries are used to check how unbound variables affect the execution of a federated SPARQL query. The first query $Q1$ contains the UNION pattern presented in Example 2 in P_1 (i.e. the pattern that queries the local dataset). The second query $Q2$ is the query presented in Example 3. That query contains a single graph pattern for querying the local dataset (P_1) and the previous UNION pattern in the remote SERVICE call (P_2).

In addition, we downloaded two datasets from the Bio2RDF domain: the Mouse Genome Database (MGI) and the Database of Human Gene Names (HGNC). The MGI dataset consists of 2,454,589 triples and the HGNC of 919,738 triples and we created 8 queries for these two datasets. Each query has two SERVICE patterns P_1 and P_2, the first one (P_1) querying the local endpoint hosting the MGI dataset and the second (P_2) querying the remote endpoint, hosting the HGNC data.

The first 4 queries (B0– B3) plus query B7 do not contain blank nodes in the interim results or unbound join variables while queries B4– B6 contain variables that may be unbound. These three queries will allow us to study the behaviour of the proposed strategies with unbound join variables. The results obtained for these last queries may be unsound, i.e. they differ in the amount of results returned to the users, according to the theoretical results presented in Section 3.

---

[10] http://bio2rdf.org

Table 2. Result size of P_1 (local) and P_2 (remote) for our example queries. $|P|$ is the result size of executing first P_1, next P_2 and finally do the join locally.

	Cardinality		#Triple patterns			
Query	$[\![P_1]\!]_G$	$[\![P_2]\!]_G$	$\|P_1\|$	$\|P_2\|$	$\|P\|$	Comment
B0	27	1	1	1	1	
B1	27	33562	1	1	1	
B2	17817	33562	2	1	17547	
B3	16753	2	2	3	2	
B4	250924	23	1	2	6	P_1 contains one non strongly bound join variable
B5	16753	8771	2	2	3274	P_2 contains one non strongly bound join variable
B6	268743	27132	3	7	23873	P_1 and P_2 with non strongly bound join variable
B7	35636	33134	3	4	17545	Two join variables

5   Results

In this section we summarise the results we obtained from the execution of the proposed strategies using the evaluation queries for each dataset configuration. We first present the results of the strategies over the data and queries of §4 and next we present the results for the Bio2RDF dataset queries.

5.1   SERVICE Implementation Test

At the time of writing, we initially tested the current version of Fuseki (version 1.0.1) but due to a bug in the evaluation of FILTER expression we had to settle for a previous version not containing that error. This behaviour could be not observed with Fuseki version 0.2.7 which returned the correct results.

Overall, our evaluation confirmed that the SPARQL engines do not properly deal with unbound join variables for their SERVICE implementation. Table 3 shows the number of returned results for our two queries and the three tested systems. We observe that for all queries the FILTER, UNION and symmetrical hash join strategies returns the correct number of results in Sesame and Virtuoso. Considering Fuseki, all evaluation strategies fail to return the correct results except for in the symmetrical hash join strategy. We contacted the lead developer of the Fuseki system to verified that the SERVICE evaluation strategy is similar to a nested loop approach as the results indicated. Interestingly, Fuseki does not differ from Sesame and Virtuoso in the execution of SERVICE queries since they all return the same amount of results. That means that all three systems seem to implement a Nested Loop Join algorithm for implementing the SERVICE operator.

5.2   Performance of Alternative Strategies

The next evaluation task had the goal to see how the different strategies behave with real world data and different queries.

Table 3. Returned amount of results for theorem queries and synthetical data for different SPARQL engines: the table shows result size differences in the query evaluation for the different strategies by the SPARQL servers

	Q1 (Example2)			Q2 (Example3)		
	Fuseki	Sesame	Virtuoso	Fuseki	Sesame	Virtuoso
SERVICE	2	2	2	2	2	2
VALUES	2	1	1	2	2	2
FILTER	2	1	1	2	1	1
UNION	2	1	1	2	1	1
NESTED	2	2	2	2	2	2
SYMHASH	1	1	1	1	1	1

Implementation restrictions & solution. In our initial tests we observed two technical exceptions with the used systems and libraries.

HTTP GET *vs* HTTP POST *queries:* At first, we used HTTP GET requests to send the queries to the local and remote endpoints. However, the servers threw an exception if the created query URL exceeds the maximum or allowed URL length. This happened for queries with thousands of interim results for P_1. Our solution is to use HTTP POST requests with the query in the request body.

Large FILTER *and* UNION *expressions:* The second exception happened due to internal stack overflows in the ARQ library while parsing the FILTER (or UNION expression, caused by large numbers of filter statements for P_2. We mark such exception with a "+". Our technical solution for these exception is to split the results for P_1 into batches which can be handled by the remote endpoint. If such an exception occurred in our test we also evaluate the strategy with batch processing.

Results. The runtime in ms for the various strategies and queries are presented in Table 4 for Fuseki, Table 5 for Sesame and Table 6 for Virtuoso. We use the superscript "−" to indicate an incorrect number of results. Results marked with superscript "*" indicate a 500 Server Error response error from Fuseki, 400 Bad Request from Sesame[11] or HttpException from Virtuoso. These errors indicate that a problem occurred in the server while the processing of the query was ongoing. In such cases, we report the times taken from a run with a batch size of 750 results. In this evaluation we use the symmetrical hash join with pagination strategy (SYMHASHP) with a batch size of 750 instead of the SYMHASH strategy since the former is more suitable for queries with larger amounts of results. Those queries that have as result to mean that were automatically stopped from the client after 30 minutes. The bold results present the best runtime for each query across the strategies.

Overall the FILTER and VALUES evaluation strategies provide in general the fastest query times for Fuseki (cf. Table 4). We can also see that the internal SERVICE evaluation strategy has similar runtimes as our nested loop implementation. This is no surprise since Fuseki uses a nested loop style evaluation strategy. The UNION strategy is used for large remote queries which we needed to break down into batches to be

---

[11] Sesame's 400 Bad Request errors indicate that the query contained to many patterns.

Table 4. Query times in ms (Fuseki 0.2.7). The best strategy for a Fuseki server is to either use a FILTER strategy injecting the values in the FILTER expression or use the VALUES operator. The SYMHASHP is the third best strategy.

	B0	B1	B2	B3	B4	B5	B6	B7
SERVICE	1436	642	31620	39119	62243^*	858681^-	60276^*	to
FILTER	439	360^+	$\mathbf{7235^+}$	6022^+	13633^+	$\mathbf{3638^+}$	26577^+	62947^+
UNION	730	678^+	10657^+	15033^+	22269^*	7732^*	60814^*	63335^+
VALUES	**211**	**227**	8247	5223	16728^*	899667^-	19289^*	**11646**
NESTED	758	643	52160	55445	to^-	922805^-	to	to
SYMHASHP	403	16462	17563	**1937**	**9494**	13082	53592	28759

accepted by the remote endpoint. However, comparing the runtimes with the FILTER evaluation strategy, which also required use of batch processing, we measured approximately two times slower performance. It is important to notice that queries B4 to B6 returned some type of error when using the strategies SERVICE, UNION, VALUES and NESTED. These queries contain one or more non strongly bound join variables which that not only increase the complexity of the query evaluation but also return wrong results. We observed that for query B4 using the NESTED strategy and removing all timeouts the amount of results returned was 5,361,421 (it should return 6 results) and it took more than 12 hours to finish (query marked with the superscript $^-$). Query B5 also took longer using the SERVICE, NESTED and VALUES strategies, and returned 4,576,843 results, when it should return 3,274 results. The most reliable strategies were FILTER and SYMHASHP, which managed to finish all query executions.

Table 5. Query times in ms (Sesame). The best strategy for Sesame is to use either SERVICE or FILTER strategies.

	B0	B1	B2	B3	B4	B5	B6	B7
SERVICE	**77**	320	**1555**	73	618852^-	to	to	**1968**
FILTER	149	596	4340^+	4788^+	7815^+	3230^+	15746^+	7032^+
UNION	260	645	6415	10807	12502	5443^*	43648	13673
VALUES	167	**153**	4289	2893	8095^*	2276^*	8482^*	7042
NESTED	443	385	52051	62083	to^-	to	to	89487
SYMHASHP	101	14520	15037	1203	**4662**	5409	20915	21242

The results of our evaluation with the Sesame system shows a different picture compared to the Fuseki test (cf. Table 5). Overall, the internal SERVICE implementation provides the best performance for 4 out of the 8 queries. This is surprising since our previous experiment suggested that Sesame implements the SERVICE operator as a Nested Loop Join. However, the results in Table 5 show that the SERVICE strategy outperforms the NESTED strategy by order of magnitudes. The results indicate that Sesame uses some internal optimisations (e.g., based on statistics) which results in the observed runtime difference. For the other 3 queries, the FILTER strategy showed the fastest query answering time for queries B5 and B6 while the SYMHASHP strategy was the fastest for query B4. It is important to note that the only evaluation strategies that managed to finish executing were the FILTER and SYMHASHP strategies, while we observed the same problems regarding the non strongly bound join variables: query B4 returned 5,361,421 results in the SERVICE and NESTED strategies (the NESTED strategy needed almost 12 hours to complete). Again, the most reliable strategies were FILTER and SYMHASHP.

Table 6. Query times in ms (Virtuoso 7.10). The best strategy for a Virtuoso Server is a SYMHASHP, specially for low selective patterns (queries B6 and B7).

	B0	B1	B2	B3	B4	B5	B6	B7
SERVICE	45*	41*	60*	35*	61*	56*	54*	75*
FILTER	159	159+	**1731**	31720+	26329+	31324+	68749+	37444+
UNION	267	237+	30904+	72495+	55321+	3737*	7134*	11990+
VALUES	137	**117**	6611	7561	260736−	781657	to	13291−
NESTED	559	500	88240	128399	2721065*	to	to	196280
SYMHASHP	**102**	1905	2733	**2205**	**5525**	**2306**	**8149**	**3407**

Again, the results from the evaluation using the Virtuoso Open Source server are very different from the evaluation for other stores. The best strategy when using Virtuoso is a SYMHASHP strategy, which is the fastest in almost all queries. Only in query B1 the strategy VALUES and in query B2 the strategy FILTER strategy were faster. As before, a similar situation happens when running the queries containing non strongly bound join variables. In this case the VALUES strategy for query B4 returned 23 results, which differs from the 6 results that the FILTER and SYMHASHP strategies return. Again, the SYMHASHP and the FILTER strategies are the only strategies that were able to finish all query executions.

6 Related Work and Conclusions

Although there is a lot of theoretical work on distributed query processing and query planning, both in the database world [5] and in the context of the semantic Web [10,12,7], this is indeed one of the first works that considers *practical* limitations of existing SPARQL endpoints when executing already established federated query plans using SPARQL1.1's federated query extension. For instance, FedX [12] describes a similar evaluation strategy to our UNION strategy (called *bound join*), but does not consider the corner cases we discuss in Theorems 1+2 above. Likewise, whereas various works have addressed equivalences and optimisations for local SPARQL query patterns [8,11,6], few have considered SERVICE patterns.

In summary, in this paper we have, firstly, illustrated that querying remote SPARQL endpoints with SERVICE patterns is a non-trivial task due to the limitations that the servers hosting these endpoints impose; the most common restriction is a result size limit that prevents users from obtaining complete results to their queries. Secondly, we have also shown some results in terms of defining equivalences for SPARQL queries involving SERVICE patterns that may help remedy these limits in practice. Thirdly, our evaluation should give some hints on which strategies are practically feasible in a particular setting, depending on the data, the local SPARQL engine and the engine running at the involved endpoints in a federated query. It is important to notice that only the FILTER and SYMHASHP strategies returned results for all queries in all systems. In addition, these strategies were sound, i.e. returned correct results for all queries since they do not "inject" any new value in the remote query (instead they either filter the unwanted results out or perform the join locally). The NESTED strategy (along with the SERVICE strategy) not only failed to return results in several queries but also returned incorrect results when non strongly bound join variables were present (confirming thus the theoretical results obtained). We believe that the investigation of the issues around executing federated SPARQL queries in practice deserves increased attention if we seriously intend to make the the the Semantic Web vision work.

Acknowledgements. Thanks to Aidan for his last bulletproof reading and to Martín for his support in finding the missing variable bindings.

References

1. Buil-Aranda, C., Arenas, M., Corcho, O., Polleres, A.: Federating Queries in SPARQL 1.1: Syntax, Semantics and Evaluation. J. Web Semantics 18(1) (2012)
2. Buil-Aranda, C., Hogan, A., Umbrich, J., Vandenbussche, P.-Y.: SPARQL Web-Querying Infrastructure: Ready for Action? In: Alani, H., et al. (eds.) ISWC 2013, Part II. LNCS, vol. 8219, pp. 277–293. Springer, Heidelberg (2013)
3. Harris, S., Seaborne, A.: SPARQL 1.1 Query Language (January 2012)
4. Jayram, T.S., Kolaitis, P.G., Vee, E.: The containment problem for real conjunctive queries with inequalities. In: 25th ACM SIGACT-SIGMOD-SIGART Symposium on Principles of Database Systems (PODS), pp. 80–89 (2006)
5. Kossmann, D.: The state of the art in distributed query processing. ACM Comput. Surv. 32(4), 422–469 (2000)
6. Letelier, A., Pérez, J., Pichler, R., Skritek, S.: Static analysis and optimization of semantic web queries. ACM Trans. Database Syst. 38(4), 25 (2013)
7. Montoya, G., Vidal, M.-E., Acosta, M.: A heuristic-based approach for planning federated sparql queries. In: Workshop on Consuming Linked Data (COLD) (2012)
8. Pérez, J., Arenas, M., Gutierrez, C.: Semantics and complexity of SPARQL. TODS 34(3) (2009)
9. Prud'hommeaux, E., Buil-Aranda, C.: SPARQL 1.1 Federated Query (March 2013)
10. Quilitz, B., Leser, U.: Querying distributed rdf data sources with sparql. In: Bechhofer, S., Hauswirth, M., Hoffmann, J., Koubarakis, M. (eds.) ESWC 2008. LNCS, vol. 5021, pp. 524–538. Springer, Heidelberg (2008)
11. Schmidt, M., Meier, M., Lausen, G.: Foundations of SPARQL query optimization. In: ICDT 2010, Lausanne, Switzerland (March 2010)
12. Schwarte, A., Haase, P., Hose, K., Schenkel, R., Schmidt, M.: FedX: Optimization techniques for federated query processing on linked data. In: Aroyo, L., Welty, C., Alani, H., Taylor, J., Bernstein, A., Kagal, L., Noy, N., Blomqvist, E. (eds.) ISWC 2011, Part I. LNCS, vol. 7031, pp. 601–616. Springer, Heidelberg (2011)

A   Proof for Theorem 1(i)

Proof. We now show that there is a 1:1 correpsondence between those solution mappings of P_1 joining with (SERVICE c P_2) and the ones joining with $\mu^B(P_2)$.

The theorem trivially holds for $c \in I \setminus dom(ep)$, i.e. if c is not the IRI of a SPARQL endpoint, cf. [1]. Otherwise, let now $\mu \in [\![P]\!]_G$, then we know for each mapping[12] $\mu_i \subseteq \mu \in [\![P_1]\!]_G$ there is a mapping $\mu_j \subseteq \mu \in [\![P_2]\!]_{G_c}$ such that for each variable $v \in dom(\mu_i) \cap var(P_2)$ it holds that $\mu_i(v) = \mu_j(v)$ $in I \cup L$: since (a) blank nodes from the local graph queried by P_1 are always disjoint with blank nodes from the remote endpoint P_2 and (b) all join variables (i.e., $var(P_1) \cap var(P_2)$) are strongly bound in P_2, which means that indeed all $v \in dom(\mu_i) \cap var(P_2)$ are also in $dom(\mu_j)$.

It is now easy to see that for each such solution μ_j there is a solution $\mu_j' \in [\![\mu^B(P_2)]\!]_{G_c}$ with $dom(\mu_j') = dom(\mu_j) \setminus dom(\mu_i)$ and that corresponds to μ_j on all variables in $dom(\mu_j')$, which proves that $[\![P]\!]_G \subseteq [\![P_1]\!]_G \bowtie [\![\mu^B(P_2)]\!]_{G_c}$.

On the other hand, there are no additional mappings in $[\![\mu^B(P_2)]\!]_G$ that do not correspond to a μ_j which follows from Lemma 1 and the construction of $\mu^B(P_2)$, which concludes the argument.   □

We leave Theorem 1(ii) – which can be shown with similar arguments – without proof and directly skip to the proof of the more general Theorem 2.

B   Proof of Theorem 2

Proof. Without making any assumptions about (strong) boundedness of variables, again, we want to show that there is a 1:1 correspondence between the solution mappings of P_1 joining with (SERVICE c P_2) and the ones joining with (SERVICE c $P_2^{\mathrm{FILTER}'_{P_1}}$). Again, the theorem trivially holds for $c \in I \setminus dom(ep)$, i.e. if c is not the IRI of a SPARQL endpoint. Otherwise, let now $\mu \in [\![P]\!]_G$, then we know for each $\mu_i \subseteq \mu \in [\![P_1]\!]_G$ there is a compatible mapping $\mu_j \subseteq \mu \in [\![P_2]\!]_{G_c}$ such that for each join variable $v \in var(P_1) \cap var(P_2)$ it holds that either: (i) $v \notin dom(\mu_i)$, (ii) $v \notin dom(\mu_j)$, or (iii) $\mu_i(v) = \mu_j(v)$. We now treat these cases separately to show that $\mu_j \in [\![P_2^{\mathrm{FILTER}'_{P_1}}]\!]_{G_c}$ in each case:

(i): since the FILTER expression in $P_2^{\mathrm{FILTER}'_{P_1}}$ only considers variables in $dom(\mu_i)$ the FILTER leaves bindings for v in P_2 unaffected.

(ii) : the FILTER expression in $P_2^{\mathrm{FILTER}'_{P_1}}$ evaluates to true, due to $\neg bound(v)$

(iii) : the FILTER expression in $P_2^{\mathrm{FILTER}'_{P_1}}$ evaluates to true, due to $v = \mu(v)$

In total, we have shown that each $[\![P]\!]_G \subseteq [\![P_1]\!]_G \bowtie [\![P_2^{\mathrm{FILTER}_{P_1}}]\!]_{G_c}$.

For the other direction, it is easy to see that $[\![P_2^{\mathrm{FILTER}_{P_1}}]\!]_{G_c} \subseteq [\![P_2]\!]_{G_c}$, i.e. again, the rewritten query cannot deliver any additional results on the service side, which proved the opposite direction.   □

Again, the proof for $P_2^{\mathrm{UNION}'_{P_1}}$ follows similar arguments.

---

[12] Slightly abusing notation, when we write here $\mu_i \subseteq \mu$, we mean that μ_i is a submapping of μ, i.e. that $dom(\mu_i) \subseteq dom(\mu)$ and that $\mu_i(v) = \mu(v)$ for all $v \in dom(\mu_i)$.

Toward the Web of Functions: Interoperable Higher-Order Functions in SPARQL

Maurizio Atzori

Math/CS Department,
University of Cagliari,
Via Ospedale 72,
09124 Cagliari (CA), Italy
atzori@unica.it

Abstract. In this work we address the problem of using any third-party custom SPARQL function by only knowing its URI, allowing the computation to be executed on the remote endpoint that defines and implements such function. We present a standard-compliant solution that does not require changes to the current syntax or semantics of the language, based on the use of a `call` function. In contrast to the plain "Extensible Value Testing" described in the W3C Recommendations for the SPARQL Query Language, our approach is *interoperable*, that is, not dependent on the specific implementation of the endpoint being used for the query, relying instead on the implementation of the endpoint that declares and makes the function available, therefore reducing interoperability issues to one single case for which we provide an open source implementation. Further, the proposed solution for using custom functions within SPARQL queries is quite expressive, allowing for true higher-order functions, where functions can be assigned to variables and used as both inputs and outputs, enabling a generation of Web APIs for SPARQL that we call *Web of Functions*. The paper also shows different approaches on how our proposal can be applied to existing endpoints, including a SPARQL-to-SPARQL compiler that makes the use of `call` unnecessary, by exploiting non-normative sections in the Federated Query W3C Recommendations that are currently implemented on some popular SPARQL engines. We finally evaluate the effectiveness of our proposal reporting our experiments on two popular engines.

1 Introduction

During the years, the Web enlarged its initial scope of place where to publish static interlinked hypertexts. Standards such as HTTP enabled an incredible diversity of applications. Recently, Linked Data has shown the huge potential of having the Web as an unbounded, decentralized and free crowdsourced data store where everyone can access and contribute. Nowadays, structured data can be shared by a simple URI, in a similar way to HTML pages, where URIs can link each others by using the RDF model, forming a huge graph. Each data publisher provides a part of this graph, and through endpoints those subgraphs

P. Mika et al. (Eds.) ISWC 2014, Part II, LNCS 8797, pp. 406–421, 2014.
© Springer International Publishing Switzerland 2014

can be effectively queried by means of a powerful standard (by W3C) query language, the SPARQL. When it was announced, Sir Tim Berners-Lee declared that "SPARQL will make a huge difference" making the Web machine-readable. More recently, as also detailed later in the paper, a number of researchers worked on extending the relations between SPARQL and the Web of Data, allowing for instance dynamic exploration of the linked data by dereferencing the URIs appearing in the query, and therefore not relegating SPARQL to be a language for local data only.

In our work, we further embrace this research line, but instead of dealing with the data, we focus on the computational power and expressivity of functions that can be used within a query. While extending the language with user-defined custom functions (sometimes called extension functions) represented by URIs is a native feature of the language, the mechanism only works on the single endpoint featuring that specific function. Instead, in this paper we envision a Web where also functions can be openly published, making them available to all the users of any other endpoint. We address the problem of practically realizing such *Web of Functions* with a Remote Procedure Call (RPC) approach, that is, users can call a function by only knowing its corresponding URI, as it is the case for the Web of Data, while the implementation and the computational resources are made available by the function publisher, as it happens with RPC and usual Web APIs. In other words, we present a first step toward a new generation of Web APIs available within any endpoint, to be used in SPARQL queries, and strictly coupled with the Web of Linked Data. Our contribution enables the Web of Functions with a surprisingly strong backward compatibility, since *(a)* it does not require any change to current SPARQL specifications, *(b)* it does not require a special implementation of the endpoint that declares and publish a custom function and *(c)* only requires the definition of a `call` function on the querying endpoint. Regarding the last point, we provide an open source implementation for the required function, along with two other approaches making no requirements on the querying endpoint, based on W3C SPARQL Federated Queries (FED). The approaches are proved to work on Apache Jena and on any other endpoint that implements the non-normative parts described in the FED Recommendations.

Organization. In Section 2, we review the related work. Section 3 introduces the problem and the desiderata through simple examples. Section 4 describes our solution based on a function to implement remote calls. In Section 5 we show how to deploy the remote call functionality on existing endpoints, including Section 5.3 where we show a pure SPARQL approach that under some hypothesis can realize the Web of Functions with backward compatibility, through a SPARQL-to-SPARQL compiler. In Section 6, we discuss notable aspects and limitations of the approach. In Section 7 we show our outcomes experimenting our prototype implementation on two popular engines and finally, in Section 8, we draw the conclusions and identify possible future work in this research area.

2   Related Work

In [1], Gregory Williams defines an approach to make the extension functions interoperable. The paper suggests to act on the engine implementation of the endpoint in order to allow each SPARQL engine to run code, specifically javascript code, downloaded from third-party servers at query time. This allows any kind of functions to be run on the SPARQL endpoint containing the data. Although effective, that approach requires modifications of the way SPARQL functions are published, with mandatory dereferenceability of functions, the development of a code interpreter on each endpoint, other than security and other performance issues already discussed in the original paper. Work in [1] is definitely an interesting research proposal and present a non-backward-compatible way of implementing the Web of Functions, with high costs in terms of SPARQL engine codebase modifications. In contrast, our approach already works off-the-shelf in existing SPARQL engines, as it is totally compliant with current SPARQL standards, without requiring any changes in the existing SPARQL endpoint codebase, relying on RPCs made possible by the Federated Queries part of the SPARQL 1.1 standard.

Another interesting and related line of research is the one of query execution through link traversal, in Olaf Hartig et al. [2–5], including SQUIN[1], a query interface for the Web of Linked Data based on these studies. In the same area of research is DIAMOND [6, 7]. In our opinion these papers show the growing trend of joining tools like endpoints and the SPARQL query language thought for local usage, with the larger Web of Linked Data. We believe our work can be considered in this research streamline, although focusing on functions instead of data.

In our paper we also deal with the expressivity of SPARQL. Existing work that focuses on its computational power and expressivity can be found in [8]. In [9] we propose a simple function that enhances the computational power of SPARQL by introducing recursive SPARQL functions.

In [10] a recent proposal to combine REST scalability with Linked Data expressivity is presented. The work is focused on the use of JSON-LD. While powerful and related, their approach seems not to consider SPARQL endpoints as a querying source. Our work is instead focused on envisioning a Web of Functions where functions are callable from any endpoint, while minimizing (or avoiding at all) technology changes to existing engine installations by leveraging the federated queries mechanism [11].

3   Problem Definition

In this Section we detail the problems in current custom functions that we are addressing in this paper. In our opinion, there are two main issues that limit the free use of "public" (that is, shareable, third-party) custom functions inside SPARQL queries: interoperability and expressivity.

---

[1] http://squin.org/

3.1   Limited Interoperability

The first problem is that user-defined functions are not interoperable. In fact, current official SPARQL extension function mechanism is based on the exploitation of unspecified behavior in case of function errors, a sort of trick on the semantics of the `PrimaryExpression` SPARQL 1.1 grammar rule, where expected error values are instead used as an extension point to implement custom functions in specific engines, including Virtuoso, Jena, Sesame and others. Specific implementations of SPARQL endpoints can therefore compute a function instead of throwing an error, allowing the execution of custom user-defined functions missing in the SPARQL specification. The specification correctly states that "SPARQL queries using extension functions are likely to have limited interoperability", as the custom function will only run on the endpoint implementing that specific function. The custom function seems to be confined to the endpoint that implements it.

In order to better show the problem, let us stick to the following running example and have some fun stealing names from cryptography. Suppose we are Alice, the owner of the domain `alice-server.org`, with semantic data exposed as linked open data and through an endpoint at `http://alice-server.org/sparql`. We want to query our data using a complex function that is not part of standard SPARQL. That function has been already implemented in Bob's endpoint, `http://bob-server.org/sparql`, and he called it `http://bob-server.org/fn/complexFunction`.

The desiderata for Alice would be to run on her own endpoint a query similar to the following:

```
PREFIX bob: <http://bob-server.org/fn/>
SELECT *
WHERE {
    # within Alice data, find useful values for ?arg1, ?arg2 and ?arg3
    ...
    # now use Bob's function
    FILTER(bob:complexFunction(?arg1, ?arg2, ?arg3) )
}
```

Note that this is perfectly compliant with the syntax of SPARQL, but nonetheless it is not going to work on Alice's endpoint because it does not recognize the semantics of `bob:complexFunction`. On the other end, if she runs the query on Bob's endpoint, the function will be working but Alice data would be inaccessible. A simple trick could be to use federated query on Bob's endpoint to get Alice data and then use `bob:complexFunction`. Unfortunately, this is not working in the general case where we also want to use functions from other function providers, such as `carol:otherFunction`. Therefore, custom functions such as `bob:complexFunction` and `carol:otherFunction` are totally acceptable from a syntactic point of view, but unfortunately they are not interoperable, i.e., difficult or impossible to be used by other endpoints such as Alice's. Another important thing is that, in our view, functions should be utilizable by just sharing the URI, not also the endpoint address. This is a principle in the Web of

Linked Data, where anyone can access and refer to data by just referring to its URI. Our desiderata requires the same principle, applied to functions. While the syntax of SPARQL already allows functions to be represented as URIs, they are not usable unless the endpoint that defines their semantics is also known and, even worse, currently the same URI may have different semantics on different endpoints.

3.2 Limited Expressivity

As far as we have seen, the syntax of SPARQL is ready for open functions. In fact the query shown above, that Alice would like to run, validates. Nevertheless, in terms of expressivity, the SPARQL language lacks of basic syntax to handle higher-order functions (HOF) effectively. First let us review the previous query example in terms of language expressivity. Function names are URIs, and therefore can be assigned to variables. Functions can be called passing variables, therefore the syntax allows functions to accept functions as input, and also to return functions. Further, although our examples always use functions as FILTER expressions for the sake of readability, it is well-known that SPARQL does not relegate functions to this usage, for instance we can use

```
BIND( bob:complexFunction(?arg1, ?arg2, ?arg3) AS ?result )
```

assigning the result of a function call to a variable. This may apparently and surprisingly put SPARQL in the class of languages that natively support higher-order functions. Unfortunately expressivity is strongly limited as we are going to show in the following example.

```
SELECT *
WHERE {
    # within Alice data, find useful values for ?arg1, ?arg2 and ?arg3
    ...
    # now Alice also binds ?f to a URI that represents a function
    # for instance, suppose ?f is bound to alice:fn
    BIND(alice:fn AS ?f)
    ...

    # now Alice wants to call the ?f function with arguments
    FILTER( ?f(?arg1, ?arg2, ?arg3) )
}
```

As before, in the last line we want to call a function with 3 arguments, but here the function is assigned to a variable, whose value is known only at runtime. This is not valid syntax in SPARQL 1.1 recommendation. This is not only a syntactic sugar restriction, it strongly limits the expressivity of function usage in SPARQL, since e.g., we cannot call a function which is the result of another function call. Here another related example of unfeasible query:

```
PREFIX alice: <http://alice-server.org/fn/>
SELECT *
WHERE {
    # within Alice data, find useful values for ?arg1, ?arg2 and ?arg3
```

```
    ...
    FILTER( alice:memoize(alice:fn) (?arg1, ?arg2, ?arg3) )
}
```

The function `alice:memoize`, that is supposed to memoize the input function `alice:fn` by caching the computed result, returns an (unnamed) function that should be called with the three arguments. Notice that in this example all the functions are local on purpose (i.e., not referring to Bob's endpoint) to better show that this is not a problem of interoperability.

In the following Section, we propose our simple solution to handle both limitations while sticking on the current syntax of SPARQL, i.e., without proposing unlikely future language extensions and changes.

4 A Function to Rule Them All

We found a simple and elegant solution to the problem of expressivity just described, that also strongly reduces the problem of interoperability to one single case. Let us show how the proposed approach can be applied in practice, and later we will detail how the remaining interoperability issue can be solved.

Given a query such as:

```
{
    ?arg a :UsefulThing # some interesting stuff
    FILTER( fn:thirdPartyFunction(?arg) )
}
```

involving a custom function, we propose to write the last line as:

```
    FILTER( wfn:call(fn:thirdPartyFunction , ?arg)  )
```

where the prefix `wfn` is a loosely short for "Web of Functions", defined as:

```
    wfn : <http://webofcode.org/wfn/>
```

The simple expedient of using `wfn:call` to call a function solves the expressivity problem of Section 3.2. In fact, now we can handle functions in variables:

```
    ?function a :UsefulFunction # match to a function
    FILTER( wfn:call( ?function , ?arg)  )
```

as well as nested calls. Please notice that since the expressivity problem of Section 3.2 originates from a syntax limitation in SPARQL, any solutions will have to deal with the syntax of the query. We believe that our proposal of using a "call" function can be considered, concerning the syntax, an acceptable solution to the problem. In fact, it is similar to already well-known functions (e.g., *apply* or *funcall* in other functional languages) and, more importantly, it does respect the syntax of SPARQL as per current W3C recommendations, therefore a viable solution even for existing endpoints.

If this proposed way of formulating a query involving function calls is used, then the only required custom function to be implemented on an endpoint is `wfn:call`. In other words, its use solves the expressivity issue and reduces the interoperability issue to one special case, the function `wfn:call` itself.

In the following, we describe what we expect from the execution of the call function, in order to implement it. Then, in Section 5 we devise three different approaches to implement this function, including a pure SPARQL implementation, detailed in Section 5.3, that works under some assumptions.

4.1   Semantics of WFN:CALL

The function `wfn:call`, as we have seen, is a custom function that takes one argument, which is a constant or a variable containing an IRI representing a function, and then zero or more other arguments (either constants or variables). Whenever the function is called, it takes the first argument, the function URI, and call it passing all the remaining arguments. The semantics is therefore the same of *funcall* in the Lisp language.

Remember that given an IRI, there is no explicit semantics of what code should be run, since as we already mentioned, it is left to the specific endpoint implementation. In our approach, calling a function means to execute a SPARQL query over the endpoint that defines it. Here is the tricky part, as there is no way in SPARQL to know the correct endpoint that defines a custom function given a function IRI. We propose three possible answers to this problem:

Explicit Reference List. The endpoint has a user-defined list of *(function URI, endpoint URI)* pairs, therefore when a function should be called, the correct endpoint is found by matching that function URI. This approach requires a static configuration – while restrictive, this has the benefit of reducing the risks of running functions by only allowing known trusted endpoints.

Dereferenceable Functions. Whenever a function should be called, it is dereferenced. The entity should be of type `sd:Function` and also have a property `sd:endpoint` that points to the endpoint URL that implements the dereferenced function. Here we are reusing the official `sd` prefix defined in the SPARQL Service Description recommendation. Dereferecing functions is a feature already mentioned and proposed in literature (e.g., see [1]), but currently not described in the recommendation nor used on a widespread basis. A disadvantage of this approach is that it cannot be implemented using pure SPARQL since dynamic dereferencing (that is, the URI to be dereferenced is contained in a variable) is not allowed in SPARQL. Anyway, we suggest to make function URIs dereferenceable even when this approach is not used to implement `wfn:call`. We also notice that some RDF attributes available through function dereferenceability may also inform on the computational complexity and other function characteristics (number of arguments, returned type, etc.). In this paper we only focus on the problem of running remote custom functions without proposing a specific ontology for functions and algorithms.

Function-to-Endpoint IRI pattern. By sticking on a URI pattern, we may force that given a function URI, there is a deterministic way to find its endpoint. We propose to remove all the ending chars different from "/" and then append the string "sparql". That is, if the function IRI is `alice:myFunction` then the computed endpoint URI will be `alice:sparql`. To the best of our knowledge, this is an original proposal that solves the problem. It also allows similar functions (determined by the URI prefix) to be implemented by the same endpoint and viceversa; also, the computation is fast and can be implemented in pure SPARQL as we are going to show in Section 5.3.

As we have seen, all of these 3 strategies to finding the endpoint associated to a function URI have pros and cons. In the following, unless otherwise noted, we assume that the *Function-to-Endpoint IRI pattern* strategy is used.

By using our running example, if Bob wants to share a custom function, he can create an endpoint such as `http://bob-server.org/fn/sparql` where his custom functions, for instance `bob:complexFunction` and `bob:anotherCoolFn`, are implemented. So, now that we know which endpoint should be queried for a given IRI function, the `wfn:call` can query the correct endpoint and execute the custom function. It will proceed by following these protocol steps:

1. compute the endpoint URI by using one of the alternatives mentioned earlier;
2. make a SPARQL query to the remote endpoint using the given parameters as arguments for the remote custom function, binding the results to a variable;
3. get the returning value, and use it as a returning value for the call function; in case of error, the same error must be thrown by the call function, as if the function was run locally.

For nested calls, the inner calls should be computed first, as usual. This also means that every remote call will not contain any reference to the custom function `wfn:call` in the arguments since it should be already resolved.

5   Implementing and Executing the WFN:CALL Function

Once we reduced all the interoperability issues arising from the use of custom functions to one single case, it remains to solve the interoperability issue of the function `wfn:call`. In other words, we need to assure that the `wfn:call` function will be recognized and run by the querying endpoint.

We devise three approaches here to implement the `wfn:call` on an endpoint: (1) through the extensible testing function on the querying endpoint; (2) through a middleware third-party endpoint implementing the function acting as a proxy between the querying endpoint and the remote endpoint that implements the custom function; and (3) through a SPARQL-to-SPARQL compiler (a query rewriting tool).

In the following we detail all of these three solutions, enlightening both positive aspects and disadvantages.

5.1 Native Support on the Querying Endpoint

The simplest way to allow the use of wfn:call is to implement it in the SPARQL engine. This can be done by vendors or by the user, as a custom function, and this is exemplified in the upper path of Fig. 1. We implemented that function in Java[2] on an Apache Jena/Fuseki triplestore, as shown later in the Experiments section. Notice that such implementation should be implemented only on the querying endpoint. For instance, the following call:

```
VALUES (?arg1 ?arg2 ?arg3) {("1st" "2nd" "3rd") }
FILTER( wfn:call(bob:complexFunction, ?arg1, ?arg2, ?arg3) )
```

will be caught by the SPARQL processor (also known as ARQ in Apache Jena) and executed by a Java class[3] that extends FunctionBase. The Java implementation will use one of the strategies in the previous section to compute the endpoint's URI associated with the bob:complexFunction function. Then, it will run on Bob's endpoint a query such as the following[4]:

```
SELECT ?result
WHERE {
    BIND( <http://bob-server.org/fn/complexFunction>("1st","2nd","3rd")
    AS ?result)
}
```

obtaining the result computed in the remote endpoint. Notice that at the time of running the Java code, arguments are bound and therefore their values can be used in the query.

This solution will work, with the only drawback of requiring a native implementation of wfn:call on the endpoint. The next approaches show that under some hypothesis it is not necessary to implement it on the querying endpoint.

5.2 Proxy-Based Federated Query

If we cannot rely on a native implementation in our endpoint (e.g., we do not have privileges to register a custom function), we can still use the wfn:call implemented on a third-party commodity endpoint by using the SPARQL 1.1 Federated Query mechanism, under a reasonable hypothesis discussed later in this subsection.

---

[2] Available at http://atzori.webofcode.org/projects/wfn/

[3] See https://jena.apache.org/documentation/javadoc/arq/com/hp/hpl/jena/sparql/function/FunctionBase.html for details; in OpenLink Virtuoso it will require a C program, and current version forces the use of the prefix bif (built-in function).

[4] The actual query is slightly more complex in order to be run on those endpoints (such as Virtuoso) that do not support the use of BIND without a previous graph pattern matching; on some other endpoints (e.g., Apache Jena) this is a valid SPARQL query.

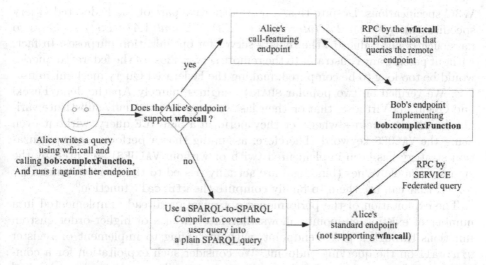

Fig. 1. The workflow of the user query in case *(a)* of an endpoint supporting `wfn:call` and *(b)* of a standard endpoint, not supporting the extension. In the second case, the tool described in our paper can convert the query into a standard one, that can be run on any endpoint.

This approach is based on rewriting each part of the query where the call function appears. For any occurrence of `wfn:call`, starting from inner nested calls and continuing to outer calls, the expression is substituted with a `SERVICE` call to the commodity call-featured server. For instance, let us take Alice's query (PREFIXes are removed for the sake of readability):

```
SELECT ?arg1
WHERE {
    # within Alice data, find useful values for ?arg1, ?arg2 and ?arg3
    ...
    # now want to use remote Bob's function
    FILTER( wfn:call(bob:complexFunction, ?arg1, ?arg2, ?arg3) )
}
```

The query will not be changed except for the last FILTER line, that will be replaced with the following lines, exploiting the federated query mechanism:

```
SERVICE wfn:commodityEndpoint {
    BIND ( bob:complexFunction(?arg1, ?arg2, ?arg3) AS ?tmp_result1 )
}
FILTER( ?tmp_result1 )
```

This simple expedient allows the part of the query using the call function to be computed against a commodity endpoint known to feature it.

There is a hidden hypothesis under which this federated query will work. The tricky part is that function arguments (`?arg1, ...`) are bound, but such bindings are not guaranteed to be passed to the remote server according to normative

W3C specifications. Despite this, a non-normative part of the Federated Query specifications (section 2.4 *Interplay of SERVICE and VALUES*[5]) suggests to pass such bound values to the remote server for optimization purposes. In fact, without passing any constraint to the remote server, most of the federated queries would be too long to be computed, making the Federated Query mechanism useless. We verified on two popular SPARQL engines, namely Apache Jena/Fuseki and OpenLink Virtuoso, that on their last versions they actually substitute variables with their values whenever they perform a SERVICE query, without even using the VALUES keyword. Therefore, assuming that a performance optimization strategy has been implemented (with or without VALUES) and used by the engine, variable values (bindings) are actually passed to the remote commodity server, that can use them to finally compute the wfn:call function[6].

The exploitation of the performance optimization already implemented in a number of existing endpoints allows therefore the use of higher-order custom functions through a proxy endpoint, without having to implement or register wfn:call on the querying endpoint. We consider such exploitation for a completely different problem (implementing remote calls on SPARQL) an original contribution of this paper.

5.3   A Pure SPARQL Approach Based on SPARQL-to-SPARQL Query Compiling

In both previous approaches we had to implement wfn:call (in the querying endpoint or in the proxy endpoint). Here we are going to show how SPARQL can be turned into a fully HOF-featuring language without relying on the implementation of a call function nor introducing changes to the current SPARQL syntax, We found existing SPARQL specification mechanisms that can be used to implement it as a query rewriting tool. This way we can construct a SPARQL-to-SPARQL compiler able to rewrite a SPARQL query that uses wfn:call into another that does not, therefore usable on current endpoints not implementing the call function.

Firstly, we show that through the *Function-to-Endpoint IRI pattern* approach described above we can dynamically compute the endpoint address given a function IRI, by using only SPARQL, which is not possible in general by dereferencing, and very limited by using, instead, a predetermined list of known IRI. Secondly, we generate a pure SPARQL query usable within a SPARQL query from any endpoint by exploiting the federated query mechanism. Thus, we propose a standard-compliant technique to allow easily shareable third-party functions to be used within SPARQL queries from any existing endpoint, assuming the implementation of two non-normative parts in the Federated Query specifications. We stress that, unlike other proposals, this is possible without changing SPARQL specifications nor any codebase of existing engine implementations, since the compiled query

---

[5] See http://www.w3.org/TR/sparql11-federated-query/#values
[6] In case of VALUES, the proxy can read the bindings and rewrite the query to be sent to the final endpoint, without using the VALUES keyword

is a standard SPARQL 1.1 query where `wfn:call` does not appear, and other custom functions are called remotely against the appropriate endpoint. Of course, the assumption that non-normative parts are implemented does not always hold, and therefore approaches in previous sections are still interesting. Anyway, we verified that on the popular Apache Jena/Fuseki engine the two non-normative parts required for this approach actually hold, and therefore this pure-SPARQL approach may have a practical impact on some existing installations.

The SPARQL-to-SPARQL compiler works as described next. As in the previous proxy-based approach, any occurrence of `wfn:call` will be replaced with a SERVICE call. For Alice's query:

```
SELECT ?arg1
WHERE {
    # within Alice data, find useful values for ?arg1, ?arg2 and ?arg3
    ...
    # now want to use remote Bob's function
    FILTER( wfn:call(bob:complexFunction, ?arg1, ?arg2, ?arg3) )
}
```

the compiler will not change the query except for the last FILTER line, this time without using any proxy endpoint, relying on the Bob's endpoint directly:

```
SERVICE bob:sparql {
    BIND ( bob:complexFunction(?arg1, ?arg2, ?arg3) AS ?tmp_result1 )
}
FILTER( ?tmp_result1 )
```

Now let us show the case where the function URI is not known at compile time. The query that Alice wants to run may contain a variable ?f bound to a function:

```
# now Alice wants to call the ?f function with arguments
FILTER( wfn:call(?f, ?arg1, ?arg2, ?arg3) )
```

To solve this, we propose the use of another non-normative Section of the W3C Federated Query Specification (Section 4 titled *SERVICE Variables*[7]), that allows to use SERVICE against dynamically computed endpoints. Thus, in this case the compiler will convert the previous FILTER line into the following:

```
# dynamically compute the endpoint URI
BIND( URI(REPLACE( STR(?f) ,"/[^/]*$" , "/sparql" ) )
        AS ?tmp_endpoint1)

SERVICE ?tmp_endpoint1 {
```

---

[7] See `http://www.w3.org/TR/sparql11-federated-query/#variableService`. We verified that at least on Apache Jena this non-normative part has been implemented. Note that the query is valid SPARQL, since the syntax for SERVICE VAR is normative, but some vendors may require user configuration or have a different semantics for SERVICE variables.

```
    BIND ( wfn:call(?f, ?arg1, ?arg2, ?arg3) AS ?tmp_result1 )
}
```

```
FILTER( ?tmp_result1 )
```

Here we are featuring a query that has to deal with the expressivity syntactic issue of Section 3.2. Therefore, this time wfn:call must appear in the query to maintain syntactic compatibility with SPARQL standard. Anyway, it should be noted that it is performed on the remote server publishing the custom function, that we may assume it is a call-featuring engine. Also notice that the implementation of the wfn:call in Bob's engine is straightforward (a simple query rewriting), since at the time of execution the variable ?f is always instantiated by Alice's endpoint, and it is assumed to point to a Bob's function.

This last example also helps us to show the implications of the different alternatives in the previous section, namely Explicit Reference List, Dereferenceable Functions, and Function-to-Endpoint IRI pattern. Having an Explicit Reference List with a known URI can be used to convert, within the query, a function URI into a SPARQL endpoint URI, after importing the list by using, e.g., the FROM clause. Although working, in this approach it is not clear who should be in charge of maintaining such a centralized list. We believe it is in contrast with the decentralized architecture of the Web of Linked Data. Dereferenceability of function URIs is a generally desirable behaviour, but unfortunately the SPARQL language does not seem to support dereferencing a URI contained in a variable[8], therefore a pure SPARQL compiler would not be possible. Instead, as we have shown, the last approach based on Function-to-Endpoint URI pattern can work in a SPARQL-to-SPARQL tool without drawbacks except for the acceptable constraint on the relation between function's and endpoint's URIs.

6   Discussion on the Proposed Approach

In the following, we discuss some notable aspects arising when using custom functions through the "function-as-a-service" RPC approach we have presented.

Decoupling Functions and Data. Since the basic problem addressed in this paper is about having data and functions in different servers, we should note that decoupling them takes consequences on the possible interactions. For instance, the result of a function that computes the palindrome of a given string only depends on the input string. Such palindrome function has no interaction problem. We notice that almost all the standard SPARQL functions behave like this. On the contrary, a function computing the length of a minimum path between two IRIs also needs the whole graph to get the result, not only the two given IRIs. The same limitation occurs when dealing with blank nodes, which are not sharable across SPARQL endpoints by definition. A consequence is that functions handling RDF collections (e.g., rdf:List of *W3C RDF Schema 1.1*) cannot be

---

[8] Legacy, non standard solutions may exist on specific engines; for instance, the Virtuoso engine supports the input:grab-var pragma to dereference the content of a variable.

computed with the call function, since only a reference to the first element is transferred (not the whole collection). Although in a true Linked Open Data this is still feasible, because by dereferencing the IRIs the server implementing such a function can fetch the whole graph, this may lead to reduced performance. Also notice that dereferenceability is not mandatory for this approach: the server implementing the function can run a SPARQL query against the first endpoint to get the other data needed to answer[9].

Performance. Being outsourced, performance on the computation of custom functions depends on other servers. The approach also has an intrinsic performance limitation, requiring the input data to be passed to the external server, and then getting the answer back. Our experiments show that performances are acceptable in many cases, whenever the number of function calls (determined by the number of possible arguments matching locally) is not too large.

The system used to implement the federated query protocol can also contribute to improve the performances. For instance, function calls can be compacted to a single query with the VALUES keyword used to specify multiple set of function arguments, reducing delays due to network latency.

True HOF. Our HOF approach allows functions to be used as input and output. In fact, there is no technical constraint that avoids custom functions to be created at runtime. For instance, we implemented a function compose that given two other functions returns a dynamically-generated function URI that, whenever used, returns the composition of the two given functions [12].

Security. Our approach based on computing functions on someone else's server, which is declaring the function and providing the implementation, drastically reduces Denial of Services and more serious security threats feasible in other approaches [1], where on the contrary the calling endpoint engine does run unknown code dynamically downloaded from another server. Since we are using only existing standards, most of the security issues known and related to already accepted mechanisms, such as federated queries. Anyway, we remark that enhancing expressivity necessarily also leads to enhanced capabilities for attackers, allowing for instance new kinds of Denial of Services (DoSs) attacks derived by the composition of functions. We suggest an implementation with user-configurable timeouts, that will kill any external function call after a determined period of time. While this paper is not focused on security issues related to querying untrusted federated endpoints, this should mitigate a number of possible attacks.

Privacy. Whenever we use a remote custom function, we are providing arguments to a remote (potentially untrusted) endpoint server. Likewise SPARQL Federated Queries, privacy issues must be taken into account before sharing sensitive data with untrusted servers.

---

[9] Although this may introduce interoperability problems in case the data is not shown by the endpoint.

7   Experimental Evaluation

In order to verify the effectiveness of our approaches, we implemented `wfn:call` on the Apache Jena/Fuseki endpoint, using the *Extensible Value Testing* mechanism of SPARQL, available at `http://atzori.webofcode.org/projects/wfn/`.

7.1   Time Performance of `wfn:call`

Running a function through a Remote Procedure Call mechanism introduces network delays that must be evaluated. We computed the concatenation of two strings on 3 different settings: (a) locally, i.e., without the use of `wfn:call`, (b) remotely, against a Jena server, and (c) remotely, against a Virtuoso server. Results are shown in Table 1. Differences are negligible considering that times are in milliseconds. We also performed the experiment on a slower network connection, obtaining no sensible differences, requiring approx $5s$ for every setting. Therefore, we conclude that `wfn:call` is effective in terms of performance, executing queries in the same order of magnitude (x3.1) even in the worst-case setting.

Table 1. Time performance in different query settings

Setting	Time (ms)	Overload (times)
local execution of fn:concat	46	x1 (ref)
execution of fn:concat on a remote Jena server	71	x1.5
execution of fn:concat on a remote Virtuoso server	144	x3.1

7.2   Experiments on the Current Feasibility of a SPARQL-to-SPARQL Compiler

According to Lee Feigenbaum, Co-Chair of the W3C SPARQL Working Group, "SPARQL 1.1 defines a mechanism to communicate results from one endpoint to another, but this is not currently widely deployed". We ran a number of queries against the latest versions[10] of Apache Jena/Fuseki and and OpenLink Virtuoso to verify their implementation of the Federated Query protocol and non-normative parts. We found that both engines optimize federated queries sending bindings to the remote endpoint, although they use substitution instead of the suggested `VALUES` clause. For each engine, we found a federated SPARQL query that can take the place of the `wfn:call` function. Further, only Apache Jena implements `SERVICE VAR` where variables can contain references to remote endpoints. More information available at the above web site.

8   Conclusions and Future Work

We have shown how the current specification of the SPARQL language allows the use of higher-order custom functions, which are also interoperable. This is

---

[10] Jena v. 2.11.1, Fuseki v. 1.0.1, Virtuoso Opensource Single Server Edition v. 07.10.3209 – all running on a Linux box.

possible through the use of a specific function, or by query rewriting techniques developed in the paper without introducing mandatory language extensions on some engines. We believe this may be the first step toward a novel view of the Web as a place holding code and functions, not only data as the Linked Data is greatly doing. The Semantic Web already shifted URIs from pages to conceptual entities, primarily structured data. We believe that among these concepts there should be computable functions. In other words, Semantic Web and its SPARQL language should include web services as first class resources, not only static Web of Data, enabling what could be called the *Web of Functions*. As a future work we plan to explore this research direction by also including the *property functions* (sometimes called magic properties) and possible integrations with user-friendly SPARQL interfaces such as SWiPE [13].

Acknowledgments. This work was supported in part by the RAS project CRP-17615 *DENIS* and by MIUR PRIN 2010-11 project *Security Horizons*.

References

1. Williams, G.: Extensible SPARQL Functions with Embedded Javascript. In: ESWC 2007 Workshop on Scripting for the Semantic Web, SFSW 2007 (2007)
2. Hartig, O., Bizer, C., Freytag, J.-C.: Executing SPARQL Queries over the Web of Linked Data. In: Bernstein, A., Karger, D.R., Heath, T., Feigenbaum, L., Maynard, D., Motta, E., Thirunarayan, K. (eds.) ISWC 2009. LNCS, vol. 5823, pp. 293–309. Springer, Heidelberg (2009)
3. Hartig, O.: An Introduction to SPARQL and Queries over Linked Data. In: Brambilla, M., Tokuda, T., Tolksdorf, R. (eds.) ICWE 2012. LNCS, vol. 7387, pp. 506–507. Springer, Heidelberg (2012)
4. Hartig, O.: SPARQL for a Web of Linked Data: Semantics and Computability. In: Simperl, E., Cimiano, P., Polleres, A., Corcho, O., Presutti, V. (eds.) ESWC 2012. LNCS, vol. 7295, pp. 8–23. Springer, Heidelberg (2012)
5. Hartig, O.: SQUIN: a traversal based query execution system for the web of linked data. In: ACM SIGMOD Conference, pp. 1081–1084 (2013)
6. Arenas, M., Gutierrez, C., Miranker, D.P., Pérez, J., Sequeda, J.: Querying Semantic Data on the Web? SIGMOD Record 41(4), 6–17 (2012)
7. Miranker, D.P., Depena, R.K., Jung, H., Sequeda, J.F., Reyna, C.: Diamond: A SPARQL Query Engine, for Linked Data Based on the Rete Match. In: Artificial Intelligence Meets the Web of Data Workshop, Co-located at ECAI 2012 (2012)
8. Angles, R., Gutierrez, C.: The Expressive Power of SPARQL. In: Sheth, A.P., Staab, S., Dean, M., Paolucci, M., Maynard, D., Finin, T., Thirunarayan, K. (eds.) ISWC 2008. LNCS, vol. 5318, pp. 114–129. Springer, Heidelberg (2008)
9. Atzori, M.: Computing Recursive SPARQL Queries. In: 8th IEEE International Conference on Semantic Computing, ICSC, pp. 258–259 (2014)
10. Lanthaler, M.: Creating 3rd generation web APIs with hydra. In: 22nd International World Wide Web Conference, WWW (Companion Volume), pp. 35–38 (2013)
11. Aranda, C.B., Arenas, M., Corcho, Ó., Polleres, A.: Federating queries in SPARQL 1.1: Syntax, semantics and evaluation. J. Web Sem. 18(1), 1–17 (2013)
12. Atzori, M.: call: A Nucleus for a Web of Open Functions (submitted for publication)
13. Atzori, M., Zaniolo, C.: SWiPE: Searching Wikipedia by Example. In: 21st World Wide Web Conference, WWW (Companion Volume), pp. 309–312 (2012)

Explass: Exploring Associations between Entities via Top-K Ontological Patterns and Facets

Gong Cheng, Yanan Zhang, and Yuzhong Qu

State Key Laboratory for Novel Software Technology, Nanjing University,
Nanjing 210023, P.R. China
{gcheng,yzqu}@nju.edu.cn, ynzhang@smail.nju.edu.cn

Abstract. Searching for associations between entities is needed in many areas. On the Semantic Web, it usually boils down to finding paths that connect two entities in an entity-relation graph. Given the increasing volume of data, apart from the efficiency of path finding, recent research interests have focused on how to help users explore a large set of associations that have been found. To achieve this, we propose an approach to exploratory association search, called Explass, which provides a flat list (top-K) of clusters and facet values for refocusing and refining the search. Each cluster is labeled with an ontological pattern, which gives a conceptual summary of the associations in the cluster. Facet values comprise classes of entities and relations appearing in associations. To recommend frequent, informative, and small-overlapping patterns and facet values, we exploit ontological semantics, query context, and information theory. We compare Explass with two existing approaches by conducting a user study over DBpedia, and test the statistical significance of the results.

Keywords: Association exploration, clustering, exploratory search, faceted search, ontological association pattern.

1 Introduction

Searching for associations (a.k.a. relationships) between two entities is needed in many areas. For instance, a security agent may be interested in the associations between two suspected terrorists. A historian may study the associations between two politicians in history. Researchers may be curious about the associations between each other in an academic network.

Carrying out association search over unstructured data on the Web, e.g. web-page text [15], is not an easy task because direct relations between entities need to be extracted from ambiguous text, and finding indirect associations may even have to integrate information from multiple sources. In recent years, association search has been facilitated by the availability of graph-structured data on the Semantic Web, which exactly describes entities and the relations between them, and can relatively be easily integrated from different sources. In such an entity-relation graph, associations between two entities are explicitly captured by the paths that connect these two vertices. Association search is then transformed into path finding [3], and it faces two challenges when entity-relation graphs

P. Mika et al. (Eds.) ISWC 2014, Part II, LNCS 8797, pp. 422–437, 2014.

become very large: how to efficiently find associations, and *how to help users explore a large set of associations that have been found.* The latter challenge will be addressed in this paper.

We meet this challenge by realizing exploratory search for associations. Exploratory search [16] is designed to serve complex and uncertain information needs, which is often the case in association search. It aims to help users explore, process, and interpret a large set of search results via continuous and exploratory interaction, mainly based on statically defined facets or dynamically generated clusters [9]. Distinguished from existing work on exploratory association search [10,19], our contribution is summarized as follows.

- Our approach to association exploration, called Explass, provides a flat list (top-K, rather than a hierarchy [19]) of clusters for refocusing. Each cluster is labeled with an ontological association pattern (or pattern for short), which makes up of classes and relations and preserves the path structure of association. It can give users a conceptual summary of the associations in the cluster.
- To obtain clusters, i.e. to recommend patterns, we propose to firstly mine all the significant patterns that are highly relevant to the query context by formulating and solving a data mining problem, and then find top-K ones that are as frequent and informative as possible while sharing small overlap between each other by formulating and solving an optimization problem.
- In this novel solution, the frequency of a pattern reflects its relevance to the query context. The informativeness of a pattern is learned from the entity-relation graph according to information theory. The overlap between patterns is identified based on ontological semantics and query context.
- Further, Explass integrates patterns with facet values, which are classes of entities and relations appearing in associations, and can be used to refine the search as filters. Rather than showing all of them [10], we adapt the above solution to recommend top-K ones. We will show that patterns and facets are complementary in terms of usage in association exploration.
- We implement a prototype of Explass based on DBpedia. To investigate how patterns and facets help users explore associations in practice, we compare Explass with two existing approaches by conducting a user study, and test the statistical significance of the results.

The remainder of the paper is structured as follows. Section 2 discusses related work. Section 3 presents an overview of Explass. Section 4 gives some preliminaries. Section 5 and 6 describe the recommendation of patterns and facet values, respectively. Section 7 reports a user study. Section 8 concludes the paper.

2 Related Work

Definitions of Association. Given an entity-relation graph, association between entities has various definitions. Anyanwu and Sheth [3] defined four types of associations, in which path-based association has received the most attention and is adopted by this paper. Among other definitions, in REX [6], an association conforms to a certain constrained graph pattern, and is obtained by combining paths. In Ming [12], an association between a set of entities is a connected subgraph containing all of them. In this paper, *we will not address these different definitions, and will only deal with path-based association.*

Association Discovery and Ranking. Discovering path-based associations boils down to finding paths in an entity-relation graph, which is a challenge when the graph is large, and has attracted considerable interest [7,11]. However, *what we focus on in this paper is a problem that follows, namely how to help users explore a large set of associations that have been found.* So far, major efforts addressing this issue were made to appropriately rank associations so that more important ones could be shown earlier. Existing ranking methods exploit various structural features of an association [1,2], consider query relevance [20], and produce personalized results [5]. *Complementary to ranking, another line of research builds on exploratory search, and our approach belongs to this category.*

Exploratory Association Search. Exploratory search [16] serves complex and uncertain information needs, and expects search systems to facilitate cognitive processing and interpretation of a large set of search results via continuous and exploratory interaction that goes beyond lookup and ranking. Facets and clustering are two popular methods for realizing this [9]. Facets are usually statically defined, whereas clustering lets search results speak for themselves. Both facets and clustering have been widely adopted in Web search and, in particular, in entity search [14,17]. Recently, they have also been adopted in association search [10,19]. Among existing attempts, RelFinder [10] employs classes of entities and relations appearing in associations as facet values for refining the search and filtering associations. RelClus [19] organizes associations inclusively into a hierarchy of clusters for refocusing, where each cluster is labeled with a pattern. In this paper, *we realize exploratory association search in a new way. Our Explass integrates both clusters (i.e. patterns) and facets (i.e. classes and relations)* and, in particular, *it provides a flat list (top-K) of informative patterns*, thereby avoiding deep and complicated hierarchical organization as well as very general and meaningless high-level patterns met on RelClus. Technically, different from [10,19], *we give our attention to the recommendation of patterns and facet values, and consider their frequency, informativeness, and overlap by exploiting ontological semantics, query context, and information theory.* We will compare Explass with RelFinder and RelClus in a user study.

3   Overview of Explass

Before formally introducing Explass, in this section, we illustrate the exploration operations it supports. A prototype based on DBpedia is available online.[1]

As illustrated in Fig. 1, after obtaining a set of associations between two entities, Explass recommends a set (top-K) of path-structured patterns (cf. Sect. 5)

---

[1] http://ws.nju.edu.cn/explass/

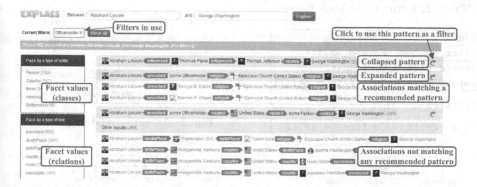

Fig. 1. A prototype of Explass based on DBpedia

and a set (top-K) of facet values (cf. Sect. 6) for further exploration. Firstly, all the associations matching a recommended pattern are clustered and placed under this pattern, which provides a conceptual summary of these associations. It is followed by the number of these associations in parentheses, and is expandable/collapsible to show/hide them for refocusing. Associations not matching any recommended pattern are placed at the end. Secondly, a pattern can also be used as a filter to refine the search. After that, search results will be limited to those matching this pattern, and all the recommendations will be re-computed. Filters in use can be canceled. Thirdly, classes of entities and relations appearing in associations comprise facet values, each of which is followed by the number of associations to expect if using this class/relation as a filter to refine the search and limit search results to those containing its instance/occurrence.

4 Preliminaries

Table 1 and Fig. 2–4 comprise a running example in this paper.

Let $\Sigma_E, \Sigma_C, \Sigma_R$ be the sets of all entities, classes, and relations (i.e. properties connecting entities), respectively. An entity is an instance of one or more classes, as illustrated in Table 1. For each class c, let $I(c)$ be the set of all its instances. Classes are organized into a class hierarchy describing the subclass-superclass relation denoted by $\sqsubseteq_C$, as illustrated in Fig. 3. At the top of the class hierarchy, ENTITY represents a superclass of all other classes, and every entity is an instance of this class. Similarly, a relation hierarchy describing the subrelation-superrelation relation denoted by $\sqsubseteq_R$ is illustrated in Fig. 4, the top of which is called RELATED.

Entities and the relations connecting them form an *entity-relation graph*, as illustrated in Fig. 2, which is formalized as a labeled directed graph $G = \langle V, A, s, t, l_V, l_A \rangle$, where

- V is a finite set of vertices,
- A is a finite set of directed arcs,

Table 1. Entities and Their Classes

Entity	Class
Alice, Bob	Person, ENTITY
PaperA, PaperB, PaperC, PaperD	ConfPaper, Publication, ENTITY
ArticleA	JArticle, Publication, ENTITY
ConfA, ConfB	Conference, ENTITY

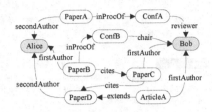

Fig. 2. An entity-relation graph

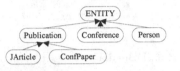

Fig. 3. A class hierarchy

Fig. 4. A relation hierarchy

- $s : A \mapsto V$ returns the source vertex of each arc,
- $t : A \mapsto V$ returns the target vertex of each arc,
- $l_V : V \mapsto \Sigma_E$ returns the unique label of each vertex, which is an entity, and
- $l_A : A \mapsto \Sigma_R$ returns the label of each arc, which is a relation.

An *association* from an entity e_S to an entity e_E comprises the labels of the vertices and arcs (i.e. entities and relations) in a path in G from e_S to e_E where no vertices are repeated and arcs not necessarily go the same direction. To differentiate between the two directions of an arc, the label r of each "reverse" arc going from e_E to e_S is substituted by a pseudo-relation $\hat{\ }r$. In particular, $\hat{\ }r_i \sqsubseteq_R \hat{\ }r_j$ if and only if $r_i \sqsubseteq_R r_j$; and for the top relation, $\hat{\ }\texttt{RELATED} = \texttt{RELATED}$. Then formally, corresponding to a path $v_0 a_1 \cdots a_n v_n$ from $e_S = l_V(v_0)$ to $e_E = l_V(v_n)$ which is an alternating sequence of vertices and arcs, an association of length n from e_S to e_E is an alternating sequence of relations and entities, $r_1 e_1 \cdots e_{n-1} r_n$, beginning and ending with a relation, and subject to

- for $1 \leq i \leq n-1$, $e_i = l_V(v_i)$, and
- for $1 \leq i \leq n$, if $s(a_i) = v_{i-1}$, then $r_i = l_A(a_i)$; otherwise, $r_i = \hat{\ }l_A(a_i)$.

For instance, the entity-relation graph in Fig. 2 contains five associations of length 3 from `Alice` to `Bob`:

$$Z_1 : \hat{\ }\texttt{secondAuthor PaperA inProcOf ConfA reviewer}$$
$$Z_2 : \hat{\ }\texttt{firstAuthor PaperB inProcOf ConfB chair}$$
$$Z_3 : \hat{\ }\texttt{firstAuthor PaperB cites PaperC firstAuthor} \qquad (1)$$
$$Z_4 : \hat{\ }\texttt{secondAuthor PaperD } \hat{\ }\texttt{cites PaperC firstAuthor}$$
$$Z_5 : \hat{\ }\texttt{secondAuthor PaperD } \hat{\ }\texttt{extends ArticleA firstAuthor}$$

An *ontological association pattern* (or pattern for short) provides an abstraction of association by substituting entities with classes they belong to and optionally substituting relations with their superrelations. More formally, a pattern of length n is an alternating sequence of relations and classes, $r_1 c_1 \cdots c_{n-1} r_n$, beginning and ending with a relation. An association $Z = r_1 e_1 \cdots e_{n-1} r_n$ *matches* a pattern $P = r'_1 c'_1 \cdots c'_{n-1} r'_n$, denoted by $Z \in M(P)$, if

- for $1 \le i \le n-1$, $e_i \in I(c'_i)$, and
- for $1 \le i \le n$, $r_i \sqsubseteq_R r'_i$.

For instance, both Z_1 and Z_2 in Eq. (1) match several different patterns such as

$$P_1 : \hat{}\texttt{author ConfPaper inProcOf ENTITY RELATED}. \tag{2}$$

To also allow entities to appear in a pattern, for each entity e, a pseudo-class $psc(e)$ is introduced that has e as its only instance, i.e. $I(psc(e)) = \{e\}$, and is a subclass of every other class that e belongs to. Then, Z_1 also matches

$$P_2 : \hat{}\texttt{author } psc(\texttt{PaperA}) \texttt{ inProcOf ENTITY RELATED}. \tag{3}$$

5 Pattern Recommendation

Given $\mathcal{Z}$, a set of associations from an entity e_S to another e_E found in the entity-relation graph G, we aim to recommend up to K patterns for exploring $\mathcal{Z}$. We firstly mine all the significant patterns that are highly relevant to the query context, and then find up to K of them that are as frequent and informative as possible while sharing small overlap between each other.

We assume the associations in $\mathcal{Z}$ are all of length n. Otherwise, we can group them by length, and recommend patterns for each group and show all of them.

5.1 Mining Significant Patterns

Given $\mathcal{Z}$ and a pattern P, to characterize the relevance of P to the query context, we define the *frequency* of P w.r.t. $\mathcal{Z}$ as

$$freq(P) = \frac{|hits(P)|}{|\mathcal{Z}|}$$
$$hits(P) = \{Z \in \mathcal{Z} : Z \in M(P)\}, \tag{4}$$

which is in the range $[0, 1]$. For instance, given $\mathcal{Z}$ comprising the five associations in Eq. (1), the frequency of P_1 in Eq. (2) is $\frac{2}{5}$ because it is matched by Z_1 and Z_2, i.e. by 2 out of the 5 associations.

We aim to find all the *significant patterns*, denoted by $\mathcal{P}_{\mathcal{Z}}$, namely those having a frequency higher than a threshold $\tau \in [0, 1]$. We formulate it as a frequent closed itemset mining problem (FCIMP), which has been extensively studied in the field of data mining [8]. A tricky issue in the formulation is how to encode the path structure of association and pattern.

Specifically, each association in $\mathcal{Z}$ corresponds to a "transaction" (which is a set of "items") in FCIMP, and an "item" is a position-relation pair in $\{1, 3, \ldots, 2n-1\} \times \Sigma_R$ or a position-class pair in $\{2, 4, \ldots, 2n-2\} \times \Sigma_C$. An association $Z = r_1 e_1 \cdots e_{n-1} r_n$, as a "transaction", contains a position-relation pair $\langle 2i-1, r \rangle$ if $r_i \sqsubseteq_R r$, and contains a position-class pair $\langle 2i, c \rangle$ if $e_i \in I(c)$. For instance, Z_1 in Eq. (1) contains $\langle 1, \hat{}\texttt{secondAuthor} \rangle$, $\langle 1, \hat{}\texttt{author} \rangle$, $\langle 1, \texttt{RELATED} \rangle$, $\langle 2, psc(\texttt{PaperA}) \rangle$, $\langle 2, \texttt{ConfPaper} \rangle$, $\langle 2, \texttt{Publication} \rangle$, $\langle 2, \texttt{ENTITY} \rangle$, etc.

Then, we use CHARM [18] to find all the frequent closed "itemsets" being subsets of at least $\tau |\mathcal{Z}|$ "transactions". From such a frequent closed "itemset", we try to obtain a pattern by selecting, if possible, one position-relation or position-class pair for each position in $\{1, 2, \ldots, 2n-1\}$ and arranging these relations and classes in ascending order of their positions. Once achieved, it can be proved that the pattern obtained is a significant pattern, and all the significant patterns can be obtained in this way. The proof is straightforward and is omitted due to lack of space.

5.2   Finding Frequent, Informative, and Small-Overlapping Patterns

Among all the significant patterns, we aim to find up to K ones that are as frequent and informative as possible while sharing small overlap between each other. In the following, firstly we define the informativeness of a pattern and the overlap between two patterns. Then we formulate and solve an optimization problem to integrate frequency, informativeness, and overlap.

Informativeness. A significant pattern may provide little information and become meaningless, e.g. one comprising only ENTITY and RELATED. However, we prefer to recommend informative patterns. To quantify the informativeness of a pattern, we measure the informativeness of each class and relation in the pattern.

As to classes, the idea is that a class having fewer instances is more specific and thus more informative. We formulate it using information theory. Specifically, for each class c, let $pr(c)$ be the probability that a random entity belongs to c. By estimating it based on the entity-relation graph $G = \langle V, A, s, t, l_V, l_A \rangle$, we measure $sinf(c)$, the self-information of the event that c is indeed observed as a class of some entity:

$$sinf(c) = -\log pr(c)$$
$$pr(c) = \frac{|\{v \in V : l_V(v) \in I(c)\}|}{|V|}. \tag{5}$$

For instance, given G in Fig. 2, $sinf(\texttt{ConfPaper}) = -\log \frac{4}{9}$ because 4 out of the 9 entities in G belong to ConfPaper. Further, we normalize $sinf(c)$ into the range $[0, 1]$ as the *informativeness of class* c:

$$sinf_N(c) = \frac{sinf(c)}{\log |V|}. \tag{6}$$

As to relations, the idea is similar but more complex because a relation has two ends (i.e. connecting two entities), called the source end and the target end, and each of them can be treated as a random variable. We separately process the two ends and integrate the results. Firstly, we treat the target end of a relation r as a random variable and measure its entropy, denoted by $\overrightarrow{eta}(r)$, which quantifies the expected value of the self-information of its outcomes (i.e. all possible entities appearing at the target end of r, denoted by $\overrightarrow{val}(r)$). By estimating $\overrightarrow{pr}(r, e)$, the probability of observing each outcome e based on $G = \langle V, A, s, t, l_V, l_A \rangle$, we have

$$\overrightarrow{eta}(r) = - \sum_{e \in \overrightarrow{val}(r)} \overrightarrow{pr}(r, e) \log \overrightarrow{pr}(r, e)$$

$$\overrightarrow{val}(r) = \{e \in \Sigma_E : \exists a \in A, (l_A(a) \sqsubseteq_R r, t(a) = e)\} \quad (7)$$

$$\overrightarrow{pr}(r, e) = \frac{|\{a \in A : l_A(a) \sqsubseteq_R r, t(a) = e\}|}{|\{a \in A : l_A(a) \sqsubseteq_R r\}|}.$$

For instance, given G in Fig. 2, $\overrightarrow{val}(\texttt{firstAuthor}) = \{\texttt{Alice}, \texttt{Bob}\}$ because only Alice and Bob (2 times) appear at the target end of firstAuthor, and Bob appears 2 out of the 3 times so that $\overrightarrow{pr}(\texttt{firstAuthor}, \texttt{Bob}) = \frac{2}{3}$. Further, we normalize $\overrightarrow{eta}(r)$ into the range $[0, 1]$:

$$\overrightarrow{eta}_N(r) = \frac{\overrightarrow{eta}(r)}{\log |\{a \in A : l_A(a) \sqsubseteq_R r\}|}. \quad (8)$$

The source end of r is processed analogously, and its normalized entropy is denoted by $\overleftarrow{eta}_N(r)$. To integrate $\overrightarrow{eta}_N(r)$ and $\overleftarrow{eta}_N(r)$, we calculate their harmonic mean in the range $[0, 1]$ as the *informativeness of relation r*:

$$eta(r) = \frac{2 \cdot \overrightarrow{eta}_N(r) \cdot \overleftarrow{eta}_N(r)}{\overrightarrow{eta}_N(r) + \overleftarrow{eta}_N(r)}. \quad (9)$$

Finally, the *informativeness of a pattern* $P = r_1 c_1 \cdots c_{n-1} r_n$ is obtained by adding up the informativeness of the classes and relations it contains:

$$inf(P) = \sum_{i=1}^{n-1} sinf_N(c_i) + \sum_{i=1}^{n} eta(r_i). \quad (10)$$

Overlap. Patterns sharing considerably large overlap are redundant and will not be recommended together. We identify two types of overlap between patterns.

Firstly, given two patterns $P = r_1 c_1 \cdots c_{n-1} r_n$ and $P' = r'_1 c'_1 \cdots c'_{n-1} r'_n$, we check the subclass-superclass and subrelation-superrelation relations in all their corresponding positions. Based on the following two functions:

$$ss_C(c_i, c_j) = \begin{cases} 1 & \text{if } c_i \sqsubseteq_C c_j \text{ or } c_j \sqsubseteq_C c_i, \\ 0 & \text{otherwise,} \end{cases}$$

$$ss_R(r_i, r_j) = \begin{cases} 1 & \text{if } r_i \sqsubseteq_R r_j \text{ or } r_j \sqsubseteq_R r_i, \\ 0 & \text{otherwise,} \end{cases} \quad (11)$$

we define the *ontological overlap* between P and P' in the range $[0, 1]$ as

$$ovlp_O(P, P') = \frac{\sum_{i=1}^{n-1} ss_C(c_i, c_i') + \sum_{i=1}^{n} ss_R(r_i, r_i')}{2n - 1}. \tag{12}$$

For instance, the ontological overlap between P_1 in Eq. (2) and P_2 in Eq. (3) is $\frac{5}{5}$ because $\sqsubseteq_C$ or $\sqsubseteq_R$ holds in all the 5 positions.

Secondly, we check to what extent P and P' are matched by common associations in $\mathcal{Z}$. By using the Jaccard similarity, we define the *contextual overlap* between P and P' in the range $[0, 1]$ as

$$ovlp_C(P, P') = \frac{|hits(P) \cap hits(P')|}{|hits(P) \cup hits(P')|}, \tag{13}$$

where $hits$ is given by Eq. (4). For instance, given $\mathcal{Z}$ comprising the five associations in Eq. (1), the contextual overlap between P_1 in Eq. (2) and P_2 in Eq. (3) is $\frac{1}{2}$ because P_1 is matched by Z_1 and Z_2, and P_2 is matched by Z_1.

Optimization. In $\mathcal{P}_\mathcal{Z}$, the set of significant patterns mined from $\mathcal{Z}$, we aim to find up to K ones that are as frequent and informative as possible while sharing small overlap between each other. It can be formulated as a multidimensional 0-1 knapsack problem (MKP) [13]. Specifically, each $P_i \in \mathcal{P}_\mathcal{Z}$ corresponds to a candidate "item" to be selected whose "profit" is $freq(P_i) \cdot inf(P_i)$ and whose "weight" is 1, when the "capacity" of the "knapsack" is K. For each pair of patterns sharing considerably large ontological or contextual overlap, an additional constraint is introduced to require that they are not selected together.

More formally, we number the patterns in $\mathcal{P}_\mathcal{Z}$ from P_1 to $P_{N=|\mathcal{P}_\mathcal{Z}|}$, and introduce a series of binary variables x_i to indicate whether pattern P_i is selected. Then we formulate a MKP as:

$$\text{maximize} \sum_{i=1}^{N} x_i \cdot freq(P_i) \cdot inf(P_i)$$

subject to

$$\sum_{i=1}^{N} x_i \leq K, \tag{14}$$

$$\sum_{i=1}^{N} x_i w_i^{j,k} \leq 1 \text{ for } j, k = 1, \ldots, N \text{ s.t. } j \neq k \text{ and}$$

$$ovlp_O(P_j, P_k) \geq \mu_O \text{ or } ovlp_C(P_j, P_k) \geq \mu_C,$$

$$x_i \in \{0, 1\} \text{ for } i = 1, \ldots, N,$$

where $\mu_O, \mu_C \in [0, 1]$ are thresholds, and

$$w_i^{j,k} = \begin{cases} 1 & \text{if } i = j \text{ or } i = k, \\ 0 & \text{otherwise.} \end{cases} \tag{15}$$

MKP is NP-hard [13]. To find a reasonably good feasible solution within reasonable running time, we use a greedy algorithm that considers the "items" (i.e. patterns) one after another and puts an "item" into the "knapsack" if adding this "item" would not violate any constraint. We use the following greedy heuristic to order the "items" in descending order:

$$g(P_i) = \frac{freq(P_i) \cdot inf(P_i)}{w(P_i)}, \tag{16}$$

where $w(P_i)$ returns the total "weight" of P_i in all the constraints. That is, priority is given to patterns that are more frequent, more informative, and share considerably large overlap with fewer patterns in $\mathcal{P}_\mathcal{Z}$.

6   Facet Value Recommendation

We also aim to recommend up to K classes of entities and K relations appearing in the associations in $\mathcal{Z}$ as facet values. In accordance with the recommendation of patterns, we adapt our solution described in Sect. 5 to recommend facet values that are as frequent and informative as possible while sharing small overlap between each other. To achieve this, we only need to redefine frequency, informativeness, and overlap for facet values. In this section, we will do this only for classes due to lack of space. Relations can be processed in an analogous way.

Firstly, given $\mathcal{Z}$ and a class c, similar to Eq. (4), we define the frequency of c w.r.t. $\mathcal{Z}$ as

$$freq(c) = \frac{|hits(c)|}{|\mathcal{Z}|} \tag{17}$$
$$hits(c) = \{r_1 e_1 \cdots e_{n-1} r_n \in \mathcal{Z} : \exists e_i \in I(c)\}.$$

For instance, given $\mathcal{Z}$ comprising the five associations in Eq. (1), the frequency of Conference is $\frac{2}{5}$ because its instances ConfA and ConfB appear in Z_1 and Z_2, respectively, i.e. in 2 out of the 5 associations.

Secondly, the informativeness of c has been given by Eq. (6).

Thirdly, two classes c and c' share ontological overlap if one of them is a subclass of the other, i.e. $ss_C(c, c') = 1$ according to Eq. (11). Contextual overlap between classes is defined similar to Eq. (13) by using $hits$ given by Eq. (17). When formulating a MKP, for each pair of classes sharing ontological or considerably large (i.e. $\geq \mu_C$) contextual overlap, an additional constraint is introduced to require that they are not selected together.

7   User Study

To investigate how patterns and facets help users explore associations in practice, we invited twenty university students to carry out association exploration tasks over DBpedia by using Explass and two existing approaches to association exploration. By analyzing subjects' responses to questionnaires and their behavior during the experiment, we mainly aimed to test the following two hypotheses.

H1. For association exploration, providing a flat list (top-K) of frequent, informative, and small-overlapping patterns (as on Explass) is more satisfying than an inclusive hierarchy of patterns (as on RelClus [19]).

H2. Patterns and facets are notably complementary in terms of usage in association exploration, and thus providing both of them (as on Explass) is more satisfying than only one of them (as on RelFinder [10] and RelClus [19]).

7.1 Data Sets

We used DBpedia in our experiment. Specifically, the entity-relation graph was obtained from the *mapping-based properties* data set, excluding RDF triples containing literals. Classes of entities were obtained from the *mapping-based types* data set. Class and relation hierarchies were obtained from the *DBpedia ontology*. The *short abstracts* and *images* data sets were used to provide a textual description and an image for each entity, respectively, which will be detailed later.

7.2 Tasks

To the best of our knowledge, there were no benchmark association exploration tasks available for evaluation. So we established a set of association exploration tasks to be used in our experiment as well as in future research. Our association exploration tasks were derived from the 100 training queries[2] provided by the multilingual question answering challenge of the QALD-3 evaluation campaign, which mentioned a total of 72 distinct entities in DBpedia. The names of these entities (e.g. *Abraham Lincoln*) were submitted to Google Search, some triggering Google's Knowledge Graph to return related entities that "people also search for" (e.g. *George Washington, John F. Kennedy*). For each search, among the entities returned that could also be found in DBpedia, the first one (e.g. *George Washington*) was selected, and then an association exploration task was defined in the following way.

> Suppose you will write an article about the associations between *Abraham Lincoln* and *George Washington*. Use the given system to explore their associations and identify several themes to discuss in the article.

In this way, 30 distinct tasks were defined. However, three were removed because in each of these tasks, the number of associations of length 1–4 (which was the setting for the systems in the experiment) found between the two entities was less than one hundred, making the task not very challenging; and one was removed because the two entities belonged to different classes, making this task inconsistent with the others. Finally, the remaining 26 tasks[3] were to be used in the user study, one of which was specifically for tutorials.

---

[2] http://greententacle.techfak.uni-bielefeld.de/~cunger/
qald/3/dbpedia-train.xml

[3] http://ws.nju.edu.cn/explass/tasks.txt

Table 2. Pre-task Questions and Responses about Exploration Context

Question	Response: Mean (SD)			$F(2, 38)$
	Explass	RelClus	RF	(p-value)
I think this task is difficult.	3.30	3.80	3.35	2.372
	(1.22)	(0.77)	(1.27)	(0.107)
I'm familiar with the domain of this task.	1.75	1.30	2.00	2.684
	(0.97)	(0.47)	(1.08)	(0.081)

7.3 Participant Approaches

We (re-)implemented three association exploration approaches over DBpedia to be compared in the user study: Explass, RelClus [19], and RF (based on [10]).

In all these systems, subjects started with two entity names, which were then mapped to two entities by the autocomplete functionality. Of each length from 1 to 4, up to one thousand associations between the two entities were found. When presenting them, each entity involved was accompanied by its image (if available, as illustrated in Fig. 1), and hovering the mouse over an entity activated a pop-up showing its textual description. Both images and pop-ups were to help subjects quickly understand entities and thus understand associations.

However, these systems organized associations in different ways, and supported different sets of exploration operations.

- Explass, as described in this paper, recommended a total of up to 10 patterns (giving priority to patterns of a short length), and up to 10 classes and 10 relations as facet values. We set τ, μ_C, μ_R to $0.1, 0.7, 0.7$, respectively.
- RelClus [19] organized associations inclusively into an expandable/collapsible hierarchy of clusters for refocusing. Each cluster was labeled with a unique pattern matched by all the associations in the cluster.
- RF reproduced the core feature of RelFinder [10], namely faceted association exploration. However, we did not reproduce the visualization technique adopted by RelFinder in order to make it comparable with the other two systems. Besides, in order to be comparable with Explass, RF also recommended up to 10 classes and 10 relations according to Sect. 6, and the parameters were set to the same values as in Explass.

7.4 Procedure

Subjects were instructed not to use their prior knowledge of the tasks, and they were not permitted to use tools other than the given system. Each subject carried out two random tasks using each of the three systems arranged in random order, and all the six tasks were different. Before using each system, a tutorial was given to demonstrate its functionality. The subject was then given the first task as a warmup. After that, she was given the second task and responded to two pre-task questions in Table 2 about exploration context. She had to complete this

Table 3. Post-task Questions and Responses about Exploration Effectiveness

| Question | Response: Mean (SD) | | | $F(2, 38)$ | LSD post-hoc |
	Explass	RelClus	RF	(p-value)	($p < 0.05$)
Q1: The system helped me get an overview of all the information.	4.25 (0.85)	3.80 (0.77)	3.05 (0.94)	14.989 (0.000)	Explass, RelClus > RF
Q2: The system helped me easily find information relevant to this task.	4.30 (0.57)	3.25 (0.79)	3.15 (0.99)	18.769 (0.000)	Explass > RelClus, RF
Q3: The system helped me easily compare and synthesize all kinds of relevant information.	4.00 (0.86)	3.25 (0.85)	2.60 (0.99)	14.901 (0.000)	Explass > RelClus > RF
Q4: The system provided me with much support for carrying out this task.	4.10 (0.72)	3.45 (0.94)	2.85 (0.88)	16.172 (0.000)	Explass > RelClus > RF
Q5: The system provided me with sufficient support for carrying out this task.[a]	3.85 (0.88)	3.20 (1.11)	2.65 (0.75)	11.636 (0.000)	Explass > RelClus, RF

[a] Different from Q4, this question targets the functions that are expected but missing.

task in ten minutes, during which all her operations were recorded. Finally, she responded to five post-task questions in Table 3 about exploration effectiveness (which were inspired by [4]), responded to the widely-used system usability scale (SUS), and commented on the system. Questions were responded using a five-point Likert item from 1 for strongly disagree to 5 for strongly agree.

7.5   Results and Discussion

Exploration Context. Pre-task questions in Table 2 capture subject-perceived task difficulty and domain familiarity. Repeated measures ANOVA revealed that the differences in subjects' mean ratings with different systems were not statistically significant ($p > 0.05$), which supported that tasks were carried out with different systems in comparable contexts in terms of task difficulty and domain familiarity. So these two factors can be excluded from the following discussion.

User Experience. Post-task questions Q1–Q5 in Table 3 capture subjects' exploration experience with different systems. Repeated measures ANOVA revealed that the differences in subjects' mean ratings were all statistically significant ($p < 0.01$). LSD post-hoc tests ($p < 0.05$) revealed that, according to Q1, Explass and RelClus provided a better overview of all the associations than RF due to the use of patterns. According to Q2 and Q3, compared with RF and

Table 4. SUS Scores

Mean (SD)			$F(2,38)$	LSD post-hoc
Explass	RelClus	RF	(p-value)	($p < 0.05$)
76.13	68.00	62.75	9.062	Explass > RelClus, RF
(12.53)	(17.93)	(14.93)	(0.001)	

Table 5. Average Number of Exploration Operations Performed per Task

Operation	Explass	RelClus	RF
Refocusing by expanding or collapsing a pattern	9.55	19.60	n/a
Refining the search by a pattern filter or canceling it	0.35	n/a	n/a
Refining the search by a facet value filter or canceling it	5.35	n/a	9.60

RelClus, Explass helped subjects more easily find, compare, and synthesize associations by using frequent, informative, and small-overlapping patterns and facet values. Finally, according to Q4 and Q5, Explass provided subjects with more comprehensive support for exploring associations than RF and RelClus.

Table 4 summarizes SUS scores of different systems. Repeated measures ANOVA revealed that the difference in SUS score was statistically significant ($p < 0.01$). LSD post-hoc tests ($p < 0.05$) revealed that Explass was more usable than RF and RelClus.

User Behavior. Table 5 summarizes the average number of exploration operations performed per task on different systems. On Explass, both patterns and facets were frequently used, indicating that they were notably complementary in terms of usage. However, patterns were mostly used to refocus but rarely used to refine the search. Besides, compared with RelClus whose hierarchical organization of patterns needed to be explored step by step, fewer pattern operations were performed on Explass mainly due to its flat organization of patterns.

User Feedback and Discussion. We summarized all the major comments that were made by at least five subjects. On RelClus, 6 subjects (30%) said a hierarchy of clusters labeled with patterns provided a good overview of all the associations and helped refocus on a particular theme, but 11 subjects (55%) said patterns at a high level were often too general to be useful, and they were often confused about the deep and complicated hierarchies. On RF, 5 subjects (25%) said recommended classes and relations were useful filters, but 8 subjects (40%) said they needed a better overview for summarizing associations. On Explass, 14 subjects (70%) said recommended patterns provided a good summary of associations and helped refocus on a particular theme when recommended facet values helped filter associations, but 11 subjects (55%) said some very large clusters could be divided into small ones.

These comments were consistent with subjects' experience and behavior reported previously. All of these collectively supported our hypotheses H1 and H2.

- As to H1, Explass better leveraged patterns than RelClus because, firstly, RelClus may provide a deep and complicated hierarchy of patterns, whereas Explass recommended a size-controllable flat list (top-K) of patterns. Secondly, RelClus may provide very general and meaningless patterns, whereas Explass considered the informativeness of patterns in recommendation.
- As to H2, patterns and facets were complementary because frequent, informative, and small-overlapping patterns provided an overview that meaningfully summarized significant subsets of associations covering diverse themes to be refocused on, when facets provided useful filters for refining the search.

8 Conclusion and Future Work

We have realized exploratory association search in a new way by recommending top-K patterns and facet values, which have been shown to be notably complementary in terms of usage: patterns for summarizing and refocusing, and facets for refining and filtering. Compared with RelClus, our Explass provides a flat list (top-K) of clusters, which avoids deep and complicated hierarchies as on RelClus but sometimes produces very large clusters. Whereas such a large cluster could be divided into small ones by using this pattern as a filter to refine the search and obtaining its subclusters, such an operation was rarely performed by subjects in the user study, indicating that our design of user interface still needs to be carefully improved. In the future, we will also extend the notion of pattern to support the exploration of associations between more than two entities, or more generally, the entire entity-relation graph.

To recommend appropriate patterns and facet values, our novel solution has considered their frequency, informativeness, and overlap, and has exploited ontological semantics, query context, and information theory. Though it was proposed to deal with associations, the solution or its components may also be applied to recommend facet values for entity search. In the future, we will compare it with existing methods in this direction.

Acknowledgments. The authors would like to thank all the participants and reviewers. This work was supported in part by the NSFC under Grant 61100040, 61223003, and 61170068, and in part by the JSNSF under Grant BK2012723.

References

1. Aleman-Meza, B., Halaschek-Wiener, C., Arpinar, I.B., Ramakrishnan, C., Sheth, A.P.: Ranking Complex Relationships on the Semantic Web. IEEE Internet Comput. 9(3), 37–44 (2005)
2. Anyanwu, K., Maduko, A., Sheth, A.: SemRank: Ranking Complex Relationship Search Results on the Semantic Web. In: 14th International Conference on World Wide Web, pp. 117–127. ACM, New York (2005)

3. Anyanwu, K., Sheth, A.: ρ-Queries: Enabling Querying for Semantic Associations on the Semantic Web. In: 12th International Conference on World Wide Web, pp. 690–699. ACM, New York (2003)
4. Arguello, J., Wu, W.-C., Kelly, D., Edwards, A.: Task Complexity, Vertical Display and User Interaction in Aggregated Search. In: 35th International ACM SIGIR Conference on Research and Development in Information Retrieval, pp. 435–444. ACM, New York (2012)
5. Chen, N., Prasanna, V.K.: Learning to Rank Complex Semantic Relationships. Int'l J. Semant. Web Inf. Syst. 8(4), 1–19 (2012)
6. Fang, L., Das Sarma, A., Yu, C., Bohannon, P.: REX: Explaining Relationships between Entity Pairs. Proc. VLDB Endowment 5(3), 241–252 (2011)
7. Gubichev, A., Neumann, T.: Path Query Processing on Very Large RDF Graphs. In: 14th International Workshop on the Web and Databases (2011)
8. Han, J., Kamber, M., Pei, J.: Data Mining: Concepts and Techniques. Morgan Kaufmann, Waltham (2011)
9. Hearst, M.A.: Clustering versus Faceted Categories for Information Exploration. Commun. ACM 49(4), 59–61 (2006)
10. Heim, P., Lohmann, S., Stegemann, T.: Interactive Relationship Discovery via the Semantic Web. In: Aroyo, L., Antoniou, G., Hyvönen, E., ten Teije, A., Stuckenschmidt, H., Cabral, L., Tudorache, T. (eds.) ESWC 2010, Part I. LNCS, vol. 6088, pp. 303–317. Springer, Heidelberg (2010)
11. Janik, M., Kochut, K.: BRAHMS: A Workbench RDF Store and High Performance Memory System for Semantic Association Discovery. In: Gil, Y., Motta, E., Benjamins, V.R., Musen, M.A. (eds.) ISWC 2005. LNCS, vol. 3729, pp. 431–445. Springer, Heidelberg (2005)
12. Kasneci, G., Elbassuoni, S., Weikum, G.: MING: Mining Informative Entity Relationship Subgraphs. In: 18th ACM Conference on Information and Knowledge Management, pp. 1653–1656. ACM, New York (2009)
13. Kellerer, H., Pferschy, U., Pisinger, D.: Knapsack Problems. Springer, Heidelberg (2004)
14. Lee, J., Hwang, S.-W., Nie, Z., Wen, J.-R.: Query Result Clustering for Object-level Search. In: 15th ACM SIGKDD International Conference on Knowledge Discovery and Data Mining, pp. 1205–1214. ACM, New York (2009)
15. Luo, G., Tang, C., Tian, Y.-L.: Answering Relationship Queries on the Web. In: 16th International Conference on World Wide Web, pp. 561–570. ACM, New York (2007)
16. Marchionini, G.: Exploratory Search: From Finding to Understanding. Commun. ACM 49(4), 41–46 (2006)
17. Oren, E., Delbru, R., Decker, S.: Extending Faceted Navigation for RDF Data. In: Cruz, I., Decker, S., Allemang, D., Preist, C., Schwabe, D., Mika, P., Uschold, M., Aroyo, L.M. (eds.) ISWC 2006. LNCS, vol. 4273, pp. 559–572. Springer, Heidelberg (2006)
18. Zaki, M.J., Hsiao, C.-J.: CHARM: An Efficient Algorithm for Closed Itemset Mining. In: 2nd SIAM International Conference on Data Mining, pp. 457–473. SIAM, Philadelphia (2002)
19. Zhang, Y., Cheng, G., Qu, Y.: Towards Exploratory Relationship Search: A Clustering-based Approach. In: Kim, W., Ding, Y., Kim, H.-G. (eds.) JIST 2013. LNCS, vol. 8388, pp. 277–293. Springer, Heidelberg (2014)
20. Zhou, M., Pan, Y., Wu, Y.: Conkar: Constraint Keyword-based Association Discovery. In: 20th ACM International Conference on Information and Knowledge Management, pp. 2553–2556. ACM, New York (2011)

Expressive and Scalable Query-Based Faceted Search over SPARQL Endpoints

Sébastien Ferré

IRISA, Université de Rennes 1,
Campus de Beaulieu, 35042 Rennes cedex, France
ferre@irisa.fr

Abstract. Linked data is increasingly available through SPARQL endpoints, but exploration and question answering by regular Web users largely remain an open challenge. Users have to choose between the expressivity of formal languages such as SPARQL, and the usability of tools based on navigation and visualization. In a previous work, we have proposed Query-based Faceted Search (QFS) as a way to reconcile the expressivity of formal languages and the usability of faceted search. In this paper, we further reconcile QFS with scalability and portability by building QFS over SPARQL endpoints. We also improve expressivity and readability. Many SPARQL features are now covered: multidimensional queries, union, negation, optional, filters, aggregations, ordering. Queries are now verbalized in English, so that no knowledge of SPARQL is ever necessary. All of this is implemented in a portable Web application, Sparklis[1], and has been evaluated on many endpoints and questions.

1 Introduction

Linked data is increasingly available through SPARQL endpoints, but exploration and question answering is often tedious for SPARQL practitionners, and largely remains an open challenge for regular Web users. Semantic search can be evaluated according to a number of criteria such as expressivity or scalability. Maximizing any of those criteria in isolation is relatively easy, and what remains a challenge is to reconcile them as far as possible. We consider such a reconciliation as a key to the effective access to semantic data, and hence to the wide adoption of semantic data. Indeed, an easy-to-use system may not satisfy advanced users with more complex information needs, and everybody can become an advanced user in some domain (e.g., profession, hobby). Similarly, an expressive system that does not scale is only of limited use. We shortly define the criteria that motivated this work, and identify for each of them the existing approach that seems to best fulfill it.

Expressivity measures the diversity and complexity of questions that can be answered. It seems clear that the leading approach for maximizing that criteria is formal query languages, and prominently SPARQL.

---

[1] Sparklis http://www.irisa.fr/LIS/ferre/sparklis/osparklis.html

P. Mika et al. (Eds.) ISWC 2014, Part II, LNCS 8797, pp. 438–453, 2014.

Guidance measures the level of assistance given to users in their search. It involves interactivity, suggestion, immediate feedback, and dead-ends prevention. We here retain Faceted Search (FS) [11,24]. First, FS is increasingly adopted in e-commerce and multimedia collections. Second, FS has already been adapted to semantic search (see Section 2).

Readability measures the ease for users to read and understand the textual components and controls of the user interface. Natural Language (NL) is obviously more readable than formal languages like SPARQL. If formal queries are used in a system, they should therefore be verbalized into NL, which has already been proposed for SPARQL [22].

Scalability measures the ability of a system to be responsive on large datasets. Most of the scalability effort in the semantic web has gone into RDF stores and SPARQL engines. It therefore seems reasonable to leverage their power.

Portability measures the cost of applying a system to a new dataset. Some systems require manual configuration, and others need an appropriate ontology. SPARQL endpoints have the advantage to provide a standard API.

Guidance and readability are two aspects of *usability* that we address in this paper. Other aspects that we do not consider here are *a smooth learning curve* or *personalization*. Another important criteria for semantic search that is not addressed in this paper is *openness*. It measures the ability to explore distributed linked data (querying several endpoints, following `owl:sameAs` links). In a previous work, we have introduced *Query-based Faceted Search* (QFS) [6,5] as a way to reconcile the expressivity of formal query languages with the guidance of faceted search. The obtained user interaction is similar to query builders that guide users in the construction of queries, but with a more fine-grained guidance that is based on actual data rather than on syntax and data schema.

The first contribution of this paper is to further reconcile QFS with the readability of NL. Questions and system suggestions are verbalized in (a fragment of) English so that no knowledge of SPARQL is ever necessary for users. This makes QFS a kind of Natural Language Interface (NLI) except that questions are not freely input by users, but produced through a user-system dialog. The second contribution is to further reconcile QFS with the scalability and portability of SPARQL endpoints. Question answers and system suggestions are entirely computed by generating and sending SPARQL queries to the endpoint. Portability is ensured by strictly conforming to the SPARQL standard. Compared to previous work, we also improve QFS expressivity. In addition to arbitrary basic graph patterns, unions, and negations, we now also cover multidimensional queries (tables as results), optionals, common filters, aggregations, and orderings. All those contributions are implemented in a Web application, Sparklis, that only needs the URL of the desired endpoint as input.

The main limitation to our work is that it only provides bare views of linked data, without any pre- or post-processing, and therefore exposes any data noise and heterogeneity to users. It uses neither linguistic knowledge (e.g., lexicons), nor external resources (e.g., full-text indexes) to make it more readable and efficient. We made this choice for the sake of portability, genericity, and simplicity, but nothing prevents to customize and improve our approach by using dataset-specific knowledge and resources.

Section 2 is an overview of different approaches and systems in semantic search (Section 2). Section 3 recalls the key principles of QFS to reconcile expressivity and guidance. Section 4 and 5 present the contributions of this paper: NL verbalization and QFS over SPARQL endpoints. Section 6 provides the results of a few evaluations of Sparklis w.r.t. the above criteria. Finally, Section 7 concludes and sketches future work.

2   Related Work

There are mainly two approaches to make semantic search more usable: user interaction (UI) and natural language (NL). UI systems reuse and adapt UI paradigms to semantic data: hypertext browsing (e.g., Fluidops Information Workbench[2]), query builders (e.g., SemanticCrystal [16]), faceted search (FS) [24], or OLAP [2]. Query builders generally offer more *expressivity*, but lack *readability* because based on formal languages. Moreover, their guidance is mostly based on syntax, and sometimes on a data schema, but not on actual data, like in FS. Most FS-based systems do not claim for a contribution in term of *expressivity*, and contribute either to the design of better interfaces and visualizations, or to methods for the rapid or user-centric configuration of faceted views: e.g., Ontogator [19], mSpace[3], Longwell[4]. Similarly, OLAP-based systems emphasize visualization, and require substantial amount of configuration to extract cubic views over RDF graphs: e.g., Cubix [21], Linked Data Query Wizard [14]. Therefore, their contributions are somewhat orthogonal to ours, and could certainly complement them. A few FS-based systems extend faceted search *expressivity*: e.g., SlashFacet [13], BrowseRDF [23], gFacet [12], VisiNav [9], SemFacet [1], OpenLink FS[5], Vinge Query&Explore[6]. While more expressive than classical FS, those systems are still much less expressive than SPARQL 1.1, and approximately cover basic graph patterns. None of them support union, negation, or aggregation. All except Vinge Query&Explore present only lists of results, rather than tables. That expressivity is reflected by the frequent choice to use trees and graphs to represent the query. Those representations have a good match with SPARQL graph patterns, but do not scale well to express union, negation, or aggregations, unlike natural language.

Natural Language Interfaces (NLI) [18] use NL in various forms, going from full natural language (e.g., PowerAqua [17]) to mere keywords (e.g., NLP-Reduce [16]) through controlled natural languages (e.g., Ginseng [16], SQUALL [4]). Systems based on full NL or keywords devote the most effort to bridging the gap between lexical forms and ontology triples (mapping and

---

[2] Fluidops Information Workbench `http://iwb.fluidops.com/`

[3] mSpace `http://mspace.fm/`

[4] Longwell `http://simile.mit.edu/wiki/Longwell`

[5] OpenLink FS `http://dbpedia.org/fct/facet.vsp`

[6] Vinge Query&Explore `http://www.vingefree.com/querybyexplore/`

Table 1. Navigation scenario in Sparklis over DBpedia

step	query
1	Give me something
2	Give me **a Writer**
3	Give me a Writer **that has a nationality**
4	Give me a Writer that has nationality **Russians**
5	Give me a Writer that has nationality Russians **and that has a birthDate**
6	Give me a Writer that has nationality Russians and whose birthDate **is after 1800**
7	Give me a Writer that has nationality Russians and whose birthDate is after 1800 **and that is the author of something**
8	Give me a Writer that has nationality Russians and whose birthDate is after 1800 and that is the author of **a Book**
9	Give me a Writer that has nationality Russians and whose birthDate is after 1800 and that is the author of **a number of** Book
10	Give me a Writer that has nationality Russians and whose birthDate is after 1800 and that is the author of **the highest-to-lowest** number of Book
11	Give me a Writer that has nationality Russians **or something** and whose birthDate is after 1800 and that is the author of the highest-to-lowest number of Book
12	Give me a Writer that has nationality Russians or **Russian_Empire** and whose birthDate is after 1800 and that is the author of the highest-to-lowest number of Book

disambiguation), and process only the simplest questions, i.e., they generate SPARQL queries with only one or two triples. Most of them support none of aggregations (e.g., counting), comparatives, or superlatives, even though those features are relatively frequent.

Some systems integrate the UI approach in NLIs to alleviate the *habitability problem* [16], in which users have not a precise knowledge about what can be understood by the NLI system, and therefore can be frustrated by syntax errors or empty results. Those systems (e.g., Ginseng [16], Atomate [25]) can be seen as query builders based on a controlled natural language. They improve the former with readability, and the latter with guidance, but they still lack the fine-grained guidance of FS that is necessary to fully solve the hability problem.

3   Query-Based Faceted Search

In this section, we recall the key principles of Query-based Faceted Search (QFS) [6,5], and how they enable to reconcile *expressivity* and *guidance*. QFS guidance relies on the interaction loop of Faceted Search (FS). FS guides users in the iterative refinement of a set of items. The key to QFS expressivity is to replace the *set of items* by a *structured query*, and to define the *focus* as a syntactic part of the query. System suggestions at each navigation step are therefore defined as *query transformations*, rather than as *set-based operations*.

442   S. Ferré

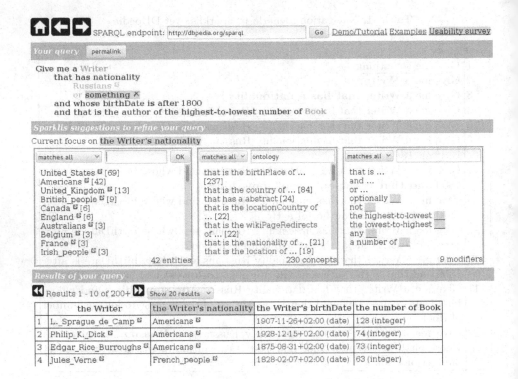

Fig. 1. Sparklis screenshot at step 11 of scenario in Table 1

In short, we propose *query-based* FS as a generalization of classical *set-based* FS. It is a generalization because a set of items can be derived unambiguously from a query and focus (by query evaluation), while many queries may correspond to a given set of items. We have previously demonstrated that set-based FS has strong limits in terms of expressivity, which disappear with query-based FS [6]. In particular, it becomes possible to navigate to arbitrary Boolean combinations of elementary queries.

Table 1 shows the successive queries, as verbalized in Sparklis (see Section 4), of a QFS navigation scenario that leads the user in 12 steps to a list of "Russian writers born since 1800, and ordered by decreasing number of written books". That scenario is only one of several possible scenarios leading to the same results: e.g., the birth date could have been constrained before the nationality. At each step, the bold part represents the newly inserted query element, chosen by the user at the previous step among system suggestions, and the underlined part represents the query focus that is used for the next query transformation. The query focus is moved simply by clicking on different parts of the query. The query elements that are suggested for insertion at query focus can be entities (e.g., `Russian`), classes (e.g., `a Book`), properties in both directions (e.g., `is the author of`, `has birthDate`), filters (e.g., `after 1800`), and various modifiers (e.g., `number of`, `or`). Figure 1 is a Sparklis screenshot at step 11, during the specification of an alternative nationality for the writer (Russian_Empire as a synonym of Russians). The user interface is made of three parts: top, middle, bottom. The top part shows the current query, and highlights the current focus, here something. The first branch of disjunction is transparent to reflect the fact that it is ignored during the construction of the second branch. The bottom part is the result table of the current query, with a column for each entity/value in the query (here: writer, nationality, birth date, and number of books). Note that QFS has relational results (tables) whereas classical FS has sets (lists). The focus column, here the nationality, is highlighted. The middle part contains relevant query elements for insertion at the query focus. It is split in three lists. The first list contains entities (URIs) and values (literals) found in the focus column. It also enables the construction of filters over values. The second list contains *concepts* (classes and properties) that apply to entities/values found in the focus column. The third list contains modifiers that are applicable to the query focus, such as Boolean connectors, aggregation operators, and ordering. Each list provides auto-completion for quickly locating a query element (see Section 5.2). In addition to selecting a query element to insert it at query focus, the query part under focus can be deleted by clicking the red cross in the query.

4   NL Verbalization and SPARQL Translation

In this section, we improve previous work on QFS by verbalizing queries in NL for user display, and by translating them in SPARQL for evaluation by SPARQL endpoints. The current query and focus play a central role because they represent the full state of the navigation process. Results and suggestions are entirely computed from them. Their internal representation must be designed to facilitate three processes: (1) NL verbalization, (2) SPARQL translation, and (3) application of query transformations. Using SPARQL for internal representation would make (2) trivial, but (1) difficult as shown by previous work [22]. Using NL for internal representation would make (1) trivial, but (2) and (3) would be tedious because of the many peculiarities of NL. Our choice, inspired by state-of-the-art in the compilation of high-level programming languages, is to use Abstract Syntax Trees (AST) as an intermediate representation between NL and SPARQL. AST leaves are entities, values, and concepts. AST nodes correspond at the same time to NL syntactic structures, such as noun phrases (NP) or verb phrases (VP), and to SPARQL features, such as triple patterns or unions. The query focus, as a syntactic part of the query, is represented as a distinguished node of the AST of the query.

NL verbalization is performed by mapping AST leaves and nodes to NL expressions. Entities and concepts are verbalized by the local name of their URI, i.e. the part after the last sharp or slash. This choice was made for the sake of portability and efficiency, but future work will consider the use of RDFS labels and lexicons, e.g. represented in Lemon [20]. One or a few syntactic patterns are associated to each type of AST nodes. For example, syntactic patterns for relative clauses based on a property p are: that has p *NP*, whose p *VP*, and that

Table 2. Mapping from Sparklis query elements to SPARQL features

query element	SPARQL feature
concept name, `relation`	triple pattern
entity name	URI in triple pattern
value	literal in triple pattern
a, the	variable in triple pattern, and after `SELECT`
any	variable not put after `SELECT`
and, that	join
or	`UNION`
optionally	`OPTIONAL`
not	`FILTER NOT EXISTS`
matches	`REGEX()`
higher than, after, between, ...	comparators $(<, \leq, ...)$
language	`lang()`
datatype	`datatype()`
highest-to-lowest	`ORDER BY DESC()`
lowest-to-highest	`ORDER BY ASC()`
number of	`COUNT()`
list of	`GROUP_CONCAT()`
total, average, ...	`SUM(), AVG(), ...`

```
PREFIX n1: <http://dbpedia.org/ontology/>
PREFIX n2: <http://dbpedia.org/resource/>
SELECT DISTINCT ?Writer_1 ?birthDate_3 (COUNT(DISTINCT ?Book_4) AS ?number_of_Book_5)
WHERE { ?Writer_1 a n1:Writer .
        { ?Writer_1 n1:nationality n2:Russians . }
        UNION { ?Writer_1 n1:nationality n2:Russian_Empire . }
        ?Writer_1 n1:birthDate ?birthDate_3 .
        FILTER ( str(?birthDate_3) >= "1800" )
        ?Book_4 a n1:Book .
        ?Book_4 n1:author ?Writer_1 . }
GROUP BY ?Writer_1 ?birthDate_3
ORDER BY DESC(?number_of_Book_5)
```

Fig. 2. SPARQL translation for the last query in the scenario of Table 1

is the p of NP. The choice of the pattern can depend on whether the object of the property is better verbalized as a NP or a VP. An example of that is visible in Table 1, when comparing steps 5 and 6: that has a birthDate becomes whose birthDate is after 1800 after the insertion of the filter. To render the correct precedences of Boolean connectors, indentation is used in the display of the verbalized query (see Figure 1). That makes the query more readable, and avoids the use of brackets. Finally, syntax coloring is used to differentiate the different kinds of query elements: class names (orange), property names (purple), entity names (blue), values (green), modifiers (red).

SPARQL translation is based on Montague grammars [3], which were invented to bridge the gap between NL and formal languages. Those are founded on lambda calculus, and are fully compositional in the sense that the meaning of a sentence is the direct result of the composition of the meaning of its parts. Here, the "meaning" of a sentence or any of its parts is represented with SPARQL patterns. For example, a VP is translated to a function from entities to graph patterns, while a NP is translated to a function from graph patterns to graph patterns. Note that, unlike translating from SPARQL to NL, translating from ASTs to SPARQL is deterministic, and can be performed very efficiently. Figure 2 shows the SPARQL translation of the final query in the above navigation scenario, as produced by Sparklis. Table 2 maps elements of Sparklis queries to SPARQL features, and hence provides an overview of the expressivity of Sparklis compared to SPARQL. Remember that QFS interaction loop allows to build arbitrary combinations of those query elements, provided that those combinations make sense in the dataset, i.e. return results. For example, it is possible to use two aggregations in a same query, to perform ordering on an aggregated value, to follow arbitrary long property paths, or to define Boolean combinations of filters on a same variable. The main missing features compared to SPARQL 1.1 are: arbitrary expressions, only simple filters are available; subqueries, which are for example necessary to express nested aggregations; iterated property paths (operators + and *); named graphs (GRAPH) and federated search (SERVICE); CONSTRUCT and DESCRIBE queries; updates. Technical details about query/focus internal representation and SPARQL translation can be found in a research report [7].

5   Scalable QFS over SPARQL Endpoints

In this section, we improve previous work on QFS by entirely defining the computation of results and suggestions on top of SPARQL endpoints, rather than with in-memory RDF stores. We also take care to make it scale to the largest endpoints by limiting the number of results and suggestions. To preserve guidance completeness, results and suggestions beyond that limit can be found with an intelligent auto-completion mechanism.

NL verbalization, SPARQL translation, and the application of query transformations are computationally cheap, and are all done entirely on the client side. The computation of results from the SPARQL query uses one HTTP request to the SPARQL endpoint at each step, and therefore costs the same as when using a classical query editor in an incremental way. Therefore, the only significant additional cost of QFS, compared to direct querying in SPARQL, is the computation of suggestions, i.e. the three lists in the middle of Figure 1. Indeed, the three lists must be computed at each navigation step.

5.1   Computation of Suggestion Lists

The first suggestion list contains possible entities/values at the focus. For example, in the query Give me a Writer that has a nationality (step 3), nationalities of a writer are possible entities. Those entities/values are exactly those in the focus column of the result table, and can therefore be computed efficiently on client side. The third list contains applicable modifiers. There are only a dozen modifiers, and their applicability can be decided efficiently by looking at the query/focus. The second list contains concepts that possibly apply to entities/values in the first list. Here, a client-side computation is incompatible with portability, because it would require a client-side knowledge of the dataset, such as an ontology or indices. Moreover, ontology-based suggestions would be less precise because they would provide general rules (e.g., "books generally have authors"), rather than concrete facts (e.g., "only 10 of those 200 books have a defined author"). In heterogeneous datasets, like DBpedia, ontology-based guidance would often lead to empty results, and hence user frustration. Computing suggested concepts therefore require to query the SPARQL endpoint, and is actually the main issue for the scalability of QFS.

Assuming SPARQL variable ?f is bound to a possible entity or value at focus, the possible classes can be obtained as the bindings of variable ?c in the triple pattern ?f a ?c. Similarly, possible properties can be obtained with the triple pattern ?f ?p [], and inverse properties with the pattern [] ?p ?f. The question is how to use those triple patterns into SPARQL queries so as to efficiently get lists of suggestions. There are several ways to do it. For the binding of ?f, the SPARQL translation of the query can be reused, or the entities/values of the focus column can be used into a large UNION pattern. Relative to the three kinds of suggestions (classes, properties, inverse properties), three queries can be used, or a single query using an UNION pattern. We made extensive experiments [7] to compare the efficiency of the different options, and came to the conclusion that the best option is generally to use three queries, one for each kind of suggestion, and to avoid the recomputation of the main query by using an UNION pattern over all focus entities/values: f1, f2, ...

```
Q1: SELECT ?c WHERE { {f1 a ?c} UNION {f2 a ?c} UNION ... }
Q2: SELECT ?p WHERE { {f1 ?p []} UNION {f2 ?p []} UNION ... }
Q3: SELECT ?p WHERE { {[] ?p f1} UNION {[] ?p f2} UNION ... }
```

In principle, each triple pattern is efficiently evaluated by RDF stores using classical indices, because it contains one resource (URI or literal), and one unbound variable.

It remains to define the computation of suggestions at the initial step, when the query is still empty, and therefore no focus entity/value is available. That computation is crucial to provide guidance from the beginning. In a first stage, we use the following efficient SPARQL queries to retrieve classes and properties:

```
Q1: SELECT DISTINCT ?c WHERE { ?c a rdfs:Class }
Q2: SELECT DISTINCT ?p WHERE { ?p a rdf:Property }
```

In SPARQL endpoints whose RDF graph does not contain the schema itself, the above queries return empty results. We then resort to the following queries which are less efficient, but have the advantage to reflect actual data.

```
Q1': SELECT DISTINCT ?c WHERE { [] a ?c }
Q2': SELECT DISTINCT ?p WHERE { [] ?p [] }
```

Although not mentioned for the sake of generality, all above SPARQL queries come in practice with a LIMIT clause to better control response times. We discuss in the next section the impact on the *completeness* of the guidance, and how it is addressed in Sparklis.

5.2 Intelligent Auto-Completion

There are two important properties for QFS guidance: safeness and completeness. A *safe* guidance avoids dead-ends (i.e., empty results) by providing only relevant suggestions, i.e. suggestions that match actual data. A *complete* guidance fulfills the expressivity potential by providing *all* relevant suggestions. In a previous work [6], we formally proved the theoretical safeness and completeness of QFS. However, in practice, scalability requires to put limits on the number of query results and suggestions, and SPARQL endpoints also enforce such limits. Therefore, partial results and suggestions are unavoidable with large datasets. A previous work [7] has shown that partial results have generally a small impact on frequent concepts, but a high impact on infrequent concepts and entities/values. That impact is significant at the beginning of a search when result sets are large, and tends to disappear when the query becomes specific.

Our objective is to reconcile scalability in the computation of suggestions, and completeness in guidance. The solution that we have found and implemented in Sparklis is based on *intelligent auto-completion*. Auto-completion is a well-known user interface mechanism that provides guidance and feedback, and has already been adapted to semantic contexts [15,8]. Sparklis auto-completion is directly available at the top of each suggestion list, and dynamically filters suggestion lists at each keystroke for immediate feedback. It is intelligent in two ways. First, the filter condition depends on the user-selected filter operator. If that operator is matches all, then the suggestion must contain all keywords, in any order and insensitive to the case. If that operator is between, then the suggestion must be between the two given values, using numerical comparisons. Second, Sparklis auto-completion uses a cascade of three stages to ensure completeness. At stage 1, the partial list of suggestions is filtered on the client side, which can be done efficiently. At stage 2, if the filtered list gets empty, the list of suggestions is re-computed by sending to the SPARQL endpoint a new query that includes the user filter (depending on the filter operator). This means that the same partial query results are used, but a constraint is put on the expected classes and properties. At stage 3, when the filtered list is still empty, new queries are again sent to the SPARQL endpoint, using the full SPARQL query instead of the partial results, in addition to the user filter. This ensures that all query results are used in the computation of suggestions. Given the increasing cost of stages 2 and 3, they are triggered only when the user has entered a full keyword (trailing space), so as not to do it at every keystroke.

6   Evaluations

We present three evaluations to assess the portability, the expressivity and scalability, and the usability of QFS, based on its implementation as a Web application: Sparklis. The experimental data of those evaluations are available at http://www.irisa.fr/LIS/ferre/pub/iswc2014/.

6.1   Sparklis: QFS as a Web Application

Sparklis is entirely based on Web standards. It uses SPARQL endpoints for RDF storage and querying, HTTP requests to query them, JavaScript (JS) for the application code, and HTML5/CSS3 for the user interface. Queries to SPARQL endpoints are sent directly from the client browser, using AJAX requests. It makes Sparklis independent from a server, hence trivial to deploy, and efficient because all application code runs on the client. For code safety and development speed, the JS code is compiled from a high-level language (OCaml using js_of_ocaml[7]). The source code counts about 4000 lines of code, and the minimized JS code weights about 260k.

6.2   Portability to SPARQL Endpoints

We first assess the portability of Sparklis on permanent SPARQL endpoints found on the Web. The web site *SPARQL endpoints status*[8] maintains a list of SPARQL endpoints, along with dynamic information about their availability, performance, and expressivity. We took a sample of 57 active endpoints, and tried Sparklis on each of them. We report on three aspects: success/failure of the connection, performance, and usability. Out of the 57 endpoints, 3 connections failed because of the endpoint server (e.g., HTTP 500 error, POST requests not accepted), 24 were successful, and surprisingly 30 connections failed because of the *same-origin policy*. That policy, enforced by Web browsers, forbids scripts to send HTTP requests to other origins (e.g., http://dbpedia.org/) than the script origin (http://www.irisa.fr/ for Sparklis). It is crucial for the security of many Web applications, but it is not relevant for SPARQL endpoints, which act as public web services. Fortunately, there is a simple solution, but it is the responsability of each endpoint administrator to apply it. It suffices to add the line Access-Control-Allow-Origin: * in the HTTP response headers.

Out of the 24 successful connections, 22 were responsive enough to allow for fluid exploration of the dataset. The initial step typically took between 1 and 3 seconds, and 7 seconds in the worst case. In terms of contents, 10 endpoints contained only facts about concepts, ontologies, and datasets; 10 endpoints contained concrete facts about various topics (e.g., Austrian skiers, Chile administration, Nobel prizes); and 4 endpoints appeared empty. The 4 latter endpoints appeared empty because of a bug in some RKBEXPLORER-based

---

[7] http://ocsigen.org/js_of_ocaml/
[8] http://sparqles.okfn.org/

endpoints related to UNION: an union of empty results is not empty, and contains unbounded bindings. On a few endpoints, our random explorations have led to interesting results. For example, on http://data.ox.ac.uk/sparql/, we got the list of Oxford colleges along with their logo, and a picture. On http://data.nobelprize.org/sparql, we found the laureates of the Peace Nobel prize in decreasing year, people with several prizes (e.g., Marie Curie had 2), and the shocking gender imbalance (44 women vs 803 men). For 6 endpoints, URI local names of entities are opaque codes (e.g., numbers) that hinder the readability of suggestions and results. It does not prevent to access and use the real names of entities, but it requires additional navigation steps.

6.3   Expressivity and Scalability over DBpedia QALD Questions

We here assess the practical expressivity and scalability of Sparklis using questions from the QALD-3 challenge[9]. QALD (Question Answering over Linked Data) primarily targets Natural Language Interfaces (NLI) where natural questions are answered in one interaction step. We instead use QALD questions as the expression of information needs that are satisfied through multi-step interaction (QFS). For each of the 100 training questions over DBpedia, we evaluated the minimum interaction time to answer the question, when possible, starting from the empty query (Give me something). Because we here evaluate the scalability and efficiency of Sparklis, and not the usability (see next section), we strived to minimize the exploration and thinking user time by using the gold standard SPARQL queries provided by QALD as a guide in the selection of suggestions. Therefore, the measured times represent the optimal interaction time for a trained and focused user. In real use, interaction times will increase according to unfamiliarity with Sparklis and the dataset, and to lack of focus in search (exploratory search).

Expressivity. With Sparklis, we could answer 90/100 questions. Out of the 10 failed questions, 9 correspond to missing information in DBpedia (aka. OUT OF SCOPE questions). The other failed question is because a YAGO class could not be found due to timeouts from the endpoint. Unlike DBpedia classes that are quickly found among suggestions, YAGO classes are numerous and difficult to get. A few gold standard queries could not be constructed, but the answer was still easy to get. For example, the question asking *whether Natalie Portman was born in the US* cannot be reached because she was born in Israel, but as Sparklis immediately shows the actual birth place, the answer was obviously *No.*

Scalability. Figure 3 shows the distribution of the wall-clock interaction time for the 90 successful questions[10]. Half of the questions can be answered in less than 27s (median time). The most complex QALD questions can be answered in less than 2min. We found those results quite satisfactory given the billions of triples of DBpedia. The simplest questions generally involve an entity and

---

[9] http://www.sc.cit-ec.uni-bielefeld.de/qald/

[10] Note that the responsiveness of DBpedia endpoint may vary over time.

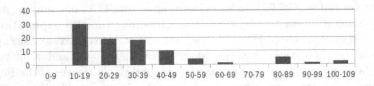

Fig. 3. Histogram of wall-clock interaction times for 90/100 QALD-3 questions

a property (e.g., *Give me the homepage of Forbes*), or a class, a property, and a value (e.g., *Give me all books written by Danielle Steel*). The more complex questions combine unions, string matching, numerical comparisons, counts, or ordering. For example, question (*Which telecommunications organizations are located in Belgium?*) has 3 unions and 2 string matching because there are different ways to express *telecommunications* and *located in Belgium* due to data heterogeneity, and it requires 14 navigation steps.

For comparison, we shortly describe the performance of the best NLI participant to the QALD-3 challenge: CASIA [10]. CASIA produced correct answers for 29 questions, and partially correct answers for 8 questions. The average computation time over the 100 questions is 83s. With regard to faceted search, we found no system capable of exploring DBpedia and responsive enough.

6.4   First Usability Experiments

We have so far conducted three usability experiments of QFS. In the first experiment [6], we asked 20 graduate students to answer 18 questions about genealogical data using Sewelis, a desktop version of QFS. The dataset was small, but the questions already involved complex graph patterns, disjunction, and negation, and the subjects had no previous knowledge about SW technologies. The results showed that, after a short training, all subjects were able to answer simple questions, and most of them were able to answer complex questions. The average time per question ranged from half a minutes to six minutes. The main observed difficulty was in understanding the notion of focus. The SUS questionnaire showed that subjects did not find the system *unnecessarily complex*, and that they *would learn to use it very quickly*.

In the second experiment [7], the developer of the former version of Sparklis, Scalewelis, took part in the QALD3 challenge on DBpedia questions. He was of course expert in the use of Scalewelis, but he was unfamiliar with the DBpedia dataset. He tried to answer the 100 test questions, and submitted them. Because Scalewelis was less expressive than Sparklis, he could answer "only" 70 questions. Out of them, 32 were correct and 1 was partially correct. Most errors were because there are often several representations of the same meaning in DBpedia, which produce different answers: e.g., "being an actor" is represented either by the pattern `?x a dbo:Actor` or by `[] dbo:starring ?x`. Also, most properties come in two versions: one in DBpedia ontology, and one among DBpedia properties. Scalewelis was ranked third out of six participants, with recall

(33%) and precision (33%) very similar to best NLI approaches. This experiment demonstrated that QFS is a promising approach for question answering, albeit it is based on interaction rather than on NL understanding.

In the third experiment, which is still ongoing as an online survey we ask anonymous Web users to try and answer 12 questions over DBpedia, after viewing a tutorial video[11]. Only 6 people have filled the survey yet, but they have different profiles, and results are already instructive. On average, they have built correct queries for 7.8 questions. For non-IT people (2/6), the average goes only slightly down to 7. For people having some knowledge of SPARQL (2/6), it goes up to 10 questions. An expert user, who can write SPARQL queries, had 9 correct answers, made 2 errors related to disjunction, and skipped a single query (which was skipped by all users). (S)he found Sparklis much easier to use than SPARQL, and declared: "I like use this system and I find it is easy to use unlike other semantic web search engines". An advanced user, who can do some programming but never heard about SPARQL, had 8 correct answers, made 2 errors by using string matching instead of numerical comparison, and skipped 2 queries. (S)he found it difficult to find the right concepts (classes and properties), but declared that "there are no inconsistencies in the suggestions", and that "the system is really usable". A regular user, who know neither SPARQL nor programming, had still 6 correct answers (involving comparisons, negation, and ordering), 3 incorrect answers, and 4 skipped queries. (S)he expressed difficulties with focus position and interaction logic, but declared that "for some questions, it would take me hours to do the same in Excel, while here a few clicks are enough!". No user managed to answer the question *Which U.S. states do not possess gold minerals?* because it requires to find one among the many YAGO classes (see Section 6.3). Most expert and advanced users (4/5) managed to answer the complex question *Give me all bridges crossing the Saint Lawrence river, ordered by decreasing length, and with an optional depiction.* whose answer is an ordered three-dimensional table (bridge, length, and depiction). The SUS questionnaire gives results consistent with our first experiment, and answers mostly differ on the expected amount of learning depending on user background.

7   Conclusion

We have improved Query-based Faceted Search (QFS) with NL verbalization for readability, and with SPARQL endpoint-based computation of results and suggestions for scalability and portability. This makes it an appealing approach for semantic search as it reconciles the expressivity of formal languages, the guidance of query builders and faceted search, the readability of natural language interfaces, the scalability of the most powerful RDF stores and SPARQL engines, and the portability to many SPARQL endpoints thanks to a strong conformance to W3C standards. Our evaluations have shown that our QFS implementation, Sparklis, can be used effectively on various endpoints, without configuration, can

---

[11] Survey form and video are online at http://tinyurl.com/kxozx9r

answer most QALD questions and more, and was evaluated positively in first usability experiments.

Our priorities for future work concern expressivity, readability, and visualization. We aim to cover all SPARQL features while avoiding to make user interaction more complex. Note that union, negation, aggregation, and ordering all simply add modifiers as suggestions, and we expect the same for other SPARQL features. User interaction in QFS is *FS + query + focus* so that usability is mostly a matter of readability and visualization. We plan to improve readability by using ontology lexicons [20] in NL verbalization, when available, and visualization by producing graphical views (e.g., diagrams, charts, maps) from tables of results [21,14].

Acknowledgement. We are grateful to Joris Guyonvarc'h for his master work that contributed to this work by designing, implementing, and experimenting a first version of QFS over SPARQL endpoints. Interesting technical details not present in this paper for space reasons can be found in a technical report [7]. We also thank the reviewers for their thorough analysis, and encouraging comments.

References

1. Arenas, M., Grau, B., Kharlamov, E., Marciuška, Š., Zheleznyakov, D., Jimenez-Ruiz, E.: SemFacet: Semantic faceted search over YAGO. In: World Wide Web Conf. Companion, pp. 123–126. WWW Steering Committee (2014)
2. Codd, E., Codd, S., Salley, C.: Providing OLAP (On-line Analytical Processing) to User-Analysts: An IT Mandate. Codd & Date, Inc., San Jose (1993)
3. Dowty, D.R., Wall, R.E., Peters, S.: Introduction to Montague Semantics. D. Reidel Publishing Company (1981)
4. Ferré, S.: SQUALL: a controlled natural language for querying and updating RDF graphs. In: Kuhn, T., Fuchs, N.E. (eds.) CNL 2012. LNCS, vol. 7427, pp. 11–25. Springer, Heidelberg (2012)
5. Ferré, S., Hermann, A.: Semantic search: Reconciling expressive querying and exploratory search. In: Aroyo, L., Welty, C., Alani, H., Taylor, J., Bernstein, A., Kagal, L., Noy, N., Blomqvist, E. (eds.) ISWC 2011, Part I. LNCS, vol. 7031, pp. 177–192. Springer, Heidelberg (2011)
6. Ferré, S., Hermann, A.: Reconciling faceted search and query languages for the Semantic Web. Int. J. Metadata, Semantics and Ontologies 7(1), 37–54 (2012)
7. Guyonvarch, J., Ferre, S., Ducassé, M.: Scalable Query-based Faceted Search on top of SPARQL Endpoints for Guided and Expressive Semantic Search. Research report PI-2009, IRISA (2013), http://hal.inria.fr/hal-00868460
8. Haller, H.: QuiKey – an efficient semantic command line. In: Cimiano, P., Pinto, H.S. (eds.) EKAW 2010. LNCS (LNAI), vol. 6317, pp. 473–482. Springer, Heidelberg (2010)
9. Harth, A.: VisiNav: A system for visual search and navigation on web data. J. Web Semantics 8(4), 348–354 (2010)
10. He, S., Liu, S., Chen, Y., Zhou, G., Liu, K., Zhao, J.: CASIA@QALD-3: A question answering system over linked data. In: C.U., et al. (eds.) Work. Multilingual Question Answering over Linked Data, QALD-3 (2013), http://www.clef2013.org

11. Hearst, M., Elliott, A., English, J., Sinha, R., Swearingen, K., Yee, K.P.: Finding the flow in web site search. Communications of the ACM 45(9), 42–49 (2002)
12. Heim, P., Ertl, T., Ziegler, J.: Facet graphs: Complex semantic querying made easy. In: Aroyo, L., Antoniou, G., Hyvönen, E., ten Teije, A., Stuckenschmidt, H., Cabral, L., Tudorache, T. (eds.) ESWC 2010, Part I. LNCS, vol. 6088, pp. 288–302. Springer, Heidelberg (2010)
13. Hildebrand, M., van Ossenbruggen, J., Hardman, L.: /facet: A browser for heterogeneous semantic web repositories. In: Cruz, I., Decker, S., Allemang, D., Preist, C., Schwabe, D., Mika, P., Uschold, M., Aroyo, L.M. (eds.) ISWC 2006. LNCS, vol. 4273, pp. 272–285. Springer, Heidelberg (2006)
14. Hoefler, P., Granitzer, M., Sabol, V., Lindstaedt, S.: Linked data query wizard: A tabular interface for the semantic web. In: Cimiano, P., Fernández, M., Lopez, V., Schlobach, S., Völker, J. (eds.) ESWC 2013. LNCS, vol. 7955, pp. 173–177. Springer, Heidelberg (2013)
15. Hyvönen, E., Mäkelä, E.: Semantic autocompletion. In: Mizoguchi, R., Shi, Z.-Z., Giunchiglia, F. (eds.) ASWC 2006. LNCS, vol. 4185, pp. 739–751. Springer, Heidelberg (2006)
16. Kaufmann, E., Bernstein, A.: Evaluating the usability of natural language query languages and interfaces to semantic web knowledge bases. J. Web Semantics 8(4), 377–393 (2010)
17. Lopez, V., Fernández, M., Motta, E., Stieler, N.: PowerAqua: Supporting users in querying and exploring the semantic web. Semantic Web 3(3), 249–265 (2012)
18. Lopez, V., Uren, V.S., Sabou, M., Motta, E.: Is question answering fit for the semantic web?: A survey. Semantic Web 2(2), 125–155 (2011)
19. Mäkelä, E., Hyvönen, E., Saarela, S.: Ontogator - a semantic view-based search engine service for web applications. In: Cruz, I., Decker, S., Allemang, D., Preist, C., Schwabe, D., Mika, P., Uschold, M., Aroyo, L.M. (eds.) ISWC 2006. LNCS, vol. 4273, pp. 847–860. Springer, Heidelberg (2006)
20. McCrae, J., Spohr, D., Cimiano, P.: Linking lexical resources and ontologies on the semantic web with lemon. In: Antoniou, G., Grobelnik, M., Simperl, E., Parsia, B., Plexousakis, D., De Leenheer, P., Pan, J. (eds.) ESWC 2011, Part I. LNCS, vol. 6643, pp. 245–259. Springer, Heidelberg (2011)
21. Melo, C., Mikheev, A., Le Grand, B., Aufaure, M.A.: Cubix: A visual analytics tool for conceptual and semantic data. In: Int. Conf. Data Mining Workshops, pp. 894–897. IEEE Computer Society (2012)
22. Ngomo, A.C.N., Bühmann, L., Unger, C., Lehmann, J., Gerber, D.: Sorry, I don't speak SPARQL: translating SPARQL queries into natural language. In: WWW, pp. 977–988 (2013)
23. Oren, E., Delbru, R., Decker, S.: Extending faceted navigation to RDF data. In: Cruz, I., Decker, S., Allemang, D., Preist, C., Schwabe, D., Mika, P., Uschold, M., Aroyo, L.M. (eds.) ISWC 2006. LNCS, vol. 4273, pp. 559–572. Springer, Heidelberg (2006)
24. Sacco, G.M., Tzitzikas, Y. (eds.): Dynamic taxonomies and faceted search. The information retrieval series. Springer (2009)
25. Van Kleek, M., Moore, B., Karger, D., André, P., Schraefel, M.: Atomate it! end-user context-sensitive automation using heterogeneous information sources on the web. In: Int. Conf. World Wide Web, pp. 951–960. ACM (2010)

Querying Heterogeneous Personal Information on the Go*

Danh Le-Phuoc, Anh Le-Tuan, Gregor Schiele, and Manfred Hauswirth

INSIGHT Centre for Data Analytics,
National University of Ireland, Galway

Abstract. Mobile devices are becoming a central data integration hub for personal information. Thus, an up-to-date, comprehensive and consolidated view of this information across heterogeneous personal information spaces is required. Linked Data offers various solutions for integrating personal information, but none of them comprehensively addresses the specific resource constraints of mobile devices. To address this issue, this paper presents a unified data integration framework for resource-constrained mobile devices. Our generic, extensible framework not only provides a unified view of personal data from different personal information data spaces but also can run on a user's mobile device without any external server. To save processing resources, we propose a data normalisation approach that can deal with ID-consolidation and ambiguity issues without complex generic reasoning. This data integration approach is based on a triple storage for Android devices with small memory footprint. We evaluate our framework with a set of experiments on different devices and show that it is able to support complex queries on large personal data sets of more than one million triples on typical mobile devices with very small memory footprint.

Keywords: mobile database, personal information system, RDF store.

1 Introduction

The availability of an up-to-date, comprehensive and consolidated view of a user's social context not only enables novel applications such as distributed social networks [16], semantic life [8], or a semantic desktop [18] but is increasingly becoming an essential requirement for many mobile applications. As an example, consider a typical mobile user who has access to contact information of his acquaintances via Facebook, LinkedIn, Google+ and his phonebook. Each of these data sources may contain different types of information about this user, e.g., personal and professional information, phone numbers or message and call histories, and they may exhibit different levels of quality. Consequently, a contact management application should be able to link and integrate all this information

---

* This publication has emanated from research supported in part by a research grant from Science Foundation Ireland (SFI) under Grant Number SFI/12/RC/2289 and by Irish Research Council under Grant No. GOIPD/2013/104 and European Commission under Grant No. FP7-287305 (OpenIoT) and Grant No. FP7-287661 (GAMBAS) and Grant No. FP7-ICT-608662 (VITAL).

P. Mika et al. (Eds.) ISWC 2014, Part II, LNCS 8797, pp. 454–469, 2014.

and automatically extract and integrate the right pieces of information from the whole set of data sources available. Similarly, a messaging widget should be able to integrate the messages from different services in order to track the user's conversations across all messaging service platforms.

However, the creation and continuous maintenance of such a view is a challenging task. The reason for this is twofold: First, despite the steady increase in computation and communication capabilities, mobile devices are battery powered. As a result, developers typically spend a considerable fraction of their development time on minimizing the amount of computation and bandwidth utilization to reduce the impact of their applications on the device's energy profile. Second, despite the popularity of some mainstream social networking services, the creation of a truly comprehensive view on the user's context usually requires the integration of considerable amounts of data from a user-specific set of services. As a result, developers must provide mechanisms to deal with the integration of complementary as well as overlapping and possibly inconsistent data sets.

Existing solutions typically use one of the following two approaches: Either they may use a powerful and well-connected cloud infrastructure to perform the data integration [12] or they may focus on the integration of an application-specific set of data types from a (possibly) limited set of services [13]. The first approach requires the provisioning of access credentials to the centralised/cloud-based data integration infrastructure which may then access, process and store the user's information. This remotely processing approach for mobile applications raises several privacy and security concern as security credentials leave the device and privacy is given up (entrusted to the cloud/remote servers without control by the users and without means to enforce it). Therefore, granting access on the mobile device is under the full control of the user is desired in ongoing security and privacy debates in many countries in respect to the cloud. To this end, the second approach is the preferable choice. However, it is not cost-effective as it requires developers to repeatedly make complicated design decisions. Furthermore, it may be also inefficient, especially in cases where multiple applications require access to the same data resulting in duplicate data retrieval and integration.

In this paper, we present an alternative approach for data integration by introducing a comprehensive framework that takes care of data retrieval, identity consolidation, disambiguation, storage and access, locally on mobile devices. To reduce privacy and security concerns, the framework does not require any remote storage and processing. It is solely executed on the mobile device of a user. In contrast to application-specific approaches, our framework is generic with respect to the supported types of data. It is extensible with respect to the supported services and it is open with respect to application support. To achieve this, the framework (1) leverages Linked Data to facilitate the storage of arbitrary types of data, (2) employs a plug-in model to connect to different services and (3) provides a generic query processor with support for SPARQL to be open with respect to application support. As a validation of the usefulness of the framework and to verify the efficiency of the framework, we present the results of an extensive experimental evaluation.

The remainder of this paper is structured as follows: In the next section we describe our approach for data consolidation and integration on mobile devices. After that we present the design and implementation of our framework, and evaluate its performance. Finally, we discuss related work and finish the paper with our conclusions and discuss directions for possible future work.

2   Integration of Heterogeneous Personal Information

To integrate the personal data from different data sources, several approaches proposed a unified data model for transforming heterogeneous data formats to RDF driven by agreed-upon vocabularies (FOAF, SIOC, vCard,etc) [2]. RDF statements are used to link and describe people, their social relationships, the content objects relevant to them, etc. However, a person can have multiple identifiers (IDs) on different data spaces. When they are integrated in a single data space, these IDs have to be interlinked and unified to represent a unique person. To uniquely identify someone across various data spaces, there are some rules that have to be set to infer and ensure uniqueness of that person. Along with some explicit properties like *owl:sameAs*, there are some implicit rules defined from properties indicating that two IDs are "talking" about the same person [2]. For instance, in practical, an *"inverse-identification"* property is used as an indirect identifier, e.g., foaf:phone, foaf:mbox_sha1sum. Therefore, having multiple identifiers poses several challenges for aggregating personal data from heterogeneous data spaces to store in RDF and to make it useful on resource constrained devices.

To demonstrate why it is challenging to enable a unified, integrated view of heterogeneous personal information sources on mobile devices, let us take a closer look on the example depicted in Figure 1. The data shown in this figure is

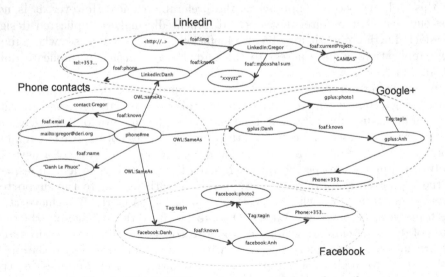

Fig. 1. Simple RDF graph integrated from data silos

acquired and transformed to RDF from Facebook, Google+, LinkedIn and phone contacts of a user's mobile phone in a similar fashion as proposed in [16,2].

The explicit *owl:sameAs* statements are added to link a user's IDs from different data spaces. In addition, two RDF nodes, *facebook:Anh* (Facebook identifiers) and *gplus:Anh* (Google+ identifiers), represent one person because they have the same inverse-identification property *foaf:phone* with the same value < *phone* : +35389... >. Similarly, two RDF nodes, *linkedin:Gregor* (LinkedIn identifier) and *phone:Gregor* (identifier given by the phone's contact application) also represent one person because the *sha1sum* value of his email has the same value as his *foaf:mbox_sha1sum* in LinkedIn. In essence, this RDF graph implicitly represents "different" pieces of information of three people who have different RDF statements attached with different RDF nodes representing each of them. However, if we store the simple RDF reification[1] of this graph in a standard RDF store, the SPARQL query processor will not be able to return complete information about a person. For instance, the query *"SELECT ?friends WHERE {phone:me foaf:knows ?friend}"* can only return one friend with the identifier *contact:Gregor* from the explicit statement in the phone contacts. Standard SPARQL is not able to infer the implicit statement *{phone:me foaf:knows facebook:Anh}* because *phone:me* and *facebook:me* is the same person.

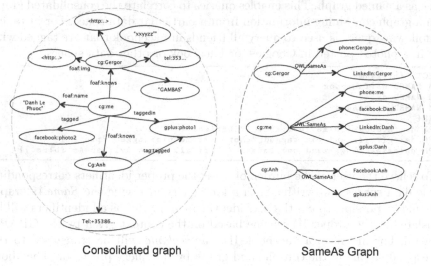

Consolidated graph   **SameAs Graph**

Fig. 2. Consolidated and SameAs graph

The solution for this problem is to use entailment regimes[2] instead of simple entailment in the above graph. This requires a modification in the SPARQL query processor to employ a reasoner to infer implicit RDF statements for basic graph pattern matching operators. However, this approach is not practical because it needs a considerable amount of memory and a fairly powerful CPU for the reasoning process. Another alternative solution is to use an ID consolidation

---

[1] http://www.w3.org/TR/rdf-primer/

[2] http://www.w3.org/TR/sparql11-entailment/

approach [12,6] to compute all implicit RDF statements, then store them in an RDF store and query it with a standard SPARQL query processor. However, this approach is hard to adopt for resource constrained mobile devices. On top of that, having all possible explicit RDF statements in an RDF store is expensive for both updating and querying the data stored in the storage. It is even more expensive for incrementally updating the RDF store because the data needs to be synchronized with the original data sources [15,17].

To remedy these problems, we propose to create a unified integration view by managing additional graphs to query all personal information desired. Firstly, we manage a "consolidated graph" that contains the aggregated personal information from different data spaces. As illustrated on the left of Figure 2, the consolidated graph provides an aggregated view of personal information, so that a standard SPARQL query processor can provide complete answers relevant to a person. Note that, this consolidated graph uses only one ID scheme that provides a single ID for one person. However, the integration view also has a *SameAs graph* that links consolidated IDs with their counterparts given in other data spaces as shown on the right of Figure 2.

To store and manage the provenance information of the data acquired from difference data spaces, the integration view also stores the data from each data space as a named graph. This enables queries to correlate the consolidated graph with a graph containing information from a particular data space. For instance, the following query is used to query all friends in Facebook that are tagged with "me in a photo" posted in Google+ or Facebook or other data spaces.

```
SELECT ?fbfriend
FROM NAMED ds:facebook
FROM NAMED ds:cg
FROM NAMED ds:sameas
WHERE{
GRAPH ds:facebook{fb:me foaf:knows ?fbfriend}
GRAPH ds:cg{?cgfriend pim:tagged ?photo. ?cgme pim:tagged ?photo.}
GRAPH ds:sameas{?cgfriend owl:sameAs ?fbfriend. ?cgme owl:sameAs fb:me.}}
```

To relieve the user of the burden of using the proper identifiers corresponding to the data spaces and writing such a long query involving the *SameAs* graph, it should be possible to use the user identifiers in queries as all identifiers will be translated to the proper ID scheme based on the context given by the GRAPH keyword. For instance, a Facebook ID *Facebook:me* will be translated to the corresponding one in the consolidated graph by the query processor. The above query could be written in a shorter form as follows:

```
SELECT ?fbfriend
FROM NAMED ds:facebook
FROM NAMED ds:cg
WHERE{
GRAPH ds:facebook{fb:me foaf:knows ?fbfriend.}
GRAPH ds:cg{?cgfriend pim:tagged ?photo. fb:me pim:tagged ?photo.}}
```

To create and maintain the unified view composed from such graphs, we would need a data integration platform that requires several features specifically designed for mobile devices. The first feature is the data aggregation from heterogeneous data sources. After data is aggregated, it has to be consolidated to create constituent graphs for the integrated view. To store and query data from these graphs, the platform also needs a fully-fledged RDF store tailored to the needs of resource-constrained devices. On top of that, the data in this RDF store has to be accessed in a controlled manner to meet the security and privacy concerns of personal data. These requirements drives the design and implementation decisions of our framework in the following section.

3   System Design and Implementation

To enable querying heterogeneous personal information with the unified view described in previous section, we design the system architecture to meet aforementioned requirements in following. We also describe the implementation of the core component, RDF store for mobile devices, that dictates the expected performance of the whole system in context of resource constraints.

3.1   System Architecture

Figure 3 shows the overall system architecture which we will discuss in the following.

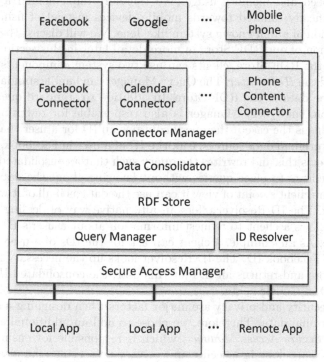

Fig. 3. System architecture overview

As discussed before, there are different sources for personal information like Facebook or Google Calendar that developers should be able to integrate into our framework. To do so, our framework allows developers to create *Connector* classes and plug them into the framework using the *Connector Manager*. Each Connector is tailored towards a specific information source. So far, we provide a core set of Connectors, namely for Facebook, Google+, Google Calendar,LinkedIn and the local mobile phone content. If developers need to access additional information sources, they can easily implement new connectors for them using the existing ones as a blueprints.

Each connector pulls relevant information from its information source and pushes it towards the *Data Consolidator*. The Data Consolidator consolidates and integrates data from different connectors into the corresponding RDF graphs for each data source. The Data Consolidator also computes the aggregated graph and SameAs graph as described in Section 2. These RDF graphs are stored as an integrated view into the RDF Store.

The *RDF Store* is a core component of our system as it manages triple data directly on the mobile phone instead of on an external server. RDF triples can be stored, indexed and retrieved. The store contains the actual personal data as well as all metadata needed for data consolidation, e.g., user IDs in different data sources and how they relate to each other. The RDF Store has major influence on our system performance and thus must be highly efficient both in terms of execution speed and memory usage. We therefore implemented a RDF store that is specifically tailored towards mobile devices instead of using a feature reduced version of a well known system like Jena. We will discuss the design and implementation of our RDF Store in more detail later in this section.

To access the RDF Store, clients can use two system components, the *Query Manager* and the *ID Resolver*. The Query Manager can handle standard SPARQL queries on the data in the RDF Store. In addition to standard query planning and execution, the Query Manager is also responsible for rewriting queries if necessary. This is the case if the query contains an ID for a user that originates in one of the original data sources, e.g., the ID of a user in Facebook. The Query Manager detects this and rewrites the query such that a consolidated ID is used. This allows clients to place queries without knowing about the data consolidation. From the client's point of view it can use the data as if all of it was available on Facebook. The ID Resolver offers an alternative way of dealing with multiple IDs. It allows a client to request information about a user's ID in different data sources. As an example, a client can ask for the IDs of a user for which it provides the Facebook ID. The ID Resolver looks up the necessary metadata in the RDF Store and returns all IDs for this user, the consolidated ID as well as the user's ID in Google+, etc.

Clearly, security and privacy are major factors when designing a system that manages personal data. Therefore, we chose to add an additional system component, the *Secure Access Manager*, which is responsible for ensuring that all client accesses are done in a secure and privacy-preserving manner. The Secure Access Manager receives requests from local as well as remote client applications. It authenticates the requesting clients and checks their authorisation to access private data. Authorisation is given by the local user using so-called privacy policies. If access is granted, the Secure Access Manager forwards the request to either the Query Manager or the ID Resolver. It also forwards any results to the requesting client.

To ensure secure communication with remote clients, the Secure Access Manager uses the PIKE approach for secure peer to peer communication establishment for mobile devices [1]. PIKE includes mechanisms to initiate a secure key exchange and to establish a secure network connection with it. It is also able to set up an ad-hoc communication network between mobile devices if necessary.

3.2 High Performant and Low Memory Consumption RDF Store

As presented in Section 2, our solution for maintaining a unified integration view of heterogeneous personal information is to manage a consolidated graph for the aggregated data from different spaces and a sameAs graph to link the consolidated ID with their counterparts. Applying this approach on mobile devices requires a mobile RDF store component which is designed for update-intensive operations. To this end, we built a native and fully-fledged, persistent RDF storage and SPARQL query processor for Android devices, called *RDF On the Go* (RDF-OTG) [3]. RDF-OTG has been extensively used for managing semantic contextual information on mobile devices in PECES[4] and GAMBAS[5] projects. In our implementation, we focused on minimizing the memory footprint and designing data structures tightly coupled with the storage mechanism of mobile devices to achieve maximum efficiency in terms of low memory consumption and high update frequency. In the following we briefly describe our main optimisations to maximise performance and scalability for personal information management applications on mobile devices. A full analysis of the performance gains is given in Section 4.

Reducing memory consumption is one of the critical key targets in mobile DBMS design [10] since most mobile devices have (relatively) limited memory. To achieve that, we reduce the memory footprint of data operations on RDF data by using dictionary encoding, similar to the implementations of JenaTDB or Sesame. Each RDF node is mapped to a compact 32-bit integer with 9 bit to encode the node type and the remaining 23 bit encoding a string identifier which is kept separately on the flash memory instead of in main memory. Most operations on nodes, e.g., matchings during a query execution, can be performed on these node identifiers without accessing the actual string representation. Thus, only one integer must be kept in memory for each node, while string representations can be stored on the flash memory. This leads to a memory footprint of just up to 12 bytes per triple. This is considerably low compared to 450 bytes per triple for the Jena Memory Model as reported by the memory profiler. Note that the compact integer format is used for optimising millions rather than billions of RDF nodes which we believe this is the common scale of most mobile personal information applications. For instance,1.5 million triples are required to represent the information of 1200 user profiles (cf., Section 4). However, if necessary, this restriction could be easily removed.

---

[3] RDF-OTG is open-sourced at https://code.google.com/p/rdfonthego/

[4] http://www.nes.uni-due.de/research/projects/peces/

[5] http://www.gambas-ict.eu/

Mobile devices are equipped flash memory as the secondary storage. Flash memory has no mechanical latency, reading is faster than writing and the storage is organized in memory blocks. Instead of reading or writing individual bytes, the I/O unit always reads/writes a whole block. That leads to its erase-before-write limitation when writing a single byte in a block, i.e., the whole block must be read, modified and written again. Thus to achieve the writing requirement, our RDF store needs to optimize writing efficiency rather than reading effiency. To simplify the writing process we use the simplest version of multiple indexing framework of RDF data [4]. It contains only three cyclic orderings of a triple's components with respect to subject(S), predicate(P) and object(O): SPO, POS and OSP. Each indexing order of triples is stored in a separate table.

Due to the impact of flash memory, unmodified versions of traditional data structures do not perform well. On the other hand, flash-aware indexing structure do not work well with "narrow and long" tables as resulting from the above indexing approach. Thus, we use a two-layer indexing approach to manage these tuples of three encoded integers in their corresponding tables. In each table, tuples are sorted lexicographically, partitioned and compressed into individual fixed-size and same-length blocks to the flash I/O block size of the device. The second index layer is a sparse index, small enough to fit into main memory to enable fast lookup for the triples contained in each block. The index holds the lowest and highest node identifier in each sorted block. We also use an in-memory caching mechanism which maintains a limited number of frequently used index blocks.

If a new triple is added, it must be added to the indexes. To do so, the system loads the required index blocks into the cache. Then the triple must be allocated at the right position in the index. This is trivial if the triple should be added at the end of an existing block that still has open space. Otherwise, we would need to move all triples by one position, resulting in a large number of writes. To further reduce the number of read/write accesses, when we need to remove a block from the cache and write it back to flash, our strategy chooses a block that has thehighest chance of not being changed in the future.

4   Experimental Evaluation

The approach for data integration presented in Section 2 avoids reasoning tasks by modifying RDF triples and then storing them in a unified integration view. This solution is suitable for mobile devices since it does not require much memory for executing the reasoning tasks but it requires a highly performant mobile RDF store when the graphs have to be modified frequently to maintain the unified view. Thus, performance of the system described in Section 3 heavily depends on the performance of the back-end mobile RDF store used. In this section, we present a thorough experimental evaluation[6] of our system's performance and scalability in terms of data updating and querying. The evaluation uses two system configurations with different mobile RDF stores to evaluate its impact

---

[6] The description of how to reproduce the results can be found at
https://code.google.com/p/rdfonthego/wiki/SocialNetworkEvaluation

on system's performance and to measure the efficiency gained through our RDF store. In the following we first describe the setup of the experiments and then present and discuss the results obtained from the results.

4.1 Evaluation Setup

Our evaluation setup is as follows: To evaluate the impact of our special triple store on system performance, we compare two different system configurations. The first one uses our system as described in the last section, i.e., it uses our triple store, RDF On The Go (RDF-OTG). The original implementation of RDF-OTG was presented in [9]. Since then RDF-OTG has been completely redesigned and reimplemented for maximum performance in Section 3.2. In the experiments we use the most recent version. In the second configuration we replaced RDF-OTG by TDBoid,[7] the Android version of Jena TDB. The rest of the system remained unchanged.

To evaluate how different device profiles with different resources and capabilities impact on the performance, we use three classes of Android devices in the experiments: a HTC desire, a Samsung Galaxy Nexus, and a Nexus 7 Tablet. Their configuration details are described in Table 1.

Table 1. Android devices

HTC desire	Samsung Galaxy Nexus	Nexus 7 Tablet
AndroidOS 2.3.3	AndroidOS 4.2.2	AndroidOS 4.2.2
998Mhz CPU	1200Mhz CPU	1300Mhz CPU
404MB physical RAM	694MB physical RAM	974MB physical RAM
32MB DVM heap size	96MB of DVM heap size	64MB of DVM heap size

For the evaluation dataset, we use a social network data generator [11] to generate three social networks, one for Facebook, one for Google+ and one for LinkedIn. From these we extract relevant data profiles for a person, i.e., the profiles of that person and his/her friends, and feed them into our system. The data generator generates random inverse-identification properties, e.g, mbox_sha1sum, phone from the same dictionary for three social networks so the overlaps are random. With this dataset, we conducted the following four experiments:

Update throughput: In the first experiment we tested how much new data the system can incrementally update with a certain underlying RDF store corresponding to each hardware configuration. We simulated the process of data growing by gradually adding more data to the system. We measured the throughput of inserting data (triples/second) until the system crashed or until we reach 1 million triples (whichever happened first).

Query processor comparison: In the second experiment we tested the performance and functionalities of TDBoid and RDF-OTG using 8 typical queries with on the maximum data sizes that both TDBoid and RDF-OTG could support. The queries are chosen to cover all query patterns and different complexities. Note that, each query accesses to the aggregated view which already involves

---

[7] https://code.google.com/p/androjena/

data from multi-sources and queries 7 and 8 are to show the ability to refer back to the original data sources. The list of the queries in SPARQL language is given in the Appendix.

Memory consumption: In the third experiment, we measured the memory consumption of two system configurations while performing the queries. The experimental application ran the different queries repeatedly and recorded the maximum memory heap that the operating system allocated for it. To evaluate the impact of the data size on memory consumption, the test was conducted on the Nexus 7 Tablet with five datasets with different sizes. Note that the memory consumption is device-independent. We used the same queries set as in the second experiment.

Scalability: In the last experiment we evaluated the scalability of RDF-OTG by measuring the query response time of the above 8 queries on the maximum data sizes that each of the above devices could store.

4.2 Evaluation Results

Figure 4 shows the results of our first experiment, in which we measured the update performance of RDF-OTG and TDBoid when adding more and more triples to the store. As we can see, in general, the writing throughput of RDF-OTG is roughly twice as high as TDBoid's. This shows the advantage of our

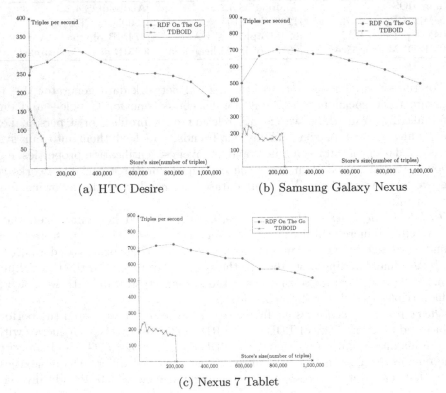

(a) HTC Desire

(b) Samsung Galaxy Nexus

(c) Nexus 7 Tablet

Fig. 4. Updating throughputs

optimizations for flash memory compared to the design used in TDBoid, which was originally designed for normal magnetic disks.

In addition, while throughput decreases for larger data sizes in the store, RDF-OTG is able to add more triples to the store for all scenarios with acceptable rates (approx. 200 triples/sec for the HTC Desire and approx. 500 triples/sec for the two more powerful devices), even if nearly one million triples were already in the store. TDBoid on the other hand, is not only slower, but it also cannot cope at all with such data sizes and reaches its upper capacity limit at 100k triples on the HTC Desire, 220k triples on the Galaxy Nexus and around 200k triples on the Nexus 7.

In our second experiment we measured the performance of evaluating different queries (as discussed earlier) on existing data sets. The results are shown in Figure 5. Unfortunately, TDBoid does not return any results for Query 7 and 8 because it does not support queries involving named graphs. Therefore, we omitted these two queries from the graphs below. In addition, due to the limitation in the number of triples that TDBoid can handle, we had to reduce the number of profiles contained in the test data for each of the devices: 45 profiles for the HTC Desire, 180 profiles for the Galaxy Nexus and 112 profiles for the Nexus 7.

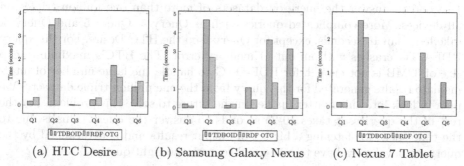

(a) HTC Desire   (b) Samsung Galaxy Nexus   (c) Nexus 7 Tablet

Fig. 5. Comparing the query response times of RDF-OTG and TDBoid

The results show that the query performance of RDF-OTG is much higher than TDBoid's for the Galaxy Nexus and the Nexus 7. However, for the HTC Desire, the performance is comparable or even worse for RDF-OTG. The reason for this is that we specifically optimized our system for flash memory. However, the HTC Desire uses an external SD card for storing data instead of internal flash memory. This induces a much higher cost to I/O operations on the HTC Desire. Since TDBoid is originally designed for (relatively slow) magnetic disks, it is able to handle this better than RDF-OTG. However, to do so, TDBoid uses a lot of main memory, which explains its restricted scalability.

The results of the third experiment for measuring the memory consumption for querying are presented in Table 2. Due to the limited scalability of TDBoid exhibited in the inserting throughput test, the tests with TDBoid could only be executed on data sizes of 100,000 and 200,000 triples. The results of the experiment demonstrate the great improvement in memory footprint optimization of our system. With the same dataset, RDF-OTG requires only one third of the memory that TDBoid needs. For instance, RDF-OTG requires 4MB for the 100,000 triple dataset and 8MB for 200,000 triples to perform the queries while TDBoid requires 11MB and 26MB for the same setup. The efficiency in memory usage also enables RDF-OTG to support much larger datasets. Even with a dataset of 1.5 million triples, the heap size of a system configured with RDF-OTG is lower than 64MB (the JVM maximum heap size of the Nexus 7 tablet).

Table 2. Memory consumption of mix queries/size of data

	100k	200k	500k	1m	1.5m
RDF-OTG	4MB	9MB	17MB	34MB	46MB
TDBOID	11MB	26MB	N/A	N/A	N/A

Our last experiment evaluated the scalability of our system. Due to the scalability limitations that we found in earlier experiments, we omitted TDBoid in this experiment and focused on RDF-OTG. Table 3 shows the query response times of the 8 queries on the three devices. As we can see, our system is able to handle datasets of 1 million triples (900 profiles) on the HTC Desire, and 1.5 million triples (1200 profiles) on the Galaxy Nexus and Nexus 7 without any problems. For simple queries like Query 1 and Query 3, it takes less than 1 second to answer the query on datasets of more than one million triples on all devices. More complicated queries such as Query 4, Query 5 and Query 6, take less than 10 seconds, except for Query 5 on the HTC Desire. For this query RDF-OTG crashes with an out of memory error. The HTC's maximum heap size of 32MB is not enough for RDF-OTG to handle the large number of intermediate results generated for this query from the one million triple dataset.[8] We plan to look into this matter further in the future to solve this problem. For the rest of the queries, it takes 10-25 seconds to answer the query. This is due to the time spent for fetching a big set of output results and is determined by the query, so developers have to be careful to "ask the right queries."

Table 3. Query response time (seconds) on maximum datasets for RDF-OTG

	Q1	Q2	Q3	Q4	Q5	Q6	Q7	Q 8
HTC (900 Prof/1M tr)	0.114	19.035	0.402	3.714	failed	6.093	22.652	24.345
GALAXY (1.2K Prof/1.5M tr)	0.322	14.705	0.341	3.490	7.858	1.713	16.111	19.223
NEXUS 7 (1.2K Prof/1.5M tr)	0.113	11.638	0.242	2.458	6.649	1.579	12.769	17.044

5   Related Work

Semantic Web and RDF have long been used as a solution for modeling and integrating heterogeneous personal data. Many works have aimed to better allow a user's access to multiple data silos by using Semantic Web technologies to satisfy the requirements of data portability in terms of identification, personal profiles and friend networks [2]. SemanticLife [8] is one of the early attempts to employ ontologies for modeling personal digital information. Then there is a series of

---

[8] 34MB would be required as shown in our third experiment.

work on Semantic Desktop such as the Gnowsis Semantic Desktop [14] or the Social Semantic Desktop [5] to provide semantic Personal Information Management (PIM) tools. Additionally, other integrated platforms such as Haystack [12] and Semex [6] provide a wide range of tools and functionalities for PIM. However, they all aim at a standard computer environment and do not take into account mobile devices and their specific problems.

Since then several works have tried to achieve the same functionalities on mobile devices. But the adaptations necessary for the mobile setting proved to be challenging. The first line of work followed the approach of connecting mobile devices to a centralized infrastructure where all processing and storages are delegated to [3,4]. This line of early work has a lot of security, connection and performance issues. To address them, there are emerging efforts to ship processing and storage of personal information to mobile devices. For instance, [16] tries to store the personal data retrieved from distributed social networks on the phone. However, most of these works still have certain dependencies and use unsecured data exchanges with intermediate parties.

However, these early works have shown the clear interest of using Semantic Web technologies for integrating personal data on mobile devices and the also have shown the need for mobile RDF data processing engines. But these existing works ignore the fact that existing triple storage technologies from normal computers *can not* be directly applied to the mobile setting. For example, the early adoption of Jena to J2ME [7] is micro-Jena [9] which only works on in-memory data on Symbian mobiles. The Android version of Jena, TDBoid, is far better due to newer hardware capabilities but it has a lot of limitations in respect to performance and scalability as we have shown in our experiments in Section 4. We believe this paper is the first to systematically investigate and address the issues of security, integration, performance and scalability of integrating heterogeneous personal information data.

6 Conclusions

In this paper, we presented a comprehensive framework for the integration of personal data from heterogeneous data sources, such as different social networks, on mobile devices. Our framework builds upon Linked Data technologies to be generic with respect to the supported data types and data requests, offers a plug-in model to be extensible for additional data sources and relies solely on a user's mobile device, without the need for storing or processing any data on an external, possibly untrusted, server infrastructure. The performance and scalability issues are addressed by our RDF triple store for Android devices, RDF On the Go, which is specifically optimised for mobile devices and flash memory usage. It offers full support for RDF triples and SPARQL queries and is able to handle more than a million triples on typical mobile devices efficiently. Complex queries are supported and can be executed in reasonable time, even for such large data sets but with very small memory footprint.

---

[9] http://poseidon.ws.dei.polimi.it/ca/?page_id=59

References

1. Apolinarski, W., Handte, M., Iqbal, M., Marron, P.: Pike: Enabling secure interaction with piggybacked key-exchange. In: PerCom (2013)
2. Bojars, U., Passant, A., Breslin, J.G., Decker, S.: Social network and data portability using semantic web technologies. In: SAW 2008 (2008)
3. d'Aquin, M., Nikolov, A., Motta, E.: Building sparql-enabled applications with android devices. In: ISWC 2011 (2011)
4. David, J., Euzenat, J.: Linked data from your pocket: The android rdfcontentprovider. In: ISWC 2010 (2010)
5. Decker, S., Frank, M.R.: The networked semantic desktop. In: WWW Workshop on Application Design, Development and Implementation Issues in the Semantic Web (2004)
6. Dong, X.L., Halevy, A.: A platform for personal information management and integration. In: Proceedings of VLDB 2005 PhD Workshop (2005)
7. Hayun, R.B.: Java ME on Symbian OS: Inside the Smartphone Model, vol. 30. John Wiley & Sons (2009)
8. Hoang, H.H., Andjomshoaa, A., Tjoa, A.M.: Towards a new approach for information retrieval in the semanticlife digital memory framework. In: WI (2006)
9. Le-Phuoc, D., Parreira, J.X., Reynolds, V., Hauswirth, M.: Rdf on the go: An rdf storage and query processor for mobile devices. In: ISWC 2010 (2010)
10. Nori, A.: Mobile and embedded databases. In: SIGMOD 2007 (2007)
11. Pham, M.-D., Boncz, P., Erling, O.: S3g2: A scalable structure-correlated social graph generator. In: Nambiar, R., Poess, M. (eds.) TPCTC 2012. LNCS, vol. 7755, pp. 156–172. Springer, Heidelberg (2013)
12. Quan, D., Huynh, D.F., Karger, D.R.: Haystack: A platform for authoring end user semantic web applications. In: Fensel, D., Sycara, K., Mylopoulos, J. (eds.) ISWC 2003. LNCS, vol. 2870, pp. 738–753. Springer, Heidelberg (2003)
13. Rekimoto, J.: Timescape: A time machine for the desktop environment. In: CHI 1999 (1999)
14. Sauermann, L.: The gnowsis-using semantic web technologies to build a semantic desktop. Diploma thesis, Technical University of Vienna (2003)
15. Schandl, B., Zander, S.: Adaptive RDF graph replication for Mobile semantic web applications. Ubiquitous Computing and Communication Journal (2009)
16. Tramp, S., Frischmuth, P., Arndt, N., Ermilov, T., Auer, S.: Weaving a distributed, semantic social network for mobile users. In: Antoniou, G., Grobelnik, M., Simperl, E., Parsia, B., Plexousakis, D., De Leenheer, P., Pan, J. (eds.) ESWC 2011, Part I. LNCS, vol. 6643, pp. 200–214. Springer, Heidelberg (2011)
17. Tummarello, G., Morbidoni, C., Bachmann-Gmür, R., Erling, O.: Rdfsync: efficient remote synchronization of rdf models. In: Aberer, K., et al. (eds.) ISWC/ASWC 2007. LNCS, vol. 4825, pp. 537–551. Springer, Heidelberg (2007)
18. Weippl, E.R., Klemen, M.D., Fenz, S., Ekelhart, A., Tjoa, A.M.: The semantic desktop: A semantic personal information management system based on rdf and topic maps. In: Collard, M. (ed.) ODBIS 2005/2006. LNCS, vol. 4623, pp. 135–151. Springer, Heidelberg (2007)

Appendix: Queries Used in the Experiments

```
PREFIX foaf:   <http://xmlns.com/foaf/0.1/>
SELECT ?per ?property ?info
WHERE {?per foaf:mbox 'mailto:Thierry59@gmx.com'. ?per ?property ?info.}
```

Query 1: Return all information of a person by given mbox

```
PREFIX foaf:  <http://xmlns.com/foaf/0.1/>
PREFIX db:  <http://dbpedia.org/resource/>
SELECT ?firstname ?lastname ?mbox ?friend ?birthday ?gender
WHERE {
    ?person foaf:based_near db:Bulgaria. ?person foaf:firstName ?firstname.
    ?person foaf:lastName  ?lasttname. ?person foaf:mbox  ?mbox.
    ?person foaf:birthday  ?birthday.?person foaf:gender  ?gender. }
```

Query 2: Extract some informations of people who are nearby Bulgaria

```
PREFIX sibv:    <http://www.ins.cwi.nl/sib/vocabulary/>
PREFIX sioc:    <http://rdfs.org/sioc/ns#>
PREFIX dbpo:    <http://dbpedia.org/ontology/>
PREFIX fbp:     <http://www.facebook.com/person/>
SELECT DISTINCT ?location
WHERE { ?user sioc:account_of fbp:p151.
    ?photo sibv:usertag ?user.
    ?photo dbpo:location ?location. }
```

Query 3: Request all the locations that a person has taken a photo

```
SELECT DISTINCT ?properties
WHERE {?person rdf:type foaf:Person. ?subject ?predicate ?person.}
```

Query 4: Request incoming property of a person

```
PREFIX foaf:    <http://xmlns.com/foaf/0.1/>
PREFIX rdf: <http://www.w3.org/1999/02/22-rdf-syntax-ns#>
SELECT DISTINCT ?properties
WHERE {{?person rdf:type foaf:Person. ?subject ?predicate ?person.}
UNION  {?person rdf:type foaf:Person. ?person  ?predicate ?object.}}
```

Query 5: Request incoming and outcoming properties of person

```
PREFIX foaf:        <http://xmlns.com/foaf/0.1/>
PREFIX rdf:         <http://www.w3.org/1999/02/22-rdf-syntax-ns#>
PREFIX sioc:        <http://rdfs.org/sioc/ns#>
PREFIX sibv:        <http://www.ins.cwi.nl/sib/vocabulary/>
PREFIX fbp:         <http://www.facebook.com/person/>
SELECT  DISTINCT ?photo
WHERE{
fbp:p39 foaf:knows ?person. ?user sioc:account_of ?person.
?user sibv:like ?photo. ?photo rdf:type sibv:Photo.}
```

Query 6: Request all the photos that are liked by a person

```
PREFIX foaf:        <http://xmlns.com/foaf/0.1/>
PREFIX rdf:         <http://www.w3.org/1999/02/22-rdf-syntax-ns#>
PREFIX sioc:        <http://rdfs.org/sioc/ns#>
PREFIX fbph:        <http://www.facebook.com/photoalbum/>
SELECT  ?per {
GRAPH <facebook> {?per rdf:type foaf:Person.}
GRAPH <master> {?user sioc:account_of ?per. ?user sioc:creator_of fbph:pa103.}}
```

Query 7: Request the photo on Facebook by LinkedIn account

```
PREFIX foaf:        <http://xmlns.com/foaf/0.1/>
PREFIX rdf:         <http://www.w3.org/1999/02/22-rdf-syntax-ns#>
PREFIX sioc:        <http://rdfs.org/sioc/ns#>
PREFIX sibv:        <http://www.ins.cwi.nl/sib/vocabulary/>
SELECT ?user ?c
{
GRAPH <facebook> {?c rdf:type  sibv:Comment. ?user sioc:creator_of ?c.}
GRAPH <master> {?user sioc:account_of <http://linkedin.com/person/p174>}
}
```

Query 8: Request the LinkedIn account of a friend on Facebook

The Web Browser Personalization
with the Client Side Triplestore

Hitoshi Uchida[1,2], Ralph Swick[2], and Andrei Sambra[3]

[1] Canon Inc., Tokyo, Japan
[2] World Wide Web Consortium, MIT CSAIL, Cambridge, MA USA
{uchida,swick}@w3.org
[3] Decentralized Information Group, MIT CSAIL, Cambridge, MA USA
asambra@mit.edu

Abstract. We introduce a client side triplestore library for HTML5 web applications and a personalization technology for web browsers working with this library. The triplestore enables HTML5 web applications to store semantic data into HTML5 Web Storage. The personalization technology enables web browsers to collect semantic data from the web and utilize them for enhanced user experience on web pages as users browse. We show new potentials for web browsers to provide new user experiences by personalizing with semantic web technology.

Keywords: semantic web, HTML5, triplestore, inference, web browser.

1 Introduction

1.1 Silos of Current Web Services

It is becoming common to manage our personal data on diverse web services in which we can create documents and presentation materials, manage personal schedules, send and receive emails, manage personal photo albums not only with web browsers on laptop PCs but also dedicated smart phone applications. It is also becoming common to synchronize PC data to cloud storage services which enable users not only to backup but also to open the synchronized files with smart phone applications on the go. Thanks to social network services, our daily lives became more communicative with friends and family by instantaneously sharing messages and schedules and postings.

However, current web systems don't provide enough options for users to mash up and utilize personal data which are distributed among those services users depend on in daily lives. A practical way to reuse our personal data among services is to exchange them with one of authorization protocols such as OAuth[1]. Through a handshake between OAuth client and OAuth provider, they exchange an access token which grants a permission to allow OAuth client to access user data in the OAuth provider. However, the traditional approach using the authorization protocol causes privacy issues for reuse of user data on other services.

---

[1] http://tools.ietf.org/html/rfc6749

P. Mika et al. (Eds.) ISWC 2014, Part II, LNCS 8797, pp. 470–485, 2014.
© Springer International Publishing Switzerland 2014

Without disclosing our private data to 3rd party services, we can't reuse and mash up among them. It is also difficult to understand how securely our privacy is protected. After granting the access for user data to the 3rd party services, in general, users don't pay attention to which user data are still opened and accessible for 3rd party services they previously authorized. In addition it is difficult for users to understand what is happening during the handshake because the architecture of general authorization protocols depends on HTTP redirection through client web browsers. If our favorite services don't support the authorization protocol, we can't reuse personal data between services without migrating or copy-and-pasting them manually.

1.2   The User Data Centralization on 3rd Party Services

Web browsers are becoming more functional on not only rendering rich graphical web pages but also using latest innovative technologies such as real-time transfer protocols of WebSocket[1] and SPDY[2], video streaming interface WebRTC[3] and client side Web Storage[4]. However, we strongly depend on 3rd party services to use and manage our personal web data. By disclosing our private data to those 3rd party services, we get the benefits of reuse of our web data. We depend on their functionality to control our web data and security levels because current web browsers lack functionality for us to control personal web data. Though Web Storage can store user data in web browsers, this capability is used by web applications and not directly by users. We are always tied up with the architecture of current web system where web browsers mainly work as web application execution engine. Web browsers are users' personal tools and they should give more control for our personal data on the web without strongly depending on 3rd party services and disclosing our privacy.

1.3   What We Want to Achieve

The prior use cases and applications using semantic web were mainly server side. The major architecture was to store application data as triples with standardized formats like RDF[5] and provided endpoints which enabled client applications to retrieve the stored application data with a dedicated query language such as SPARQL[6]. However, there are a few challenges to apply semantic web to client side web applications, especially for the new HTML5[2] platform which is dramatically changing the existing web infrastructure.

In this paper we introduce a client side triplestore library, *triplestoreJS*[3], and semantic web browser plug-in, *Semantic Spider*[4], working with the triplestore. The *Semantic Spider* site[5] describes the detailed architectures and demonstrates

---

[2] http://www.w3.org/TR/html5/

[3] http://www.w3.org/2013/04/semweb-html5/triplestoreJS/

[4] https://chrome.google.com/webstore/detail/
semantic-spider/ckdnmkbanbampnifpddcfdphonmfibkb

[5] http://www.w3.org/2013/04/semweb-html5/spider/

how it works. The source code of *triplestoreJS* and *Semantic Spider* is available in a Github public repository[6]. The triplestore is a wrapper application programming interface (API) for HTML5 Web Storage and enables HTML5 web applications to store semantic data triples into a web browser local store and search these stored triples with a dedicated triplestore API. The triplestore is expected to meet enough processing performance to enable web applications to work with it at reasonable speed. The semantic web browser plug-in is an HTML5 application working with the triplestore and currently works on Google Chrome as an extension. The fundamental architecture is to extract semantic data from web pages which a user visits in daily web browsing and save these data into the triplestore of the plug-in. In addition to the semantic data extracted from the web pages, the plug-in also collects personal semantic data from major social networking services (SNS). The collected semantic data represents the user interests precisely, and allows the web browser integrating the plug-in to work with the personal semantic data. This architecture to centralize user data into the web browser local storage has the potential to resolve privacy issues caused by the traditional approaches of permitting services to share data among themselves. We hope this challenge to apply semantic web technology into an actual web browser will provide new inspirations and expand the use cases.

2 Related Works

One of the well-known cases using semantic web for knowledge bases is *DBpedia*[7]. *DBpedia* is a crowd sourced community effort to extract knowledge information from Wikipedia and make the information accessible on the Web in structured form. Client applications can retrieve the extracted information with semantic web tools using RDF/JSON/CSV/HTML as data format and SPARQL as query language and can become more intelligent by integrating the knowledge bases. Currently the English version of *DBpedia* describes 4 million things, out of which 3.22 million are classified in a consistent ontology, including 832,000 persons, 639,000 places, 372,000 creative works, 209,000 organizations and so on. DBpedia is also available in localized versions in 119 languages. Because Wikipedia is growing and maintained by contributors from all over the world, *DBpedia* will be one of the central knowledge sources for intelligent applications. It is easy to create an encyclopedia application continuing to support new words and keep up to date with the internationalization support.

Another well-known case using semantic web for knowledge bases is search engines. Though a search engine crawler analyzes web pages to identify embedded data for web search, it also extracts semantic data RDF and RDFa[7] and microdata[8] which annotate the web contents. The semantic data provides machine readable information which helps client applications like the crawler to precisely understand the data types and composing properties of the web contents from the standardized structure format. All of latest major web sites

---

[6] https://github.com/shishimaru/triplestoreJS
[7] http://dbpedia.org/

integrate semantic data into their HTML pages. They expect that the crawler analyzes their web sites more precisely and collects higher quality information which will be useful for web search processing. Currently the major consumer of the semantic data integrated into web sites is the crawlers of the search engines. Though the number of web pages continues to increase with the additional semantic data to annotate the web contents, general users don't directly feel the full benefit in web browsing.

The Tabulator Extension[9] is a browser plug-in that visualizes RDF semantic data in tabular form which is retrieved from a server. Users can browse and edit the visualized RDF data in the web browser and reflect the modification against the originating server with SPARQL update messages. *Piggy Bank*[10] is also a browser plug-in which stores extracted semantic data during web browsing into the web browser and provide a user interface to review them on any web sites. However, these prior tools are for semantic web engineers; general users of web browsers don't get clear benefits how semantic web can change our lives on the web. Therefore, we demonstrate how we can utilize potential semantic web for enhancing browsing experiences as section 4.2-4.5.

There are existing development efforts in semantic web JavaScript libraries for web applications. *Green Turtle*[8] and *microdatajs*[9] are RDFa and microdata parsers in JavaScript, respectively. *sparql.js*[10] is a JavaScript SPARQL library which enables web applications to retrieve semantic data with sending SPARQL messages to SPARQL endpoints. *rdf-store.js*[11] is a comprehensive semantic web JavaScript library which supports JSON-LD/Turtle/N3 parsers and a persistent storage using HTML5 LocalStorage and a SPARQL query. Because the persistent storage is based on W3C RDF Interfaces API which is a set of basic primitives and a low level interface, it is for advanced developers who understand the semantic web well. In the other hand, because our *triplestoreJS* is based on an extension of RDFa API[12] whose architecture integrates the W3C DOM API general web developers are familiar with, the learning curve is gentler and it is easier to start web application development with the library.

3   A Triplestore for HTML5 Web Storage

We developed a triplestore wrapper library *triplestoreJS* in JavaScript which stores subject-property-value triples into HTML5 Web Storage[13]. Web Storage is a new persistent data storage of key-value pairs for web applications and enables to store application data into local storage of a web browser. The API of *triplestoreJS* is an extension on the RDFa API and provides operations to store and search triples. Though Web Storage is based on key-value and isn't

---

[8] https://github.com/alexmilowski/green-turtle
[9] https://github.com/foolip/microdatajs
[10] http://www.w3.org/2001/sw/wiki/SPARQL_Javascript_Library
[11] https://github.com/antoniogarrote/rdfstore-js
[12] http://www.w3.org/TR/rdfa-api/
[13] http://www.w3.org/TR/webstorage/

optimized for storing triples, *triplestoreJS* is organized for storing and searching the subject-property-value model. *triplestoreJS* also conceals the routine work to resolve CURIEs within RDFa. Therefore, it can reduce the development cost for web applications which store triples into a browser storage. Performance measurements of the triplestore are described in section 5.

3.1   A Save Operation

Web applications can store specified triples into Web Storage with a dedicated triplestore API. Because the Web Storage is based on the key-value model using string data type, the triplestore stores a subject as a key and a JSON string of the corresponding RDF properties and values as a value.

```
var st = new Triplestore();
/*
 * 'setMapping(prefix, URI)' registers a pair
 * of prefix and URI for CURIE processing.
 */
st.setMapping('foaf', 'http://xmlns.com/foaf/0.1/');
/*
 * 'add(subject, property, value)' method saves a triple.
 * If the subject already has a value for the property,
 * the new value is appended as additional values of the property.
 */
st.add('http://example.org/people#bob', 'foaf:name', 'Bob');
st.add('http://example.org/people#bob', 'foaf:homepage',
       'http://old.org');
/*
 * 'set(subject, property ,value)' method overwrites
 * all old values of the property with new one.
 */
st.set('http://example.org/people#bob', 'foaf:homepage',
       'http://new.org');
```

3.2   A Search Operation

Web applications can search the stored triples with simple APIs, getProperties(subject), getValues(subject, property) and so on. If the property parameter of getValues(subject, property) is null, all values which associate with the subject are returned.

```
//returns ['http://xmlns.com/foaf/0.1/name',
//         'http://xmlns.com/foaf/0.1/homepage']
var properties = st.getProperties('http://example.org/people#bob');
//returns ['Bob']
var name = st.getValues('http://example.org/people#bob', 'foaf:name');
//returns all values ['Bob', 'http://new.org']
var values = st.getValues('http://example.org/people#bob', null);
```

4 A Web Browser Enhanced with Personal Semantic Data

We integrated *triplestoreJS* into Google Chrome as a Chrome extension to evaluate the potential to apply semantic web technology into the actual web browser experience. Especially, our challenge is to address how to utilize the personal semantic data collected during web browsing to enhance current and future user experience during browsing operations. The Chrome extension is an HTML5 application and has its own Web Storage.

4.1 Collecting Personal Knowledge Bases from the Web

Any web contents annotated with RDFa or microdata are extracted from web pages users visit and are stored into the web browser automatically via the *triplestoreJS* as shown Figure 1. An automatic save function works when one of following conditions is met:

- When a user stays at a page longer than a specific period, e.g. 5 minutes
- When a user visits a page more than a specific frequency, e.g. 5 times

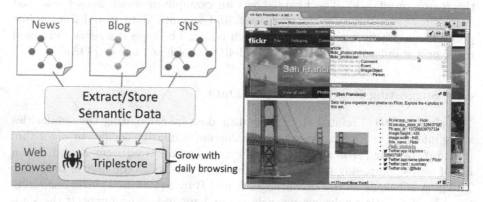

Fig. 1. Architecture for collecting personal knowledge bases

Fig. 2. Screenshot of a search function for stored semantic data

If a subject and the properties are already stored and now new additional properties of the subject are found in other web pages, the additional properties are appended to the subject. In this manner, the users' database of semantic data will grow based on their web browsing and the plug-in can provide more personalized functions with the stored personal semantic data.

Besides semantic data extraction from web pages, the plug-in supports login to Google and Facebook to gather user profile information, contact lists of friends, personal schedules and postings by the user and friends. Those user data and SNS data are converted into triples with standard vocabularies from schema.org[14] and Friend-of-a-Friend (FOAF)[15]. Therefore, after storing the user data from

---

[14] http://schema.org/
[15] http://www.foaf-project.org/

those services, the internal representations can be equally combined with general semantic data stored from web pages.

If a stored triple has an expiration date and time, it will be removed automatically from the triplestore as the browser does for cookie or cache expiration. When a user visits a web page, the plug-in monitors HTTP traffic and handles *Expires* header in HTTP response. When the semantic data is stored, the expiration information is also stored at the same time. Even if the auto-save function is always enabled by the user, this auto-remove function reduces the growth of stored semantic data in the triplestore.

The stored semantic data can be synchronized among browsers. If a user would like to copy stored favorite semantic data into another browser, the user can indicate which items she would like to synchronize. The plug-in stores the specified items into a dedicated Chrome synchronization storage and a plug-in working in another browser merges them into the local triplestore. The plug-in executes the synchronization process only when the activity on the browser is idle so as not to slow the browsing operation.

Figure 2 is a screenshot of the visualized stored semantic data. The user interface has three components: keyword search field, item type search field, and the search result field. The figure shows an example in which a user searched items whose types were '*flickr_photos:set*' and semantic data stored from online photo album Flickr is shown in the search result. The type is a service oriented name or a standardized URI or a term defined in schema.org or FOAF.

4.2   Suggesting Related Semantic Data

The plug-in detects related stored semantic data by calculating the similarities using inference processing based on the *Jaccard* similarity coefficient algorithm [13]. Suppose that A is a list of words composing a stored item X and B is a list of words composing a new item Y found in a web site the user is browsing. The plug-in calculates the similarity of A and B by equation (1) after sanitizing them by eliminating noise words such as numbers and determiners. If the similarity is above a pre-defined threshold, the plug-in recognizes the item X has a relationship with item Y. If the web site has several items of semantic data, the plug-in calculates the similarity for all combination of item X and Y. We used 0.5 as the pre-defined threshold for *Jaccard*.

$$J(A, B) = |A \cap B|/|A \cup B| \tag{1}$$

One use case for this similarity function is to make a personal online photo album by mashing up user data distributed on the web. Figure 3 represents a possible architecture for the use case. Generally the online photo album should contain some relationships with other user data. For example, if the photo was taken while traveling, then the corresponding schedule would be also registered in a calendar service. If the photo has persons, some of them may be friends who are registered in SNS services. An SNS friend may post a new message for the online album representing her impression.

In step 1 of figure 3, the plug-in collects those personal user data from the web and stores into the local triplestore. In step 2, the plug-in finds related semantic data from the personal triplestore by calculating the *Jaccard* similarities and suggests this data to mash up with the online multimedia. Then the plug-in generates an HTML fragment including the detected semantic data and inserts this fragment into the web page. Figure 4 is a screenshot of the behavior of this use case on a Google+ photo album. The plug-in suggests the related schedule item of the trip containing the date and location and creator, a comment item for the album posted by a Facebook friend, the friend's SNS profile item containing the name and account id and organization, the album item containing the title and date and number of photos. The suggestion window created by the plug-in is minimized by default and toggled with the ESC key. One common issue for photo albums is how to easily add annotations to photos because this is a tedious work and we need to consider the contents of the annotation itself. In section 4.3, we introduce an annotation function which assists users to annotate photos with the suggested semantic data.

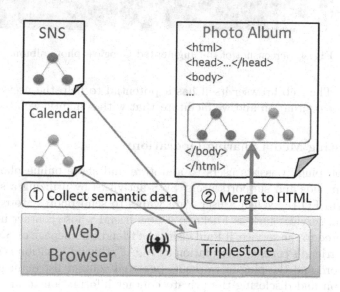

Fig. 3. Architecture of the personalized photo album

In the current architecture, to mash up user data on several services users needed to authorize those services to allow access to user data. The access to user data always raises underlying privacy issues. If some of the services don't support an authorization protocol, users can't mash up and utilize their personal web data. The challenge for mashing up personal data continues to grow as users manage data in more dedicated services and the kinds of data become diverse: from an office domain like documents and calendars and emails to a social network domain like friend networks and published postings and photos

Fig. 4. Screenshot of the augmented Google+ photo album

and videos. The web browser itself has a potential to help the users to resolve the data access situation and we facilitate that with semantic web technology.

4.3 Assisting Media Sharing Operations

Our Chrome plug-in assists users to annotate and share online photos/videos with their friends and supports users' SNS activities by utilizing a stored contact list from FOAF. When a user Paul wants to send photos stored in online photo album services such as Flickr to a new friend whose contact information isn't registered to the service, if Paul visits the friend's homepage or SNS page including the friend's contact information as FOAF, this information is stored into the triplestore and the plug-in works as personal contact list manager without depending on and disclosing the private contact information to 3rd party services. Figure 5 illustrates this architecture. In step 1, the plug-in collects FOAF data from SNS services and Blog sites and stores the data into the triplestore. In step 2, when a user indicates to the plug-in to share a specified online photo with the SNS friends, the plug-in shows the stored contact information of the SNS friends overlaid on the photo album site. If the user selects one of contacts, then the plug-in sends the photo using the specified contact information.

For example, in a personal photo album of a trip to New York City on Flickr, when a user selects a photo with right click to share with an SNS friend and select 'share' from the menu provided by the plug-in then a stored contact list is overlaid on the web site as showed in Figure 6. When the user selects one of these contacts, the plug-in asks the user to select related semantic data to annotate

Fig. 5. Architecture of the assisted media sharing

Fig. 6. Screenshot of showing a contact list

Fig. 7. Screenshot showing suggested tags for annotating a photo

Fig. 8. Screenshot showing the photo sharing with a Google+ friend

the photo to be shared. In Figure 7, a schedule name of a trip to New York stored in Google Calendar and photo album items stored in Flickr are suggested for annotating the photo. If the schedule name is selected, the user can send the photo through Google+ or Facebook or email with the annotated travel schedule as showed in Figure 8. The receiver can see the shared photo with the annotated travel schedule.

4.4   Assisting Text Input Operations

When a user is inputting a search keyword into text fields in web sites, the plug-in suggests candidates from stored semantic data. Though newer online services also suggest popular keywords or users' prior input histories, keyword suggestion provided by this plug-in is independent of any 3rd party services and derived from the users' personal semantic data collected from their web browsing and representing their interests. It is difficult for 3rd party services to collect this personalized data, however the plug-in learns them from the user's activities and we utilize this stored data for the keyword suggestion.

The keyword suggestion works in any text fields on web pages. Figure 9 shows how this works on online photo albums mashed up with personal schedules of stored semantic data. In step 1, the plug-in stores the user's personal schedules from calendar services into the triplestore. In step 2, when the user starts to input a search keyword in a search field on the online photo album, the plug-in finds items whose name are matched with the search keyword and generates an HTML fragment including the names of the matched items and appends it close to the search field the user inputs.

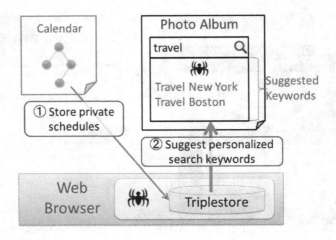

Fig. 9. Architecture of the keyword suggestion combining calendar and photo album

Figure 10 is the screenshot of the behavior on an online photo album Flickr. If a user manages his photo albums based on travel names like 'Travel New York' and starts to search with a keyword 'Travel' on a search field in Flickr, then because personal schedules from Google Calendar can be collected as semantic data by the plug-in, the corresponding matched travel names are suggested for the candidate.

The plug-in recognizes semantic tagging on HTML input fields; If a text field in a web page is annotated with an attribute *@itemtype* with microdata or *@type* with RDFa which constrains the type of semantic data, the plug-in understands the annotation and suggests only keywords whose types of semantic data are matched with the specified type. For example, if the text field is described with the following markup, only keywords which are related to information whose type is 'http://schema.org/Event' are suggested.

```
<input type="text" itemtype="http://schema.org/Event">
```

Suggested keywords

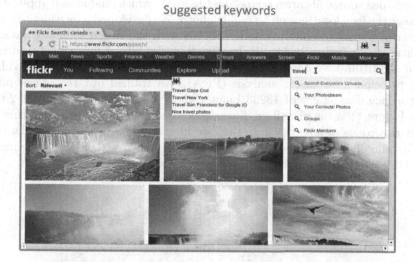

Fig. 10. Screenshot of the search keyword suggestion on Flickr

It is difficult for a general web service to suggest such keywords which are derived from other web services because the service needs to support at least one authorization protocol to get permission to access user data and collect user interests and preferences from other web services beforehand. Our plug-in architecture allows the web browser to securely collect user interests from web browsing without changing services, therefore this keyword suggestion can be realized and works on any web pages.

4.5 Annotating Online Photos

Major online photo album services provide face annotation functionality which shows the name of the identified person if his or her name and face image are registeredin the services beforehand. Some online photo album services support online machine learning which enables users to register new face images on their online photos and learn with the new faces and improve the accuracy of the face annotation.

Our plug-in supports a face annotation function which works on any online photo with the stored personal semantic data without disclosing the user's private information to the photo album services. The plug-in collects profile information of friends and family from any web pages distributing FOAF data and from SNS services like Google+ and Facebook through a login functionality the plug-in provides. If a user visits a blog site managed by a friend distributing FOAF data, the plug-in can easily collect profile data when visiting the blog. After storing FOAF data, the plug-in annotates online photos with the stored FOAF data using face identification processing we developed. For face detection, we used open source libraries *ccv.js*[16] and *face.js*[17] which enable web applications to detect the face locations on an online photo. We developed a face identification JavaScript library to annotate online photos with the stored semantic data.

Matthew A. Turk and Alex P. Pentland[14] describe a fundamental identification algorithm by comparing characteristics of the face to known individuals using principal component analysis (PCA). We trained our recognizer offline using a face database[18] of 13233 images and created a training result *Eigenfaces*. Figure 11 is the visualized *Eigenfaces* we acquired. We serialized this into JavaScript codes to integrate into the face identification processing of the plug-in. The plug-in compares each face of an online photo with SNS profile images from the stored semantic data using the serialized *Eigenfaces*.

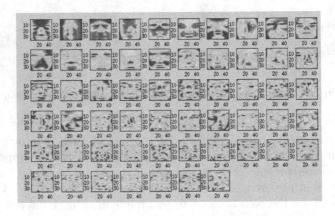

Fig. 11. Screenshot of visualized *Eigenfaces* trained with 13233 face images

Figure 12 is a screenshot of the face annotation functionality on an online photo. The gray rectangle represents the detected face location obtained from *face.js*. If a user moves a mouse pointer to one of the gray rectangles, then the corresponding FOAF data collected from the web is overlaid on the photo. In figure 12, a Google+ account is suggested for the selected SNS friend and the user can share the online photo with the friend through Google+. Without depending on the functionality of 3rd party online services and disclosing our SNS friends' information to them, the face annotation can be realized with stored personal semantic data within client side scripts in real-time.

5   Evaluation

We measured the processing performance of the client side triplestore library used by the plug-in. For performance measurement we used semantic data col-

---

[16] http://libccv.org/
[17] https://github.com/wesbos/HTML5-Face-Detection
[18] http://vis-www.cs.umass.edu/lfw/

Fig. 12. Screenshot of face annotation with stored FOAF data

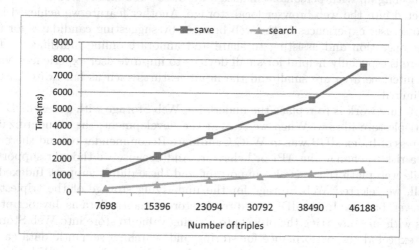

Fig. 13. The result of performance measurement based on the number of triples

lected from Google+ and Facebook and web sites including RDFa or microdata. The average number of properties per item was 9.5.

For the 'save' operation, we measured the performance by saving triples, a subject and properties and corresponding values into the triplestore. For the 'search' operation, we measured the performance by searching all values of specified subjects and properties. The searched data is the data stored by 'save' operation. Graph 13 shows the measured performance based on the number of triples. The horizontal axis is the number of triples and the vertical axis is the total time to complete each operation. For example, in case of 7698 triples, the average time to save was 1125 milliseconds, and the average time to search was 245 milliseconds. As we can see from the graph 13, the performance is linear with the number of triples. We think the core operations 'save' and 'search' using semantic data collected from actual web services meet sufficient performance for web applications to work on a general HTML5 platform.

6   Conclusion and Future Work

In this paper we introduced a client side triplestore library *triplestoreJS* for the HTML5 platform and a web browser personalization technology working with this library. Where existing examples of semantic web development were mainly server side applications and used for background development tools, general users didn't directly see benefits in daily web browsing. The motivation for general web developers to integrate semantic data into their web sites was to expect higher ranking on search results. We directly enhance user experience in the web browser by utilizing personal semantic data collected during prior browsing activity.

One of the features we achieved is to make online services more informative by mashing up with personal semantic data discovered on the web and securely collected into the web browser local storage. Another feature we achieved is to enhance user experiences in the web browser by suggesting candidates for text input operation and assisting to share and annotate online multimedia. This feature is especially helpful for small devices to improve user experiences whose user interface area are small and the input features such as hardware buttons are limited.

A future work is to replace the underlying Web Storage with IndexedDB[19] in the triplestore library. When we started the development, the standardization progress of IndexedDB was in W3C Candidate Recommendation and there was still a risk to change the API or behavior. And because we thought supporting mobile web platforms was also important and these didn't support IndexedDB at all, we selected Web Storage for the underlying storage of the triplestore. However, because IndexedDB can directly store semantic data as JavaScript objects without converting the objects to a string value to store into Web Storage, it is expected the performance for storing and searching semantic data can be improved. A performance comparison of the triplestore between Web Storage and IndexedDB will be also addressed.

We hope the work introduced in this paper will inspire new applications of semantic web technologies in HTML5 and will expand the use cases and be a promising bridge between them.

References

1. Pimentel, V., Nickerson, B.G.: Communicating and Displaying Real-Time Data with WebSocket. Internet Computing 16, 45–53 (2012)
2. Cardaci, A., Caviglione, L., Gotta, A., Tonellotto, N.: Performance Evaluation of SPDY over High Latency Satellite Channels. In: Dhaou, R., Beylot, A.-L., Montpetit, M.-J., Lucani, D., Mucchi, L. (eds.) PSATS. LNICST, vol. 123, pp. 123–134. Springer, Heidelberg (2013)

---

[19] http://www.w3.org/TR/IndexedDB/

3. Singh, V., Lozano, A.A., Ott, J.: Performance Analysis of Receive-Side Real-Time Congestion Control for WebRTC. In: Proc. of IEEE Packet Video, vol. 2013 (2013)

4. West, W., Pulimood, S.M.: Analysis of privacy and security in HTML5 web storage. Journal of Computing Sciences in Colleges 27, 80–87 (2012)

5. Broekstra, J., Kampman, A., van Harmelen, F.: Sesame: A generic architecture for storing and querying rdf and rdf schema. In: Horrocks, I., Hendler, J. (eds.) ISWC 2002. LNCS, vol. 2342, pp. 54–68. Springer, Heidelberg (2002)

6. Quilitz, B., Leser, U.: Querying distributed RDF data sources with SPARQL. In: Bechhofer, S., Hauswirth, M., Hoffmann, J., Koubarakis, M. (eds.) ESWC 2008. LNCS, vol. 5021, pp. 524–538. Springer, Heidelberg (2008)

7. Dietzold, S., Hellmann, S., Peklo, M.: Using javascript rdfa widgets for model/view separation inside read/write websites. In: Proceedings of the 4th Workshop on Scripting for the Semantic Web (2008)

8. Heinrich, M., Gaedke, M.: WebSoDa: a tailored data binding framework for web programmers leveraging the WebSocket protocol and HTML5 Microdata. In: Auer, S., Díaz, O., Papadopoulos, G.A. (eds.) ICWE 2011. LNCS, vol. 6757, pp. 387–390. Springer, Heidelberg (2011)

9. Berners-Lee, T., Chen, Y., Chilton, L., Connolly, D., Dhanaraj, R., Hollenbach, J., Sheets, D.: Tabulator: Exploring and analyzing linked data on the semantic web. In: Proceedings of the 3rd International Semantic Web User Interaction Workshop, vol. 2006 (2006)

10. Huynh, D.F., Mazzocchi, S., Karger, D.R.: Piggy bank: Experience the semantic web inside your web browser. In: Gil, Y., Motta, E., Benjamins, V.R., Musen, M.A. (eds.) ISWC 2005. LNCS, vol. 3729, pp. 413–430. Springer, Heidelberg (2005)

11. Cai, M., Frank, M.: RDFPeers: a scalable distributed RDF repository based on a structured peer-to-peer network. In: Proceedings of the 13th International Conference on World Wide Web, pp. 650–657. ACM (2004)

12. Buraga, S.C., Panu, A.: A Web Tool for Extracting and Viewing the Semantic Markups. In: Wang, M. (ed.) KSEM 2013. LNCS (LNAI), vol. 8041, pp. 570–579. Springer, Heidelberg (2013)

13. McAuley, J.: Machine grouping for efficient production. Production Engineer 51, 53–57 (1972)

14. Turk, M., Pentland, A.: Eigenfaces for recognition. Journal of Cognitive Neuroscience 3(1), 71–86 (1991)

CrowdTruth: Machine-Human Computation Framework for Harnessing Disagreement in Gathering Annotated Data

Oana Inel[1,3], Khalid Khamkham[1,3], Tatiana Cristea[1,3], Anca Dumitrache[1,3],
Arne Rutjes[2], Jelle van der Ploeg[2], Lukasz Romaszko[1,3], Lora Aroyo[1],
and Robert-Jan Sips[3]

[1] VU University Amsterdam
k.khamkham@gmail.com, {anca.dumitrache,oana.inel,lora.aroyo}@vu.nl,
tatiana.cristea@student.vu.nl, lukasz.romaszko@gmail.com
[2] IBM Services Center Benelux, The Netherlands
arne.rutjesISC@nl.ibm.com, j.van.der.ploegISC@nl.ibm.com
[3] CAS Benelux, IBM Netherlands
Robert-Jan.Sips@nl.ibm.com

Abstract. In this paper we introduce the *CrowdTruth* open-source software framework for machine-human computation, that implements a novel approach to gathering human annotation data for a variety of media (e.g. text, image, video). The CrowdTruth approach embodied in the software captures human semantics through a pipeline of four processes: *a*) combining various machine processing of media in order to better understand the input content and optimize its suitability for micro-tasks, thus optimize the time and cost of the crowdsourcing process; *b*) providing reusable human-computing task templates to collect the maximum diversity in the human interpretation, thus collect richer human semantics; *c*) implementing 'disagreement metrics', i.e. *CrowdTruth metrics*, to support deep analysis of the quality and semantics of the crowdsourcing data; and *d*) providing an interface to support data and results visualization. Instead of the traditional inter-annotator agreement, we use their disagreement as a useful signal to evaluate the data quality, ambiguity and vagueness. We demonstrate the applicability and robustness of this approach to a variety of problems across multiple domains. Moreover, we show the advantages of using open standards and the extensibility of the framework with new data modalities and annotation tasks.

Keywords: crowdsourcing, gold standard data, machine-human computation, data analysis, experiment replication, information extraction.

1 Introduction

The unprecedented amount of information available on the Web in terms of text, images and videos opens incredible opportunities and challenges for machines to interpret such data adequately. Machines are typically good in handling massive

P. Mika et al. (Eds.) ISWC 2014, Part II, LNCS 8797, pp. 486–504, 2014.

scale, e.g. indexing huge amounts of data and humans in interpreting text, images and audio-visual content. Automated approaches for semantic interpretation are typically founded on a very simple notion of truth, while in reality the principled approach is that truth is not universal and is strongly influenced by human perspectives and the quality of the sources.

The Semantic Web had already made a huge leap by adding both diversity and machine-readable semantics of data on the Web. However, the scale of the Web provides unlimited amounts of new perspectives and interpretation contexts. Using crowdsourcing platforms such as CrowdFlower[1] or Amazon Mechanical Turk[2] (MTurk) for gathering human interpretation on data has become now a mainstream process. In the NLP field [1], crowdsourcing has been used for nearly a decade, as the low level language understanding tasks map well into micro-tasks. In the AI field [2], this has become a scalable way to gather a cheaper annotated data for gold standards that is used to train and evaluate machine learning systems. However, as we have observed previously [3], the introduction of crowdsourcing has not fundamentally changed the way gold standards are created: humans are still asked to provide a semantic interpretation of some data, with the explicit assumption that there is *one correct interpretation*. Thus, the diversity of interpretation and perspectives is still not taken in consideration.

In previous work, we have introduced the *CrowdTruth methodology, a novel approach for gathering annotated data from the crowd.* Inspired by the simple intuition that human interpretation is subjective [4], and by the observation that disagreement is a natural product of having multiple people performing annotation tasks, this methodology can provide useful insights about the task, a particular annotation, or a worker. We proposed rejecting the traditional notion of ground truth in gold standard annotation, in which annotation tasks are viewed as having a single correct answer, and adopting instead a disagreement-based crowd truth [5]. In [4, 6–8] we have validated *CrowdTruth* in the context of measuring the quality of workers, annotation units, and tasks. We showed experimental evidence that these measures are inter-dependent, and that existing crowdsourcing approaches that measure only worker quality are missing important information, as not all the annotated units are created equal.

This paper presents the open-source *CrowdTruth software framework* that implements the CrowdTruth methodology in a machine-human computing workflow for collecting, processing and evaluating crowdsourcing data. In this workflow, the capacities of both humans and machines are optimally combined for the output of high quality gold standard for machines to learn from. Such framework can be helpful to the Semantic Web community considering the growing number of crowdsourcing applications in this field, as well as the growing need for gold standard training and evaluation data. Significant benefits brought up by the CrowdTruth framework over the current state-of-the-art crowdsourcing frameworks such as CrowdLang [9] and Jabberwocky [10] are the deeper analysis of the annotated data and the data visualization tools. In contrast to

---

[1] https://crowdflower.com/

[2] https://www.mturk.com/mturk/

GATECrowd [11], the presented framework has the advantage of manipulating a variety of input media types. Moreover, the added value of the framework is increased due to the PROV[12] model integration. Thus, its generic and domain-agnostic features are essential inside CrowdTruth, as they offer a straightforward solution to (1) visualize the entire process cycle of a media unit, (2) assess the clarity of a media unit as well as (3) replicate the same process for different other media units. The open source CrowdTruth framework is available for download at `https://github.com/laroyo/CrowdTruth`, the service at `http://crowdtruth.org` and documentation as `http://crowdtruth.org/info`.

2   CrowdTruth Use Cases

Before diving into the CrowdTruth framework and its components in Section 5, we introduce the use cases in the context of which the system has been developed and tested. To ensure data diversity, each use case introduces either a new domain, content modality or a new annotation task. All the data and the experiments can be viewed in *CrowdTruth* through the *Media* section. New content can be inserted for immediate execution of new experiments through the *Upload Media* option, as described in Section 4. Below we describe the four use cases:

- IBM Watson *medical text* annotation for *factor span extraction* (FactSpan) and *relation extraction* (RelEx)
- IBM Watson *newspapers text* annotation for *event extraction* (MRP-Events)
- Sound & Vision *video* annotation for *event extraction* (NISV-Events)
- Rijksmuseum *image* annotation for *flower names extraction* (Rijks-Flowers)

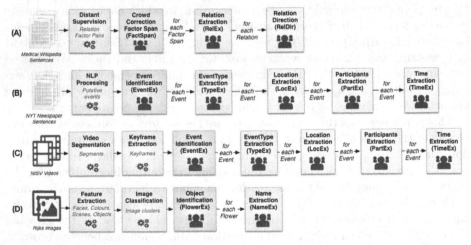

Fig. 1. CrowdTruth Annotation Workflows for Text, Images and Videos

The main experiments initiating the implementation of this framework were focussed on providing gold standard to the IBM Watson system for relation and factor extraction in medical texts. Thus, the best illustration on how the CrowdTruth Framework works can be currently observed in the *RelEx* and

FactSpan use cases. For this, we have defined (as depicted in Fig. 1) workflow A, where medical sentences are shown to the crowd for annotation in three micro-tasks. In the context of the MRP project at IBM, we have also experimented with newspaper text and annotations for event and named entities extraction (workflow B). Workflows C and D, show the annotation tasks on Rijksmuseum Amsterdam images and Sound & Vision videos we have performed within the context of two research projects. In the following section, Section 3, we provide a detailed description of the annotation tasks for all use cases.

3   CrowdTruth Annotation Tasks

The CrowdTruth use cases introduce about 14 distinct annotation templates across three content modalities (text, image, video) and three domains (medical, news, culture). Each of those templates has also a number of variations, depending on the target result quality. Ultimately, CrowdTruth framework is aimed to provide its template collection as a continuously extendible *library of annotation task templates*, which can be reused and adapted for new data and use cases. The implementation of CrowdTruth does not pose restrictions for the creation of new templates. To see more detailed description for all tasks and their templates, visit this page: http://crowdtruth.org/templates/examples. The templates themselves are accessible through the *Jobs* section in *CrowdTruth*, by selecting the *Create New Job* option. Depending on the type of content chosen, only the applicable sub-set of templates will be presented.

3.1   Medical Text Annotation: IBM Watson Medical Use Cases

– **FactSpan: Factor Span Correction.** The crowd is given a *sentence* with two highlighted *factors* (either a word or a word phrase). For each factor, the crowd is asked to determine whether it is complete. If it is not, the workers highlight the words in the sentence that would complete the factor.
– **RelEx: Relation Identification.** The crowd is given a *sentence* with two highlighted *factors* and a set of 12 target *relation types*. The crowd is asked to select all the relations expressed in the sentence between the given factors.
– **RelDir: Relation Direction Identification.** The crowd is given the output of *RelEx* - a *sentence*, two highlighted *factors*, and a *relation* between the factors - and are asked to choose the direction of the relation. Since this is an easy task, we use golden units (instances with known answers - e.g. "*Aspirin* treats *headaches*") to decrease the spam rate. The advantage of this method is that CrowdFlower immediately rejects untrustworthy workers.
– **RelExDir: Relation & Direction Identification.** The crowd is given the combined task of relation and direction identification on the *FactSpan* output. As with *RelEx*, the crowd is shown a *sentences* with two highlighted *factors* and is asked to check all the relations that apply between them. The relations set contains the initial 12 relations and their inverses (23 in total).

3.2   Newspaper Text Annotation: IBM Watson MRP Use Case

- **EventEx: Event and Event Type Identification.** The crowd is given a *sentence* with a highlighted *putative event* (word phrase that could potentially express an event, i.e. verbs or nominalized verbs) and is asked whether it refers to an event. For each event the crowd is asked to choose the event type expressed in the sentence from an *EventType* taxonomy (see Table 1).
- **LocEx, TimeEx, PartEx: Event Location, Participants & Time Identification.** The crowd is given a *sentence* with a highlighted *event* from the *EventEx* output, and is asked (1) to indicate whether the sentence contains *location*, *time* or *participant* for this *event*, (2) to highlight the words in text that refer to those and (3) to select their types (see Table 1).

Table 1. Event Role Fillers Taxonomies

Role Filler	Taxonomy
Event	Purpose, Arriving or Departing, Motion, Communication, Usage, Judgment, Leadership, Success or Failure, Sending or Receiving, Action, Attack, Political
Location	Geographical (Continent, Country, City); Land Area (Island, Mountain, Beach); Water Area (Ocean, River, Lake, Sea); Road/Railroad (Road, Street, Railroad); Building (Educational, Government, Residence, Commercial, Industrial, Military, Religious)
Period	Before, During, After, Repetitive, Timestamp, Date, Year, Week, Day, Part of Day
Participant	Person, Organization, Geographical Region, Nation, Object

3.3   Image Annotation: Rijksmuseum Amsterdam Use Case

- **FlowerEx: Depicted Flower Identification with Bounding Box.** In the pre-processing we identify the images with the highest chance of depicting flowers. We ask the crowd to identify all the flowers in them (by surrounding each flower with a box), and to fill in their names, the total number of flowers and the number of different flower types depicted.

3.4   Video Annotation: Sound and Vision Use Case

- **DescEventEx: Event Identification in Video Description.** The named entities are extracted during pre-processing form the video description text. The crowd is asked to confirm or reject any machine annotations on this text, and highlight all the events and their role fillers.
- **VidEventEx: Event Identification in Video.** The crowd is given a video or a video segment and is asked to annotate events that are *depicted* (literally mentioned) or *associated* (related to some spoken events/role fillers).

4   CrowdTruth Data Model

Essential to maintaining all the data resulting from the annotation tasks in Section 2 is the definition of a data model, which complies with three main requirements: (1) to be abstract enough to store different content modalities, i.e. text, images, videos, (2) to be specific enough, i.e. semi-structured, to still be able to query the data, and (3) to capture the provenance of the data. The MongoDB[3]

---

[3] http://www.mongodb.org/

document-oriented NoSQL database does not rely on predefined schemas, rather the structure of the data stored can be defined dynamically at any point in time. Such flexibility is a key requirement because when collecting crowdsourcing data, we often do not know upfront the appropriate structure. An example of this are the various online content processing APIs that return results in a JSON format but with different structures. MongoDB allows us to store any of these JSON results in documents without any conversion because of its BSON storage design. However, storing data without defining structure makes it difficult to query. Thus, we defined a data model that is abstract enough to be able to store any type of data, yet specific enough to be able to query this data (Figure 2).

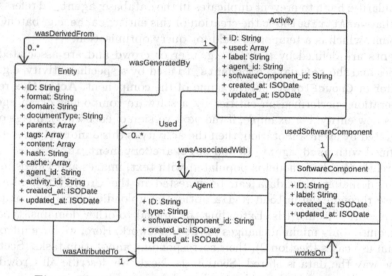

Fig. 2. The CrowdTruth Data Model and Data Provenance

The CrowdTruth MongoDB deployment hosts one database, with four collections **Entities**, **Activities**, **Agents** and **SoftwareComponents**. For every collection we define **Models** in the framework which map to their respective collections. The models are used by the Moloquent Object Document Mapper, which allows easy creation, reading, update and deletion of data. The four collections are connected with the core provenance relations as defined by W3C PROV. Each collection is defined by **created_at** and **updated_at** timestamps.

In PROV entities are described with their provenance, that might refer to other entities (i.e. an image is an entity whose provenance refers to other entities such as an annotation on the image, the software component or the agent that created the annotation). Entities can have different attributes and can be described from different perspectives, e.g. a text unit, the same unit after annotation and the aggregation of all annotations on this unit are three distinct entities for which we save provenance. The advantage of using the PROV model inside the CrowdTruth data model is the ability to capture each of the stages performed by the framework (i.e. data pre-processing, gathering human and machine annotations, analyzing the results). Moreover, by capturing all those stages it helps to evaluate the improvement of final results over partial results.

In CrowdTruth **Entities** represent data units and are defined by `format`, e.g. text, image, video with possibility to add other modalities; `domain`, e.g. medical, news, art, also extensible with additional domains; `documentType`, e.g. IBM-medical-sentence, NYT-news-article, Rijks-image; `parents` refers to the parent identifiers to capture the provenance of each data unit, e.g. `wasDerivedFrom` relation and parents are typically generated upon creation of an entity by an activity; `content`, which contains the JSON structure specific to that documentType; `tags`, e.g. unit, segment, frame, which typically can indicate an aggregation level or granularity; `hash` to prevent duplicates in the database; `agent_id` refers to the agent that `wasAttributedTo` the creation of this entity; `cache`, e.g. batchCount, jobsCount, which is a temporary field for query optimisation.

Agents are defined by a `type`, e.g. user or crowd and are associated with activities and the `softwareComponents_id` used by a specific activity, e.g. `File Uploader` or `CrowdFlower`, i.e. the name of the component. **Activities** refer to the operations performed on entities by a software component or an agent to create a new entity. For example, if the next version of each video, image or text is generated by event annotation, then the activity is this `annotation`. Activities are defined with `used`, `agent_id` and `softwareComponent_id`.

Currently the data model is populated with text, images and videos in three different domains. New data can be ingested in the CrowdTruth MongoDB database through the `Upload Media` option by uploading local files or pulling online resources from APIs. Extending the upload to other domains, types and APIs requires only minimal changes to the framework. Here, we have introduced the main use cases (Section 2), their corresponding annotation tasks (Section 3) and the way the data is stored (Section 4). Next, we describe all CrowdTruth components involved in the end-to-end workflow.

5   The CrowdTruth Framework

The *CrowdTruth* software framework integrates a set of open source components providing an end-to-end workflow for collaborative machine-human computing for annotation of different data modalities (e.g. text, videos, images). To ensure extensibility and openness the framework is implemented using open web standards. It is built on top of an open source PHP framework *Laravel*[4], which uses the MVC pattern to decouple application logic, data and presentation. It leverages built-in packages for authentication, routing, creation of templates and APIs. External packages are used to extend the framework, e.g we use an Object Document Mapper *Moloquent* to query any MongoDB storage. We also developed open source SDKs for CrowdFlower and MTurk to optimise the communication with those platforms. Data ingested and produced through the framework can be exported in different formats. For more details see the documentation[5].

---

[4] http://laravel.com/

[5] http://crowdtruth.org/info

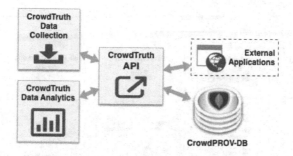

Fig. 3. The CrowdTruth Main Components and Open API

Fig. 3 illustrates the framework components. It provides *CrowdTruthPROV-DB*, a provenance-preserving storage of crowdsourcing data, *CrowdTruth Data Collection* services for job configuration, creation and results retrieval, including a library of reusable and extensible micro-task templates, and *CrowdTruth Analytics*, a set of data visualisation and analysis tools. The *CrowdTruth API*[6], is an open API for external applications to query the data in the framework or to ingest their own data. Such an API allows for community building in terms of sharing data, analysis metrics, crowdsourcing templates and optimised job settings. Many of the crowdsourcing templates take a long time to determine their most effective form, thus sharing previous experiences is extremely valuable. Figure 4 provides an overview of the overall framework workflow:

- After input data ingestion, specific *Data Pre-processing* is typically applied to filter out and specify the appropriate input to reach an optimal crowdsourcing task. For examples, the sentence word count property allows for filtering of sentences between a specific word count range.
- The *Job Configuration* component takes the aforementioned filtered input in the form of a batch, and creates a job with specific job settings such as: the crowdsourcing template that is to be used, payment options, and the running platform for the job.
- The *Data Collection* component provides an almost live update of the crowdsourcing results from the annotation platforms, as these results are pushed from CrowdFlower and polled at regular intervals from MTurk. The results are stored in the database along with their provenance.
- *Post-processing* allows for deep analysis of the quality of the crowdsourcing results on three levels: Worker, Annotation and Unit. The *CrowdTruth Metrics* are able to identify the low quality workers, the suitability of a unit for a task and the clarity of the annotations.
- The *Data Analytics* component provides visualizations tailored for use with the CrowdTruth metrics. As such, it provides functionalities for evaluating results through graphical views at both individual and aggregated levels.

The following sub-sections describe each component in more detail.

---

[6] http://crowdtruth.org/api/examples

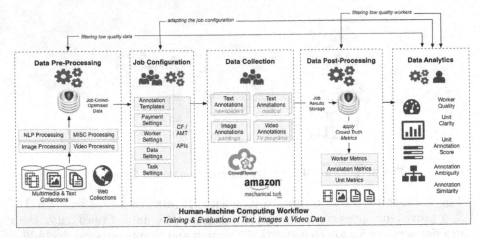

Fig. 4. CrowdTruth Overall Architecture

5.1 Data Pre-processing Components

The pre-processing components allow for various processing of the input data to optimize its use in specific crowdsourcing tasks. Before running a *flower name annotation task* we pre-process images to know which ones have high probability of depicting a flower and we send only those for crowd annotations. This saves both cost and time and makes the micro-task more engaging for the workers. Figure 5 depicts the three **pre-processing workflows** for all content modalities. The left side (A) of the figure shows the workflow for **video and image pre-processing** and the right side (B) shows the workflow for **text pre-processing**. They all share the same MongoDB storage (depicted in the centre of the figure). The video pre-processing makes also use of a physical storage. Following, we provide details on the three pre-processing workflows in this figure.

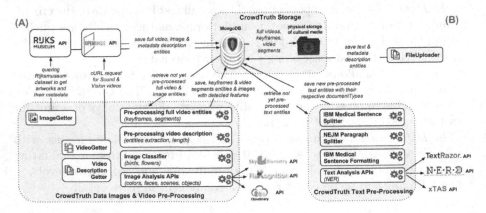

Fig. 5. CrowdTruth Pre-processing Workflows for Text, Images and Videos

To **ingest images in CrowdTruth framework** we use `ImageGetter`, which calls the open API of the Rijksmuseum Amsterdam[7] by querying, e.g. for a number of paintings or drawings described with a specific keyword, like 'birds'. It is straightforward to extend it with additional APIs of other online collections. The **Image pre-processing** is performed by three external APIs - Rekognition[8], Cloudinary[9], Skybiometry[10], and a local classifier. Each of them contributes complimentary and redundant annotations with their corresponding confidences, e.g. Rekognition provides depicted objects, faces; Cloudinary detects faces, colour histogram, while Skybiometry detects faces with their position and gender. The local classifier is trained for flowers and birds. The pre-processing is finalised by storing the image URLs and metadata in the MongoDB database as parent entities together with separate children. The children entities contain information about the software agent used and its configuration, as well as the features received by calling the aforementioned APIs and the classifier.

To **ingest videos in CrowdTruth framework** we use OpenImages[11] API by querying for videos from the collection of the Netherlands Institute for Sound and Vision. Figure 5 on the left (A) depicts the workflow for *video pre-processing*. After returning the requested number of videos from OpenImages, we create an entity for each item, containing all the metadata features. The item is linked through the provenance model to an activity `OpenImagesGetter` and an agent, e.g. CrowdTruth user. Next, each video is downloaded and saved in the public storage of the framework together with its description as Metadata Description entity. For maintaining the provenance consistency, the Metadata Description entities are linked to an activity `VideoDescriptionGetter`, an user_id and the full video as the parent entity.

To optimise the crowd annotations, videos need to be pre-processed to a length reasonable for a micro-task, e.g. up to a minute. Thus, we perform video segmentation. Similarly as with the images, we would like to have some indication of the featured topics and objects in each video. For this we extract keyframes, which are processed as images to detect the depicted objects. Both pre-processing are implemented using the open source FFmpeg[12] framework. Additionally, to detect main concepts we process the video description and transcript and extract the named entities. The new entities get stored in the database with their particular activity, user and parent entity.

We **ingest text in CrowdTruth framework** using a local component `FileUploader`, as we are provided with large amounts of IBM Watson medical data to experiment with. The text pre-processing is depicted in the right part (B) of Figure 5. Text annotation tasks typically require specific formatting of the text in order to anchor the human annotation around specific word(s) or phrase(s). Similarly as with the videos, the text needs to be fitted to a length

---

[7] http://www.rijksmuseum.nl/api
[8] http://rekognition.com/
[9] http://cloudinary.com/
[10] http://www.skybiometry.com/
[11] http://www.openbeelden.nl/api/
[12] http://www.ffmpeg.org/

suitable for a micro-task, e.g. sentences or short paragraphs. Additional filters to maximise the quality of the sentences have also been implemented, e.g. detection of UMLS[13] medical relations, semicolon or comma-separated list in sentences. For detailed examples of those **special filters** consult the dedicated document section `http://crowdtruth.org/info/special_filters`.

Additionally, for the *Event extraction from newspapers* task, we have ingested a set of NYTimes article URLs and extracted the date when the article was published and its content. Pre-processing activities for these texts are (1) sentence splitting, (2) length-based selection on the sentences for removing too short sentences which are meaningless, (3) putative events extraction using the Stanford Parser[14] (mainly for verbs) and NomLex, a dictionary for nominalizations. Next, (4) the putative event is marked in the sentence with capital letters and surrounded by square brackets; and (5), for each event or event role filler (participants, location, time) we align their types to a set of predefined (existing but simplified) ontologies (Table 1).

5.2 Job Configuration and Data Collection Components

The Job Configuration component provides functionality for (1) creation of batches of media units to be used in a job, (2) job template configuration and (3) job settings (Fig. 6). Each job can be duplicated or adapted for different data, settings and template which is saved in a JSON format and further translated to the dedicated crowdsourcing platform format. The platform components are written in the form of Laravel packages. In the documentation there is information on how to write your own package, by extending an abstract class, calling your API and adhering to our data model standard. After configuring the job's title, reward and other settings, the user creates the job. The request is routed through the respective package, where any necessary conversion is done, to the platforms' API. If this succeeds, one job per platform is stored in our database.

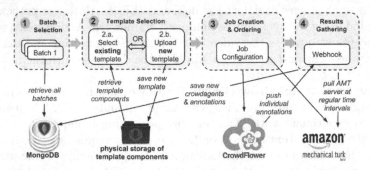

Fig. 6. CrowdTruth Job Configuration and Data Collection Workflow

The **Collection of Annotated Data** in CrowdTruth is a workflow of four main steps as depicted in Figure 6. It starts with the steps described for the

---

[13] `https://uts.nlm.nih.gov/home.html`
[14] `http://nlp.stanford.edu/software/lex-parser.shtml`

Job Configuration component: batch creation, template selection and job creation and ordering. Finally, in the *Results Gathering* phase the crowdsourcing results from both CrowdFlower (webhook call when a new judgement is received) and MTurk (poll the mTurk server at regular intervals to check for new judgements) are pulled into CrowdTruth framework. Results are saved in the MongoDB database in the PROV model, along with each additional information provided by the platforms.

5.3 Data Post-Processing and Data Analytics Components

Data visualization plays a central role in the CrowdTruth framework. It provides tools for deep analysis of crowd data based on the core notion of CrowdTruth, to harness disagreement. Ultimately, it should implement the instantiation of the triangle of reference [3] for the range of tasks supported in the framework. The *Data Analytics* component is developed using the Highcharts JS library and interacts with the CrowdTruth API. In the backend the requests are processed into optimized aggregated queries for the MongoDB database. Thus, the data is protected and the process is optimized by efficiently querying the DB and partially executing in the backend the necessary computations. On one hand the interface is more responsive, increasing the framework usability. On the other hand, the visual components are synchronized and communicate between themselves, e.g. general and specific information views, as well as their table views.

The visual components depict the three main sections of the framework: media, workers and jobs. The views facilitate the visualization and analysis of imported and generated data by the framework (media, workers, jobs). The visualization of new data is possible as long as it conforms to the defined data model. All the charts are created through a facade object which specifies the settings of the graphs. Thus, the charts are easily adaptable by changing the settings of the objects to be created. Beside the barchart views, which are specific to each section, all the other components of the views share the same implementation making the framework robust to changes and easily extensible.

The core of the CrowdTruth framework are the disagreement metrics [6, 5] that evaluate evaluate the crowdsourced data in a variety of annotation settings, such as event extraction, video and image annotation, medical relation and factor extraction. These metrics are implemented in Python and similarly to the visualization component use the API to get the data from the server. The basic assumption of the framework and metrics is that each individual unit that can be interpreted (e.g. sentence, image, video) is annotated by multiple workers, and their annotations are aggregated together and used in the following ways:

Annotation Vector: The most important step in adapting the CrowdTruth metrics to a new task is designing the annotation vector so that the results can be compared using cosine similarity. For each worker i submitting their solution to a micro-task on a MediaUnit u, the vector $W_{u,i}$ records their answers. If the worker selects an answer, its corresponding component would be marked with '1', and '0' otherwise. The size of the vector depends on the number of possible answers per task. The output for open-ended tasks (e.g. FactSpan) was inter-

Table 2. Annotation vectors for the various crowdsourcing tasks

Task	Annotation vector
FactSpan	9-component vector: 3-words-left-of-factor, 2-words-left-of-factor, 1-words-left-of-factor, factor, 1-words-right-of-factor, 2-words-right-of-factor, 3-words-right-of-factor, OTHER, Answer-Validation
RelEx	16-component vector: 12 components - each corresponding to a relation including NONE and OTHER, and Answer-Validation-NONE, Answer-Validation-OTHER
RelDir	3-component vector: each possible direction of a relation and no relation
RelExDir	23-component vector: each relation with its inverse (if it exists)
EventEx	14-component vector: each event type, OTHER and NONE
PartEx, LocEx, TimeEx	the size of the vector corresponds to the number of defined types for Location, Time, Participants + OTHER and NONE
Passage filtering	2 annotation vectors: one to account for disjoint passage-answer pairs, and one for multiple-choice justifications
Passage alignment	fixed-size vectors for each question-passage pair, with a component for each type of relation that can exist between the terms

preted to fit into a fixed-size vector, for the purpose of reusing the disagreement metrics. An explanation of how the Annotation vectors were adapted for various crowdsourcing tasks is available in Table 2.

MediaUnit Vector: This vector accounts for all worker submissions on a unit, for a given task. For every unit u, we compute the MediaUnit vector $V_u = \sum_i W_{u,i}$ by adding up the annotation vectors for all workers on the given task. Along with the Annotation vector, this is used as a core component for analysing disagreement in the crowd.

The crowdsourcing system contains 3 components: the Worker, the Unit, and the Annotation. Ambiguity can occur as part of each of these components (e.g. a spammer can generate disagreement for the Worker component) or can propagate inside the system (e.g. an unclear Unit can generate disagreement among workers). Therefore, we analyse how ambiguity and disagreement occur for each system component using the Annotation and MediaUnit vectors and a set of specialized metrics for Worker, Annotation and Unit. We use the cosine similarity coefficient as the basis of most of these metrics, in order to determine the similarity of vectors. In the following section, we show both their definition and examples of visualisation in the CrowdTruth Analytics (see Fig. 7, 9, 10).

5.4   Worker Metrics

These metrics are used to measure disagreement at the level of the worker, in order to differentiate between spammers and high quality contributors.

Worker-unit disagreement measures the cosine distance between a worker's Annotation vector and the MediaUnit vector (subtracting the worker vector), for each Worker-Unit pair. The average of this metric across all units in a set gives a measure of how much a worker disagrees with the crowd on a per-unit basis. Consistent low unit disagreement scores can indicate a low quality worker.

Worker-worker disagreement is equal to $1 - avg(\kappa)$ for a particular worker. Since κ is a pairwise metric, for each worker we average the κ scores between that worker and all the others. Similarly to the previous metric, the worker-worker disagreement metric measures how close a worker performs to the group of workers solving the same tasks. sagreement with the majority of workers is an indicator of low quality work.

Average annotations per unit is measured for each worker as the number of annotations they choose per unit averaged over all the units they annotate. Since in many tasks workers are allowed to choose "all annotations that apply", a low quality worker can appear to agree more with the crowd by repeatedly choosing multiple annotations, thus increasing the chance of overlap. A high score here can indicate low quality workers. All three metrics are used to determine worker quality in the pie chart on the left in Fig. 7.

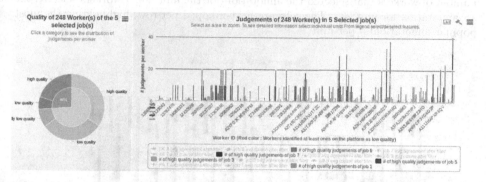

Fig. 7. Screenshot of CrowdTruth Analytics for Worker Quality and Annotations (jobs comparison); more details can be obtained by clicking on a worker (bar chart), or a type of worker (pie chart)

5.5   Unit Metrics

These metrics are used to determine the clarity of the input unit that is given to the crowd. An ambiguous unit (e.g. a sentence that is difficult to read) could generate disagreement, therefore tampering with the quality of the results.

Unit-annotation score is the core CrowdTruth metric. It is measured for each annotation on each unit as the cosine similarity of the unit vector for the annotation with the MediaUnit vector. For instance, in Fig. 8, unit 735 has complete agreement between annotators for annotation sS. Therefore, the unit-annotation score for unit 735 and annotation sS is equal to 1. Unit 733 has more disagreement, so its unit-annotation score for annotation sS is equal to 0.63.

Unit clarity is defined for each unit as the maximum annotation score for that unit. This metric is used to determine the quality of the unit which is given as input to the crowd. If all the workers selected the same annotation for a unit (e.g. unit 735 in Fig. 8), the max annotation score will be 1, indicating a clear unit. In contrast, unclear units will have low clarity scores (e.g. unit 732 has a clarity score of 0.5). Unit clarity is shown in Fig. 9, among other worker and annotation metrics. This view is the most comprehensive tool to compare sub-sets of MediaUnits (containing one ore more units) with each other.

Rel: 15 Workers/sent pair														Sentence Clarity
Sentence ID	sT	sP	sD	sCA	sL	sS	sM	sCl	sAW	sSE	sIA	sPO	sNONE	sOTH	
225527731	0	0	0	1	0	11	0	0	0	0	0	0	0	0	0.91
225527732	0	0	0	0	0	7	2	0	2	2	0	1	0	0	0.50
225527733	0	0	0	1	0	7	1	0	1	0	0	0	0	1	0.63
225527734	0	0	0	0	0	1	0	0	2	0	0	0	0	9	0.75
225527735	0	0	0	0	0	13	0	0	0	0	0	0	0	0	1.00

Fig. 8. Annotation vectors of RelEx task on 5 units, with 15 workers contributing per unit. Rows are individual units, columns are the annotations. Cells contain the number of workers that selected the annotation for the unit, i.e. 7 workers selected the sS annotation for unit 732. The cells are heat-mapped per row, highlighting the most popular annotation(s) per unit.

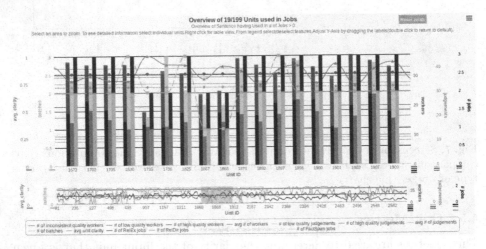

Fig. 9. Screenshot of CrowdTruth Analytics for Units; more details about the unit jobs, workers and annotations can be obtained by clicking on a unit bar

5.6   Annotation Metrics

These metrics are used to measure the quality of the pre-defined annotation types that are part of the task (e.g. whether or not relations in $RelEx$ have overlapping meanings). This can then be used to distinguish between disagreement that is the result of low quality workers, and the disagreement from badly designed tasks, in order to improve future crowdsourcing.

Annotation similarity is defined as the *causal power* [13], which is the pairwise conditional probability $P(A_j|A_i)$ adjusted for the prior probability of A_i. We want to know if annotation A_i is annotated in a unit and how often annotation A_j is as well, but only if A_j is significantly more likely to be annotated when A_i is as well. A high similarity score for a pair of annotations indicates the annotations are confusable to workers: their semantics may be similar or routinely expressed in similar ways in language, or the semantic specification may be confusing or vague. For example when annotations for two relations often appear together in sentences, this could mean the relations are confusing, overlapping in meaning, etc. In Fig. 8, the sCA and sS annotations appear to have this form of similarity.

Annotation ambiguity is defined for each annotation as the maximum annotation similarity for the annotation. If an annotation is clear, its score is low. Annotation that is strongly associated with other may create problems for the task, as well as for training machines that need to discern between them.

Annotation clarity is defined for each annotation as the max unit-annotation score for the annotation over all units (of a given type). If an annotation has a low clarity score this may indicate unattainable NLP targets and problems with the semantic specification. For instance, in Fig. 8, sM is one example of a low-clarity annotation, since few workers ever picking this annotation.

Annotation frequency is the number of times the annotation is annotated at least once in a MediaUnit. The latter three metrics are shown in Fig. 10.

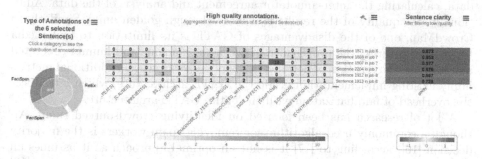

Fig. 10. Screenshot of CrowdTruth Analytics for Annotations on Selected Units in Selected Jobs; click on the pie chart to see the annotation distribution per micro-task

6 Related Work

The amount of knowledge that crowdsourcing platforms like CrowdFlower or Amazon Mechanical Turk hold fostered a great advancement in human computation [14]. Although the existing paid platforms manage to ease the human computation, it has been argued that their utility as a general-purpose computation platform still needs improvement [9]. Both paid platforms support the task creation, distribution to the workers and gathering of the results and provide some quality management tools. However, the quality measures that they apply are inferior to our CrowdTruth metrics, as lots of tainted judgements are still accepted. Even if CrowdFlower's job monitoring support improves the analysis of the data, the provided set of quality metrics is limited. Moreover, the missing links for interconnecting the units, workers and annotations across one or multiple jobs hinder the data exploration and visualization.

Since the development of crowdsourcing has become more intensive, much research has been done in combining human and machine capabilities in order to obtain an automation of the process. Some state-of-the-art crowdsourcing frameworks are CrowdLang [9], CrowdMap [15], GATECrowd [11]. CrowdLang represents a general approach of integrating both human and automatic computation for different use cases and media modalities. However, it restricts the users to work with its own internal programming language, while the overall framework availability for usage or testing is still low. Further, CrowdMap represents an implementation of a workflow model for crowdsourcing mappings between ontologies. The main drawback of the framework is the fact that its parameters are tuned to get the best results for ontology alignment tasks, and it is not easily extendable to other types of media formats or tasks. Furthermore, both frameworks lack in proper visualization of the annotated data.

A more general solution for language processing is represented by GATE-Crowd, a crowdsourcing plugin for the GATE framework. It facilitates the pre-processing of data for crowdsourcing tasks, communicates with Crowdflower for gathering the annotated data and aggregates the results. The plugin takes advantage of the GATE toolbox functionalities for collecting and processing the data, calculating the inter-annotator agreement and analysis of the data. Additionally, the quality of the results is insured through golden units. Similarly to CrowdMap, one of the disadvantages of GATE is its limitation to text media types. By capturing the provenance between the machine and human generated annotations, the creation of new metrics is possible. However, additional metrics imply existing implementation inside the GATE architecture, which introduces the overhead of familiarization with the entire GATE architecture.

A lot of research has been focused on identifying crowdsourced spam. Although a commonly used algorithm for removing spam workers is the majority decision [16], according to [17] it is not an optimal approach as it assumes all the workers to be equally good. Alternatively, expectation maximization [18] estimates individual error rates of workers. First, it infers the correct answer for each unit and then compares each worker answer to the one inferred to be correct. However, [6] shows that some tasks can have multiple good answers, while most spam or low quality workers typically select multiple answers. For this type of problem, some disagreement metrics [5] have been developed, based on workers annotations (e.g. agreement on the same unit, agreement over all the units) and their behavior (e.g. repetitive answers, number of annotations).

7   Conclusions and Future work

In this paper, we introduced the CrowdTruth open-source software framework as an end-to-end collaborative machine-human computing workflow for text, images and video annotations across different domains and use cases. *CrowdTruth framework* implements the novel *CrowdTruth Methodology* for gathering annotated data, which rejects the notion that human interpretation can have a single *ground truth*, and is instead based on the observation that disagreement between annotators can signal ambiguity of the content or annotation task. The CrowdTruth methodology is based on the *triangle of reference* [3] whose implementation in the framework allows for easy adaptation to new micro-tasks. We have validated this, as the initial set of metrics was developed for the medical text use case of IBM Watson and we easily applied them to new tasks, such as event extraction in newspaper text, question-answer alignment and video and image annotations.

We presented the details of the entire human-computing and machine processing workflow, as well as the specifics of each framework component. We demonstrated how such a framework can be beneficial to the Semantic Web community by adding human semantics to existing content interpretations, as well as by supporting the growing trend for crowdsourcing tasks, and continuous need for gold standard data. Detailed documentation http://crowdtruth.org/info and code https://github.com/laroyo/CrowdTruth are provided online. Data export from the CrowdTruth framework is provided in different formats and at different phases of the workflow. The CrowdTruth framework is implemented using open standards, and an important gain is achieved by the usage of the PROV model, compared to existing crowdsourcing platforms and frameworks. This ensures a monotonically increasing behaviour curve in terms of media unit clarity and micro-task template suitability for each media unit that is intended to gather annotations. As future work, we plan to gather more use cases to extend the system with new data, micro-task templates and domains. Additional visualisations are also explored to increase the usability and effectiveness of the CrowdTruth metrics.

References

1. Snow, R., O'Connor, B., Jurafsky, D., Ng, A.Y.: Cheap and fast—but is it good?: evaluating non-expert annotations for natural language tasks. In: Proceedings of CEMNLP 2008, pp. 254–263. Association for Computational Linguistics (2008)
2. Ambati, V., Vogel, S., Carbonell, J.G.: Active learning and crowd-sourcing for machine translation. In: LREC, vol. 1, p. 2. Citeseer (2010)
3. Aroyo, L., Welty, C.: Truth is a lie: Crowdtruth and the 7 myths of human annotation. AI Magazine (2014)
4. Aroyo, L., Welty, C.: Crowd Truth: Harnessing disagreement in crowdsourcing a relation extraction gold standard. In: WebSci 2013 (2013)
5. Aroyo, L., Welty, C.: Measuring crowd truth for medical relation extraction. In: AAAI2013 Fall Symp. on Semantics for Big Data (2013)
6. Soberón, G., Aroyo, L., Welty, C., Inel, O., Lin, H., Overmeen, M.: Measuring crowd truth: Disagreement metrics combined with worker behavior filters. In: Proc. of CrowdSem 2013 Workshop, ISWC 2013 (2013)
7. Inel, O., Aroyo, L., Welty, C., Sips, R.J.: Exploiting Crowdsourcing Disagreement with Various Domain-Independent Quality Measures. In: Proc. of DeRiVE 2013 Workshop, ISWC 2013 (2013)
8. Aroyo, L., Welty, C.: Harnessing disagreement for event semantics. In: Proc. of DeRiVE 2012, ISWC 2012, p. 31 (2012)
9. Minder, P., Bernstein, A.: Crowdlang-first steps towards programmable human computers for general computation. In: Human Computation (2011)
10. Ahmad, S., Battle, A., Malkani, Z., Kamvar, S.: The jabberwocky programming environment for structured social computing. In: Proceedings of ACM Symposium on UI Software and Technology, pp. 53–64. ACM (2011)

11. Bontcheva, K., Roberts, I., Derczynski, L., Rout, D.: The gate crowdsourcing plugin: Crowdsourcing annotated corpora made easy. In: Proc. EACL (2014)
12. Groth, P.: Moreau (eds.), L.: PROV-Overview. An Overview of the PROV Family of Documents. W3C Working Group Note NOTE-prov-overview-20130430, World Wide Web Consortium (April 2013)
13. Cheng, P.: From covariation to causation: A causal power theory. Psychological Review 104 (1997)
14. Quinn, A.J., Bederson, B.B.: Human computation: a survey and taxonomy of a growing field. In: Proc. of the SIGCHI, pp. 1403–1412. ACM (2011)
15. Sarasua, C., Simperl, E., Noy, N.F.: Crowdmap: Crowdsourcing ontology alignment with microtasks. In: Cudré-Mauroux, P., et al (eds.) ISWC 2012, Part I. LNCS, vol. 7649, pp. 525–541. Springer, Heidelberg (2012)
16. Hirth, M., Hoßfeld, T., Tran-Gia, P.: Cost-optimal validation mechanisms and cheat-detection for crowdsourcing platforms. In: Innovative Mobile and Internet Services in Ubiquitous Computing, pp. 316–321. IEEE (2011)
17. Raykar, V.C., Yu, S., Zhao, L.H., Valadez, G.H., Florin, C., Bogoni, L., Moy, L.: Learning from crowds. The Journal of Machine Learning Research 99 (2010)
18. Dawid, A.P., Skene, A.M.: Maximum likelihood estimation of observer error-rates using the em algorithm. Applied Statistics, 20–28 (1979)

Joint Information Extraction from the Web Using Linked Data

Isabelle Augenstein

Department of Computer Science, The University of Sheffield, UK
i.augenstein@sheffield.ac.uk

Abstract. Almost all of the big name Web companies are currently engaged in building 'knowledge graphs' and these are showing significant results in improving search, email, calendaring, etc. Even the largest openly-accessible ones, such as Freebase and Wikidata, are far from complete, partly because new information is emerging so quickly. Most of the missing information is available on Web pages. To access that knowledge and populate knowledge bases, information extraction methods are necessitated. The bottleneck for information extraction systems is obtaining training data to learn classifiers. In this doctoral research, we investigate how existing data in knowledge bases can be used to automatically annotate training data to learn classifiers to in turn extract more data to expand knowledge bases. We discuss our hypotheses, approach, evaluation methods and present preliminary results.

1 Problem Statement

Since the emergence of the Semantic Web, many Linked datasets such as Freebase [5], Wikidata [31] and DBpedia [4] have been created, not only for research, but also commercial purposes. These have shown significant results in improving search, email, calendaring, etc. With new information emerging very quickly, cost-efficient methods for maintaining those datasets are very important. Since most of the missing or new information is available on Web pages, the cheapest method for automatically populating knowledge bases is to process those pages using information extraction (IE) methods. However, IE methods require training data to learn classifiers. Because manually creating training data is expensive and time-consuming, we propose to use *self-supervised learning* or *distant supervision*, a method proposed in recent years which utilises data already present in datasets to train classifiers [19]. Distant supervision is based on the assumption that if two entities participate in a relation, every sentence that contains those entities expresses that relation. Although distant supervision approaches are promising, they have so far ignored issues arising in the context of Web IE, specifically:

(i) *Incorrect labelling*: Distant supervision approaches automatically create training data by heuristically annotating sentences with relations between entity pairs contained in a knowledge base. This heuristic causes problems because some entity pairs are ambiguous and knowledge bases are incomplete.

(ii) *Unrecognised entities*: One subtask of relation extraction (RE) is entity recognition and classification (NERC). While existing NERC systems can be used, they are based on a restrictive set of entity types and are trained for different domains and thus often fail to recognise entities of diverse types on heterogenous Web pages.

P. Mika et al. (Eds.) ISWC 2014, Part II, LNCS 8797, pp. 505–512, 2014.
© Springer International Publishing Switzerland 2014

(iii) *Data sparsity*: Existing distant supervision approaches only learn to extract relations from text and only from sentences with contain explicit entity mentions. Since not all information on Web pages is contained in text and entities are not always refered to by their proper name, but also by using pronouns, this limits the number of extractions. The goal of this work is to research novel methods, which do not require manually labelled training data, for Web information extracting to populate knowledge bases.

2   Relevancy

The contribution of this PhD research will be two-fold: the output of the Web information extraction can be validated manually and then used to populate knowledge bases, also, the Web information extraction system can be run as a service to do extraction on the fly for a given user query. This will be of interest for *Web companies* interested in expanding their knowledge graphs or improving results for search, *The Linked Data and Semantic Web community*, because it will allow to generate annotations and triples automatically across domains and reduce manual effort for populating ontologies, *The Natural Language Processing community*, because it will improve the state of the art in information extraction, and *the Machine Learning community*, because it will increase the real-world application and improve accessability of distant supervision.

3   Research Questions

Our overall research question is: is distant supervision a feasible approach for Web information extraction? How does it perform compared to unsupervised and semi-supervised methods? To answer this, the following research questions will be investigated:

1. **Seed Selection:** Is it possible to improve the precision and recall of distant supervision by strategically selecting training data? If so, by how much?
2. **Joint NERC and RE:** Is it possible to train an extraction model for joint distantly supervised entity classification and relation extraction? Will this achieve a higher precision and recall than a pipeline model which uses a state of the art supervised NERC as input for a distantly supervised relation extractor?
3. **Joint text, list and table extraction:** Does training a joint distantly supervised model for free text, list and table extraction from Web pages achieve higher precision and recall than using a pipeline model which combines those strategies?

4   Related Work

Web IE approaches to populate knowledge bases which try to minimise manual effort either use *semi-supervised* or *unsupervised* learning. *Semi-supervised bootstrapping* approaches such as NELL [6], PROPERA [20] and BOA [11] use pre-defined natural language patterns to extract information, then iteratively learn new patterns. While they can be used for Web IE for the purpose of populating knowledge bases, they are rule-based, not statistical approaches, and as such make hard judgements based on prominant extraction patterns instead of soft judgments based on weights for features.

Extraction patterns often have a good performance on narrow domains, but are less suitable for heterogenous domains, because they are less robust to unseen information or infrequent expressions. *Open information extraction* approaches such as TextRunner [34], Reverb [10], OLLIE [16] and ClausIE [8] are unsupervised approaches, which learn relation-independent extraction patterns from text. Although those patterns can be mapped to ontologies later, this is an error-prone process. In addition, those approaches often produce uninformative or incoherent IE patterns. *Automatic ontology learning and population approaches* such as FRED [22] and LODifier [3] extract ontology schemas and information for those schemas by performing deep semantic processing using a pipeline of text processing tools. Because those tools are trained on newswire, they are not robust enough to process noisy Web pages. Existing *distant supervision* system have so far only been developed for extraction from newswire [33], Wikipedia [19] or biomedical data [24]. They therefore fail to address issues arising when processing heterogenous Web text, such as dealing with grammar and spelling mistakes and recognising entities of diverse types.

While there is no system that incorporates all of the aspects discussed in Section 3, there are approaches which address the three invidual aspects.

Seed Selection: A few strategies for seed selection for distant supervision have already been investigated: at-least-one models [13][29][23][33][17], hierarchical topic models [1][25], pattern correlations [30], and an information retrieval approach [32]. At-least-one models assume that "if two entities particpate in a relation, at least one sentence that mentions these two entities might express that relation". While positive results have been reported for those models, Riedel et al. [23] argue that they are challenging to train because they are quite complex. Hierarchical topic model approaches group relations by assuming that the context of a relation is either specific for the pair of entities, the relation, or neither. Min et al. [17] propose a hierarchical model to only learn from positive examples to address the problem of incomplete negative training data. Takamatsu et al. [30] use a probabilistic graphical model to group extraction patterns. Xu et al. [32] propose a two-step model based on the idea of pseudo-relevance feedback. Our approach to filter unreliable training data is based on a different assumption: instead of trying to address the problem of noisy training data by using more complicated multi-stage machine learning models, we want to examine how data already present in the knowledge base can be even further exploited for simple statistical methods.

Joint NERC and RE: While RE approaches typically use a separate NERC, previous works have shown that applying text processing models in a pipeline fashion causes errors made by one component to be propagated to the next one, which has a significant impact on precision [26][27][14][15]. Approaches such as Integer Linear Programming [26][27] and Markov Logic Networks [9] have been proposed to solve both tasks at the same time. Existing distant supervision systems are based on pipeline models using supervised NERC models. This is partly because, in order to jointly solve both tasks in one fully distantly supervised model, the NERC has to be distantly supervised too.

Joint Text, List and Table Extraction: Most existing Web extraction approaches focus on either text, list or table extraction. There are a few approaches which combine those [28][6][7][12][21][18], but they do so by using separate classifiers for the different tasks, even apply them to different corpora, then combine the results. We argue that by considering text, tables and lists in isolation, important information gets lost. We want to research how solving those tasks at the same time and also making use of Web page-level features could improve the precision and recall of Web information extraction systems.

5 Hypotheses

Our research hypotheses are as follows:

1. **Seed Selection:** Removing ambiguous training examples, as well as possible false positives using statistical methods will help to improve the precision of distant supervision approaches.
2. **Joint NERC and RE:** State of the art supervised NERCs are trained for the news domain and will therefore have relatively low precision and recall on Web pages. Distantly supervised NERCs will perform better on Web pages than supervised NERCs trained on the news domain. Joint NE and relation extraction models will achieve a higher precision than pipeline models. Using fine-grained ontology-based NE classes instead of broad NE classes will lead to a higher RE precision.
3. **Joint text, list and table extraction:** A distant supervision model trained on combined feature vectors for text, list and table features will perform better than three separate models. Semi-structured (list and table) extractors have a substantially higher precision than unstructured (free text) extractors, which can be exploited by giving a higher weight to semi-structured features. Existing semi-structured extractors only consider lists and tables in isolation. Using the local and global context of lists and tables on Web pages as features will improve the precision of semi-structured extractors.

6 Approach

We develop a distantly supervised IE system in order to test our different hypotheses. A high-level overview of our approach in provided in Figure 1. Our approach consists the following components: a user integration component, a seed selection component, a feature extraction component and a multi-task learning component.

User Integration: The user can select what information about an entity of a specific class to extract, e.g. all members and albums of the band "The Beatles". For evaluation purposes, those user queries will be generated automatically. Web pages for the user query are then retrieved. After the information is extracted, it is presented to the user.

Seed Selection: The seed selection component decides which of the triples in the knowledge base to use for automatically annotating training data. We use several statistical measures to choose positive and negative training data. Our main idea is to select triples which have a relatively low ambiguity and are therefore very specific to the relation. As an example, The Beatles released an album called "Let it Be", which also contains the track "Let it Be". If a sentence contained both "The Beatles" and "Let it Be" it would be unclear if the sentence represents the relation "has album" or "has track". We would therefore discard "Let it Be" as training data because it has a high ambiguity.

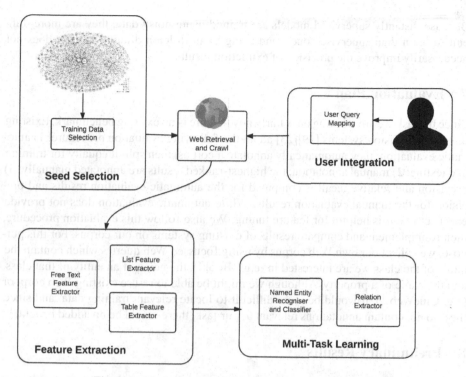

Fig. 1. Architecture of the Joint Web Extraction approach

Further, if two entities appear together in a sentence which are not related in the knowledge base, we use them as negative training data. Because knowledge bases are prone to be imcomplete, this assumption leads to further noise. Our approach is to devise statistical measures based on background data to determine how likely it is for two unrelated entities to be false positives, i.e. missing from the knowledge base. We then only select pairs of entities as negative training data which are likely to be true negatives.

Feature Extraction: The feature extraction component extracts features for entities and relations in text, lists and tables on Web pages. Instead of merely considering those sources in isolation, we use the local and global context of lists and tables on Web pages as features. The local context would for example be the text appearing immediately before a list or table, whereas the global context would be the title of a Web page or words appearing on the Web page as a whole. We will also use annotations on Web pages as features, for example formatting information, which might indicate entity boundaries, and existing semantic annotations, which might help to extract relations.

Multi-task Learning: The multi-task learning component learns to extract entities and relations at the same time. Further, selectional restrictions for the subject and object of a relation obtained from the knowledge base are enforced, e.g. the subject of "has album" has to be a musical artist and the object has to be an album. We use an existing multi-task model for this. Our main contribution is to devise a distantly supervised NERC and to test if multi-task models also perform better than pipeline models if they are distantly supervised. So far, joint models have only been researched for supervised approaches.

Because distantly supervised models are trained using noisy data, they are more difficult to learn than supervised ones, and using them to learn difficult models does not
neccessarily improve the precision of extraction results.

7 Evaluation Plan

Since the task we are working on is fairly novel, there is no existing benchmark. Existing
distant supervision systems [19][23] adopt the following evaluation procedure: 1) automatic evaluation: they automatically annotate a corpus, then split it equally for training
and testing; 2) manual annotation: the highest-ranked results are annotated manually; 3)
precision and relative recall is computed for the automatic evaluation results and precision for the manual evaluation results. While automatic evaluation does not provide
exact results, it is helpful for feature tuning. We also follow this evaluation procedure,
then re-implement and compare results of existing systems on our corpus. For this purpose, we collect our own Web corpus by using focussed Web queries which contain the
name of the class we are interested in (e.g. 'Book'), the name of an entity of that class,
and the name of a property. Although we might be able to re-use existing Web corpora
(e.g. ClueWeb [1]), it would be more difficult to locate relevant training data, and since
they do not contain annotations relevant to our task, there would be no added benefit.

8 Preliminary Results

We have already performed experiments to test our first research question, results are
partly documented in Augenstein [2]. We find that statistical methods for discarding
highly ambiguous seeds can result in an error reduction of about 35%, however, detecting and discarding unreliable negative training data is a lot more challenging. Further,
using existing NERC tools results in a low recall, since Stanford NERC is trained on
a different sort of text, news, and uses standard NE classes (person, location, organisation, mixed). It often fails to recognise entities which should fall into the 'mixed' class,
such as 'track' or 'album'. Recall improves significantly when using our own NER in
addition to Stanford NERC, which indicates that further experiments on distantly supervised NERC for RE might be useful. Lastly, we find that the distant supervision
assumption is quite restrictive: It requires both subject and object of a relation to be
mentioned in the same sentence explicitly. Using existing coreference resolution tools
does not significantly improve recall, however, we find that performing RE across sentence boundaries by relaxing the distant supervision assumption results in three times
the number of extractions.

9 Reflections

Our approach aims at learning to extract information from the Web in a novel way. Traditional approaches use supervised learning to train models for extracting entities and
relations. Our approach is based on distant supervision, a method that has gained popularity recently, which leverages on Linked Data to train extraction models and does not

---

[1] http://lemurproject.org/clueweb12/

require manually labelled training data. Distant supervision has so far only been applied to RE from text and not been used for Web information extraction. We argue that Web IE is more challenging than the well-researched task of IE from newswire since Web content often contains noise such as spelling or grammar mistakes, but it is also more useful for gathering information, since most content is available on the Web. While existing approaches focus on standard NE classes, we argue that it would be beneficial to extend this approach to NE classes of any domain and for this purpose investigate distantly supervised NERC for RE. Preliminary results suggest this would substantially increase the number of extractions [2]. We further find that filtering unreliable training data using statistical methods results in an error reduction of about 35% [2].

Acknowledgements. We thank Fabio Ciravegna and Diana Maynard for helping to develop this research plan, Ruben Verborgh and Tom De Nies for their writing tips, as well as the anonymous reviewers for their valuable feedback. This research is partly supported by the EPSRC funded project LODIE: Linked Open Data for Information Extraction, EP/J019488/1.

References

1. Alfonseca, E., Filippova, K., Delort, J.Y., Garrido, G.: Pattern Learning for Relation Extraction with a Hierarchical Topic Model. In: Proceedings of ACL, Jeju, South Korea (2012)
2. Augenstein, I.: Seed Selection for Distantly Supervised Web-Based Relation Extraction. In: Proceedings of SWAIE (2014)
3. Augenstein, I., Padó, S., Rudolph, S.: LODifier: Generating Linked Data from Unstructured Text. In: Simperl, E., Cimiano, P., Polleres, A., Corcho, O., Presutti, V. (eds.) ESWC 2012. LNCS, vol. 7295, pp. 210–224. Springer, Heidelberg (2012)
4. Bizer, C., Lehmann, J., Kobilarov, G., Auer, S., Becker, C., Cyganiak, R., Hellmann, S.: DBpedia-A crystallization point for the Web of Data. Web Semantics: Science, Services and Agents on the World Wide Web 7(3), 154–165 (2009)
5. Bollacker, K., Evans, C., Paritosh, P., Sturge, T., Taylor, J.: Freebase: A Collaboratively Created Graph Database For Structuring Human Knowledge. In: Proceedings of ACM SIGMOD, pp. 1247–1250 (2008)
6. Carlson, A., Betteridge, J., Kisiel, B., Settles, B., Hruschka, E.R., Mitchell, T.M.: Toward an Architecture for Never-Ending Language Learning. In: AAAI (2010)
7. Carlson, A., Betteridge, J., Wang, R.C., Hruschka Jr., E.R., Mitchell, T.M.: Coupled Semi-Supervised Learning for Information Extraction. In: Proceedings of WSDM (2010)
8. Del Corro, L., Gemulla, R.: ClausIE: Clause-Based Open Information Extraction. In: Proceedings of the 22nd International Conference on World Wide Web, pp. 355–366 (2013)
9. Domingos, P., Kok, S., Lowd, D., Poon, H., Richardson, M., Singla, P.: Markov logic. In: De Raedt, L., Frasconi, P., Kersting, K., Muggleton, S.H. (eds.) Probabilistic ILP 2007. LNCS (LNAI), vol. 4911, pp. 92–117. Springer, Heidelberg (2008)
10. Fader, A., Soderland, S., Etzioni, O.: Identifying relations for open information extraction. In: Proceedings of EMNLP, pp. 1535–1545 (2011)
11. Gerber, D., Ngomo, A.-C.N.: Extracting Multilingual Natural-Language Patterns for RDF Predicates. In: ten Teije, A., Völker, J., Handschuh, S., Stuckenschmidt, H., d'Acquin, M., Nikolov, A., Aussenac-Gilles, N., Hernandez, N. (eds.) EKAW 2012. LNCS (LNAI), vol. 7603, pp. 87–96. Springer, Heidelberg (2012)
12. Govindaraju, V., Zhang, C., Ré, C.: Understanding Tables in Context Using Standard NLP Toolkits. In: Proceedings of ACL (2013)

13. Hoffmann, R., Zhang, C., Ling, X., Zettlemoyer, L.S., Weld, D.S.: Knowledge-Based Weak Supervision for Information Extraction of Overlapping Relations. In: Proceedings of ACL, pp. 541–550 (2011)
14. Kate, R.J., Mooney, R.J.: Joint Entity and Relation Extraction using Card-Pyramid Parsing. In: Proceedings of CoNLL, pp. 203–212 (2010)
15. Li, Q., Heng, J.: Incremental Joint Extraction of Entity Mentions and Relations. In: Proceedings of ACL (2014)
16. Mausam, M.S., Soderland, S., Bart, R., Etzioni, O.: Open Language Learning for Information Extraction. In: Proceedings of EMNLP-CoNLL, pp. 523–534 (2012)
17. Min, B., Grishman, R., Wan, L., Wang, C., Gondek, D.: Distant Supervision for Relation Extraction with an Incomplete Knowledge Base. In: Proceedings of HLT-NAACL, pp. 777–782 (2013)
18. Min, B., Shi, S., Grishman, R., Lin, C.Y.: Ensemble Semantics for Large-scale Unsupervised Relation Extraction. In: EMNLP-CoNLL, pp. 1027–1037. ACL (2012)
19. Mintz, M., Bills, S., Snow, R., Jurafsky, D.: Distant supervision for relation extraction without labeled data. In: Proceedings of ACL, vol. 2, pp. 1003–1011 (2009)
20. Nakashole, U., Theobald, M., Weikum, G.: Scalable Knowledge Harvesting with High Precision and High Recall. In: Proceedings of WSDM, pp. 227–236 (2011)
21. Pennacchiotti, M., Pantel, P.: Entity Extraction via Ensemble Semantics. In: Proceedings of EMNLP, pp. 238–247 (2009)
22. Presutti, V., Draicchio, F., Gangemi, A.: Knowledge Extraction Based on Discourse Representation Theory and Linguistic Frames. In: ten Teije, A., Völker, J., Handschuh, S., Stuckenschmidt, H., d'Acquin, M., Nikolov, A., Aussenac-Gilles, N., Hernandez, N. (eds.) EKAW 2012. LNCS (LNAI), vol. 7603, pp. 114–129. Springer, Heidelberg (2012)
23. Riedel, S., Yao, L., McCallum, A.: Modeling Relations and Their Mentions without Labeled Text. In: Balcázar, J.L., Bonchi, F., Gionis, A., Sebag, M. (eds.) ECML PKDD 2010, Part III. LNCS (LNAI), vol. 6323, pp. 148–163. Springer, Heidelberg (2010)
24. Roller, R., Stevenson, M.: Self-Supervised Relation Extraction using UMLS. In: Kanoulas, E., Lupu, M., Clough, P., Sanderson, M., Hall, M., Hanbury, A., Toms, E. (eds.) CLEF 2014. LNCS, vol. 8685, pp. 116–127. Springer, Heidelberg (2014)
25. Roth, B., Klakow, D.: Combining Generative and Discriminative Model Scores for Distant Supervision. In: Proceedings of ACL-EMNLP, pp. 24–29 (2013)
26. Roth, D., Tau Yih, W.: A Linear Programming Formulation for Global Inference in Natural Language Tasks. In: Proceedings of CoNLL, pp. 1–8 (2004)
27. Roth, D., Yih, W.T.: Global Inference for Entity and Relation Identification via a Linear Programming Formulation. In: Introduction to Statistical Relational Learning, pp. 553–580 (2007)
28. Shinzato, K., Torisawa, K.: Acquiring Hyponymy Relations from Web Documents. In: HLT-NAACL, pp. 73–80 (2004)
29. Surdeanu, M., Tibshirani, J., Nallapati, R., Manning, C.D.: Multi-instance Multi-label Learning for Relation Extraction. In: Proceedings of EMNLP-CoNLL, pp. 455–465 (2012)
30. Takamatsu, S., Sato, I., Nakagawa, H.: Reducing Wrong Labels in Distant Supervision for Relation Extraction. In: Proceedings of ACL, pp. 721–729 (2012)
31. Vrandečić, D., Krötzsch, M.: Wikidata: A Free Collaborative Knowledge Base. Commun. ACM (to appear, 2014)
32. Xu, W., Hoffmann, R., Zhao, L., Grishman, R.: Filling Knowledge Base Gaps for Distant Supervision of Relation Extraction. In: Proceedings of ACL, pp. 665–670 (2013)
33. Yao, L., Riedel, S., McCallum, A.: Collective Cross-document Relation Extraction Without Labelled Data. In: Proceedings of EMNLP, pp. 1013–1023 (2010)
34. Yates, A., Cafarella, M., Banko, M., Etzioni, O., Broadhead, M., Soderland, S.: TextRunner: Open Information Extraction on the Web. In: Proceedings of HLT-NAACL: Demonstrations, pp. 25–26 (2007)

Entity Linking with Multiple Knowledge Bases: An Ontology Modularization Approach

Bianca Pereira

Insight Centre for Data Analytics
National University of Ireland, Galway
bianca.pereira@insight-centre.org

Abstract. The recognition of entities in text is the basis for a series of applications. Synonymy and Ambiguity are among the biggest challenges in identifying such entities. Both challenges are addressed by Entity Linking, the task of grounding entity mentions in textual documents to Knowledge Base entries. Entity Linking has been based in the use of single cross-domain Knowledge Bases as source for entities. This PhD research proposes the use of multiple Knowledge Bases for Entity Linking as a way to increase the number of entities recognized in text. The problem of Entity Linking with Multiple Knowledge Bases is addressed by using textual and Knowledge Base features as contexts for Entity Linking, Ontology Modularization to select the most relevant subset of entity entries, and Collective Inference to decide the most suitable entity entry to link with each mention.

Keywords: Entity Linking, Linked Data, Ontology Modularization.

1 Problem Statement

Natural language understanding, in particular, the recognition of entities in text, has been the basis for different computer-based applications such as Semantic Search, Recommendation Systems, Sentiment Analysis, and Social Media Monitoring just to mention a few.

Among the biggest challenges in the recognition of entities are the synonymy and ambiguity. Synonymy is given by the existence of different names (mentions) in text to the same real world entity. For instance, *IBM* and *International Business Machines* are two mentions for the same real world entity. Ambiguity, moreover, occurs when one mention may refer to more than one real world entity. The mention *Jackson*, for instance, may refer to more than 500 different entities[1].

Entity Linking is the task of *grounding entity mentions in documents to Knowledge Base entries* [7]. It is investigated as way to solve both synonymy and ambiguity by linking mentions in natural language text with entity entries in a given Knowledge Base, where those entries provide a unique identifier for each

---

[1] http://en.wikipedia.org/wiki/Jackson_(name)

P. Mika et al. (Eds.) ISWC 2014, Part II, LNCS 8797, pp. 513–520, 2014.

real world entity. One example is the interlinking between the mention *Michael Jackson* and the Wikipedia[2] link http://en.wikipedia.org/wiki/Michael_Jackson providing information about which real world entity the mention is referring to.

Cross-domain datasets such as Wikipedia, DBPedia[3] and YAGO[4] are the most used Knowledge Bases for Entity Linking. This happens mainly because of the high number of domains they cover. Even so, those Knowledge Bases can benefit from expanding them using other Knowledge Bases. Wikipedia, for instance, has data about almost 5 million entities in different domains. Internet Movie Database[5] (IMDB) contains more than 8 million entities in the cinema domain, and Music Brainz[6] has 30 million entities in the music domain. Those two databases contain seven times more entities than whole Wikipedia even when only two domains are considered.

The focus of this work is to enrich the understanding of entities in natural language text through Entity Linking using multiple Knowledge Bases.

2   Relevancy

Entity Linking enables the improvement of a broad number of applications, such as: the enrichment of the reader experience when applied in Wikification; the query for documents based on real world entities instead of keywords, when applied to Semantic Search; the recognition of sentiments related to entities when applied to Sentiment Analysis or Reputation Management; and the enrichment of the analysis of textual data in Big Data Analytics Solutions. The recognition of entities through Entity Linking can also be used for a series of Information Extraction (e.g. Relation Extraction and Attribute Extraction) and Natural Language Processing approaches (e.g. Coreference Resolution across texts).

The use of multiple Knowledge Bases for Entity Linking improves even more those applications. It increases the range of entities they can work with. The combination of private and public Knowledge Bases can even be applied to understand enterprise textual data (such as reports, intranet texts, and Customer Relationship Management descriptions) improving the value of the data for business.

3   Related Work

There are relatively few work on using multiple Knowledge Bases for Entity Linking. Tools such as AlchemyAPI[7] and Zemanta[8] are two examples but due

---

[2] http://www.wikipedia.org/

[3] http://dbpedia.org/

[4] http://www.mpi-inf.mpg.de/departments/databases-and-information-systems/research/yago-naga/yago/

[5] http://www.imdb.com

[6] http://musicbrainz.org

[7] http://www.alchemyapi.com/

[8] http://www.zemanta.com/

to their commercial characteristic, the methods they use are not described in detail. In the research side, there is the work from [2] and [12] dealing with more than one Knowledge Base for Entity Linking.

[12] performs Entity Linking using Relational Databases. The authors present an adaptive solution that can use any database under Boyce-Codd Normal Form (BCNF) as Knowledge Base. They used IMDB and a sports database for evaluation of their approach.

[2] focuses on large scale Entity Linking using Linked Data. DBPedia, Freebase[9], Geonames[10] and New York Times Linked Data[11] are used as Knowledge Bases. The authors assume all Linked Data datasets are already linked to each other. Their algorithm relies on the existence of textual descriptions in the Knowledge Base and in a crowd-sourcing step to improve the results.

[2] uses TF-IDF over the textual descriptions in the Knowledge Base to choose the best entity to be linked with each mention. [12] uses text in entity attributes in the Knowledge Base as information for disambiguation. Both solutions use only the words around each mention as context for disambiguation (*local context*). Despite the state-of-the-art in Entity Linking shows the improvement in using more information as context for disambiguation [11], those contexts (*local and global*) were not applied for Entity Linking with Multiple Knowledge Bases.

State-of-the-art solutions describe the number of candidates for each mention (i.e. the ambiguity of a mention) as the main drawback for Entity Linking [4,3,6]. In other words, as bigger the Knowledge Base and the number of candidates per mention as much time it may take to find a solution. While current approaches rely in approximate algorithms, this PhD research proposal aims the use of Ontology Modularization to limit the number of entity entries considered for linking. Ontology Modularization has been used to improve manual annotation of image and text [1,13]. To the best of our knowledge this is the first time Ontology Modularization is used for Entity Linking.

4   Research Questions

The problem of Entity Linking using multiple Knowledge Bases leads to the following research questions:

RQ1 What are the textual features most relevant for Entity Linking?
RQ2 What are the Knowledge Base features most relevant for Entity Linking?
RQ3 Is it feasible to create an Entity Linking approach using multiple Knowledge Bases with comparable performance to Knowledge Base-specific approaches?

---

[9] http://www.freebase.com/
[10] http://www.geonames.org/
[11] http://data.nytimes.com/

5   Hypotheses

Our work is based on several hypotheses related to the research questions listed in Section 4:

H1 Verbs and mentions appearing near a given mention measures the relevance of a candidate entry to be linked with this mention. (local context)

H2 Mentions appearing in the same paragraph are more relevant for disambiguation than those appearing far in the text. (global context)

H3 Mentions and verbs in text can be directly mapped to entities and relationships in the Knowledge Base.

H4 Comparable performance with Knowledge Base-specific Entity Linking can be achieve through the division of the Knowledge Base in context-specific modules.

6   Preliminary Results

Our first experiments envisioned the creation of a baseline approach for Entity Linking with Multiple Knowledge Bases.

The first experiment analyzes the feasibility on using solely Linked Data Knowledge Bases as sources for entity mentions in text. This experiment evaluates different heuristics to automatically discover properties that carry lexical information for entity entries in the Knowledge Base. The results are available in [10] and they shows that even simple heuristics can identify the correct properties. It demonstrates that Linked Data Knowledge Bases can be used as dictionary for mentions.

The second experiment verifies if current linking methods developed for a specific Knowledge Base can be used with different ones. We adapted the work presented in [3] to use Jamendo[12] and Linked Movie Database[13], two publicly available Linked Data datasets. As those datasets do not have full text descriptions for all entities, the mapping between text around mentions and textual descriptions could not be used, as well as the computation of TF-IDF. Even without this context the results were quite encouraging with f-score of 54% for Disambiguation with Jamendo and 87% with Linked MDB. Those results are presented in [9].

Due to the positive results from the second experiment, the third one envisions the use of DBPedia in order to compare with related work. Using AIDA-CoNLL[4], an annotated corpora, as gold standard, the best accuracy was 32% while related work [8] reports accuracy ranging from 34% to 82.3% in the same corpora. Thus, the next step is to evaluate how much each textual and Knowledge Base features contribute to find the best linking. This analysis will help us discover why the results with DBPedia were so low when they were good with the other Knowledge Bases. More information about future evaluations are given in Section 8.

---

[12] http://dbtune.org/jamendo/
[13] http://linkedmdb.org/

7   Approach

Natural language text often contains a human-readable description of a set of entities and their relationships. We consider Knowledge Base as a machine-readable description of entities and their relationships. This approach aims to use a model that better represents both descriptions in order to identify the best pair (mention, Knowledge Base entry) that refers to the same real world entity.

There are many formats of Knowledge Bases that can be used for Entity Linking. Linked Data datasets explicit the semantic of the data and enable the easy extension of the Knowledge Base by direct linking entries in different datasets. Because of this, this work focus only on the use of Linked Data datasets as Knowledge Bases.

A series of constraints were identified during the development of our baseline:

– There is no annotated corpora associated to the Knowledge Base.
– The Knowledge Base does not contain textual description for entities.
– All information available for Entity Linking comes only from the textual source and the Knowledge Base.

This approach is divided in three sequential steps (Figure 1). The Mention Recognition step deals with the identification of entity mentions in text. The Candidate Selection step collects a list of candidate entity entries in the Knowledge Base to link with each mention. And the Disambiguation step selects the most suitable candidate to be linked with each mention. The solution applied for each one of these steps is explained in the following subsections.

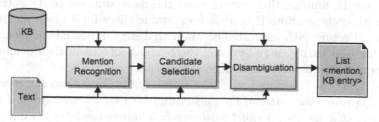

Fig. 1. Entity Linking pipeline

7.1   Mention Recognition

Mention Recognition is the first step for Entity Linking. This step deals with the recognition of entity mentions in text. The text is given as input and the expected output is a list with all mentions appearing in it. Using the text *"Mick Jackson wrote Blame it on the Boogie, a great success of The Jackson's."* as input text, the expected output is the list M = {"Mick Jackson", "Blame it on the Boogie", "The Jackson's"}.

Each entry in the Knowledge Base is considered as an entity entry if there is lexical information attached to it. In other words, a given entry is considered an entity entry only if its name is expressed in the Knowledge Base. Based on this, the Knowledge Base is used as a dictionary to identify mentions in the text.

If one surface form in the text matches a dictionary entry then the surface form is recognized as a mention.

7.2   Candidate Selection

Given all mentions recognized by the Mention Recognition step, the Candidate Selection step selects a set of candidate entries for each mention. In this context, candidate entry is a Knowledge Base entry with a probability higher than zero to be linked with a given mention. The biggest issue in candidate selection is the high number of possible candidates for a single mention. For instance, the word *Jackson* may refer to more than 500 entity entries in Wikipedia[14]. Considering a Knowledge Base with all people in the world, the number of candidates for the word Jackson turns the process of Linking unfeasible. Due to that, the Candidate Selection should return only the most relevant subset of candidates for the given text.

The contribution of this work in the candidate selection is in the use of Ontology Modularization. The process of Candidate Selection is given by the division of the Knowledge Base in contextual modules. Each contextual module keeps a maximum limit on the number of candidates for each surface form. The key idea is that entities in the same context are semantically related in the Knowledge Base. Thus, by looking for candidates in the Knowledge Base, the module that contains candidates for the highest number of mentions is more likely to represent the context of the text.

7.3   Disambiguation

Finally, the Disambiguation step chooses the most suitable entity entry to be linked with each mention. If there is no suitable entry for a given mention this step should return NIL instead. The main challenge in disambiguation is identifying the best entity entry by using the textual content in the document and the information provided by the Knowledge Base.

Considering the following text: *"The Battle of the Boogie was the event where Michael Jackson, the writer of the music, and Michael Jackson, from The Jackson 5, were in a dispute for chart positions."*. A human reader easily understands who are the two Michael Jacksons in the text. By that, she uses hers background knowledge and the context given by the words in the text to infer the difference between both. The aim of this approach is to have an algorithm that mimic this process. It collects the textual context (Research Question RQ1 and Hypotheses H1 and H2) and maps it to the context provided by the Knowledge Base (Research Question RQ2 and Hypothesis H3). A Collective Inference model will be used to merge both contexts and identify the best (mention,entry) link [5].

The contribution of this work is in using only content words near mentions (Hypothesis 1) and lexical cohesion in the text (Hypothesis 2) as textual contexts. And the mapping between those content words (nouns, adjectives, and verbs) to semantic information in the Knowledge Base (entities, attributes, and relationships) rather than to textual descriptions.

---

[14] http://en.wikipedia.org/wiki/Jackson_(name)

8   Evaluation Plan

There are some corpora already linked to Wikipedia and Wikipedia-related Knowledge Bases [4,11]. Those corpora can be used as gold standard for Entity Linking and they enable the comparison with state-of-the-art approaches [8]. The unique problem is that such corpora do not enable the evaluation using other Linked Data datasets as Knowledge Bases. Given that, the first step for the evaluation will be the development of a set of Guidelines for Annotation and the annotation of a corpus with links to different Knowledge Bases.

8.1   Mention Recognition

In the Mention Recognition step, the evaluation will measure the coverage of the Knowledge Base as a dictionary to recognize mentions. This evaluation will use a manually annotated corpora as gold standard and precision, recall, and f-measure as measures for evaluation.

8.2   Candidate Selection

The best method for generation of modules is the one which returns all the best possible candidates as part of the candidate set. The annotated corpora will be used as gold standard for evaluation and the accuracy will be used as the measure to evaluate the Ontology Modularization method.

8.3   Disambiguation

For disambiguation it is necessary to evaluate: the contribution of each textual feature, the contribution of each Knowledge Base feature, and the contribution of the methods for collective inference using both textual and Knowledge Base contexts. The first two contributions can be measured separately by generating a ranking of candidates for each mention in text and measuring the precision@N, recall@N, and f-measure@N. In other words, measuring if the best entity entry given by the gold standard appears in the first top N positions in the ranking. This separation of each feature enables the comparison with features used in related work. The evaluation of methods for collective inference will be made by choosing the best features from text and Knowledge Base and measuring the results using precision, recall and f-measure. It also enables the comparison with related work.

9   Reflections

Despite the increasing number of research papers in Entity Linking there are only a small number of works considering the use of more than a single Knowledge Base. In this PhD research proposal the goal is to solve the problem of Entity Linking with Multiple Knowledge Bases. This will be done by using different textual and Knowledge Base features, and Ontology Modularization to select entities in the same semantic context. The main contributions are in enabling: a higher number of Knowledge Bases to be used for Entity Linking, the use of

Linked Enterprise Data in Entity Linking context, and the use of more types of entities for Entity Linking and applications based on the use of entities.

In conclusion, this work will improve upon previous approaches by enabling the use of multiple Knowledge Bases for Entity Linking.

Acknowledgments.. The author would like to thanks Georgeta Bordea for the kind review of early drafts of this paper as well as Emir Munoz and Andre Freitas for the insightful discussions. This work has been conducted under the supervision of Paul Buitelaar and was partially funded by the EC for the FP7 project EuroSentiment under Grant Agreement 296277 and in part by a research grant from Science Foundation Ireland (SFI) under Grant Number SFI/12/RC/2289 for the INSIGHT project.

References

1. d'Aquin, M., Schlicht, A., Stuckenschmidt, H., Sabou, M.: Ontology Modularization for Knowledge Selection: Experiments and Evaluations. In: Wagner, R., Revell, N., Pernul, G. (eds.) DEXA 2007. LNCS, vol. 4653, pp. 874–883. Springer, Heidelberg (2007)
2. Demartini, G., Difallah, D.E., Cudré-Mauroux, P.: 21st International Conference on World Wide Web
3. Han, X., Sun, L., Zhao, J.: Collective entity linking in web text. In: 34th Annual ACM SIGIR Conference (2011)
4. Hoffart, J., Yosef, M.A., Bordino, I., Furstenau, H., Pinkal, M., Spaniol, M., Taneva, B., Thater, S., Weikum, G.: Robust disambiguation of named entities in text. In: Empirical Methods in Natural Language Processing 2011, pp. 782–792 (July 2011)
5. Jensen, D., Neville, J., Gallagher, B.: Why collective inference improves relational classification. In: ACM SIGKDD 2004, pp. 593–598 (2004)
6. Kulkarni, S., Singh, A., Ramakrishnan, G., Chakrabarti, S.: Collective annotation of Wikipedia entities in web text. In: ACM SIGKDD (2009)
7. McNamee, P., Dang, H.T.: Overview of the tac 2009 knowledge base population track. In: Text Analysis Conference, vol. 17, pp. 111–113 (2009)
8. Moro, A., Raganato, A., Navigli, R.: Entity linking meets word sense disambiguation: a unified approach. Transactions of the Association for Computational Linguistics 2 (2014)
9. Pereira, B., Aggarwal, N., Buitelaar, P.: AELA: An Adaptive Entity Linking Approach. In: World Wide Web Companion (2013)
10. Pereira, B., da Silva, J.C., Vivacqua, A.: Discovering names in linked data datasets. In: 1st International Workshop on Web of Linked Entities (2012)
11. Ratinov, L., Roth, D., Downey, D., Anderson, M.: Local and Global Algorithms for Disambiguation to Wikipedia. In: 49th Annual Meeting of the Association for Computational Linguistics: Human Language Technologies (2011)
12. Sil, A., Cronin, E., Nie, P., Yang, Y., Popescu, A.-M., Yates, A.: Joint Conference on Empirical Methods in Natural Language Processing and Computational Natural Language Learning, pp. 116–127
13. Wennerberg, P., Schulz, K., Buitelaar, P.: Ontology modularization to improve semantic medical image annotation. Journal of Biomedical Informatics 44(1), 155–162 (2011)

Populating Entity Name Systems for Big Data Integration

Mayank Kejriwal

University of Texas at Austin
kejriwal@cs.utexas.edu

Abstract. An Entity Name System (ENS) is a thesaurus for entities. An ENS is a fundamental component of *data integration* systems, serving instance matching needs across multiple data sources. Populating an ENS in support of co-referencing Linked Open Data (LOD) is a Big Data problem. *Viable* solutions to the long-standing *Entity Resolution* (ER) problem are required, meeting specific requirements of *heterogeneity, scalability* and *automation*. In this thesis, we propose to develop and implement algorithms for an ER system that address the three key criteria. Preliminary results demonstrate potential system feasibility.

Keywords: Entity Name System, Data Integration, Entity Resolution.

1 Problem Statement

Linked Open Data (LOD) has grown exponentially since 2007 [2]. Many entities on the LOD cloud refer to the same logical entity and need to be resolved by linking them using *owl:sameAs* [10]. Given that LOD currently contains billions of triples in *independently* developed data sources, the *Entity Resolution* (ER) problem needs to be both *scalable* and to account for schema or *structural heterogeneity* between sources. Given that the Deep Web is about 500 times larger than the Surface Web [12], an ER solution that works with both RDF and relational (the dominant data model in the Deep Web) would need to also account for *data model heterogeneity*. The continuous growth of LOD mandates *automatic* linking of entities without excessive reliance on domain expertise.

   In this thesis, we develop and implement algorithms for an ER system meeting certain requirements of heterogeneity, scalability and automation. We describe these requirements, and propose novel techniques to satisfy them in a *MapReduce* based framework for both RDF and relational data models.

2 Relevancy

The primary motivation of the proposed system is *data integration* [7]. A complete data integration system relies on the population of an ENS component, to resolve equivalent entities occurring in multiple data sources. The generic ER problem is pervase, however, both in the relational database community as

P. Mika et al. (Eds.) ISWC 2014, Part II, LNCS 8797, pp. 521–528, 2014.

record linkage [8], and in the linked data community as *instance matching* or *link discovery* [10]. The importance of the problem is growing in concert with the Semantic Web, and with Web-scale efforts such as the Okkam ENS [3]. Thus, our solution would not be limited in potential application to data integration alone. Furthermore, the advantage of having a MapReduce [6] implementation is that the prototype can be deployed scalably as a *cloud* workflow on dynamically provisioned clusters. Scalability has emerged as an important issue in recent works on both data and ontology matching [9].

3   Related Work

The longevity of the ER problem has led to a considerable body of work on the subject. In this section, we selectively assess some recent literature from the framework of addressing automation, heterogeneity and scalability criteria. We first survey some techniques developed in the relational community, followed by related efforts in the Semantic Web community.

The ER problem has emerged in several different communities, with a profusion of terminology. Elmagarmid et al. surveys it broadly in the relational setting [8]. Typically, ER is conducted as a sequence of two steps. The first step, *blocking*, attempts to mitigate $O(n^2)$ complexity of pairwise comparison of n records by clustering 'similar' entities into overlapping *blocks* using an inexpensive *blocking scheme*. The second step takes a block as input and applies a similarity function only to pairs of entities *within* blocks. Christen provides a good survey of blocking methods [4]. Intuitively, blocking captures the *scalability* aspect.

Till quite recently, a domain expert had to *manually* specify a blocking scheme. In 2006, two independent *supervised* blocking scheme learners (BSLs) were proposed. These BSLs would learn a blocking scheme from *provided* training examples [1],[20]. Given that there was no unsupervised blocking, employing these methods implied choosing between scalability or automation, but not both. Recently however, we presented an *unsupervised* BSL [16]. In the context of this thesis, the solution addressed an impending *automation* issue.

The importance of scalability is further highlighted by an increased interest in parallel and distributed ER systems [19], with a good example of a MapReduce-based system being Dedoop [18]. Dedoop expects domain expertise or training examples, and cannot deduce blocking schemes on its own. We attempt to build our own MapReduce-based system for this thesis that integrates our automatic BSL. The ultimate goal is to ensure the system is both automated and scalable.

All works mentioned above (including our own) assumed the relational setting, and additionally, *structural homogeneity*. Elmagarmid et al. defines this as input tables restricted to having the *same* schemas [8]. Applying and extending these methods to structurally heterogeneous datasets is still relatively open, and addressed in this thesis as one *heterogeneity* contribution.

Because of the prevalence of RDF, the Semantic Web community has developed its own solutions to the ER problem. Research in this area was propelled in large part by the Silk system [13]. Ferraram et al. survey some recent ER methods in the Semantic Web [10]. Two important systems that have gained recent attention are RDF-AI [23] and Knofuss [21].

From the lens of our three criteria, we note that no automatic MapReduce-based instance matching system currently exists in the Semantic Web. As for heterogeneity, while it is addressed *within* the community [22], linking instances of two *different* models is relatively unaddressed. In this thesis, we present techniques to link tables and RDF graphs in a *unified* framework. In current literature, data models are explicitly assumed to adhere either to RDF or relational. This discussion shows that, while ER research is continuing to converge, no system currently fulfills all three criteria in a combined framework.

We also note that *DataSpace Support Platforms* (DSSPs) abstractly address some of the same three criteria as in this thesis [14]. To quote from an influential work on DSSPs, the framework assumes a '*large* number of *diverse*, interrelated sources' [11]. The authors also described how human attention should be judiciously used to continuously improve performance. Therefore, DSSPs embody scalability, heterogeneity and automation requirements that we address in this thesis. Traditionally, DSSPs were proposed in the context of *query answering* [11]. This thesis adapts similar principles to ER.

4   Research Questions

Based on the reviewed work, we identified three open research questions to motivate the thesis proposal and to respectively address heterogeneity, automation and scalability:

- In our context, a practical ER system must be designed to work with both RDF and relational models, given the growth of both LOD [2] and the Deep Web [12]. The first research question investigates whether existing ER techniques are even *well-defined* for input pairs where one input is RDF and the other, relational (*data model* heterogeneity). We also ask if current relational record linkage techniques can properly address *structural heterogeneity*.
- Assuming dataspace-like principles [14], a full ER pipeline must properly accommodate *uncertain* domain expertise. A research question is if we can anticipate the possible *forms* of domain expertise likely to be available, and incorporate the expertise in a judicious, performance-enchancing manner. A stronger research question is if we can eliminate supervision altogether.
- Given the dependencies among proposed methods, the last research question asks if a full ER pipeline can be implemented in a MapReduce-based prototype while still fulfilling the other two criteria.

The first two questions identify heterogeneity and automation issues. The third questions the possibility of scalably integrating these techniques in MapReduce. We choose MapReduce specifically because of its proven fault-tolerance advantages and the convenience of scaling and deploying MapReduce programs on the cloud [6].

Subject	Genre	Platform	Company
World Series of Poker	Card game	Wii; Personal Computer	Activision
Uno Rush	Card game	Xbox 360	*null*

(a)   **(b)**

Fig. 1. An example of the property table representation of an RDF fragment. The keyword *null* and delimiter *;* are reserved. Each field value in the property table has set semantics.

5   Hypotheses

To answer each of these questions, we present the following hypotheses:

- Abstractly, RDF-tabular heterogeneity exists because there are two data models involved, and *also* because the RDF model may not have accompanying schema information (as RDFS or OWL). We hypothesize that this heterogeneity is partially reconciled by *logically* representing RDF in a *property table*, which was originally a *physical* data structure for efficient triple store implementations [25]. We detail the rationale (and potential issues) in Section 6. Figure 1 shows an example.
- We can employ principles from our unsupervised BSL [16] to generate our *own* (noisy) training samples using inexpensive heuristics. We hypothesize that robust machine learning classifiers (e.g. SVMs) will be able to learn from these noisy samples in a self-supervised fashion. We also propose a *knowledge base* (KB) to flexibly incorporate available domain expertise. The hypothesis is that after N ER tasks, the KB will be sophisticated enough that the $N + 1^{th}$ task requires no user corrections at all, for reasonable N.
- We design a full ER prototype with *two* MapReduce phases and *one* serial module, with the aim of bounding time and space complexity of each compute node by a sub-quadratic function. Moreover, we would ideally want the *number* of compute nodes to scale linearly with input dataset size.

6   Approach

We enumerate some approaches for testing the outlined hypotheses:

- Using a *property table* has several advantages that allow us to use it for ER. First, the property schema is built *dynamically* and populated at run-time, which makes it appropriate for non-static LOD datasets. Secondly, property tables are physical data structures that are already used in the Jena framework for implementing triple stores [25]. This gives the approach a *systems-level* advantage, since we can link RDF data already present in Jena triple stores, without processing, moving or re-storing the data. Note that some

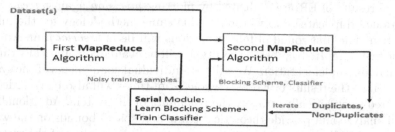

Fig. 2. An in-development prototype for unsupervised ER, with the KB excluded. We do not describe the full details of this schematic in this document; an implemented, evaluated version (with an integrated KB) will be a key deliverable of the proposed thesis

interesting *inverse mapping* issues arise when representing RDF as property tabels. For example, R2RML explores mappings in the relational to RDF direction [5]. Property tables explore mappings in the inverse direction, with a view towards performing ER between two models. This is an important theoretical consequence that we will investigate during the course of the thesis. Another open issue is how to incorporate available schema information (as OWL/RDFS files) of the RDF datasets in the property table.

- We will adapt the noisy training set generator from our previous work [16], to bootstrap the system and make it self-supervised. We will implement the KB as an ontology, and try a variety of techniques, including rules, transfer learning and online algorithms to evaluate the best way of accommodating uncertain domain expertise.
- The schematic of the prototype is shown in Figure 2. Intuitively, a first MapReduce phase can be used to *generate* noisy training samples, while a second MapReduce phase is used to perform two-step ER, based on a blocking scheme and classifier trained in a *serial* module. If available, domain expertise can also be utilized in the serial module. In the first set of empirical evaluations, we will disallow domain expertise. After deriving initial insights, we will attempt integrating an adaptive KB into the unsupervised prototype.

7 Evaluation Plan

Both the ER and machine learning literature have well-defined criteria for evaluating success of our proposed methods. Henceforth, we assume RDF datasets are represented as property tables.

- The *blocking* phase of ER is traditionally evaluated separately using three metrics: Pairs Completeness (PC), Reduction Ratio (RR) and Pairs Quality (PQ). In our first set of evaluations, we measure the quality of our noisy training samples as well as unsupervised blocking. In essence, we are evaluating the impact of proposed *automation* and *heterogeneity* techniques on the blocking problem.

- Final results of ER are evaluated by plotting *precision* against *recall* of the obtained duplicates. We will follow this same methodology for the full ER system. The first round of full evaluations will be in a *serial* framework.
- The first[1] MapReduce-based prototype will be evaluated empirically through a Hadoop implementation. We will test individual components of the system, as well as the results of ER as a whole. Run-times will also be recorded and plotted to empirically evaluate the *scalability* of the system. Additionally, we will analyze and provide theoretical (time and space) bounds on the various phases. Ideally, we would want to prove near-linear scaling of the system.
- We will evaluate the KB through plotting *learning curves* showing precision-recall f-scores against *units* of domain expertise. The specific nature of these units will depend on the finalized KB approach. Because it is the most uncertain of the current thesis proposal, this evaluation is the last in our sequence.

We will carry out all these experiments on a range of at least three real-world, representative test suites. At least one of these has already been identified and published by us in a related work [24]. We have also identified good sources of government data.

8   Preliminary Results

We observed in Section 3 that, although unsupervised techniques have been developed for several ER phases, learning a blocking scheme remained supervised till quite recently. In a 2013 work, we devised an approach for unsupervised learning of blocking schemes on structurally homogeneous datasets [16]. To deal with lack of training data, we devised an inexpensive token-based algorithm to generate our own *noisy* training set. We showed that for a *few* retrieved

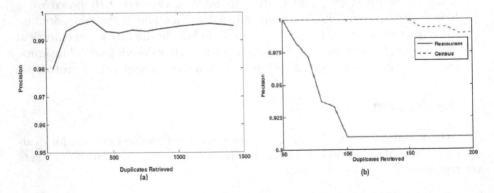

Fig. 3. Precision of duplicates automatically retrieved from three benchmark datasets ((a) shows *Cora* and (b) *Restaurant* and *Census*), using an inexpensive heuristic. Precision of non-duplicates (up to 5000 samples) was 100% for all benchmarks

---

[1] The first version is unsupervised, and does not employ the KB (Figure 2)

examples, the noise levels are low. Figure 3 shows some selected results from this work. On all three benchmarks, precision was well over 90%; on *Cora*, it was almost perfect. In our blocking scheme learner [16], we used feature-selection based techniques to compensate for these noise levels. Final blocking results (not shown here) were competitive compared to a *supervised* set-covering baseline[1]. This shows that noisy training set generation is a viable procedure as long as noise levels are low, and the algorithmic design takes the noise into account.

We have since extended this work to account for structural heterogeneity and link discovery [17], and are also in the process of using it for a full self-supervised ER pipeline. Additionally, we have also developed some theoretical results on heterogeneous blocking in a recent report, and are continuing to update it [15].

9 Reflections

In this thesis, we propose solutions to the ER problem that address three key criteria of automation, heterogeneity and scalability in a unified framework. To address automation, we generate noisy training samples in an unsupervised procedure, and incorporate limited domain expertise by building and updating a flexible *knowledge base*. We extend methods to explicitly account for *structural* heterogeneity, and use the physical property table representation of RDF *logically* to address *data model* heterogeneity. Proposed methods will be implemented in a MapReduce-based prototype to address *scalability* and cloud deployment.

One potential area of concern is the *noise* in the generated training samples. The system will therefore have to be *robust*. Another threat could be scaling the property table for highly heterogeneous RDF datasets, and incorporating OWL schema information in the property schema. We continue to investigate these issues, both empirically and also in a theoretical framework.

Acknowledgments. I want to thank my advisor, Dr. Daniel P. Miranker, for his support. I am also grateful to the reviewers for their constructive feedback.

References

1. Bilenko, M., Kamath, B., Mooney, R.J.: Adaptive blocking: Learning to scale up record linkage. In: Sixth International Conference on Data Mining, ICDM 2006, pp. 87–96. IEEE (2006)
2. Bizer, C., Heath, T., Berners-Lee, T.: Linked data-the story so far. International Journal on Semantic Web and Information Systems 5(3), 1–22 (2009)
3. Bouquet, P., Molinari, A.: A global entity name system (ens) for data ecosystems. Proceedings of the VLDB Endowment 6(11), 1182–1183 (2013)
4. Christen, P.: A survey of indexing techniques for scalable record linkage and deduplication. IEEE Transactions on Knowledge and Data Engineering 24(9), 1537–1555 (2012)
5. Das, S., Sundara, S., Cyganiak, R.: R2RML: RDB to RDF Mapping Language (2012)

6. Dean, J., Ghemawat, S.: Mapreduce: simplified data processing on large clusters. Communications of the ACM 51(1), 107–113 (2008)
7. Doan, A., Halevy, A., Ives, Z.: Principles of data integration. Access Online via Elsevier (2012)
8. Elmagarmid, A.K., Ipeirotis, P.G., Verykios, V.S.: Duplicate record detection: A survey. IEEE Transactions on Knowledge and Data Engineering 19(1), 1–16 (2007)
9. Euzenat, J., Shvaiko, P., et al.: Ontology matching, vol. 18. Springer (2007)
10. Ferraram, A., Nikolov, A., Scharffe, F.: Data linking for the semantic web. In: Semantic Web: Ontology and Knowledge Base Enabled Tools, Services, and Applications, p. 169 (2013)
11. Halevy, A., Franklin, M., Maier, D.: Principles of dataspace systems. In: Proceedings of the Twenty-fifth ACM SIGMOD-SIGACT-SIGART Symposium on Principles of Database Systems, pp. 1–9. ACM (2006)
12. He, B., Patel, M., Zhang, Z., Chang, K.C.-C.: Accessing the deep web. Communications of the ACM 50(5), 94–101 (2007)
13. Isele, R., Bizer, C.: Learning expressive linkage rules using genetic programming. Proceedings of the VLDB Endowment 5(11), 1638–1649 (2012)
14. Jeffery, S.R., Franklin, M.J., Halevy, A.Y.: Pay-as-you-go user feedback for dataspace systems. In: Proceedings of the 2008 ACM SIGMOD International Conference on Management of Data, pp. 847–860. ACM (2008)
15. Kejriwal, M., Miranker, D.P.: N-way heterogeneous blocking. In: TR-14-06 (2013)
16. Kejriwal, M., Miranker, D.P.: An unsupervised algorithm for learning blocking schemes. In: Thirteenth International Conference on Data Mining, ICDM 2013. IEEE (2013)
17. Kejriwal, M., Miranker, D.P.: A two-step blocking scheme learner for scalable link discovery. In: Under Review at ISWC OM Workshop (2014)
18. Kolb, L., Thor, A., Rahm, E.: Dedoop: efficient deduplication with hadoop. Proceedings of the VLDB Endowment 5(12), 1878–1881 (2012)
19. Mamun, A.-A., Mi, T., Aseltine, R., Rajasekaran, S.: Efficient sequential and parallel algorithms for record linkage. Journal of the American Medical Informatics Association, amiajnl–2013 (2013)
20. Michelson, M., Knoblock, C.A.: Learning blocking schemes for record linkage. In: Proceedings of the National Conference on Artificial Intelligence, vol. 21, p. 440. AAAI Press, MIT Press, Menlo Park, Cambridge (1999, 2006)
21. Nikolov, A., Uren, V., Motta, E., De Roeck, A.: Handling instance coreferencing in the knofuss architecture (2008)
22. Nikolov, A., Uren, V., Motta, E., de Roeck, A.: Overcoming schema heterogeneity between linked semantic repositories to improve coreference resolution. In: Gómez-Pérez, A., Yu, Y., Ding, Y. (eds.) ASWC 2009. LNCS, vol. 5926, pp. 332–346. Springer, Heidelberg (2009)
23. Scharffe, F., Liu, Y., Zhou, C.: Rdf-ai: an architecture for rdf datasets matching, fusion and interlink. In: Proc. IJCAI 2009 Workshop on Identity, Reference, and Knowledge Representation (IR-KR), Pasadena, CA, US (2009)
24. Tian, A., Kejriwal, M., Miranker, D.P.: Schema matching over relations, attributes, and data values. In: Proceedings of the 26th International Conference on Scientific and Statistical Database Management, p. 28. ACM (2014)
25. Wilkinson, K., Sayers, C., Kuno, H.A., Reynolds, D.: et al. Efficient rdf storage and retrieval in jena2. In: SWDB, vol. 3, pp. 131–150 (2003)

Semantic Complex Event Processing
for Decision Support

Robin Keskisärkkä

Linköping University, Linköping, Sweden
robin.keskisarkka@liu.se

Abstract. An increasing amount of information is being made available as online streams, and streams are expected to grow in importance in a variety of domains in the coming years (e.g., natural disaster response, surveillance, monitoring of criminal activity, and military planning [7,22]). Semantic Web (SW) technologies have the potential to combine heterogeneous data sources, leveraging Linked Data principles, but traditional SW methods assume that data is more or less static, which is not the case for streams. The SW community has attempted to bring streams to a semantic level, i.e., Linked Stream Data, and a number of RDF stream processing engines have been produced [1,4,13,20]. This thesis work aims at developing and evaluating techniques for creating aggregated and layered abstractions of events. These abstractions can be used by decision makers to create better situation awareness, assisting in identifying decision opportunities, structuring and summarizing decision problems, and decreasing cognitive workload.

Keywords: RDF stream processing, Semantic CEP, decision support, situation awareness.

1 Introduction/Motivation

Traditionally, authorities and citizens have relied on official communication channels to achieve situation awareness, but today online communication channels are increasingly being used [11,25]. As an example, analysis of social media has been used to assess influenza outbreaks [12], and to assist disaster relief [23]. But while humans can handle complex recognition and analysis tasks with great accuracy, performance suffers greatly as workload increases, which introduces a bottleneck for large scale data analysis tasks.

The information available as online streams is expected to grow in importance across many domains, e.g., natural disaster response, surveillance, monitoring of criminal activity, and military planning [7,22]. Online streams are already used in domains such as electronic trading and market feed processing [18].

The Semantic Web (SW) community has attempted to bring streams to a semantic level, i.e., Linked Stream Data, but in handling continuously delivered data traditional SW technologies fall short [14]. The streaming data is characterized by being received continuously in possibly unbounded streams [4]. Since no

P. Mika et al. (Eds.) ISWC 2014, Part II, LNCS 8797, pp. 529–536, 2014.

final answer can typically be returned, queries must be executed repeatedly as new data becomes available. The traditional methods for querying Linked Data build on the assumption of data as more or less static, but streaming data is often outdated quickly and needs to be consumed on the fly [24]. Also, the rate and quantity of the incoming data in itself may require data to be processed continuously. To tackle this problem a number of streaming engines and query language extensions, targeted at querying streaming and static RDF data, have been developed. These systems have largely been inspired by data stream management systems, e.g., CQL [2], which use query operators to isolate portions of streams based on timestamps.

The purpose of Complex Event Processing (CEP) is to (semi-)automatically create "actionable" abstractions from streams of events [16]. In order to support flexible abstractions and pattern matching of heterogeneous data streams semantics must be introduced, and Semantic CEP is targeted specifically at *semantically* interpreting and analyzing data using the Linked Data principles and SW technologies.

The abstraction task can be described as process in which sets of *low-level* events are aggregated into *high-level* events, by means of some event pattern. An event is defined here as "anything that happens, or is contemplated as happening", while a complex event is defined as "an event that summarizes, represents, or denotes a set of other events" [16].

A simple view of decision making is as a process in which an answer is selected among a set of alternatives, but a more sophisticated view includes many other aspects, such as identifying that there is a decision to be made in the first place. Empirical studies have demonstrated that human judgment and decision making relies heavily on intuitive strategies, rather than on strict reasoning rules [6]. These strategies reduce cognitive load, but also make decisions more sensitive to biases. The purpose of Decision Support Systems (DSS) is to assist decision makers in the activity of making a decision by providing a set of tools to aid decision makers in the process of modeling and analyzing data, identifying decision opportunities, imposing structure on data, and supporting the choice processes [17, Chapter 1]. Another way of supporting the decision making process is to abstract portions of a decision-making situation and to model the available information in ways which retain only the essential relationships to reduce cognitive load and problem complexity. The abstractions additionally help make knowledge easier to transfer across problems and domains.

2   Related Research

The SW community is relatively new in the field of stream processing, but a considerable amount of research has previously been done on continuous query processing over streams, e.g., in projects such as the STREAM prototype developed at Stanford [2], StreamBase[1], and ESPER[2]. This research has largely

---

[1] http://www.streambase.com/
[2] http://esper.codehaus.org/

made up the foundation for the state-of-the-art RDF stream processing (RSP) systems that have been implemented to date.

There are no official standards for how RDF data streams are to be represented or published. In [4] an RDF stream is defined as an ordered sequence of tuples, consisting of an RDF triple and a timestamp. Triples with the same timestamp are treated as if they occurred at the same time. However, RDF streams can be represented in a number of ways, e.g., data elements can be RDF graphs rather than triples, intervals can be used instead of timestamps, and timestamps/intervals could be represented in the stream itself rather than as parts of streamed tuples [9].

In CEP streams consist of simple (atomic) and complex (composite) events. To represent events in a general sense a number of vocabularies have been proposed [21]. A common model for complex events can simplify querying and abstraction into higher level events, but it may also result in additional overhead.

2.1 State of the Art

DSSs normally have narrow application scopes and are typically not generalizable to different decision-making contexts. Over the last decade SW technologies have been used in DSS to solve tasks such as information integration and sharing, web service annotation and discovery, and knowledge representation and reasoning. For a more in-depth review of SW technologies in DSS refer to [5].

The next sections briefly describe four RDF Stream Processing (RSP) systems that represent current state of the art. These are followed by discussion of frameworks using a CEP engine in combination with Linked Stream Data.

CQELS was created to address the problem of scalable query processing of Linked Stream Data [13]. The query language is an extension of SPARQL 1.1, supporting query patterns for the defining logical and physical windows over streams. The engine is a native implementation and returns results in near real-time, and for some queries the CQELS engine outperforms similar approaches (C-SPARQL and ETALIS) by orders of magnitude [13].

C-SPARQL is an RSP engine with a query language that extends SPARQL 1.0 to support the definition of physical and logical windows over streams, as well as aggregation operators. Queries are executed periodically at a rate decided by the system, and the engine can report duplicates of results if the windows of two query executions overlap.

EP-SPARQL is a language for event processing developed for ETALIS to handle SW applications [1]. The language is based on SPARQL 1.0, but extends the language with a number of binary temporal operators. Instead of defining windows over streams functions exist to access duration, start time, and end time, and using these windows can be defined inside filter expressions.

INSTANS is a query engine capable of continuous execution of selected parts of SPARQL 1.1 Query and Update [20]. It avoids repeated computation of the same data, and makes results available immediately when a query patterns is matched. INSTANS additionally supports the detection of missing events by employing a timer that can be registered for events. Modeling of time and windows must be expressed manually in RDF (e.g. as suggested in [8]).

2.2 Framework Approaches

The Streaming Linked Data (SLD) framework [3] was designed to allow publishers to stream data to a central server, where streams can be queried, stored and replayed, decorated with additional information, and republished as new streams. It assumes that streams are published using the HTTP protocol and uses a built-in RSP engine (C-SPARQL).

Another framework project is the Super Stream Collider (SSC) [19]. It to supports the registering of streams and queries, but relies instead on the CQELS engine. SSC supports streams published using Web Sockets. Web Sockets are highly efficient and allow for real-time and high speed full-duplex communication, and guarantees that data will arrive in the order it was originally streamed.

A different approach was proposed in the framework in [15]. This framework focuses on bridging the gap between Linked Data and rule-based CEP engines. This is accomplished by translating events into the format required by a specified engine, specifically for Drools Fusion[3]. The obvious benefit of this approach is that a mature and well-used CEP engine can be employed, but it also means that translations need to be provided back and forth between internal engine formats and Linked Data.

3 Problem Statement and Contributions

Current decision support systems do not assist users in making any high-level abstractions of situations, rather they only summarize or visualize data. The main hypothesis of this thesis work is that the combination of Linked Data, SW technologies, and CEP make it possible to create useful abstractions based on event patterns in real-time.

Existing vocabularies for expressing complex events will be evaluated and possibly extended. Additionally, ways of querying event streams, and representing boundaries of complex events, will be investigated. The work aims to develop ways of expressing more declarative descriptions of queries and complex events using Ontology Design Patterns (ODPs)[4], and reusable query templates, to enable more generalizable event pattern descriptions.

Social media streams are becoming an increasingly important asset in achieving situation awareness in many domains and will be also be leveraged in this

---

[3] http://drools.jboss.org/drools-fusion
[4] http://ontologydesignpatterns.org/

work. Social media streams require systems that can handle incomplete, unreliable, incorrect, and even contradictory data. To handle this it should be possible to employ external applications, e.g., for natural language processing.

The novelty of this approach, compared with traditional CEP, lies in bringing in semantics for the explicit use in decision support, and in taking advantage of Linked Data concepts to abstract heterogeneous data streams. Complex events will be described using a vocabulary that supports layered abstractions of events. By automating various abstraction steps in tractable fashion, the goal is to support decision makers, e.g., by decreasing cognitive workload, assisting event detection, and increase situation awareness.

4   Research Methodology and Approach

Part of the research work involves developing a framework for experimenting with streams, and enabling different RSP engines to be plugged in. This approach is similar to the examples described in Section 2.2. The framework will make it possible to experiment with and benchmark different engines, vocabularies, and queries with minimum overhead. The framework will include adapters for various types of live and recorded streams and support generation of new streams from queries, which will enable the development of various types of stream decorations.

Declarative descriptions will be used to simplify the creation and maintenance of queries, and complex events, and to make some changes to queries possible with minimal user intervention. Appropriate ODPs and query templates will have to be developed. Query templates may require an extension of SPIN[5] (or similar).

5   Preliminary or Intermediate Results

We have previously proposed a number of approaches to representing event object boundaries in various types of RDF streams [9]. While none of the approaches have been evaluated in use, it was shown that if events are described by single RDF graphs boundaries are manageable. In the context of abstracted event objects, consisting of multiple hierarchically ordered graphs, the boundary issues become more complex. Supporting a general view of aggregated and composite event objects will require both a suitable vocabulary, and a clear standard for how RDF streams are represented and communicated.

In [21] we presented a vocabulary that can be used to structure, integrate, and interchange events, regardless of the underlying vocabulary. The model supports multiple time-related parameters, e.g., sampling time, time of entry in the stream, and time of arrival. It also supports the use of payloads, and the encapsulation of event objects. Another important aspect of this vocabulary is that is was defined with querying ability in mind.

---

[5] http://spinrdf.org/

The requirements and challenges for social media monitoring have also been discussed [10]. In the paper we identified a set of requirements against the current state-of-the-art RSP engines, and highlighted some of the strengths and weaknesses of the systems. While a number of the challenges can be addressed by providing various stream decoration techniques, others are more difficult to address. Only INSTANS is designed to make timestamps available as triples, meaning that it would be difficult for the other engines to support multiple timestamps. The fact that timestamps are not available as triples also creates difficulties with regard to how timestamps should be handled in the case of complex events.

6   Evaluation Plan

The hypothesis of this thesis work will be evaluated within the project *Visual Analytics for Sense-making in CRiminal Intelligence analysis* (VALCRI). The project will enable us to develop and test models for representing complex events, as well as various ways of expressing generalized event patterns, in a real-world setting. The project officially started in late May 2014, and preliminary data and data stream logs have recently been made available.

A survey regarding sate-of-the-art detection of criminal activities will be used as a reference for developing event patterns, query templates, and ODPs. The event patterns and ODPs will be developed in cooperation with the Pacific Northwest National Laboratory. In particular, it will be important to develop event patterns for detecting events from low-frequency signals.

The event patterns will (hopefully) be tested in cooperation with domain experts, acting both as users of the systems and as validators of the generated abstractions. Additionally, validation may be possible based on the data logs themselves, as they contain anonymized records of criminal reports.

7   Reflections

This thesis work aims to develop techniques to assist decision makers in dealing with systems involving large scale heterogeneous real-time data streams by creating high-level abstractions of events. Abstractions in decision making situations can reduce problem complexity and cognitive workload, improve situation awareness, mitigate decision biases, and help to create predictions of future states.

It is clear that streaming data is becoming increasingly important in many domains, but for Semantic CEP to become effective on a broad scale community consensus is required, and there is a need for establishing standard vocabularies, query languages, and stream formats.

When producing declarative descriptions of event patterns the degree to which they can be made scalable is at present not known. All patterns may not be expressible using the available RSP engines and corresponding query languages, e.g., if windows need to be expressed in the past, or a stream has to be referenced with different windows in the same query.

The representation of complex events risks greatly affecting streaming performance of the engines, and the querying of complex events may introduce considerable overhead and memory problems. Current state-of-the-art RSP engines are still not fully mature, meaning that they are still quite limited in the number of streams and queries they can handle efficiently. One possible scenario is therefore that the systems will only be able to execute a very limited amount of the more complex event pattern queries, or that the queries will result considerable delays.

Acknowledgement. The thesis work is financed by *Visual Analytics for Sensemaking in CRiminal Intelligence analysis* (VALCRI), *Semantic Technologies for Decision Support* (STeDS), and *Center for Industrial Information Technology* (CENIIT).

References

1. Anicic, D., Fodor, P., Rudolph, S., Stojanovic, N.: EP-SPARQL: A Unified Language for Event Processing and Stream Reasoning. In: Proceedings of the 20th International Conference on World Wide Web (2011)
2. Arasu, A., Babu, S., Widom, J.: The CQL Continuous Query Language: Semantic Foundations and Query Execution. The VLDB Journal 15(2), 121–142 (2006)
3. Balduini, M., Della Valle, E., Dell'Aglio, D., Tsytsarau, M., Palpanas, T., Confalonieri, C.: Social Listening of City Scale Events Using the Streaming Linked Data Framework. In: Alani, H., et al. (eds.) ISWC 2013, Part II. LNCS, vol. 8219, pp. 1–16. Springer, Heidelberg (2013)
4. Barbieri, D.F., Braga, D., Ceri, S., Valle, E.D., Grossniklaus, M.: Querying RDF streams with C-SPARQL. SIGMOD Record 39(1), 20–26 (2010)
5. Blomqvist, E.: The Use of Semantic Web Technologies for Decision Support - A Survey. To appear in: Semantic Web Journal (2012)
6. Druzdzel, M.J., Flynn, R.R.: Decision Support Systems. In: Bates, M.J., Maack, M.N. (eds.) Encyclopedia of Library and Information Science, 3rd edn. Taylor & Francis, Inc., New York (2010)
7. Goodwin, J.C., Russomanno, D.J.: Ontology integration within a service-oriented architecture for expert system applications using sensor networks. Expert Systems 26(5), 409–432 (2009)
8. Gutierrez, C., Hurtado, C.A., Vaisman, A.: Introducing Time into RDF. IEEE Transactions on Knowledge and Data Engineering 19(2), 207–218 (2007)
9. Keskisärkkä, R., Blomqvist, E.: Event Object Boundaries in RDF Streams: A Position Paper. In: ISWC 2013 Workshop: Proceedings of OrdRing 2013 - 2nd International Workshop on Ordering and Reasoning, Sydney, Australia. CEUR workshop proceedings (October 2013)
10. Keskisärkkä, R., Blomqvist, E.: Semantic Complex Event Processing for Social Media Monitoring - A Survey. In: Proceedings of Social Media and Linked Data for Emergency Response (SMILE) Co-located with the 10th Extended Semantic Web Conference, Montpellier, France. CEUR workshop proceedings (May 2013)

11. Kwak, H., Lee, C., Park, H., Moon, S.: What is Twitter, a social network or a news media? In: Proceedings of the 19th International Conference on World Wide Web, pp. 591–600. ACM, New York (2010)
12. Lampos, V., De Bie, T., Cristianini, N.: Flu detector: tracking epidemics on twitter. In: Balcázar, J.L., Bonchi, F., Gionis, A., Sebag, M. (eds.) ECML PKDD 2010, Part III. LNCS (LNAI), vol. 6323, pp. 599–602. Springer, Heidelberg (2010)
13. Le-Phuoc, D., Dao-Tran, M., Xavier Parreira, J., Hauswirth, M.: A Native and Adaptive Approach for Unified Processing of Linked Streams and Linked Data. In: Aroyo, L., Welty, C., Alani, H., Taylor, J., Bernstein, A., Kagal, L., Noy, N., Blomqvist, E. (eds.) ISWC 2011, Part I. LNCS, vol. 7031, pp. 370–388. Springer, Heidelberg (2011)
14. Le-Phuoc, D., Parreira, J.X., Hausenblas, M., Hauswirth, M.: Unifying Stream Data and Linked Open Data. Tech. rep., DERI (2010)
15. Liu, D., Pedrinaci, C., Domingue, J.: A Framework for Feeding Linked Data to Complex Event Processing Engines. In: ISWC 2010 Workshop: The 1st International Workshop on Consuming Linked Data (COLD), vol. 665. CEUR Workshop Proceedings, Shanghai (2010)
16. Luckham, D.C.: The Power of Events: An Introduction to Complex Event Processing in Distributed Enterprise Systems. Addison-Wesley Longman Publishing Co., Inc., Boston (2001)
17. Marakas, G.: Decision support systems in the 21st century, 2nd edn. Prentice Hall, Upper Saddle River (2003)
18. Morris, G.W., Thomas, D.B., Luk, W.: FPGA accelerated low-latency market data feed processing. In: Proceedings of the 17th IEEE Symposium on High Performance Interconnects (2009)
19. Quoc, H.N.M., Serrano, M., Le-Phuoc, D., Hauswirth, M.: Super Stream Collider–Linked Stream Mashups for Everyone. In: Proceedings of the Semantic Web Challenge Co-located with the 11th International Semantic Web Conference, Boston, MA, USA (November 2012)
20. Rinne, M., Abdullah, H., Törmä, S., Nuutila, E.: Processing Heterogeneous RDF Events with Standing SPARQL Update Rules. In: Meersman, R., et al. (eds.) OTM 2012, Part II. LNCS, vol. 7566, pp. 797–806. Springer, Heidelberg (2012)
21. Rinne, M., Blomqvist, E., Keskisärkkä, R., Nuutila, E.: Event Processing in RDF. In: ISWC 2013 Workshop: Proceedings of the 4th Workshop on Ontology and Semantic Web Patterns (WOP 2013). CEUR Workshop Proceedings, Sydney (2013)
22. Sequeda, J.F., Corcho, O.: Linked Stream Data: A Position Paper. In: ISWC 2009 Workshop: Proceedings of the 2nd International Workshop on Semantic Sensor Networks (2009)
23. Slagh, C.L.: Managing Chaos, 140 Characters at a Time: How the Usage of Social Media in the 2010 Haiti Crisis Enhanced Disaster Relief. Master's thesis, Georgetown University, Washington, DC (2010)
24. Stonebraker, M., Çetintemel, U., Zdonik, S.: The 8 requirements of real-time stream processing. SIGMOD Record 34(4), 42–47 (2005)
25. Teevan, J., Ramage, D., Morris, M.R.: #Twittersearch: a comparison of microblog search and web search. In: Proceedings of the Fourth ACM International Conference on Web Search and Data Mining, pp. 35–44. ACM, New York (2011)

Enriching Ontologies with Encyclopedic Background Knowledge for Document Indexing

Lisa Posch

GESIS – Leibniz Institute for the Social Sciences
Unter Sachsenhausen 6-8
D-50667 Cologne, Germany
lisa.posch@gesis.org

Abstract. The rapidly increasing number of scientific documents available publicly on the Internet creates the challenge of efficiently organizing and indexing these documents. Due to the time consuming and tedious nature of manual classification and indexing, there is a need for better methods to automate this process. This thesis proposes an approach which leverages encyclopedic background knowledge for enriching domain-specific ontologies with textual and structural information about the semantic vicinity of the ontologies' concepts. The proposed approach aims to exploit this information for improving both ontology-based methods for classifying and indexing documents and methods based on supervised machine learning.

1 Introduction

The amount of scientific publications available on the Internet is increasing rapidly. Without efficient methods for document classification and indexing, it is increasingly time consuming and difficult for researchers to find relevant publications. Traditionally, scientific institutions performed the task of facilitating search for relevant literature by manually indexing and classifying new publications, with the goal of maintaining an ideally complete domain-specific database. However, this task is becoming progressively more difficult to perform, as manual indexing is time consuming, tedious and expensive.

In the recent decades, researchers of different domains have attempted to tackle this problem by developing a wide range of methods for automatic text classification and indexing. Most of these methods are based on machine learning algorithms or on algorithms which use ontologies as background knowledge. While existing approaches allow rapid classification and indexing of a large number of documents, the quality of the results is not comparable to the performance of expert human indexers. Therefore, it is an ongoing challenge to improve the methods for automatic classification and indexing.

The main goal of this thesis is to build upon existing methods to construct an improved framework for automatic classification and subject indexing of documents. The proposed approach leverages encyclopedic background knowledge for enriching existing domain-specific ontologies and classification systems with

P. Mika et al. (Eds.) ISWC 2014, Part II, LNCS 8797, pp. 537–544, 2014.

additional textual and structural information about the semantic vicinity of the ontologies' concepts. Specifically, I plan to investigate whether this encyclopedic background knowledge is useful for improving the results of ontology-based classification and indexing methods as well as methods based on machine learning.

This paper is structured as follows: Section 2 gives a brief overview of related research on subject indexing and classification. My research questions and hypotheses are stated in Section 3. Section 4 discusses the proposed approach and Section 5 describes the evaluation process. The datasets which I plan to apply my approach to are introduced in Section 6; preliminary experiments on one of these datasets are presented in Section 7. Finally, Section 8 concludes this work.

2   Related Work

Most of the approaches to classification and indexing of documents are based on either machine learning algorithms or on methods which use ontologies as background knowledge. This section briefly summarizes the main techniques which have been used to address the challenge of automatically classifying and indexing documents.

Subject indexing refers to assigning topical keywords to documents (usually from a controlled vocabulary such as a thesaurus), while *document classification* assigns a document to one or more semantic categories. The difference between these tasks, however, is negligible, as the aim of both is to produce appropriate connections between documents and semantic entities [10]. *Semantic annotation* refers to attaching meta-data to resources, usually in the context of the Semantic Web [12]. Both subject indexing and document classification can therefore be seen as a form of semantic document annotation.

Machine Learning Based Methods: Both supervised and unsupervised machine learning methods have been applied to document classification and indexing. A popular method for representing documents in supervised learning is the *bag-of-words* approach, which represents documents by the words they contain, disregarding the order in which they occur. Instead of single words, also sequences of words (*n-grams*) can be used to represent a document. The words or n-grams can be weighted by different schemes such as term frequency or TF-IDF [14]. While TF-IDF is unable to capture the semantic structures in documents, methods such as *latent semantic analysis (LSA)* [5] and *probabilistic LSA (pLSA)* [8] try to overcome this weakness. Recently, also encyclopedic background knowledge has been leveraged for representing documents. For example, *explicit semantic analysis (ESA)* [6] represents the meaning of documents as weighted vectors of Wikipedia-based concepts. While originally intended for computing semantic relatedness, it has also been applied successfully to text classification (e.g. [7]).

One commonly used method for unsupervised text classification and indexing are *topic models*. Topic models are statistical models which aim to discover latent topics in documents. The simplest one is *Latent Dirichlet Allocation (LDA)*, which was introduced by Blei et al. [3]. A supervised version of LDA, *sLDA*, was later presented by Blei and McAuliffe [2]. *Labeled LDA*, another supervised topic model, was introduced by Ramage et al. [13]. Labeled LDA constrains the latent topics which are to be learned to the labels of the documents in the training dataset. Topic models have also been used to create features for training supervised classifiers [2].

Ontology-Based Methods: An ontology is a *"formal, explicit specification of a shared conceptualization."* [15] Ontologies have been used as background knowledge for semantic annotation of documents (e.g. [9], [4]), mostly in the context of the Semantic Web. Jonquet et al. [9] presented the Open Biomedical Annotator, which is an ontology-based Web service for annotating documents with biomedical ontology concepts. The annotation process consists of two main steps: The first step, *concept recognition* produces direct annotations by matching textual meta-data of the documents to ontology concepts. In the second step, the set of direct annotations is *expanded* by using semantic relations of the ontology and by using existing mappings to other ontologies. I plan to build upon and extend this approach by incorporating textual and structural encyclopedic background knowledge.

3   Research Questions and Hypotheses

My research aims to investigate ways in which encyclopedic background knowledge, in the form of textual and structural information about the semantic vicinity of ontology concepts, may be useful for improving the classification and indexing of documents. In particular, I plan to address the following research questions:

1. How does the effectiveness of automatic indexing and classification techniques which exploit encyclopedic background knowledge compare to the effectiveness of techniques which do not use encyclopedic background knowledge?
2. How does the effectiveness of automatic indexing and classification techniques which exploit encyclopedic background knowledge change with different strategies of incorporating the background knowledge?
3. In which ways can encyclopedic background knowledge be useful for effectively combining the sets of keywords and classes suggested by machine learning methods with those suggested by ontology-based methods?

I hypothesize that encyclopedic background knowledge about the semantic neighborhood of the defined concepts in an ontology can be successfully leveraged for modeling a more comprehensive representation of said concepts and that the enhanced representation of these concepts is likely to contribute to a more accurate classification and indexing of documents.

4   Proposed Approach

This section describes the proposed approach for classifying and indexing documents using encyclopedic background knowledge. The approach leverages non-domain-specific encyclopedic background knowledge to enrich existing domain-specific ontologies (and classification systems) with additional information about the concepts contained in the ontology. This additional information includes encyclopedic textual information about concepts which are semantically closely related to concepts contained in the ontology, as well as structural information about the nature of the semantic relations between the concepts. I believe that this information can be useful for automatic classification and indexing of documents, contributing to a more accurate assignment of semantic classes and topical keywords by ontology-based as well as supervised methods.

To the best of my knowledge, this is the first attempt to enrich existing domain-specific ontologies and classification systems with non-domain-specific encyclopedic background knowledge with the aim of improving automatic indexing and classification of documents. The two main steps of my approach are described in more detail in the rest of this section.

4.1   Enriching an Existing Domain-Specific Ontology

The first step of the approach consists in enriching an existing domain-specific ontology with encyclopedic background knowledge. This can be achieved by first mapping the concepts contained in the ontology to the concepts contained in an encyclopedia and subsequently modeling the semantic neighborhood of the ontology's concepts. Wikipedia constitutes an attractive option for using as the encyclopedia of choice, as it has often shown to be useful for a wide range of applications in domains such as natural language processing, information retrieval and ontology building [11]. The mapping could be achieved either manually or by employing automatic mapping techniques.

For modeling the semantic neighborhood of the ontology's concepts, it is necessary to identify which encyclopedic entries lie in the semantic vicinity of the ontology's concepts, as well as the nature of the semantic relations to the ontology's concepts and between the encyclopedic entries. If Wikipedia is chosen as the encyclopedia, this task can be achieved by employing ontologies extracted from Wikipedia such as Yago [16] or DBpedia [1]. One of the main challenges in this step is to adequately map the entire ontology, and to appropriately deal with ontology concepts which do not match any encyclopedia concept (e.g., by linking them to several related encyclopedia concepts).

4.2   Using the Enriched Ontology with Existing Classification and Indexing Methods

The second step of the approach is to investigate whether the enriched ontology is useful for classifying and indexing documents. To achieve this, I plan to integrate it into existing ontology-based methods and supervised machine learning methods.

Ontology-Based Methods: In an approach building upon the one used by the Open Biomedical Annotator [9], encyclopedic background knowledge is likely to be useful in both concept recognition and the identification of semantically related ontology concepts to extend the keyword set. Concerning the concept recognition task, the textual information from encyclopedic entries in semantic vicinity of ontology concepts can be used to better identify matching concepts in the text (i.a. by alleviating the problem of vocabulary mismatch). Regarding the extension of the keyword set, the structural information from the encyclopedia can provide support nodes and support relations, which could prove useful for making a better decision on which additional ontology concepts to include in the keyword set.

Supervised Machine Learning Methods: The textual information of the encyclopedic articles in the semantic vicinity of a category or ontology concept is likely to be able to diminish the problem of sparseness in training datasets, by providing additional training examples. A potential limitation for the usefulness of these additional training examples is that the type of language used in the documents may differ significantly from the language used in the encyclopedia.

Combination of Ontology-Based and Supervised Methods: Encyclopedic background knowledge could be useful for effectively combining the keywords suggested by supervised machine learning with those suggested by the ontology-based approach. The resulting keyword sets could be combined, for example, by starting out with the intersection set and including further keywords from the union of both keyword sets. Which keywords are chosen for indexing would depend on the semantic distance, calculated on the enriched ontology, to the keywords in the intersection set.

5   Evaluation

To evaluate the utility of the enriched ontology for the various methods, I plan to use three methods which I describe in this section. Each method will be employed to compare indexing and classification methods which use the enriched ontology with the corresponding methods which do not use the enriched ontology.

Evaluation based on existing manually created keyword sets: The results of the different models will be compared to existing manually defined keywords provided by expert indexers. Standard metrics such as precision, recall and F1-Score can be used to quantify the effectiveness of the models.

Comparison with inter-expert semantic similarity: Semantic similarity measures can be employed for calculating the semantic distance between different sets of suggested keywords. The semantic distance between the keyword sets produced by different human expert indexers (for the same document) will be measured. This semantic distance will then be compared to the semantic distance between the keyword set produced by the model and the keyword sets produced by the different human expert indexers. The choice of the semantic similarity measure can be based on a preceding evaluation of the accuracy of the results of different measures, conducted by domain experts.

Recommendation-based evaluation by expert indexers: The keyword sets produced by the model will be presented to human expert indexers, along with the document to be indexed. The human annotators will then judge which

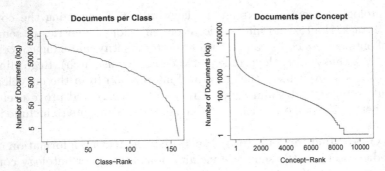

Fig. 1. Distribution of documents (log-scale) in the different classes from the classification system for the social sciences and concepts from the thesaurus for the social sciences in the SOLIS dataset.

suggested keywords, in their opinion, are appropriate, which ones are wrong and which ones are missing. Based on this evaluation, standard metrics can be calculated, as well as the semantic distance to the keyword set after correction.

6   Datasets

I plan to apply my approach to and evaluate it on the following datasets: the Social Science Literature Information System (SOLIS), the Social Science Open Access Repository (databases containing German social science publications), the German Education Index (German educational science publications), and PubMed Central (English biomedical and life sciences publications). The first dataset which I will apply my approach to is SOLIS, a collection of meta-data (including abstracts) of roughly 450,000 social science publications which are fully manually classified and indexed by human expert indexers according to the classification system and the thesaurus for the social sciences.

7   Preliminary Results

This section briefly describes the supervised classification experiments which I conducted on the SOLIS dataset. The results presented in this section are not to be seen as preliminary results of my proposed approach, but rather as a motivation for why an improved approach is necessary.

Experimental Setup: I conducted the classification experiments on a subset of the SOLIS database which consists of all documents that were published after the year 2003. It contains 144,259 documents and 306,879 class labels (from the classification system for the social sciences). Figure 1 shows the skewed distribution of classes and ontology concepts assigned to documents. A skewed class distribution is often a problem when applying supervised classification methods, due to the lack of training documents in the sparse classes.

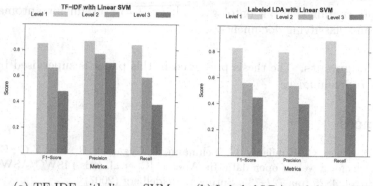

(a) TF-IDF with linear SVM.   (b) Labeled LDA with linear SVM.

Fig. 2. Results of supervised machine learning targeting three semantic specificity levels of the classification system

After applying standard preprocessing techniques (removing stopwords and stemming), I calculated two sets of features on the textual information of the documents: *TF-IDF features* and *Labeled LDA topic distributions*. Identifying the categories assigned to a document constitutes a multi-label classification task, where there can be multiple correct classes for each document. I used the *One-vs-Rest* strategy for this task, which trains a separate classifier for each class and fits this class against all other classes. The classification system for the social sciences is hierarchically organized, so it is possible to conduct classification at different levels of semantic specificity. Three classification models, one for each of the three top semantic levels in the classification hierarchy, were trained for both feature sets. Support vector machines with linear kernels were used for all classification experiments, and all classifiers were trained on a 67% split of the subset and tested on the remaining 33%.

Results and Discussion: The results of the experiments are presented in Figure 2. Generally, Labeled LDA features produced a higher recall, while TF-IDF features resulted in a higher precision. While both feature sets achieve an acceptable F1-Score when targeting only first-level hierarchy categories, the effectiveness of the classifiers targeting more semantically fine-grained categories is unsatisfactory. This shows that a more elaborate approach is necessary for effectively classifying social science documents.

8   Conclusion

Subject indexing of unstructured text continues to constitute a challenging field of research. The PhD thesis presented in this paper focuses on a new approach to enriching ontologies and classification systems with the background knowledge of encyclopedias. From such background knowledge, textual and structural information about the semantic vicinity of ontologies' concepts can be extracted. This additional knowledge, by providing a more comprehensive representation of concepts contained in an ontology, is likely to be useful for automatically indexing and classifying documents.

Acknowledgments. The thesis presented in this paper is supervised by Prof. Dr. Markus Strohmaier.

References

1. Auer, S., Bizer, C., Kobilarov, G., Lehmann, J., Cyganiak, R., Ives, Z.G.: Dbpedia: A nucleus for a web of open data. In: Aberer, K., et al. (eds.) ISWC/ASWC 2007. LNCS, vol. 4825, pp. 722–735. Springer, Heidelberg (2007)
2. Blei, D.M., McAuliffe, J.D.: Supervised topic models. In: Neural Information Processing Systems (2007)
3. Blei, D.M., Ng, A.Y., Jordan, M.I.: Latent dirichlet allocation. The Journal of Machine Learning Research (2003)
4. de Melo, G., Siersdorfer, S.: Multilingual text classification using ontologies. In: Amati, G., Carpineto, C., Romano, G. (eds.) ECiR 2007. LNCS, vol. 4425, pp. 541–548. Springer, Heidelberg (2007)
5. Deerwester, S.C., Dumais, S.T., Landauer, T.K., Furnas, G.W., Harshman, R.A.: Indexing by latent semantic analysis. Journal of the American Society for Information Science (1990)
6. Gabrilovich, E., Markovitch, S.: Computing semantic relatedness using wikipedia-based explicit semantic analysis. In: Proceedings of the 20th International Joint Conference on Artificial Intelligence (2007)
7. Gupta, R., Ratinov, L.A.: Text categorization with knowledge transfer from heterogeneous data sources. In: Proceedings of the 23rd Conference on Artificial Intelligence (2008)
8. Hofmann, T.: Probabilistic latent semantic indexing. In: Proceedings of the 22nd Annual International ACM SIGIR Conference on Research and Development in Information Retrieval (1999)
9. Jonquet, C., Shah, N.H., Musen, M.A.: The open biomedical annotator. Summit on translational bioinformatics (2009)
10. Lancaster, F.W.: Indexing and abstracting in theory and practice. University of Illinois Press (1991)
11. Medelyan, O., Milne, D., Legg, C., Witten, I.H.: Mining meaning from wikipedia. International Journal of Human-Computer Studies (2009)
12. Oren, E., Möller, K., Scerri, S., Handschuh, S., Sintek, M.: What are semantic annotations. Technical report (2006)
13. Ramage, D., Hall, D., Nallapati, R., Manning, C.D.: Labeled lda: A supervised topic model for credit attribution in multi-labeled corpora. In: Proceedings of the 2009 Conference on Empirical Methods in Natural Language (2009)
14. Salton, G., Buckley, C.: Term-weighting approaches in automatic text retrieval. Information Processing & Management (1988)
15. Studer, R., Benjamins, R., Fensel, D.: Knowledge engineering: principles and methods. Data & Knowledge Engineering (1998)
16. Suchanek, F.M., Kasneci, G., Weikum, G.: Yago: a core of semantic knowledge. In: Proceedings of the 16th International Conference on World Wide Web. ACM (2007)

Detecting and Correcting Conservativity Principle Violations in Ontology Mappings

Alessandro Solimando

Dipartimento di Informatica, Bioingegneria, Robotica e Ingegneria dei Sistemi,
Università di Genova, Italy
alessandro.solimando@unige.it

1 Problem Statement

Ontologies play a key role in the development of the Semantic Web and are being used in many diverse application domains such as biomedicine and energy industry. An application domain may have been modeled according to different points of view and purposes. This situation usually leads to the development of different ontologies that intuitively overlap, but that use different naming and modeling conventions.

The problem of (semi-)automatically computing mappings between independently developed ontologies is usually referred to as the *ontology matching problem*. A number of sophisticated ontology matching systems have been developed in the last years [5, 30]. These systems, however, rely on lexical and structural heuristics, and the integration of the input ontologies and the mappings may lead to many undesired logical consequences. In [13] three principles were proposed to minimise the number of potentially unintended consequences, namely: *(i) consistency principle*, the mappings should not lead to unsatisfiable classes in the integrated ontology, *(ii) locality principle*, the mappings should link entities that have similar *neighbourhoods*, *(iii) conservativity principle*, the mappings should not introduce new semantic relationships between concepts from one of the input ontologies. Violations to these principles may hinder the usefulness of ontology mappings. Our aim is to develop effective and efficient detection and correction techniques for violations of the conservativity principle for ontology alignments.

2 Relevancy

Given the formal semantics of ontologies, logical defects in the alignment between them may hinder their usefulness and lead to undesired results. The practical effects of these logical violations highly depend on the intrinsic nature and characteristics of the ontology-based system.

When ontology-to-ontology mappings are used, for instance, in an ontology-based data access (OBDA) [27] or an ontology-based data integration system (OBDI) [35], a high quality alignment is mandatory. In such scenarios, any violation of the consistency or conservativity principles will directly affect the

P. Mika et al. (Eds.) ISWC 2014, Part II, LNCS 8797, pp. 545–552, 2014.

quality of the query results, since queries will be rewritten according to the ontology axioms, the ontology-to-ontology mappings and the ontology-to-database mappings. On the contrary, an ontology-based information retrieval (IR) system may better tolerate some logical defects.

A definition of effective techniques for assessing and re-establishing the logical soundness of ontology-to-ontology alignments would be key for any critical ontology-based system using them, directly or indirectly. When such detection and repair techniques are also efficient, ontology matchers may use them for: (i) pruning the usually large search space when computing mappings, (ii) computing high quality alignments by minimising the number of logical violations. *LogMap* [12] and *AML* [28] ontology matchers, for instance, have already successfully applied these ideas by including detection and repair techniques for the consistency principle in the mapping computation process.

Our work follows a classic approach to ontology alignment debugging, where the repair can only affect the alignment, considering as immutable the matched ontologies [12, 14, 21, 28]. This is not the only possible approach to the problem. The work presented in [10, 17, 18], for instance, considers the violations of the conservativity principle as possible false positives, based on the potential incompleteness of the input ontologies. Hence, the correction strategy may also insert subsumption axioms to the input ontologies, to enrich their concept hierarchies. Authors in [26] also suggest that fixing the input ontologies may be an alternative for mapping removal.

Nonetheless, there are also important application scenarios in which the aligned ontologies have to be considered as not modifiable. One such example is the EU Optique project.[1] Optique aims at facilitating scalable end-user access to big data in the oil and gas industry (based on an OBDA system). Currently, in the Optique use case, the input ontologies are not modifiable. The query formulation ontology is a domain ontology based on the Norwegian Petroleum Directorate (NPD) Fact-Pages[2] [31] and it is currently preferred by Optique end-users to feed the visual query formulation interface [34]. NPD ontology is not intended to be modifiable by end-users, because it includes knowledge already agreed on by the community. The other is a bootstrapped ontology *directly* linked to the information represented in the database.

In general, our approach aims at developing a technique suitable for any ontology-based system, where the used ontologies are not directly controlled by the system and can be only used as they are. For instance, the authors in [20] apply ontology matching in a multi-agent system scenario in order to allow the exchange and extension of ontology-based *action plans* among agents.

3   Related Work

The three principles mentioned in Section 1 have been actively investigated in the last years (*e.g.*, [11, 12, 13, 21, 22, 23, 28]).

---

[1] http://www.optique-project.eu/
[2] http://factpages.npd.no/factpages/

In particular, the conservativity principle problem, although indirectly, has been actively studied in the literature. Schlobach [29] originally introduced the *assumption of disjointness* to address the repair of ontologies underspecified in terms of negative constraints (disjointness axioms, in particular). A serious obstacle for the practical success of the techniques based on such assumption is the usually prohibitive number of candidate disjointness axioms to be inserted. Meilicke *et al.* [22] applied this assumption in the context of repairing ontology mappings, and limited the number of disjointness axioms to be inserted by using learning techniques [36]. These techniques, however, typically require a manually created training set. In [7] the authors present an interactive system to guide the expert user in the manual enrichment of the ontologies with disjointness axioms. Clearly, this method is not suitable for scenarios in which no user intervention is possible.

Our approach aims at minimising the subset of candidate disjointness axioms that need to be inserted, without compromising the repair effectiveness. However, in order to be applicable to completely automatic repair scenarios, our method needs to work independently from any manual intervention.

Ontology matching systems have also dealt with the conservativity principle in order to improve the precision (w.r.t. a reference mapping set) of the computed mappings. For example, systems such as *ASMOV* [11], *Lily* [37] and *YAM++* [24] have implemented different heuristics to avoid violations of the conservativity principle. Another relevant approach [2] presents a set of sanity checks and best practices when computing ontology mappings. A preliminary analysis shows that the provided heuristics fail at preventing and solving many violations [32, 33].

Unfortunately, for many of the mentioned approaches, the covered ontology fragment is not clear, and their effectiveness can only be experimentally verified, thus limiting the comparability of different contributions. Conservativity principle highly benefited from the definition of formally grounded methods, instead of heuristics approaches, as the results of *OAEI* in the years demonstrate. To this aim, our main goal is to define an elegant way to detect and solve conservativity principle violations by reducing the problem to a consistency principle violation problem, in the Horn propositional fragment. However, in the literature an efficient and automatic technique for enriching ontologies with disjointness axioms, at the basis of the aforementioned reduction, is still missing.

4   Research Questions

After analysing the related work on the subject, we still consider as open the following research questions: *(RQ.i)* Which consequences may have an alignment violating the conservativity principle in different application scenarios? *(RQ.ii)* Is there a relationship between the violations affecting an alignment and its correctness or completeness? *(RQ.iii)* Which algorithms can be used to compute a repair for an alignment violating the conservativity principle? *(RQ.iv)* Which is the trade-off between completeness and runtime for these algorithms? *(RQ.v)* Which are the consequences of applying ontology alignment evolution techniques on an alignment violating the conservativity principle? *(RQ.vi)* How can conservativity principle violations detection and repair support interactive alignment revision?

5   Hypotheses

(H.i) Conservativity principle violations may harm the correctness of ontology-based systems in relevant application scenarios such as OBDA and OBDI *(RQ.i)*. *(H.ii)* Conservativity principle is tighly coupled with the notion of conservative extension [16], an extremely challenging decision problem, and would therefore benefit from approximated repair techniques for achieving scalability on reduced DL fragments (*e.g.*, in the $\mathcal{EL}$ family). This principle could be partly reduced to the consistency principle, but a multi-strategy repair is needed to address the uncovered violation kinds *(RQ.iii,RQ.iv)*. *(H.iii)* Ontology alignment evolution algorithms usually propagate violations, this could also affect the optimality of the update strategies *(RQ.v)*. *(H.iv)* The detection and repair techniques can be coupled with existing user-driven ontology enrichment of negative constraints [7] and ontology revision techniques [25] *(RQ.vi)*.

6   Approach

Addressing the conservativity principle violation requires a detection and repair technique. For violation detection, we propose a complete technique, based on an efficient interval labelling schema [1] for the input/aligned ontologies. Given that not all the violations are independent, we plan to provide a discrimination between direct and derived violations, that would rely on a graph representation [32] of the aligned ontology. This refined notion of violation will offer a fine grained violation rate estimation.

For conservativity violations affecting atomic concepts not involved in a subsumption relationship nor sharing any descendant, the problem can be reduced to a consistency repair by inserting a disjointness axiom between the two concepts. A classic approach for debugging ontologies is to compute a repair by computing a (minimal) *hitting set* over the set of justifications [9] (minimal sets of axioms entailing a consequence). Computing all the justifications for a given entailment is a costly reasoning service, and all the scalable debugging algorithms propose approximate repair computations [15, 21, 24, 26]. To address the scalability problem when dealing with large ontologies and mapping sets, our method actually relies on the (Horn) propositional projection of the input ontologies, but does not ensure completeness [33]. We plan to cover expressive fragments such as $\mathcal{EL}$ terminologies (*e.g.*, using the hyper-graph representation of [4]). Currently, we have adapted the infrastructure provided by *LogMap* matcher[12, 14]. However, other mapping repair systems, such as *Alcomo* [21] or *AML* [28], could be considered. Note that, to the best of our knowledge, these mapping repair systems have only focused on solving violations of the consistency principle.

Instead, for the violations affecting concepts involved in a subsumption relationship, the graph representation [32] will again be used, exploiting the property that part of these violations form a cycle (one half represents the previous subsumption relationship, the other one representing the violation). The detection and repair strategies work on the strongly connected components (SCCs) of the graph representation of the aligned ontology, exploiting the well-known relation between SCCs and directed cycles. The approximate repair aims at removing all the cycles corresponding to a violation by computing a solution to an ad-hoc variant of the *Feedback Arc Set* problem [6], encoded as a logic program [32].

The idea of enriching the input ontologies with additional disjointness axioms is not new. The novel aspects of our approach are an automatic and efficient identification and addition of a small set of disjoint axioms, using interval indexing. As already discussed in Section 3, another contribution would be the first method addressing the conservativity principle with a theoretical foundation of the concrete ontology fragment covered by both the detection and repair techniques. Another innovative aspect is the combination of graph-theory and logic programming for addressing the violations that cannot be reduced to the consistency problem. Finally, to the best of our knowledge, despite the attention that ontology alignment debugging and ontology alignment evolution [8, 19] techniques have received in the literature, a combined analysis of the possible interrelation between the two fields is still missing.

7 Preliminary Results

Violation Rate: A preliminary analysis [32, 33] suggests that conservativity principle violations not only deeply affect the alignments computed by the top-level ontology matchers, but also widely affect agreed reference alignments, as emerged from the evaluation of the *Ontology Alignment Evaluation Initiative*[3] (*OAEI*) dataset. Also manually curated alignments, such as *UMLS-Metathesaurus* [3] (*UMLS*), a comprehensive effort for integrating biomedical knowledge bases, suffer from these violations.

Conservativity to Consistency Principle Reduction: The repair algorithm of [33] relies on a reduction of the conservativity to the consistency principle, with promising results. We tested the algorithm on the reference alignments of *OAEI 2013*. The complete detection algorithm takes only 275 seconds to process the aligned ontology SNOMED-NCI (the biggest *OAEI*'s test case). Repair efficiency and effectiveness are also promising. Almost all the violations for the five main tracks of the *OAEI 2013* are fully repaired.

Repair Algorithms: For what concerns the two orthogonal repair techniques, the preliminary results show their efficiency and effectiveness in isolation [32, 33]. From the theoretical standpoint, the two techniques address different kinds of conservativity principle violations, but the concrete effect of combining them still needs to be explored in practice. Moreover, their suitability for an automatic use in an ontology matching process has to be experimentally verified.

8 Evaluation Plan

The evaluation phase will provide a quantitative measurement of the hypotheses underlying the different aspects of our proposal:

---
[3] http://oaei.ontologymatching.org/

(H.i) will be investigated using the new track of *OAEI 2014*,[4] that will be addressing the problem of ontology alignment for query answering. The effect of the violations and their repair will be tested using the same metrics proposed by the organisers. To this extent, another interesting evaluation is the comparison with alternative approaches (see Section 3) w.r.t. the same task.

(H.ii) has been already successfully addressed in [33]. The preliminary analysis consisted in the detection of the initial number of violations for the *OAEI* reference alignments, the runtime for computing a repair, the size of the repair and the number of unsolved violations. In [32], a similar analysis has been performed on the alignments computed by *OAEI* participants. In addition, an analysis of the repair effect in terms of the completeness and correctness of the alignments has also been conducted.

(H.iii) The state of the art ontology mapping evolution algorithms will be tested using the publicly available snapshots of SNOMED-CT, FMA and NCI ontologies, and UMLS alignments between them (as already done in [8]). The used metric will be the number of violations with and without a repair step on the source (and possibly the target) alignment. The effect in terms of completeness and correctness against the repaired and original reference alignment will be measured using the standard notions of *precision, recall* and *f-measure*.

(H.iv) The practical effect of coupling the automatic detection and repair techniques with a user-driven ontology disjointness addition will be conducted by means of a user survey. In addition, we plan to also evaluate completeness and correctness against a manually defined gold-standard using standard IR metrics.

Finally, the acceptable trade-off between the completeness of the detection and repair algorithms and their runtime will be tested by integrating the implemented techniques into an existing ontology matcher.

9   Reflections

Despite the increasing number of contributions addressing ontology alignment debugging, the conservativity principle has received little attention. A possible explanation is that the negative effects of violations to the consistency principle are already evident for any ontology alignment application scenario, and therefore were considered at an earlier stage. Our claim (Section 5) is that conservativity principle would affect more advanced application scenarios, such as OBDA and OBDI. To this aim, in our opinion, it is extremely significative the introduction of a novel track addressing ontology-based query answering in *OAEI 2014*, given the importance of this venue for ontology matching researchers.

Finally, as discussed in Section 7, we have already been able to accumulate encouraging results for what concerns the violation rate, and the efficiency and effectiveness of our detection and repair techniques. This constitute a reasonable guarantee for the feasability of our approach.

Acknowledgements. The author thanks Ernesto Jiménez-Ruiz and Giovanna Guerrini for their invaluable help.

---

[4] http://www.om2014.ontologymatching.org/

References

1. Agrawal, R., Borgida, A., Jagadish, H.V.: Efficient Management of Transitive Relationships in Large Data and Knowledge Bases. In: ACM SIGMOD Conf. on Manag. of Data (1989)
2. Beisswanger, E., Hahn, U., et al.: Towards valid and reusable reference alignments-ten basic quality checks for ontology alignments and their application to three different reference data sets. J. Biomed. Semant. 3(suppl. 1), S4 (2012)
3. Bodenreider, O.: The Unified Medical Language System (UMLS): integrating biomedical terminology. Nucleic Acids Research 32, 267–270 (2004)
4. Ecke, A., Ludwig, M., Walther, D.: The Concept Difference for $\mathcal{EL}$-Terminologies using Hypergraphs. In: DChanges Workshop (2013)
5. Euzenat, J., Meilicke, C., Stuckenschmidt, H., et al.: Ontology Alignment Evaluation Initiative: Six Years of Experience. J. Data Sem. 15, 158–192 (2011)
6. Even, G., Naor, J.S., Schieber, B., Sudan, M.: Approximating Minimum Feedback Sets and Multicuts in Directed Graphs. Algorithmica 20(2), 151–174 (1998)
7. Ferré, S., Rudolph, S.: Advocatus Diaboli - Exploratory Enrichment of Ontologies with Negative Constraints. In: ten Teije, A., Völker, J., Handschuh, S., Stuckenschmidt, H., d'Acquin, M., Nikolov, A., Aussenac-Gilles, N., Hernandez, N. (eds.) EKAW 2012. LNCS (LNAI), vol. 7603, pp. 42–56. Springer, Heidelberg (2012)
8. Groß, A., Dos Reis, J.C., Hartung, M., Pruski, C., Rahm, E.: Semi-automatic adaptation of mappings between life science ontologies. In: Baker, C.J.O., Butler, G., Jurisica, I. (eds.) DILS 2013. LNCS (LNBI), vol. 7970, pp. 90–104. Springer, Heidelberg (2013)
9. Horridge, M., Parsia, B., Sattler, U.: Laconic and Precise Justifications in OWL. In: Sheth, A.P., Staab, S., Dean, M., Paolucci, M., Maynard, D., Finin, T., Thirunarayan, K. (eds.) ISWC 2008. LNCS, vol. 5318, pp. 323–338. Springer, Heidelberg (2008)
10. Ivanova, V., Lambrix, P.: A Unified Approach for Aligning Taxonomies and Debugging Taxonomies and their Alignments. In: Cimiano, P., Corcho, O., Presutti, V., Hollink, L., Rudolph, S. (eds.) ESWC 2013. LNCS, vol. 7882, pp. 1–15. Springer, Heidelberg (2013)
11. Jean-Mary, Y.R., Shironoshita, E.P., Kabuka, M.R.: Ontology Matching With Semantic Verification. J. Web Sem. 7(3), 235–251 (2009)
12. Jiménez-Ruiz, E., Cuenca Grau, B.: LogMap: Logic-based and Scalable Ontology Matching. In: Aroyo, L., Welty, C., Alani, H., Taylor, J., Bernstein, A., Kagal, L., Noy, N., Blomqvist, E. (eds.) ISWC 2011, Part I. LNCS, vol. 7031, pp. 273–288. Springer, Heidelberg (2011)
13. Jiménez-Ruiz, E., Cuenca Grau, B., Horrocks, I., Berlanga, R.: Logic-based Assessment of the Compatibility of UMLS Ontology Sources. J. Biomed. Semant. 2(suppl. 1), S2 (2011)
14. Jiménez-Ruiz, E., Cuenca Grau, B., Zhou, Y., Horrocks, I.: Large-scale Interactive Ontology Matching: Algorithms and Implementation. In: Eur. Conf. on Artif. Intell. (ECAI) (2012)
15. Jiménez-Ruiz, E., Meilicke, C., Grau, B.C., Horrocks, I.: Evaluating Mapping Repair Systems with Large Biomedical Ontologies. In: Description Logics, pp. 246–257 (2013)
16. Kontchakov, R., Wolter, F., Zakharyaschev, M.: Can you Tell the Difference Between DL-Lite Ontologies? In: Int'l Conf. on Knowl. Representation and Reasoning (KR) (2008)
17. Lambrix, P., Dragisic, Z., Ivanova, V.: Get My Pizza Right: Repairing Missing Is-a Relations in $\mathcal{ALC}$ Ontologies. In: Takeda, H., Qu, Y., Mizoguchi, R., Kitamura, Y. (eds.) JIST 2012. LNCS, vol. 7774, pp. 17–32. Springer, Heidelberg (2013)
18. Lambrix, P., Liu, Q.: Debugging the Missing Is-a Structure Within Taxonomies Networked by Partial Reference Alignments. Data Knowl. Eng (DKE) 86, 179–205 (2013)
19. Martins, H., Silva, N.: A user-driven and a semantic-based ontology mapping evolution approach. In: ICEIS (1), pp. 214–221 (2009)

20. Mascardi, V., Ancona, D., Barbieri, M., Bordini, R.H., Ricci, A.: CooL-AgentSpeak: Endowing AgentSpeak-DL Agents with Plan Exchange and Ontology Services. Web Intelligence and Agent Systems 12(1), 83–107 (2014)
21. Meilicke, C.: Alignments Incoherency in Ontology Matching. Ph.D. thesis, University of Mannheim (2011)
22. Meilicke, C., Völker, J., Stuckenschmidt, H.: Learning Disjointness for Debugging Mappings between Lightweight Ontologies. In: Gangemi, A., Euzenat, J. (eds.) EKAW 2008. LNCS (LNAI), vol. 5268, pp. 93–108. Springer, Heidelberg (2008)
23. Melnik, S., Garcia-Molina, H., Rahm, E.: Similarity Flooding: A Versatile Graph Matching Algorithm and Its Application to Schema Matching. In: IEEE Int'l Conf. on Data Eng. (2002)
24. Ngo, D., Bellahsene, Z.: YAM++: A Multi-strategy Based Approach for Ontology Matching Task. In: ten Teije, A., Völker, J., Handschuh, S., Stuckenschmidt, H., d'Acquin, M., Nikolov, A., Aussenac-Gilles, N., Hernandez, N. (eds.) EKAW 2012. LNCS (LNAI), vol. 7603, pp. 421–425. Springer, Heidelberg (2012)
25. Nikitina, N., Rudolph, S., Glimm, B.: Interactive ontology revision. Web Semantics: Science, Services and Agents on the World Wide Web 12, 118–130 (2012)
26. Pesquita, C., Faria, D., Santos, E., Couto, F.M.: To repair or not to repair: reconciling correctness and coherence in ontology reference alignments. In: Ontology Matching (OM) (2013)
27. Poggi, A., Lembo, D., Calvanese, D., De Giacomo, G., Lenzerini, M., Rosati, R.: Linking Data to Ontologies. In: Spaccapietra, S. (ed.) Journal on Data Semantics X. LNCS, vol. 4900, pp. 133–173. Springer, Heidelberg (2008)
28. Santos, E., Faria, D., Pesquita, C., Couto, F.: Ontology Alignment Repair Through Modularization and Confidence-based Heuristics. arXiv:1307.5322 preprint (2013)
29. Schlobach, S.: Debugging and Semantic Clarification by Pinpointing. In: Gómez-Pérez, A., Euzenat, J. (eds.) ESWC 2005. LNCS, vol. 3532, pp. 226–240. Springer, Heidelberg (2005)
30. Shvaiko, P., Euzenat, J.: Ontology Matching: State of the Art and Future Challenges. IEEE Transactions on Knowl. and Data Eng. (TKDE) (2012)
31. Skjæveland, M.G., Lian, E.H., Horrocks, I.: Publishing the Norwegian Petroleum Directorate's FactPages as Semantic Web Data. In: Alani, H., et al. (eds.) ISWC 2013, Part II. LNCS, vol. 8219, pp. 162–177. Springer, Heidelberg (2013)
32. Solimando, A., Guerrini, G.: Coping with Conservativity Principle Violations in Ontology Mappings. Tech. Rep. DIBRIS-TR-14-01, University of Genova (January 2014), ftp://ftp.disi.unige.it/person/SolimandoA/cycleMappingDbgExt.pdf
33. Solimando, A., Jiménez-Ruiz, E., Guerrini, G.: Detecting and Correcting Conservativity Principle Violations in Ontology-to-Ontology Mappings. Tech. Rep. DIBRIS-TR-14-05, University of Genova (May 2014), ftp://ftp.disi.unige.it/person/SolimandoA/conservLogMap.pdf
34. Soylu, A., Skjæveland, M.G., Giese, M., Horrocks, I., Jimenez-Ruiz, E., Kharlamov, E., Zheleznyakov, D.: A Preliminary Approach on Ontology-Based Visual Query Formulation for Big Data. In: Garoufallou, E., Greenberg, J. (eds.) MTSR 2013. CCIS, vol. 390, pp. 201–212. Springer, Heidelberg (2013)
35. Tian, A., Sequeda, J.F., Miranker, D.P.: QODI: Query as Context in Automatic Data Integration. In: Alani, H., et al. (eds.) ISWC 2013, Part I. LNCS, vol. 8218, pp. 624–639. Springer, Heidelberg (2013)
36. Völker, J., Vrandečić, D., Sure, Y., Hotho, A.: Learning Disjointness. In: Franconi, E., Kifer, M., May, W. (eds.) ESWC 2007. LNCS, vol. 4519, pp. 175–189. Springer, Heidelberg (2007)
37. Wang, P., Xu, B.: Debugging Ontology Mappings: A Static Approach. Computing and Informatics 27(1), 21–36 (2012)

Author Index